Minerva and the Muse

Minerva and the Muse

A LIFE OF MARGARET FULLER

JOAN von MEHREN

University of Massachusetts Press / Amherst

Copyright © 1994 by The University of Massachusetts Press
All rights reserved
Printed in the United States of America

LC 94-18663
ISBN 0-87023-941-4

Designed by Susan Bishop
Set in Adobe Minion by Keystone Typesetting, Inc.
Printed and bound by Braun-Brumfield, Inc.

Library of Congress Cataloging-in-Publication Data
Von Mehren, Joan, 1923–
Minerva and the muse : a life of Margaret Fuller / by Joan von
Mehren.
p.   cm.
Includes bibliographical references (p.   ) and index.
ISBN 0-87023-941-4 (alk. paper)
1. Fuller, Margaret, 1810–1850—Biography.   2. Women authors,
American—19th century—Biography.   3. Feminists—United
States—Biography.   I. Title.
PS2506.V66   1995
818'.309—dc20   94-18663
[B]

British Library Cataloguing in Publication data are available.

For my Mother and for Arthur

Contents

Illustrations follow page 182

Acknowledgments

SINCE the vast majority of Fuller source materials is at Houghton Library at Harvard and the Boston Public Library, I owe special thanks to Rodney G. Dennis and Leslie Morris, Curators of Manuscripts at Houghton, Laura Monti, Curator of Rare Books and Manuscripts at the Boston Public Library, and their staffs for their help and guidance.

I gratefully acknowledge the assistance of the following: Catherine Craven and Virginia Smith of the Massachusetts Historical Society; Carl A. Starce of the Long Island Historical Society; Wendy Wick Reaves, Curator of Prints, National Museum of American Art; Sandor B. Cohen of the New Jersey Historical Society; William Loos, Curator of the Rare Book Room, Buffalo and Erie County Public Library; Elizabeth Shenton of the Schlesinger Library; Mary Smith of Widener Library; the late Dr. Lola L. Szladitz, Curator of the H. W. and A. A. Berg Collection at the New York Public Library; Jacques Suffel, Director of the Archives Lovenjoul, Chantilly, France; Dr. John Treherne of Downing College, Cambridge; Professor Kurt Lipstein and Dr. Richard Gooder of Clare College, Cambridge; Gesine Bottomley of the Institute for Advanced Study, Berlin; and the staffs of the Istituto per la Storia del Risorgimento in Rome, the Bibliothèque Nationale, the Bibliothèque Arsenal, and the Musée Adam Mickiewicz in Paris, the Adam Mickiewicz Museum and Library in Warsaw, the British Museum in London, the Library of Cambridge University, Fruitlands Library and Museum in Harvard, Massachusetts, and the Athenaeum Library of Boston.

Thérèse Marx-Spire, a George Sand scholar, interrogated George Lubin for me on Sand's relationship with Fuller and answered many questions about French socialism in the 1840s. Professor Wilhelm Vosskamp of Bonn University instructed me on *Wilhelm Meister* and Goethe's theories on Bildung. For help with the knotty problem of the Ossoli marriage and the canon law, I am grateful to Professor Charles Donahue of Harvard Law School and Avvocato Giovanni Ughi of Milan. Andrzej Burzyuski translated for me in Warsaw. Dr. Sylviane Colombo helped me with Italian translations and made many useful suggestions. In 1988 and 1989 I benefited greatly from the seminars chaired by Helena Lewis on "Writing Biography" at Harvard's Center for Literary and Cultural Studies.

Others who have been very kind with their time have been Constance Fuller Threinen, John Mansfield, Barbara Hanawalt, Louise and James Scott, Yen Tsai Feng McNiff, Terry Martin, Erica Chadbourn, Wilma Cannon Fairbank, Sue Trautman, Sayre Sheldon, Marie Olesen Urbanski, Anne Jackson Lindbeck, Carol Houck Smith, Felicia Lamport Kaplan, Sara Blackburn, Tine Kjoerup Christensen, Ruth Smith, Benjamin R. Sears, and my editors, Janet Benton, Barbara Palmer, and Pamela Wilkinson.

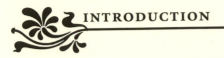

Margaret Fuller: Should She Be Famous?

IN 1902, when a mass magazine held a poll to select twenty American women to present as candidates for the Hall of Fame for Great Americans at University Heights in New York City, Margaret Fuller came in sixth, behind Harriet Beecher Stowe but ahead of Mary Lyon, Frances Willard, and Maria Mitchell, all of whose names were engraved in high relief on one of the hall's 150 bronze tablets three years later. Even so, Fuller's placing in the poll—she garnered more votes than Pocahontas, Betsy Ross, Louisa May Alcott, and Abigail Adams—attests to her celebrity at the turn of the century. A 1902 book on the Hall of Fame considered the twenty "most eligible women" for the honor and included thumbnail biographical sketches of each of them. The researcher did a careless job on Fuller:

Sarah Margaret Fuller was born in Cambridgeport, Mass., in 1810. Early in life she won friends among the leading writers and philosophers of the day, her unusual mental qualities enabling her to meet them as equals. In 1844, she came to New York and joined the staff of the *Tribune*, displaying in her writing a wide philanthropic purpose and occupying a high position in literary and artistic circles. In 1847, while on a visit to Europe, she was married to Giovanni Angelo Ossoli, Marquis Ossoli, and became an ardent supporter of the struggle for [Italian] independence. On her return to New York she renewed her literary work, winning fresh renown as an author and a reformer.[1]

The glaring error in this account is the ending. On Fuller's return to New York in the summer of 1850, the bark *Elizabeth*, in which she was traveling with Giovanni Ossoli and their two-year-old son, was caught in a hurricane and went aground less than a hundred yards off Fire Island. After several hours of waiting on board for rescue, the entire family was drowned when the ship broke up. In the course of the following week, Horace Greeley published a stirring elegy to Fuller in the *New-York Daily Tribune* and sent his star reporter, Bayard Taylor, to Fire Island to cover the story; Ralph Waldo Emerson sent Henry Thoreau to canvass the beaches in search of any remains of Fuller or Ossoli, whose bodies were never recovered; by the end of the week the *Tribune* reported that Fire Island citizens "often exclaimed" that had they known that so much "interest was taken in the lady on board" extra measures to save her might have been undertaken.[2]

At the time rumors of scandal were circulating over the relationship of the forty-year-old Fuller to the handsome twenty-nine-year-old Marchese Ossoli, who lacked any pretension to learning or intellectual power. While serving as foreign correspondent to the *Tribune* during the 1848–49 revolutionary years in Italy, Fuller had kept secret this part of her life as well as the existence of their son. He was a year old when she wrote her family and friends that she was a mother and should be addressed as Margaret Fuller Ossoli. She provided no details of a marriage, leading even her staunchest friends to speculate as to whether she had bothered to take the marriage vows.

Yet, in claiming that Fuller won fresh renown after her return, the author of the Hall of Fame sketch was not entirely wrong—although her posthumous reputation was rather less as an author or reformer than as a commanding personality. Henry James, who recalled hearing Washington Irving tell his father the story of Fuller's death in the summer of 1850, wrote thirty years later that she had become "a sort of a legend," such that "people who had known her well grew at last to be envied."[3] Disparate groups kept her name alive: former students from her teaching career in Boston and Providence; literary associates from her New England days when she edited the Transcendentalist journal, the *Dial;* many of the some 200 women who participated at one time or another in her Boston Conversations, group sessions in which Fuller encouraged educated women to articulate and identify subjects of concern; members of the New York literary establishment who admired her writings. But, by the time the Hall of Fame poll took place, Fuller's generation was long gone. Only Julia Ward Howe and Thomas Wentworth Higginson appeared in person or sent telegrams on the few occasions when Fuller's memory was honored.

Although the Hall of Fame pollsters did not identify their voters demographically, most of those who gave Fuller their vote in 1902 were probably members of the Ossoli clubs (often called culture clubs) that were scattered across the country or activists in the woman suffrage movement. In 1881 Elizabeth Cady Stanton and Susan B. Anthony wrote in the *History of Woman Suffrage* that Fuller "possessed more influence on the thought of American women than any woman previous to her time."[4]

Her book, *Woman in the Nineteenth Century* (1845), appeared at a time when women's rising educational levels and growing expectations provided a ready audience for an appeal to women to direct their energies to exploring the self, developing autonomy, and expanding their intellectual and personal horizons. Measuring women's position in the new republic against the ideals of the American Revolution and religious values of human equality, Fuller analyzed the possibilities for realistic change, calling on women as a group to raise themselves out of their condition of dependence to one of self-reliance. Her program emphasized the development of intellectual discipline, critical intelligence, and self-awareness—qualities she categorized as Minerva-like powers— as a needed balance to woman's already overdeveloped emotional, intuitional, divinatory, or Muse-like qualities. She believed that bringing into harmony

Minerva and the Muse would endow woman with the power to subdue cultural opposition and take her place as man's equal in society.

Fuller presented her arguments in sermon form, taking care to avoid aggressive language; yet the subversive message of the book coupled with her unconventional personality marked this witty, wily, self-absorbed, and highly energetic woman as a species unto herself. James Russell Lowell caricatured her cruelly in his *Fable for Critics;* Edgar Allan Poe, after asserting in 1846 that she "unquestionably" possessed "high genius," dubbed her "a very inconsistent old maid" a year and a half later. On the other hand, Julia Ward Howe, who reigned in Boston cultural circles like Queen Victoria, was a Fuller champion. Admitting that Fuller was derided for "her unlikeness to the popular or fashionable type of the time," Howe asked whether the "trait which occasioned so much animadversion was not the concomitant of one of Margaret's most valuable qualities," "a belief in her own moral and intellectual power, which impelled her to examine and decide all questions for herself, and which enabled her to accomplish many a brave work and sacrifice."[5]

Howe's approval may have influenced votes for Fuller's Hall of Fame candidacy, but Fuller, for all her much criticized self-esteem, would have been surprised even to find herself as a candidate for a national pantheon. When she decided to return to the United States with her personal history still very much a matter of suspicious rumor, she was resigned to public opprobrium. At the age of fifteen, however, she had hungered for renown. She wrote to the Marquis de Lafayette, then touring the country, "Should we both live, and it is possible to a female, to whom the avenues of glory are seldom accessible, I shall recal my name to your recollection." Soon afterward, she announced to her former school headmistress, "I am determined on distinction," and outlined the program she was pursuing to realize her goal.[6]

By her late twenties, she faced overwhelming obstacles to realizing her ambitions. In a time when mental hygiene books warned that overstraining the mental faculties was especially dangerous for women and could lead to premature death, she worried that her fantasies of future glory indicated that she was abnormal. Authorship was an acceptable vocation for women, but the gender restrictions on subject matter, language, and form stifled her. She wanted to "write like a man of the world of intellect and action" and not "like a woman of love and hope, and disappointment." To do so, she felt compelled to keep "behind a curtain" all that she knew about "human nature."[7] She articulated the dilemma. "One should be either private or public. I love best to be a woman; but womanhood is too tightly bound to give me scope. At hours, I live truly as a woman; at others, I should stifle; as on the other hand, I should palsy when I would play the artist."[8] To escape her dilemma she developed a public persona and a public voice that served her in the public domain. The Minerva side of

Fuller, the accomplished, intellectual critic and scholar that Howe defended, masked a sensitive, perceptive, affectionate, and highly intuitive Muse side in constant pursuit of intimacy. This aspect of her nature finds expression in her private life, in her correspondence, journal entries, poems, and a few mystical essays.

Within a few years of her death, her family and friends, concerned to preserve her memory, destroyed or mutilated much of her personal correspondence and papers and thus made it possible for the legend that Henry James wrote of in 1879 to be transposed into a myth that persisted in spite of a few good biographies that should have dispelled it. The interest in women's history in the 1960s provided new approaches to the study of Fuller's achievement; scholars and biographers, now more aware of her importance, began to reexamine and reorder the sources. Robert N. Hudspeth's landmark achievement, the editing of her letters, with five volumes now completed, and the bibliographical scholarship of Joel Myerson signaled a Fuller revival which has now become a minor industry. New editions of her essays and books, fresh examinations of her poetry, the publication of her *Tribune* dispatches from Europe in one volume, and the appearance of some of her private journals, resurrected from dusty boxes, and new scholarship on many of the figures who peopled her life (many of them women) have provided authors with a wealth of fresh material. In late 1992, when the manuscript for this biography was completed, the first volume of Charles Capper's two-volume *Margaret Fuller: An American Romantic Life* appeared, demonstrating in its detail, and the breadth of its historical and social context, the richness of this new hoard of information. *Minerva and the Muse: A Life of Margaret Fuller* is more strictly focused on Fuller herself, the charting of her character; on the strategies she used to balance her private and her public life, how she engaged in living, theorizing, and writing the story of a woman's life in a different way. It traces her uncertainties about vocation, her search for intimacy and means of expression, and how her private life informed her evolving ideology about personal development and democratic culture.

Robert Hudspeth noted recently that, before Fuller left New York for Europe, she remarked in an important essay evaluating the state of American literature in 1845, "we are sad that we cannot be present at the gathering of the harvest. And yet we are joyous, too, when we think that though our name may not be writ on the pillar of our country's fame, we can really do far more towards rearing it, than those who came at a later period and to a seemingly fairer task." Thanks in some part to Fuller, the task has indeed become fairer. She, who felt deeply estranged from her country at the time of her death, would be surprised to find that in recent years she has been granted " 'canonical' stature" and that her name is being written eagerly on numerous pillars of fame.[9]

Fuller liked to experiment with ways of harmonizing and balancing opposing elements: humanism and idealism, culture and nature, intuition and tradition, rich and poor, male and female, Minerva and the Muse, past and future. As an experiment in biography, why not try to re-create a life of Fuller by fusing the form and some of the mannerisms of women's biography of the nineteenth century with the attitudes, values, and insights of the end of the twentieth century? This seemed a way not only to take a leaf from her book but to bridge the distance between past and present that she tried to imagine 150 years ago.

CHAPTER 1

*How is it that I seem to be this Margaret Fuller? What does
it mean? What shall I do about it?*

The Protected Years

IN 1831, when Margaret Fuller was twenty-one, she had a mystical experience on
a dreary November afternoon. Bored with the Thanksgiving Day church service, at odds with her family, and seeing no possible future for herself other
than growing old as the old-maid, elder sister in a large family, she ran off into
the woods and fields along the Charles River in Cambridge, Massachusetts, to
nurse her misery. She could not "bear" herself any longer, she wrote, and she
could not see how she could return to a life in which she had "no place." She ran
until she was exhausted. A few moments after she sat down to rest, the sun came
out, and she recalled

how, [as] a little child, I had stopped myself one day on the stairs, and asked, how came I
here? How is it that I seem to be this Margaret Fuller? What does it mean? What shall I do
about it? I remembered all the times and ways in which the same thought had returned. I
saw how long it must be before the soul can learn to act under these limitations of time
and space, and human nature; but I saw also that it *Must* do it.[1]

Her soul's quest for meaning became Margaret's continual concern, and she
recorded her experiences in diaries, journals, essays, book reviews, short stories, and a constant convoy of letters to her many friends.

"Writing is worthless except as a record of a life," she came to believe, and
during the several months of mystical withdrawal that preceded her thirtieth
birthday, she wrote a number of partly fictionalized autobiographical fragments in which she sought to explain her high-strung, nervous personality, her
alternating moods, and her ambition, as well as the headaches and back trouble
that dogged her at every crisis of limitation.[2]

She pictured herself as the victim of a domineering father whose rigorous
intellectual training ignored her natural bent to follow her instincts, to grow at
her own pace and lose herself in poetic imaginings. Instead of being allowed to
grow up unfettered as her mother had done (she described her mother as a free
spirit "bound by one law with the blue sky, the dew, and the frolic birds"),
starting at the age of three and a half, Margaret was given daily lessons in
mathematics, grammar, history, and classical languages. Her father had graduated from Harvard, and he believed that the regimen he had followed in order
to pass the entrance examinations not only trained the mind but developed the
moral qualities he wished for his children: "Common Sense," "hardihood,"

"earnest purpose," and "an indomitable will." The pressure to satisfy her father's demands went against the grain, Margaret maintained; it often exhausted her and forced her to find relief in fantasy and dreams. "Poor child!" she lamented as she looked back on that period, "I had no natural childhood."[3]

By the time Margaret was entering her thirties, the child-rearing methods of her parents had been discredited among the progressive thinkers of New England. By then, Fuller herself had taught professionally for a few years and had observed firsthand the advantages of a less strenuous regime.

If we had only been as well brought up in these respects! It is not mother's fault that she was ignorant of every physical law, young, untaught country girl as she was; but I can't help mourning, sometimes, that my bodily life should have been so destroyed by the ignorance of *both* my parents.[4]

Even though her parents were both fifth-generation descendants of English yeoman stock who immigrated to the Massachusetts Bay Colony in the middle of the seventeenth century and both were country-bred in modest circumstances in villages not far from Boston, they thought of themselves as coming from different backgrounds.

Timothy Fuller, Jr., her father, was born in 1778 on the island of Martha's Vineyard where his family had taken refuge during the Revolution; after the war, he was brought up on a farm on the side of Mount Wachusett in Princeton, Massachusetts, north of Worcester. Her mother, Margarett Crane, lived until her marriage at twenty in Canton, a town to the southwest of Boston in the Old Colony, as the area surrounding Plymouth was called. She was the daughter of Peter Crane, a gunsmith, who was known for his superior workmanship in iron and steel; he was a close friend of the Paul Revere family, who had moved their copper foundry to Canton in 1802. Although Peter Crane never saw action during the Revolution, he was a member of the Twenty-fourth Regiment of the Massachusetts Line and occasionally served as its chaplain. His wife, Elizabeth Jones Weiser, was remembered in Canton as a sweet, religious woman who spent her days reading pious texts and singing devotional hymns.[5]

The important difference in the heritage of Margaret Fuller's parents was education. Her grandfather, Timothy Fuller, Sr., was an ordained clergyman who had graduated from Harvard in 1763. Even though he lost his Princeton pulpit in 1776 for lack of sympathy with the revolutionary cause and failed to reclaim it after the war, he continued to carry the distinction of a learned man during the years he made his living as a farmer in Princeton where he had accumulated a large parcel of land before he ran into difficulty. His wife, Sarah Buckminster Williams, was the daughter of a respected Congregational minister, Abraham Williams, of Sandwich, a distinguished early supporter of the Revolution and one of the founding members of the American Academy of Arts and Sciences. An educated woman, Sarah Williams was learned enough to help prepare her five sons for Harvard and her five daughters to earn their livings as schoolteachers.

None of the Cranes went to college or was educated in the classics or higher mathematics. Before she married Timothy Fuller, Jr., on May 28, 1809, Margarett Crane had taught for a few months in the village school at Canton. She could compose a good letter with vivid descriptions and crisp expressions, and with most of the words properly spelled, and she freely admitted after her marriage that it was "ridiculous" to "continue in ignorance with all the means of emancipation" at hand. But as household tasks increased, she found it impossible to implement her plans for self-improvement. "[B]ooks accumulate & time *diminishes* & cares increase," she wrote her husband shortly after their fourth child was born.[6]

Though a letter written after their marriage mentions a chance first meeting on the Boston Bridge, according to the family tradition Timothy Jr. met Margarett Crane at church on a visit to Canton in 1808. He married her soon afterward, even though, according to their son Richard, "Father was not blind to worldly advantages of family and position; and such were readily within reach of a rising young lawyer, whose talents had already become favorably known." By the standards of the time, Margarett Crane was her husband's inferior in education and social position, but her lighthearted, instinctual, affectionate, and sometimes frivolous nature was a complement to her husband's dogmatic puritanism. Their daughter Margaret, in her autobiographical sketch, put her finger on the attraction when she wrote of her parents: "His love for my mother was the green spot on which he stood apart from the commonplaces of a mere bread-winning, bread-bestowing existence." Margarett Crane was a handsome, willowy, blue-eyed blonde who, at five feet, ten inches, stood several inches taller than her compact husband, whose idea of a joke was to quip that he liked to look up to her "with high favor." Outside of the family circle, joking did not come easily to Timothy. He took himself far too seriously. In his Harvard diary (1798–1801), where he articulated his ambitions and goaded himself with noble resolutions and self-rebukes, he recognized his social ineptitude. He chided himself for his pride and his fear of losing his dignity and yearned to appear to the world as an amiable fellow.[7]

He seems never to have accomplished this, but he did achieve another ambition: success in the great world. In 1813, twelve years after he graduated from college, he was elected to the Massachusetts Senate, and in 1817, when he was thirty-nine, he was elevated to the Congress of the United States. Education was the key to success in the new country that had become independent during his boyhood, and he intended to pass on to his children the reliable virtues of self-discipline, hard work, and devotion to study that had brought about his rise in the world.

His own childhood had not been as secure as the one he hoped to provide for his offspring. Born in exile on an offshore island where his father preached throughout the New England phase of the Revolution, at the age of five he returned with the family to Princeton. But after a few months the Fullers moved again. This time, his father, who had studied law on his own during the Martha's Vineyard years, decided to sue the town of Princeton for his back pay and argue for his reinstatement. During the months that Timothy Sr. engaged in this pursuit, he settled his family in Middleton where his great-grandfather, Thomas Fuller, his first American forebear, had built a house near the Mill Pond in 1638. This temporary home was conveniently near Salem, the seat of the Supreme Judicial Court of the Commonwealth. The effort not only failed but Fuller was ordered to pay the trial's expenses. Not surprised by the outcome, he paid the sum and took his family back to Princeton. Except for a few calls to fill empty pulpits for short periods in remote parts of New England, he was deprived for the rest of his life of his vocation. But his trained mind and strong character were recognized by his neighbors when he was elected in 1788 as the town's delegate to the state convention for the ratification of the Constitution. There he demonstrated again his independence from majority opinion when he voted against the document because it recognized slavery. In 1796 he once more uprooted his family and moved to farmland in Merrimack, New Hampshire, where he died after a long illness in 1805.[8]

A 1790 diary kept by Elizabeth Fuller, the family's third daughter, when she was fifteen hints that the Fuller children grew up with a shared resentment of Princeton's treatment of their father. That the matter rankled to the end is evident in the sermon preached at Timothy Sr.'s funeral in 1805 where his fortitude in the shadow of an unjust humiliation is praised as a Christian virtue. It is not difficult to suppose that Timothy Jr. was motivated strongly to erase any suggestion of dishonor from the family name.[9]

He was a model son, postponing college until the Merrimack farm was established and taking jobs as a schoolteacher during all his vacations. A member of Phi Beta Kappa, he graduated second in his class; he always thought that he would have been first if he had not participated in a student riot in his junior year. After graduation, he spent a year as a schoolteacher, helping to raise money for the education of his younger brothers. While at college he had become a confirmed Jeffersonian, a decision that several of his close friends viewed as unnecessarily rash at a time when most members of the educated classes were expected to be Federalists, but Timothy Jr.'s allegiance proved fortunate. In 1803 he began reading law in the Worcester offices of Levi Lincoln, the leading Jeffersonian in the state—during Jefferson's first term, Lincoln served as attorney general of the United States and was secretary of state at the end of the second term. By the time Timothy Jr. opened his own office on Court Street in

Boston in 1805, he had already connected himself to the network of Jeffersonian Democratic Republicans in the Commonwealth, and the party was beginning to gain ground.[10]

During the last two months of his father's final illness he spent half his time by his father's bedside reading sermons, and for four years thereafter he devoted himself to the fatherless family, showing special concern for his youngest brother, Elisha, who was only eleven when his father died. During the same period, Timothy Jr. extended his legal business, developed his political skills, and became a sought-after orator for patriotic occasions. By the time he fell in love with Margarett Crane in 1809, his brothers Henry and William were Harvard undergraduates; another brother, Abraham, was settled in a lucrative business career; three of his sisters—Deborah, Nancy, and Martha—were married; and Elisha was seriously parsing Virgil. Timothy was almost thirty-one when he felt free to marry. A few months after the wedding, Timothy bought a fine, three-story, Federal-style house on Cherry Street in Cambridgeport for $6,000, a sizable sum. It was close enough to the bridge that led to his Court Street office across the river in Boston that he could walk to work in less than an hour. On May 23, 1810, a year after the wedding, Margarett Crane Fuller gave birth to their first child. Timothy named her Sarah Margaret after his mother and his wife, but later on, when the child was nine and on her way to developing a strong identity, she insisted on dropping the Sarah and being called "Margaret alone."[11]

During Margaret Fuller's early childhood, she was surrounded with love and affection. Her parents doted on her and were in love with each other. "Yours with *romantick* & unreasonable & unalterable affection" was the way Timothy signed a letter to his wife in their sixth year of marriage. On their eighth wedding anniversary, Margarett Crane Fuller wrote her husband, "I would run ten times as far to see you now as you say I did eight years ago." In honor of his daughter's birth, Timothy was said to have planted the three elm trees that stood in front of the Cherry Street house for over a century and a half. "I long to embrace my *pair* of M[argaret]s," he wrote his wife when their daughter was six months old. During the winter months of separation when Timothy served in Congress, he suggested that they consecrate their affection with a special ritual. "Hereafter we can appoint a certain hour of every Sabbath to employ ourselves in reading the same book and passages in the bible. We shall then experience a livelier sympathy, than the lovers, who fixed on the same hour to gaze at the moon."[12]

The commodious Cambridgeport house had space for a large family, and there were constant visits from aunts, uncles, and cousins and frequent buggy rides across the fields to visit the Cranes in Canton. Over the years that country village became a second home. When Margaret was two and a half, a sister, Julia Adelaide, was born. Fourteen months later, when the baby died, a gloom descended over the household that remained with Margaret as her first memory, all the more striking because the happy household was transformed into a house of sorrow, of pulled curtains and whispering relatives and long-faced callers. Later in life, when Margaret felt overburdened and discouraged, she fantasized how growing up with a sister close in age would have cushioned her role as the eldest daughter. Grief for herself lay at the heart of her recollection of her sister's death many years later. "This has made a vast difference in my lot," she wrote at age thirty, only hinting at the store of self-pity that sometimes overwhelmed her after her father's death. If she had been able to share the burden with Julia Adelaide, Margaret believed, her life would have taken "a gentler and more gradual course."[13]

For the two years following Julia Adelaide's death, Margarett Crane Fuller suffered a period of delicate health. Looking back, she remembered how much she enjoyed being with Margaret at this time, taking pleasure in her "intelligence, rich fancy, buoyant spirits, and extreme activity." From the first, Margaret's "superior intelligence, and ready invention" were evident. She loved reading, riding, gathering flowers, and "singing with feeling expression," and was noticeably adept at imitating unusual sounds. There was one other characteristic that Margaret's mother noticed: "At this early age she showed great sensitivity to reproof not so much as tears shed at the time, but silent reserve. Nothing like obstinacy do I ever remember, but a determination to examine the reasons of restraint or rebuke, and when not convinced acting according to her convictions when not acted upon by affection."[14]

By the age of five, Margaret had blossomed into a beautiful little girl. James Freeman Clarke, who was to become one of her most intimate friends, remembers visiting the Cherry Street house at this time and being met by a "joyful child, with light flowing locks and bright face, who led me by the hand down the back-steps of her house into the garden."[15]

Although Margaret was to leave behind a vivid trail of responses to her father's role in her life, she was relatively reticent about her mother. This has led most biographers to portray Margaret as very much her father's child. But running beneath the surface of her self-revelations is evidence that her close identification with her mother in her early years created a deeply embedded realm of sympathy and understanding that not only countered the impact of her father's strict training but laid the groundwork for her later preoccupation with the position of women in the new republic. One sparse phrase in the bare paragraph she wrote about her mother in her "Autobiographical Romance" hints at her approval of the streak of independence in her mother that sometimes disrupted the family harmony. "[A] creature not to be shaped into a merely useful instrument," she added to the description that would otherwise have read as an encomium to a perfect model of the true, self-denying woman of the period.[16]

An identification with mothering itself was Fuller's most obvious inheritance. For many years before she had a child of her own, she yearned for motherhood and adopted a maternal relationship with students and friends, even encouraging one to call her "Mother." Most of the men she loved had characteristics considered feminine according to the gender prescriptions of the time. And when she finally chose a lover, she noted with satisfaction that he had a temperament very like her mother.

Associating her "flower-like" mother with growing flowers, preserving seeds, and turning wild spaces into cultivated gardens, she portrayed her as a woman of unfettered nature, a prelapsarian Eve, unburdened with the anguished self-awareness that constantly threatened her own peace of mind. "Of all the persons whom I have known, she had in her most of . . . that spontaneous love of every living thing, for man, and beast, and tree, which restores the golden age." When Fuller in later years experimented with a literary genre she called her "flower-pieces," she explained that these attempts to reach and express hidden, feminine sources in her psyche through flower symbolism could be traced to the "connexion" with flowers she had inherited from her mother. "She has the love, I the interpretation," she explained.[17]

Margarett Crane Fuller was fiercely loyal to her husband, but she did admit in writing of Margaret's childhood that "[h]er Father's habit had always been implicit obedience to parents and in all essentials he required this of her." It was just about the time Julia Adelaide died, when Margaret was three and half, that her father began teaching her to read and write. At four and a half, he began to drill her in arithmetic. On the first of January, 1815, he wrote in his diary:

enjoy myself in my family with my wife and our little Sarah Margaret, who is now four & a half years old, and reads tolerably in any common book. I have lately purchased for her Miss Edgeworth's "Parent's Assistant" which she reads & understands the stories in a very great degree. I have devoted some time this morning to teaching her the figures/digits which had not before been taught.[18]

The birth of Margaret's first brother, Eugene, in May 1815, just before her fifth birthday, brought an end to Margaret's close relationship with her mother. Now her father introduced English and Latin grammar simultaneously. A year later, she was translating simple passages from Virgil. Timothy was proud of her quickness and enjoyed showing her off and boasting of "my *promising* and *precocious* daughter." In early childhood, reading became for her "a habit and a passion," and her most available comfort and escape.[19]

Beginning reading and writing at an early age and even starting Latin instruction at six were not unusual at the time, not only in the college town of Cambridge but in many parts of the country. Margaret's biographer, Thomas Wentworth Higginson, who was a Fuller family friend, drew attention to this practice in his reminiscences. He remarked that his sister began to read at three and that on his own sixth birthday he received a note from the daughter of a professor who wrote: "I am glad you are six years old. I shall be four in March."[20]

By the time Fuller looked back on her childhood, she had suffered enough losses to need to cast blame somewhere for what seemed in the retrospective light of thirty to be a betrayal. Her notable success in following her father's educational regime had failed to yield the expected result, a secure and favored place in an ordered republican society. As a convinced Jeffersonian, Timothy Fuller believed that for the first time in history virtue and talent were to be rewarded and sanctioned by a national government. By the time he took his daughter in hand, he had paid his dues for membership in Jefferson's natural aristocracy; his years of virtuous self-denial were already rewarding him with public office and the promise of honor and wealth. To qualify Margaret to continue in the high rank he had earned for her as a daughter of the republic, she was to be carefully trained from early childhood. "My love to the little Sarah Margaret," he wrote when she was three. "I love her if she is a good girl." A year later he sent his love and added, "She must be goodnatured & learn to read, & sing when desired." This was the refrain that continued even when she had graduated to the college textbooks he had used at Harvard. When she was ten, he offered to buy her a piano if she would promise to excel in it. "To excel in all things should be your constant aim," he wrote; "mediocrity is obscurity."[21]

Another brother, William Henry, was born in the summer of 1817, but the most important change in Margaret's life that year came in the fall when her father was elected as representative to the United States Congress from the Middlesex district of Massachusetts. For the next eight years, from the time Margaret was seven until she was fifteen, her father spent four to six months of every year in Washington, D.C.

During the first winter Timothy was in Washington, the Fuller family stayed with the Cranes in Canton, but thereafter, during the winter, the Cambridge-port house was a house of women and small children. "You known, dear Timo, how difficult it is to manage one woman," his wife wrote. "I have the care of three." She called herself "Lady F. at the head of the Rt. Hon. T. Fuller's Establishment." Abby, her musical sister, who ran a singing school in Canton, was the most constant and best-loved of the winter guests. One winter, Elizabeth Jones Weiser Crane was ill and came with Abby so she would be assured of good care. During several winters, Timothy's unmarried sisters, Sarah and Elizabeth, were imported to help with the children's education in Timothy's absence, but they were less popular. Margarett Crane Fuller complained that Elizabeth, who was the children's arithmetic teacher, was "obstinate" and "refractory," and Margaret thought she tattled on family members to Timothy. Other frequent visitors were the Boston families of Margarett Crane Fuller's stepsister, Nancy Weiser Kuhn, and Timothy's sister, Martha Fuller Whittier.[22]

By the time Timothy left for Washington, his brother Henry had finished

Harvard and law school and had joined Timothy in the Court Street law office. Since Timothy did not trust Margarett Crane Fuller with financial responsibilities, he charged Henry and another brother, the businessman Abraham, with overseeing his family's expenses. This arrangement caused many quarrels in the Cherry Street house while Timothy was away. Margarett Crane Fuller complained that her brothers-in-law often came to sit by her fire all evening and then would accuse her of spending too much money for firewood. Even though Margaret was to remember later the tediousness of these "petty conflicts," she grew up in the midst of a close-knit clan; most of the members were self-assertive, argumentative, and vitally responsive to one another. In her later life she was attracted to similarly independent people and challenged them to responsiveness and vigorous interaction. By the time Margaret was growing up in Cambridge, her father and his brothers were establishing a family reputation in Cambridge that was not entirely favorable. While it was conceded that Fullers were gifted, energetic, and impressively knowledgeable, they were known to be opinionated, pushing, and "without a particle of tact."[23]

Because the four fireplaces in the Cherry Street house provided the only heat during the winter nights, Margaret slept with her mother. Often the maid—at first, Betsy, and later, Hannah—slept with them too, and the other children slept in the same room in trundle beds. Almost every two years another baby was born: Eugene was five and William Henry three when Ellen Kilshaw Fuller was born in 1820; she was followed by Arthur Buckminster in 1822 and Richard Frederick in 1824. By 1826 and 1828, when James Lloyd and Edward Breck were born, Margaret had another room. Along with learning Latin and rhetoric and memorizing chronologies, Margaret grew up with the care of young children. Like her mother, who was once described by a friend as "apt to get into raptures when speaking of children," Margaret was always fond of them and had years of experience in the Fuller home school before she took up teaching as her first career.[24]

During Timothy's long absences, he was by no means forgotten in the Cambridgeport household. During his first few winters away, he wrote home every day and required daily replies. He ordered his wife's letters to be dated and numbered, and he liked them to contain descriptions of everyone in the family as they appeared in the parlor in the evening when they sat together while she wrote her daily letter to him and read his letters to all assembled. The paternal voice in the letters was authoritative but affectionate, solicitous, and caring. Enclosing small gifts for the children—dandelions, almonds, raisins, and even cake from the president's levee—he drew pictures of lips kissing and tears falling to express his affection. He had a soft heart too for the ragged children on the muddy roads of Washington who begged from the congressmen all winter. In seeing them as society's responsibility, he was ahead of his time. "The want of education in national religion and industry is the greatest source of vice, want and misery," he wrote. "Society might avert these evils in a great mission, and is therefore justly charged with the fatal consequences of its own passive indolence."[25]

But when he thought his authority at home was being threatened, he could turn sarcastic. In the spring of 1820 when Margarett Crane Fuller made plans to go to Canton to help nurse her ailing father, leaving the children at home in the care of one of his sisters and the housemaid, Timothy asked her if she was considering giving up housekeeping and expressed shock that she would contemplate such a radical action without his "request or consent." When he forbade her another such visit in the winter of 1821, she answered coolly that she would accept his "advice," even though she was longing to see her parents and wanted to help her "good sister" who had been long confined to the household. Shame was another tactic. "Shall I go home and leave the field of battle while my colleagues remain in the ranks of their country?" he asked, when she complained of his long absences. "Answer me, like Cato's daughter and the Wife of Brutus."[26]

Impressed with the important figures he met in Congress and the foreign dignitaries in the diplomatic corps who entertained him, Representative Fuller sent home tantalizing descriptions of the official social world of which he was now a part: Eliza Monroe, the president's wife, gave a splendid party opening the new White House, rebuilt after the British burned it during the War of 1812. During a stopover in New York, he had met the authors James Fenimore Cooper and Catharine Sedgwick. Once he spent an evening with the controversial feminist, Frances Wright. He envied Henry Clay's powerful oratory and admired the cautious intelligence of the secretary of state, John Quincy Adams.

Although Timothy spent most of his free time in Washington in a dreary boardinghouse and his moments in the presence of the famous were only fleeting, his cautious awe of life in high places was so abundantly clear that Margaret could not help feeling the lure of celebrity. She met only one person during her childhood who struck her as an inhabitant of the desirable world of beauty and self-assurance that fascinated her father and that was portrayed in many of the books she was reading. Ellen Kilshaw was a young Englishwoman, the daughter of a Liverpool manufacturer, who came to stay with friends in Cambridgeport for a few months in 1817. Her beauty, her elegant clothing and crisp accent, but above all her Englishness impressed all the Fullers. When she came to call at the Cherry Street house for the first time, Margaret was overwhelmed with shyness and hid. But Ellen made a pet of her, treated her as a personage with a unique personality and intelligence, and when she returned to England left behind the aura of a lady of style and sensitivity.

The Fullers solidified the Kilshaw friendship with a lively correspondence and the hope that one of Timothy's brothers would marry her: Timothy writing in the voice of a sophisticated man of affairs; Margarett Crane as a devoted mother and wife, somewhat piqued at her husband's interest in Kilshaw; and Margaret as an enthralled admirer of the family's one European contact and friend. Later Margaret would trace to Ellen Kilshaw her first experience of a galvanizing friendship and the first that would personify the "modern European influences" that she would cultivate and promote in her later life. The contrast between a woman like Ellen Kilshaw and "the shrewd, honest eye, the homely decency," of the New England villagers of Cambridgeport led Margaret to yearn for a broader life than seemed to be in store for her.[27]

Life in the Port, as everyone called Cambridgeport, did not provide much variety or excitement. When Timothy bought the Cherry Street house in 1809, the Craigie Bridge from Lechmere Point to Boston had just been finished, and there was a prospect that the area, which was situated across from the Boston docks, would develop into an independent port city like Hoboken. Early in the century, developers brought in gravel to fill the marshes and began building a network of wharves and canals, laying roads, and subdividing the huckleberry patches into a gridwork of housing lots. In 1805, when the United States Congress declared Cambridge an official port of entry, the Cambridgeport Proprietors, as the developers called themselves, built a meetinghouse and a school, fenced off a burial ground, and bought a fire engine. But the Embargo Act of 1807 and the War of 1812 brought shipping to a halt in Boston. By the time the war was over, the dream of a second shipping center was doomed. Grass was beginning to grow in the streets; wharves were rotting under heaps of kelp; only a few curriers made use of the canals; and the single vessel tethered at Cambridgeport was a wide-bottomed sloop that Harvard College sent down to the state of Maine to bring back firewood. During Margaret's childhood years, the Port developed into a drowsy commercial suburb of produce warehouses, lumberyards, and factories.[28]

Kept busy at home most of the time and not allowed to play in the surrounding marshland with the neighborhood children, Margaret grew up conscientious and self-conscious. The first winter Timothy was in Washington, Margarett Crane Fuller noticed that Margaret was "awkward in company" and suspected that "reading so many books and fragments of books enfeebles her mind." She was tall for her age, and by the time she was eight people were beginning to treat her as if she were much older. When she was nine, she wrote her father: "I want to ask you a question. Whether my manners ought to increase with my growth or with my years. Mamma says people will judge of me according to my growth. I do not think this is just for surely our knowledge does not increase because we are tall."[29]

If Margaret was making a veiled bid here for her father to lessen his demands and remember that she was still a child in spite of her size and accomplishments, she had cause. As her brothers grew older, his letters abounded in pleasurable references to their antics while she was continually exhorted to greater responsibility and maturity. Guilt about his long absences may have played its part in Timothy Fuller's steady stream of Franklinesque maxims and Enlightenment advice. The barrage increased after Margarett Crane Fuller reported in the late winter of 1819 that her greatest "sin of omission" during his absence was neglect of their daughter's "disposition and the cultivation of her mind."[30]

A complex relationship was developing between father and daughter. "She says she hopes yet to be *all* that we wish her to be," her mother wrote in the same letter in which she regretted her neglect. With the understanding that the family's status and future hopes depended on Timothy Fuller's prominence and ambition, the family structure was geared to his long absences. From the nation's capital he sent his daily decrees governing even the minutest details of household management. Margaret, having entered the family romance with the need to view her father as a god on the domestic scale, had seen him elevated from her tutor and mentor to a worldly power carrying great weight in the small world around her. The colorful world brought to life in the evening rituals of letter reading in the parlor held an inviting promise—that they might all participate in such a world someday.[31]

During Timothy's absences, his brothers were instructed to hear Margaret's lessons once or twice a week, but that plan never worked out with any consistency. After exhausting the books in Timothy's library—the French political philosophers, Shakespeare, Cervantes, Molière, Smollett, and Fielding—she borrowed books from neighbors and friends and from the local lending library. When she developed a taste for novels, Timothy, who disapproved of "mere narrative" and wanted to restrict her diet to history, travel, biography, ordered that she ask for permission every time she was tempted. Although she tried to obey, her appetite was far too ravenous to wait upon the mail.[32]

During Timothy's months back home, he would assign her a daily lesson, and she would prepare to recite for him in the evening regardless of the hour. Expected to "give the thoughts in as few well-arranged words as possible, and without breaks or hesitation," she was continually kept on her mettle. Her father's stern demands and lack of patience, and her anxiety to satisfy his "high standard," kept her "on the stretch" and often exhausted her. In the process Margaret developed a well-stored mind, a remarkable facility with the spoken word and with foreign languages, and the exhilarating sense that she was very alive under tension. Later she would come to regard complacency or self-satisfaction of any kind—in religion and politics, in personal relations, and in the habits of daily life—as a kind of moral delinquency.[33]

In the summer of 1809, when the Reverend Abiel Holmes, the pastor of the Congregational Church in Old Cambridge, the settlement surrounding Harvard College, joined with a group of Harvard professors to start a day school in Cambridgeport with a Harvard graduate as the master, Timothy decided to send Margaret and Eugene.

The Port School, as it came to be called, offered little change in Margaret's educational program. Its advantage for her was that Edwards Dickinson, the master, would correct her themes and translations on a regular basis and hear her recitations when he had time. The Port School met on the second floor of a building around the block from the Fullers' Cherry Street house. A one-room school with the boys' benches facing the girls' benches, there was a wide disparity in the ages of the seventeen children in the entering class. At five, Richard Henry Dana, who would later gain fame as the author of *Two Years before the Mast*, was, along with Eugene, one of the youngest scholars. Margaret's contemporaries included her neighbor Harriet Fay, a dainty blonde beauty whom everyone admired for her ladylike charms, and Abiel Holmes's son, Oliver Wendell.

Some people said later that Oliver Wendell Holmes (his friends called him Wendell) modeled the title character of his novel *Elsie Venner* after Margaret. If so, during his school days at least, he did not see her as a heroine. He thought she was nice-looking, but she was taller than he was and acted so superior, in his estimation, that he took a dislike to her. Later in life, he guessed that he was probably "jealous" of her and "never did her quite justice. It began when we were children," he explained. "We used to go to school together, and she got ahead of me." She came to the school with the reputation for "being smart," he wrote later, and the trouble started when she used the word "trite" in one of her compositions. "Alas! I did not know what *trite* meant. How could I ever judge Margaret fairly after such a crushing discovery of her superiority?" He made fun of her mannerisms and her appearance—her virago temper when she rushed to the defense of a mistreated schoolmate, and "the aqua-marine lustre" in her eyes, and "her long, flexile neck, arching and undulating in strange undulating movements which one who loved her would compare to a swan, and those who loved her not to the ophidian who tempted our common mother."[34]

For "being smart," Margaret was forced to face ridicule frequently in her life. Although she learned to face it down, she never became thick-skinned. When she was ten, her mother found among "little scraps of her writing" a note that she preserved: "On the 23rd of May 1810 was born one foredoomed to sorrow and pain and like others to have misfortunes. She had feeling which few have and which is the source of SORROW Is to everyone who possesses it."[35]

A few months after Margaret started going to the Port School, she added a postscript to a letter to her father: "I do not like Sarah, call me Margaret alone, pray do!" Expressing annoyance at her suggestion, Timothy replied that the change would require "an act of the General Court" and would be "disrespectful & unkind" to his mother. But Margaret persisted with everyone outside the family. "If you ever write to me leave out that name Sarah," she wrote her friend Mary Vose a few months later: "Out upon it I will not be content to be called by it till I am sixty years old Then I will take it for it is a proper, good, old maidish name. I will be willing to sit down and knit stockings look cross and be called Miss Sarah Fuller for the rest of my life."[36]

There is a double irony in the fact that at the time Timothy Fuller refused his daughter's request to call her "Margaret alone" he was reading the book that above all others available to him at the time ought to have sensitized him to his daughter's drive to establish her individuality. On January 22, 1820, he wrote his wife, "I have been reading a part of Mary Wollstonecraft's 'Rights of Women' & am so well pleased with it that if I find nothing more exceptional than what I have yet seen, I will purchase it for you. It will tend to give us some very sensible & just views of education." One irony is that the book, *A Vindication of the Rights of Woman*, which shocked Britain with its radical views when it was published in 1792, led him to worry lest Margaret's education had neglected "a knowledge of household affairs, sewing etc."[37] Wollstonecraft had argued that equal education and status for women were not only a personal benefit to which every individual had an inherent right but one that would benefit the future of the race indirectly, because most women, as wives and mothers, influenced the rising generation in incalculable ways. It was probably this secondary argument that caught Timothy's attention, because, soon afterward, he geared Margaret's education to the usual one for young women in comfortable circumstances based on the probability that she would be married by the time she was twenty and the hope that she would make a good match.

But a greater irony is that Wollstonecraft had written her book in response to the news that in the aftermath of the French Revolution the French government was planning to reorganize the French educational system along democratic lines but without including women in the program. Yet in the United States thirty years later, without particular regard to Wollstonecraft, her argument put forth to focus attention on women's importance to republican society had become commonplace; it fit so completely the needs and aspirations of the new society that it had altered fundamentally the position of women in America. One of the hallmarks of the new republican middle class of America was its view that women were "the principal civilizing agents in a new and raw society" and the guardians of decency and virtue. By putting woman on a pedestal and creating an idealized role for her, the new society had turned Wollstonecraft's reasoning on its head.[38]

As an enlightened man with genteel aspirations, the prevailing attitude toward women worked to temper Timothy Fuller's inbred patriarchalism. He usually treated the women in his family with kindness, and at times showered his wife with husbandly love, but his didactic rationalism could not cede any claim to moral superiority in the family, nor did he believe that women should be treated with particular delicacy. When Margarett Crane Fuller announced her pregnancy by writing that she was "suffering other qualms than those of conscience," he scoffed at her modesty. "[W]hy should you be more fastidious than the Princess Charlotte or the Duchess of Berrè—whose condition is announced with triumph to the whole nation?"[39]

Timothy's aim was to form Margaret into the ideal woman of the ideal republic. He now wrote: "*All* accomplishments, & the whole circle of the virtues & graces should be your constant aim, my dear child." He fussed about her shortsightedness and badgered her not to blink her eyes when she entered a room. Her mother was instructed to help her learn to dance properly, to point her toes and hold out her dress. To improve her posture, Timothy recommended the technique that had produced the "remarkably straight and well formed" daughters of his Washington friend, Major Boberdeau; they were trained to march around the house beating drums harnessed over their shoulders so as to hold their heads back. She had drawing lessons, pianoforte lessons, singing and penmanship instructions. Her mother showed far better sense than Timothy at this time. Margarett Crane Fuller wrote him in December 1820 that their constant attention to Margaret's appearance was making her so self-conscious that she had become "unwilling to expose herself." One had to show good judgment "in mixing encouragement and disapprobation in the education of children," she counseled him. "I see in Sarah M. much to be proud of & much to correct, but I wish above all things to preserve her confidence & affection & not appear to be a severe judge, but a judicious *tender* mother to her and each of our children." She wrote him proudly that at a recent party Margaret was called "very handsome," that she had lately spent a Sunday in town tutoring a family friend, Mr. Balch, in French pronunciation, and that Dr. Abiel Holmes had spoken "in very flattering terms" to her of Margaret's "talents and acquirements in literature."[40]

In spite of the attention that her father showered on her, Margaret wrote later that she always felt deprived of his love. "When I recollect how deep the anguish, how deeper still the want, with which I walked alone in hours of childish passion, and called for a Father often saying the Word a thousand times till it was stifled by sobs, how great seems the duty that name imposes," she wrote a friend later.[41] This complaint, coupled with the superficial facts of the Fuller family configuration, could lead, as it has, to the Freudian explanation of an unresolved Electra or Oedipus complex that drove her development well into her adulthood. But the plot of Margaret Fuller's affective life is complex, and she has left behind only accidental and much mutilated evidence. That a constant and passionate search for intimacy with both men and women was an overriding force in her psyche is clear. That she became a woman with a strong libido and sense of purpose is also evident. She herself was continually probing the source of her energies and trying to give them a name.

In her "Autobiographical Romance" she makes two seemingly unrelated comments that may set the pattern in the carpet. "He hoped to make me the heir of all he knew," she wrote by way of putting a gloss of generosity on her father's martinet methods.[42] If Timothy was unconsciously viewing her as a son and heir or, more subtly, if she had come to view herself in that role, the father–daughter relationship could take on an abnormal weight. If her father unconsciously thought of her as an extension of himself or as a son, he would not be able to express affection in the terms a daughter would solicit from him. And if she, in compliance with such expectations, responded like a son while hoping to win the right to be a daughter, the relationship could settle into a course that would explain why Margaret could never feel she was getting enough love from her father and why her father, expecting her to equal his attainments and even surpass them, could never express to her the kind of father–daughter love she needed since he was never satisfied with himself.

If this pattern helps explain some of the later emotional problems of Margaret's life, notably the perplexities of coming to terms with what she viewed as the male impulses in her nature, another comment on her father's emotional life may provide corroboration. "In the more delicate and individual relations, he never approached but two mortals, my mother and myself," she wrote, staking a claim of intimacy with him equal to her mother's and excluding the outside world.[43] If she felt herself designated to provide the intellectual companionship her mother was unable to provide, to be a surrogate for qualities her mother lacked, that could further complicate her situation.

In her fictionalized and speculative "Autobiographical Romance," Margaret analyzed her relation to her parents in terms of a sharp duality. Her father represented "available intellect" and "that coarse but wearable stuff woven by the ages,—Common Sense," whereas her "natural bias" of character, which she described as "fervent, of strong-grasp, and disposed to infatuation, and self-forgetfulness," found its expression in daydreams and imaginative journeys in her mother's secluded garden. Here she liked to fancy herself a royal foundling and a future queen. Later, when she became engrossed in romantic concepts while still searching for her father in herself, she studied theories of the androgyne and the Isis myth for possible sources of feminine power and capability. Later still, she looked outward and found the source of her discontent in the arrangements of society. But throughout her life she pursued these questions and many others with restless energy and a determined drive.[44]

Rebellion was brewing in the Cherry Street household during the winter of 1820–21. "I am wholly at a loss how to manage S. Margaret," her mother wrote her father in November. "She is so impertinent." She described Margaret's continual teasing to go off on her own to Boston when she was needed at home. Two months later, she reported that Margaret turned up her lip whenever anyone called her "a child." Timothy responded by threatening to send Margaret to work in a factory if she did not behave. Her mother wrote that the threat brought on a flood of tears. Margarett Crane Fuller was restless and moody herself at this time, and mother and daughter were probably reacting to one another. Soon after Timothy left for Washington in the fall of 1820, his wife wrote that she did not intend "to be left behind again" and added, "I have long thought that the constant care of children narrowed the mind." A new baby— named after Ellen Kilshaw—had been born in August. Soon afterward Hannah, the maid, left, and Margarett Crane Fuller wrote that she could "scarcely find time" to write letters. She promised to take care of the house like a "faithful steward" but threatened, "I intend some time to leave you in the same situation I am placed in just to see how much real patience and philosophy you possess."[45]

During his three years in Congress, Timothy had not made much of a mark. "I am rather too indolent or unenterprising for the slight skirmishes," he wrote to his wife, "& the great questions require too much trouble and thought." Three of his speeches had been published and praised. They all took humane positions on important issues. He opposed an early law requiring extradition of fugitive slaves; he deplored the inhumanity of the Seminole War; and he opposed the Missouri Compromise, insisting that no compromise was possible on the evil of slavery. He had not drafted any important legislation, but he was now on the Naval Committee and in line to be chairman. This gave him a measure of social status in Washington, and his prospering legal business made it possible for him to buy a carriage and to outfit Margarett Crane Fuller for a Washington social season.[46]

The Crane relatives in Canton agreed to take care of the younger children during the winter of 1821–22, and Margarett Crane Fuller began making arrangements for Margaret to attend a boarding school in Jamaica Plain, which Margaret described as a school for improvement "in elegant accomplishments."[47] But Timothy, in an about-face, without notifying either Margaret or her mother, had his brother Henry enroll Margaret in the Boston Lyceum for Young Ladies, the girls' school with the most demanding curriculum in Boston where the privileged families of Boston had been sending their daughters for over a decade. Margaret's second cousin, Susan Williams, was a student there and had impressed Margaret with her enthusiasm for Dr. Park's School, as it was called. After Margaret started in September 1821, she had a long walk to and from the school on Beacon Hill's Mount Vernon Street every day until mid-November, when her parents left for Washington and she moved into the Boston home of her father's sister, Aunt Martha Fuller Whittier.

For the next year and a half, Margaret had an education comparable to the best preparatory programs available to young men. The curriculum covered Latin, French, Italian, ancient and modern history, geometry and trigonometry, natural history, and geography. The school's headmaster, Dr. John Park, used a classroom reward system that he found brought results. Each week the student who had consistently excelled in each class received a medal; twenty-one medals won for a scholar an Eye of Intelligence, the school's highest honor.

In December Margaret wrote her parents that she hoped she would have the Eye before their return in April.[48]

She was disappointed when her cousin, the only student she knew beforehand, fell ill and could not continue. All the other girls seemed to be "sisters." She felt left out and wrote her mother, "[I]t is hard for me to stand unconnected; and all girls who have no intimate friends are not so much beloved."[49]

She could not admit to her parents that she had become the butt of teasing by a clique of city girls who ridiculed her country mannerisms, her awkwardness, her shortsightedness, her arch way of talking, her plain clothes, and her eagerness to excel in her schoolwork. Later, it was thought by some that the "petty persecutions" of her schoolmates honed the "formidable" wit and the "indiscriminate sarcasms" with which she met attacks for several years afterward. One of her lifelong friends thought that the experience laid the groundwork for her book *Woman in the Nineteenth Century,* because she then felt the insults, "and laid up for future reflection, how large a place in woman's world is given to fashion and frivolity." But an examination of the hundreds of family letters exchanged between Washington and Cambridge during her childhood would indicate that she had appropriated and honed to her own style the system of verbal aggression and defense of the Fuller family. She herself would admit frankly in her twenties that she had been insufferable during her adolescence. But this confession came some years after she had passed through her teens when her only defense was her stubborn pride.[50]

She could no more complain to her parents than she could give satisfaction to her tormentors. She had been bred to the Roman virtues—"The Will, the Resolve of Man!"—and she refused to give quarter. As she wrote later to a friend who hurt her feelings, "I take my natural position always, and the more I see, the more I feel that it is regal.—Without throne, sceptre, or guards, still a queen!"[51]

Her bravura did not win many friends, but it kept up her courage, and she needed that through her stormy adolescence.

CHAPTER 2

I am determined on distinction.

A Varied Education

MARGARETT Crane Fuller's social season in Washington lasted only a few weeks. On December 8, 1821, Peter Crane died in Canton, and when the news reached Washington a week later, Timothy was tempted to delay telling his wife, so she could enjoy a reception at the home of the French minister, M. Hyde de Neuville. But the loss of her father and the worrisome news that followed soon after—that Eugene and William Henry had come down with measles—sent Margarett Crane Fuller back to Canton. During the New Year recess Timothy accompanied her home, and as she was pregnant with her sixth child she stayed in Canton through the winter before moving back to Cambridge where Margaret rejoined the family and resumed her daily trudge over the bridge to school in Boston.

Timothy continued to supervise Margaret's welfare. During her stay in Boston, he wrote his sister Martha that he wanted her to be sure that Margaret had stout boots, that she rode to school in a hansom cab in bad weather, and that she always had a fire in her room in the evenings. She was sharing a bedroom with her Grandmother Fuller who had rarely visited in Cambridgeport, so the arrangement gave Margaret a chance to know her father's mother, who had continued to live at the Merrimack farm year-round until her old age. Sarah Williams Fuller was suffering what was to be her final illness; she died in March 1822.

Margaret's school day lasted from nine until two, and homework assignments required several more hours of home study. In spite of her proficiency in Latin and her eagerness to learn, she had never before followed a balanced curriculum geared to her level; she had to study hard to excel, especially in those subjects in which she had not had steady instruction, such as geography, history, Italian, and French. Before becoming an educator, Dr. Park had served as a naval medical doctor in Haiti and spoke French fluently. Learning French and Italian from him at this time gave her a firm background in two of the languages that would be important in her later work when, as literary editor of the *New-York Daily Tribune,* she undertook to introduce European literature to American readers.[1]

At dancing school on winter afternoons Margaret found relief from competition. Cotillions, gavottes, garlands of two, three, and twelve, and country dances of all kinds were favored by all classes. Dance evenings with light suppers were the commonest social entertainment in Boston and Cambridge. Family groups of all ages attended, and Margaret enjoyed the exercise and conviviality immensely.

In December 1822, when Margaret had been at Dr. Park's School for a year and a half, Timothy decided that she must change schools. The apparent reason was that her eyes, which had troubled her for the last year, had become painful. (She was shortsighted, but eyeglasses were not yet generally in use.) She was to transfer to the Port School where she could study at her own pace and where she could look after Eugene and William Henry.

When Timothy announced his decision, he warned her to be careful not to give Dr. Park the impression that the move implied any "dissatisfaction" on his part, and she was to be "prudent" and "a little reserved" when she entered the Port School, and "by no means display your attainments and incur dislike." Although Dr. Park had previously told Margarett Crane Fuller that he had never had a student of Margaret's achievements, he did not single her out when she left but took the occasion of her departure and that of another student to combine "fine compliments" with "advice" about religion and conduct through life.[2]

At twelve, Margaret was showing signs of an adolescent willfulness and tactlessness that had begun to worry her parents, her aunts, and her uncles. Soon after she left Dr. Park's School, her father gave her permission to hold a ball at the Cherry Street house so as to cement her school friendships. With great anticipation she set about planning her party for January 15, 1823. She sent out ninety invitations, but by the evening of the twelfth, she had only a handful of acceptances. Even the help of her popular Uncle Elisha, who acted as master of ceremonies and caller of the complex cotillion steps, failed to save the evening. A few days later her mother described the party as "well-over." The weather had been bad that night; many guests sent their regrets, and several merely failed to come, but, according to Frederic Henry Hedge, whose sister was present, the basic cause of the disaster was Margaret's behavior—she "gave great offence" by playing up to her Boston schoolmates to the "indignation of her little world of Cambridge." Because of this display of favoritism, Margaret was "sent to Coventry for a time," and only his sister Mary would speak to her, Hedge said.[3]

Henry Hedge—he dropped the Frederic—had recently returned from five years' study in Germany where he had been sent at the age of twelve because, although he had completed all the entrance requirements for Harvard, his father, Levi Hedge, professor of logic and metaphysics, considered him too young to enter. As George Bancroft (who later became a distinguished historian and Democratic political figure) was about to depart for a period of European study at Harvard's expense, Professor Hedge had asked Bancroft to supervise a German secondary education for his son. After studying at the famous German gymnasia at Ilfeld and Schulpforta, young Hedge was now back home and enrolled at Harvard. As the Hedges were Fuller family friends, Henry had many opportunities to be with Margaret. She was, he remembered, so "precocious" mentally and physically that she easily passed for eighteen and was mixing with the college students. Attracted by her wit and exuberance, he was especially impressed with her articulateness and with what he called her "political h[ea]d"— her faith and hope in the future of the nation. Whenever he argued in favor of "European ways," she vigorously defended American political institutions. Henry Hedge, whom Margaret and others nicknamed "Germanicus," became one of her most steadfast friends, but he was not attracted to her physically. His description of her at the age of thirteen as "a blooming girl of a florid complexion and vigorous health" was his judicious way of avoiding mention that she was having skin trouble, putting on weight, and behaving in a bumptious manner.⁴

Margaret remembered later that when she developed "a flush in the forehead" her father blamed the condition on her excitability and her excess vitality. "My parents were much mortified to see the fineness of my complexion destroyed," she recalled. "My own vanity was for a time severely wounded, but I recovered and made up my mind to be bright and ugly."⁵

In the face of a confusion of messages as to what was expected of her, Margaret's air of bravado increased. She read her parents' anxiety over her looks as a sign of a failure that no exercise of mind or will could overcome. Only by continuing to excel intellectually could she fulfill at least one of her father's requirements, and she took to flaunting her ready wit and mental attainments. Though her exuberance and high spirits attracted attention, many in small-town Cambridge looked upon her as a defiant and uncontrolled young woman. Henry Hedge and others remembered that Timothy, even in the presence of her friends, constantly interrupted her with corrections. She rebelled by taking advantage of his absences to follow her own caprices, to stay out too late at parties, and to speak disrespectfully to her mother and aunts when they tried to discipline her. Margarett Crane Fuller's letters concentrated more and more on her inability to handle her daughter. Soon the Fuller family contingent in Cambridge and Boston were complaining that Margaret was making a spectacle of herself.

Timothy implored her to be a model for the younger children, and he put a crimp in her social life by requiring that she write for his permission before accepting evening invitations. Although she was continuing to read voraciously such books as "Bacon's Essays" and "Paley's Internal Evidence" and claimed to be working on Latin translations, by the beginning of the winter of 1823–24 Margaret was aware that the family had decided she should be committed to a regular routine. Hoping to be able to continue her social life, she begged her father to send her to the school in Boston that Ralph Waldo Emerson, a recent Harvard graduate, had a short while ago taken over from his brother William.

But Timothy had already made up his mind that she should be sent to Miss Prescott's Young Ladies' Seminary in Groton, a country boarding school with a reputation for inculcating good manners and "female *propriety*."[6]

Timothy explained that he would prefer to keep her at home if he could depend on her help in educating the younger children, but he was sending her away for her "*own sake*." The family consensus was that she lacked "a discreet, modest, unassuming deportment," qualities which were "indispensable to endear any one, especially a young lady to her friends, & to obtain the world's good word." He hoped that "a few months with a good country lady" would set her right. She should view the experience as "a fair opportunity to begin the world anew, to avoid the mistakes & faults that had deprived her of some esteem" in the past, and to "convince" Miss Prescott that she was "determined to be as near perfection as possible." Her father's final demeaning thrust was to assert that he would be "very much gratified" to find her deportment exhibit "as much true tact" as her two close friends, Elizabeth Ware and Harriet Fay, and her cousin Susan Williams. Margaret replied with sarcasm. "I always hold, that, those who love me, will wish to have me with them." A few days after she arrived in Groton on May 12, 1824, she wrote her father, "I feel myself rather degraded from Cicero's Oratory to One and two are how many It *is* rather a change, is it not?" Her roommate was "a very disagreeable girl," but she had found a "chum" and was enjoying the beautiful countryside.[7]

Within a few weeks, she settled into the school routine and came to enjoy it. Open-air exercise was encouraged, and she became a leader in walking expeditions. Margaret grew increasingly fond of Susan Prescott, the headmistress, who treated her with kindness and understanding, and she made one close friend in Mary Soley from Charlestown. By the time she returned to Cambridgeport a year later, she was less rebellious and more willing to accept criticism, but she still had a quick temper and a sarcastic tongue, and her deportment could not be depended upon to be modest and unassuming.

In her early thirties Fuller traced her emotional problems to her restless temperament. She saw herself as by nature more intense, emotional, and headstrong than was the accepted norm among New England women. She wrote a short story, "Mariana," which many friends thought was based on a personal experience at Miss Prescott's school. Describing her heroine as one of "ardent and too early stimulated nature" with a "touch of genius and power that never left her," Fuller shows Mariana—a willful, charismatic, energetic young woman—being forced painfully into conformism until, like a victim of brainwashing, she expresses prayerful gratitude to her schoolmates for curing her of the disease of self-expression. When the story was published, Fuller confessed that the character portrayed "one phase" of her character, a side that people could admire "at poetic distance" but would find alarming in real life.[8]

Soon after Margaret returned to Cambridge, she wrote Susan Prescott, for whose sympathetic instruction she remained grateful, that she was now driven by "ambition" and the belief that "nothing," not even "perfection, is unattainable." She was "determined on distinction," she insisted, even though she knew it would take years to attain her goal. "I know the obstacles in my way. I am wanting in that intuitive tact and polish, which nature has bestowed upon some, but which I must acquire." That she was a rough-hewn stone had been hammered into her by everyone, but she was confident that nature had not been stingy with her when it came to "powers of intellect," and all "hindrances may be overcome by an ardent spirit."[9]

She had set herself a strenuous schedule of exercise, French and Italian language study, pianoforte practicing, and morning Greek lessons at the Port School. Her aim was not only to become a social success but to develop her inner resources. This zealous onrush of good intentions may have been inspired by General Lafayette's visit to Boston shortly after Margaret's return from Groton. Lafayette, who was making a triumphal tour of the United States on the fiftieth anniversary of the American Revolution, came to lay the cornerstone of the Bunker Hill Monument on June 17, 1825, the fiftieth anniversary of the crucial battle. All the survivors of the original regiment paraded behind him through Boston and up the hill where the regiment's chaplain, the reverend Mr. Thaxter, gave the convocation and Daniel Webster the oration.

For days before the general's arrival, the excitement had been mounting to a fever pitch. Crowds of patriots were coming in from the countryside. "Everything that has wheels and everything which has legs," said a stage driver, "used them to get to Boston." Ever since the previous August, Lafayette had been traveling from city to city, usually bareheaded and on horseback, to unprecedented popular acclaim. All over the country, his profile in miniature appeared on boots, hats, watch ribbons, and gloves. As the adulation reached a crescendo, "to be Lafayetted" became part of the American language. The supreme moment in the tour was in December when Lafayette had visited Mount Vernon and bent down to kiss the iron casket of his old companion, George Washington. For New Englanders, the Bunker Hill ceremony was to be an equally holy occasion. As Timothy's Fuller's daughter, Margaret was a guest at the official reception on the eve of the ceremony.[10]

As the great day approached, fifteen-year-old Margaret could hardly contain herself. On the day of the reception, Margaret, overcome with the momentousness of the coming hour, wrote the general a personal note:

Sir,
I expect the pleasure of seeing you tonight. . . . I cannot resist the desire of saying "La Fayette I love I admire you"; I am sure that this expression of feeling, though from one of the most insignificant of that vast population whose hearts echo your name, will not be utterly inconsequent to you; I am sure that not one of that people in whose cause you consumed, amid the toils and hardships of a camp, the loveliest years of human exis-

tence and from whom you are now receiving a tribute of gratitude unparalleled in the annals of history as your extraordinary life, is inconsequent to you. I expect the pleasure of seeing you tonight. . . . Sir the contemplation of a character such as yours fills the soul with a noble ambition. Should we both live, and it is possible to a female, to whom the avenues of glory are seldom accessible, I shall recal my name to your recollection

Accept the sincere homage of a youthful heart and dear friend of my country, farewell

Sarah Margaret Fuller[11]

The Lafayette visit provided Margaret with an experience she never forgot. At the end of the ceremony at Bunker Hill, the general made a toast prophetic not only of the future of the century but of her future as well: "Bunker Hill, and the holy resistance to oppression which has already enfranchised the American hemisphere. The next century jubilee's toast shall be: 'To Enfranchised Europe!' "[12]

Twenty-four years later, when Margaret was something of a hero herself—a foreign correspondent for the *New-York Daily Tribune* in Rome during its battle to become enfranchised—she would call on her fellow Americans to come to the aid of the besieged Romans as Lafayette had once done for them. "I saw him when traversing our country, then great, rich and free. Millions of men who owed in part their happiness to what, no doubt, was once sneered at as romantic sympathy, threw garlands in his path."[13]

When Margaret returned from Groton, her father was no longer in Congress. During her absence, he took a calculated risk and decided not to run for a fourth term. Ever since 1820, he had been looking for ways to help John Quincy Adams—the secretary of state in the Monroe administration—win the presidency in the 1824 election. Even though Adams had told him clearly that he never involved himself in "caballing, bargaining, place-giving," Timothy hoped to be rewarded with a federal appointment, preferably in the diplomatic corps.[14]

In the course of the four years preceding the election, Adams called on Timothy Fuller only once for help; the rest of the time he went out of his way to avoid him, but Timothy did what he could to keep Adams aware of his support. In the summer of 1823 he took Margarett Crane Fuller and Margaret out to Quincy to visit old President John Adams; he hoped to discuss the coming election, only to find that conversation was impossible because the ninety-year-old Adams was sitting for his portrait by Gilbert Stuart. During the summer before the election Timothy went out again, this time alone, and was delighted to be told that he was a "known advocate." Before the election he authored and circulated a broadside advertising John Quincy Adams's superior claims to the job over Jackson, Crawford, and Clay.[15]

But nothing came of his efforts. In the November election, no candidate won a clear majority. In February 1825, the House of Representatives vote gave the prize to Adams amidst virulent outcries that Clay had sold out his votes in a deal to become secretary of state. Timothy stayed on in Washington through the inauguration and until Clay had finished making appointments to foreign ministries and missions. In April, when he knew he would not be tapped for a federal position, he hoped he would be asked to fill a vacancy on the Supreme Judicial Court of Massachusetts, but he was passed over there as well. On his return home, he ran successfully for the Massachusetts House and was immediately chosen as Speaker. (Until 1833 Election Day for state offices was the last Wednesday in May.)

Years later, Margaret's favorite brother, Richard, who was born while she was at school in Groton, said that it was part of the family lore that Timothy had "expected a mission to Europe, as a token of the appreciation of his influential labors on behalf of the successful candidate. But the President did not 'remember Joseph.' " Richard also said that Timothy had led Margaret to believe that she would certainly be going with him on his foreign missions. Instead, when she returned home in the spring of 1825, she took up once again the position of big sister and family governess.[16]

Margaret took the younger children to the Port School and studied Greek there herself. A few times a week she rode on horseback out to Watertown to study with the author Lydia Maria Francis, who ran an unconventional school out of the home of her brother, Convers Francis, the Unitarian minister. Maria Francis supervised Margaret's readings in literature: Together they read Rousseau and Byron, Mme. de Staël, Epictetus, Milton, John Locke, and Castilian ballads. Years later, when Margaret was visiting the library of the Chamber of Deputies in Paris, she would hold reverently in her hands a few manuscripts of Rousseau and claim that his soul "pervaded" the nineteenth century, that he was "the precursor" of all that was most valued in her time, an example of the power of genius.[17]

At twenty-three, Maria Francis was already a local celebrity. Her novel *Hobomok* (1824), the story of the marriage of a Pequod Indian and a white woman, had turned her into a literary lion overnight. The daughter of a Medford baker (the inventor of the well-known Medford biscuit), she was, for the moment, the darling of the Boston intellectuals for having written a book with an authentic American setting at a time when they were anxious for the development of an American literature. "She is a natural person,—a most rare thing in this age of cant and pretension," Margaret described her to Susan Prescott.[18]

Maria, who later became prominent in the antislavery movement, was an avowed romantic when she and Margaret embarked on their ambitious reading program. "I was all absorbed in poetry and painting,—soaring aloft on Psyche wings, into the etherial regions of mysticism," was her self-description, and Margaret was delighted to take flight with her. The tumultuous excitement of romantic literature, its ardent individualism and emotional license, fed Margaret's rebelliousness and gave intellectual sanction to her inchoate feelings; she found in Maria Francis a model of an intelligent, enthusiastic young woman, as ambitious as herself. A letter Margaret wrote to Susan Prescott in Groton signals her awakening to serious questioning of those commonsense voices of authority favored by her father and an increasing attention to the new voices expressing feelings and anxieties that matched the yearnings of her inner life.

I am studying Madame de Stael, Epictetus, Milton, Racine, and Castilian ballads, with great delight. There's an assemblage for you. Now tell me, had you rather be the brilliant De Stael or the useful Edgeworth?—though De Stael is useful too, but it is on the grand scale, on liberalizing, regenerating principles, and has not the immediate practical success that Edgeworth has. I met with a parallel the other day between Byron and Rousseau, and had a mind to send it to you, it was so excellent.[19]

When Maria became engaged in October 1828 to David Child, Margaret worried that the marriage would end their friendship. Maria assured her that they would "have many and pleasant years of acquaintance yet," but when Maria married, moved to Boston, and began publishing the *Juvenile Miscellany,* the first American periodical for children, they saw very little of each other for several years until Maria joined Margaret's first Conversation class in Boston in 1839.[20]

In the spring of 1826, the Fullers moved from their Cherry Street house in shabby Cambridgeport to a fine mansion in Old Cambridge close to Harvard College. If Timothy could not be a foreign diplomat, he at least had the means to live like one. Shortly after the Revolution, Francis Dana, Sr., the first United States minister to Russia, had built the stately mansion on a terraced height overlooking the Charles River, with the Brighton hills across the river and Mount Auburn beyond. A tree-lined carriageway in an orchard of pear trees led up to the entrance. The Fullers now lived in comfort. They had their own carriage and a staff of helpers: Silver, the houseman; a seamstress, Polly; and steady kitchen and cleaning help. The older children, Eugene, William Henry, and Ellen, were in a nearby fee school, but Margaret was expected to help with the younger children, Arthur, Richard, and the baby, Lloyd.

Even before they moved, Timothy had tried to get Margarett Crane Fuller to agree to invite President and Mrs. Adams to dinner. She had always put him off, but now that they were living in the Dana Mansion, there was no excuse. John Quincy Adams's acceptance of an invitation to dine with the Fullers on September 26, 1826, was a great event for the Fuller family—a sure sign of the president's respect. Adams had spent the better part of the summer in Quincy arranging the affairs of his father, whose death on July 4, within two hours of the death of Thomas Jefferson, had stunned the nation. (Many believed there was a divine significance in the coincidence: two ancient rivals, reconciled in their old age, dying on the fiftieth anniversary of the Declaration of Independence. Nathanial Bowditch, Boston's famous mathematician, computed the odds that two signers of the Declaration would live fifty years and die on the same day at one in 200 million.)

For the people of Cambridge, the evening was a historic occasion. According to Thomas Wentworth Higginson, it was "one of the most elaborate affairs of the kind that had occurred in Cambridge" since prerevolutionary days. But there was malicious gossip. People were disappointed when the president excused himself after the dinner and before the dancing; Margaret was remembered as looking awkward in a tight pink dress that was unbecoming to her florid complexion and accentuated her robust figure.[21]

Having a father in the public eye did not help allay Margaret's self-consciousness, especially since her father supervised her social life and her choice of clothing and carefully monitored her public behavior. Nor did it help that her father and his brothers, while admired for their talents and conscientiousness as they rose to prominence, had a family reputation for pushiness, tactlessness, and exaggerated self-esteem. William Henry Channing, who later became one of Margaret's staunchest friends—and one of her biographers—was a Harvard student at the time the Fullers moved into the Dana Mansion. His sister Susan had been at Dr. Park's school with Margaret, and she verified the speculations about Margaret's painful experiences there. William remembered admiring Margaret's "fluency and fun," but her "decisive tone, downrightness, and contempt of conventional standards" kept him at bay, and he knew several people who shunned her because of her habit of asking personal questions and assuming a confidential manner on slight acquaintance.[22]

But if she was not a universal favorite, there were some who admired her confident independence. Thomas Wentworth Higginson quoted a contemporary of Margaret's describing "a social library in one of the village shops," where Margaret would go, "wearing a hooded cloak; she would take off the cloak, fill the hood with books, swing it over her shoulders, books and all, and so carry it home." "We all wished," said Higginson's informant, "that our mothers would let us have hooded cloaks, that we might carry our books in the same way."[23]

Her remarkable conversation style had already become her hallmark. Henry Hedge made an effort to describe how she created her remarkable effect.

Her conversation, as it was then, I have seldom heard equalled. It was not so much attractive as commanding. Though remarkably fluent and select, it was neither fluency, nor choice diction, nor wit, nor sentiment, that gave it its peculiar power, but accuracy of statement, keen discrimination, and a certain weight of judgment, which contrasted strongly and charmingly with the youth and sex of the speaker.[24]

While the Fullers occupied the Dana Mansion, a faithful group of friends gathered around Margaret; they saw so much of each other for the next few years that they were believed to have a circle of their own with Margaret at the center. She was still friendly with her childhood Cambridge friends, Harriet Fay and Elizabeth Ware, as well as two young Boston women whom she had known as long as she could remember, Elizabeth Randall, the daughter of the Fuller family doctor, and Amelia Greenwood, whose brother, Francis Pitt Greenwood, was a respected Boston clergyman, a minister at King's Chapel. The beautiful Almira Penniman of Brookline was another girlhood friend who was often at the Dana Mansion as was Ellen Sturgis, the daughter of a wealthy merchant, who was admired for her skill as a poet.

One of Margaret's distant cousins, George Davis, a member of the class of 1829 at Harvard, frequently brought his classmates to the Dana Mansion. Among them was George Hillard, later a prominent Boston lawyer known for his polish and wit, and Joseph Angier, who had a reputation for being a ladies' man. During the winter of 1828–29, James Freeman Clarke, whose parents were family friends of the Fullers, often joined them with his sister Sarah, who was already an accomplished painter.

The friends enjoyed picnics, horseback and sleigh rides, many evening dances, and endless literary talk. It was a time of rebellion at Harvard College when the students, responding to the dramatic changes in the country's political climate and an influx of new ideas from Europe, complained that the curriculum was outdated and boring and had nothing to do with their concerns. Earlier in the decade, at a time when a German university education was considered the finest in the world, a stellar group of Americans, with postgraduate degrees from Göttingen University, had returned to Harvard to teach, bringing a flurry of expectation that the curriculum would be modernized. The classicist Edward Everett, whose eloquence had impressed many students, was now in the House of Representatives, having replaced Timothy Fuller. The historian George Bancroft, after annoying the college authorities with his foreign ways, was in the western part of the state, running the Round Hill School. With him had gone Joseph Cogswell, who had taught geology and mineralogy and had reorganized the college library. George Ticknor, professor of belles lettres, French, and Spanish was still at the college, but his efforts to reorganize academic studies had been blocked. On the faculty also were two recent European arrivals, Charles Follen, the first instructor of German at Harvard, and Pietro Bachi who taught Italian, but their offerings were considered peripheral to major requirements for graduation.

George Davis and James Freeman Clarke were part of a group who petitioned the college for a change of textbooks, and they were active participants in the political parties that formed around the agitation. They complained that the college gave them no incentive to study other than to get above their classmates in rank. Like the many students who agreed with them, they ignored their regular assignments and pursued an alternative education on their own, seeking out books that galvanized their interest. The mood of the country that led to Andrew Jackson's election as president in 1828, and the voices of change and romantic unrest that inspired European writers, lured the Harvard students from what they considered a provincial education. They were responding to natural, individualistic, eccentric writers like Sir Thomas Browne,

Ben Jonson, Charles Lamb, Wordsworth, Coleridge, and Macaulay; historians and travel writers who had unique outlooks and unusual experiences; and writers like Germaine de Staël who could synthesize a culture. Years later, James Freeman Clarke wrote that he would always remember the heady excitement of going with George Davis to Boston's private library, the Athenaeum, to read Thomas Carlyle's articles in the *Edinburgh Review,* the *Foreign Review,* and *Fraser's Magazine.* Thomas Carlyle's "new and profound views of familiar truths" made them feel they "saw angels ascending and descending in a Jacob's dream." They felt they had known Carlyle all their lives. Attracted by the "wild bugle-call" of Thomas Carlyle's "romantic articles on Richter, Schiller, and Goethe," day after day they would go to Boston to sit under the statue of Laocoon and read the same article over and over.[25]

At the time, women could not have an Athenaeum reading card, but Margaret responded to her friends' enthusiasms and pursued her own alternative education, finding elsewhere books that would satisfy the group's taste and stimulate her personal fascination with ideas and attitudes that questioned the status quo. Quick at picking up the new ideas, articulating them freshly, and animating the group into debate and conversation, she presided over her own salon in the Dana Mansion. During this time she was reading voraciously in English, French, and Italian literature—"beautiful" Jane Austen, Benjamin Disraeli, Edward Bulwer-Lytton, William Godwin, Voltaire, Dante, Petrarch, Ariosto, and the American Charles Brockton Brown.

A few years later, when she became friends with Ralph Waldo Emerson, he noticed some lapses in her education. Though he found her "rich in culture" and "well read in French, Italian," and though she "knew German books more cordially than any other person," her reading in English literature was "incomplete." He took it on himself to encourage her to read more Shakespeare and introduced her to Chaucer, Ben Jonson, George Herbert (who became a great favorite), Beaumont, Fletcher, and Bacon, all of whom she would have been familiar with if she had been able to attend college.[26]

Fuller's early education was unsystematic and lacked consistency in supervision, but its basis was a solid classical training within a framework of standards based on her father's Enlightenment principles. Even after she began to read eclectically in modern literature, she was never to lose her high regard for the achievements of the Greeks and the Romans. In addition, her father, the lawyer, trained her continually in analytical skills, emphasizing the importance of logic and correct use of language. She was always to save one theme she wrote for him in her teens, an analysis of the motto "Possent quia posse videntur," because, she wrote, "it shows very plainly what our mental relation was." In it, she accepted the general proposition that within reasonable boundaries one should be able to do whatever one can imagine oneself capable of doing, but one is always subject to "the power of circumstance." Yet even that limitation, she asserted—in the voice of her father—can be put to heroic use by the great, the good, and the wise.[27]

She thought that her reputation as a talented intellect was somewhat overblown. A few years later she wrote a friend that she supposed that people who spoke of her as unusually gifted "were dazzled by a superficial brilliance of expression" that she was sometimes "excited into." But she assumed her close friend was able "to see perfectly the want of depth and accuracy and the ceaseless fluxuation" of her mind.[28]

Though Margaret's lack of inhibition annoyed many Cambridge people, her obvious intelligence, curiosity, and hunger for learning and friendship won her the affection of one of the town's most admired women, Eliza Rotch Farrar, who came to Cambridge in 1828 as the second wife of the widower John Farrar, Harvard's professor of mathematics and astronomy. Mrs. Farrar said later that she was first attracted to Margaret because of her "remarkable intellect," but the two became fast friends during a period early in Eliza's marriage when she was depressed and Margaret "forced her way to" Eliza and reasoned with her over life's "trials and disappointments." Something in Margaret's earnest awkwardness and sincerity led Eliza Farrar to take her permanently in charge.[29]

Born in France during the French Revolution, Eliza Farrar had an exciting background by Cambridge standards. She had met many of the English woman authors whom Margaret had grown up reading—Letitia Barbauld, Amelia Opie, and Elizabeth Fry—and, as a young woman, she had even caught a glimpse of Lord Nelson and Lady Hamilton walking down the street together in Bath. Benjamin Rotch, Eliza's father, a Nantucket Quaker in the whaling business, had gone to France to develop commercial relations in the whale oil business. Forced by the Revolution to move to England, the family settled first in a London suburb and later in a lavish country home in Wales. But when Benjamin Rotch went into bankruptcy in 1819, family poverty forced Eliza to come to New Bedford to live with her grandparents as a companion.

Their deaths in the late 1820s freed her to marry, but soon afterward family quarrels erupted over the Rotch fortune, and the matter dragged on for months, depressing and embarrassing Eliza. During this low period in Eliza Farrar's life, Margaret became something of a household fixture at the Farrar home on Professors' Row. Having no children of her own, Mrs. Farrar, who was only two years younger than Margarett Crane Fuller, treated Margaret like a daughter and even included her in the family life of the Rotch clan in New Bedford. Through her, Margaret met many of the people who became the most important influences in her later life: Ralph Waldo Emerson, Harriet Martineau, Anna Barker, and Sam Ward.[30]

But even more important to Margaret's future, Eliza's trust and affection, offered when she urgently needed the attention of a respected adult outside her immediate family, gave Margaret the assurance to tone down her behavior without sacrificing her individuality. With Eliza Rotch Farrar behind her, people were encouraged to look beyond Margaret's superficial eccentricities for the qualities that endeared her to the most charming hostess in Cambridge. Taking advantage of Margaret's veneration, Eliza offered instruction on hair styles and dress and on decorous and tactful behavior. Margaret could not have had a more qualified teacher, a sensible, down-to-earth Quaker woman who had grown up in Europe and had escaped the false gentility of much of women's education there at the time, as well as the provincial American ideas of propriety that turned people away from Margaret Fuller.

But Mrs. Farrar, as Margaret always addressed her, understood that public opinion could not be totally disregarded, and Margaret may have served as something of an experiment. In 1836 Farrar published one of the most successful manners books of the century; titled *A Young Lady's Friend, by a Lady,* it went through six editions. While Mrs. Farrar's book talked more common sense than most of the other social etiquette books of the time, the message called for greater self-control and self-abnegation than Margaret's impulsive temperament could consistently bear. Nevertheless, all of the town observers credited Mrs. Farrar with making great headway with Margaret's deportment and appearance.

During these years Margarett Crane Fuller did not assume the social leadership that her husband's distinction and her fine mansion might have encouraged among "the Square Gentry," as she "whimsically styled" the leaders of social life in Old Cambridge in one of her letters. Timothy often took Margaret to the official functions his station required, and during these years she looked to some of the more socially secure Cambridge older women as models. Years later, when Margaret wrote a plan for a narrative with similarities to her "Autobiographical Romance," she noted that the protagonist (whose mother "died early") "elected a Mother" at the age of seventeen, seemingly because the real mother's death had left the child with the need to search continually for "the rainbow of beauty and love" in personal relationships. Farrar was the first of the mother-figures that Margaret would elect. As an author and the most respected hostess in Old Cambridge, she came closer than any other local woman to holding a public position while maintaining private respect. For Margaret, ambitious for "distinction," as she had described herself, Mrs. Farrar, more than any other available model, held the keys to success.[31]

When Fuller was in her midtwenties and had begun to feel in greater control of herself, she admitted to the British author Harriet Martineau that at nineteen she had been "the most intolerable girl that ever took a seat in a drawing room." By the time she made this confession, she was no longer a bumptious, overweight adolescent but a slender, meticulously dressed young woman of middle height whose plain appearance was redeemed by her thick blonde hair, fine teeth, and expressive eyes. She had courteous manners, but her intensity gave the impression that at any moment she might lose control and burst forth with the unexpected. For as long as she lived, and afterward too, almost everyone who knew Fuller well groped for words when they tried to describe her; nearly all of them were compelled, sooner or later, to use the word "force."[32]

Although she tried all her life to subdue her tumultuous nature, she never completely succeeded. In large part, this was because her family situation, her high intelligence and restless temperament, the ideas issuing from Europe in the first half of the nineteenth century, and, as she was to point out continuously herself, "the power of circumstances" all conspired to confirm her view that a life of conformity to what was expected of a New England woman in antebellum America was a life of complacency and boredom. "Who would be a goody that could be a genius?" she asked Ralph Waldo Emerson a few years later. It was out of her private struggle with this problem that she developed her remarkable public career.[33]

Our family star has taken an unfavorable turn; father had always luck in aid of his efforts till now; now his fortunes begin to decline and we shall never be lucky any more.

An Unfavorable Turn

WHEN the Fullers first settled in Cambridge, they became members of the Congregational church in Old Cambridge where Abiel Holmes served as minister, but in 1814 when Thomas Brattle Gannett came to Cambridgeport as the first minister of the new Congregational church, they transferred their membership and soon became pillars of the new society. Timothy Fuller served on the Church Committee and, according to his son Richard, "Every Sabbath he used to read the Bible with the family and address the throne of grace." Before his marriage, while living in Boston, he was a member of the Brattle Street Church of his distant cousin, Joseph Stevens Buckminster, whose sermons later became legendary for their "domestication of European graces in ungainly New England." Buckminster was the first of the Boston pastors to warn that America's promise of unlimited economic prosperity presented unique spiritual dilemmas. To counter the danger that the love of luxury or of money should "overwhelm the rising generation," he advised that "the love of literature and intellectual pursuits should be greatly encouraged; for though the passion for knowledge is no proof of a principle of virtue, it is often a security against the vices and temptations of the world." It was a message that Timothy Fuller took to heart; Margaret, from her early childhood, was trained to view the pursuit of knowledge as sanctioned by religion.[1]

This emphasis was only one of the many distinguishing elements that gradually led to a splitting of Congregational societies during the first two decades of the century into orthodox and liberal wings, a split that had its origins in major changes in the society at large as well as in doctrinal differences that had been developing for two generations centering on the Trinity, on free will and salvation, on the role of divine mediation, and on the interpretation of Christ's miracles as testimony to God.[2]

During Margaret's late teens and early twenties, this controversy played out poignantly in Cambridge. The Old Cambridge congregation of Abiel Holmes, the father of Oliver Wendell, split into two factions, the liberals and the orthodox. Lucinda Willard, the daughter of a Harvard president, wrote in 1828 that the disagreements between the two sides were "the great and mighty subject" of Cambridge, "which can be called the little peaceful village no longer, as husband is against wife and mother against daughter as it were."[3]

The members of the liberal parish committee—they called themselves Unitarians—established their position by substituting the Harvard College hymnbook for Isaac Watts's old standby. Many of the liberals withdrew their children from the orthodox Sunday School and sent them to a new school conducted by Eliza Cabot Follen in connection with the Harvard Chapel (by the twenties, Harvard was solidly in the Unitarian camp). Abiel Holmes warned his parishioners against this "opposition school" and would not allow any guest preacher representing the Unitarian heresy to occupy his pulpit. In May 1829 the liberals gained the majority and terminated Holmes's contract. Oliver Wendell Holmes, who lived at home while at Harvard, had little to say about his father's tribulations. In one of the few letters he wrote during his college years, he described Harvard as his "Godless college"—then crossed out the adjective and replaced it with "heretic."[4]

While Margaret Fuller was growing up, William Ellery Channing, the eloquent preacher of the Federal Street Church in Boston, was the dominant voice of the Unitarians. In 1819 he set out in a sermon the three tenets of Unitarian belief: the primacy of reason in the interpretation of the Scriptures; the unity and moral perfection of God; and the spiritual leadership of Jesus. In 1825, when the American Unitarian Association was formed, the movement as a whole took on an official identity, but Thomas Brattle Gannett's church in Cambridgeport had been Unitarian in spirit from its inception.

Margarett Crane Fuller's religious practices were more pious and emotional than those of her husband, and she even went to evangelical camp meetings from time to time. She attended the Unitarian church but had no exclusive attachment to it. "I wish to confine my children to no particular creed," she wrote her son Arthur when he was sixteen and wanted to become a Baptist. "I want to see the fruits of well-regulated lives, growing out of the pure principles of Jesus and I care not by what name they are called."[5]

Timothy Fuller, on the other hand, in his constant exhortations to Margaret to strive for perfection echoed Channing's "perfectibilitarian message," which taught that "Christianity should be comprehended as having but one purpose, the perfection of human nature, the elevation of men into nobler beings." Salvation was a step-by-step ascendancy to perfection, a raising of the soul from moral evil to perfection—a process that was the beginning and end of Christianity and required the mediation of Christ. "Have you faith in your souls as capable of ascending to sinless purity"? Channing asked.[6]

Channing's vision of perfectibility depended on a bedrock of infinite aspiration. It flourished in the Boston of the 1820s, and its spirit lay at the heart of the forthright statement that Fuller wrote in early 1830 when her friend George T. Davis asked her to comment on "the most important of subjects." She preferred to finesse any absolute commitment, but of all her Harvard College friends, Davis had the greatest claim to an answer. While noticeably omitting Christ's all-important role as mediator, she saw her religion in true Channingesque terms as an ongoing education, an "Eternal Progression" of her spirit.

I have not formed an opinion. I have determined not to form settled opinions at present. Loving or feeble natures need a positive religion, a visible refuge, a protection, as much in the passionate season of youth as in those stages nearer to the grave. But mine is not such. My pride is superior to any feelings I have yet experienced: my affection is strong admiration, not the necessity of giving or receiving assistance or sympathy. When disappointed, I do not ask or wish consolation,—I wish to know and feel my pain, to investigate its nature and its source; I will not have my thoughts diverted, or my feelings soothed; 'tis therefore that my young life is so singularly barren of illusions. I know, I feel the time must come when this proud and impatient heart shall be stilled, and turn from the ardors of Search and Action, to lean on something above. But—shall I say it?—the thought of that calmer era is to me a thought of deepest sadness; so remote from my present being is that future existence, which still the mind may conceive. I believe in Eternal Progression. I believe in a God, a Beauty and Perfection to which I am to strive all my life for assimilation. From these two articles of belief, I draw the rules by which I try to regulate my life. But, though I reverence all religions as necessary to the happiness of man, I am yet ignorant of the religion of Revelation. Tangible promises! Well defined hopes! are things of which I do not *now* feel the need. At present, my soul is intent on this life, and I think of religion as its rule; and, in my opinion, this is the natural and proper course from youth to age. What I have written is not hastily concocted, it has a meaning. I have given you, in this little space, the substance of many thoughts, the clues to many cherished opinions. 'Tis a subject on which I rarely speak. I never said so much but once before. I have here given you all I know, or think, on the most important of subjects—could you but read understandingly.[7]

She realized that "most people" would misinterpret her "religious opinions" and "deprecate" her for "believing, even 'temporarily' in Deism," but she would answer that she did not "*dis*believe or even *carelessly set aside* Revelation; I merely remain in ignorance of Christian Revelation because I do not feel it suited to me at present."[8]

By January 1830 Davis, who had been one of Fuller's closest friends among the Harvard class of 1829, no longer came regularly to see her. Margaret had believed that their earlier rapport amounted to far more than a casual college friendship, that the frankness and honesty they had shared required more honorable responses and reactions than an unexplained retreat. Her statement of her religious attitude at the age of nineteen has to be read as an effort of sincerity and personal disclosure to a friend of several years in answer to a deeply personal question, but the answer is laced with statements about her own character and resolve at a time when she was testing Davis's commitment to her.[9]

Distantly related to Fuller on her Grandmother Sarah Williams Fuller's side of the family, Davis had grown up in Sandwich on Cape Cod, but his father's people came from the Carolinas, and his New England relatives assumed that his southern blood explained his debonair, irreverent manner. Delicate-looking with a smooth baby face, he appeared, according to his classmate George Hillard, as if "summer suns" had never "scorched him" nor "winter winds had blown upon him," and in a college reunion photograph taken years later the paleness and softness are still evident. His classmates admired him for his feats of memory and his skill as a raconteur. (When Thackeray visited the United States in 1852, he met Davis, who was then a Whig congressman, and pronounced him the best conversationalist in the country.)[10]

His wit, vivacity, and broad-mindedness greatly attracted Margaret, and, of all the young men she knew, she thought he was the one who most appreciated her talents. What she liked most about him was his independence. He went his own way, established his own standards, and asked little of others. She wrote him that he had certain resemblances to the admirable qualities in the otherwise disreputable Lovelace in Richardson's *Clarissa*—"the resemblance to you which I mentioned is in his levity, nay! brilliant vivacity and airy self-possession under circumstances of the greatest difficulty, doubt and mortification."[11]

When he stopped coming by to see her at the Dana Mansion after he graduated from college in the summer of 1829, she was hurt. Enrolled at the law school, he was spending much of his time reading law in Greenfield in the western part of the state. They corresponded a bit, met at the homes of others, but, without any explanation, he seemed to be distancing himself. The disappointment settled in her; she brooded over it, and she was forced to admit that he did not return her strong feelings.

The realization came at a sad time. In September 1829, just after the class dispersed—commencements then came in late August or early September—Margaret's youngest brother, Edward Breck, the ninth and last Fuller child, died while she was holding him in her arms. He had been born two days before her eighteenth birthday, on May 21, 1828, and died eighteen months later. Her mother had put him under Margaret's special care; his death was thus not only a keen loss but a failure as well, and it came just at the time when she had begun to fear that the friendship with George had been only a college dalliance.[12]

Fortunately, she had a confidante in George's friend James Freeman Clarke, who was courting her good friend, Elizabeth Randall, and suffering repeated rebuffs. James, who was in his first year of Harvard Divinity School, lacked George's wit and breadth of learning, but he was earnest and idealistic. An undistinguished student during his first three Harvard years, he caught fire in his senior year when he discovered Coleridge. *Aids to Reflection, Biographia Literaria,* and *The Friend,* woke him up, he wrote later, to the idea that the workings of the human mind and spirit, the ways of perceiving beauty, truth, morality, values, and motivation, were subjects he could ponder and study.

Instead of going to law school, as he had originally planned, he went to Harvard Divinity School so he could study metaphysics, but soon after he started he began to have doubts about his choice of vocation. He was afraid he would never develop the commanding presence and pulpit eloquence necessary to reign over a New England congregation.

When he turned to Margaret for encouragement and company, she took on the role of confessor and comforter, but she warned him, when he accused her of not being as forthcoming as he wished, that she was wary of intimate friendships because inevitably most of "the sympathy" and "the interest" ended up on her side. In a direct reference to George Davis, she told James that she had recently had a disappointing experience, and "those emotions, so necessarily repressed, have lost their simplicity, their ardent beauty," and she could never be as trusting and open as before. At a time when they both were at a crossroad in their lives, they found safety and encouragement in each other's company.[13]

During the fall of 1830, James and Margaret were thrown even closer together when he was forced to drop out of divinity school. His father, Dr. Samuel Clarke, was a pharmacist who ran a shop out of the family home on School Street in Boston and could barely make ends meet when James was a boy. As a result, James's step-grandfather, James Freeman, the Unitarian minister of King's Chapel in Boston, had taken him into the Freeman home in Newton and given him a first-class education. But Grandfather Freeman warned in advance that he would pay James's expenses for only one year of divinity school. When that year was over, the Clarke family was even worse off than usual. To help out financially, James's mother, Rebecca Hull Clarke, had opened a Boston boardinghouse. His older brother, Sam who had been running the family pharmacy, had just come down with a mysterious nervous disease and was bedridden. James had to leave school and look for work. While he was exploring possibilities, Timothy Fuller proposed him for an opening as the master of Margaret's old day school, the Port School. To add to James's sorrows, soon after he started as schoolmaster his father collapsed and died of a cerebral hemorrhage while James was at his side.

Throughout the rest of the year, Margaret and James were constant companions, exchanging books, gossip, confidences, and even analyzing each other's dreams. James would bring books from the Athenaeum or Harvard Library, and Margaret borrowed from friends and used the lending libraries. They went together to parties at the Farrars, the Hedges, and the Wares, and at the home of James's musical cousin, Helen Davis (no relation to George), who lived in a handsome Bullfinch mansion overlooking the Cambridge Common. James and Margaret were together so much that his Grandfather Freeman feared it was a serious romance and expressed his foreboding that James would "go & marry that woman & be miserable all the days of his life."[14]

When James encouraged Margaret to write down "portraits" of their friends, she obliged with a study of George in which she denied ever being in love with him. She preferred to call it an "attachment." She expressed gratitude for his "great effect" on her mind and paid tribute to his talents and considerable charms: his ability to excite her to "boundless gayety," his "scintillating, arrowy wit," and his "mirth [that] unsettled all objects from their foundations." He was "brilliant, versatile, and cold."[15]

Margaret may well have suspected that James would show her "portrait" to George, and she may have written it as a means of indirect communication with him. It was a common practice among all ages at the time to share letters, essays, and stories with close friends, a sign of intimacy and trust awarded those within one's circle of romantic friendship. Margaret's talent for writing character sketches of her friends and her love for analyzing people were among her ties with George. James's sister Sarah later recalled that when present with George and Margaret she "should have thought the plan was to pull people to pieces to see what they were made of, and then divert themselves with the fragments."[16]

Margaret could take a detached view of George when analyzing him for James, but she was unable to overcome her love for him. In February 1831, after they had met by chance one evening, she wrote him a confused and abject letter in which she dropped her customary mask of self-sufficiency and revealed her vulnerability as she tried to reestablish their friendship with an earnest confession.

My cousin and (at this moment) dearest friend. I expressed to you last night either nothing of what I felt or something directly opposite to it. I did not know what I said; I was so troubled and surprised that you could still excite a new sensation. I feel that but for you I should be free at last in the common or worldly sense of the word. You are the only person who can appreciate my true self. . . .
O would to heaven my cousin that I could act out my present feelings and show gratitude to the person who has embellished my life with one sweet emotion. Alas! I dare not hope it. You alone can see me as I truly am.[17]

George did not respond with any encouragement to this or the few similar letters that followed. When Margaret continued to suffer, James tried to comfort her by pointing out that ever since George had begun law school he had been cold and stand-offish with all his old friends. When Margaret saw him at a party in Cambridge in the spring of 1832, she refused to shake his hand when he offered it. By this time she had undoubtedly heard the rumors that he was all but engaged to Harriet Tidd Russell, a young Boston woman who was at school in Greenfield, where Davis clerked in a law firm.

James decided it was time to bring about a reconciliation between his two friends. When confronted, George told James that he was suffering from private pains he was unwilling to discuss, that his demeanor of lighthearted humor was a ruse to "conceal his real sadness." As for Margaret, he could not understand why she could not let their relationship "take care of itself," the way everyone else was doing. He complained that she was too prone to misrepresent things; she deduced "important consequences" from "the smallest things" and "twisted everything to suit" her own idea.[18]

This at least cleared the air. Margaret told James that she could see now that she was not being singled out for special treatment, and it was only "her vanity [that] always made her suppose she would be different to him from everyone else." For several years George kept a hold over her imagination. When they renewed their friendship later, she wrote him that she had thought at first that she would never be able to forgive the "insincerity and heartlessness" of his treatment of her when he had encouraged her to believe that he cared for her and when she had always been straightforward with him.[19]

By 1830, when Margaret was trying to recapture George's affection, the romantic movement had taken hold in middle-class America, greatly affecting close human relationships, turning them into personal dramas played out privately between the participants or within the confines of family or close friendships. This was true for same-sex relationships as well as those between the sexes. The idea of a romantic self, of a unique and deeply personal essence that transcended the social roles of gender, class, or social position, expressed itself in the private realm of romantic love. It was one of the many mechanisms that helped to form individualism in American culture. Introspection and obsessive involvement with one's own inner life and that of one's lover were a dominant activity. Exchanges of self-revelation and disclosure were major steps in courtship, a process that encouraged identification with another self, nurturing sympathy and understanding across gender boundaries in a private arena where the stricter boundaries of public roles were laid aside. To be insincere or deceptive was a cardinal sin in friendship or romantic courtship because the hiding of one's true self obstructed the progress of intimacy. When Margaret accused George of insincerity, it was not a charge to be taken lightly.[20]

Jealousy and possessiveness were the unpleasant consequences of so anxious a process. Even in less intense involvements such as the romantic friendship between Margaret and James in this early period, these emotions threatened to wreak havoc. Margaret caused James weeks of anguish in the winter of 1831 by neglecting to deliver a letter he asked her to give to Elizabeth Randall. James had wanted the letter delivered because his infatuation with Elizabeth had come to an impasse, and he assumed it was because he was unable to express himself freely in her presence. The letter explained his behavior and asked for her indulgence. It was only after he had suffered several weeks of anxiety waiting for the answer that Margaret confessed she had never delivered the letter. She explained that she had felt justified in her action because she knew Elizabeth well enough to be sure that the letter would make no impression on her. Only on second thought had she decided there would be a purpose in delivering the letter after all—it would cure James of falling back on the excuse that the reason Elizabeth was indifferent to him was that she was unaware of his feelings for her. At this time James was so respectful of Margaret's judgment that he not only accepted her explanation but even agreed she had a right to behave as she had done because she had told him often that Elizabeth was "altogether unsuited" to him.[21]

In their letters to each other, James and Margaret endowed each other with the qualities they dreamed of for themselves; Margaret revealed her own fantasies when she told James that he had the makings of a great man, a "genius" of the nineteenth century, someone who was self-possessed, strong-minded, sensitive to beauty and spiritual values, and fully capable of expressing his ideals directly in thought and action:

[T]here was something in the unshrinkable confidence with which you now and then pursued with all your strength the flying footsteps of truth; in your putting by vanities confessedly dear to you; in your incapacity to be happy without some *imaginative* love in whose atmosphere your fancy might breathe and plum herself that made me think you might have been the Being I wished to see.[22]

When Margaret expressed her fears that she would never find an outlet for her talents and ambitions, James assured her that she had no cause for complaint:

Whatever you may have suffered from the extent of your desires, you have also enjoyed, to a degree equal to your suffering, in the consciousness of your powers. I cannot pity such a destiny, Margaret. . . . [T]o one whose only evil is that her powers immeasurably transcend her sphere, I in truth have little pity to offer.

But even as he encouraged her onward in noble language, he pronounced her in his journal as "Not happy." Her remarkable power ends "in nothing—it produces no commensurate effects," he continued, and the reason for this, he concluded wisely, was "she has no field of action."[23]

Margaret despaired that her only destiny for the coming years was to fulfill the task her father required of her—to help educate her sister and her younger brothers. In the fall of 1830 Eugene had entered Harvard at the age of fifteen. William Henry balked at settling down to prepare for college, so Timothy found him a job as a clerk at Fullerton and Craigin, merchants in Boston. Ellen, Arthur, and Richard were at Miss Ellis's School in Cambridge, but Margaret was expected to hear their recitations daily as her father had done for her. The youngest child, Lloyd, was five now and a handful. Her father had promised her a trip to Europe when the children were educated, but if he expected her to be the family governess until Lloyd was in his teens, she would be in the harness for a long time.

It was a discouraging prospect now that her circle of friends was dispersing. Harriet Fay had married William Greenough and moved to Falmouth on Cape Cod. Almira Penniman Barlow was in Lynn, the wife of the Unitarian clergyman, David Barlow. Elizabeth Ware had married another clergyman, George

Putnam, and Margaret's beloved schoolmistress, Susan Prescott, stopped corresponding after marrying John Wright and moving to Lowell. Henry Hedge was
married to Lucy Poor and had a temporary living as the minister of the Unitarian church in Arlington.[24]

That summer (1831) Margaret fell into a depression. She craved sleep and
slept for long hours, sometimes through the day. She was put under the care of
a Dr. Robbins. It was an upsetting time in the Fuller household. Timothy
suddenly announced that he was disgusted with political life. He wanted to
move to a country town, where, like his hero Thomas Jefferson, he would
devote himself to writing. Although his law business was steady—he claimed to
be earning twenty dollars a day—he was losing ground as a man of affairs, and
his political career had been faltering.

In 1827 and 1828 he had been a candidate for the Harvard Board of Overseers
and had lost both times. In Massachusetts his old political party, the National
Republicans (earlier called the Democratic Republicans), was splitting into
factions, some of whom joined with the conservative Whigs. Unable to join the
Democrats because of his personal distaste for Andrew Jackson, he joined the
Antimasons, a new upstart party that served in Massachusetts as a refuge for
old-style republicans like Timothy Fuller and middle-class populists who could
not identify either with the Jacksonian rabble or with the Whigs and National
Republicans, who were dominated by property interests. In 1828, largely because of disarray in the Democratic party, the Antimasons had been gaining
power in the state. That year Timothy was president of the Antimason convention. Although there was a behind-the-scenes agreement that he would be
nominated to run for governor, at the last minute he heard that the former
president, John Quincy Adams, now a Massachusetts congressman, had "proposed and earned the substitution" of another candidate. Unabashed, Timothy
ran again for the Massachusetts House on the Antimason ticket and was elected
for a two-year term. But he was shrewd enough to see that he had no permanent political future. He had long had a hankering to move back to the country,
and, now in his fifties, he was ready to make the change. He put the Dana
Mansion up for sale; on August 22, 1831, it was bought for $8,000 by the
Reverend John H. Hopkins, an Episcopal minister.[25]

In 1832 he ran unsuccessfully on the Antimason ticket for lieutenant governor while scouring the countryside for his retreat. Meanwhile, the family
waited in the home of his brother Abraham, the Brattle House, at the end of
Tory Row in Old Cambridge. It was one of the town showplaces, then twice the
size it is now and surrounded with a formal garden of parterres, terraced walks,
a grove of fruit trees, and a park with a fish pool, bridges, and a fountain. Years
later, Margaret would recall as a prophecy a discussion with her brother Eugene
in the garden in which he said, "Our family star has taken an unfavorable turn;
father had always luck in aid of his efforts till now; now his fortunes begin to
decline and we shall never be lucky any more."[26]

For Margaret the Brattle House was a gilded cage; she called it "a prison." Her mother was miserable over the loss of her beautiful home and found it nearly impossible to raise her young family in the house of her fastidious brother-in-law. If Timothy was a difficult man to please, his younger brother, Abraham, was the one man in town who surpassed him. Thomas Wentworth Higginson recalled that Uncle Abraham was given to "dictatorial domineering" and had a local reputation for being "the narrowest and most arbitrary of all the paternal race."[27]

Unable for financial reasons to go to college because of the death of the Reverend Timothy Fuller, Sr., in 1804, Abraham went to work for an importer, who was warehousing scarce goods in anticipation of the Embargo of 1807–9. When the plan succeeded beyond expectations, the employer retired, leaving the business in Abraham's hands. By his midthirties, he was one of the rich men of Cambridge. A lifelong bachelor, he fancied himself a desirable catch. "He buzzed about the subject of marriage like a moth around a candle," his nephew Richard wrote later, "but never got into it, as he was afraid of being 'taken in.' "[28]

During the year and a half that Margaret lived under Uncle Abraham's roof, she concentrated on learning German together with James, who returned to divinity school in the fall of 1831. They decided that they would have to know the language to keep up with the new ideas coming out of Europe. James was troubled by Margaret's unhappiness, but he saw no way he could help her. After a September visit, he wrote in his journal that he was "puzzled" by her. "I am disposed to believe her the most remarkable of women, yet I am not sure but that I am to a certain degree imposed upon." She continued to fascinate him, but he worried that she was too dominating. George Davis told him that he too felt "constraint" when in Margaret's presence, and James thought the reason for this was that their "vanity" made them unwilling to reveal their incapacities to her. "I feel the expansion of her mind, & the decision of her opinions, & my own weakness and wants."[29]

Looking back on these "bitter months" in the Brattle House, Margaret wrote that "a treble weight" was pressing down on her, "the weight of deceived friendship, domestic discontent and bootless love." She was seldom free of the "great burden of family cares," and her mind was "pressed almost to bursting" with the excitement of learning German.[30]

On Thanksgiving Day, 1831, Timothy forced her to go to church, and she sat seething in her pew; the service's tone of cheerful gratitude and complacency jarred on her nerves—she was in no mood to give pious thanks. As soon as she could slip away, she ran outside and kept running, out beyond the town limits into the bleak November fields and through "the meditative woods." She ran herself into a state of exhaustion that resulted in the mystical experience described in Chapter 1, the first of several, which would almost always occur at times when she felt overburdened with unresolvable conflict or was suffering an overwhelming loss. The flash of insight she always remembered later was that she would have to school her soul to "learn to act" under life's limitations. She perceived that "there was no self; that selfishness was all folly, and the result of circumstance." "It was only because I thought self real that I suffered," she realized. "I had only to live in the idea of the All, and all was mine. This truth came to me, and I received it unhesitatingly; so that I was for that hour taken up in God." Admitting that she had only received a glimpse—"a touch," as she put it—of the "only haven of Insight," Margaret accepted the revelation that her hungry ego accounted for much of her misery.[31]

Coming a year and a half after her no-nonsense religious discourse to George Davis in which she placed herself squarely in the midst of the material world, this mystical experience represents a considerable leap, although she continued to relate learning and acting to religious experience. The "glimpse" may have slowly and unconsciously nourished some of Fuller's poems and flower pieces written a few years later, but in 1831, as she embarked on her twenties, the most noticeable change in her attitude and activity was a general seriousness and sobering, a cautiousness, and a consciousness of limitation.

She found a stimulating and steadying outlet in the study of German. Reading the recent German philosophers, novelists, and poets had become a craze among the Harvard students in the late 1820s. The enthusiasm was especially pronounced among the divinity students, all of whom were preparing for Unitarian leadership. Many of them were looking for ways to revitalize their creed's services and help Unitarianism meet the challenge of the immensely popular evangelical movement that was sweeping across many areas of the country with astounding success.

Searching for ways to include greater emotion and intensity of feeling in their religion, they found inspiration in the essays of Carlyle and Coleridge that pointed to the contemporary German writers as heralds of a new faith, a fresh and exciting way to reconcile rationality and feeling. "Close thy Byron—Open your Goethe!" Carlyle commanded. Margaret and James took him literally. At a time when it was almost impossible to buy a German book in Boston, James found a full set of Goethe's works, and the two threw themselves into learning to read them.[32]

James was astonished at her progress. Within three months she had read Goethe's *Faust, Torquato Tasso, Iphigenie, Hermann und Dorothea, Elective Affinities,* and *Memoirs.* She had also dipped into works by Tieck, Körner, and Richter, and was most of the way through Schiller's principal dramas and his lyric poetry. It was not only the amount of reading she was accomplishing that impressed James but "how comprehensive and understanding" her mind was. Her ability to trace ideas "through minds and works" carrying "the initiative idea everywhere" made him feel as if his own mind was a "sheet of white paper" in comparison. *Wilhelm Meisters Lehrjahre,* the novel in which Goethe set forth his doctrine of self-culture, appealed so much to the two that they adopted as their own the goal of the book's main character: "The cultivation of my individual self, here as I am, has from my youth upwards been constantly (though dimly) my wish and my purpose." It seemed to them a noble and idealistic aim, because, in James's words, "it recognized something divine, infinite, imperishable in the human soul,—something divine in outward nature and providence, by which the soul is led along its appointed way."[33]

From *Wilhelm Meisters Lehrjahre* and another of Goethe's novels, *Hermann und Dorothea,* they developed a code language in which they shared their experiences, using the names of Goethe's characters to refer to themselves or their friends in predicaments similar to those in the books. A lifetime aim of "extraordinary generous seeking," taken from *Wilhelm Meisters Lehrjahre,* became Margaret's motto. At a time when she felt she was marking time, it provided her with a purpose and a justification for the intensity with which she tried to extract the last ounce of meaning from every encounter and experience. The two even exchanged dreams. Margaret wrote of "a horrid dream":

I have often undergone in the visions of night the anguish of bereavement or hope deferred and I have sometimes thought that at those times I learned to read strange secrets in the hearts of others which real life never made familiar to my own. This might account for my understanding so well and sympathizing so little. And some believe the soul lives most in sleep.[34]

Goethe's doctrine gave a foreign gloss to the central idea in the teachings of William Ellery Channing that both Margaret and James had been brought up on—the idea that the soul was a "dynamic organism capable of cultivation to an ever-increasing harmonious growth." If an individual "does what he can to unfold all his powers and capacities, especially his nobler ones . . . [s/he] practices self-culture." Both Margaret and James believed that their earnest pursuit of learning and wider experience was sanctioned by their religion.[35]

So she could have a record of her response to each new writer, Margaret kept a reading journal; at one moment she was refreshed with the mysticism of Novalis, at another, stirred by the patriotism of Körner; she admired Schiller's insight into character, but she always returned to Goethe. The German romantic poets and dramatists encouraged her participation in the cult of romantic friendship, her exploration of the occult, her fascination with mystical pietism, her preoccupation with her inner life, and the high value she put on literature and art. But they also encouraged her extremism, her subjectivism that at times became morbid, and the disdain she sometimes expressed for the practical world of day-to-day politics and moneymaking.

No matter how far she wandered among the authors of the German school, she always returned to Goethe, who denied any alliance with the romantics. In him she found the broad humanism, the tolerance, and the open-mindedness to new ideas that liberated her thinking and molded her aspirations. In April 1832 she wrote in her journal: "He [Goethe] comprehends every feeling I have ever had so perfectly, expresses it so beautifully; but when I shut the book, it seems as if I had lost my personal identity."[36]

In the autumn of 1833 she began to translate Goethe's *Torquato Tasso*, the drama of a self-tortured Renaissance poet caught in an identity crisis, who finds his way to self-respect with the help of two women, a highly educated unmarried princess and a mother-educated married commoner. There was much in the conflict that echoed Fuller's predicament, especially in the scene she highlighted between the poet and the princess in which they express their envy of a life of action in the outside world.

When Margaret sent an early draft to James, to whom she had recently wept while describing her dejection, he encouraged her to dedicate herself to writing as a career. "Margaret, you are destined to be an author. I shall yet see you wholly against your will and drawn by circumstances, become the founder of an American literature!" But the compliment brought a troubled reply.

I know not whether to grieve that you too should think me fit for nothing but to write books or to feel flattered at the high opinion you seem to entertain of my powers. . . . Whether I was born to write I cannot tell but my bias towards the living and practical dates from my first consciousness and all I have known of women authors' mental history has but deepened the impression.
But I feel too variously on this subject to hope to be understood—I have often told you that I had two souls and they seem to roll over one another in the most incomprehensible way. Tastes and wishes point one way and I seem forced the other.[37]

"Tastes and wishes point one way and I seem forced the other" was to become her theme song for years to come. Every time she was on her way to an accommodation with her situation, circumstances would intervene and turn her in another direction. The struggle to reconcile her two souls—to satisfy her parents' and society's expectations on the one hand and her own personal goals for self-fulfillment on the other—was dominating her inner life. Poised tensely between two ways of being, she was afraid to make any definite decisions when she had so little control over her life; it was safer not to make any promises to herself or to anyone else. In the meantime, she told James that she was resigning herself "to the stream of events and take the day at its due worth. It is at such times I can learn."[38]

Whenever possible, Margaret escaped the tensions of the Brattle House by visiting Mrs. Farrar. Having recovered her spirits, she had written two successful children's books, *A Children's Robinson Crusoe* (1830) and *Lafayette* (1831), and was now entertaining constantly. She encouraged Margaret's friendship with her young cousin, Anna Barker, who visited Cambridge during the summers on her way to and from Newport, where her mother, Eliza Hazard Barker, had been brought up and where the family still kept a summer cottage. Three years younger than Margaret, Anna was a natural and beautiful young woman with so charming a manner that even sensible Eliza Farrar viewed her as a "beautiful enchantress." Her father, Jacob Barker, was a Quaker merchant and politician who was a founder of Tammany Hall and had helped finance the American war effort in the War of 1812. Not in the least ashamed to call himself an "adventurer," he was flamboyant and combative, but was greatly admired for his business acumen.[39]

Even though Margaret saw Anna only for a few days or, at most, for two or three weeks a year, she chose her for her dearest friend. She put her on a pedestal, wrote poems to her, called her pet names, such as her "divinist love." She told all her other friends about their special attachment and for the next few years arranged her summers so as to spend as much time as possible in Anna's company. In return, Anna was affectionately responsive. When James Clarke met Anna a few years later in New Orleans, he wrote to Margaret, "lovely she is, how she idolizes you, how happy it must make you to be loved by her so much."[40]

In her possessiveness toward Anna, in her proud flaunting of their friendship, in the excitement she expressed before and after Anna's visits, something more compelling was going on than in her warm and lasting friendships with Elizabeth Randall, Ellen Sturgis, Amelia Greenwood, Almira Penniman Barlow, and Mary Soley. For the next ten years, the relationship with Anna, protected by months of absence from the ruthlessness of daily give-and-take, served as Margaret's most cherished romantic love. Their interchange of letters in these early years has not survived, but Margaret's poems and terms of endearment, especially her later characterization of her love for Anna as "the same love we shall feel when we are angels," suggest that Anna's attraction, while based on the power of opposites (the beautiful Anna, the brilliant Margaret), was possibly sustained by Margaret's need, as Bell Chevigny has suggested, "to resolve her sexual identity by transcending sex itself." This licensed highly charged statements of attachment to her men friends as well. During her adolescent years, Fuller's expressions of affection to her men and women friends were not remarkably different.[41]

Although the rules of propriety forbade public display of attractions and passions between the sexes, affectionate behavior and language between women were accepted as girlishly pure, a sign of sensibility and emotional responsiveness. Though sexual feelings clearly played their part in the custom of amorous display, they were generally regarded as innocent, permissible, and unthreatening—of a different order than those between man and woman. In her role as social arbiter, Eliza Farrar was aware of the complications lurking in the practice, but she did not forbid private intimacies between her young charges. In her best seller *A Young Lady's Friend,* she cautioned:

All kissing and caressing of your female friends should be kept for your hours of privacy, and never indulged in before gentlemen. There are some reasons for this, which will readily suggest themselves, and others, which can only be known to those well acquainted with the world, but which are conclusive against the practice.[42]

In one of Margaret's letters to James, she had said that "some *imaginative* love in whose atmosphere your fancy might breathe and plum[e] herself" was desirable for a young person of passion. Margaret chose Anna Barker as her imaginative love, in whose aura she breathed and plumed herself; she awarded her an important role in her inner life and identified with her possessively to the extent that when the stability of their romantic friendship was threatened years later Margaret experienced a major crisis in her life.[43]

In the spring of 1832 Timothy found a satisfactory farm for sale in Groton. It belonged to his friend Judge Samuel Dana of the Massachusetts Supreme Judicial Court. For most of the summer they haggled about the price of the twenty-eight-acre parcel of land with homestead, outbuildings, woodlot, and pasture. When the sale went through it was decided that the Fullers would take possession in time for spring planting in 1833.

Although Margaret had plenty of time to prepare for what was coming, the final decision was devastating for her. She would be separated from everything that satisfied her hunger for new experiences and for intellectual and social stimulation. She wrote James that she feared being thrown back on her own resources as never before.

[T]he time is probably near when I must live alone, to all intents and purposes,—separate entirely my acting from my thinking world, take care of my ideas without aid,—except from the illustrious dead,—answer my own questions, correct my own feelings, and do all that hard work for myself.[44]

Elizabeth Palmer Peabody, an intellectual young woman in Boston whom Margaret knew, had just made a stir with her translation of Joseph De Gérando's book, *Self-Culture,* a French treatise expounding on the doctrine of moral progress through self-education that Goethe had explored in *Wilhelm Meister.* With the hope that she too might be able to begin her literary career as a translator, Margaret spent her last few Cambridge months working on her *Torquato Tasso* translation. James was translating Schiller's *Maid of Orleans.* Together they studied English verse forms so as to make their translations scan.

By the time the Fuller family was ready to move to Groton in early April 1833, Margaret had almost completed her translation. She had also begun her first attempt at fiction, "Camillus and Lelio," in which Camillus speaks in Fuller's voice of "restlessness" and "ungratified ambition" and "the religion which should console, is ever commenting on the unused talent." When she sent it to James, he commented in his journal, "Is this anything more than a desire of finding something to love?" He promised to keep in touch with her by sending every few weeks a letter journal of his activities and thoughts.[45]

When the family finally departed for Groton in a train of buggies and carts,

Margaret managed to get permission to stay on in Cambridge for a few extra days so she would not miss two great events of the Boston cultural season: the appearance at the Tremont Theatre—beginning April 16—of Eliza Farrar's personal friend, Fanny Kemble, the world-renowned actress, in her role as Shakespeare's Juliet, and the thrilling display at the Boston Athenaeum of its collection of plaster casts of famous sculptures (including an *Apollo Belvedere*) for the first time at night, thanks to the installation of a recent innovation, the gaslight.

But a few days before the opening night at the Tremont Theatre and the gala evening at the Athenaeum, a Groton farmhand, while tossing logs on a pile, accidently hit ten-year-old Arthur Fuller. The boy was in bed, feverish with a concussion and blind in both eyes. Margaret was summoned immediately. She scribbled James a hasty goodbye and, after she was settled in Groton, she wrote him that she was trying to accommodate herself to her new home. Elizabeth Randall was giving her lessons on the guitar, and she was now able to sing, "Far from my thoughts vain world begone." It was better in many respects than living with Uncle Abraham in the Brattle House.

I can walk out or into it and never think of a prison—I have got some splendid far blue hills to look at and it does not hurt me now to think of distant things—I extend my arms and utter forth apostrophes. . . . I know no poverty but have no tickets in the lottery to make me anxious and all things are bearable except suspense and remorse.[46]

Yet earning money—think of that. 'Tis but a little but 'tis a beginning. I shall be a professional character yet.

Vain World Begone

MARGARET never understood her father's decision to move to Groton. She said she "secretly wondered how a mind which had for thirty years been so widely engaged in the affairs of men could care so much for trees and crops." Only the younger boys could possibly benefit, but even that advantage seemed blighted when Arthur's accident resulted in the loss of sight in one eye.

Timothy, no longer in a position to legislate Jeffersonian principles in the wider community, now planned to live as a farmer-scholar as Jefferson himself had done in his retirement from public life. Convinced that "the endurance and industry" of farm life would harden his children and make them able candidates for Jefferson's natural aristocracy, he imposed a rigorous routine: early hours, cold baths, and simple meals of bread and milk.[1]

The square farmhouse, though less dignified than the Dana Mansion or the Brattle House, was large and comfortable; it sat on a rise at the north end of Farmer's Row with a wide view toward both Mount Monadnock and Mount Wachusett. During the first spring and summer they built a new barn, seeded five acres in corn, beans, pumpkins, and potatoes, and fenced another ten acres as pasturage for three cows, a yoke of oxen, and the family horse, Old Charley. With Margaret's help, Margarett Crane Fuller planted a herbaceous border along the walk from the side piazza all the way to the road. Margaret ran the home school, served as the family seamstress, and helped her mother in the dairy.[2]

At the bottom of the hill, Timothy built a rustic arbor in a section of the woodlot and christened it Margaret's Grove, but she found herself another hideaway, a quarter of a mile from the house on the side of the river. "The birds and the wind . . . and the thick carpet of last year's dried oak leaves do their best to make me feel at home." She called it Hazel Grove.[3]

In early May, after a quarrel with her mother, she rushed off to her grove and began a Groton journal with an Italian inscription: "Scrivo sol per sfogar l'interna" ("I write only to vent my inner life"). She devoted a soliloquy to a confession of her faults—"Thou art too vain, too selfish"—and the unlikelihood that she would ever marry; she ended with a prayer.

> But Oh—might I but see a little onward
> Father, I cannot be a spirit of power

> I am not fitted for a spirit of love
> Since thou hast torn me from the path which nature
> Seemed to appoint—oh deign to ope another
> Where I may walk with heart, with hope assured.

Experimenting with romantic moods and verse forms, she sought inspiration in lightning storms, moonlit nights, and eclipses of the moon. Meditating on the Muse of poetry, she filled her notebooks with prayers for wisdom, beauty, and goodness.[4]

She immersed herself in Goethe and identified with his thinking. Confident that he would have been able to show her a way out of her difficulties, she wished she could see him and tell him her "state of mind" (Goethe died in 1832). He would have shown her "how to rule circumstances instead of being ruled by them." When she was reading Goethe's *Second Residence in Rome,* she wrote:

I shut the book each time with an earnest desire to live as he did—always to have some engrossing object of pursuit—I do sympathize deeply with a mind in that state—while mine is being used up by ounces. . . . I am being dejected and uneasy when I see no results from my daily existence, but I am suffocated and lost when I have not the bright feeling of progression.[5]

She was not completely cut off from her friends. Elizabeth Randall's family spent their summers in the nearby village of Stow, and other friends often came to visit. There were a number of Fuller family friends living in Groton, Lawrences and Danas and the Reverend Charles Robinson. James faithfully sent her his diary and occasionally rode over to see her from his grandparents' home in Newton.

To comments he made in his April–May letter journal that there was "no all-comprehensive idea," that "Every man leant on his favorite one," she responded aggressively, revealing her restlessness and her yearning for some bedrock philosophy on which to rely.

Now this is just my case. I *do* want a system which shall suffice to my character, and in whose applications I shall have faith. I do not wish to *reflect* always, if reflecting must be always about one's identity, whether "*ich*" am the true "*ich*" etc. I wish to arrive at that point where I can trust myself, and leave off saying, "It seems to me," and boldly feel, It *is* so to me.[6]

But her adherence to the mixture of Unitarian self-culture and Goethe's quest philosophy of continual "generous seeking" outlawed resting in any one safe position. She was also reading the collected works of Friedrich von Hardenberg, the German mystic and novelist who called himself Novalis. His theories of apprenticeship in life and literature opposed Goethe's ideal. Trained in medicine and mathematics, he had formulated an aesthetics that called for using the "slumbering religious sense" to raise the self to ever-higher levels of consciousness. His mystically erotic hymns, lyric poems, and novels influenced her mystical contemplations. She called him "a wondrous youth," and in her Novalis journal she explained her fascination: "For mysticism is by no means fanaticism. . . . In its pure significance it implies merely a steadfast listening to a still, small voice of the soul in preference to the trumpet calls of the outside world." Novalis offered her mysticism as a method to use in exploring her inner life.[7]

After his graduation from divinity school, James Clarke planned to take over as minister of the small Unitarian congregation in Louisville, Kentucky. In search of a challenge, he wanted to strengthen the feeble beginnings of Unitarianism on the other side of the Appalachian Mountains in the new West where the church had recently established outposts in St. Louis, Buffalo, and Cincinnati, as well as Louisville. In mid-July, just days before his departure, he came out to Groton for two days to say goodbye. Expecting that their parting would be marked by some recognition of what they had meant to each other during the past three and a half years, Margaret gave him a "Brahmah lock book," a diary of fine leather with a lock, but James bade her a perfunctory farewell, leaving her deeply disappointed.[8]

After James left, Margaret began to brood about him. Angry that he took their friendship so lightly, she thought it was futile to continue giving so much of herself when she was merely taken for granted. She could not admit that she was in love with him, but she wanted him to clarify where they stood with one another.

As soon as she knew that he had arrived in Louisville, she wrote him confessing her anger over his lack of response when she tried to share her feelings with him:

[W]hen borne beyond myself I have related to you some page of feeling and you would hear me with cold gravity, then rise and leave me. O how I hated that impulse which showed me a slave for I gave my heart's blood unpaid—a child—an infant *still*, for I sinned against my own conviction and violated my character. . . . I longed—(may I say it without irreverence) to give you my blessing when you departed—to express the nature of my hopes and expectations for you in appropriate words, to compress all I had ever thought and felt toward you. . . . But your manner repressed me and it was well I believe for thousands of things styled extravagances in the workingday world were in my head to do.

Having made her point, she confessed, "Now that I have lost you, I think of you constantly," noting that she sometimes carried on imaginary conversations with him in her haunt in the woods. But James, who was discovering that the western settlers were not hungering for liberal Christianity (he never had more than thirty in his church on Sunday), disregarded her distress. In November she threatened to discontinue their correspondence because of the "tone" of his letters.[9]

"Surely *we* cannot afford to waver from our firm faith in our perfect appreciation of each other," he replied. In January she repeated her threat in a muddled letter that equated her feelings for James to those she had once held for George Davis.

since he [George Davis] could willingly forfeit the attachment of the only person on earth who knew him thoroughly, I could never confide again in an attachment founded on similar causes. . . . I will never be to you as George is to me a walking momento haunting your day-dreams—But a second shock to my faith and my pride were not bearable—now I must be prepared, steeled against the assaults of fate—'Tis not that I think you capable under any circumstances of selfishness. I know your heart, dear James, it is not *that* I distrust. But your path and mine will gradually diverge and an intimacy, so intellectual, so unimaginative suffers from absence and in lessening ceases to be any-thing. . . . I am three and twenty. I believe in love and friendship, but I cannot but see that circumstances have appalling power and that those links which are not riveted by situation, by interest (I mean not merely worldly interest but the instinct of self-preservation) may be lightly broken by a chance touch.[10]

Margaret's fear of losing James was aggravated by dissension at home. William Henry's career as a store clerk was proving unsteady, and Eugene disappointed his parents at the end of his junior year at Harvard by failing to win a part in the Exhibition, the annual event at which students with high records displayed their accomplishments in poems and orations. To Margaret's chagrin, Eugene's poor grades were in the very subjects that she had prepared him in for college. Throughout that first Groton summer she tutored him. "[H]e is a sweet youth," she wrote, and "may perhaps be a good and happy man—but he has no ambition." She wanted to admire him as a man of accomplishment but had given up all hope of that.[11]

In the autumn, when Eugene was back in college and Timothy needed the younger boys in the fields, she was allowed to make a long visit to Cambridge. Helen Davis gave a party for her; Dr. Felton, professor of Greek at Harvard, lent her his copy of Flaxman's etchings; she heard George Bancroft's lecture in praise of *Wilhelm Meister;* she enjoyed conversing with William Eliot, who was about to take over a parish in St. Louis. Eliza Farrar said she would try to get the *Tasso* translation published. (It was later said that they contrived a plan to send it to a British publisher under the guise that the author was British, but the plan fell through.) Henry Hedge asked her to join a literary club he hoped to form in imitation of the German literary circles—"a few friends meet together, converse on various topics relating to Literature, Art & Life, read essays or tales which we have composed."[12] The highlight of her visit was an invitation from James's mother and sister to accompany them to New York in a group including Elizabeth Randall and Almira and David Barlow. Other than brief visits to relatives in southern Maine, the New York expedition was Margaret's first journey beyond the outskirts of Boston and Groton.

Waiting for Timothy's permission and money for the trip kept her in a heightened state of anticipation until the last minute. In New York she visited

Anna Barker, who was staying with New York relatives. "I went through the second chapter in my acquaintance with this 'fairy-like musick' very happily," she wrote of Anna to James. "I made some amusing acquaintance, heard wealth of good stories and collected quantities of those most desirable articles—new ideas." She saw a "real Titian" and won the affection of James's discriminating sister Sarah, a professional painter who had studied with Washington Allston and had shown her paintings at the Boston Athenaeum. "We began as usual by expressing our certainty that we should never get along together," Sarah wrote James, "and that, being conceded, we did get along most swimingly."[13]

At the end of November she returned home to the forced seclusion of the New England winter. By December 24 she could boast that for a whole month, "my father has not once seemed dissatisfied with me." As she had set up a schoolroom for the younger children and William Henry was between jobs that winter, she persuaded her father to let him come home so he could benefit from further instruction. The work was draining. "Four pupils are a serious and fatiguing charge for one of my some what ardent and impatient disposition," she wrote.[14]

Her plan for the winter was to study the history and geography of modern Europe, the elements of architecture, the works of Alfieri, the historical and critical works of Goethe and Schiller, and the outline of the history of the United States. Her father was devoting his evenings to writing a biography of Jefferson. She joined him in reading Jefferson's letters and in studying the lives of Benjamin Franklin and Benjamin Rush. "I rejoice if only because my father and I have so much in common on this subject," she wrote. "All my other pursuits have led me away from him; here he has so much information and ripe judgement."[15]

While granting the benefits of studying with her father, she still indulged in fiction. That winter she read and analyzed in her journal the recent novels of Benjamin Disraeli. She identified with Contarini Fleming, the fanatically-ambitious hero of Disraeli's autobiographical novel of that name, because he had many childhood fantasies of future fame and glory, very similar to her own. "My childhood was full of presentiments like that of Contarini Fleming," she wrote, "but I differ from the author who thinks himself a natural human—I know I was not and would gladly extirpate the causes of this factitious state of being instead of combining a system of philosophy in conformity with it."[16]

A disturbing book that connected mental disorder with early intellectual training added to her concern about the connection between her ambition and her uneven temperament: Amariah Brigham's *Remarks on the Influence of Mental Cultivation and Mental Excitement on Health*. Brigham, the first superintendent of the country's first major mental hospital (in Utica, New York) and founder of the journal which became the present *American Journal of Psychiatry*, criticized the obsession of Americans with education. Driven by the belief that they could raise their station in life by cultivating their minds, but ignorant of the dangerous consequences of mental "overexcitement" in early childhood, Americans were starting the process much too early. The dangers were especially great in the case of women, Brigham warned. Because they were "endowed with quicker sensibility and [a] far more active imagination than men," it was important that their "exquisite sensibility" should never be allowed to become "excessive" from too much mental stimulation. Critical of "the folly and false vanity of parents, who are ambitious of holding forth their children as specimens of extraordinary talent" by imposing on them intellectual tasks which "frequently pave the way to decided paroxysms of convulsions," Brigham concluded that "early forcing' could even be the cause of premature death."[17]

"Many observations in this book give me new light on myself," Margaret wrote in her journal. "From my own experience merely, I should go great lengths with him." She recalled her childhood "attacks of delirium" after late sessions of reciting Latin to her father, and a period of sleepwalking and frightening "spectral illusions," all symptoms, according to Brigham, of "premature development of the mind." She could not see any advantage in her "precocity." In her journal she pleaded, "O Amariah, can it be that I am doomed in accordance with thy fiat to be driven down the stream of time ere my summer is well begun. . . . Forbid it—my own energies—Amariah! I defy thee." For the rest of her life she held to her self-diagnosis from Brigham's book that "early forcing" was the root cause of many of her difficulties and that there was an "inevitable reaction of body on mind." Persuaded that she would have been healthier and happier "had sense, intellect, affection, passion been brought out in natural order," she now had an explanation for the intensity of her feelings and her overexcitable nature.[18]

While making every effort to adapt to the farm routine, Margaret dreamed of escape. At the beginning of the winter she wrote James asking him what he would think of her going west to teach in a school. "I wish to earn money to go to Italy," she explained. She wanted to make plans for "the bye and by." When he did not answer, she wrote again. "[T]he schoolmistress plan" was not "a mere chimera. . . . I cannot yet give up my beloved plans of travel and I can think of no other way of fulfilling them." At the end of February, James sent a discouraging reply: "This western country is a wild country and I would advise no female friend of mine to come to it in any capacity which would bring her into such collision with the natives as you would be as a teacher," he cautioned. Cincinnati, where Catharine Beecher had recently founded the Western Teachers Training School, was the only civilized place. He mentioned a Cincinnati school where Margaret might apply, but he did not encourage her to come.[19]

Margaret did not dare broach the matter with her father, but her mother, when told, pointed to her uncertain health and appealed to Margaret not to leave her alone in charge of the women's work on the farm. "This excellent woman and beloved friend has of late been subject to violent illnesses of a sort which requires great attention. Unless her heath should improve I ought not to leave her and assume such a responsibility that I could not return if she wanted me," Margaret wrote James. "But all may be changed again. . . . I would like to have some defined plan to which I may turn if circumstance (O unspiritual diety, I must again call thee) should render it desirable." Whereas her father held Margaret to the farm by his strict laws of family duty, her mother's dependence on her held her there just as surely.[20]

From the time Margaret was seven, when Timothy first went off to Washington for several months of every year, the responsibilities of the elder daughter had been impressed on her. While her mother's frailty was a given of the family self-image, Margaret was cast in the role of the all-capable woman who could read Virgil while rocking a cradle. "I had too much strength to be crushed," she wrote of herself in her "Autobiographical Romance." She was trained in "Roman virtue," she believed.[21] It was unthinkable to abandon her mother now. It might also have been unthinkable to break with the family to which she was so strongly bound. It was a decision Margaret could not bring herself to make.

Throughout her childbearing years, Margarett Crane Fuller had suffered frequent bouts of illness—she was thought to have a weak heart—and Margaret often worried about her mother's health. She had a recurrent dream of her mother's death and burial. After the dreams, while still half-asleep, she would lie sobbing, caught up, as she described it, in grief and dread. On a conscious level, Margaret interpreted the dream as a warning that she should protect her mother and shield her from shocks. The closest Margaret could bring herself to unburdening all this to James was to tell him that she lived under "painful domestick circumstances" which were likely "to become much more difficult." She found it impossible to be "frank"; she could only pray "that my talents with which Heaven has endowed me may be ripened to their due perfection and not utterly wasted in fruitless struggles with difficulties which I cannot overcome."[22]

In late April 1834 she wrote James again, asking him to make inquiries as to what sort of compensation she could expect if she were to take a teaching position in Cincinnati.

Money, Money, root of all evil—how much have I not suffered already with things connected with its absence or superfluity. A money talk always makes me wish to shuffle off this mortal veil more than anything. However, it is hardly proper for a lady to talk to a gentleman on such topicks even between you and me, who have always been more bluntly Citoyen and Citoyenne to one another than two young persons brought up in *tolerably* polished society ever were—[23]

They agreed to discuss her Cincinnati plans when he came home for the summer, but Margaret's short temper was to prevent that discussion. Soon after James returned, Margaret caught sight of him at a party talking with Harriet

Russell, George Davis's fiancée. (The engagement of Harriet and George had been announced in September 1832.) Margaret expected that James would rush to greet her as soon as he saw her. Instead, he merely acknowledged her presence and continued his conversation with Harriet. His indifference made her snap. She was about to go to Newport to stay with Anna Barker and had intended to invite James to visit them there, but she told him after the party that she did not want to see him anymore.

When James was safely back in Louisville, he wrote a letter of apology. Acknowledging that he had been "impolite," he explained that he had been unable on the spur of the moment to return to "the old confessional vein" after a year "deprived of all sympathy." He understood that she was "hurt," but he thought it was less because of his distant manner than annoyance that he "should really prefer the talk of such a child as you think Harriet" to conversing "with the friend of so many treasured hours." For the first time he articulated clearly to Margaret how he felt toward her.

There are many things you alone can appreciate and understand. I do not wish like George to be independent of your influence. I do not wish to separate what is yours from what is mine in the web of my character. I feel grateful for the high intellectual culture and excitement of which you have been to me the source. . . . I beg you not to determine rashly, from a Pride of Understanding, that our friendship is over. . . . Do not determine that if we are not *all* to each other we shall be nothing. I will never find such another as you, and I think you will not meet with exactly such another friend as

Yours truly[24]

It was not a love letter, but she was satisfied that James had finally gone to the trouble to pay attention to her cries for clarification. She forgave him, even though she had been justified, she wrote him, in being annoyed. She hoped they could "begin a new era" and "alter the *nature*" of their "friendship without annihilating its soul." She proposed as a model Mrs. Farrar's close relationship with the Reverend Orville Dewey, who had been Mrs. Farrar's minister in New Bedford. "I am willing to resume correspondence with you," Margaret wrote, "and time will decide whether we can resist the changes in one another. Time only can do it—I shall therefore say nothing further on the subject."[25]

Margaret's happy visit in Newport with Anna made it easier to excuse James. Anna's parents, brothers, and sisters came and went while Margaret and Anna rode horseback, galloped across the beaches, climbed the rocks, listened to the sea, and joined in the obligatory social rituals of resort life. She was fascinated to meet Eliza Farrar's friend Fanny Kemble, the English actress, who was in Newport with her new husband, the southern planter Pierce Butler (whose ruthlessness to his slaves Fanny was to chronicle later).

After two weeks in Newport Anna returned with Margaret for a two-week visit to the Farrars. It was by far the longest period Margaret was ever to spend near Anna. "I love Anna passing well," she wrote when she returned home; "a delightful harmony reigned between us—we were surprisingly dear & I am sure dear to each other—and it is a real grief to me that I must live so far from the light of those sweet eyes."[26]

After her vacation the return to farm life was depressing. In October she wrote Almira Barlow that she was "more and more dissatisfied with this world" and could not find a "home" in it. In the summer and fall of 1835 another group of her friends were marrying: Mary Soley to a wealthy Rhode Islander, William Bradford DeWolfe; Amelia Greenwood to a good-humored doctor, George Bartlett; and on Thursday morning, October 16, George Davis married Harriet Russell. Harriet wrote Margaret "a pretty note" inviting her to the wedding; Margaret returned her regrets in a manner "neat and appropriate."[27]

During the fall of 1834 Margaret's home school was all but defunct. Ellen was in a local school for girls, and Arthur and Richard were in a school in nearby Stow where Eugene was teaching. He had surprised everyone by winning a part in his senior class Exhibition. William Henry, after quarreling with his father, had taken flight to the West Indies. With only the obstreperous Lloyd to teach, Margaret took the time, at Timothy's urging, to write a long letter to the *Boston Advertiser and Patriot* rebutting an attack on the character of Brutus made by the young Democratic historian George Bancroft in an article in the *North American Review*. Bancroft had claimed that it was only Brutus's success as an assassin that had made him a hero. In Margaret's letter, written very much in her father's voice and published on November 27—and signed merely "J"— she took issue with Bancroft's characterization of Brutus as a man of "head-strong, unbridled disposition," as "time-serving," "treacherous," and "the dupe of more sagacious men." Depending largely on Plutarch, she questioned Bancroft's authorities and concluded with a charge that would be leveled against her within a few years.

[A]s the avenues to the temple of Fame become more and more thronged with eager devotees there is a class who seek notoriety by broaching new opinions on topics and characters . . . as well settled as the relation the earth bears the sun. They labor to set aside the verdict of our forefathers; and industriously collect from the annals of the past, rubbish beneath which they seek to bury the shrines of our old religion.[28]

Fuller wrote Henry Hedge that she considered the affair "highly flattering." During the winter of 1834–35, she was keeping in close touch with Hedge. She was a regular reader of the Unitarian journals and was interested in church controversies less for theological distinctions than for what they revealed about new channels of thought. In March 1833 Hedge had published in the Unitarian journal, the *Christian Examiner*, an article which he claimed later was the "*first word*" in America to state the case for "Transcendentalism," the new philosophical outlook that was arousing curiosity and some alarm in the Unitarian community.[29]

The "transcendental philosophy" derived from the German philosopher Immanuel Kant, whose monumental work, *Critique of Pure Reason* (1781), challenged the rationalist philosophy of John Locke. Whereas Lockean philosophy described the mind as a blank slate accumulating impressions, ideas, and sensations, the transcendental philosophy distinguished between two powers of the mind: One, the understanding, was directed to the phenomenal world, and the other, reason, was an active and creative capacity that arranged and ordered these impressions in the light of "the free intuition" or "interior consciousness," thus explaining our knowledge of phenomena inaccessible to our five senses—phenomena such as God or creation. (Kant had called this creative operation of the mind "transcendental" because its workings defied analysis by rational means.)[30]

Hedge explained that the transcendental philosophers wrote for those who "seek with faith and hope for a solution to questions that philosophy meddles not with,—questions which relate to spirit and form, substance and life, free will and fate, God and eternity." He defended "the Newness," or the "New School," as a few Americans were now calling it, for extending "the kingdom of human knowledge," for giving a fresh impulse to scientific research, increasing moral liberty, and encouraging the investigation of "every corner of biblical lore." In short, its "quickening power" was influencing every department of science and art.[31]

The New School also begged the question of the divinity of Christ and the authenticity of biblical history. Fuller now felt the need to come to grips with some of her uncertainties. She turned to Henry Hedge for advice. The ideas of her infidel and deist friends and "skeptical notions" of her own were haunting her. She wanted "to examine thoroughly . . . the evidences of the Christian religion."[32]

Hedge cautioned her that "the evidence that Christianity comes from God is a matter of experience, not of the historicity of any of the books of the *Bible*," but that if she insisted she might start with Johann Gottfried Eichhorn's *Einleitung ins Alte Testament* since there was no equivalent in English. While she waited to get a copy of Eichhorn, she read Jahn's *History of the Hebrew Commonwealth* and was studying the Old Testament in Old German in hopes that "it would seem fresh in a foreign language." Her wish was "to be a Christian . . . not in sickness and adversity but in health and in full possession of my reasoning powers." She had no doubts whatsoever about the immortality of the soul but found it difficult to believe consistently in the loving, benevolent God of the Unitarians.

[I]t so often seems to me that we are ruled by an iron destiny—I have no confidence in God as a Father, if I could believe in Revelation and consequently in an over-ruling Providence many things which seem dark and hateful to me now would be made clear or I could wait—My mind often burns with thoughts on these subjects and I long to pour out my soul to some person of superior calmness and strength and fortunate in more accurate knowledge. I should feel such a quieting reaction. But generally I think it is best I should go through these conflicts alone. The process will be slower, more irksome, more distressing, but the result will be all my own and I shall feel greater confidence in it.[33]

While she wrestled with the great question of faith, her home school had grown; she was earning money for the first time in her life. In the middle of the winter Eugene had gone off to Culpeper County, Virginia, to teach in a school run by a relative of the Higginsons. Margaret hoped that a wider knowledge of the world would instill in him "a steady and honorable ambition," but she feared that he was still in need of parental "checks"—his job in Stow had terminated when he swallowed some lamplighter by mistake. Arthur and Richard were now back in her schoolroom; she had three Fullers and three neighborhood children as pupils.

"Yet earning money—think of that," she wrote James. " 'Tis but a little but 'tis a beginning. I shall be a professional character yet." For months she had made no further mention of going west to teach, but when she read about the student rebellion over the slavery issue at Lane Seminary in Cincinnati, she wrote James, "My desire to go to the West is revived by the doings at Lane Seminary— That sounds from afar so like the conflict of keen life—."[34]

For over a year the students at the Cincinnati theological school had been holding meetings debating the two most widely held proposals to solve the slave problem: abolition versus colonization. Many were openly fraternizing with blacks and holding tutoring sessions. When the students voted overwhelmingly for emancipation, the trustees banned all public meetings and fired Professor John Morgan, who was known to have incited the students to take a stand on the sensitive issue. In protest, over fifty students left Lane Seminary en masse and joined Morgan at nearby Oberlin College where the professor had been welcomed. Margaret yearned to be part of some similar dramatic action. She wrote James despairingly that in Groton the antislavery activity was in the hands of the idle elderly and manifested itself only in "incessant lectures."[35]

Out of the blue, at the end of the winter Margaret received two unexpected requests that offered her a chance to publish. On the same day—February 20, 1835—both Henry Hedge in Cambridge and James Clarke in Louisville wrote asking for her help. Each announced that he was about to publish a new periodical, and both begged her for contributions.

Henry Hedge was on his way to take over the Unitarian parish in Bangor, Maine. To keep in touch with his Boston and Cambridge friends, he was proposing a journal to propagate the new ideas coming out of Europe. He envisioned "a periodical of an entirely different character of any now existing," he explained to Margaret, "a journal of spirit, not philosophy, in which we are to enlist all the Germano-philosophico-literary talent in the country." He asked Margaret to send him anything "transcendental," either an essay or literary criticism. Hedge judged that this would be the best way of influencing "our generation and converting the heathen of this land." George Ripley, another young Unitarian minister who was writing on "the Newness," would be his coeditor. They had already recruited a galaxy of advanced thinkers: Ralph Waldo Emerson, James Marsh, William Henry Furness; and they even planned to invite Thomas Carlyle. Margaret wrote back that she was "honoured" to be deemed worthy of lending a hand, but she was "merely Germanico" and not "transcendental." But after Hedge settled in Maine she heard nothing further of his ambitious plans.[36]

James and his friends—the Unitarian ministers in the West—were ready to go to press with their publication in one or two months. "We mean to make this a first rate affair," James wrote, "and to combine literature and other miscellaneous matters with religious discussions. I mean it to have a Western air and spirit, a free and unshackled spirit and form." He demanded "a bundle of good long (or short) articles" as soon as possible. Margaret replied that she was ready with two book reviews and had another in her head; she had in addition perfected plans for six historical tragedies, but her attempts at writing them had "served to show the vast difference betwixt conception and execution." Another idea was "a series of tales illustrating Hebrew history." How was she ever going to find "the peace and time" to follow up her ideas?[37]

On April 1 Margaret sent off her first packet of manuscript to the *Western Messenger*. In answer to her request for a professional evaluation, James wrote that she was not "distinct enough, not enough plainness and detail." One of her essays was "a perfect labyrinth." Her language was "too elevated"; he wanted "a various and conversational" tone. She suffered from being "too lofty." Western people, he reminded her, "are no reading people, but an observing and talking people, and an *acting* people." Their "thoughts are sudden, strong, frequently deep; never long pursued." He told her she could be "as transcendental" as she pleased.[38]

"Why you call me 'Transcendental' I don't know," Margaret protested. "As far as I know myself I am at present 'all no how' except on matters of taste." She asked for help in launching "a scheme" to establish herself as a translator. She would begin with some French short stories. "My aim is *money*," she announced. "I want an independent income very much." But she needed someone to help her find a publisher. For all her "aspirations after independence," she still did not have the nerve, she confessed, "to walk into the Boston [publishing] establishments" and ask them to buy her work. What she needed was a friend to encourage her and to bolster her confidence, someone "at once efficient and sympathizing." She could never get through to James—who had his coterie of fellow ministers and old school friends to help him—how difficult it was for her to establish her "sphere of action" all by herself.[39]

James managed to persuade Ephraim Peabody, the editor-in-chief of the

Western Messenger, to publish Fuller's first literary criticism in the magazine's first issue in June 1835. (Peabody's objection was that the article was "undignified" and unsuited to a western audience.)[40] The article was a review of two recent biographies, one of the pastoral poet, George Crabbe, and the other of the popular writer on religious subjects, Hannah More.

Identifying with her two subjects, Margaret emphasized how important it was for both More and Crabbe to have had sympathetic guides to steer them in the right direction at the outset of their careers. Hannah More had a favored place in the "grand theatre" of the literary society of late-eighteenth-century London. Just to imagine the excitement of More's life was enough, Fuller wrote, to make her "guilty of the child-like folly of wishing for a monarchy." More's life was most interesting when she was moving back and forth between Garrick's London, where she was received "in the most brilliant circle of that brilliant capital," and her home in Bristol. Stimulated by the new ideas of the metropolis, she could retreat to the provincial town to write. The most important lesson Fuller found in the life of George Crabbe was "the genuine power of the much-mistaken human will." Moved by the description of Crabbe's "forlorn" years in London, when he was living on "fourpence" and enduring a series of "repulses" and "disappointments" without complaint, she recommended the book "to the consideration of all those sorrowful geniuses who are forever telling their friends and themselves what they might have done if some slight check, forsooth, had not blighted the hopeful bud."[41]

Fuller's first published literary criticism, though lively, was almost entirely subjective. The language was stilted, and her allusions were literary and forced. Although brisk and full of ideas, the review suffered from an excess of preaching. She had read too much in church journals and the didactic *North American Review* and listened to too many sermons and political speeches to be free of their influence.

Her review of Edward Bulwer's novels appeared in the August issue. Although the young Bulwer (later Bulwer-Lytton) was generally dismissed in America as an author who wrote about the dissolute society of upper-class Britain, she defended her right to choose him as a subject on the grounds that "every author" requires someone to "buckler him against the hostile" as well as explain him to "the careless millions." Bulwer-Lytton was worthy of examination because of the moral progress his novels displayed.[42]

Later in the year, when James Freeman Clarke had become editor of the *Western Messenger,* he published two more of Fuller's book reviews; the more ambitious was of Henry Taylor's popular patriotic play, *Philip van Artevelde,* in which she began to articulate a theory of criticism and aesthetics that would develop in sophistication over the next decade. Here she chose as her standard the conventional one of her time, the comparison of the work with one or more works of the same genre already accepted in the literary canon. To clarify her standards she went to some lengths to distinguish between the terms "classical" and "romantic," coming down in favor of the former in spite of her personal inclinations. But the romantic found its outlet in her prophecy of the role the arts could play in a future day when the new American democracy would come into its own, when there would be "an American mind" as well as an American system of government, a time when American culture would be on a par with the more developed nations of the world. "Then—ah, not yet! shall our literature make its own laws and give its own watchwords; till then we must learn and borrow from that of nations who possess a higher degree of cultivation though a much lower one of happiness."[43]

Unlike most of the members of the literary establishment of the time, she was interested not in the making of a national literature but rather in developing the attitudes and values conducive to self-culture. Margaret's dream of a future golden age would not come until the "broad West" swarmed with "an active, happy and cultivated people," until the South was freed from "the incubus" of slavery, and until the East had thoroughly absorbed the cultural riches of the Old World and used them to develop a uniquely American culture.[44]

Nevertheless, now just twenty-five, she was in demand as a contributor to the first journals in the country dedicated to a distinct American style, form, and subject matter. Groton was not Bristol, and Boston was not London. Nor were Henry Hedge and his phalanx of young literary ministers or James Freeman Clarke and his western experimenters any substitute for Hannah More's brilliant company of David Garrick, Joshua Reynolds, and Samuel Johnson. But Margaret Fuller, full of misgivings and eager for improvement, had begun her career as a woman of letters.

In May 1835, when the Farrars invited her on a summer expedition up the Hudson River to Trenton Falls—"the North River trip," one of the decade's most fashionable tourist jaunts for New Englanders and New Yorkers—she abandoned for the moment her literary plans. Thrilled by the chance to meet new people and see the romantic scenery of the Hudson and beyond, she wrote in her journal, "All my plans of study and writing this summer are dashed by the prospect of this delightful journey. . . . I think now I shall live down all the obstacles in time."[45]

Because she had already promised to take over the management of the Groton house for the summer so her mother could go to Canton, the immediate obstacle she had to overcome would be Timothy's opposition. In the letter home begging for a reprieve, she retrogressed to the tone of the petitioning schoolgirl. The voice she felt obliged to assume was a far cry from the worldly frankness of her intimate letters to James Freeman Clarke, the tone of professional equality that marked her correspondence on theology and philosophy with Henry Hedge, or the easy friendliness she shared with her woman friends. She knew that Timothy was most susceptible when she played the docile daughter, dependent on him for every favor and advantage.

And now I have something to tell you which I hope—Oh I *hope*—will give you as much pleasure as it does me.—Mr and Mrs Farrar propose taking me with several other delightful persons to Trenton Falls this summer. The plan is to set out about the 20th July—go on to N York, then up the North River [the Hudson] to West point, pass a day there—then to Catskill, pass a day there then on to Trenton and devote a week to that beautiful scenery—I said I had scarcely a doubt of your consent as you had said several times this winter you should like to have me make a pleasant journey this summer. Oh I cannot describe the positive extacy with which I think of this journey—To see the North River at last and in such society! Oh do sympathize with me—do feel about it as I do— The positive expences of the journey we have computed at forty seven dollars—I shall want ten more for spending money—but you will not think of the money—*will* you? I had rather you would take *two hundred* dollars from my portion than feel even the least unwilling. *Will* you not write to me immediately and say you love me and are very glad I am to be so happy???[46]

Although capable of impulsive acts of generosity, Timothy kept a tight hold on the family purse strings; he distrusted extravagance lest it lead to willful indulgence. He believed that children should be trained in "self-denial" rather than "accumulation"; when they were given candy, they were told to see how long they could go without eating it. No one in the family had any idea of how much money Timothy had; they assumed they were comfortably off and that the stringencies imposed on them were all part of their upbringing. To wheedle money out of her father, Margaret, at twenty-five, knew that the best strategy was to assume her guise as "Margaret Goodchild."[47]

Apparently, her campaign succeeded. After paying for her trip with an arduous June and early July on the farm, she went off with the Farrars on a journey that she looked back on for years "as the last period of tranquility" in her life. The high point was traveling with seventeen-year-old Samuel Gray Ward, who was soon to become another member of her pantheon. She had met Sam fleetingly a few times at the Farrars where he was boarding while attending Harvard; when he joined them on the Hudson River sailing cruise, she did not expect to "like him much," but by the time they reached Trenton Falls (a three-hour buggy ride north of Utica) and were taking moonlight walks in the woods together, she had adopted him as another of her objects of imaginative love.[48]

Sam's background as the son of Thomas Wren Ward, scion of a wealthy shipping family and American representative of the British bank, Baring Brothers, freed him from ambition for money and social prestige. Though clearly intelligent, he was not jockeying for class rank at college. Instead, he believed, as he wrote later in an essay, "every day" should be considered "more or less a *jour de fête*." Sam had a studio in the family townhouse on Park Street in Boston where he sketched and painted as a hobby. For Margaret, who revered literature and art as the highest of endeavors, Sam's interest in art added to his charms. At the experimental Round Hill School in Northampton where he prepared for college, he had been introduced to Italian and German literature. In Cambridge earlier he had been "so far deterred by her formidable reputation both for scholarship and sarcasm" that he "did not venture to attempt any intimacy," but a half-century later, when he recalled the Trenton Falls trip in his reminiscences, Sam wrote that in the course of their three weeks together he discovered that beneath Margaret's "defensive outside" was a "proud and sensitive nature" and "a personality of rare gifts and solid acquirements, a noble character and unfailing intellectual sympathy." After "the barrier of reserve on both sides vanished," she put him forever in her debt for introducing him "to the new world of literature and thought." It was just the right moment in his development, Sam recalled, and he considered himself fortunate to have become her friend.[49]

On the way home from Trenton Falls, Margaret learned that Anna was in Newport. Sam, who had many Newport friends, offered to escort her there. From his kindness and admiration she began to construct a mental image of him and their relationship that was to grow out of proportion in the coming years. A gentlemanly young man of impeccable manners who struck everyone as much older than his years because of his perfect composure, Sam had no idea of the importance of the role he was beginning to play in Margaret's imagination.

After Margaret returned to Cambridge, the Farrars invited her to remain for another two weeks so she could meet the celebrated British writer Harriet Martineau, who was making a year-long tour of the United States and was expected to arrive in Cambridge in time for the Harvard commencement ceremonies on August 18, 1834. Greeted and entertained at every stopover, inundated with letters of introduction, Martineau had already toured the South and West of the United States by the time she reached Cambridge. The leading literary editors of the day were aware that she was gathering material for a book of judgment on the new North American democracy, and they were following the tour anxiously. Everyone went to great lengths to make a good impression.

A round-faced, snub-nosed, nervous woman of thirty-three who had been deaf since childhood, she used an ear trumpet and required undivided attention when she spoke. When she was in her early twenties, her father, a Norwich manufacturer of bombazine and camlet, suddenly died, leaving the family with no means of support. To help out, Harriet began writing for a Unitarian church journal—just as Margaret was starting to do at much the same age. When, at twenty-seven, Harriet read Jane Haldimand Marcet's influential book, *Conversations on Political Economy,* she got the idea that launched her into fame. She wrote a series of popular pamphlets designed to portray social and economic injustices in novelette form. Among her targets were the Corn Laws, primogen-

iture, and penal colonization. Her first pamphlet, *Life in the Wilds,* a tale set in
South Africa, sold out in ten days. By the time she left for America she had
thirty-four titles to her credit. In a very short time Martineau commanded
worldwide attention. Queen Victoria praised her *Taxation Tales;* King Louis
Philippe read her books aloud to his family and ordered them translated for use
in French schools; it was said that the czar of Russia was a fan.[50]

Fuller was afraid that Martineau would not be interested in someone of so
little importance as herself and was astonished and grateful to be received "so
kindly as to banish all embarrassment at once." After a week the two became
friends. Harriet wrote later that she admired Margaret's "candour," her honest self-criticism, and "the philosophical way in which she took herself in
hand." Margaret hoped that she had found in Harriet the friend she was looking
for—"an intellectual guide," someone who would show her how to proceed in
her vocation as an author. "She has what I want," Margaret concluded, "vigorous reasoning powers, invention, clear views of her objects, and she has been
trained to the best means of execution." Harriet promised that they would meet
again before she returned to Europe.[51]

While Fuller was enjoying a social summer, a short romance she had au-
thored appeared in the *Galaxy,* a weekly newspaper of light reading edited by
John Neal, a colorful literary entrepreneur from Portland, Maine. "Lost and
Won: A Tale of Modern Days and Good Society" was clearly influenced by the
Bulwer-Lytton novels of British fashionable life that Fuller had been reading the
past winter. Since the story was unsigned, she had no reason to fear that anyone
would suspect that she was the author. But the mother of her old friend Harriet
Fay chanced upon the story and immediately saw in it a roman à clef derived
from the braggadocian claims of Joe Angier (a classmate of George Davis and
James Clarke) concerning his attempts to flirt with Harriet Russell after her
engagement to George Davis had been announced. Mrs. Fay shared her discovery and strong suspicion that Fuller was the most likely author with several
acquaintances, including Helen Davis, a cousin of James and Sarah Clarke. On
September 15 James, who was visiting in Newton where his grandfather was
terminally ill, wrote Margaret congratulating her on her "admirably sketched"
tale and told of all the speculation it had generated about the real identity of the
characters. He wrote that he had "procured several copies, and showed them to
many individuals." He was sending copies to Harriet and George.[52]

Unaware of Mrs. Fay's part in the developments, Margaret was incensed that
James would be so disloyal and insensitive as to advertise her authorship within
the family, let alone to spread the word. In the light of Fuller's own recent
disappointments in love, the story can be read as more strictly autobiographical, as a moral tale of the transfer of her own affections from the Lovelace-like
Davenant, based on the less admirable qualities in George Davis, to the steady,
responsible Fred, who resembled James Freeman Clarke. In either case, she

found herself caught in an embarrassing situation. She wrote James a letter berating him so severely that he had his sister Sarah write the reply. Sarah assured Margaret that James had discussed "Lost and Won" only with George and one other person. They would do everything they could to stifle the gossip and make sure that Harriet's behavior was viewed by all as entirely honorable.

Margaret, in the meantime, had developed a serious illness that began with an intense headache and fever that came on while she "meditated literary plans with full hope." Encouraged by Harriet Martineau, she believed that if she "could command leisure" she "might do something good." But the illness raged for nine days, weakening her so much that she "looked upon Death very near."[53]

The family diagnosed Margaret's illness as "brain fever," but several years later she told her Brook Farm friend, Georgiana Bruce, that her illness had been "typhoid fever." The conditions were present for a psychosomatic reaction, a form of "conversion hysteria" brought on by the two previous years of over-work, her frustrating sense of confinement, and the guilt she felt for yearning to be free of her family. If so, the trigger could well have been her discovery that even an innocent attempt to distill fiction from her personal experience could backfire, catching her in yet another conflict—this time, between her public ambitions and her private duty to honor her friends' privacy, a problem that was becoming ever more evident as she started out as a writer.[54]

Her condition frightened Timothy into comforting her with greater tender-ness than ever before. Usually "so sparing in tokens of affection" but fearing that she might not recover, he came into her room one morning and said, "My dear, I have been thinking of you in the night, and I cannot remember that you have any *faults*. You have defects, of course, as all mortals have, but I do not know that you have a single fault." The words seemed "so strange from him who had scarce ever in my presence praised me and who, as I knew, abstained from praise as hurtful to his children—affected me to tears," she wrote.[55]

Only a few days later the memory was to take on the significance of a benediction. On the thirtieth of September, Timothy came home from the fields feeling so ill that he was carried up to bed, where he lay in pain for twenty hours, enduring alternate attacks of chills and perspiration. The local doctor diagnosed him as suffering from Asiatic cholera; an autopsy later confirmed the opinion. From the beginning of the attack Timothy expressed the view that death was near. With the family surrounding him, kissing him and whispering farewells, he died on October 2, 1835. Margaret closed his eyes and for the rest of her life held the date in reverence. For years afterward Margarett Crane Fuller told of "how Margaret brought the younger children together around the life-less form of her father, and, kneeling, pledged herself to God that if she had ever been ungrateful or unfilial to her father, she would atone for it by fidelity to her brothers" and her sister.[56]

[Y]ou know we women have no profession except marriage, mantua-making and school-keeping.

A Trial to Fortitude

FULLER was surprised to find that soon after her father was buried her grief gave way to "an awful calm." Thinking of the anger and rage he had caused her, she walked around the property looking at all the improvements he had made and wondering what had obsessed him to give up the comforts of town life to come here to kill himself with backbreaking work. Now she became aware of how deeply she resented his having thrust her mother and herself into a life for which they were unprepared. She thought of all the family suffering that had resulted from Timothy's "collisions with his elder sons" and how "embittered" and "over anxious" he had been during the last years of his life. She walked down to the spot he called Margaret's Grove and regretted that she had never shown the least appreciation of his effort to provide her with a private place to read and write.

I contented myself with, 'when you please, Father,' but never went; what would I not now give, if I had fixed a time, and shown more interest. A day or two [ago] I went there. The tops of the distant blue hills were topped in delicate autumn haze. Soft silence brooded over the landscape. Nothing sustains me now but the thought that God . . . must have some good for me to do.[1]

They had so often been at odds that she now wondered if the reason for her calm was that she was released from the continual pressure to conform to his wishes and meet his moods. Her brother Richard later wrote that hers "was a strong and original nature that required much experience of life to shape it" and that their father had not always "well comprehended nor adequately sympathized with . . . the struggle of chaotic elements" in her. With the realization that neither Eugene nor William was likely to step in and take Timothy's place and that her mother would lean almost entirely on her, she wrote in her journal that she quickly became used to the idea of being "an orphan." In her use of the telling word "orphan" she accepted—but not without enough anger for the resentment to reappear in dreams—that her mother had been inadequate in filling her needs as she was growing up. With the death of her father, for all her tenderness toward her mother, she considered herself to all intents and purposes parentless. Hoping to turn the situation into a challenge, Margaret wrote in her journal that she now realized that all her thrashing about in search of her ideal and for a clear purpose in life had been a form of vanity; her nearest duty was now to her family. If self-sacrifice were her only option, she would dedicate herself to it with single-minded earnestness.[2]

Both George Davis and James Clarke came out to Groton to offer their condolences. With them both, Fuller made her peace. She also "exchanged a letter" with Harriet Davis, putting "matters on a more amicable footing." A few weeks later, James's grandfather, James Freeman, died while James was on his way back to Louisville. Sobered by the deaths, Margaret wrote James a straightforward letter. "I am sensible that I must in great measure give you up," she wrote. She admitted that she had often been "presumptuous" in her expectations of him. Confessing that she would probably never "become more tenderly attached to any other man," she wrote that she hoped he would soon find someone to love. "[Y]ou would flourish so beneath it, and repay it so generously," she wrote, releasing him for the first time from any romantic obligation to her.[3]

During the winter she had another unexpected mystical experience in the course of a night spent at the bedside of a neighbor dying of tuberculosis; the impoverished young woman's illness, it was said, was brought on by the means she had used to induce a miscarriage. While despairing over the moral depravity ascribed to this "crime for the sake of sensual pleasure," Fuller was overwhelmed with "a sadness of deepest calm." At dawn when she returned home, "exalted and exhausted," she shut herself up in her father's room where she fasted for a day, read the Bible and Wordsworth intermittently, and "comprehended the meaning of an ascetic life."[4] Later she described the experience to a friend.

O, it has ever been thus, from the darkest comes my brightness, from Chaos depths my love. . . . The change from my usual thoughts and feelings was as if a man should leave the perfumed, wildly grand oft times poisonous wildernesses of the tropics . . . for the snowy shroud . . . from which Phenix like rises the soul into the tenderest Spring.[5]

She had entered a state of mourning that worked its way into her psyche, connecting her father's death with all the past losses in her life. Sadness and morbidity, as depression was called in her time, became her great enemy and refuge as she struggled with her sense of duty. Fortunately, within weeks of his death she was presented with two invigorating prospects during a visit to Cambridge to meet again with Harriet Martineau. The Farrars invited her to accompany them to Europe in the summer. Martineau would be traveling with them as far as England; Sam Ward might join them for part of the trip; Anna Barker had also been invited. To Fuller the invitation seemed the chance of a lifetime; the career that seemed most open to her was that of cultural go-between bringing the new ideas developing in Europe to the attention of American readers. But the realization of her dream depended on the family financial position, which was unclear.

While she waited, she threw herself compulsively into the second prospect. During her Cambridge visit, Martineau encouraged her to turn her fascination with Goethe into a full-length book. Martineau told her that the time was ripe for a biography of the German poet, dramatist, and philosopher, who had died in 1832 and whose ideas and personality still dominated European literature. "I have confidence in her judgement for she has knowledge of the public mind and cannot be biased to partiality for me," Fuller wrote as she made up her mind to embark on the first American biography of the man she called "one of the Master Spirits of this world."[6]

"It is a great work. I hope nobody will steal it from me," she worried as she gathered all of Goethe's works around her and started systematic study. In March 1836 she reported to James: "I am thinking now—really thinking, I believe; certainly it seems as if I had never done so before—If it does not kill me, something will come of it . . . for never was my mind so active and its subjects are God—the universe—Immortality."[7]

With no guide to help her work her way into German philosophical writing, she was soon ranging through the list Henry Hedge had provided. As she became immersed in her studies, she wondered if she had not been "very arrogant" even to think of such an undertaking. The more she read Goethe, the more difficult she found his philosophy and the more she began to question apparent discrepancies between his public stance and his private morality. She was troubled when she came upon references to irregularities in his relations with women. "I want to know the facts about Goethe and Lili [Lili Schöne-mann]," she wrote Henry Hedge. "This somewhat passée affair troubles me; I want to know did he give her up from merely interested (ie selfish) motives." The problem became more serious when her research revealed that Goethe had fathered a son by Christiane Vulpius and had lived with her for twenty years before marrying her; even then, according to available information, he had married her only to legitimize the son. (In fact, Christiane Vulpius had borne several children before the marriage.)[8]

"I had no idea that the mighty 'Indifferentist' went so far with his experimen-talising in *real life*," she wrote James Freeman Clarke. Acknowledging that this was a subject "on which *gentlemen* and *ladies* talk a great deal but apart from one another," she begged James not to "mince matters" and tell her what he knew about the affair. If she had been too hasty in assuming Goethe's personal life had been purer than was actually the case, she wanted to know it, though she would not, she vowed, let such information influence her view of his works.[9]

"[O]n the subject of Goethe's license," James answered, "his moral code was not of the strictest kind." She thought of writing Thomas Carlyle or even Goethe's Weimar friend, Friedrich von Müller; he might be "pleased at the idea of a life of G. written in this hemisphere." When her efforts drew a blank, she wrote James again in April, "How am I to get the information I want, unless I go to Europe?" All through the winter of 1835–36 and well into the spring she was kept on tenterhooks.[10]

Everything depended on how much money Timothy had left to his family. The meticulous Timothy, who had so often criticized his daughter for careless-ness, who had constantly preached the doctrine of orderliness, had died with-out a will. Although the law of Massachusetts permitted widows to administer the estate, Uncle Abraham and Uncle Henry immediately took over as execu-tors. It was a period of renewed suffering, for they treated Timothy's family as indigent relatives who were completely dependent on them. As no one could find any records of Timothy's holdings either in the office or at home, Uncle Abraham badgered Margaret and her mother to search out old bills and rec-ords. In order to evaluate the property, they had to slaughter and salt the cow and two hogs and put aside the year's harvest of corn and English grain until a price could be put on them. The family was forced to apply to Abraham even to use the produce they had on hand.

Humiliated by Abraham's treatment, Margaret wrote that she had often regretted being "of the softer sex, and never more than now." Were she the eldest son, she could be "guardian" to her brothers and sister, "administer the estate and really become the head of the family." Regretting that she had taken "refuge" in the "serene world of literature and the arts," she made up her mind to learn how to "advise and act."[11]

In January 1836 Timothy's will was filed with an inventory establishing the worth of his estate at $18,098.50, most of it tied up in notes and land. As the estate had no cash available and the only income was the "trifling" rents from the Cherry Street house and two "unprofitable" farms, one in Easton and another in Salem, Abraham continued to control the family finances. He ad-vised the most stringent economies, and the family sold the sleigh and cut down to one newspaper.[12]

Fuller realized that the chance of seeing Europe with her "heart's sister," Anna Barker, was unlikely. In reply to a letter in which Anna projected the joys of their trip together, she sent a sonnet.

TO ANNA
In answer to her letter of January 6, 1836

How beauteous the dream thy hopes portray!
Oh my heart's sister and my fancy's love
Shall the same gale to both of us convey
The fragrance of the Italian orange grove?
And break the Bay of Naples into smiles?
Shall we together in the mighty heart
Of empire once so proud, revere the Past?
Or mid the wonders of the busy mart
Of England's greatness present life contrast

With all those glories of an earlier day?
Upon the waters of romantic Rhine,
More happy than its bard, shall I convey
My feelings to thy "gentle hand in mine,"
Without the aid of words? Can all this be?
Never, sweet friend, 'till "life be Poesy."[13]

In February she wrote George Davis that all her plans were "painfully un-
decided." The trip promised to be "equally delightful and profitable," but still it
was true that on her return she would have to "maintain" herself, and, she
added, "you know we women have no profession except marriage, mantua-
making and school-keeping." Continuing the sardonic voice she often used
with Davis, she added that, if she did not go, "staying behind will be a pretty
trial to my fortitude and quite finish my moral education—indeed at the expense of my intellectual but this last is quite a secondary affair—Tis said."[14]

All through the spring the probate judge delayed his decision on the division
of the Fuller property. Uncle Abraham kept urging Margarett Crane Fuller to
rent the farm and take a cheaper place in town. She was forced to beg Abraham
for money to have Timothy's remains removed to the family plot in Cambridgeport and for new clothes for William Henry, who had returned from
his West Indies escapade. Ellen, now fifteen, had blossomed into a slender,
blonde beauty, much admired by Margaret's men friends. Margarett Crane
Fuller wished she could afford to send her away to a first-class school.

Margaret still refused to give up hope. She wrote Eugene, telling him how
much it would mean to her to go to England and meet "the best literary society"; she implored him to return home "with the spirit of a *man*" and do for his
mother "what a daughter cannot," giving him some of the spine-stiffening talk
to which Timothy had subjected her.[15]

By the time Eugene arrived home in April (to read law in the office of a
Groton attorney, George Farley), Fuller was still waiting to hear if she could
afford the trip. In early May, Uncle Abraham consulted with Eliza Farrar. She
told him that they planned to be away for a year and a half and expected the cost
to come to five dollars a day. After computing that Margaret would require
$1,825 for the first twelve months plus an additional $300 to $500 for her "out-
fit," he wrote her a letter explaining the family financial situation. If her father's
personal estate were to be settled within two years, there would be $1,400 for
each child, but part of that would not be available for three more years. He
added that he was forced to discount an additional $9,000 because it was tied
up in unproductive real estate which was unsalable in the foreseeable future.[16]

With Margarett Crane Fuller receiving the widow's share of one-third and
the seven children dividing the remainder, Margaret's full share would limit her
to six months in Europe at best, and she would be without a nest egg for the rest
of her life; the trip would also put her in the untenable moral position of living

in luxury while the rest of the family was pinching every penny. In such a situation it was clear that she would not see England, the Rhine, or the Bay of Naples until—as she had written Anna—"life be Poesy." On her twenty-sixth birthday, May 23, she realized that she could not make the journey. "Circumstances have decided that I must not go to Europe, and shut upon me the door, as I think, forever, to the scenes I could have loved," she wrote. The disappointment sapped her confidence, and she did not see how she could now "produce a valuable work" on Goethe, but she remembered his advice on how to proceed during times of doubt: "Try to do thy duty, & thou wilt know what is in thee." Making allowance for all she had gone through in the last months, she reasoned: "I may be renewed again, and feel differently. If I do not soon, I will make up my mind to teach. I can thus get money, which I will use for the benefit of my dear, gentle, suffering mother,—my brothers and sister. This will be the greatest consolation to me."[17]

During the winter and spring Margaret had been writing reams of occasional poetry. She sent Anna poems describing their last meeting in Newport and a moonlight boat ride they had taken together; in a sonnet she described her terrible illness of the previous September and her constant wish for death during her suffering. In April she sent Sam Ward a sheaf of poems commemorating their journey to Trenton Falls; she celebrated the palisades of the Hudson, their mountain climb at Catskill, the trip on the Mohawk River, and, in three versions, the beauty of the falls at Trenton: "early in the morning," "afternoon," and "by moonlight." Romantic celebrations of nature's power to deepen friendship and of shared experiences to activate the inner life, her verses were also a way of communicating to her friends their singular importance, one of the rituals of romantic friendship that the German writers she admired had practiced.[18]

In May she wrote an elegy on the death of Charles Chauncey Emerson, a twenty-eight-year-old lawyer she had met only once or twice. But she knew his fiancée, Elizabeth Hoar, a close friend of both Elizabeth Randall and Sarah Clarke, and was moved by the circumstances of his death on May 9 from tuberculosis. "Lines—On the Death of C.C.E." appeared on the front page of the *Boston Daily Centinel* on May 17, 1836. Tuberculosis was the particular scourge of the Emerson family. Less than two years before, Charles's older brother, Edward, had died of it in Puerto Rico where he had gone for his health. In 1831 tuberculosis had claimed Ellen Tucker Emerson, the bride of his brother Ralph Waldo, after only sixteen months of marriage. One of the stanzas of Margaret's elegy was directed to Elizabeth Hoar.

> Sad friends are bending o'er his bier;
> *One* droops—a more than friend:—
> Kind heaven! *her* hour of agony,
> Thy sympathy attend!

The next verse was written for Ralph Waldo Emerson, whom Margaret had met only fleetingly at the Farrars during the Harvard commencement activities just before her father's death. She had heard enough praise of him from her friends to wish for an opportunity to meet him. His reputation for eloquence as a public lecturer and his personal history set him apart. He had attracted notice in October 1832 when he resigned as pastor at the South Church in Boston because he found he could not administer the communion service—his rejection of Christ's absolute authority had set him on the way to his new formulation of the relationship of the individual to the divine. After his resignation, he went to Europe where he met Coleridge, Carlyle, Wordsworth, John Stuart Mill, and General Lafayette. On his return he began a new career as a public lecturer and was now remarried and settled in Concord. As his reputation as an original thinker spread in the Unitarian community, Margaret's curiosity to know him personally grew stronger. She was careful in her choice of words when she referred to him.

> And vainly sterner could repress
> Their manly sorrow now:—
> None can assuage grief's dread excess,
> Omnipotence! but thou.[19]

Waldo Emerson clipped the poem and pasted it in one of his blotting books. As it was signed only with the initial "F," he may not have guessed who had written it, but he certainly would have recognized her name by now because several of his friends had been telling him of Fuller's interest. In March, Eliza Farrar told Waldo that while she was in Europe she would like to have "Miss Fuller cared for spiritually." Charles Emerson, on hearing this, made a joke of it; he interpreted the request as a hint that his fiancée Elizabeth Hoar should be encouraged "to draw that lady into the potent circle of enchantments of Criticism & the First Philosophy" in Concord, where Hoar lived not far from the Emersons. Harriet Martineau also put in a good word for Fuller. "I introduced her to the special care of R. Waldo Emerson and his wife," Martineau recalled in her autobiography, "and I remember what Emerson said in wise and gentle rebuke of my lamentations for Margaret that she could not go to Europe, as she was chafing to do, for purposes of self-improvement. 'Does Margaret Fuller,— supposing her to be what you say,—believe her progress to be dependent on whether she is here or there?' "[20]

Years later, Elizabeth Palmer Peabody claimed the distinction of prodding the Emersons into inviting Fuller for a visit beginning July 21, 1836, just before the Farrars set sail for Europe with Harriet Martineau and Sam Ward. Lidian Jackson Emerson agreed to the visit but expressed concern that her husband might not get along with Margaret. At the end of July she wrote Peabody that everything was going better than expected.

Miss Fuller is with us now—and you will be glad to hear that we find real satisfaction—Miss F. Mr. E. & myself. . . . We like her—she likes us—I speak in this way—because you know we came together almost strangers—all to one another and the result of the experiment—as Miss F. herself said in her letter to you on the subject of nearer acquaintance with us—was doubtful—the tendencies of all three being strong & decided—and possibly not such as could harmonize.[21]

Winning Mr. Emerson's friendship was not as easy as Lidian Emerson made it sound. Emerson weighed the hours jealously that he spent outside of his study, and it taxed all of Margaret's abilities to convince him that time in her company was well spent. He wrote later that after the first half-hour of talking with her he did not expect that they would "get far." Although she was nicely dressed and behaved in a ladylike manner, he found nothing "prepossessing" about her appearance, and he did not like her habit of blinking her eyes. He had heard that she irritated people with her "overweening sense of power" and that the satirical tone of her conversation made one uncomfortable. But in spite of himself he found himself laughing more than he liked. Flattered by her efforts to "establish[ ] a good footing" between them, he let her draw him into hours of "amusing gossip."

She studied my tastes, piqued and amused me, challenged frankness by frankness, and did not conceal the good opinion of me she brought with her, nor her wish to please. She was curious to know my opinions and experiences. Of course, it was impossible long to hold out against such urgent assault. She had an incredible variety of anecdotes, and the readiest wit to give an absurd turn to whatever passed; and the eyes, which were so plain at first, soon swam with fun and drolleries, and the very tides of joy and superabundant life.[22]

When Fuller came to the large, comfortable Emerson house on the Cambridge Turnpike, a half-mile from Concord village, Lidian Jackson and Waldo Emerson had been married ten months and had settled into the orderly and hospitable domestic routine that was one of the bonds of their long and stable but occasionally troubled marriage. When she married, Lidian (her given name was Lydia, but Waldo renamed her) was thirty-three, a few months older than her husband, who had been a widower for four years when he proposed to her by mail after a slight acquaintance. She assented immediately because, as she told their daughter years later, she thought their union had been ordained in heaven.

Lidian would have preferred to live in her native Plymouth, but when Waldo married her he had already decided that in order to live as he planned—as an independent poet and philosopher—he needed to be in Concord among what he called "the quiet fields of my fathers." His ancestors had founded Concord, and he had spent many childhood summers in the Old Manse, the house his grandfather had built overlooking the Battleground. Convinced that he would be crippled living anywhere else, he wrote her, "I must win you to love it. I was born a poet, of low class without doubt yet a poet. . . . Plymouth is streets." He had to live in the open countryside.[23]

Because Waldo and Lidian were aware of the disadvantages of their isolation in a country town, a three-hour stagecoach ride from Boston, they agreed before they married that they would arrange the household for long visits from favored friends. The house, which they later called Bush, had two guest rooms and the use of a third when Waldo's mother, Ruth Haskins Emerson, was away visiting. She lived with Lidian and Waldo, as she had with Ellen and Waldo, with definite housekeeping duties. There were usually two regular maids, and temporary help was employed when needed.

Their independent way of life was possible only because Emerson had inherited some $23,000 from his first wife, Ellen Louise Tucker; the income came to about $1,200 a year. Augmenting this with fees from itinerant preaching and lecturing and avoiding all extravagance, they were able to live in modest comfort.

While Fuller was staying with the Emersons, she had the red room across the hall from Emerson's study. At first her frequent interruptions annoyed him, but by the end of two weeks he was enthusiastic. He wrote his brother William in New York that Margaret was "quite an extraordinary person for her apprehensiveness, her acquisitions & her powers of conversation. It is always a great refreshment to see a very intelligent person. It is like being set in a large place. You stretch your limbs & dilate to utmost size."[24]

She was very good company, and they had a wonderful time together, so much so that Emerson discounted all the talk he had heard that she was "sneering, scoffing, critical, [and] disdainful." This was no more than "a superficial judgment," he wrote later. Even her gossipy "satire" was no more than "the pasttime and necessity of her talent, the play of superabundant animal spirits."[25]

While Fuller was visiting, Amos Bronson Alcott, a stocky, self-involved schoolmaster from Boston, joined them for a few days. The two men had become friendly the summer before when Emerson visited Alcott's Temple School in Boston and became interested in Alcott's original experiments in early-childhood education. Alcott brought the news that Elizabeth Palmer Peabody, who had been his assistant teacher at the school, had just notified him that she was resigning. He had another young woman in mind as Peabody's replacement, Anna Thaxter of Hingham, but if she did not wish the job he promised to hire Fuller.

With Eugene living at home now while reading law in Groton, and with the teenagers, Arthur and Richard, on hand to help her mother with the farm duties, Fuller felt free to move to Boston where she could live with her Uncle Henry for the winter. Margarett Crane Fuller was now in continual battle with Uncle Abraham over family expenditures, but she had wheedled enough to send Ellen to Miss Urquhart's School in Boston, and, if all went well, Eugene would start law school at Harvard in January.

Fuller marked her decision to enter teaching professionally by attending the annual meeting of the American Institute of Instruction at Worcester in the last week of August where Alcott caused an uproar during a debate on the question, "Is the necessity of moral education, as the ground of all human culture, felt as it ought to be by teachers and by the community in general[?]" When Alcott argued vehemently that the answer to the question was "man is a God on earth," the phrase triggered strong objections and charges of blasphemy. The *Boston Daily Register* reported the outcry, and it was a foreboding of the unfavorable publicity that was to plague Alcott in the months to come.[26]

Alcott had an idealistic educational philosophy. "I aim at reform," he wrote, "to unmake and reconstruct the consciousness of men—to gather all their intellectual conceptions around the august Idea of spirit." He was a Platonist, and he believed, in marked contrast to the old Puritan view that all children were born "sin-defiled," that they were born pure, innocent, and absolutely good. To teach them was a matter of drawing out their innate goodness and making them aware of their godliness.[27]

During its first year and a half, his Temple School, which met on the top floor of the Masonic Temple overlooking Boston Common, had flourished, growing rapidly from ten to forty students. Elizabeth Palmer Peabody taught geography, Latin, and astronomy and was the school's recruiter of new students; Alcott called them "disciples." She also kept a diary of the school's activities and a transcript of Alcott's Socratic "conversations" with the students—his method of awakening the moral consciences of his pupils by "leading" them to an awareness of spiritual reality. As a means of advertising the new method, Peabody's first diary had been published as a book, *Record of a School*.

When Peabody pointed out that Alcott's method was sometimes so suggestive as to be manipulative, and that it indoctrinated the children in his brand of thinking rather than leading them to express their innate ideas, trouble began between the two. Annoyed further when Alcott kept postponing paying her salary, Peabody took a leave of absence during the summer of 1836 and turned the school diary over to her sister Sophia, who agreed to stand in for her.

Once Elizabeth returned to the Peabody family home in Salem, people questioned her about rumors of impropriety at Mr. Alcott's school. When she read over her notes for a sequel to *Record of a School* and those of Sophia with a special eye to the criticisms, she was shocked to realize the extent to which Alcott's questions plumbing the mysteries of birth, divine and human, danced gingerly around the exploration of sex. The examples were plentiful. In connection with the birth of John the Baptist, the Annunciation, and the birth of Jesus, Alcott asked the children to define words like "conceive," "quicken," and "deliver." Intent on making his pupils aware of the animal as well as the spiritual nature of man, one day he demanded, "I want all of you to account for the origin of the body. How is the body made?"[28]

When freckle-faced, six-year-old Josiah Quincy, the grandson of Harvard's president, answered that "the naughtiness of people" had something to do with it, Sophia Peabody dutifully wrote his comment in her notebook. When Elizabeth read this, she wrote Alcott, telling him that she could not continue at the school; she implored him to suppress the many indiscretions in the transcripts. "Why did prophets and apostles veil this subject in fables and emblems if there was not a reason for avoiding physiological inquiries &c?" she asked him. "However, you as a man can say anything; but I am a woman, and have feelings that I dare not distrust, however little I can *understand* them or give an account of them."[29]

Although Fuller never included Elizabeth Palmer Peabody in her circle of intimates, they had a cordial enough friendship for her to be aware of Peabody's differences with Alcott. While waiting for a firm offer from him, she began to give private lessons, ending up with five young women scholars and one of the Bond children, a blind boy, to whom she read English history and Shakespeare's plays. In November she decided to try a teaching experiment, using as her model the series of evening classes for adult women that Peabody had been pioneering in Boston since the winter of 1833. For a nominal fee, Peabody gave lessons in history and the classics, calling them, variously, Reading Parties, Historical Conversations, and Conferences (she made fifty dollars from her 1832 Reading Party). In October Fuller advertised her "classes for ladies in German, Italian and French literature," at a charge of fifteen dollars for twenty-four lessons of two hours each. On her behalf Emerson even approached three Harvard foreign-language instructors, Hermann Bokum, Francis Sales, and Pietro Bachi, who all agreed "to teach pronunciation of German, French, & Italian to any ladies who should read those languages" with her during the winter.[30]

Fuller soon had some twenty young women studying with her, two of whom would become close friends. Jane Tuckerman, the daughter of Gustavus Tuckerman, a prominent Boston businessman, was to become one of Margaret's lifelong correspondents and would occasionally serve as her secretary. But the friendship that took the firmest hold that year was with seventeen-year-old Caroline Sturgis, the younger sister of Ellen Sturgis, whom Margaret had known for several years.

Caroline was the daughter of Captain William Sturgis, one of "the great Merchants," as his distant relative, the philosopher George Santayana, later called him because, rising from cabin boy to captain by the time he was nineteen, Sturgis accumulated a large fortune in the China trade while enjoying the adventure of fighting pirates and learning to speak the languages of the Pacific Indians. Now a partner in the Boston trading firm of Bryant and Sturgis, which handled "more than half of the trade out of Boston with the Pacific coast of the Oregon Territory and with China," he lived with his wife and five daughters in a fine town house on Summer Street around the corner from Avon Place where Margaret's Uncle Henry lived and where she was boarding that winter.[31]

Caroline, a dark, intense, introverted young woman who cultivated an off-hand demeanor, inherited some of her father's adventurous and romantic spirit. Independent and scornful of convention, she was moody and unpredictable, and people compared her to a gypsy. Of the daughters, she was the artist, and Ellen, who also attended Margaret's language class, was the poet. The drowning of their older brother, William, in 1826 shadowed their family life. Captain Sturgis would not allow the boy's name to be mentioned in his presence, and Elizabeth Davis Sturgis, their mother (a relative of George Davis), went into a depression after his death and never recovered enough to take up family life fully.

Unlike most of Fuller's other friends who were embedded in the rituals of family life, Caroline was much freer to go her own way, hatch her own plans, and make her own decisions. She was also quite often at loose ends. Before she joined Fuller's class in the winter of 1836, she had gone to a girls' school in Hingham and had attended one of Peabody's classes in 1835. Peabody had been struck with her intellectual curiosity. "C[aroline] S[turgis] is a deep enthusiast," Peabody wrote of her while she had her in the class. "I never knew such a devouring desire of the higher knowledge."[32]

As Fuller's student, Caroline was unusual in her cool ability to evade Fuller's attempts to enthrall or dominate her. The friendship was based on mutual admiration, and the distance between them that the difference in their ages and roles would normally require all but disappeared in the course of a year. They bickered and argued and tested each other as if they had been intimate equals for a long time.

Another of Fuller's students was Mary Channing, the daughter of William Ellery Channing, the minister of the Federal Street Church. Now in his fifties, he was revered as a saint by Unitarians for his noble sermons, his delivery, and his gentle, earnest character—Fuller said his sermons "purged as by fire." Anxious to acquire some German and learn about Goethe, whom he much doubted "on the moral score," he invited Margaret to read with him one evening a week during the winter. Because in recent years Channing had been stressing in his sermons moral reform, political ethics, and the obligations of his comfortable parishioners to the disadvantaged, Fuller called him "our philanthropist."[33]

The German lessons were frequently interrupted by evening callers and conversations on general subjects, such as the upcoming presidential election, the annexation of Texas, the possibility of the dissolution of the Union, and the effect on the country of the enormous influx of immigrants. Fuller spent one evening trying to quell the fears of the literary essayist Richard Henry Dana, Sr., who deplored the effects on the tempo of life of such new industrial and scientific inventions as the railroad train. (His son, Richard Henry Dana, Jr., who had dropped out of college to go to sea, had recently returned to Harvard and was beginning to write *Two Years before the Mast.*)

When one of the younger Unitarian ministers in the city, George Ripley, pastor at the Purchase Street Church, sought Fuller out to talk about recent themes in German theology, he advised her not to allow Channing to influence her; the old man was behind the times. Ripley was married to Sophia Dana, a niece of the original owner of the Dana Mansion and a brilliant schoolteacher in her own right. Sophia shared her husband's enthusiasm for reform. From the time George Ripley began reading German philosophy, theology, and poetry, his views had become increasingly liberal. In the fall of 1836, just as Fuller was settling down for the winter in Boston, he published an article arguing that Christian truths can be explained without resorting to the miracles for confirmation. This claim evoked a fierce response from Andrews Norton, Ripley's former professor of sacred literature at the Harvard Divinity School, who now dominated theological circles. Thus began the long battle between Transcendentalists and conservative Unitarians, a battle in which Fuller was seen as an articulate and conspicuous member of the Transcendentalist faction, even though she was never comfortable with the label.[34]

With the help of Peabody, Fuller published three literary essays during the spring and fall of 1836 in the *American Monthly Magazine,* a new journal devoted to "original Papers, Reviews of latest works, Literary Intelligence, and notices of Science and Arts." In the spring the publisher, Park Benjamin, had approached Peabody with a request to see some of her work as well as some of Fuller's recent writings. Biographies always fascinated Fuller; her review of *The Life of Sir James Mackintosh* by his son, Robert James Mackintosh, gave her a chance to project her subjective concerns and her fascination with the ingredients of genius and greatness in her analysis of the shortcomings of the Whig philosopher and statesman, who was "almost a great man" but failed because he lacked sufficient "earnestness of purpose." In diagnosing Mackintosh's inability to concentrate his powers, she focused on two circumstances that had afflicted his life as well as hers, "the want of systematic training in early life" and the "detrimental" effects of having "uncommon talents for conversation." A second article, "Present State of German Literature," a review of a book on the subject by Heinrich Heine, presented the case for reading the modern Germans as an antidote to the utilitarianism of American culture.[35]

The third essay, "Modern British Poets," which appeared in two parts, was sweeping and ambitious in its claims and evaluations. The editors specifically disavowed responsibility for Margaret's opinions, announcing that the editors disagreed completely with many of her judgments and "almost entirely" with "the view taken of Lord Byron." But, even so, it gave them "pleasure" to present their readers with an article "of so much power and beauty, from so bold and original a hand." Predicting that nine contemporary British poets were candidates for posterity, Fuller confidently explained each one's strengths and weaknesses. She dared to defend Byron, whose reputation for sexual promiscuity and melancholic posings made him a distasteful example of European license. She also praised Shelley, who had put himself outside the pale for many readers because of his outspoken atheism, and she predicted that Coleridge, Wordsworth, and Southey were the contemporary poets who would become immortal because of their "universality." She was finding her way into the field of literary criticism that had hardly begun in the United States.[36]

She hoped that her work on Goethe would establish her as an author, but she had very little time to work on his biography during the winter of 1836–37. At the beginning of December she started at Alcott's Temple School, where she taught until one o'clock in the afternoon every day in the large square schoolroom dominated by a floor-length Gothic window. Busts of Plato, Socrates, Shakespeare, and Milton sat on pedestals; in the corners were bouquets of fresh flowers. Alcott had taken out extensive loans to supply his school with the best of furniture, the finest equipment; he wanted everything arranged to encourage openness and trust.

Fuller was expected to give lessons in Latin, French, and Italian and keep the record of the conversation classes. After a few weeks Alcott jotted in his diary that he was impressed with her "imaginary power," with her "free and bold speculation," and especially with her "rare good sense," and he predicted that she was likely "to add enduring glory to female literature."[37] Fuller was less enthusiastic about Alcott. He made her uneasy. She wrote in her journal that she felt a certain "distrust" of Mr. Alcott's mind. "There is something . . . in his philosophy which revolts either my common-sense or my prejudices, I cannot be sure which."[38]

In the classroom Fuller took matters into her own hands and interrupted Alcott when she thought he was misinterpreting the children's remarks and leading them "into an allegorical interpretation . . . when their own minds did not tend towards it." In March she gave up keeping the dangerous record. Her care to keep Alcott out of risky territory may have been what lay behind a note he made on her character in a March journal entry. He wrote that he had discovered that, along "with the gift of genius," she was given "that of prudence."[39]

Her prudence was of little help to him after February when, following the publication of two volumes of his *Conversations on the Gospels,* he became the object of a virulent newspaper attack. Even before his public censure, parents were withdrawing their children; the January term had begun with twenty-five students, fifteen fewer than the semester before. In late January Alcott noted that his "best talkers" were leaving him and that there was "no promise of others to supply their places." He heard that many Boston ministers were saying that he was an "interloper."[40]

Bronson Alcott, a Connecticut farmboy, had less than a year of formal education beyond the one-room schoolroom where he learned to read and write. He
was wholly self-educated. Tall, blue-eyed, with a rough-hewn, cavernous face,
bushy eyebrows, and a protruding lower lip, he yet had a bearing that an
Englishman later described as "the manners of a very great peer." Although he
had never been to a college or a divinity school, he had moved into the sphere of
religious education by adapting his teaching methods to his spiritual philosophy. But in 1837 there was too much religious controversy, too much nervousness in the theological air of Boston, for him to get away unscathed.[41]

On March 21 Nathan Hale, the influential editor of the *Boston Daily Advertiser,* reviewed Alcott's *Conversations on the Gospels* and pronounced his teaching method "a signal failure" that ought to be abandoned. Eight days later,
Joseph T. Buckingham, editor of the *Boston Courier,* attacked Alcott in an
editorial: If Alcott were indeed honest and sincere, "he must be half-witted, and
his friends ought to take care of him without delay." He was not only guilty of
blasphemy but dangerous to society as a corrupter of youth. Court proceedings
should be considered.[42]

Andrews Norton was quoted as saying of *Conversations on the Gospels* that
"one-third was absurd, one-third blasphemous, and one-third obscene." When
Dr. Channing, who had supported Alcott when he first set up his school,
expressed dismay over the book, Alcott felt betrayed. There were rumors that a
mob was forming with plans to storm one of his Friday evening meetings with
Sunday School teachers.[43]

Having dispatched letters of protest to both the attacking newspapers after
the first outburst, Emerson wrote Alcott, "I hate to have all the little dogs
barking at you." Fuller, in spite of her misgivings about Alcott, respected his
sincerity and his great generosity of spirit. The personal nastiness of the press
reaction aroused her to fury. When a rumor reached her that Henry Hedge was
providing ammunition to the opposition in a review for the Unitarian bi-
monthly, the *Christian Examiner,* she threw all her prudence to the wind: "I do
not believe you are going to cut up Mr Alcott. There are plenty of fish in the net
created solely for markets &c no need to try your knife on a dolphin like him."
Hedge ought "to act as a mediator." She could not believe that he would lend his
wit "to the ugly blinking owls who are now hooting from their snug tenements . . . at this star of purest ray serene."[44]

Hedge backed down and agreed not to "increase the uproar." James Freeman
Clarke wrote a spirited defense in the *Western Messenger* where he was now the
editor; he compared Alcott to Socrates, who was also "accused of not believing
in Gods in which the city believes," of "introducing other divinities," and of
"corrupting the young."[45]

Chandler Robbins, the editor of the Unitarian biweekly, the *Christian Register,* tried to help. In April he ran three articles sympathetic to Alcott, but by then

it was too late. With only eleven pupils left, Alcott had to give up his lease on the top-floor rooms of the Masonic Temple. The school moved to the basement. To pay his creditors, he sold at auction the busts, the globes, and most of the custom-designed desks. Realizing that he would have to sell 150 books from the library he had accumulated, he consoled himself that he was already "imbued with the spirit that had produced them."[46]

The previous fall, Emerson's first published book, *Nature,* had appeared; it took God out of the churches and all but unfrocked the ministerial profession. *Nature* was just the latest in a series of disturbing books written by young Unitarian ministers in recent months that challenged mainstream Unitarianism: George Ripley's *Discourses on the Philosophy of Religion,* William Furness's *Remarks on Four Gospels,* and Orestes Brownson's *New Views of Christianity, Society, and the Church* all had challenged not only Unitarian belief but the very idea of organized religion and, indeed, the structure of society itself.

When the revered Dr. Channing had introduced the concept of man's likeness to God ("man has a kindred nature with God, and may bear most important and ennobling relations with him"), he had not foreseen how dangerously it could be developed in the hands of the younger theological thinkers.[47] As the controversy sharpened, the more conservative of the faithful were shocked. Could this mean that women and men had no need of the Bible, church history, religious institutions, or even the assurances of Revelation in order to comprehend the Divinity? Did it mean that any individual could find God all alone, with no help from anyone else? The young ministers seemed to be moving in just this direction.

By the spring of 1837 the more conservative Unitarians were blaming the threat to their theological position on subversive foreign literature: Coleridge, Carlyle, and the Germans. Viewing the challenge as an annoying eruption of the younger clergy within their own ranks, they began to call it "transcendentalism"—the better to isolate it. It was one thing for one of their own ordained ministers to assert the independence of the human spirit from human institutions; it was quite another for an outsider like Alcott, a man of little formal education, to tinker boldly with the sensitive issues of liberal religion.

By the end of March, Alcott had so few students that he could no longer pay Fuller's salary. Exhausted after the winter of "incessant toil" and worried about her health, she left the school, intending to devote herself to her writing, but a disciple of Alcott's, a young man named Hiram Fuller (no relation), headmaster of the Greene Street School in Providence, offered her a teaching position at an annual salary of $1,000, beginning the first week in June. The Greene Street School was about to move to its new quarters, an elegant Greek temple furnished with carpeted floors, upholstered desk seats, and cut-glass water urns in every classroom. If she had only her own interests to consider, Fuller thought she would be better off continuing with her Boston reading classes; they provided enough income for her own support, and she could then control her time and have the leisure to forward her literary career. Looking back on the winter, she remarked, "I was so new to a public position and so desirous to do all I could I took a great deal more upon myself than I was able to bear," and declared herself "as ill placed as regards a chance to think as a haberdasher's prentice or the President of Harvard University."[48]

On her way back to Groton from Boston at the end of April, she stopped for a few days with the Emersons in Concord and met for the first time their adored new son, Waldo, now six months old. She read aloud Benjamin Disraeli's new novel, *Vivian Grey,* to the elder Waldo and made him "very merry," but he grumbled when she forced lessons in German pronunciation on him.[49]

Nevertheless, he allowed it was "a great convenience" to have her help. He had taught himself German and had read widely in the recent literature. While scorning Goethe's "velvet life" as a member of the Weimar court, he recognized that there was "something gigantic about the man." He had fifty-five volumes of Goethe's works in his library, and he believed that Fuller's work on Goethe was important. As part of her research she had begun a translation of Johann Eckermann's *Conversations with Goethe,* and Emerson helped her make arrangements with George Ripley, who was editing the newly initiated series, Specimens of Foreign Standard Literature, to publish it. With an extra good word from Emerson, by mid-May Margaret also had Ripley's assurance that he would publish her biography of Goethe.[50]

On May 10, a week after Fuller returned to Groton, the panic of 1837 began; the New York banks refused to redeem paper bank notes in hard money, and the crisis soon spread throughout the country. A depression had begun that was to last for the next five years. The scarcity of money made relations with Uncle Abraham even more strained. Margarett Crane Fuller was insistent that fifteen-year-old Arthur prepare for college at Leicester Academy, pointing out that he was "unfortunate in the loss of an eye that makes his situation one of great difficulty." She was just as forceful in her desire to have seventeen-year-old Ellen continue her education so she would be prepared "if she be obliged to teach for a living."[51]

The thousand-dollar salary that Hiram Fuller offered Margaret to come to Providence was more than most ministers or college professors were earning. How could she refuse? "I shall teach the elder girls my favorite branches, for four hours a day,—choosing my own hours, and arranging the course," she wrote. On balance she decided that it would be "unwise" to give up the handsome salary. "I have not yet written the Life of Goethe but have studied and thought about it a good deal," she wrote James Freeman Clarke in the middle of May. "Three years are given me to write it in and it can be rec'd as much sooner into the series as I may wish. . . . I am now beginning to work in good earnest."[52]

She expected that for the next year she would be living a quiet life in the

backwater city, teaching in the mornings and working on her literary manuscripts the rest of the day. Before she left she wrote Elizabeth Palmer Peabody
breezily that she thought she would be spared much "matronizing" except "to
let my candle shine with its usual lustre" and be an example "to the maidens of
Providence." She did not think she was cut out to be a governess. Hired to teach
"History, *languages*, literature" would be her "Ideal"; but as usual she took the
precaution of hedging her hopes. She promised to write Peabody later to tell
how "far the real corresponds."[53]

CHAPTER 6

I keep on "fulfilling all my duties" . . . except to myself.

Schoolkeeping in Providence

DURING the year and a half that Fuller taught at the Greene Street School in Providence, she boarded with Susan Aborn, the mother of one of her colleagues. At first the Aborn house was in the city proper, but later, in March 1838, the family moved to a larger house a little outside of town. Although there were relatives and grandchildren in the house, another teacher, Georgianna Nias, and her children, as well as other boarders, Fuller was happy with the arrangement. She worked hard at her teaching, but she never felt at home in Providence. Culturally, she thought it "might as well be Borneo." She complained about the quality of the students. Even those with "well-disposed hearts," she wrote Alcott, had minds that had been too long "absolutely torpid." She missed the "lively minds" of her Boston children, but even more, she missed her Boston life and friends.[1]

Hiram Fuller had asked Bronson Alcott to dedicate the school's new building on June 10, 1837, but Alcott, realizing that he might be a liability, suggested Emerson in his place. Emerson took the opportunity to criticize American education for its "desperate conservatism," but the speech brought little response; a single letter to the *Providence Journal* described the speech as "transcendental and scarcely intelligible in parts." The letter reflected the current view that those who subscribed to the principles deemed transcendental dealt in vague abstractions and were impractically idealistic.[2]

Fuller had understood she was employed to teach only the older girls, but she found herself in charge of 60 of the school's 150 students. Teaching Latin, composition, elocution, history, natural philosophy and ethics, and, later, a course in the New Testament, she found it challenging to adapt to her pupils' "various ages and unequal training," but she put her faith in her philosophy of education: "Activity of mind, accuracy in processes, and . . . search after the good and beautiful, 'that's the ground I go upon,'" she wrote Emerson. Her teaching style was sometimes confusing to the younger children, but she made a strong impression on many of the older girls. In the classroom she was regarded as strict and demanding, witty and authoritarian, at times unreasonable but always formidable, challenging, and impressive.[3]

Mary Ware Allen, who was attracted to the school from Northboro, Massachusetts, because of Fuller's reputation, wrote in her journal a few days after her arrival, "I love Miss Fuller already, but I fear her." A few weeks later she noted that she would go out of her way to avoid offending Miss Fuller. "She is very critical and sometimes cuts us into bits. When she cuts us all in a lump, it is quite pleasant, for she is quite witty; but *woe* to the one whom she cuts by herself." On one occasion the class rose up against Fuller when she lashed out at the popular Juliet Graves for a careless paraphrase of *Romeo and Juliet.* When the class protested in a round-robin letter, Fuller's reply came as a surprise. Freely admitting that she had been in "miserly" spirits, she apologized for being "too rough." She would like, she told them, to make up for it in any way they might suggest. While insisting on class discipline and high standards— she divided her Latin classes relentlessly on the basis of achievement—she often drew on her formidable conversational talent to enliven her classroom performance.[4]

For most of the year and a half she lived in Providence, she struggled to repress her resentment that the family situation forced her to live away from Cambridge and Boston. With few diversions and no close friends at the outset, she hoped to keep a daily schedule that would allow her to work on her Goethe biography and the translation of Eckermann's *Conversations with Goethe.* During the summer term she started her day at five in the morning so as to have two hours of her own work done before breakfast. She had most of the afternoon and the evenings to herself and hoped to be able to control her time, so as to live "very rationally."[5]

"I now begin really to feel myself a citizen of the world," she wrote Emerson after she was settled. He had loaned her several books to help with her research and had written to Thomas Carlyle for help in getting more information on Goethe. The Emersons invited her to spend a few days of her end-of-term vacation with them in August. She was to ride back with them after the Harvard commencement and join the next day in a picnic meeting of Mr. Hedge's Club, an informal discussion group that had been meeting since the previous September whenever Henry Hedge came to town from Bangor—hence the club's name. They discussed questions dealing with the religious and cultural climate of the country. Bronson Alcott, "the most insatiable talker of them all," recorded in his journals conversations on eclecticism, culture, comedy, music, futurity, faith, incarnation, and miracles. It was Margaret's initiation into the group that was to be later known as the Transcendentalists.[6]

Most of the members were present on August 31, 1837, in the First Parish Church in Cambridge when, on the day following commencement, Ralph Waldo Emerson gave the Phi Beta Kappa Address on the conventional subject for the occasion: the role and importance of the life of the mind, of "Man Thinking," in America. But Emerson's unconventional treatment, especially his prediction that American life and attitudes were about to change radically, was disturbing to many in the audience. The pivotal sentence was: "Our day of dependence, our long apprenticeship to the learning of other lands, draws to a close." He heralded a new spirit of change at work in the country, one that would save women and men from the dehumanizing effects of the major institutions in the land. He saw these "auspicious signs" of a new consciousness in the "literature of the poor, the feelings of the child, the philosophy of the street, the meaning of the household life, and the topics of the times."[7]

Years later, Oliver Wendell Holmes dubbed the address "our intellectual Declaration of Independence," and James Russell Lowell said it was "an event without any parallel in our literary annals," but at the time those who most appreciated his message were his close friends, many of whom, including Fuller, accompanied him back to Concord.[8]

On September 1, 1837, Lidian entertained seventeen Hedge's Club members all day, giving them a full tea as well as a dinner; she had an extra plank made for the dining room table for the occasion. Along with Fuller, the newcomers were Elizabeth Hoar, whom the Emersons cherished as a "sister," and Sarah Alden Ripley, a learned woman whose school in nearby Waltham had prepared a generation of students for New England colleges. In addition to a "noble great piece" of beef, Lidian's menu included

a boiled leg of mutton with Caper sauce and for side dishes ham and tongue (not cut up.) For vegetables there were corn—beans tomatoes macaroni cucumbers lettuce & *applesauce* and for puddings a ground rice with currants & a biscuit-pudding with raisins—or rather *two* of each. Besides which an array of soft custards graced the board. I gave them only pears nuts and raisins for dessert.[9]

A week later Fuller attended the next meeting of the club at the Clarke family home in Newton—James was back home on his annual leave. At this meeting Sarah Clarke and Elizabeth Palmer Peabody joined the group. Other than the women members and Bronson Alcott, the club members were young Unitarian ministers. Some were dissidents teetering on the brink of resigning the ministry, but the majority were seeking ways to invigorate Unitarianism from within. They called themselves, variously, the Aesthetic Club, the Symposium, and Hedge's Club. As they became better known as a group, outsiders began to speak of the "Transcendental Club." The members resisted this tag; they found it insulting as well as misleading, for all were not idealists of the German variety, nor did they have any party platform. In an effort to set the record straight, James Freeman Clarke suggested the name "the Club of the Like-Minded," because "no two of us thought alike." Fuller had no use for the "Transcendentalist" label, but she soon discovered that she was tainted by her association with those who were causing comment in Boston.[10]

During her vacation, she had arranged with Captain Sturgis to have Caroline come to Providence for the coming winter as a special pupil; the plan was that Caroline would live in the Aborn house and follow an independent reading program under Fuller's supervision. When Fuller left Boston for Providence in early September she thought Caroline would be joining her in December. But when she began to make arrangements for Caroline to board in the Aborn house, Caroline wrote that she would be staying home that winter. The only hint of explanation was that in Boston people were calling Margaret Fuller a Transcendentalist. Margaret snapped back:

As to transcendentalism and the nonsense which is talked by so many about it—I do not know what is meant. For myself I should say that if it is meant that I have an active mind frequently busy with large topics I hope it is so—If it is meant that I am honored by the friendship of such men as Mr Emerson, Mr Ripley or Mr Alcott, I hope it is so—*But* if it meant that I cherish any opinions which interfere with domestic duties, cheerful courage and judgement in the practical affairs of life, I challenge any or all in the little world which knows me to prove such deficiency from any acts of mine since I came to woman's estate.[11]

Considering herself almost a total hostage to family responsibilities, Fuller found it particularly galling for anyone to suggest that she was shirking her obligations. She knew that in the public mind a Transcendentalist was someone who was dreamy and unpractical, living in a vague poetic ether—someone who was "a little beyond," as her friend Almira Penniman Barlow put it with a wave of her hand heavenward.[12]

Not to have Caroline in Providence was a great disappointment. Yet when it became clear—after a spirited exchange of letters—that nothing was to be done, Fuller closed the matter to further discussion and wrote Caroline that she would see her during the winter holiday. "I do not wish to be needlessly agitated by exchanging another letter on this topic—I will let you know when I am in Boston and see you there at least once."[13]

Fuller disassociated herself forcefully from the popular conception of transcendentalism, yet she was fierce in its defense when Harriet Martineau's account of her American travels, *Society in America,* appeared in the fall of 1837. After dubbing Boston "the headquarters of Cant," where the current fad was a "spiritualism" based on "the principle that human beings are created perfect spirits in an infant body," Martineau ridiculed Bronson Alcott and the Temple School for basing its teaching on such "outrageous absurdities" and offering its pupils "every inducement to falsehood and hypocrisy."[14]

Fuller took it upon herself to write Martineau, berating her for the book's "want of soundness" and her "crude, intemperate tirade." Bronson Alcott was "a true and noble man" whom Harriet "should have delighted to honor" instead of assailing. Margaret expressed the hope that her bluntness would not jeopardize their friendship, but she felt compelled to clarify their differences of opinion. Behind the scolding tone of her letter lay resentment that her British friend's judgments had been at times superficial, that the measuring stick of the British reformer might not always be the right instrument to assess the progress of the new nation in the making.[15]

The ferocity of Fuller's letter surprised Martineau; she admitted in her journal that she felt chastened. Afterward their correspondence continued, but the two were more wary of each other. Years later, in Martineau's autobiography, she explained that "the difference" between Fuller and herself developed because Fuller's dedication to transcendentalism caused her to fritter away her talent. Transcendentalism was nothing more than "a rainbow arch . . . to be puffed away . . . with the first breeze of reality," and Margaret's early promise had been sidetracked, Martineau believed, as she became more deeply involved with those who talked philosophical inanities while ignoring such serious social issues as the abolition of slavery.[16] To Fuller, an effort that aimed at humanizing the whole cultural attitude of the country while it was still in its formative stage was basic to the nation's future and would help establish a climate in which humane social policies would result with less conflict. Was not this a serious and worthy reform?

Martineau was unaware of the degree to which Fuller labored under the weight of family cares. Uncle Abraham continued to bully her mother; he accused Margarett Crane Fuller of trying to raise her children above their station in life and threatened to take the guardianship of the younger children away from her. He even suggested that she should relieve her financial burden by allowing one of the childless Fuller relatives to adopt Richard.

"Do not suffer the remarks of that sordid man to give you any uneasiness," Margaret instructed her mother. All the children were to be educated as their father would have wished. "Fit out the children for school, and let not Lloyd be forgotten. You incur an awful responsibility by letting him go so neglected any longer." Lloyd was eleven, and it had become clear that he was not only a slow learner but a behavior problem. "I am not angry but I am determined," Margaret continued. "I am sure that my Father, if he could see me, would approve the view I take." If necessary, she would give an extra private language class in Providence to earn more money; she would live as cheaply as possible. "It will not even be a sacrifice to me," she wrote her mother; "I am sated and weary of society; and long for the oppor[tunit]y for solitary concentration of thought for my book."[17]

When Uncle Abraham came up with funds sufficient only for Arthur and Lloyd's schooling for the fall semester, she had Ellen come to Providence so she could direct Ellen's studies personally until enough money had been saved for her schooling and, in order to spare her mother the cold and tedium of the Groton farm during February, she had her come to visit. At the beginning of the winter, after Ellen had left for a school in Jamaica Plain, Margaret began teaching a weekly evening class in German for a group of prominent Providence women and men.

As she put more demands on herself, she had less time to spend on her writing. Periodic bouts of illness plagued her. For the rest of her life she would blame her unreliable health on the tensions and responsibilities that fell on her shoulders after her father's death. She was too gregarious and eager for new experiences to keep to the strict schedule she had set for herself early in the summer, and she found that social activity enlivened her and quelled her anxieties and fits of despondency. In August, "to the horror" of her employer, Hiram Fuller, a confirmed Democrat, she attended a Whig party caucus to sample the renowned oratory of the local Whig congressman, Tristam Burges. "It is rather the best thing I have done," she wrote Emerson. Party politics had no interest for her, but experience of the life of action, even when she was limited to the role of observer, certainly did. The closest she came to making a political statement in the classroom was a remark dutifully recorded by the most methodical of her students, Ann Brown, who wrote in her journal on March 15, 1838:

Miss Fuller wished us to have a distinct idea of the two classes of people, one called Conservatives the other Liberals or reformers. The first are those who wish to keep things as they are, and are afraid of improvement. The latter are those who wish to alter things, and bring the poor more on a level with the rich and this class are never the most numerous.[18]

Throughout the fall and winter, Fuller sampled most of the city's cultural offerings, including a lecture by the visiting English Quaker leader, Joseph John Gurney, whose "self-complacency" and "bat-like fear of light" so surprised and annoyed her that she prayed for *his* soul during the meditation period. In January 1838 she followed a course of lectures on Shakespeare's dramas given by her Boston literary friend, Richard Henry Dana, in Providence's new culture center, Shakespeare Hall. After sampling the sermons in several Providence churches, she found in the Unitarian antislavery activist, the Reverend Edward B. Hall, a minister who allowed her to take communion on her "own terms." It was the first time she had taken communion, she wrote, but she did not explain what her terms were. Within the next year she would take the sacrament three times, signaling the deepening need for reliance on a higher authority that followed her father's death. Whatever were Hall's terms, they must have been liberal enough for Fuller to interpret her dedication to a Christian life in her own way. Two years later she would write to a young friend, "I deem if the religious sentiment is again to be expressed from our pulpits in its healthy vigor it must be by those who can speak unfettered by creed or covenant; each man from the inner light."[19]

In October, James Freeman Clarke stopped over for several days on his way back west. For years he had been fascinated with new developments in mesmerism, animal magnetism, and especially phrenology, the "science" of reading a person's character from the configuration of bumps on the head. (In the early 1830s James kept a "phrenology journal" that included the observation from a lecture by the founder of the "new mental science," Johann Kaspar Spurzheim, that education could never make the two sexes the same because female heads are "long and narrow" and male heads are "thick and wide.")[20]

Providence at the time had the reputation for being a center for such experiments and demonstrations, and James persuaded Margaret to submit to a session with Miss Loraina Brackett, a partially deaf, dumb, and blind woman, said to possess extraordinary clairvoyant powers, but Margaret wrote Caroline afterward that even though "the blind somnambulist" had successfully located the exact spot of her headache and soothed the pain away she did not think it took clairvoyance to advise her that her headaches would be less frequent if she talked and wrote less.[21]

Although her first experience was not convincing, she kept an open mind and, though careful not to go on record as a true believer, she thought that there were many unsolved mysteries about the workings of the human mind that the experiments with mental phenomena might be able to clarify. From her own experience in personal relations, she believed in intuitional communication and thought that women especially had what she came to call an "electrical" gift of instinctive insight, possibly related in some way to mesmerism. Phrenology had less appeal for her, but her interest in self-improvement led her to test it occasionally because its proponents claimed that, once a person's characteristics were established, one could decide which to develop and which to curb.

The most successful promoters of phrenological science in America were the Fowler brothers, Orson and Lorenzo, who traveled about the country with their charts and plaster casts of the human head. When Orville Fowler visited the Greene Street School in mid-November, he examined the heads of both Margaret and Ellen. Margaret kept no record of Fowler's findings but, later in that month, the poet Sarah Helen Whitman, who was to become famous as Edgar Allan Poe's "Helen," was present with Margaret at a Providence dinner party when Margaret let down her hair for the popular lecturer and journalist John Neal, who had added phrenology to a long list of accomplishments that included fencing, drawing, lawyering, and auctioneering.

Whitman recalled many years later that Margaret's bumps revealed that she was the victim of contradictory forces: Her "Parentiveness" was at odds with her "Ideality," while her "Amativeness" struggled with her "Adhesiveness." In Margaret Fuller, according to Whitman's report, the "man, woman, scholar, teacher, child, mother and lover" all struggled for dominance.[22]

John Neal had come to Providence to lecture to the students at the Greene Street School on "the destiny and vocation of Woman." A large, handsome man, he had lived as a journalist for three years in London in the home of Jeremy Bentham and was now the editor of the Portland, Maine, literary weekly, the *Yankee*. For more than a decade he had been referring to the status of women in America as a form of "slavery" and advocating woman's suffrage and equal property rights for both sexes. Fuller admired his "*manly* view" of the subject and observed how unusual it was.[23]

Constantly noting the opportunities she was missing by living so far from Boston, she was especially frustrated when she learned too late that the British author Anna Jameson, well known as a good friend of Goethe's daughter-in-law, Ottilie von Pogwisch von Goethe, had passed through Boston and had met several of her friends. She lost no time in writing Jameson in hopes of arranging a meeting in New York or beginning a correspondence, but Jameson did not reply, and Fuller was left as before: at a loss about how to continue with her biography of Goethe when she was denied the resources needed to explore his complex personality. Nevertheless, she spent what little free time she had for scholarly pursuits on her translation of Eckermann's *Conversations with Goethe*.

Because of her Transcendentalist connections in Boston and her reputation as a learned woman, she was invited to join the Coliseum Club, a group of prominent Providence women and men who met throughout the winter months in each other's homes to socialize and read original research papers. The mainstays of the club were Mary Ann and Albert Gorton Greene; they were too conservative to agree with Margaret on most questions but liked her so much that they later named a daughter after her. Sarah Helen Whitman and Rhoda Mardenbrough Newcomb, a Goethe scholar, were already avowed Transcendentalists and became good friends. Whitman later likened Fuller's reception by the Providence literati to the reaction of "some watcher of the skies when a new planet swims into his ken." "She brought with her a flood of light on all the new and exciting topics of the day. She came enveloped in a halo of Transcendentalism—a nebulous cloud of German mysticism and idealism."[24]

On April 19, 1838, Fuller presented a twenty-four-page essay as part of a club debate on "progress in society." Greatly influenced by Emerson and making use of his theories of compensation and correspondence, but without his optimistic reliance on "the new consciousness" forming in the country, she attacked the utilitarianism and materialism of the age and the forces she saw as swallowing up "the claims of the individual man." In the country's heady self-confidence she saw much to deplore. The sorry relation of women to society, especially "women of genius," was an obvious area where modern society lagged far behind earlier ones. "I might easily be tempted to write a volume on this subject," she noted prophetically.[25]

If society was not progressing, all the more reason for her to keep her aspiring soul on the path of Eternal Progression. More than anything else that winter, Margaret regretted not hearing Emerson's new lecture series on human culture at the Masonic Temple in Boston. "I want to see you and still more to hear you. I must kindle my torch again," she wrote him in March. He had become one of her household gods—"an image in my oratory," she called him. Bestowing on him the nickname "Sanctissime," she made him her father confessor. She poured out her frustration with trying simultaneously to teach, engage in a reasonable social life, and make progress with her writing:

I have behaved much too well for some time past; it has spoiled my peace. What grieves me too is to find or fear my theory a cheat—I cannot serve two masters, and I fear all hope of being a worldling and a literary existence also must be resigned—Isolation is necessary to me as to others. Yet I keep on 'fulfilling all my duties' . . . except to myself.[26]

Courting Emerson's sympathy and encouragement, leaning on him as mentor, parish priest, friend, and hero, she approached him with the hope that he would be able to make up for Timothy's fatherly shortcomings. Although characteristically protective of his energy and time, Emerson responded generously. On March 13 he met her in Boston, took her to a painting exhibition, and discussed with her the French philosopher Victor Cousin and Carlyle's recently published *French Revolution.* Upon her return to Providence, she wrote James Freeman Clarke that Emerson "is to me even nobler than he was, wise, steadfast, delicate. One who will never disappoint my judgement nor wound my taste."[27]

In June the Emersons invited Fuller and Sturgis to visit them together. Having overcome whatever prejudices Captain Sturgis held against her, Fuller had spent part of her March vacation at the Sturgis summer home in Brookline. The two were now thought of as inseparable friends. Although Emerson had known Sturgis slightly for several years, he had recently discovered in her qualities he found particularly attractive. During the winter he had seen her on a few social occasions in Boston, and they had begun a correspondence. Sturgis's rejection of her conventional role as a socialite for the company of bookish people caught Emerson's attention. In his lecture that winter on "Heroism," Caroline was in his mind when he wrote: "The fair girl who repels interference by a decided and proud choice of influences, so careless of pleasing, so willful and lofty, inspires every beholder with somewhat of her own nobleness."[28]

Like Fuller, Sturgis too had begun to look up to Emerson as a guide and spiritual advisor. During their joint visit, she worked on her drawings and poems, and Fuller concentrated on her introduction to Eckermann's *Conversations.* Emerson was full of praise for the book and asked, "Can I see it again? & again as it grows?" He advised her to curtail her social life. She had to "live with more moderation" and avoid being "the servant of a visiting-card box"; she should adopt as a motto, "Ten people are a great deal better than a hundred."[29]

Fuller tried but found it impossible to take his advice. During her vacations, her first thought was to visit her old friends. In June, before she visited the Emersons with Sturgis, she had spent a few days in New Bedford with Eliza Rotch Farrar's Aunt Mary. After Concord she rejoined Aunt Mary for a few days at her Newport summer cottage, the Glen. Then, as soon as her late-summer break began in August, Fuller rushed to Boston, where she had a reunion with

Sam Ward, now two years older and much more mature than when she had seen him last, just before he had sailed off with the Farrars for Europe in the summer of 1836.

During the year and a half that Sam was traveling and studying in Europe, he had corresponded with Margaret occasionally and had sent her several books. He had encouraged his younger sister, Mary, to join the German reading classes Fuller gave in Boston during the winter of 1836–37. "I am sure you will find her a most delightful acquaintance and with a universality of knowledge that will surprise you," Sam wrote his sister.[30]

He had instructed Mary to share with Fuller some of his sketches of travel scenes, but he did not get in touch with her until months after his return to the United States. In the spring of 1838 he began his banking career in the New York office of Jonathan Goodhue. There is no record of Margaret and Sam meeting until August when they arranged a rendezvous at the Athenaeum gallery. Margaret arrived ahead of Sam, and while waiting she pondered what it would be like if she could devote all her time to writing. When Sam came, they decided to go on a carriage drive into the country. "Nature seemed to sympathize with me today," she wrote in her journal that evening. "She was not too bright, she was not too wild and I was with the only person who ever understood [me] at once in such a mood." She surely realized that she was not a central person in Sam's life, yet his admiration, his kindness and gallantry, and his very remoteness— like Anna's—allowed him to serve as the perfect foil for her fancies. She continued to construct in her inner life a secret and mysterious affinity between them.[31]

She could hardly have known at this time that Sam had fallen in love with Anna Barker. During his Grand Tour in Europe, Sam had separated from the Farrars, stayed with friends in Paris for a time, and later traveled with Professor George Ticknor of Harvard in Italy and Germany. He rejoined the Farrars at Interlaken in Switzerland in August 1837 and found that Anna, whom he had seen only a few times before, was now one of the party. "It was at once as though we had been friends," he wrote years later in his reminiscences.[32]

According to Mrs. Farrar, everywhere Anna went she attracted attention. In Rome, the Danish sculptor Thorvaldsen presented her with a medallion of himself; in Florence, the American sculptor Hiram Powers did a bust of her. Sam was strongly attracted to Anna, but he understood that at twenty-one he was too young to contemplate marriage. Before he could encourage a romance, he would have to prove himself in business.[33]

At the end of Fuller's August break, she stopped over again in Concord on her way back to Providence. This was her first visit after Emerson's explosive Divinity School Address, delivered on July 15. In it he went further than ever before in his repudiation of institutional Christianity: He challenged his audience to go forth and love God directly, without the mediation of formal religion. In the weeks that followed, he was attacked on all sides. Dean Palfrey of the divinity school decreed that what was not "folly" in Emerson's talk was "downright atheism" and threatened to withdraw the students' right to invite their own speakers. And the contentious former dean, Andrews Norton, published a special address in reply to Emerson: *A Discourse on the Latest Form of Infidelity.*[34]

The fierce opposition to Emerson's views constituted a persecution that sanctified him even more in Fuller's eyes. She wrote Jane Tuckerman that she had "excellent times with Mr Emerson, seeing his [light] shine out through all this fog. I have fine friends certainly; how dignified they look, while dirt is being thrown at them!" In a letter to James Freeman Clarke she said that Emerson's enemies were now "baying" at him. " 'Tis pity you could not see how calmly he smiles down on the sleuth hounds of public opinion."[35]

Starting the new term at the Greene Street School in the fall of 1838 was a letdown, and the family financial situation was worsening. In the spring, Margarett Crane Fuller put the children on notice that their "pecuniary affairs" were "far from encouraging." They would receive "no dividend from the 2000 dollars bank stock" and might even lose the principal. They were owed $120 in back rents on the Merrimack farm, and Bishop Hopkins, who had bought the Dana Mansion, was defaulting on his payments. "Our house rents go for repairs and we are fast consuming our personal property. We must be up and doing while it is still called *today* or we shall have nothing to bestow on education."[36]

Eugene, who had started law school at Harvard in January 1838, dropped out in August. He hoped to set up his own practice in Charlestown. The plan now was to concentrate the family education money on Arthur, who was enrolled in Sarah Alden Bradford Ripley's famous college preparatory school in Waltham. Margarett Crane Fuller considered running a boardinghouse in Providence for out-of-town Greene Street School students; it would be less expensive to live there and have the younger boys attend Brown University. But Margaret was too dissatisfied with her Providence life to assume a long-term commitment to teaching under Hiram Fuller, with whom she was increasingly at odds. There was also among the conservative middle-class parents of Providence a growing dissatisfaction with the school's experimental methods. Richard, who had been handling the farm alone for part of the past winter, would soon be ready to prepare for college. The only solution, it seemed, was to sell the Groton farm and rent cheaper quarters. In September, Fuller notified Hiram Fuller that she would be leaving Providence in December. The sale of the Groton property would ease the immediate financial pressure and give her some free time to finish her books. John Sullivan Dwight was using two of her translations in his forthcoming *Select Poems of Goethe and Schiller,* but she was way behind schedule with her two Goethe manuscripts.

James Freeman Clarke published two of her poems in the *Western Messenger* in 1836 and 1837. She did not mind when the first one, "Thoughts: On Sunday Morning when Prevented by a Snowstorm from going to Church," appeared, but when she discovered that a deeply personal one, "Jesus the Comforter," alluding to her father's death was published, she expressed great annoyance, even though she had not sent it with any restrictions. While in Providence she provided Clarke with two book reviews, which he published in the winter and spring of 1838: an essay on the poems of the revered young German soldier-poet, Karl Theodor Körner, whose war songs and early death in battle for the German fatherland had won him fame, and a review of the historical novel by the Unitarian minister William Ware, *Letters from Palmyra.*

In both she focused more narrowly than in her articles a year earlier for the now defunct *American Monthly.* She wholeheartedly praised Körner's fervor and heroic sacrifice in the cause of liberty, moralizing romantically that his example proved that, "as often seen in life, what seemed calamity was misinterpreted." Although she considered *Letters from Palmyra* inferior to several recent European examples of the genre and, for a historical novel, "modern" rather than ancient in its "atmosphere," she praised it for being "full of life." In a resounding rebuke to the conservative Unitarians who were baying at Emerson—some of whom would be reading her article in a Unitarian journal—she congratulated the author, a Unitarian minister, for retaining a heart in which "the fire on the altar of beauty has not been quenched by the mists of a timid and formal morality, a morality founded rather upon fears as to the social contract, than on the piety inspired by a human nature made in the likeness of a divine nature."[37]

In May, when Clarke asked her to write an article on "Animal Magnetism," she replied that she had "no interest" in the subject, but she wanted him to clarify his remark that her recent work suffered from "sentimentalism"—she underlined that she detested sentimentality. He told her not to get upset; he only meant that she expressed too much "feeling" and not enough "argument." That her writings were too impressionistic was a criticism Emerson would later share and one she would make an effort to control.[38]

While in Providence Fuller made a useful friend in George Calvert, a Newport gentleman who had traveled extensively in Europe, knew German, and was writing on Goethe and the German romantic poets. And in the companionship of Charles King Newcomb, the eighteen-year-old son of her Coliseum Club friend Rhoda Mardenbrough Newcomb, she thought she might have discovered a poetic talent. During the summer Charles had returned home from a year of study at a Virginia Episcopal seminary where he had become fascinated with religious mysticism. His mother, afraid that he was on the brink of converting to Catholicism, implored Margaret to encourage him in a literary career; Margaret soon added Charles to her roster of sensitive young men. "I have found a new young man, very interesting, a character of monastic beauty, a religious love for what is best in Nature and books," she wrote Jane Tuckerman in September.[39]

But she had little time to spare. When Charles began to impose on her, she told him that she was surrounded with "the little imps of care" and would have to "catch and cage them" before she could take time off.[40] Ever since she had started teaching in Providence she had vacillated in her enthusiasm for teaching. At times she thought that she was learning a great deal, but she had difficulty keeping her emotions under control. The story was told of Fuller's battle of wills with a young woman scholar who refused, on principle, to read aloud in class a text defending slavery. When the student remained silent after repeated orders to obey, Margaret treated her coldly for the rest of the year. But most of Fuller's students remembered her as an inspiring teacher and filled their diaries (daily journals were required at the school) with her classroom quotations and her moral instructions. Several students mentioned that they were most influenced by her encouragement to articulate their beliefs, to live affirmatively, to seek out specific aims, and to devise strategies to fulfill them.

"She spoke upon what woman could do—said she should like to see a woman everything she might be, in intellect and character," Mary Ware Allen wrote in her journal. Evelina Metcalf noted Fuller's particular recommendation of the study of history. "She said it would be a constant and delightful resource to us and it was a study peculiarly adapted to females," that women "could and are expected to be good historians."[41]

At the beginning of the fall term she agreed to supervise three out-of-town teenage young women boarding at Mrs. Aborn's while they attended the Greene Street School. One was Lilly Gibbs, a niece of William Ellery Channing; the other two were from Louisville, the daughters of friends of James Freeman Clarke. Ellen Clarke was the daughter of James's landlord; Emma Keats was the daughter of his parishioner George Keats, the brother of the poet.

In order to check on the two young women as well as to see Margaret, James visited Providence in early December. On his way east, he had stopped in Meadville, Pennsylvania; there he became engaged on November 4 to Anna Huidekuper, a young woman as unlike Fuller as possible. (Julia Ward Howe, the author of "The Battle Hymn of the Republic" and for over thirty years one of James's parishioners in Boston, reported that Anna was extremely timid in society and "so calm in disposition" that James, on presenting his wife with a copy of Howe's book of poems, *Passion Flowers,* inscribed the flyleaf, "To the passionless.") Anna was the daughter of Harm Jan Huidekuper, a Dutch immigrant who had become a wealthy landowner, a strong Unitarian, and a frequent contributor to the *Western Messenger.* James had expected to tell Margaret about his engagement, but he found her in a bad mood—she struck him as "caustic" and made several remarks that hurt his feelings, and he thought it wiser to keep his news to himself. At a time when she was again at a crossroads,

Margaret may have sensed that she no longer had much of a place in James's life. Perhaps she was annoyed that he took her good services for granted as so often before—this time, assuming that she would be only too willing to trouble herself with the needs of his Louisville friends.[42]

Teaching was natural to her, and she would, in fact, never cease being a teacher in one guise or another. Although her Providence experience had exhausted her, she had not given up entirely on the profession. She could imagine herself running her own school in a community where she had a free hand. Just before she left Providence at the end of December, she wrote William Henry Channing, now settled in Cincinnati as pastor of the Unitarian church, that she had always had "some desire to be meddling with the West" and that Cincinnati would suit her as a good place to start a school. "I am not without my dreams and hopes as to the education of women," she added. She wrote William that it would be at least a year before she would be free.[43]

In this, as in most other matters, her instinct was to keep her options open. But before she made any new plans, she had to see if she could succeed as an author.

CHAPTER 7

A man's ambition with a woman's heart. — 'Tis an accursed lot.

Episodes in the Crusade

AT THE END of February 1839, after two months of solid work in Groton, Fuller finished her Eckermann translation, some 800 handwritten pages. After asking her editor George Ripley to "mark everything you see amiss," because she wanted to learn all she could about publishing, she turned her attention to moving.[1] Margarett Crane Fuller had sold the farm with the understanding that the Fuller family would stay on until early April. Margaret told the Emersons that she and her mother might be interested in renting a house in Concord, but by the time Emerson presented her with three possibilities (one house belonged to Henry Thoreau's aunts, Jane and Maria), the Fullers had already signed a lease for a large three-story wooden house in Jamaica Plain, close to Catherine Tilden's school where Emma Keats and Ellen Clarke were now boarders.

Willow Brook, in Bussey's Wood near today's Arnold Arboretum, was five miles from the center of Boston but close to a horsecar line and rented for only $200 a year. Years later James Freeman Clarke remembered it as "a tall, ugly, three story building" near the Forest Hill Cemetery. Margarett Crane Fuller hoped to augment the family income by taking in boarders. As the Fullers prepared for an auction of their farm utensils and household affects, Margarett Crane Fuller made it clear that her life in Groton had been "[so] painful" that she never wanted "to visit the place again."[2]

While Margaret organized her father's papers, the accumulation of forty years of diaries, themes, legal briefs, correspondence, and minutes of debates in both the United States and Massachusetts legislatures, she was moved by what she found. "Well as I knew my father, I know him hourly better and respect him more, as I look more closely into those secrets of his life which the sudden event left open in a way he never foresaw. Were I but so just, so tender, so candid towards man, so devout towards the higher Power."[3] She could now empathize with his struggles and see some of her own problems mirrored in his. In the months before he died, Timothy had built a study for himself at the end of the garden. There he had hoped to write his biography of Jefferson, but at the time of his death he had put in less than a day's work in his retreat. "If I were disposed to draw a hackneyed moral, surely there never was a fitter occasion," Margaret concluded, as she worried about her failure to realize her own youthful ambitions.

After the public auction of the Fuller household effects, leaving the house "[a]ll dust and Babel,"[4] Margaret went to visit the Emersons. They welcomed her with open arms, even though Lidian had just given birth to a daughter and Waldo's brother and sister-in-law from New York were visiting at the same time. Margaret shared a room with Elizabeth Hoar.

Elizabeth was not blind to what she called "a Mephistophelic vein" in Margaret, her unrelenting drive to influence the people around her; nevertheless, Elizabeth found her inspiring. After the visit, she described Margaret's effect on her to an old friend:

> I see so few people who are anything but pictures or furniture to me, that the stimulus of such a person is great and overpowering for the time. And indeed, if I saw all the people whom I think of as desirable, and if I *could* help myself, I do not think I should abate any of my interest in her. Her wit, her insight into characters,—such that she seems to read them aloud to you as if they were printed books, her wide range of thought and cultivation,—the rapidity with which she appropriates all knowledge, joined with habits of severe mental discipline (so rare in women, and in literary men not technically "men of science"); her passionate love of all beauty, her sympathy with all noble effort; then her energy of character and the regal manner in which she takes possession of society wherever she is, and creates her own circumstances; all these things keep me full of admiration—not astonished, but pleased admiration—.[5]

Winning Elizabeth's admiration tied Margaret even closer to the Emerson family. Only Waldo's strong-minded Aunt Mary held out firmly against her. Mary Moody Emerson had helped to bring Waldo up after his father's early death and never let him forget the strong values of the family's Puritan past. Having no home of her own, she visited for long periods with one relative after another and was the conscience of the family; any transgressor in the large Emerson clan had to answer to her for spiritual shortcomings. A tiny woman who always wore white—and, it was rumored, sometimes slept in a coffin—she did not think Margaret was a good influence on her nephew.

After Elizabeth Hoar accepted Fuller into the Emerson family circle, she wrote Aunt Mary urging her to come to Concord to get to know her. Elizabeth was sure that Aunt Mary would change her mind when she saw how Margaret affected Waldo—"her power of making him talk,—He is a ray of white light, & she a prism—If not so pure & calm, yet she has all the elements of the ray in her varied being." Aunt Mary, though she adored Waldo, was concerned about his radical departure from the old Puritan beliefs; to the last she suspected that Fuller fanned and encouraged his heresies.[6]

Once the Fuller family was settled in the big house at Willow Brook, Elizabeth Hoar came to visit. Margaret and Elizabeth enjoyed rambling in the woods around Willow Brook, and they read together from the *London and Westminster Review* some letters of Rahel Varnhagen von Ense, the romantic German woman who, without beauty or dowry, had created a salon and surrounded herself with poets and musicians, leading a life Margaret thought enviable. Being back in the environs of Boston gave her the opportunity to revive her friendships, cultivate her artistic tastes, and try to mold her life closer to her ideal.[7]

"I am as happy as I can be. My health is much improved," she wrote her Providence friend and fellow Goethe enthusiast, Sarah Helen Whitman. "My mind flows on its natural current and I feel I have earned this beautiful episode in my Crusade." She was enjoying springtime rambles and going "once or twice a week" to Boston to meet with her friends, to visit the Athenaeum's picture and sculpture galleries, and to see a special showing of Washington Allston's pictures at Harding's Gallery on School Street. "To me the gallery has been a home," she wrote Charles Newcomb at the end of May. She wrote another friend that throughout the summer she hoped to "do nothing but think and feel."[8]

A quarrel with Caroline Sturgis was the first of the shadows that came to darken her idyll. During an early June three-day visit with Sturgis at Nahant, a rocky oceanside resort north of Boston, a quarrel that had been simmering for several months reached a point where Fuller seems to have left in a huff. The trouble began during Fuller's visit in December to Boston on the way home from Providence. Sturgis's "want of affection" at the time drew comment from Fuller, but she wrote in an imperious and almost threatening tone that she did not seriously think that "there was any danger" of Sturgis's "ceasing to love" her. "There is so much in me which you do not yet know . . . that you will not be able I believe, to get free of me for some years."[9]

To consolidate their intimacy, and to educate Sturgis in some of the fine points in personal relationships, she sent her a packet of personal letters from Jane Tuckerman, Waldo Emerson, and James Freeman Clarke, drawing special attention to her Clarke correspondence, perhaps because she now had heard— and not from him—of his engagement and thus thought of him as an experiment in friendship on the wane. "There are allusions to the 3 love affairs which formed him into manhood," Fuller explained. Since the "pain and passion" had now "passed into Experience," she was sure that James would not mind her showing them. Exchanging letters and diaries was frequent among romantic young people fascinated with the psychic development of all their mutual friends. Clarke's letters were sent as "a fine picture of an intellectual friendship and an interesting history of the growth of a practical character," as well as to instruct Sturgis "on how a large class of men feel towards women."[10]

Although Fuller protested, when criticized, that she did not wish to "urge" herself on Caroline as "a heroic or a holy friend" but wanted to be received "principally through the intellect," her confiding, self-exulting, sometimes nurturing, and often judgmental letters belie these instructions. She mixed the air of a superior spiritual guide and psychological counselor with the assurance of a sibyl and, when put to the test, insisted on royal authority. She interpreted Sturgis's moods and premonitions, criticized her drawings and poems, egged her on to high aspirations, and disparaged any tendencies that could be deemed vulgar. Her possessiveness took the form of strong disapproval of some of Sturgis's young friends—in particular William Wetmore Story, the son of the Supreme Court justice Joseph Story, and Maria White, who would later marry James Russell Lowell. She disapproved of Story because he was "self-seeking"; he had played with Jane Tuckerman's affections in a way that showed he lacked "noble views"; he failed to comprehend that loving a noble person or being loved by one is " 'building the stair to heaven.' "[11]

In the spring Sturgis began to challenge some of Fuller's presumptuous stances. The quarrel in Nahant seems to have been over Fuller's attempt to extract a statement of affection from Sturgis. "At Nahant Margaret asked me if I loved her but I could not at once say yes," she wrote on one of the letters the two exchanged afterward as she tried to make amends. Fuller, in curt responses, replied as she had in Providence when she felt crossed by Captain Sturgis's restrictions; she made it clear that she did not wish to have her summer disturbed with bickering. Later in the season she explained to Emerson that she and Sturgis were "silent by mutual consent."[12]

Fuller's translation of the *Conversations with Goethe from the German of Eckermann* was published in the last week of May, just before her tiff with Sturgis. She immediately sent a copy to Emerson. The letter that came in return meant more to her, she wrote, than "a voucher from any other quarter." He wrote:

The translating this book seems to me a beneficent action for which America will long thank you. The book might be called—Short way to Goethe's character—so effectually does it scatter all the popular nonsense about him, & show the breadth of common sense which he had in common with every majestic poet, & which enabled him to be the interpreter between the real and apparent worlds.

"The Preface is a brilliant statement," Emerson added. "I like it for itself, & for its promise." At a time when to publish on Goethe, let alone to present him as one of the superior minds of the age, was certain to court suspicion of moral laxity, the translation was an act of boldness. Later plagiarized in England by John Oxenford where it was considered the standard for decades, her American translation retained its stature for many years. In 1884 Henry Hedge pronounced her preface "one of the best criticisms extant of Goethe." She avoided narrow moralizing and based her criticism on clearly stated aesthetic standards, clearing the air of the "cant" that Carlyle had taught her to target. Sarah Whitman wrote Margaret that the *Conversations* had sold out in Providence and that she was preparing a review of it for the *Boston Quarterly Review*. The *New York Review* praised the book and remarked on the "admirably written" preface. Sam Ward reported that his father had read it "with great devotion."[13]

Margaret expected to see Sam more often now that she was living so close to Boston, but she was disappointed. During the winter, after leaving his New

York banking job, he had taken a long overland trip to New Orleans, partly to assess the state of the cotton trade for his father. Margaret did not see him until the first week in June, when he stopped by briefly; it was immediately apparent that his manner toward her was changed. He was polite, but his cavalier spirit was gone. Never able to live in a state of suspense, in mid-July she wrote him a peremptory letter attempting to force the issue.

I know you have many engagements. What young man of promising character and prosperous fortunes has not one waiting his every hour? But if you are like me, you can trample upon such petty impossibilities; if you love me as I deserve to be loved, you cannot dispense with seeing me.

J'attendrai. I will not think of you, but fix my mind on work. I cannot but see that never, since we were first acquainted, have we been so far removed from one another as at present.—

We did not begin on the footing of rational good-will and mutual esteem, but of intimacy; and I should think, if we ceased to be intimate, we must become nothing to one another. We knew long ago that age, position, and pursuits being so different, nothing but love bound us together, and it must not be *my* love alone that binds us.[14]

With Fuller at such times the word "love" becomes a categorical imperative. Yet, in the atmosphere of romantic love into which she was indoctrinating several young people, the concept of noble love included the splendid and heroic qualities of loyalty, self-sacrifice, aspiration, courage, and honor that had been demeaned in the workaday world. Fuller called the young people her "children," and Sam Ward called her "Mother." With a little encouragement, Ward, an idealistic and sensitive young man with literary aspirations, could well have given her a declaration of poetic devotion and high regard, which could then conflate in Fuller's mind into the expectation of a special claim to his attention. She had looked forward to his company during her first summer of leisure since their friendship had blossomed on the excursion to Trenton Falls before her father's death.[15]

But twenty-one-year-old Sam was distracted that summer by a more compelling concern: his future with Anna Barker, with whom he had fallen in love during their European tour. Together in New Orleans, he and Anna had confessed their feelings for one another. Although there was no formal engagement announcement, they shared the private expectation that they would marry in the future. Anna planned to come to New England during the summer, and Sam was certain that when his family knew her they would approve of his choice. Because of the delicacy of the situation, both Sam and Anna took extra care to be discreet. No one outside their families was to have any knowledge of their understanding.[16]

During June, Sam made one or two formal calls at Willow Brook. He lent books and even his precious portfolio of the copies of the heads of the more prominent figures in the Vatican paintings. (While in Rome he had commissioned the artist Temmel to copy them.) But his attentions were perfunctory. In

August he went hiking in the White Mountains of New Hampshire, where by chance he met Waldo Emerson, who took to him at once and was soon calling him the pet names that Margaret had given him—"Michelangelo" and "Raphael"—as well as adding a particularly resonant one of his own: "Prince-of-the-Purple-Island." Earlier in the year Margaret too had coined a new name for Sam. When thanking Caroline, who had known Sam since childhood, for a box in which to keep Sam's letters, she enthused, "he is such an Ariel that he deserves to be ministered to of every creature's best." The new names were the first casting of roles that year in a drama that was slowly enfolding in the minds of the players. It was no accident that one player cast Sam Ward in the role of Ariel while another cast him as "Prince-of-the-Purple-Island" or that the names themselves echoed a classic fantasy of mistaken identities, mismatched loves, and self-deception.[17]

Sam and Waldo had heard a great deal about each other from Margaret. After she showed Sam's European art portfolio to Emerson in 1838, he invited Ward to Concord. Although Ward was unable to accept, the two had met briefly from time to time after Waldo's lectures and at the Athenaeum, but the White Mountains was where the two men began the friendship that blossomed during the next few years.

Fuller, in the meantime, had gone off to Bristol, Rhode Island, to visit her old friend from Miss Prescott's school, Mary Soley DeWolfe, who lived in seigneurial splendor on a thousand-acre estate on the side of Mount Hope overlooking the bay. Mary's husband, William Bradford DeWolfe, was the scion of a family that had made its fortune in the slave trade. "It gave me a sickening shuddering feeling when I thought how much blood and tears all the luxury around me has cost," Fuller wrote in her journal after her first night in the magnificent home. Yet, for all her usual sharp criticism of the materialistic complacency of the time, in the luxurious home of her girlhood friend what most interested her was how well suited her hosts were, in terms of their innate characters, to their "stagnant" and "obsolete" gentleman-farmer lifestyle. She was surprised when Mary remarked one day that she thought Fuller must have "a very contented disposition." Thinking of herself as being "so impatient and aspiring by nature," Fuller mused over this, concluding that Mary saw her as "destitute of all she thinks valuable beauty, money, fixed station in society, unsustained, uncertain as to the future." Since Mary could have no idea of Fuller's "mental compensations," she could only admire her "gay and serene manner" amidst her "vie manquee."[18]

From Bristol Fuller went on to Newport to visit the Channings for a few days, though she did not dare stay long because Anna Barker was expected in Boston in September and had promised to stay with her in Jamaica Plain. To Fuller's disappointment, Anna kept delaying her arrival. While waiting, Margaret wrote again to Sam. This letter was even more highly charged and agitated than her last. In it she mourned that "since the first flush on the cheek of June we have not once seen, felt, admired together."

You love me no more. . . . At an earlier period I would fain have broke the tie that bound us, for I knew myself incapable of feeling or being content to inspire an ordinary attachment. . . .
—You call me your best of friends, your dearest friend, you say that you always find yourself with me. I doubt not the depth of your attachment, doubt not that you feel my worth. But the confiding sweetness, the natural and prompt expression of attachment are gone—are they gone forever?[19]

It is possible that Fuller wrote this letter to vent her feelings and did not send it, but this could be the letter that forced a frank reply from Sam after Anna had come and gone. When Anna finally arrived at the end of September, Fuller was in a rush to show her off to Emerson. Having already heard so much about Fuller's "Recamier," his curiosity was strongly aroused. He met Barker on October 4 and enjoyed her company on a ride to Newton and back. His journal records the powerful effect on him of this "being, so lovely, so fortunate & so remote from my own experiences." Swept away with her "instinctive elegance," he praised her dignified manners. She was like a "princess" in her demeanor, and her conversation was "the frankest" he had ever heard. "She can afford to be sincere. The wind is not purer than she is."[20]

Although both Barker and Ward were still sworn to discretion, either Barker told Fuller about their understanding or Fuller sensed it with the aid of what she considered woman's special electrical gift. In any case, she knew that Ward was courting Barker and that they were in love. With this situation in the background, Fuller and Ward met long enough to discuss their friendship, and he wrote her a letter that dealt diplomatically with the distinction between the kind of love that he had shared with her and the kind that he felt for Barker.

I feel some difficulty in speaking frankly of the ideas suggested in your letter. They brought home to my mind the reflection how widely apart are the points from which life is surveyed by those whose personal experience of passion has been thorough, and those in whom it has (though giving brightness to the fancy and earnestness to the thoughts) remained comparatively undeveloped.
. . . Your views of life and affection are perfectly true to *you*.—I too, once knew and recognized the possibility of Platonic affection. It is possible to those who have never passed the line. . . . Before that, all the higher classes of emotion, all the nobler views of life exist; but in a shape that seems sublimated and idealized to the more experienced: to those who *have* passed that line, the higher emotions and the passions are apt to be always afterward inextricably commingled.[21]

Years later, Fuller signified her growing disillusion with Ward and her sense of betrayal by writing on this letter, "so writes the sentimental man of the world and he, once my Raffaello, would now write so too." But in the immediate aftermath of this experiment in romantic love, Fuller assumed a magnanimous stance. Releasing Ward from any obligation, she accepted the role of his noble friend, committed only to his welfare. But her release was stated with a tenaciousness that left him little room for escape. She expressed regret that he had not confided to her his love for Barker and the attendant problems.

And, though I might grieve that you should put me from you in your highest hour[,] . . . I would not complain or feel that the past had in any way bound either of us as to the present. . . . I had thought too, that in ceasing to be intimates we might cease to be friends, I think so no longer. The knowledge that I have of your nature has become a part of mine, the love it has excited will accompany me through eternity. My attachment was never so deep as now, it is quite unsustained by pride or passion, it is sufficiently disinterested for me to be sure of it.[22]

While Anna was visiting, Fuller wrote a letter of reconciliation to Caroline Sturgis, in which she mourned the end of her hopes for an ideal circle of friendship in which she would hold Caroline and her "beloved" Anna "by the hand" and Mr. Emerson would be included "for the representation of religious aspiration" and Sam Ward for the "Earth's beauty"; Fuller no longer believed her circle "would be as complete as friendship could make it."[23]

Whatever Fuller knew or did not know about Ward and Barker's attachment, she knew that the influence she had over Ward after the trip to Trenton Falls in 1835 was now a thing of the past and her friendship with Barker was irrevocably changed. In these years middle-class women viewed marriage as so strong an involvement that all other relationships were forever shadowed. As a young woman in her teens, when Maria Francis became engaged to David Child, Fuller had expressed the same anxiety, and this time she took it for granted that she would be forever an outsider. When she visited Concord at the end of October, she poured out her feelings of displacement to Emerson, portraying herself as joyfully willing to sacrifice her position in the lives of her friends to their future happiness. Emerson, in his journal and in letters to Sturgis, expressed his own disappointment in the marriage, writing that he had hoped that Barker would choose to remain unmarried and establish instead "ideal relations," choosing "[n]ot only Raphael" as her "brother" but also "that Puritan at Concord who is reputed at some time to have seen the mighty Gods." Realizing Fuller's greater stake in the change, he accepted her claim to a greater sacrifice, but he found it hard to believe that her noble attitude would be maintained; he suspected that her "dear magnanimities" could not be relied on "for the wear & tear of years." Yet he complimented her on the "sterling sincerity" she showed in revealing her feelings.[24]

Believing that she was closing the book on her episode of noble friendships with Ward and Barker, she loaned Emerson a portfolio of their letters, as well as some from Sturgis. Seeing how frank and open the participants had been with one another, instead of viewing the circle as moribund Emerson saw the opportunity for an experiment of his own, or at least that is what Fuller came to think. But before he began to add his reanimating voice to the dispersed group, Fuller

retreated into herself for a period of self-renewal, a habit that had now become
a ritual after a period of intense outward living.

She expressed her self-dedication to a holy love in a mystical poem in which
she portrayed Ward and Barker as a nightingale and a dahlia enjoying all the
pleasures of life while nearby, close to the ground, there grew "a paler flow'ret"
(herself) that was "[s]eeking an ampler urn to contain its sweetness" and "a
statelier shape to find completeness." The poem concluded:

> When at the charming of the evening dew
> The flow'ret could its secret soul disclose,
> By that revealing, touched the lovely Rose
> Forgot them both, a deeper joy to hope
> And list the love-note of the Heliotrope.[25]

A few months later Fuller wrote Emerson that the heliotrope was her favorite
flower; it signified "distinguished merit" and a "delicate sensibility." She also
adopted at this time as her talisman a gemstone, the carbuncle. The idea came
from an episode in Novalis's novel, *Heinrich von Ofterdingen,* in which a princess possesses a magic carbuncle—significantly, a gift from her mother—that
assures her of absolute power over herself; with it in her possession she could
never fall into the power of another against her will. In her journal, Fuller wrote
a brief note: "Carbuncle, says Southey are male and female. The female casts
out the light. The male has his within himself. Mine is the male."[26]

To Fuller, her bisexual and homoerotic impulses were welcome signs of the
great diversity of nature as well as the endless drive of the human soul for
wholeness, two ideas she had thoroughly absorbed from Goethe. Her homoerotic dreams were fascinating to her, signifying the split in the psyche that the
modern mind continually suffers. Sometime during 1839 she wrote that, after
going to bed with a "pain in the right side" of her head, in a dream she was
visited by an exotic female figure who sat by her side, attempting to lure a large
butterfly onto her long finger. But the butterfly settled on the left side of her
head. Resisting her attempts to drive him away, "he plunged his feet deeper and
deeper" into her brow. When she awoke, her hand was on her left brow and the
pain had transferred to that side. In another dream she was lying ill "in a room
of a large hotel." She left the room and found herself lost, wandering from room
to room, until she threw herself down exhausted in the entryway, where some
people looked at her "scornfully" but most just passed her by. Just as she came
to think she would die there,

a sweet female form approached. . . I cried out and laid my head on her bosom. . . . The
face I never saw before, but the feeling I had was the same as when Anna, in the fever,
drew me up out of the pit of blood. It is the true feeling of feminine influence, . . . the
influence of benignity, purity, and faith. As I have masculine traits, I am naturally
relieved by women in my imaginary distresses. . . . This dream seems . . . very illustrative
of the influence of the body on the mind, when will and understanding are not on the

alert to check it. Let those who undervalue the moral power of will, analyse their dreams, and see what they become.[27]

"The picturesque part of my life has now withdrawn into the past and the world for the future offers me nothing but work," Fuller wrote as she gathered her forces after her book was published. She pondered Goethe's comments on women and writing:

I think perfectly true, though in no gross or sneering sense, what Goethe & his medicin say, that women who love & marry, feel no need to write. But how can a woman of genius love & marry? A man of genius will not love her,—he wants repose. She may find some object sufficient to excite her ideal for the time, but love perishes as soon as it finds it has grasped the shadow for the substance. Divorce must take place,—for the large nature will not find one capable of continuing its consort. Nor can children of the flesh satisfy the longing of the spirit for its maternity. Such a woman cannot long remain wed, again she is single, again must seek & strive. Social wedlock is ordinarily mere subterfuge & simulacrum: it could not check a powerful woman or a powerful man.[28]

Her reading project for the summer was modern French literature. She read Balzac, Lamennais, Béranger, Jouffroy, Alfred de Vigny, and George Sand. Jouffroy's mysticism and pantheism "excited greatly my desire to be a thinker," she wrote. "If I cannot be an artist or a complete nature, surely I can be a thinker." Goethean wholeness was now her watchword, adding to her restlessness. After reading several works, she complained that "the writing of la jeune France" bored her "almost as much as Boston society."[29]

The exception was George Sand, who was to her a worthy successor to Mme. de Staël and her revered Rousseau. Sand astonished her with "her insight into the life of thought" in *Les Sept Cordes de la lyre* and *Jacques*. She could only have "learned it from some man," Fuller conjectured.

Women, under any circumstances, can scarce do more than dip the foot in this broad and deep river; they have not the strength to contend with the current. . . . It is easy for women to be heroic in action, but when it comes to interrogating God, the universe, the soul, and, above all, trying to live above their own hearts, they dart down to their nests like so many larks.[30]

Sand's *Lettres d'un Voyageur,* on the other hand, irritated Fuller. "What do I see? An unfortunate, wailing her loneliness, wailing her mistakes, writing for money! She has genius and a manly grasp of mind & woman's heart, but not a manly heart. Will there never be a being to combine a man's mind & woman's heart, & who yet finds life too rich to weep over? Never?" When she finished reading *Jacques* a second time, she wrote, "This is my ideal—the soul that, capable of the most delicate and strongest emotions, can yet look upon the world as it is with a free and eagle gaze, and without vain optimism or weak hope of a peculiar lot, can, as Jacques says *accept life*."[31] The book focused her attention on the problem that she, as a woman, found daunting—writing emotional truth from the experience of her inner life.

These books have made me for the first time think I might write into such shapes what I know of human nature. I have always thought that I would keep all that behind the curtain, that I would not write, like a woman, of love and hope and disappointment, but like a man of the world of intellect and action. But now I am tempted, and if I can but do well my present work, and if but the wild gnomes will but keep from me with their shackles of care for bread in all its shapes of factitious life, I think I will try whether I have the hand to paint, as well as the eye to see. For I cannot but feel that I have seen from the mouth of my damp cave, stars as fair, almost as many. . . . But I dare boast no more, only please fate be just and send me an angel out of this golden cloud that comes pelting showers I have bourne so long.[32]

Near the end of a scrapbook Fuller kept in 1839, she penned, "A man's ambition with a woman's heart.—'Tis an accursed lot."[33]

By the end of the year she was successfully involved in a new enterprise; she was leading a series of public Conversations designed to encourage women in self-expression and independent thinking. The idea was so successful that from the first meeting on Wednesday, November 6, 1839, Margaret Fuller's Conversations were on the winter calendar of many of the most prominent and most highly educated women in Boston. At a time when the lyceum movement was gaining popularity throughout the country, Fuller's idea was not seen as particularly bold, certainly not in Boston where Elizabeth Palmer Peabody's reading parties and other private study groups had already paved the way. Yet, largely because of her personal style, the thoroughness with which she focused on her goals, and the enthusiasm of her influential subscribers, her Conversations became a famous Boston institution. Bronson Alcott encouraged the idea. He came out to Jamaica Plain at the end of August to announce that he was planning to offer a series of conversations during the next winter in the nearby city of Lynn—he called the idea a "Ministry of Talking." He needed to earn some money somehow, for early in the summer he had chosen to close his school permanently rather than dismiss Susan Robinson, a black child he had admitted three weeks before. When he refused to bend to pressure from most of the parents, all except one family withdrew their children, and he was left with no means of support. He told Fuller of his plan to turn the conversational techniques developed in his school into a means of self-support and spiritual reform; she realized she could use the same method to further her hopes for the education of women. But her greatest resource, she knew, was the large number of women in the area who were highly educated and hungry for mental activity.

She discussed her plan first with Sophia Dana Ripley, wife of her editor, George Ripley. She had known Sophia since her days at Dr. Park's school where Sophia was the highest-ranking of the older students; they had become closer in recent years because they shared the friendship of Sarah Helen Whitman and Rhoda Mardenbrough Newcomb in Providence. (After Margaret's move to Jamaica Plain, Sophia had dubbed her "the brilliant sibyl of the plains," in recognition of the prophetic element in her conversation.) Margaret needed

Sophia's help in assembling a circle of twenty or more women eager to discuss the big issues: "What were we born to do? How shall we do it?" These were the questions, Margaret pointed out, "which so few ever propose to themselves 'till their best years are gone by." At the very least she hoped to supply "a point of union to well-educated and thinking women" where they could satisfy their "wish for some such means of stimulus and cheer, and . . . for a place where they could state their doubts and difficulties with hope of gaining aid from the experience or aspirations of others."[34]

Elizabeth Palmer Peabody offered as a meeting place the parlor of the house the Peabodys had recently acquired at 13 West Street, just off the Boston Common. Twenty-five women turned up for the first meeting, several more than Fuller had expected. Meetings were scheduled at first to begin at eleven on Wednesday mornings, but the starting time began to slip forward toward noon to accommodate the women from out of town who were dependent on the stagecoach schedules. Lidian Emerson came from Concord; she was later joined by Elizabeth Hoar and sometimes by Sarah Alden Ripley from Waltham. From Salem came the fashionable Susan Burley, the outspoken advocate of higher education for women (in 1832 she had financed a limited printing of "The Gentle Boy," written by the unknown writer Nathaniel Hawthorne and illustrated by Sophia Peabody). Mrs. Jonathan Russell, the widow of the U.S. minister to Sweden, and her daughter Ida came in from Milton. Rhoda Mardenbrough Newcomb came all the way from Providence. The veterans of Margaret's 1837–38 German class were in attendance: Caroline and Ellen Sturgis, Mary Ward, Mary Channing, Marianne Jackson, Jane Tuckerman, and Elizabeth Bliss (now Mrs. George Bancroft). Eliza Farrar, Sarah Clarke, and Belinda Randall—Elizabeth's sister—were regulars. A large contingent came from the Boston Female Anti-Slavery Society: Louisa and Anna Loring, Hope and Anna Shaw, Mrs. George Russell, Lucilla Quincy, Lydia Cabot Parker, and Anne Terry Phillips, the wife of the abolitionist orator Wendell Phillips. They came despite the rancor and division that the issue of woman's rights was beginning to cause in the antislavery community.[35]

Fuller wanted to be certain that the Conversations did not degenerate into social events or digress into gossip. Elizabeth Peabody's "abstracts" of the first few Conversations include Fuller's introductory remarks, which set the tone.

Women are now taught, at school, all that men are; they run over, superficially, even *more* studies, without being really taught anything. . . . But, with this difference; men are called on from a very early period, to reproduce all that they learn. Their college exercises, their political duties, their professional studies, the first actions of life in any direction, call on them to put to use what they have learned. But women learn without any attempt to reproduce. Their only reproduction is for the purposes of display. It is to supply this defect . . . that these conversations have been planned.[36]

In the first Conversation, Fuller proposed that the series be built around the subject of Greek mythology. Because the myths were generally well known and were expressive of an ancient and distant culture, she could use them as launching pads for a fresh approach to subjects such as the power of the human will, the sources of creative energy, the development of the arts, and the different faculties that are put to use in rational and aesthetic pursuits. She accepted the eighteenth-century view that Greek was the original language in which human understanding was expressed, so that it was only a short step to endow the myths with divine and ancient secrets waiting to be revealed. From childhood she had been thoroughly schooled in Plutarch's rendition of the myths; she was familiar with Thomas Taylor's recent translations; the previous winter she had read Heeren's *Mythology*, which presented a psychological as well as a symbolic reading of the myths. Wordsworth's *Tour of Greece* was one of her favorite books. The Greek myths gave her a means, "playful, as well as deep," to pry into subjects that most women assumed required a formal philosophical or theological education. Viewing human behavior as expressed in a mythical universe would liberate them from the proprieties of their New England upbringing and encourage them to reexamine their values on a universal scale, even to "denationalize" themselves as a way of broadening their outlook.[37]

Fuller knew that she risked being accused of being too pagan, but after the first few meetings she could joke that, although "more Greek than Bostonian" was spoken at the meetings, Mrs. Josiah Quincy saw to it that Christianity and morality were not forgotten. Sarah Clarke wrote her brother in Louisville that the Conversations were viewed from the beginning as "a kind of infidel association" and that Fuller had to exert herself to keep the Conversations from becoming "endless theological discussions."[38]

At the first meeting, Fuller inspired ten members to join in the discussion; participation increased at each successive gathering. When the first series ended in midwinter, she was immediately persuaded to start another. Stimulated by the recent donations to the Athenaeum sculpture gallery, she devoted the spring 1840 series to the subject of the fine arts.

In March 1841 she introduced an evening series as a concession to pressure to include men. The experiment was a failure because, as everyone agreed afterward, the men took over the discussion and performed for each other. By that time the Conversations had taken on a decidedly feminine character, feminine concerns addressed in feminine language in an atmosphere of feminine intimacy. The youngest participant in the series, Caroline Healey, age nineteen, kept notes; she noted that Fuller "never enjoyed this mixed class and considered it a failure so far as her own power was concerned. She and Mr. Emerson met like Pyramus and Thisby, a blank wall between." Healey also noticed that Fuller and Theodore Parker, the fiercely independent Unitarian minister in West Roxbury, were incompatible; each "required a sort of personal submission before new-comers could be admitted to a cordial understanding," and neither one of them was willing to yield ground to the other. Yet it may have been at these meetings with the men that Fuller began to formulate her theory of Minerva and the Muse. Charles Wheeler pointed out that Fuller stressed that "the predominant goddesses" represented one idea, "that of the female Will or Genius—the *bounteous giver.*" Could this be the origin of Fuller's belief that the psychology of women was ruled in part by such Muse-like qualities? Two weeks later, in a Conversation devoted entirely to Minerva, she claimed the balancing power of Minerva when she stated that "Wisdom was like woman, always ready for the fight if necessary, yet never going to it; taking reality as a basis, and classifying and arranging upon it all that Genius creates,—seeing the relations and proper values of things."[39]

Fuller kept repeating that she did not want to be forced into becoming some sort of performer, "a paid Corinne," as she put it, referring to the romantic improvisatrice heroine of Germaine de Staël's novel by the same name. Soon after she started, she pronounced herself satisfied that she had established herself as "truly a teacher and a guide," but several of her friends thought that she was too theatrical. Elizabeth Hoar found some of the Conversations "too much like a performance," and the young Caroline Healey agreed. Margaret was like a queen surrounded by her court; Caroline wished that Margaret would give up "the love of power for its own sake."[40]

Showing this band of prominent Boston women how to "question and examine, yet follow leadings," and how to shake "off a wonderful number of films" was a heady experience. Once Fuller established her reputation, she felt the pressure to be in good vein every time. Her only complaint was that she never met her match. No one dared to challenge her. "I am never driven home for ammunition; never put to any expense; never truly called out."[41]

Intellectually, she was not taxed enough, but psychologically, the two-hour sessions took their toll. Her brother Richard remembered that the Conversations "produced almost invariably torturing headaches in which her nervous agony was so great that she could not always refrain from screaming." Fuller told Eliza Farrar that she "did not care" if the effort resulted in headache because she was aroused to "such a calm consciousness of another life . . . that pain had no effect except to steal some of my time." A killing headache was a small price to pay for the excitement and pleasure.[42]

Of course, the Conversations met with criticism. According to Elizabeth Palmer Peabody, when Fuller's friends heard the "misunderstandings and ugly things" they simply ignored them. The most influential critic of the Conversations was the beautiful, headstrong, titian-haired Maria Weston Chapman, leader of the Boston Female Anti-Slavery Society. A frequent contributor to William Lloyd Garrison's *Liberator,* she wrote Fuller in 1840 suggesting that the Conversations include a discussion of abolition. Fuller replied that she could not "interrupt" her schedule but assured Maria that the abolition cause commanded her deepest respect. Though she may seem "indifferent," her own interests merely led her in a different "path." She was primarily interested, she wrote, in whether the extension of woman's rights was a part of the abolitionist platform. Garrison's society was split over the question of the active participation of women; a year earlier at the World Anti-Slavery Convention in London, American women representatives had been refused seats.[43]

Margaret had adopted Emerson's policy in regard to reform: that the place to begin is in the individual soul. She could contribute the most by changing women's perceptions of what they could do in the world. In one of his last poems, "Vermächtnis," Goethe had written that the most worthy of all pursuits was to encourage noble souls in the search for intellectual or aesthetic answers. This was the reform to which Fuller was earnestly committed in her personal and professional life.

Many abolitionists were members of the Conversations, but Maria Chapman scorned Fuller's meetings. Her annoyance may have influenced Harriet Martineau's fierce condemnation of the Conversations in her autobiography. Over the years, Chapman and Martineau became close friends; in the 1870s Martineau dictated a good part of her autobiography to Chapman and entrusted her with its editing. Martineau never attended one of the Conversations, but in condemning them she combined Chapman's scorn for the meetings with her own scorn for transcendentalism:

While Margaret Fuller and her adult pupils sat "gorgeously dressed," talking about Mars and Venus, Plato and Goethe, and fancying themselves the elect of the earth in intellect and refinement, the liberties of the republic were running out as fast as they could go, at a breach which another sort of elect persons were devoting themselves to repair.[44]

Although the Conversations lent themselves easily to satire—Emerson talked of Fuller's "Parlatorio" and her "Aulic Council of Wednesday noons"—she was acting from a strong conviction: that it was important to encourage women to begin the process of independent self-development by articulating and examining their opinions. Moreover, the Conversations were the best available means by which Fuller could translate into action her own beliefs, make use of her undisputed talent as a talker, gain the friendship of many interesting women, and earn a substantial amount of money. She charged ten dollars for the first series, making in the neighborhood of $200. During the second season, the price doubled. With two series a year and an attendance that had risen to forty-five, she was coming close to her full-time teaching salary in Providence with only a half-day's hard work a week during the winter season.[45]

Fuller supported herself with the Conversations for five years. They became a Boston institution in which over 200 women participated. In the later series, she offered subjects that were more directly concerned with the everyday lives of women. Among the topics were Education, Ethics, Culture, Ignorance, Vanity, Woman, and "Persons who never awake to life in this world."[46]

Years later, after the Civil War, Elizabeth Cady Stanton praised Fuller's Conversations as a landmark in "the vindication of woman's right to think." Many women who became leaders in the feminist movement were participants: Julia Ward Howe, Lydia Maria Child, Ednah Dow Cheney, Caroline Sturgis, and Caroline Healey Dall. The weekly discussions identified many of the ideas Margaret would use later in her landmark book on the future of women in America. As she wrote Sarah Helen Whitman in Providence, the group gave her "a real society," a circle of friends who had "patience, mutual reverence and fearlessness eno' to get at one another's thoughts."[47]

In late August 1839, only a few days before Fuller wrote Sophia Ripley about her plan for the Conversations, she sent Jane Tuckerman a letter of advice. Fuller had just returned from her trip to the DeWolfes in Rhode Island and was worried about Sam Ward's neglect. As she waited anxiously for Anna Barker's visit, she wrote Tuckerman telling her that she had recently received a "painful piece of intelligence" that gave her "an excuse for tears" (possibly a crucial letter from Ward). "That was a Black Friday," she wrote.

What demon resists our good angel, and seems at times to have mastery? Only *seems*, I say to myself, it is but the sickness of the immortal soul, and shall bye and bye be cast aside like film. I think this is the great step in life, to change the nature of our self-reliance; we find that the will cannot conquer circumstances, and that our temporal nature must vary its hue here, with the food that is given it.[48]

As she wrote this, she was on her way to taking her own advice with a vengeance.

But Oh! really to feel the glow of action, without its weariness, what heaven it must be!

The *Dial*: Discontent and Freedom

EVEN before Fuller got her Conversations underway in November 1839, she had already undertaken responsibility for another transcendental experiment that put her in the public eye. In the spring and summer, the Hedge's Club revived the idea of establishing its own journal as a platform for its progressive ideas. Since the club members were looked upon as no more than a band of heretics, the religious magazines were closed to them. The respectable, tedious *North American Review*—"the snore of the muses," according to Emerson—was out of the question; it represented just what they were clamoring against. The few ladies' magazines that accepted pieces that met their standards were published in Philadelphia and New York; their editors could not be counted on to be steadily interested in both theological commentary and experimental belles lettres, the two most likely transcendental modes of expression. After briefly flirting with a proposal from Orestes Brownson to join with his *Boston Quarterly Review,* the members decided that a separate publication was the only solution.

George Ripley was a likely choice for editor, but he was too involved in his pamphlet war with Andrews Norton, the ongoing battle that had started with Norton's attack on Emerson's Divinity School Address; to keep his hand in, Ripley volunteered as business manager. Emerson wanted the journal more than anyone else, but he was working on a new lecture series and a collection of essays and refused to complicate his life further. Without much delay it was decided that Fuller, who was regarded by most of the members as knowledgeable and competent, should be offered the job. During a weekend in Concord, on October 20, she accepted with little ado.[1]

Fuller postponed settling down to work on the *Dial* until the first week of 1840. She waited until her Conversations were running smoothly and the family routine at Willow Brook was under control. In July she had started a small boarding school in the spacious Willow Brook house with her Louisville charges, Emma Keats and Ellen Clarke, and Charlotte Newcomb, the sister of Charles, from Providence as her pupils. In August, Eugene, who had given up trying to succeed in the law, set out for New Orleans to make his fortune in business, leaving Margaret and her mother to run the family. Arthur had entered Harvard in September. Richard was studying at a Jamaica Plain day school for boys, and Ellen was at home helping with the school. In October—just at the time Margaret agreed to accept the editing job—William Henry came home from Cincinnati for a few weeks to get engaged to Fanny Hastings.

Emerson was concerned that Fuller was putting so much effort into the Conversations that she was neglecting the *Dial*. While insisting that she was the sole editor, he promised "to rhyme with might & main" for her magazine and told her that his neighbor, Henry Thoreau, had an elegy he wished to submit. She had thought that young bards and prophets would be rushing to her door, but in mid-December, when she had nothing, Emerson sent her a packet of verses and egged her on by predicting that her labors would produce "a new Age" and would "mould our opinions & we shall think what you think."[2]

She began by soliciting manuscripts from her close friends. Reminding William Henry Channing that when they had last been together in Newport he had prophesied "a new literature," she asked him what part he intended to play "in the grand symphony." She told Henry Hedge that the aim of the magazine was "to form a city of refuge for the just"; he was to supply her with "poems or philosophy or criticism" from his "sentry box" in Bangor. When she wrote James Freeman Clarke, she reminded him of his prediction ten years earlier that the two of them would join forces someday to edit a magazine. "[I]t is said this 1840 is the millennial time when it must succeed."[3]

By March, Fuller was still short of enough material for the first issue. She could make up the first number with her own writing and Emerson's contributions, but, as she wrote Henry Hedge, "the Public, I trow, is too astute a donkey not to look sad at *that*."[4]

She desperately wanted the first number to show that there were enough able writers among the much maligned disciples of Transcendentalism to sustain the journal and enough quality in their writing to command the interest of the discriminating public. "[I]f the first number justify not the magazine, it will not find justification," she wrote Henry Hedge, who had ignored her first letter. "[S]o write, my friend, write." Fuller could not believe that Hedge, who had spearheaded the Transcendental Club and had been one of the first to propose a magazine, should now ignore her pleas. But, as she was soon to learn, Hedge was only one of several young ministers who, a few years before, had wanted a journal in which to publish their dissenting views but now differed so much from each other that they shied away from appearing under the same masthead. Though this limited Fuller's ready field of authors, it also played into her hands. She still refused the title of Transcendentalist, which she viewed as a party label in an internal Unitarian debate; she wanted her journal to be "literary rather than theological," and it soon became clear that only a handful of ministers, Theodore Parker and John S. Dwight in particular, were willing to use the *Dial* as their forum.[5]

Fuller met Theodore Parker for the first time in the fall of 1839. After meeting her, he said that she resembled Mme. de Staël more than any woman he knew. In a letter to a friend that year, he described one of Emerson's lectures as made up of "fractions of Alcott, Dwight and ½ Miss Fuller." One of eleven children of a Lexington, Massachusetts, farm family and largely self-taught, Parker managed to graduate from Harvard even though poverty prevented his steady attendance at classes. The pastor of the Unitarian church in West Roxbury and wholeheartedly involved in the Unitarian theological debates, he would have liked to use the *Dial* as a forum. Fuller found his forceful character threatening. In her diary she wrote that she had no intention of letting him be a "leader" of the *Dial* "in the Heavy stern line," but his "learning and just way of thinking will make him a valuable aid."[6]

When Emerson saw how slowly she was progressing, he dug into the family archives and resurrected material written by his two deceased brothers as well as the poetry of his first wife, Ellen Tucker. He coaxed a second poem out of Henry Thoreau and two poems from Christopher Cranch, the most irreverent of the young dissenting ministers who had gone west.

By the end of March, Fuller's enthusiasm was waning. She had taken on the job in the conviction that the country needed a "perfectly free organ . . . for the expression of individual thought and character," one that would "not aim at leading public opinion, but at stimulating each man to think for himself." Now she was concerned that there was not enough interest to carry out her object. She poured out her frustration to William Henry Channing, who was becoming her most sympathetic listener:

I never, never in life have had the happy feeling of really doing anything. I can only console myself for these semblances of actions by seeing that others seem to be in some degree aided by them. But Oh! really to feel the glow of action, without its weariness, what heaven it must be![7]

For so long Fuller had seen herself cast in the role of enabling others to further their own interests while suppressing her own that, as her editing difficulties mounted, she feared she would be caught in the same trap again. She had started out with the expectation that she would be the arbiter of an energetic literary group eager to appear in print. Instead, she found herself more often used "to urge on the laggards, and scold the lukewarm."[8]

In early April even more wind was taken out of her sails when Horace Greeley's *New-Yorker* announced that a new magazine representing "the transcendental school of philosophy" would soon be published under the "Editorial direction of Ralph Waldo Emerson and associates." Thoroughly annoyed at being written off, Margaret complained that she was being "stripped" of her reputation for "talents and knowledge." Greeley's correction—published a week later—was even more demeaning; the new magazine's name was listed as the *Harbinger,* and "Miss Sophia Margaret Fuller" was to be coeditor.[9]

Emerson was impatient to get the first issue out in April. He told Fuller that she was "pretty well freighted" for her "first trip to Sea," but she was dissatisfied with the material on hand and refused to go to press. She groaned as Emerson forced on her reams of Bronson Alcott's pretentious aphorisms—his mystic "Orphic Sayings"—and when George Ripley began to interfere with her editorial decisions she wailed in her journal, "Everybody finds fault with me just now."[10]

Concerned that her friends would expect too much from the first issue, she warned William Henry Channing that it would disappoint those who expected to find "the gospel of transcendentalism" and reminded him that she brought to the editorship an entirely different background than that of the young Unitarian ministers like himself who had been editing the *Western Messenger*.

"My position as a woman, and the many private duties which have filled my life, have prevented my thinking deeply on several of the great subjects which these friends have at heart." She suspected that she differed from most of them on religious matters, but she was not afraid "to aid in enabling them to express their thoughts." She did not consider herself as utopian as most of her friends.

Yet every noble scheme, every poetic manifestation, prophesies to man his eventual destiny. . . . It is on this ground that I sympathize with what is called the "Transcendental party," and that I feel their aim to be the true one. They acknowledge in the nature of man an arbiter for his deeds,—a standard transcending sense and time,—and are, in my view, the true utilitarians.

She characterized the Transcendentalists as "a small minority" who had become aware "that political freedom does not necessarily produce liberality of mind, nor freedom in church institutions—vital religion; and, seeing that these changes cannot be wrought from without inwards, they are trying to quicken the soul, that they may work from within outwards."[11]

In her journal that winter she continued to struggle with the problem of authorship. She worried about her lack of patience in carrying out thoughts and the inadequacy of language. "The best that we receive from anything can never be written," she complained. "The best part of life can never be recorded." She questioned the "regular build" of the essay form as requiring too many worthless words between the gaps in the thought. She preferred the dialogue form as "very propitious" to good composition, and, while working on the first issue of the *Dial*, she published in the *Boston Quarterly Review* two dialogue essays under the title "Chat in Boston Bookstores," in which she puffed the poems and Shakespeare commentary of Jones Very and defended George Ripley's Transcendentalist arguments in his pamphlet war with Andrews Norton.[12]

"I have just enough talent & knowledge to furnish a dwelling for friendship, but not enough to deck with golden gifts a Delphos for the world," she wrote in one of her low moments. Using sexual symbolism to express her frustration with writing, she confessed to depressions that brought on yearnings for death.

Often, too often, do I wish to die! My spirit sinks, & my whole heart grieves. My day is poor in thought & deed; my body is a burden, not an instrument. I have few thoughts, too much feeling. Oh that I should live to write thus! I feel within myself an immense power, but I cannot bring it out. I stand a barren vine-stock, from which no grape will swell, though the richest wine is slumbering in its root. I never doubt my ultimate perfection, but I doubt where'er this life be my climate, or will ripen my fruit.[13]

At the end of April when she showed Emerson her draft of an introduction to the first issue of the *Dial*, Emerson criticized it for being too much on the defensive and then rewrote it to his liking. By this time the two were continually bickering over editorial trifles. Though Emerson insisted that he was not the editor, the success of the *Dial* was more important to him than he would acknowledge. He offered suggestions continually, and to keep Fuller's spirits up he made grandiose claims for the magazine's future. The popularity of his lecture series and the controversy aroused by his university addresses assured that his name would be associated with it. The *Dial* would test whether his prophecies were taking hold in America. Already he had written Thomas Carlyle twice about it, once claiming that his friend "Margaret Fuller's journal" would give "a better knowledge of our young people than any you have had."[14]

After George Ripley issued a prospectus announcing that the *Dial* would be published as a quarterly and sold to subscribers at three dollars a year, only thirty people subscribed; yet Emerson was so optimistic that he advised publishing 1,500 or 2,000 copies. Even if the magazine only lasted a year, he argued, the copies would have permanent value.[15]

Fuller spent most of May and June organizing and preparing the first issue. At the last minute she was forced to fill it out with odds and ends from her own journals. The response was hardly encouraging. The New York *Knickerbocker Magazine* had a heyday poking fun at Alcott's "Orphic Sayings"; otherwise, the July 1840 *Dial* was largely ignored by the important literary magazines. With the exception of the *Boston Times*, which called it "one of the most . . . ridiculous productions of the age," the Boston dailies greeted the first issue with guarded respect; a few enthusiasts of Emerson's lectures wrote letters of full-hearted encouragement. Most of the out-of-town response was downright vicious: The contributors were "zanies," and transcendentalism was "clear as mud." The most troublesome responses came from the Transcendentalists themselves. Emerson, while telling Fuller that her first issue was "good" and anointing her the "queen of the American Parnassus," sent a copy to Carlyle with an apology. Theodore Parker criticized the lack of intellectual vigor. (Behind Fuller's back he had been ridiculing her "petty jealousies, contemptible lust for power, & falling into freaks of passion.") Ripley did not think the *Dial* lived up to its "pretensions." Even Alcott, whose "Orphic Sayings" did the new journal the most damage, judged it merely "a twi-light dial."[16]

Determined to make the October issue much better, Fuller set to work immediately. By the end of July she had more than enough material for a well-balanced second issue. Her policy was to consider any contribution on any subject whatsoever that showed earnest and original thinking. Emerson was concerned that the *Dial* was becoming too literary; it should aim to be "so broad & great in its survey that it should lead the opinion of this generation on every great interest & read the law on property, government, education, as well as on art, letters, & religion." Though he foresaw the *Dial*'s future as an influential journal of public affairs, Emerson was concentrating on his essay, "Friendship." Throughout the winter, the subject drew him out of his "honorable prison" into "the pleasant element of affection with its haps and harms," as he wrote Fuller after reading the portfolio of letters between her close friends that she shared with him in the fall. While embarking on friendships with Ward, Sturgis, and Barker, he wrote her that he delighted "much" in his "new relation" to her friends. When Emerson showed her a draft of the essay, she analyzed in her journal what friendship meant to him: "Mr. E. scarce knows the instincts. And uses them rather for rejection than reception where he uses them at all. In friendship with R.W.E., I cannot hope to feel that I am his or he mine." She concluded, "His friendship is only strong preference and he weighs and balances, buys and sells you and himself all the time."[17]

Yet even as the problems of the *Dial* dominated her friendship with Emerson during the winter, he included in his letters seductive paragraphs suggesting that they turn their attention elsewhere. On seeing a bluebird during a springlike February day, he wrote of "days of passion when the air is full of cupids & devils" and philosophized, "Let us surrender ourselves for fifteen minutes to the slightest of these nameless influences" in order to be reminded "what an ignorant pretending Old Dummy is Literature." At the same time, in a flotilla of letters, he was welcoming Sam Ward as a great discovery in his life and encouraging Caroline Sturgis to an ever more lively and personal correspondence. Since impressing Emerson with her "instinctive elegance" the previous autumn, Anna Barker was in faraway New Orleans, but she too was playing a powerful but silent part as summer came to New England and everyone took a respite. "Why should there be but one 'Midsummer Nights Dream' out of all the Julys & Augusts that have darkened & glittered to the universe?" Emerson wrote Sturgis on July 21, capturing the mood of them all as they reacted to Sam Ward's return at the end of June from an overland journey to New Orleans. Sam was bedridden with a debilitating fever, probably malaria. There was talk that his romance with Anna was over. He had, in fact, proposed formally to her shortly after his arrival in New Orleans and been refused. In the course of the previous year, largely because of Emerson's influence, Ward had decided that he would be happiest living in the Emerson manner as a literary man and a scholar. The confession of this preference seems to have been one reason for Anna's refusal. Jacob Barker had been wiped out so often that he warned his children in advance that he could not promise them fortunes. If Sam insisted on being a writer, Anna would not be secure. Another reason for Anna's refusal was that she was the last single daughter in the Barker family and was made to feel it her duty to remain a companion to her parents. (In a letter to Sam's father written a few months later, Jacob Barker admitted that such was his hope.)[18]

It was a dispirited Sam who made his way back to Boston via Chicago and Cincinnati. On his way he wrote Fuller a letter describing a back-pack trek in Illinois. (She published part of it later in her book, *Summer on the Lakes.*) After arriving home, he was too sick to see his friends. When Margaret finally saw him in July, she found him "gentle celestial, not hopeful, but faithful"; she expressed the hope that their relationship would "remain as sweet and un-troubled as at present!" Believing that he was struggling with his parents over his desire to risk a literary life—an ambition in which she thought she had played a part—she had published four of his poems in the first issue of the *Dial*, along with another cryptic "Dahlia" poem of hers.[19]

Friendship was a subject to which both Fuller and Sturgis warmed. To the two of them their own relationship had provided a field for earnest study during the last few years. Their breach of the previous summer now mended, Fuller assured Sturgis that their friendship was "redeemed from 'the search after Eros'" and could now be built "with trust." They would "commune without expecting too much from each other." She would now meet with pa-tience even the "passive repulsion" that Sturgis showed at times. As one of their rituals of trust, during their vacation together at Cohasset at the end of June they shared their Emerson letters. Though they both considered his friendship one of the great prizes of their lives, they agreed that he fell far short in meeting their definition of a friend; his need for solitude and distrust of society kept him from the mutual commitments that Fuller in particular believed to be the very basis of friendship. What followed was a season in which Emerson brought upon himself a crossfire of romantic testing in which Fuller challenged him with her philosophy of friendship.[20]

On August 6 Anna Barker arrived in Jamaica Plain to visit Fuller for a few days before going to Cambridge to stay with the Farrars. On August 14 Mrs. Farrar invited both Fuller and Emerson to visit. Afterward, on the buggy ride back to Jamaica Plain from Cambridge, Fuller told Emerson that their relation-ship had disintegrated to little more than "literary gossip"; she and Sturgis both agreed that friendship with him was unsatisfactory, a matter of counting and weighing, of catechizing and criticizing rather than loving. To the diffident Emerson, who protected his vulnerability in a blanket of stoicism, the attack came as a surprise. He said only that he knew himself to be cold by nature and that all his friendships suffered from "the same hardness & fences."[21]

Mulling over the confrontation after returning home, he admitted in his journal that he would be most "grateful" if he could "melt once for all these icy barriers & unite with these lovers." But he knew he would not change:

But great is the law. (Such a one as) I must do nothing to court their love which would lose my own. Unless that which I do to build myself, endears me to them, our covenant would be injurious. Yet how joyfully would I form permanent relations with the three or four wise & beautiful whom I hold so dear, and dwell under the same roof or in a strict neighborhood.[22]

He wrote a long letter to Sturgis, defending himself against the charges Fuller had made on behalf of both of them. With the subject of friendship uppermost in his thoughts—he was still working on the revision of his essay—he invited Sturgis to come with Barker and Fuller to Concord for a long weekend; he even offered to drive them himself from Boston in a carryall. During the visit they thoroughly discussed the ins and outs of their friendships; all of them had a full opportunity to air their discontents.

That weekend's discussions were a revelation to Emerson. He confided to his journal "with a shudder of joy" that he had been overwhelmed to learn that his friends loved him for what he was and not what he did for them. "[N]ow suddenly it comes out that they have been loving me all this time, not at all thinking of my hands or my words, but only of that love of something more beautiful than the world, which, it seems, being in my heart, overflowed through my eyes or the tones of my speech." To be the object of so much reverent affection delighted him. He encouraged further letters on the subject.[23]

Amidst the intense exchange of letters that followed, a new turn of events heightened the summer's drama. Less than a week later, Anna Barker told Emerson privately that she and Sam Ward had made up their differences and had been engaged for two weeks; he was astonished both at the news and at the force of his own feelings of disappointment that the friendship circle he was just beginning to form around him would be broken up. His letters to Ward and Barker as well as to the others brimmed with strong sentiments. Instantly he realized that Fuller would be even more seriously affected than he was. The marriage of her two ideal friends would certainly leave her stranded. He advised her to be heroic and "resign without a sigh two Friends;—you whose heart unceasingly demands all, & is a sea that hates an ebb." At the same time, he wrote that he welcomed her letters and urged her to write to him "in any mood."[24]

On the surface Fuller behaved magnificently. She did not "resign" her friends in the least, but she formed what she called a "new alliance" with "Raphael and his Madonna." She claimed that for her their marriage was an edifying event, a model marriage, a holy union of the pure. Immediately after the formal announcement of the engagement on August 28, Anna and Sam set their wedding date for October 3, Sam's twenty-third birthday. (Anna was twenty-seven.)

Perhaps because Sam was leery of Jacob Barker's parental power, he did not even allow the death of his sister Mary's fiancé, on the day before the wedding date, to interfere. (Mary's fiancé was Henry Ward, Julia Ward Howe's brother. The New York Wards were close friends of the Boston Wards but were not related.) It was a small family wedding. Fuller was impressed that Barker celebrated her marriage by giving gifts to her friends. "[W]as not that like her, to give at a time when all others receive[?]" Margaret marveled.[25]

While the couple were on their honeymoon in the White Mountains of New Hampshire, they corresponded with Fuller, and immediately upon their return they came out to call. Their plans were to live in Boston on Louisburg Square in a town house that Thomas Wren Ward had given them for a wedding present. Sam had given in on the matter of his vocation; he was entering the brokerage business. Privately, Fuller viewed this as a betrayal of his talent and promise, somehow related to his personal betrayal of her. She was of two minds about the young Wards; at times she viewed their marriage as an ideal and noble union, and at others she saw the two of them as bowing ignominiously to convention. In November, when the new season of Conversation classes began, Anna joined the group and made a point of sitting next to Margaret at the weekly sessions.

The transition to the new alliance with Anna and Sam seemed to have passed peacefully, but with the withdrawal of her two most favored confidantes into the closed circle of marriage, Fuller turned her attention to her other friendships. The August weekend when Fuller, Sturgis, and Barker went to Concord to consider Emerson's "inhospitality of soul" stimulated a new round of responses that began when Fuller and Sturgis wrote Emerson conciliatory letters pledging their devotion despite his failures in friendship. He then wrote each of them a separate letter, describing the nature of his unique friendship with each, expressing his philosophy, and making it clear that he could accept no relationship that implied permanence, commitment, or bondage.[26]

Fuller's reply, a letter now missing, brought a sharp rebuke. He took particular exception to her claim in one passage that "I [i.e., Emerson] am yours & yours shall be, let me dally how long soever in this or that other temporary relation." He certainly was not hers in any sense of the word, and he wished to correct her misconception. In spite of all his gratitude to her, they met like "foreign states," he notified her. She lived on a different plane and thought "different thoughts."[27]

Describing her as a "divine mermaid or fisher of men" who surrounded herself with "a whole college" of immortals, he underlined that they differed widely in their need for a rich social life and intimated that she enjoyed power over others. He made it clear that he still thought their friendship was in process. "I am willing to see how unskilfully I make out a case of difference & will open all my doors to your sunshine and morning air," he offered calmly.

Recognizing the sexual element in the interchange that convention would not permit either of them to acknowledge to each other, he explored his private feelings in his journal:

You would have me love you. What shall I love? Your body? The supposition disgusts you. What you have thought & said? Well, whilst you were thinking & saying them, but not now. I see no possibility of loving anything but what now is, & is becoming; your courage, your enterprize, your budding affection, your opening thought, your prayer, I can love—but what else?[28]

Coming only a few days before Anna and Sam's wedding, Waldo's strong words were especially wounding. Margaret responded immediately, saying that she was all too well aware of their differences and had suffered from them. What is more, she retorted, Waldo had completely misread her character and failed in his friendship by failing to help her find her way to the religious fulfillment she was seeking.

Dear friend on one point misunderstand me less. I do not love power other than every vigorous nature delights to feel itself living. To violate the sanctity of relations, I am as far from it as you can be. I make no claim. I have no wish which is not dictated by a feeling of truth. Could I lead the highest Angel captive by a look, that look I would not give, unless prompted by true love. . . .

In me I did not think you saw the purity, the singleness, into which, I have faith that all this darting motion, and restless flame shall yet be attempered and subdued. I felt that you did not for me the highest office of friendship, by offering me the clue of the labyrinth of my own being. Yet I thought you appreciated the fearlessness which shrinks from no truth in myself and others, and trusted me, believing that I knew the path for myself. . . . If you have not seen this stair on which God has been so untiringly leading me to himself, you have indeed been wholly ignorant of me. Then indeed, when my soul, in its childish agony of prayer, stretched its arms to you as a father, did you not see what was meant by this crying for the moon; this sullen rejection of playthings which had become unmeaning?[29]

Fuller's language only encouraged Emerson to place himself at a greater distance. He replied that he could not answer her "seven chords of melody" by letter but would do so when they met. His reference to the title of George Sand's novel, *Les Sept Cordes de la Lyre*, as a way of characterizing her style gave notice that he was unsympathetic with her emotional license. (After reading several of Sand's novels at Fuller's suggestion in 1839, Emerson wrote her that Sand was "sick with the sickness of the French intellect & has not surmounted this taste for the morgue and the hells.")[30]

Soon afterward Fuller went off to spend a few days with Sturgis in the country near Newburyport. When the two women compared their latest Emerson correspondence, Fuller concluded that Emerson, while accusing her of collecting and manipulating people, had been unwittingly using the affections and loyalty of Sturgis and herself as well as the vicissitudes of Sam and Anna's romance (including its effect on her, Sturgis, and himself) as a means of furthering his study of friendship. She saw also that Emerson in his letters to Sturgis was far gentler, more comfortable, playful, and fatherly than he was to her. On October 22 she wrote him another forceful letter which—she told Sturgis—gave her "pain" to write.[31]

Her letter does not survive, but it was strong enough to bring to an abrupt end, in Emerson's words, the game of "writing romances of letters . . . all this idle happy summer." Emerson replied that he ought not to have allowed her to lead him "into any conversation or writing on our relation." He repeated that they had different constitutions, spoke in a "different rhetoric," and seemed to be "born & bred in different nations." No matter how often she claimed that she understood him perfectly, as far as he was concerned the commitments she was claiming by such assumptions did not avail. Nevertheless, he saw no reason why they should not continue their friendship. "See you not that I cannot spare you? that you cannot be spared? that a vast & beautiful Power to whose counsels our will was never party, has thrown us into strict neighborhood for best & happiest ends?" He invited her to visit him, to write to him, and to speak to him on any subject except their personal relations. He made himself clear: "Do not expect it of me again for a very long time."[32]

What kind of love was Fuller demanding from Emerson? How self-deceptive was she when she insisted that he had failed her as a friend because he had not involved himself sufficiently in her search for a satisfying spiritual path? Did Emerson's insistence on self-protection warrant her powerful response at a time when he was expounding the same philosophy of friendship to Sturgis in less confrontational language? Was there in her behavior in these exchanges the element of brash crudeness that Hawthorne was to find so offensive in later years? It has been strongly argued that Fuller brought on Emerson's reaction by openly declaring her love for him. Certainly he felt threatened by her intensity, and, in warning her that her personal feelings for him were off-limits, he may have been keeping at bay an unacknowledged attraction to her, just as she, in her anxiety over the breakup of her circle and in the name of ideal love, was channeling erotic feelings in his direction. In different degrees, they were both caught in the net created by sublimated conceptions of human relations. Regardless of the emotions that precipitated it, the debate had forced the issue of their philosophical differences. For Fuller, human interaction and intimacy with another with commitments of mutual caring were not only emotionally satisfying but among the most necessary and noblest means of deepening one's insight into the human condition as one progressed heavenward. For Emerson, much as he enjoyed his friends, this most human of pleasures was no more than one of life's elusive distractions. His "law of friendship," as he wrote Sturgis, was that "the vast spirit" was "impatient of bounds, impatient of persons, foreseeing the fall of every fondness, of every specialty." For Fuller, this was too abstract a formulation. It denied the importance of life on this earth, the dailiness of life as a preparation for heaven.[33]

It would be in keeping with Fuller's character and past behavior—and consistent with Emerson's response—for her to have taken in this crisis the strong stance she had taken with James Freeman Clarke in the episode involving Harriet Russell: to recognize her failure to induce the intimacy she desired, to consider the disappointment as a betrayal of her own considerable emotional investment, and to find a vent for her anger. It is very likely that she accused Emerson in no uncertain language of making use of her friendship for literary ends and of failing to live up to the obligations that the bond between them required. (Throughout the writing of his essay, Emerson had openly mined his letters and conversations for literary material.) Later, when Emerson described their differences, he said as much:

Our moods were very different; and I remember, that, at the very time when I, slow and cold, had come fully to admire her genius, and was congratulating myself on the solid good understanding that subsisted between us, I was surprised with hearing it taxed by her with superficiality and halfness. She stigmatized our friendship as commercial. It seemed, her magnanimity was not met, but I prized her only for the thoughts and pictures she brought me.[34]

Fuller was as distraught now as she had been years earlier when James Freeman Clarke returned from Louisville and treated her with cool matter-of-factness or, for that matter, when Sturgis had refused to submit to her demands for a confession of love in Nahant. As before, she responded by insisting on a period of withdrawal. It was painful that Emerson could score her for her aggressiveness and her ambition, the very qualities she had needed in order to make her way in the world, and—as the final insult—could imply that the development of those qualities excluded her from a devout religious life. In one of his letters describing the differences between them he had questioned the sincerity of her religious commitment with the statement, "I thought you a great court lady with a Louis Quatorze taste for diamonds & splendor, and I find you with a 'Bible in your hand.' " He accused her of "a certain willfulness" and a lack of the "pure acquiescence," which was "the only authentic mode" in which to live the religious life.[35] In his journal he puzzled over the contradictions in her behavior.

Margaret is a being of "unsettled rank in the Universe." So proud and presumptuous yet so meek; so worldly and artificial with the keenest sense and taste for all pleasures of luxurious society, yet living more than any other for long periods in a trance of religious sentiment; a person who according to her own account of herself, expects everything for herself from the Universe.[36]

The summer's experiment had left her without the social center that had become part of her identity. She had imagined that her group of friends were on their way to creating the kind of open circle of equal friendship that prevailed in literary circles in Europe. Was she trying to be an American Rahel Varnhagen or to play the role of the princess in Goethe's *Torquato Tasso*—the princess who warned the poet Tasso of the dangers of solitude and who reminded him "that the only Golden Age that matters is that which human beings constitute among themselves by moral and seemly behavior"? She had turned Emerson into her American Goethe, only to discover that he had no taste for the role. Admittedly, he was "pure" and "profound," she wrote Sturgis, but there were many who surpassed him in generosity and freedom of thought. She was tempted, she wrote in anger, "to teach this sage all he wants to make him a full-formed Angel," but she thought that the gulf between them was now too wide: His cautious reserve was the result of distrusting life too much. In her annoyance, she made a moral issue of what was temperamental in her faithful but stubborn foe.[37]

Emerson refused to take seriously the religious mode that Fuller embraced during the few weeks following the announcement of Sam and Anna's engagement. "I live, I am—*The carbuncle is found*. And at present the mere sight of my talisman is enough," she wrote Caroline in early September as she embraced "the mighty changes" in her "spiritual life." In November she described her experience to her Conversation class and to several friends as an inner calling to live as a lay nun. "[S]oon the winter winds will chant matins and vespers," she wrote William Henry Channing on October 25, "which may make my house a cell, and in a snowy veil enfold me for my prayer. If I cannot dedicate myself this time, I will not expect it again." She asked him to explain why "the religion" of her nature was so "hidden" from her peers. To Sturgis, Fuller wrote that she now found her "stern and fearless" former self transformed into someone "soft and of most delicate tenderness." Before, she had been "an Amazon" rushing into the melee, whereas now, "full of heavenly vows," she would "steal away . . . into the very heart of the untrodden mountain where the carbuncle has lit the way to veins of yet undreamed diamond." That she fell into such mystical moods at times of inner turmoil she readily admitted. Her state was marked by identification visions of the Virgin Mary and with vestal virgins watching over holy fires. She claimed that her obsession with "the realizing of ideas" had been transformed into a "nun like dedication."[38]

In her loneliness that autumn in Willow Brook, she began to translate Bettina Brentano von Arnim's *Günderode* (1840), a fictional elaboration of an attachment between two German women. She found an attractive model in the central character, Karoline Günderode, a German poet, who had withdrawn from Berlin society at the beginning of the century to live an ascetic life of religious contemplation while continuing a close friendship with a younger woman, Bettina Brentano. Fuller's letters to Caroline Sturgis at this time suggest that she was attempting to find ways to reenact the friendship of the German women in the American context.

To inspire her Conversation classes she sought out material that would provide examples of strong women and of women's friendships. In both pagan and Christian history, in allegory and in folktale, she found for her purpose virgin goddesses and nuns and laywomen who had dedicated themselves to holy or ascetic lives; they had enjoyed power and high respect and represented qualities no longer accorded to women. Without actually believing in them, Margaret found in such virgin goddesses as Isis and Diana, associated with the moon and representative of creative power, a special source of the correspondences she was seeking.

Whether or not she acknowledged it, she was playing something of a priestess role herself as leader of the Conversations and, to a degree, as editor of the *Dial*. And, like a priestess, she began to put greater emphasis on unconscious sources of power. Fascinated with Goethe's concept of the Daimon as developed in his poem cycle, "Primeval Words: Orphic," she played with the idea of a predestined fate and chance as the determinants of a human life; half seriously, she looked for meanings in chance encounters, similar names, and birthdays falling on the same day. She enjoyed seal rings with emblems and blazons to which she gave her personal translation. Her carbuncle gemstone, shooting off rays of blood-colored light, represented her quest for the idea of a universal feminine animating force, a search she viewed as religiously inspired. During her solitary winter, the quest took hold, strengthening her will to independence and leading ultimately to the central proposal in the feminist program she was to develop in her later writings.[39]

By the middle of November, Margaret was living in the big, ugly house at Willow Brook with only Lloyd for companionship. Charlotte Newcomb had returned to Providence, and Emma Keats was on her way home to Louisville with Ellen Fuller. The two had become fond friends, and Ellen, now twenty, planned to stay with the Keats family until she could find a teaching job in the West. Eugene, newly married to a young widow, Anna Eliza Rotta, had come home from New Orleans in order to bring his mother back to visit them for the winter. After William Henry's latest business venture failed in Cincinnati, he had gone with his wife Fanny to New Orleans with the hope of joining Eugene in some new scheme. Richard, who had never shone in his schoolwork, having agreed to try out a mercantile career, Uncle Henry found him a place with a dry-goods jobber in Boston. With Arthur in college, Margaret was freer than ever before.

She found it impossible to keep her vows of solitude. "I can never simplify my life; always so many ties, so many claims," she complained. Her weekly Conversation classes and especially the demands of the *Dial* kept her from losing contact with ordinary life. Even though reviewers still looked askance at her magazine and "burlesqued" its "cabalistic contents," the second number was better received than the first. Horace Greeley's *New-Yorker* reprinted whole sections, and even the prestigious New York *Knickerbocker* gave praise. New contributors were now sending in their work. When Fuller heard that John Heraud of the *Monthly Magazine* in London and George Keats in Louisville were praising her journal, she returned to the work with more gusto.[40]

She was less deferential to Emerson and now had the confidence to use her own judgment when he pressed new material on her. Without a qualm she returned Henry Thoreau's essay on bravery, "The Service," saying it required more work. She refused to publish a whole sonnet sequence of another young discovery of Emerson's, Ellery Channing, a boyhood friend of Sam Ward and a nephew of the famous William Ellery Channing; she thought his poems too imitative of Tennyson's. She also rejected—for "bad faults in style and imagery"—an essay on art submitted by William Wetmore Story, the young man who had the year before earned her ire for undervaluing Jane Tuckerman's love; he would in later years become one of Margaret's most valued friends.[41]

Challenged by Thomas Carlyle's judgment that the *Dial* was "very good as a *soul*" but lacked "body," she chose for her third issue substantial articles by Parker, Emerson, Hedge, and Hedge's neighbor, the abolitionist Thomas Stone. In publishing Sophia Ripley's article "Woman" (it analyzed the new catch phrase, "woman's sphere"), the *Dial* branched out into new territory. So as not to neglect "the soul," Fuller published poems by Caroline Sturgis, James Freeman Clarke, and Christopher Cranch. By the time she went to press for the January 1841 number, she had convinced her earlier detractors that she was in control of her magazine and that it was fulfilling its mission.[42]

Once the January 1841 issue was out, Fuller took to her bed with "nervous attacks." She had thought that the absence of family friction and a regimen of prayer and Bible reading would restore her to good health, but on January 5, 1841, she wrote in her journal that she wondered how the Trappist monks "could bear their silence." She would have thought that "each heart would have burnt out at once."[43]

In mid-February she wrote William Henry Channing in Cincinnati that her winter of spiritual dedication had changed her but not permanently: "Once I was almost all intellect; now I am almost all feeling. Nature vindicates her rights, and I feel all Italy glowing beneath the Saxon crust. This cannot last long. . . . I must die if I do not burst forth in genius or heroism."[44]

Instead of transforming her into the model of feminine acceptance that Emerson had projected as an indication of religious progress, Fuller's solitary winter had only increased her restlessness. As April approached, she had to decide where to go next; the lease on Willow Brook was up. Her mother was still in New Orleans with no definite plans to return. During the winter, Ellen had fallen violently ill in the Keats's home in Louisville and had gone to New Orleans to be under her mother's care. It had been expected that as soon as she recovered the two would return to Boston. Instead, in spite of being warned by a doctor that she had consumptive tendencies, Ellen returned to Louisville, where she was promised a teaching job.

Margarett Crane Fuller suggested one solution to the problem of where the family could settle next. She urged Margaret to invest in Brook Farm, the new community George and Sophia Ripley were starting on 175 acres in West Roxbury within walking distance of the Fuller's Willow Brook house in Jamaica Plain. For several years George Ripley, with Sophia's support, had dreamed of founding a community where people could live more integrated lives than the growing commercial culture permitted. Like most of the Transcendentalists, he believed that competition and fragmentation were the enemies of American life. In March 1841 he gave his farewell sermon at the Unitarian church on Purchase Street in Boston, telling his parishioners that "what they needed was a revolution in commercial, political, and domestic relations rather than a mild chat on Sunday mornings." By that time, Ripley was looking for five or six families willing to invest at least a thousand dollars apiece in a joint-stock company, so he could make a down payment on the land he had chosen for his experiment, the Brook Farm Institute of Industry and Education.[45]

Even though Fuller was sympathetic with the plan and admired the Ripleys for their "steadfastness and earnestness," she was no utopian; she doubted that they would be able to arrange life to "get free from all they deprecate in society."[46] Her Groton years had soured her on farm life, and she needed privacy. As the leader of the Conversations and as editor of the *Dial*, she was now a public figure in Boston. She had labored too long to sacrifice this for the obscurity of communal life. But as the Ripleys assembled the first contingent of Brook Farmers in the spring of 1841, they were happy to have Lloyd Fuller join them. Though hotheaded and moody, he was strong and able-bodied.

Fuller was now freer than she had ever been before. She decided that when her mother returned they would not keep house together—at least, not for the present. Margarett Crane Fuller would board in Cambridgeport with Thomas and Sarah Gannett. (Thomas had been the Fullers' minister when they lived in the Port.) Fuller planned to spend the next few months staying with friends. If she had no place to go, she could always take refuge at Brook Farm; they took boarders at four dollars a week with extra for tea and laundry. In the fall, when her Conversation classes began, she would use as her base an attic room in the home of her Uncle Henry and Aunt Mary at 2 Avon Place, around the corner from Elizabeth Palmer Peabody's West Street bookstore.

At the end of March 1841, Fuller moved out of Willow Brook. After selling the family cow to the Ripleys for use at Brook Farm, she went to stay for a few days with the Randalls on Winter Street in Boston. She thought of herself now as "a poor wandering pilgrim, yet no saint." She would return to the theme in the next few years, writing her friends that she "never yet [had] been at home on earth" and always felt like "a pilgrim and sojourner on earth." To feel homeless and godless in an unpredictable world was a common refrain of nineteenth-century romantics at home and abroad, but for most of Fuller's future her claim was to be literally true.[47]

CHAPTER 9

I long to fix . . . my own plans where I am clear and sure and strong.

A Sojourner on Earth

SOMETIME during this watershed period in Fuller's life—between the breakup of her friendship circle and the scattering of her family—she wrote the beginning chapters of the fictive autobiography in which she portrayed herself as the much misunderstood child of a devoted but insensitive father and an emotionally dependent mother. Simplifying the character of her complex and conflicted father into the model of the Boston State Street businessman whose values the Transcendentalists continually targeted, she strengthened the role of the narrator (herself) as the helpless victim of the social values that were threatening the future of the country. The tone of self-pity lifts completely, however, when she launches with energetic pride into a description of the breadth and depth of her early education. But the wistful sadness returns in the final episode; here she inflates her brief childhood friendship with Ellen Kilshaw into the signifying event that oriented one aspect of her life to a search for close relationships as a means of self-culture.[1]

Her friendships remained of central importance even as she began a demanding public life. The weekly Conversation classes won her considerable admiration and respect. But no new candidates for her inner circle emerged. While the constant responsibility of the *Dial* kept her in touch with a faithful group, when she sought rest or solace she returned to her old familiars. During the spring and summer of 1841, she moved back and forth visiting them. In April and May she went from the Randalls in Boston to Brook Farm and on to the Emersons in Concord. In June, while supervising the July *Dial*, she stayed with the Farrars in Cambridge. Afterward she returned to Brook Farm to take care of Lloyd, who had fallen ill.

In May, Charles King Newcomb joined the farm as a paying guest; as a favor to Margaret he had agreed to keep an eye on Lloyd. He had developed a crush on Margaret that continued after she left Providence; his sister Charlotte, Fuller's student, insinuated that he had become infatuated. To discourage him, Margaret ceased corresponding, but he found ways to command her attention. At the farm, where he went to pursue his writing career, his behavior was markedly eccentric, but everyone excused him because nonconformism was the order of the day. He decorated his room with bulrushes and pictures of saints, wore gloves to bed, slept with a veil over his face, and recited church liturgy in a singsong whisper that was heard through the thin walls. Georgiana Bruce, a fellow Brook Farmer, called him Erasmus, and when Emerson, impressed with an essay Charles wrote for the *Dial,* adopted him as one of his literary disciples, he nicknamed him San Carlos and, later, San Giovanni.[2]

From the original band of seven, including Lloyd Fuller and Nathaniel Hawthorne, who in the spring of 1840 had accompanied Sophia and George Ripley to West Roxbury, the membership at the farm had grown to almost thirty with several nonmember boarders, like Charles Newcomb and Almira Penniman Barlow, who had moved to the farm with her children after her divorce. When Margaret went to visit the farm, she usually stayed with friends who lived nearby: Sarah Blake Shaw and her husband Francis ("Frank") George Shaw, whom she had known since her childhood, or with Frank's sister, Sarah Shaw Russell, and her husband George, all of whom were staunch supporters of the Brook Farm idea and held substantial mortgages on the farm property. They lived in hillside homes on Spring Street adjoining the farm. They often invited their West Roxbury minister, Theodore Parker, and his wife, Lydia, to join them for discussion parties they called "Olympicks," where—in Parker's words— "Gunderode, Bettina, and Goethe, the 'Latest Form of Infidelity,' Fourier, Emerson's last lecture, and all kosmic questions were discussed."[3]

From Brook Farm Fuller went to Newburyport to stay a few days with Sturgis, who sympathized with Margaret's mounting family worries. In July Richard completed his year as a store clerk and announced that he could not live any longer in the "dungeon" of Boston. He wanted Margaret to make arrangements for him to prepare for college. Ellen's situation was equally unsettled. George Keats wrote that ever since Ellen's arrival in Louisville she had been a handful, keeping the Keats household in turmoil with her temper tantrums, her conniving, and her general disagreeableness. When she returned from New Orleans, she upset the family further by refusing to attend Emma's wedding. This deeply offended Emma, who had nursed Ellen through her winter illness. The Keats family felt forced to ask her to leave. She was planning to go to Cincinnati to search for a teaching position.[4]

When William Henry brought Fanny home in July for her confinement, Fuller could see that he was not prospering, nor did he bring any better news of Eugene's prospects. All Fuller heard was that her brothers needed money to start anew. Tired of the continual complications, she wrote her mother: "I confess I feel very weary of them all; there is not one except Arthur on which my mind can rest, and I long to fix it on my own plans where I am clear and sure and strong, and might find repose if not happiness."[5]

With no family home, her mother's return north presented another problem. Fuller arranged for Margarett Crane Fuller to make a long visit to the DeWolfe family in Rhode Island during the late summer. With a windfall of fifty dollars for the publication of a short story called "A Tale of Mizraim," set in ancient Egypt at the time of the Exodus, Fuller was able to buy her mother a new dress to wear during her visit to the affluent DeWolfes. The story was Fuller's first venture into plotted short fiction since the debacle over "Lost and Won." This time the setting, characters, and story line were far removed from Cambridge romantic intrigues; she was in no danger of threatening her friendships.

In the spring of 1835, when Fuller was experimenting with "embryo designs" for the *Western Messenger,* she had written James Freeman Clarke that she was thinking of writing "a series of tales illustrative of Hebrew history." Now that she was living on her own, with the heaviest burdens of family duty behind her, her imaginative life was quickening. The plot of her tale of a beautiful Jewish slave girl, the niece of Miriam and Moses, who is forced to sacrifice her love for an Egyptian prince in order to join her people on the Exodus is simple, but Fuller manages to weave into the story, along with convincing local color, a dialogue on comparative religion—Isis versus Jehovah—that demonstrates her grasp of the competing religious perspectives. Still, the story was published anonymously in a giftbook, the *Token,* and Fuller made no claim to it among her friends.[6]

Throughout the summer Sturgis was Fuller's mainstay. After a difficult two years during which Sturgis periodically had felt too much put upon, she and Fuller had settled down to a steady companionship. They agreed that when tensions mounted they would, for a time, suspend seeing each other. Sturgis apologized for her earlier abrupt withdrawals, and the two accepted each other as trusted confidantes. They spent the last two weeks of July together visiting the Emersons; in August they rented rooms in a cottage near Paradise Beach on Newport Island. They swam every day, and in the evenings they visited Channing, Farrar, or Barker relatives. In early September their truce survived a shock when Ellen wrote from Cincinnati that she was engaged to William Ellery Channing, (called Ellery to distinguish him from his famous uncle), a young poet whom Caroline had once thought she loved.

A college dropout who had been unmanageable since his mother died when he was five, Ellery had gone west in the fall of 1839 after spending five years reading at random and exasperating his family with his idleness. He planned to homestead in McHenry County, Illinois, but after a year of intolerable isolation he moved to Cincinnati.

His arrival coincided with the publication of twelve of his poems in the October 1840 *Dial.* Sam Ward, who had been Ellery's only close friend since childhood, showed Emerson a packet of Ellery's poems in January 1840; Emerson thought they showed more "inward music" and "authentic inspiration" than any he had yet seen from an American. At the time, Fuller refused them, but Emerson later included twelve in his October article on "New Poets." Ellery thought himself finally established as a poet. Ellen's love, he claimed, gave him the "home" he had long sought. He saw himself as transformed, but those who had known him a long time were not convinced.[7]

Before anyone could respond to the couple's engagement, the news came of their marriage on September 24. Aware that both Ellery and Ellen were headstrong and emotional, Fuller was depressed. "I see such perils to the happiness and good of the other, and the connextion has been so precipitately formed that I feel overshadowed by it as by a deep tragedy," she wrote Emerson.[8]

The marriage surprised Sturgis, who also thought the two were unsuited. A few summers previously, just after Ellery dropped out of Harvard, she had enjoyed a romantic interlude with him while they were both staying at Curson's Mill, a picturesque gristmill and farm on the Artichoke River near Newburyport. It belonged to distant Channing relatives who were friendly with the Sturgis family and rented out rooms. (Sturgis called the farmhouse "Bluebell," after the bluebells that grew along the river in the summer.) Since she had figured prominently in several of Ellery's poems written that summer, Sturgis thought she still had a lien on him and that she was the only one in the world who understood him. An attraction still lingered, enough to put Sturgis on the defensive when she heard the news. Writing Fuller to deny that Ellery's engagement had upset her, Sturgis expressed her sorrow that he was marrying someone who would never understand him and was not "noble enough to be his wife." She complained to Emerson, "It seems as if the best people in being married only adopt children instead of taking equal friends."[9]

Fuller's worries were based more on her assessment of Ellery's qualities as a future husband. She found it difficult to appreciate "a nature so noble, yet with no constructiveness and no force of will." All the Fullers and Channings were relieved when Ellery found an editorial job on the *Cincinnati Daily Gazette* at a salary of $400 a year with the promise of steady raises.[10]

Neither Ellery's cousin, William Henry Channing, nor his father, Dr. Walter Channing, a prominent gynecologist (the first in America to use ether for childbirth), had illusions about Ellery's ability to support a wife and family. Soon after Ellen and Ellery were married, the Channings heard that Curson's Mill might soon come on the market, and they conferred with Margaret about buying the property. There Ellery could combine farming with poetry writing closer to home. Fuller and her mother could also live on the farm with Lloyd. Even Eugene—whose business failures were now endemic—might be induced to join in the venture.

When Fuller went with Sturgis to look over the property, she thought it could be an ideal setting for a utopian community. She envisioned a neighborhood of her friends, each living on separate farms along the Artichoke River and using the picturesque mill as their meeting place. "When we wished to have merely playful chat, or talk on politics or social reform, we would gather in the mill, and arrange those affairs while grinding the corn," she wrote to William Channing. Unlike the Brook Farmers, she would not have to give up her privacy or purchase stock in what might turn out to be a risky adventure in utopian living. She wrote William Channing, who had recently become a backer of Fourierism, that she would "frame" her community "far more naturally and rationally" than those built on the model of the French socialist, Charles Fourier. But Fuller's plan was short-lived; within a few weeks it developed that the property would not be put up for sale.[11]

While Margaret and Caroline were at Bluebell, they invited Waldo Emerson to join them so he could enjoy the pastoral charms of the Artichoke River site where Caroline, Sam, and Ellery had known each other as children. Waldo came eagerly. He had set boundaries but had no wish to be excluded from intimacy with his young friends. He even wrote Fuller in August 1841 that he had discovered that the old "barrier" between them was no longer there.[12]

But only a few weeks later, when Fuller visited Bush for a few days in October, she put him off-balance again with her presumptuous claims. Emerson being preoccupied with his new lecture series, the two hardly met; when they did, Fuller felt he was only interested in using her as a sounding board, reading her his drafts and—to Fuller's annoyance—using their conversation as a stimulus to help him hit on "the best *form* of expression." Most of the day Fuller kept to her room; from time to time she sent notes to Emerson, using as her messenger young Waldo, now a handsome child of five with a beguiling imagination.[13]

One day during the October visit she wandered into Emerson's study when he was absent; the sense of his presence in the room impelled her to leave a note to assure him that his diffidence no longer upset her. She told him that she was satisfied living near him without disturbing him because she was confident nothing would interfere with their friendship. "The genial flow of my desire may be checked for the moment, but it cannot long. I shall always burst out soon and burn up all the rubbish between you and me, and I shall always find you there true to yourself and deeply rooted as ever."[14]

The familiarity of her language was disturbing and provocative. It annoyed Emerson that she could never leave well enough alone. Soon after she left Bush, he quizzed himself in his journal:

I would that I could, I know afar off that I cannot give the lights & shades, the hopes & outlooks that come to me in these strange, cold-warm, attractive-repelling conversations with Margaret, whom I always admire, most revere when I nearest see, and sometimes love, yet whom I freeze, & who freezes me to silence, when we seem to promise to come nearest.[15]

They were still uneasy with each other; Fuller still needed occasional assurances of her importance to him, and he still feared her emotional force. Years later, he wrote, "she lived at a rate so much faster than mine, and which was violent compared with mine, I foreboded rash and painful crises, and had a feeling as if a voice cried, '*Stand from under!*'"[16]

During the fall and winter of 1841–42, the Emersons were helpful and kind to Richard Fuller, who had rented a room in Concord while he was studying for the Harvard entrance examinations. To prove to his mother and Margaret that he was "a youth of promise," he lived on "a pint of milk each day, a loaf of brown bread on Saturday, and some potatoes." Fuller had hoped that twenty-four-year-old Henry David Thoreau, who was living with the Emersons as a handyman, would agree to tutor Richard. When she had gone with Thoreau on a moonlight boat ride in the spring, he had struck her as "an earnest thinker" who had the makings of "a successful and happy man," but he turned down the job. Thoreau liked Richard, but he had already made plans to spend his free time building a cabin on Flint's Pond in Lincoln. Richard relied at first on the help of the local Concord schoolmaster. When that proved insufficient, Elizabeth Hoar, who was an accomplished classical scholar, offered to supervise his studies; the experiment proved successful.[17]

During the summer, the *Dial*'s publisher, Weeks, Jordan and Co., went bankrupt. All agreed that the obvious choice for the new publisher was Elizabeth Palmer Peabody. In her West Street bookstore, she had begun a publishing business that had done a creditable job issuing both William Ellery Channing's "Emancipation Address" and Nathaniel Hawthorne's *Grandfather's Chair*. When Peabody took over as publisher, she assumed that the *Dial*'s fortunes would improve with a fresh start. Looking over the records of Weeks, Jordan and Co., she was astonished to discover that Margaret had never been paid a cent for what was now close to two years' work. She decided that Margaret should receive seventy-five dollars each quarter, a sum that was a helpful addition to her income at a time when the family was suffering another financial crisis. At the end of October, Fanny Hastings Fuller gave birth to her first child, Cornelia, just as the news arrived of her husband's bankruptcy in Cincinnati. In New Orleans, Eugene was taken ill with yellow fever—the disease was raging in the South that winter. When he recovered, he wrote home pleading for money; he was on to yet another get-rich venture, his "Havana scheme"—he had gotten permission to import books into Cuba.[18]

Margaret was now the only member of the family with a reliable income. The Conversation class was still growing in numbers, and she continued to be in demand for private lessons in foreign languages and literature. She started the winter with three private students, Caroline Sturgis, Marianne Jackson, and Anna Shaw. Later, Sam's sister Mary and a young Englishwoman, Susan Howe, joined the class. Margaret was able to support herself, but she had to be careful. At Christmastime she wrote her mother that she did not dare attend the Anti-Slavery Fair lest she be tempted to spend too much money on presents for her friends.

Her friends were of great importance as she settled down in her garret room—her "eyrie" at the home of her Uncle Henry and Aunt Mary at 2 Avon

Place.[19] Fuller's vision of living as a single working woman, free to enjoy the cultural pleasures of the city, depended in large part on the companionship of her friends. Elizabeth Randall was back in Boston for the winter. She had married Alfred Cumming of Georgia without her father's consent—the ceremony took place at Elizabeth Hoar's house in Concord—but she was now forgiven and had returned home to put herself in the care of Ellery's father because she was suffering from gynecological disorders. Her sister Belinda, Caroline Sturgis, and Sarah Clarke—all living nearby—provided Fuller with ready companionship for Boston's lectures, concerts, art exhibitions, and theatrical entertainments. In December she wrote Richard that she was in better health than at any time since Timothy died.

In the early 1840s Boston was a commercial city of 165,000 with little manufacturing or industry. Favorable social conditions kept vice, crime, and poverty at manageable levels and barely visible. The merchant princes who used Boston as a base for their far-flung ventures had turned it into a cultural hub respected throughout the nation for its school system, lyceums, musical societies, and periodicals. The influx of Irish had begun, but it would not be until the middle of the decade that the life of the city, its appearance, and its culture would begin to change dramatically in response. Living within walking distance of the vigorous cultural institutions that were earning Boston its reputation as the Athens of America, Fuller was able to visit at will the Athenaeum's sculpture and painting galleries, the baroque Tremont Theatre where the traveling troupes played, the Masonic Hall where Emerson and other lyceum lecturers held audience, and the newly furbished concert hall, the Odeon, where, under the leadership of Samuel Eliot, the Boston Academy of Music was revolutionizing musical taste in the city; indeed, with its versatile orchestra and citywide education program, it was beginning to serve as a national model.[20]

The great thrill that winter was hearing the German-born pianist Frederick Wilhelm Rackemann play Beethoven's Fifth and Pastoral Symphonies at the Academy of Music. The concert ignited a new passion that inspired at least two of Fuller's articles in the *Dial*, "Beethoven," and "Lives of the Great Composers." In December, Margaret heard Handel's *Messiah* and Haydn's *Creation* at the Handel and Haydn Society. The artistic phenomenon of the season was the free-movement dancer Fanny Ellsler, whose performance drew such raves that even Emerson stayed overnight after one of his lectures so he could see what the excitement was all about. As well as writing sketches of cultural events for the *Dial* herself, Fuller solicited material from others; in her first issue, she published an article by the young Brook Farmer John S. Dwight who later became one of the most distinguished movers and shakers in the city's music community.[21]

Anna and Sam, who lived across the Boston Common, frequently invited Fuller to their evening parties. Sam could never understand why Margaret was not a greater success in Boston society. "Had she been born thirty years later she would have come to a generation that would have appreciated her and received her with open arms," he noted later. "Being a reformer, and almost the first audible advocate of woman's rights, she found Boston, both social and literary, intensely conservative." She was taken "as a typical blue-stocking (still a word of fear at that time)." A similar "prejudice" applied to Emerson, Sam observed.[22]

Although Fuller was never taken up by the manufacturers, as Emerson called the wealthy social set in Boston, she had an appreciative circle among Boston's small avant-garde whose membership spanned the economic though not the educational spectrum. After Emerson's lecture, "Man's Relation to Nature," on January 13, 1842, Margaret held a reception for him with the Wards, Shaws, Sturgises, Charles Eames (a visiting out-of-town lecturer), and James Freeman Clarke, now back in Boston with his wife, Anna Huidekuper, and their baby son, Herman. (The Clarkes lived on Mount Vernon Street around the corner from the Wards.)

Fuller was in her element that evening, and Emerson thoroughly enjoyed himself. Less than two weeks later he suffered one of the hardest blows of his life. After four days of illness, five-year-old Waldo died of scarlet fever, leaving his father numb and his mother heartbroken. Young Waldo, born only a few weeks after Margaret's first visit to Bush in 1836, had been part of her five-year friendship with the family. She had always endowed him with unusual intelligence and believed in a charmed future for him. The day after his death, January 28, 1842, his father sent Margaret the news in six stricken sentences, ending with a cry: "Shall I ever dare to love anything again. Farewell and Farewell, O my Boy!"[23]

Shortly afterward, Emerson set off on a lecture tour to Providence and New York, partly for financial reasons and partly because he wished to escape all the daily reminders of his son—the microscope, the magnet, the globe in the study, the meadow and the sandpile where he played, the toy whistles and boats Henry Thoreau had whittled for him. Before leaving, Emerson gave Richard Fuller a letter of recommendation to present to President Kirkland when he appeared for his Harvard entrance examination.

Thanks largely to Elizabeth Hoar's superb teaching, Richard was accepted for the sophomore class. The sole drawback was the additional strain on the family purse. Since Richard had never been a strong student, Margaret wanted to arrange matters so he would not have to take time off to earn extra money. Just as she was reviewing the family finances with this in mind, Peabody discovered that Weeks, Jordan had been in debt to the *Dial* and had been misrepresenting both the size of the subscription list and the cost of publishing. When she informed Fuller that it would be impossible to pay her salary until the *Dial*'s affairs were in better condition, Fuller knew that she would have to resign as editor. A few days after Emerson returned from his lecture tour, she notified him that she had so many other obligations that she was unable to do justice to the job. If she could have earned "a maintenance" as the *Dial*'s editor and been able to give all her time to her pen, she would have been happy to continue.[24]

She felt that too much of her work on the *Dial* had been slipshod. Forced to fill up several issues with material at the last minute, she often wrote hurried reviews of books, art shows, or musical entertainments. But the situation had offered her plenty of room for experimentation, and even her inferior pieces and occasional verses show wit and originality. Her greatest stride was in the development of her theory of literary criticism. What was striking about her concept was that she envisioned critical writing as an endeavor in which the critic engaged the reader in a process gauged to awaken and stimulate thought, to involve the reader in the dynamics of self-culture. This was a radical new direction at a time when critical conventions rested on thought patterns supportive of the political and moral order. The standard critical method was to judge a new work's value in terms of its moral teaching—good or bad—by comparison with a similar established work.[25]

Her "Short Essay on Critics" in the first issue of the *Dial* categorized three types of critics—the subjective, the apprehensive, and the comprehensive—and argued for the superiority of the last. Criticism was a form of mediation in which the reader was to consider what the writer intended, how well that was accomplished, and the various ways in which the achievement might be of value in the art of life, which was to Fuller an open-ended category. This interaction was in many ways an application of her conception of the value of friendships in self-culture. The point was to discover the operative eternal idea, psychological reality, or soul, if you will, in the friend or the poem or the picture and proceed from there into generalizations on life.

Thus friendship and criticism were linked as similar human projects. Experimenting with a variety of new literary forms borrowed from European models, she made a specialty of the conversation technique of Walter Savage Landor; it adapted well to expressing opposing points of view in a lively, undogmatic manner that avoided final judgments, since living and learning were always in process. From Goethe she had absorbed the concept that Truth lay in the capacity to hold opposing views simultaneously.

The *Dial* editorship had come along just at the time when, for lack of information, she had been unable to continue with her Goethe biography. Nevertheless, her *Dial* essay on Goethe—the distillation of years of thought— was a landmark in American public recognition of his cultural importance. In it she not only challenged "the cant of coterie criticism" in defending a moral renegade but identified in terms of moral philosophy what practical-minded American readers could find in Goethe that they could put to use. For the second time she took on the formidable George Bancroft; he had written a scathing attack on Goethe's work and character in the *Christian Register*.[26]

Among the most experimental of her works are four essays in which she gave expression to her ongoing search for a universal concept of womanhood that would include the power, intelligence, and energy she had either felt within herself, seen in other women, or read about in books, qualities that seemed to be disqualifying marks in the society in which she lived but had been sources of energy elsewhere. "The Magnolia of Lake Pontchartrain," "Klopstock and Meta," "Leila," and "Yuca Filamentosa" were mystical contemplations derived from personal yearnings, from her weekly Conversations, and from her reading in Plato, Plotinus, Apuleius, Dante, Novalis, and German ballads and folktales. In "The Magnolia of Lake Pontchartrain" she described this feminine power as "[s]ecret, radiant, profound ever and never to be known. . . . All the secret powers are Mothers," she asserted. "There is but one paternal power."[27]

When possible she chose to review books that evoked a personal response, giving her a vantage point from which to discourse on literature and life. Clearly she was drawn to biography because of her fascination with people and personal relationships. Her review of Bettina von Arnim's *Günderode* was a meditation on friendship, intensified by her personal identification with aspects of both of the two women, Bettina and Günderode, whose tragic love is portrayed in the book. In her lengthy review of *Festus*, a best-selling, book-length poem on the motif of self-culture, she criticized the style and form of the work while elaborating on a theme that had directed her own life. Looking back two years later, she thought the "Magnolia" as well as some of her "little pieces" such as "The Two Herberts" had "flow and an obvious unity," but the only long piece she found satisfactory was the biographical "Lives of the Great Composers."[28]

After two years of editorial experience, she was still unable to convey in writing anything like the power she could command in a conversation. She had found neither her distinctive voice as a writer nor a subject that drove her to her best work. While still wishing to succeed as a poet or writer of fiction, she knew by now that her strength lay in criticism; she was a keen observer, and her strong moral convictions led her to pepper her critical writing with sharp insights, cutting thrusts, and occasional clever epigrams. But she had never had the leisure to write at her best.

When Fuller resigned, Emerson conceded that she had "played martyr a little too long alone," and he reluctantly decided to take over. Fuller's one regret, she wrote him, was that he would change her editorial policy. He would have "in view to make a good periodical and represent [his] own tastes," whereas she had "in view to let all kinds of people have freedom to say their say, for better, for worse."[29]

Annoyed with Elizabeth Palmer Peabody, who was publishing Fuller's partial translation of *Günderode* and had hopelessly garbled the title in the advertising flyers, her parting words to Emerson were that he should keep an eye on

Elizabeth. As publisher she had turned out to be "more exact and judicious" than one would have expected, but she was "variable in her attention."[30]

At the end of the first week in April, when Fuller's last *Dial* was published and her final Conversation for the season was over, she wrote Emerson that she looked forward to seeing the *Dial* "fresh" and "not have the thoughts of my friends indissolubly associated, with proofreading, post-office, or printer's ink." For the next two months she hid away with Aunt Abby and her Grandmother Crane in Canton.[31]

Her mother had already left with Fanny and the new baby for Cincinnati, where William Henry was starting up anew and Ellen and Ellery were living— according to their letters—in newly wedded bliss. Eugene, having abandoned his Cuban plans, had taken a job as an overseer on a Louisiana plantation at $600 a year plus his living expenses. To accommodate Lloyd, who had been complaining all year that he had to work too hard at Brook Farm, Margaret arranged with a local printer to give him a six-week trial. When the experiment failed, Margaret found herself in the embarrassing position of asking Sophia Dana Ripley to take him back at the Brook Farm school. Sophia agreed, even though Lloyd's "extreme slowness" was a constant problem. In a letter to John S. Dwight, Sophia Ripley described Lloyd as having "all the Fuller faults . . . without their merits."[32]

At the end of June, Fuller began her round of summer visits. Her first stop was at the New Bedford home of Mrs. Farrar's Aunt Mary Rotch, the heir to the Rotch whaling fortune. A Quaker woman who had left the New Bedford Society of Friends for the Unitarians when the New Lights changed many established practices in the Society's governance, including the role of women, Aunt Mary was a meticulous and fastidious hostess. Margaret admired her uncomplicated, healthy character and her sense of humor, but her orderly routine offered little excitement.

After a quiet week of afternoon tea parties, Margaret proceeded to Providence to visit Rhoda Mardenbrough Newcomb and was surprised to discover on her arrival that the city had just been placed under martial law. The streets were teeming with the ragtail leftovers from Dorr's Rebellion; militia units patrolled the streets, and the city was rife with rumors.

On the night of May 18, six weeks before Fuller's arrival, about 200 Rhode Island freemen, mostly industrial workers who were members of regular militia units, formed a makeshift army and stormed the Providence Arsenal under the leadership of Thomas Dorr, the leader of the Suffrage party. It was the last desperate act in a series of attempts by the disenfranchised in Rhode Island to establish the principle of universal manhood suffrage in the state. But the arsenal defenders had been forewarned; within a few hours the attackers were routed, and Dorr himself, fearing arrest, fled the state.

When the last contingent of Suffrage party holdouts gathered in the nearby village of Chepachet a few days before Fuller's arrival, the government, fearing another outbreak, proclaimed martial law and captured about a hundred rebels. The remainder dispersed, and no one knew if a regrouping was in the offing. When Margaret arrived, the citizens of Providence were living in a state of great tension.[33]

Fuller had experienced civil disorder in her childhood when disgruntled dockworkers set the Boston ropewalks aflame (creating evening spectacles for Cambridgeport residents who gathered on the Boston Bridge), but Dorr's Rebellion was her first experience of armed conflict. "I came into the very midst of the fuss, and, tedious as it was at the time, I am glad to have seen it," she wrote William Henry Channing. She saw what could happen when large groups lost hope in the processes of their society.

[A] city full of grown-up people as wild, as mischief-seeking, as full of prejudice, careless slander, and exaggeration, as a herd of boys in the play-ground of the worst boarding-school. Women whom I have seen, as the domestic cat, gentle, graceful, cajoling, suddenly showing the disposition, if not the force, of the tigress. I thought I appreciated the monstrous growth, of rumor before, but I never did. . . . I don't know when I have felt such an aversion to my environment.[34]

The aftermath of the Dorr Rebellion was tame in comparison to what Fuller was to experience a few years later as a participant in the revolution in Rome. But by then, though living every day amidst prejudice, mischief seeking, and troubling rumor, she would be writing home that she had never in her life felt so at one with her environment. Her fastidious distance from disorder would be a stance of the past when the insurgents were Italians fighting for a republican form of government.

It was not by chance that Fuller wrote William Channing a report on Dorr's Rebellion. Of all her friends he was the most interested in social injustice and the most instrumental in arousing her, albeit slowly, to the spirit of active reform. And of all the Harvard-bred transcendental ministers she knew well, he was the one most uncomfortable with the tenet of withdrawal from the world's affairs. When Orestes Brownson in 1840 shocked the Whig establishment by suggesting in his article, "The Labouring Classes," that there were two antagonistic classes forming in the new American democracy—the middle class and the working class—William Channing had the courage to defend him for publicizing the problem and suggesting a plan of action.

Even more than James Freeman Clarke—who carried the burden of his eminent grandfather—William Henry Channing lived in the shadow of his revered uncle, Dr. William Ellery Channing, who had served as his surrogate father after his own father's early death. He had taken to heart his uncle's exhortation to the well-heeled Unitarians of Boston to become known as Christian philanthropists, to heed the basic Christian message of the Golden Rule, to embrace the poor in their concern—in sum, to make social consciousness a major part of the Unitarian identity.

A conventional ministry could not satisfy what William Henry called his "political enthusiasm." In 1835, hoping to raise the aspirations of the poor with the message of self-culture, he went to New York as a minister-at-large and established a chapel in the Bowery. But though he preached with the voice of "an angel" (according to Sophia Peabody), he never attracted more than twenty to his Sunday service. The evangelists with more hellfire in their sermons had a far greater appeal. When the depression of 1837 brought home to him how ineffectual self-culture was in attacking the problem of poverty, William returned to Boston, disheartened but with his idealism intact.[35]

For the next few years he searched for a way to link his political and social concerns with his vocation. During the summer of 1839, while serving as an itinerant minister, he boarded with Margarett Crane Fuller in Groton and grew fond of her. At the end of the summer, while visiting his uncle at Newport, he renewed his acquaintance with Margaret, whom he had known but avoided during his student days—her garrulousness and witty sarcasm had repelled him. But his interest was aroused when he talked with her at length about the future of American literature and "her secret hope of what Woman might be and do, as an author, in our Republic." Her intensity and sincerity struck a responsive chord, and almost immediately he felt an intimacy with her: "We were strangers no more."[36]

For the rest of Margaret's life, William Henry Channing was her steadiest and most reliable male friend in America. He never excited or stimulated her as Emerson did—the sexual attraction was evidently absent—but he admired her unequivocally, tolerated her eccentricities of style and opinion, and made of her a spiritual confidante.

William's wife, Julia Allen, a wealthy New Yorker and an Episcopalian, was bringing up their children in her faith. While William moved from place to place during the early years of their marriage, Julia lived much of the time—including a good part of the three years William was in Cincinnati—with their children at her family home, Roundout, on the Hudson.

Mercurial and enthusiastic, earnest and erratic, optimistic but beset with self-doubt, William Henry Channing was far more approachable than Ralph Waldo Emerson. His temperament was much closer to Margaret's; like her, he was constantly complaining of lacking a field of action equal to his energies and his powers; like her, he was in perpetual quest of a clearer vision of the future and a definite direction in which to march. To some of his friends, notably Theodore Parker, he seemed to be always rushing about at cross-purposes.

When Margaret and William discovered each other in 1839, William, about to depart for Cincinnati, asked her to correspond with him. Certain that the

West would attract the most energetic Americans, William, like James Freeman Clarke before him, expected he would be witness to the creation of a new race and a new society as it developed in the virgin territory away from all the stale conventions of the East and of the past. William's letters to Margaret reveal his disillusionment; his despair increased as he realized that westerners were—if anything—even less willing to be liberated than their counterparts in New England. When he realized that he had been idealizing the western movement and that the liberal Unitarian message was not the Word awaited on the other side of the Appalachians, the discovery brought him to a crisis.

As he struggled with disappointment, he found little help among the Unitarians at home. Impatiently searching for a way out of his dilemma, in 1841 he impulsively resigned the ministry, proclaiming to Margaret, "You heard aright. The words are spoken. The stag is free." Although he later changed his mind and returned to the fold to work from within, for several months he was convinced that he had grown beyond the Unitarians in his aspirations for mankind. The times called for a new interpretation of Christ's message. Although the church could point the way to the panacea of the future, he believed the most effective pathway to reform of the human race was through group action and social organization. Adopting Fourierism as the answer, he turned to the French Christian socialists and foresaw on the horizon "a new moral creation of man" developing out of perfected social organizations.[37]

Throughout his religious crisis, William confided in Margaret. "For sincerely, I do think you have done more to unfold my buried nature than any friend," he wrote her in his anguish. When he formulated his new insights in a written credo, Margaret was stimulated to write down her own religious testament, in which she described her response to the two matters that William found most troubling: whether Jesus Christ was the all-embracing and final Messiah of God, and whether the true believer needed a church.[38]

For Margaret, the ideal truths of Christian experience were what was important, not the religious institutions. The religious instinct was where she centered her religious life. She accepted Jesus as a model because she had been absorbing Christian belief all her life and he constantly aided her. But at the same time "the history of the Jewish nation" presented another "great type of spiritual existence." And Moses, the Greek Apollo, Plato, Confucius, and Luther were all expressions of the Great Spirit. As for the church, she was unable "to live in it" completely because her beliefs extended beyond any one system, but that was no reason to reject it. God was a constantly evolving "spirit uncontainable and uncontained" that kept all matter evolving in a search for perfected forms. She believed that the religious experience was a constant search for a closer personal relationship with God. It was a tumultuous search, but she felt closest to religious fulfillment when she experienced "a clear note of security" in her "very Soul." "No prop will do. 'The soul must do its own immortal work,' and books, lovers, friends, meditations fly from us only to return, when we can do without them. But when we can use and learn from them, yet feel able to do without them they will depart no more."[39]

When William Channing pointed out that Margaret's credo showed how thoroughly she had "imbibed" Emerson's thought, she acknowledged that Emerson's influence had been great. But she added that her life would have been easier if she had never met him. She recounted the course of their friendship from "the first excitement of intimacy" through "the questioning season" when she was disappointed to discover how little help Emerson was to her. "He had faith in the Universal, but not in the Individual Man" was how she described their differences. His influence had been that of "lofty assurance and sweet serenity." "With most men I bring words of now past life, and do actions suggested by the wants of their natures rather than my own," she observed. "But he stops me from doing anything, and makes me think."[40]

In July she went with James Freeman Clarke and Anna on a tour of the White Mountains of New Hampshire. Thereafter, she planned a month of serious writing in the Farrar's house while they were on vacation. Brook Farm was another option, but when she returned from New Hampshire to find the Farrar holiday trip postponed, she turned first to Emerson, whom she now addressed as Waldo. She wrote that she needed a quiet place to work; could she come to Concord and "really *live*" there without being treated as a guest? He replied that he was delighted to have his house put to use for work. They would both dedicate themselves to their tasks—"speech shall be contraband & the exception not the rule." Lidian agreed but warned that Margaret would be treated like family.

Fuller stayed for over five weeks—from August 17 to September 25. By the time she left, she had learned that life in Concord was not the serene oasis she had imagined.[41]

I suppose the whole amount of the feeling is that women cant bear to be left out of the question.

Marriage Studies

WHEN George Ripley invited the Emersons to join the Brook Farm community, both Lidian and Waldo seriously considered moving to West Roxbury, but in the end the claims of their Concord life proved too strong. As an alternative, they tried to create a substitute. "Those of us who do not believe in Communities, believe in neighborhoods & that the kingdom of heaven may consist of such," Emerson explained. He wanted to create what he called a Concord university, a group of friends who would live independently and be accessible for friendly relations and the exchange of ideas. Concord would become the home, he wrote Fuller, of "poets & the friends of poets & see the golden bees of Pindus swarming on our plain cottages and apple trees."[1]

When Fuller arrived on August 17, 1842, intent on completing two articles, one on Tennyson's poetry and another on modern Greek and medieval German ballads, she found her brother-in-law, Ellery Channing, already there as a fellow guest. In July Ellery had quit his job at the *Cincinnati Gazette* and departed hastily for Boston, leaving Ellen behind with Margarett Crane Fuller to await his further instructions. Emerson had published seven more of Ellery's poems in the July 1842 *Dial*, and he assumed he was on the verge of success as a professional poet. He was looking for a Concord boardinghouse where he and Ellen could spend the winter while he completed a collection of his poems for publication. In the meantime he had already struck up a friendship with Henry Thoreau with whom he had much in common, in particular an interest in writing and a love of wandering in the nearby countryside.

With the understanding that they would honor a strict working schedule, Waldo welcomed his friends to his home. He was working on his poem "Saadi" and preparing the October *Dial* and was not in a sociable mood. On the morning after Margaret's arrival, he sat her down in the red room with "the inkhorn and pen" and left her to her work. The members of the household were expected to meet regularly only for dinner.[2]

When Bronson Alcott was forced to close his Boston school, Emerson encouraged the family to move to Concord, and they found a tenant cottage on the Hosmer estate within walking distance of Bush. Alcott immediately named it Dove Cottage after Wordsworth's home in the English Lake District, and he determined to turn himself into a full-time farmer. But even his concerted efforts could not raise the family out of poverty. In the spring of 1841 the Emersons invited the Alcotts to move in with them, but Abby Alcott objected to living under someone else's roof. "I cannot gee and haw in another person's yoke," she said. She preferred to take in sewing and piecework on shoes in order to make ends meet.[3]

The newlyweds, Sophia Peabody and Nathaniel Hawthorne, were the most recent candidates for Emerson's "university." After an engagement of five years, they were married on July 9, 1842, when, through the efforts of Waldo Emerson and Elizabeth Hoar, the beautiful old house overlooking the river next to the Concord Battleground became available. Emerson's step-grandfather, Ezra Ripley, had occupied the house for forty years. After his death in the spring, the heirs agreed to lease it to the Hawthornes.

The couple soon gave their home the name that would remain long after they had moved away. "We have been living in eternity, ever since we came to this old Manse," Nathaniel wrote soon after they were settled. During the first month, their only visitors had been Elizabeth Hoar, who had put the house in order, and Henry Thoreau, who had planted a vegetable garden. George Prescott, the milkman, delivered three pints daily "from some ambrosial cow," and Waldo Emerson had stopped by once for a moment with Ellery Channing. This was more than enough company for the Hawthornes, who showed no interest in joining the neighborhood.[4]

When Fuller came to call at the Old Manse on the Saturday after her arrival in Concord, she found the front door ajar. As she entered, the sound of her footsteps surprised the couple, who were in the parlor locked in an embrace. Sophia rushed forward to greet "Queen Margaret" (the Peabody family nickname for her) and was relieved when Nathaniel, instead of showing irritation, greeted her with a "gleaming welcome" and insisted that she remain for tea. "She was like the moon, radiant and gentle," Sophia wrote her mother.[5]

Of the three Peabody sisters, Sophia was the only one whose friendship Margaret went out of her way to cultivate. She and Elizabeth Palmer Peabody were constantly thrown together, but it made no difference to what lengths Elizabeth went to be helpful; Margaret always made it clear that she wished to keep her distance. "Not counting myself among her intimate friends, as she decidedly wished I should not," Elizabeth recalled years later that when they first met she had the distinct impression that Margaret was laughing at her, "for which there was good cause." But Peabody interpreted this as coming from a person "with a pure sense of the comic,—inevitable to an intellect sharp as a diamond." The middle sister, Mary, now Mrs. Horace Mann, was a member of the Conversations, but she and Margaret never became more than acquaintances. Perhaps it was because Sophia, the youngest, was an artist and a friend of Elizabeth Hoar and Sarah Clarke that Margaret cordially befriended her, or perhaps it was because Sophia admired Margaret in the way she wanted to be admired, as one specially gifted. Sophia put Margaret on a pedestal and had written her an adoring sonnet addressed "To a Priestess of a Temple not made with Hands."[6]

Nathaniel Hawthorne, on the other hand, thought Margaret was intellectually pretentious and fulsome. It irked him that so many people, including Sophia, revered her as a cultural sibyl. While he was at Brook Farm during its first year, he ridiculed her in letters to Sophia. When the Fuller cow joined the farm's herd, he called it "a transcendental heifer" and described it as "very fractious, I believe, and apt to kick over the milk pail." He added, "Thou knowest best, whether, in these traits of character, she resembles her mistress." On another occasion he wrote that he was "thankful" that he was unable to accept an invitation from George Bancroft to a dinner at which Margaret would be present since he avoided "literary lions and lionesses." Yet, when he finally authorized Sophia to announce their engagement after they heard the Old Manse was available, he acquiesced in Sophia's wish to have Margaret share her Concord visits with them.[7]

Nathaniel Hawthorne walked Margaret back to Bush that evening. In his happiness, he forgot his distrust and confided in her, telling her, as she wrote in her journal the next day, that "he should be much more willing to die than two months ago, for he had had some real possession in life, but still he never wished to leave this earth: it was beautiful enough."[8]

The next day, Sunday, was so glorious that at the end of it Margaret could only write, "[W]hat a happy, happy day, all clear light. I cannot write about it." She had spent the day reading in Sleepy Hollow, a woodland dell that was a short walk from Bush. While she was stretched out beside the path, Hawthorne came along. He was returning from the Emerson house where he had just dropped off a book Margaret had left at the Old Manse the day before. While they were talking about "Autumn—and about the pleasures of getting lost in the woods," about the company of crows whose cawing had been dominating the woods that quiet Sunday, and other "matters of high and low philosophy," they suddenly heard the rustling of an intruder. "[A]nd, behold, it was Mr. Emerson," Hawthorne wrote, "who, in spite of his clerical consecration, had found no better way of spending the Sabbath than to ramble among the woods. He appeared to have had a pleasant time; for he said that there were Muses in the woods today, and whispers to be heard in the breezes."[9]

Emerson took the occasion to invite the Hawthornes to dinner, but Hawthorne declined. "[I]t happens not to suit," he wrote in the family journal. He also refused Emerson's invitation to his annual party on the eve of the Harvard Phi Beta Kappa celebration later in the month. He was not to be seduced into the social life of Concord's intelligentsia.[10]

Fuller soon learned directly of his determination to protect his privacy. When she asked Sophia—at Ellery's behest—if Ellery and Ellen could board at the Old Manse during the coming winter, Sophia responded favorably, but Nathaniel thought the request was a tactless intrusion. As soon as he heard that the matter was under discussion, he wrote a firm but friendly letter to Margaret: "Had it been proposed to Adam and Eve to receive two angels into their Paradise, as *boarders,* I doubt whether they would have been altogether pleased to consent." It was probably the first time in the marriage that Hawthorne overrode a decision of his wife. He went to great pains to assure Margaret that he wanted to lighten Sophia's domestic obligations so as to free her to paint and sculpt. He also took the opportunity to lecture Margaret on the inadvisability of entering into financial arrangements with friends; the Channings would "be able to keep their own delicacy and sensitiveness much more inviolate, if they make themselves inmates of the rudest farmer's household in Concord." When Sophia wrote apologizing for the change, Margaret compared the two letters and commented, "It is a striking contrast of tone between the man and woman so sincerely bound together by one sentiment."[11]

This brief division in the Hawthorne household served to highlight the subject of marriage, which was the most commanding subject of Fuller's journal entries during her Concord visit. Even though she often regretted not being married herself, she knew that her independence had compensations and was sometimes envied by her married friends. The discussions accompanying her Conversation series of 1841 on "the ethical influences of Woman . . . on the Family, the School, the Church, Society and Literature," and of 1842 on "Woman," had sharpened her fascination with a subject that had long occupied her as she worried about her own future and empathized with her friends.[12]

In Concord, Fuller was upset by the situation in the Alcott family. In the spring, Alcott had shown signs of a breakdown; he had failed miserably as a farmer and was $6,000 in debt. To help raise his spirits, Emerson gave him $400 to finance a summer visit to England, where a small band of reformers, influenced by his *Record of a School,* had established Alcott House, a progressive school based on Alcott principles. Throughout the summer, during his absence, Abby had been proudly showing around her husband's letters, which contained fatuous outpourings of love to her. It both moved and embarrassed Margaret that Abby was forced to flaunt such specious displays of devotion from a husband whose boundless belief in his own genius had excused him from family responsibilities. While complaining that she had not been brought up to earn a living, Abby kept looking for ways to earn money and even considered sending her daughters out as domestic servants.

Ever since Alcott had been forced to close his Boston school Fuller had become increasingly fond of him, even putting his "Orphic Sayings" in her *Dial* against her better judgment, but now, unaware of the complexities of the Alcott marriage—how important her self-sacrifice and support of Bronson's reforming zeal were to Abby's personal sense of mission—she thought she saw through

Abby's proud front and wrote in her journal that Mr. Alcott's "boyish infatuation and his swelling vanity" made her ache.[13]

On the first of September, the subject of marriage dominated Margaret's
afternoon walk with Waldo.

> We got to talking, as we almost always do, on Man and Woman, and Marriage.—
> W[aldo] took his usual ground. Love is only phenomenal, a contrivance of nature, in her
> circular motion. Man, in proportion as he is completely unfolded is man and woman by
> turns. The soul knows nothing of marriage, in the sense of a permanent union between
> two personal existences. The soul is married to each new thought as it enters into it. If
> this thought puts on the form of man or woman[,] if it last you seventy years, what then?
> There is but one love, that for the Soul of all Souls, let it put on what cunning disguises it
> will, still at last you find yourself lonely—*the Soul.* There seems to be no end to these
> conversations: they always leave us both where they found us, but we enjoy them, for we
> often get a good expression.

She did not think it "worthwhile" to reply to Waldo when he said, "Ask any
woman whether her aim in this union is to further the genius of her husband;
and she will say yes, but her conduct will always be to claim a devotion day by
day that will be injurious to him, if he yields."[14]

These discussions between Emerson and Fuller had been going on ever since
1838, when Emerson was looking for subjects for his lectures. When Elizabeth
Hoar had suggested "the rights of Woman," Fuller, who was on vacation from
her Providence teaching and worrying about how her mother could manage
the education of the younger children, agreed and added that "women are
Slaves." Emerson made a note of the conversation. He touched on the subject of
marital love in his lecture, "Love," but the more Fuller emphasized that the
institution of marriage lay at the heart of the problem of woman's rights, the
more Emerson evaded the issue by relegating marriage to a minor place, a mere
incident in the life of a Soul. Fuller continued to probe.[15]

On September 9 Waldo came to Margaret's room to show her some passages
in his journal on the subject of marriage. "He listens with a soft wistful look to
what I say but is nowise convinced," she wrote when she saw how little he had
been influenced by her ideas on how the institution could be improved.[16]

Emerson resisted the idea that the marriage relation should be reformed.
"We cannot rectify marriage because it would introduce such carnage into our
social relations," he argued, "and it seems, the most rabid radical is a good Whig
in relation to the theory of Marriage." To "abrogate the laws which make
Marriage a relation for life, fit or unfit," would "not do." He was not disturbed
that the ardor of love subsided or that marriage was "a temporary relation"; it
"should have its natural birth, climax, and decay, without violence of any
kind,—violence to bind or violence to rend." As for the dissatisfactions of
marriage, he took refuge in his homemade adage: "I marry you for better not
for *worse:* I marry impersonally."[17]

A year earlier, he had explained the philosophy that allowed him to accept calmly the shortcomings of married life: "To a strong mind therefore the griefs incident to every earthly marriage are the less, because it has the resource of the all-creating, all-obliterating spirit; retreating on its grand essence the nearest persons become pictures merely. The Universe is his bride."[18] Steadfastly insisting that the ideal life was a constant ascent toward a marriage with the principle of Universal Love, he brushed aside Fuller's attempt to consider earthly marriage as the central factor in the equation. They decided to end the debate by concluding that they differed because her god was "love" whereas his was "truth."[19]

Margaret had seen Emerson's philosophy put to the test early in her visit. The first sign of trouble came when two days after her arrival she went upstairs to visit Lidian, who had been confined to her room for several days. She was suffering from a painful tooth extraction, worrying about the health of ten-month-old Edith, and still subject to depression when she thought of young Waldo. At the sight of Margaret, Lidian burst into tears; she explained that her nerves were weak because she was taking laudanum for pain. Margaret described the incident in her journal:

Presently she said something which made me suppose she thought W[aldo] passed the evenings in talking with me, & a painful feeling flashed across me, such as I have not had, all has seemed so perfectly understood between us. I said that I was with Ellery or H[enry] T[horeau] both eve'gs and that W[aldo] was writing in the study.[20]

Lidian's unexpected behavior preyed on Margaret's mind. She wondered if she had been inconsiderate or if Lidian thought she was interfering with Waldo's work. "[W]hat does it signify whether he is with me or at his writing?" she queried. Lidian "knows perfectly well" that he is interested in people only insofar as they can stimulate his thoughts. She protested that Lidian had no cause for jealousy: "As to my being more his companion that cannot be helped, his life is in the intellect not the affections. He has affection for me, but it is because I quicken his intellect. . . . I dismissed it all, as a mere sick moment of L's."[21]

Two weeks later, on September 1, the problem resurfaced with greater intensity. At dinner, when Lidian suggested that Margaret take a walk with her afterward, Margaret replied that she was already "engaged to walk with Mr. E[merson]." This brought on another flood of tears. While the whole family sat looking at their plates, Margaret tried to mend matters by telling Lidian she would be glad to go with her, only to have Lidian insist she did not want Margaret to make "any sacrifice." She had only suggested the walk because she felt "perfectly desolate, and forlorn" and thought the fresh air would do her good. While Margaret firmly brought Lidian around to agreeing that they should go together, "Waldo said not a word: he retained his sweetness of look, but never offered to do the least thing." During the walk with Lidian that afternoon and a buggy ride the next morning, Lidian poured out her problems. Afterward, Margaret analyzed the situation:

In our walk and during our ride this morning L. talked so fully that I felt reassured except that I think she will always have these pains, because she has always a lurking hope that Waldo's character will alter, and that he will be capable of an intimate union; now I feel convinced that it will never be more perfect between them two . . . for he is sorely troubled by imperfections in the tie, because he don't believe in any thing better.—And where he loved her first, he loves her always. . . . Yet in reply to all L. said, I would not but own that though I thought it was the only way, to take him for what he is, as he wishes to be taken, and though my experience of him has been, for that very reason, so precious to me, I dont know that I could have fortitude for it in a more intimate relation. Yet nothing could be nobler, nor more consoling than to be his wife, if one's mind were only thoroughly made up to the truth.—As for myself, if I have not done as much as I ought for L. it is that her magnanimity has led her to deceive me. I have really thought that she was happy to have me in the house solely for Waldo's sake, and for my own, and she is, I know, in the long account, but there are pains of every day which I am apt to neglect for others as for myself. . . . I suppose the whole amount of the feeling is that women cant bear to be left out of the question. And they dont see the whole truth about one like me, if they did they would understand why the brow of Muse or Priestess must wear a shade of sadness. . . . They have so much that I have not, I cant conceive of their wishing for what I have. . . . But when Waldo's wife, & the mother of that child that is gone thinks me the privileged of woman, & that E[lizabeth] H[oar] was happy because her love was snatched away for a life long separation, & thus she can know none but ideal love: it does seem a little too insulting at first blush.—And yet they are not altogether wrong.[22]

Now the end-of-summer rains were upon them in Concord, and the air was sultry. Everyone at Bush was housebound, and Margaret felt that she was experiencing a sense of "community," but the atmosphere was not entirely convivial. She described it as living "at swords points (though at present turned downwards)." Something she said one day caused Waldo to shadow over and avoid her for two days. At such times she thought he was offended by what he called her "worldliness."[23]

Ellery, who had been visiting her during odd hours, now became over-familiar and criticized her for making everyone around her "restless" because of her high standards. Her speech was too "disciplined," he told her. It struck him as "artificial" because it was too well thought out in advance. In her journal Margaret vowed that she would not let the criticisms disturb her.

Waldo must not shake me in my worldliness . . . nor this child of genius [Ellery] make me lay aside the armour without which I had lain bleeding on the field long since, but if they can keep closer to Nature, and learn to interpret her as souls, also,—let me learn from them what I have not.[24]

On September 2 Ellery came to her for advice. Caroline Sturgis had invited him to visit her at Naushon Island (off New Bedford). Ellen was, of course, "the flower" of his life, he protested, but he very much wanted to see Caroline again. Arguing that he had never responded before to Caroline's requests and that this would be his last chance to see her freely before Ellen returned from Cincinnati, he convinced Margaret that "the meeting would be the greatest satisfaction both to him and C[aroline]." On Friday, September 2, he left, having sworn that nothing would keep him from returning the following Tuesday, since Ellen was expected on Wednesday.[25]

It rained through the next week. Ellery did not return on Tuesday, nor was there word from Ellen. On Friday, Margaret began to panic, and the whole household joined in her concern. Margaret was certain that if Ellen arrived and found Ellery absent without explanation, "a death blow" would be dealt to their peace. She wrote frantic letters to James Freeman Clarke in Boston and to friends in New Bedford, begging for help in locating Ellery. That night, in the midst of a violent rainstorm, Ellen arrived by stagecoach. Waldo, seeing Margaret's anxiety, offered to go to Boston to seek out Ellery, but Margaret would not hear of it. While Ellen kept her up most of the night speculating on where Ellery could have gone, Margaret thought over "all these relations" and concluded:

If I were Waldo's wife, or Ellery's wife, I should acquiesce in all these relations, since they needed them. I should expect the same feeling from my husband, & I should think it little in him not to have it. I felt I should never repent of advising Ellery to go what ever happened.

When Ellery returned the next day, "Mamma [Emerson's mother, Ruth Haskins Emerson] & Lidian sympathized with me almost with tears," Margaret wrote in her journal. "Waldo looked radiant, & H[enry] T[horeau] as if his tribe had won a victory. Ellery told Ellen at once how it was, and she took it just as she ought." Knowing Ellen's temper, Margaret was greatly relieved.[26]

While Ellery was away, Sam Ward came for a two-day visit, and Margaret enjoyed his company more than at any other time since his marriage. Later in the week, Henry Hedge arrived. He stirred up discussions of "all the great themes" of the day, principally the rights of the individual versus the claims of "the Race"—the issue that was now dividing the transcendental camp. Like William Henry Channing, who had accused Emerson of trying to be "the complete Adam" all by himself with no outside help, Henry Hedge took issue with Emerson's insistence on the all-important rights of the individual. Hedge believed that the church was needed to serve as an intermediary between the individual and God and that the improvement of social institutions generally contributed to the welfare of the individual as well as the race.[27]

Fuller saw Hedge's side of the question, but she saw no reason why both points of view could not exist together. "The inspiration of the individual need not be sacrificed in favor of that of the race. We can just as well have both," she concluded. This comprehensive and balanced approach was now becoming a hallmark in her personal life, in her literary criticism, and in her aesthetic theory. The discussion with Hedge stimulated a restatement of her credo in more direct terms than ever before:

What is done here at home in my heart is my religion. . . . Let others choose their way, I feel that mine is to keep my equipoise as steadfastly as I may, to see, to think, a faithful sceptic, to reject nothing but accept nothing till it is affirmed in the due order of mine own nature. I belong nowhere. I have pledged myself to nothing. God and the soul and nature are all my creed, subdivisions are unimportant.—As to your Church, I do not deny the church. . . . I have my church where I am by turns priest and lay man. I take these simpler modes, if the world prefers more complex, let it. I act for myself, but prescribe for none other.[28]

She had, of course, been preaching, if not prescribing, her creed for years in her teaching, her writing, and her Conversations. While asserting that she was too independent to adopt any of the popular causes of the day, she had been in the vanguard of the movement to encourage women "to think" and as "fanciful sceptics" to discover the reasons for their exclusion from the opportunities for growth. She saw herself as only extending the Emersonian philosophy of "the infinitude of the private man" to women. Aimed at the individual, her reform efforts bore serious consequences for the race, but she was so accustomed to thinking of herself as dedicated to the ideal of her own growth that she did not conceive of herself as a reformer. After observing the shortcomings of the marriages of the steadfast Transcendentalists, the Emersons and the Alcotts, she knew that her philosopher friends did not have all the answers and that the subject of "Woman" needed further study.

During her last few days in Concord, Margaret went on a boat ride with the Hawthornes and accompanied Lidian on an evening visit to the churchyard to pray at little Waldo's grave. On Saturday, September 24, Lidian gave a farewell tea for her, with "rather a mob" at Bush all day. Sarah Clarke brought Caroline's sister, Ellen Sturgis Hooper; Ellen and Ellery were there with Richard; Sophia Hawthorne brought her mother, Elizabeth Palmer Peabody, Sr.[29]

By then Margaret knew she had overstayed her welcome, and after a long talk with Waldo in his study she saw it was time to go. She still felt the power of his personality, but she was determined to hold her own ground against him. In her *Dial* article, "Bettina Brentano and Her Friend Günderode," she had analyzed Bettina's idolization of Goethe and warned of the danger of such a relationship "degenerating into a mutual excitement of vanity or mere infatuation." What was necessary was "[a]n admiration restrained by self-respect," she had written. She now understood that the tensions between her philosophy and Waldo's were irreconcilable. They were buried in the difference sin their temperaments, in what he called her "worldliness," and in what she saw as religious-based belief that the pathway to spiritual understanding was through an ever-wider and more active experience of life. In her journal entry for her last day at Bush, she wrote, "Farewell, dearest friend, there has been dissonance between us, may be again, for we do not fully meet, and to me you are too much and too little by turns."[30]

She recognized that raw nerves had been touched during her five-week stay at Bush and remarked at the end of her journal that she thought she should be more attentive to Lidian and could be "of real use" to her in the future. But her visit left her uneasy. She sensed that she would never visit the Emersons again on the same free terms, and she was right.

What a woman needs is not as a woman to act or rule, but as a nature to grow, as an intellect to discern, as a soul to live freely, and unimpeded to unfold such powers as were given her when we left our common home.

The Great Lawsuit

IN THE FALL of 1842 Margarett Crane Fuller decided to rent a house in Cambridge. She wrote that she had been "so long a housekeeper" that she felt "misplaced" as a guest or a boarder, and needed to be the "center of [a] *home*" for her children. With Arthur and Richard both at the college, she could offer "shelter and affection."[1] At first Margaret found it difficult to pick up family life again in the narrow Queen Anne–style house on Ellery Street near the college. She worried that a return to housekeeping would be exhausting for her mother, and her fears seemed justified. "We spend too much; my time is invaded,— Mother makes herself sick, & does not meet the feelings of the boys," she fumed in her journal. Living on her own, Margaret had enjoyed being able to give vent to her volatile feelings whenever she wished. Now she thought she would have to keep a tight rein on herself so as not to upset her mother, but within weeks she was able to report that Margarett Crane Fuller had "learnt not to be over anxious" when Margaret gave in to her temper and tears.[2]

While in Concord in the summer, she had read over the manuscript collection of Ellery Channing's poems and now agreed with Emerson that Channing was an impressive talent. "My constellation seems full now he is added," she wrote in her journal in October, even though she was certain she would never love him as she had others. She felt that she had divined "what his final wisdom must be," but in December, when Ellery and Ellen, unable to find a place to board in Concord, joined her and her mother in Cambridge, he returned to the moody behavior for which he was known before his marriage. Encouraging him to prepare his poems for publication, Emerson offered to help with the editing, and Sam Ward promised to pay the publishing costs. The effort kept Ellery in a constant state of strain, but Margaret refused to let his temperamental behavior upset her. "Ellery has harassing cares," she wrote Elizabeth Hoar, "but, since I cannot aid, I do not dwell upon them, and I am able to prevent Mother from doing it, too, which sometimes seems to me an absolute miracle." She was equally amazed at Ellen's patience but still felt that the marriage was a "possible tragedy."[3]

Margaret contributed her share of the household expenses and spent two days of each week in Boston giving lessons and leading her Conversation classes. The 1842–43 season began with the theme, "How can constancy, a fixedness of purpose and perseverance in action be made consistent with a free development of character?" On her overnights in town she usually went to a concert or dined with friends, but she no longer craved a lively social life. In January she wrote Elizabeth Hoar that she could not explain "the unaccustomed serenity" of her mood. "The little household is so well arranged that all goes on as smooth as a wheel turns round."[4]

The Ellery Street house stood in what had once been the lower orchard of the Dana Mansion where, in their prosperous years, the Fullers had lived in high style. In 1839 the mansion had burned down; the once extensive property of Francis Dana's showplace was divided into a gridwork of streets bearing the names of Dana relatives: Ellery, Prescott, Trowbridge, as well as Dana itself. Some of Margaret's equanimity may have come from a sense of returning to the safety of that earlier home. She was again on good terms with George Davis, whom she had loved during her Dana Mansion years. In December she wrote him that her surroundings recalled the days when they had been "so much together." Her room overlooked the same view of "the river so slow and mild, the gentle hills, the sunset over Mt. Auburn." In those days, she told George, her father had often warned her of all the "ills" that could accrue from her arrogance and pride, and, although all her "cherished plans" had indeed fallen through, she did not think she had changed in any essential way. She regretted deeply that she had no children and had not yet written anything of lasting beauty, but the result had not been entirely to her disadvantage; she had been left free to think deeply and religiously. Her friendships had become of paramount importance to her, she told George.[5]

Once a week she went to the Ward's town house in Louisburg Square on Beacon Hill to read Petrarch with Anna, but her feelings toward Anna had changed dramatically. She was reminded of this one evening at the home of William Batchelder Greene, who had a collection of etchings of prominent French personalities of the revolutionary era. A large engraving of Jeanne Françoise Récamier in her boudoir fixed her attention and prompted her to write in her journal that she had often thought about the intimacy between Germaine de Staël and Récamier; their relationship recalled what she had once felt toward Anna:

It is so true that a woman may be in love with a woman, and a man with a man. It is so pleasant to be sure of it because undoubtedly it is the same love that we shall feel when we are angels when we ascend to the only fit place for the mignons where
          Sie fragen nicht nach Mann und Weib—
It is regulated by the same law as that of love between persons of different sexes, only it is purely intellectual and spiritual, unprofaned by any mixture of lower instincts, undisturbed by any need of consulting temporal interests, its law is the desire of the spirit to realize a whole which makes it seek in another being for what it finds not in itself. Thus the beautiful seeks the strong; and the strong the beautiful, the mute seek the eloquent &c the butterfly settles always on the dark flower. Why did Socrates love Alcibiades?—

why did Korner love Schneider? how natural is the love of Wallenstein for Max, that of
Me. de Stael for de Recamier, mine for Anna Barker[.] I loved Anna for a time I think
with as much passion as I was then strong enough to feel—Her face was always gleaming
before me,—her voice was echoing in my ear, all poetic thoughts clustered around the
dear image. This love was a key which unlocked for me many a treasure which I still
possess, it was the carbuncle (emblematic gem) which cast light into many of the darkest
caverns of human nature.—She loved me, too, though not so much, because her nature
was "less high, less grave, less large, less deep" but she loved more tenderly, less passion-
ately[.] She loved me, for I well remember her suffering when she first would feel my
faults and knew one part of the exquisite veil rent away, how she wished to stay apart and
weep the whole day. Then again that night when she leaned on me and her eyes were
such a deep violet blue, so like night, as they never were before, and we both felt such a
strange mystic thrill and knew what we had never known before. Now well too can I now
account for that desire which I often had to get away from her and be alone with nature,
which displeased her so, for she wished to be with me all the time.[6]

Fuller mused that she no longer felt Anna's overpowering attraction; Anna was
no longer the exclusive representation of "the Beautiful" in her life. They had
been together too seldom to form an enduring friendship. What was left between them now could only be described as "a sort of pallid, tender romance."[7]

Before Anna married Sam, there had been times when Margaret longed for
Anna's physical presence and arranged her life for weeks around the chance of
meeting with her. At that time, the excitement of a few hours with Anna could
exhaust her. Considering Anna's former power over her, Fuller realized that as
long as they had seen little of each other she and Anna were able to fulfill each
other's imaginary needs for an ideal friendship, but now time and familiarity
had done their corrosive work.

Fuller's first biographers, William Henry Channing, James Freeman Clarke,
and Ralph Waldo Emerson, quoted this journal entry out of context, but their
use of the passage as exemplary of Fuller's friendships with women would
indicate that they considered her feelings acceptable socially. It is certainly likely
that Fuller had been erotically in love with Barker, but if their physical relationship extended beyond an occasional thrilling touch, we have no evidence.
Throughout Fuller's writings the theme of opposites attracting surfaced frequently. To her it was a law of nature that two halves sought a whole. In
connecting same-sex love with the angels, as she was later to compare her
relationship with Caroline Sturgis to that of Mary and Elizabeth, the purest
women in the New Testament, she was alluding to her belief in the soul's
progress to a state of divinity that was beyond sexual definition. Yet her insistence on describing the attraction she felt for Barker and Sturgis, as well as the
relationships of several pairs of historical figures, in terms of purity and disin-
terestedness could veil an uneasiness about the source of the attraction.[8]

In spite of her disclaimers, proximity to Anna still had the power to activate
disturbing dream images. In late October, when Sam was away, she spent the

night with Anna and had a terrifying dream similar to earlier ones signifying a sense of captivity, accompanied by rejection and betrayal by friends.

Sam was away, and I slept with Anna the first time for two years. It was exquisitely painful to feel that I loved her less than when we before were thus together in confiding sleep, and she too is now so graceful and lovely, but the secret of my life is sealed to her forever. I never speak of the inmost experience, but listen to her inmost talk. I took pleasure in sleeping on Sam's pillow and before closing my eyes solicited that visions like his might come to me but I had a frightful dream of being imprisoned in a ship at sea, the waves all dashing round, and knowing that the crew had resolved to throw me in. While in horrible suspense, many persons that I knew came on board. At first they seemed delighted to see me & wished to talk but when I let them know my danger, a [sic] intimated a hope that they might save me, with cold courtliness glided away. Oh it was horrible these averted faces and well dressed figures turning from me, from captive, with the cold wave rushing up into which I was to be thrown.[9]

If this dream signified latent fears of abandonment as she shared less of her inner life with her friends, she could at least point to some progress in keeping her vow of the previous summer that she would learn what she could from her friends but take her own path. One healthy sign was her flourishing friendship with practical-minded Sarah Clarke, who admired Fuller but never lost her critical eye. Once, when her brother James mistook a *Dial* article of Margaret's on an Athenaeum art exhibit for one of hers, Sarah wrote him a furious letter, telling him she was shocked that he did not realize that Margaret's "style of judgement" was at opposite poles from her own. Sarah, who was two years older than Margaret, had felt uncomfortable with Margaret's crowd back in the Dana Mansion days, but over the years she had come to like and trust Margaret. She especially admired her "courage, ability, self-possession and grace" in conducting the Conversation classes. Like many others, Sarah Clarke was flattered by the effort Fuller put forth in her friendships; she explained Fuller's attraction thus: "Though she spoke rudely searching words and told you startling truths, though she broke down your little shams and defenses, you felt exhilarated by the compliment of being found out, or even that she had cared to find you out."[10]

In the late 1830s Clarke had studied with Washington Allston in Cambridge-port and had rented a nearby room where she painted twice a week; occasionally, her paintings were displayed at the Athenaeum. Still erratic and undependable, Sturgis repeatedly begged Fuller to visit her, but Fuller's schedule was already full. Instead of catering to Sturgis, she encouraged the friendship that had begun to blossom between Sturgis and Charles King Newcomb at Brook Farm. Sturgis had found him fascinating and attractive. She visited him and wrote to him, but by the time people were gossiping about them, she gave up— Newcomb was too listless for romantic, highly charged Sturgis. In December Fuller wrote Emerson that she and Sturgis were not "so much companions now, but dear friends."[11]

Occasionally during the fall and winter Fuller visited Brook Farm for a few days. Over the past year, Brook Farm had changed for the better, she thought. The Farmers were less driven to eccentric behavior and dress for its own sake and were settling down to a steady routine of work and study. She went to check on Lloyd's progress, to encourage Charles King Newcomb to finish his story, "Dolon," which Emerson wanted to publish in the *Dial*, and to lead a few Conversations in the evenings.

While there she met the English governess Georgiana Bruce, who had worked in Paris and in Canada before coming to Boston to join a minister's family. When the job proved unsatisfactory, Bruce took refuge at the farm where she was cooking, cleaning, and teaching in the school to earn her way. She became another of Fuller's admirers and was soon hanging on her every word and bringing her breakfast tea in the best teacup in the Hive, the farm's main building. Bruce entertained Fuller with a fund of lively stories accumulated in the course of her picaresque life. Fuller took to her at once, encouraged her to try her hand at writing, and added her to her list of correspondents.[12]

In this period of relative tranquillity, Fuller began to write "The Great Lawsuit" for the *Dial*. Every January since her father's death, she had complained of chronic flu or fever, but this year she wrote her friends that her health and spirits were better than they had ever been. Perhaps she was able to sustain an unusually buoyant attitude because she had finally found enough "lovely leisure . . . undisturbed by fears of pain to others" to write on the subject that had occupied her for years: the position of women in the new American democracy and the possibilities for change in the future. In expanded form, under the name *Woman in the Nineteenth Century*, her article would become a major document of American feminism.[13]

Several women authors whom Margaret admired had already addressed the issue. In *Society in America* (1837), Harriet Martineau had deplored the timidity and conformism of American women. Anna Jameson, whose *Winter Studies and Summer Rambles in Canada* (1838) had been criticized for its feminism, had recently written an article for the *Athenaeum* in which she described the shocking situation of laboring women in England. She was following up her article with a series of pamphlets demanding public support for better working conditions.

In the United States, women abolition leaders, notably the Grimké sisters, had for several years been arguing eloquently for a woman's right to speak in public. Catharine Beecher was leading the effort to expand public education and to train legions of women to serve as schoolteachers for the nation. The influential Sarah Josepha Hale, editor of *Godey's Lady's Book*, supported higher education for women but warned that public issues were the domain of men. In *Means and Ends; or, Self-Training*, the popular novelist Catharine Sedgwick advised women to qualify themselves for the exercise of higher powers: "When you are thus qualified, they cannot long be withheld from you."[14] Within recent years Lydia Maria Child had written a series of biographies of famous women in history. The prominence of an increasing number of women authors was in itself a sign that a new woman was in the making, Margaret wrote.

In the January 1841 *Dial*, Sophia Ripley wrote a brief essay entitled "Woman," in which she claimed that there had been "no topics, for the last two years, more generally talked of than woman, and 'the sphere of woman.'" Attacking the concept of separate spheres for the sexes as pointless, since character and intellect create a person's sphere and what is "individual and peculiar" determines it, she faulted "the present state of society" for keeping women in a state of dependency and argued cogently for the spiritual independence of woman.[15]

Fuller's much longer treatment of the topic was infused with the spirit of religious aspiration. Selecting for her essay the biblical text, "Be ye perfect," she combined the Transcendentalist argument of the unique relationship of the individual to God with a political and moral one: America's mission to develop the concept of human freedom beyond the aspirations of the American and French revolutions. "[T]his country is as surely destined to elucidate a great moral law, as Europe was to promote the mental culture of men," she wrote.[16]

Intentionally choosing a cryptic title—"The Great Lawsuit: Man *versus* Men, Woman *versus* Women"—Fuller sought to puzzle the reader into grasping her underlying point: that, in the process of living, the ideal aspirations of the individual, man or woman, are constantly in conflict with societal restrictions. At the present state of development in America the separation of the sexes into different spheres was a major stumbling block to humanity's inevitable forward progress and required correction. Arguing that so fundamental a change was a matter of altering consciousness, she set about exposing the social and psychological realities that stood in the way of her prophecy; both sexes would ultimately benefit, for "an improvement in the daughters will best aid the reformation of the sons of this age."[17]

In her exposé of patriarchy, she cited the wrongs of legal, political, and economic disenfranchisement and the strongly held bias of men against any change in the status quo: the fear that "the beauty of the home" would be destroyed, "the delicacy of the sex" violated, and "the dignity of halls of legislature destroyed" when senate chambers were "filled with cradles" and "ladies in hysterics" were at the voting booths. But she did not develop a program to correct these arbitrary barriers.[18]

Instead, using irony, ridicule, anger, and aspiration and employing many voices, she marshaled her material to assess the current climate for change in woman's situation in the culture. To break down stereotypes of feminine incapacity and instill a new "Idea of woman," she provided a panorama of empowering models of female figures, chosen from history, mythology, Scripture, literature, and the contemporary scene. Adopting the name Miranda, she introduced an idealized version of her own biography in which she represented herself as an example of a woman who understood that "the restraints upon the sex were insuperable only to those who think them so, or who noisily strive to break them." Thanks to a father who had "a firm belief in the equality of the sexes," she had been brought up to a free life of "self-dependence," "self-reliance," and "self-respect." Even though society as a whole gave only "thread-bare celebrity" to women who excelled in areas generally believed to be the province of men, she recommended that women, too long regarded as "beings of affection and habit alone," now take the time to develop the "Minerva" or intellectual side of their natures to offset the harmful effects in emotional pain and psychic exhaustion that Fuller saw as the result of permitting the intuitional and divinatory side of the feminine constitution too great a role.[19]

The heart of the program that Fuller recommended to activate a richer development of woman's nature was the theory of sexual identity that sprang from her concept of the completely developed soul as without gender. When a soul is "modified" as woman, "it flows, it breathes, it sings, rather than deposits soil, or finishes work," she explained, thus expressing what she called "the lyrical" essence of "Femality," or the Muse quality of woman. A further definition summarizes the Muse as "electrical in movement, intuitive in function, spiritual in tendency. She excels not so easily in classification, or recreation, as in an instinctive seizure of causes, and a simple breathing out of what she receives that has a singleness of life, rather than the selecting and energizing of art."[20]

As a counter to the weakening and painful effects of the overdevelopment of the Muse side of women, Fuller called for a greater emphasis on the intellectual Minerva side to free women from becoming the victims of their over-stimulated sensibilities. To harmonize the intellect and the affections, she recommended a program of self-discipline, intellectual rigor, critical reasoning, and self-awareness that included periods of isolation so as to check the harmful effects of too much emotional involvement, the common plight of the many "incarcerated souls" she knew who could be freed by greater self-reliance. She supported her theory of gender multiplicity by arguing that, since nothing in nature is "incarnated pure in any form," male and female elements "are perpetually passing into one another. Fluid hardens to solid, solid rushes to fluid. There is no wholly masculine man, no purely feminine woman." "What a woman needs is not as a woman to act or rule, but as a nature to grow, as an intellect to discern, as a soul to live freely, and unimpeded to unfold such powers as were given her when we left our common home."[21]

Fuller was particularly eloquent in asserting that the one quality ascribed to women that had never been allowed free development because of the rules of feminine decorum was the "electrical, the magnetic element," the talent for quick intuitional insights, a skill developed when aspiration and ambition are stifled. "Everything might be expected from it; she has far more of it than man."

In the development of this side of woman's nature, Fuller saw "much promise." She asked that "every arbitrary barrier [be] thrown down" and "every path laid open to woman as freely as to man." America provided "a less encumbered field, and freer air than anywhere else" for woman's growth, but the responsibility to take advantage of this situation lay with women themselves.[22]

She divided acceptable marriage styles into four main categories in ascending order of mutual spirituality, noting that marriage as an institution, even in places where the idea of "equality has become persuasive," had many shortcomings. It was often the case that "partners in work and in life, sharing together, on equal terms, public and private interests," have become "under petrified or oppressive institutions . . . warlike, paradoxical, or, in some sense, Pariahs." In a better world, women of genius and strong feelings, like Mary Wollstonecraft and George Sand, would not become "outlaws" for "breaking bonds" or be forced to "run their heads so wildly" against society's laws. But inasmuch as their personal behavior had gone beyond accepted norms, they could not be effective reformers; that role was reserved for those who lived exemplary lives.[23]

Urging women to take time out to discover "what is fit for themselves" before embarking on marriage, she quoted Emerson: "Union is only possible to those who are units." Women should be cured of the habit of dependency and realize that a satisfactory marriage was not assured in the present stage of society. Developing this idea further, she hailed the advantages of a single life as providing an opportunity for deeper perceptions and interpretations of life, the possibility of approaching apotheosis in high moral development, power and insight. Her exaltation of the single life was more than a plea for the dignity of her own position. Many of her friends and members of the Conversations were unmarried. Discussions of woman's sphere that assumed most women were wives ignored a situation that would become evident in 1845 when a Boston census would reveal that one-third of the city's women were single.[24]

In the early pages of "The Great Lawsuit," she pointed to the struggle of women abolitionists to overcome the prejudice against women speaking in public as the most prominent and laudatory example of women's organized activity on their own behalf. Previously she had privately criticized antislavery activists as a band of ineffective rabble-rousers. Now her adherence to the Emersonian precept of the autonomous individual—going it alone on a heavenward journey—was softening in the direction of proposing periods of withdrawal for spiritual refreshment and reassessment as a means of sustaining autonomy in society. Her own activity in the Conversations (where so many of the members were abolitionists) was fostering a greater openness to the idea of community action.

In early March, while Fuller was in the midst of writing "Lawsuit," Emerson summoned her to a meeting in Boston to discuss whether the *Dial* should continue. When they met after a five-month separation Emerson was aston-

ished at the changes he found in her. Five pages written in his journal toward
the end of March record his responses:

We are taught by her plenty how lifeless & outward we were, what poor Laplanders bur-
rowing under the snows of prudence & pedantry. Beside her friendship, other friendships seem trade, and by the firmness with which she treads her upward path, all mortals
are convinced that another road exists than that which their feet know. . . . She excels
other intellectual persons in this, that her sentiments are more blended with her life; so
the expression of them has greater steadiness & greater clearness. I have never known
any example of such steady progress from stage to stage of thought & of character. . . .
    . . . She rose before me at times into heroical & godlike regions, and I could remember
no superior woman, but thought of Ceres, Minerva, Proserpine, and the august ideal
forms of the Foreworld. . . .
    She has great sincerity, force, & fluency as a writer, yet her powers of speech throw her
writing into the shade. . . . You cannot predict her opinion. She sympathizes so fast with
all forms of life, that she talks never narrowly or hostilely nor betrays, like all the rest,
under a thin garb of new words, the old droning castiron opinions or notions of many
years standing. . . . Meantime, all the pathos of sentiment and riches of literature & of
invention and this march of character threatening to arrive presently at the shores &
plunge into the sea of Buddhism & mystic trances, consists with a boundless fun &
drollery, with light satire, & the most entertaining conversation in America.[25]

Whatever happened at their March meeting, it seems certain that Fuller—no
longer in thrall to Emerson—no longer unsettled him, and in turn he could
relax and sing her praises. For the first time in all their years of fencing, he came
away free to admire her without anxiety. In his unreserved enthusiasm for her
lurks the satisfaction of the teacher for the student who has learned her lesson
well and has the vitality and spirit to carry forth the flame.

Fuller encouraged him to continue the *Dial* for another year and promised to
contribute. She had already submitted for the April issue a biographical sketch
of the sculptor Canova and two book reviews, one of which was a recognition
of a new British poet, Robert Browning, who would later play a singular role in
her life. She promised "Lawsuit" for July.

While Margaret was finishing the manuscript, Anna gave birth to the Wards'
second daughter, Lydia Gray Ward. Writing Margaret about the new baby,
Waldo exhibited his characteristic attitude toward the sexes: "Though no son, a
sacred event." Margaret did not permit the comment to go unremarked. "I do
believe, O Waldo, most unteachable of men, that you are at heart a sinner on
this point. I entreat you to seek light in prayer upon it."[26]

She was rushing to complete her essay well ahead of schedule because she was
leaving for Chicago in the last week of May with the Clarke family. From Sarah
Shaw, in return for some language lessons, she had received a windfall gift of
money to help with her expenses. Caroline Sturgis would accompany them as
far as Niagara Falls. On May 9 Margaret wrote Waldo that "Lawsuit" would be
finished the following week. She wanted him to arrange for the printing so she
would not be followed with proof sheets. On May 23 Margaret left Boston by

train for the West with "Lawsuit" behind her. By the time she heard of her essay's reception, she was already in Chicago. Early in July, Emerson sent her a collection of compliments. He quoted Thoreau, whom he characterized as one "who never likes anything," as saying that "Miss F's is a noble piece, rich extempore writing, talking with pen in hand." Sarah Ripley's comment was that "Margaret's article is the cream of herself, a little rambling, but rich in all good things." Ellery approved "without qualification." Emerson himself called it "proper and noble" and "quite an important fact in the history of Woman; good for its wit, excellent for its character." Realizing that she had found a subject and a reform that thoroughly engaged her because its roots were firmly embedded in her personal experience, he prophesied wisely, "You will yourself write to this theme, whatever you write; you cannot do otherwise." Carrying his doctrine of self-realization into realms where he could not follow, she had engaged with a social reality that aroused her anger. Out of this encounter she had developed a theory of feminine psychology with novel moral implications that was designed to both explain and assuage the unbalance of power between men and women in the new republic.[27]

I trust by reverent faith to woo the mighty meaning of the scene, perhaps to foresee the law by which a new order, a new poetry is to be evoked from this chaos.

Summer on the Lakes

BY THE 1840s, Niagara Falls had become the icon of the country's Manifest Destiny. When John Quincy Adams visited in the summer of 1843, a few weeks after Fuller and her friends had departed for Chicago on the second leg of their western trip, he pronounced it "one of the most wonderful works of God" on earth, and the rainbow that arched its roaring waters whenever the sun shone was "a pledge of God to mankind."[1]

Nathaniel Hawthorne arrived in 1834, "haunted with a vision of foam and fury, and dizzy cliffs and an ocean tumbling out of the sky," but found himself cast into "a wretched disappointment" on discovering that Nature had "too much good taste" to live up to his expectations. In the same vein, Margaret Fuller approached the scene a decade later fully prepared to be swept away with "lofty emotions," only to discover that everything looked just as she thought it would. Unable to experience the sublime emotion she had been led to expect, the best she could do was tuck Niagara away in her memory.[2]

During the week, while she waited for the promised thrill, she explored all the obligatory sights but could only regret that she had not been with the first band of discoverers who had stumbled out of the primeval forest with Father Hennepin on " 'this vast and prodigious cadence of water.' " The "perpetual trampling of the waters" seized her mind and filled it with "unsought and unwelcome . . . images, such as never haunted it before, of naked savages stealing behind me with uplifted tomahawks." She faced up to this primal scene in the book she wrote after her return in which she defended the Indian as having acted "the Roman or the Carthaginian part of heroic and patriotic self-defense" when he wielded his tomahawk against "the Europeans who took possession of this country."[3]

On June 4, after Sturgis left for home, Margaret boarded a steamer with Sarah and James at Buffalo for a five-day passage through the Great Lakes to Chicago. 1843 was the year of the "Great Migration" when 1,000 settlers forged the Oregon Trail from Independence, Missouri, to the Columbia River country of Oregon. Nearly all of the Native Americans east of the Mississippi had been moved to the Great Plains, and thousands of homesteaders were rushing in from the coast and from Europe to fill the empty land. Most of the passengers on Fuller's Great Lakes steamer were easterners on their way to settle in the Mississippi Valley. Their self-seeking, fortune-hunting talk depressed her. She was convinced by now that there was "nothing real" in the expectation that the so-called freedom of thought in the West would turn the newcomer into a more rational and free-thinking human being. James Freeman Clarke's disenchantments in Louisville and William Channing's in Cincinnati had dispelled that misconception. This generation of New Englander settlers, she decided, would take "their habits of calculation, their cautious manners, their love of polemics" with them. It was unlikely that the free air of the West would change them; yet she still hoped to find some good portents for the future.[4]

When she saw from the steamboat the first Indian settlements along the St. Clair River above Detroit, she felt she was at last approaching the West. The Indians had a special claim on her attention: They were the indigenous Americans. As such she considered them the human manifestations of American nature; the American land had produced them, and their culture could unlock an understanding hidden from the newcomer. Romanticizing the Indian as the guardian of America's virgin land, she was shocked when the steamship stopped to refuel at the Manitou Islands and she watched corps of Indians cutting down trees to feed the ships' engines. "[A]lmost all the old monarch trees have already been torn to glut the steamboat," she observed. The devastation tormented her. Later, in the book she would write about her adventures, *Summer on the Lakes,* she noted that peaceful progress is "scarce less wanton than that of warlike invasion." There were no landmarks left except "the rudeness of conquest and the needs of the day." It seemed that the only value at work in the West was "go-ahead" at any price. It was hard to believe that a "race" who would "make amends to nature for the present violation of her majestic charms" could ever spring from these rapacious settlers.[5]

After stops at Milwaukee, Racine, and Southport, the steamboat arrived at Chicago where Fuller stayed alone in a boardinghouse for two weeks while the Clarke family were reunited with William Hull Clarke, who along with his younger brother Abraham had established in 1835 the city's third drugstore, now a moderately prosperous business. Chicago was then a city of 7,600 inhabitants, with most of the buildings clustered along the river. It was still possible to walk for several miles on open sandy beach along Lake Michigan, but that was one of the few pleasures Margaret discovered. Her first impression was that Chicago was "for business and for nothing else," but at least, unlike in the East, everyone was absorbed in "*material* realities." "The men are all at work for money and to develope the resources of the soil, the women belong to the men. They do not ape fashions, talk jargon or burn out life as a tallow candle for a tawdry show."[6]

She spent two weeks taking long walks and reading everything that came to hand on the Indians—Henry Schoolcraft's *Algic Researches,* Hugh Murray's *Account of Discoveries and Travels in North America,* Washington Irving's Indian stories, Anna Jameson's Indian tales, and the books of the artist George Catlin.

On June 24, soon after James left for Boston, William Hull Clarke packed Margaret, Sarah, and his mother, Rebecca Hull Clarke, into a lumber wagon "overtopped with an awning of white cotton, stuffed in every vacant space with baggage of all kinds, carpet bags and baskets of provisions,"[7] and they set out for Oregon, Illinois, a small town seventy-five miles west over the Illinois prairie, where Margaret's uncle, William Williams Fuller (the third of Timothy's four younger brothers), had settled in the 1820s. Afterward, on the way back to Chicago, Fuller had promised to investigate for her brother Arthur the possibility of establishing a school in Belvidere, Illinois, on the Kishwaukee River; Arthur was graduating from divinity school at the end of the summer and was interested in teaching. If he could succeed in Belvidere, he would be able to give the Fuller family a foothold in the West.

If Niagara was a disappointment, the covered-wagon journey was for Fuller a continuous garden of delights in which she could exercise her fancy at will. The idea of moving for days over the waving grasses of an endless prairie in the middle of the continent had a poetic appeal. "It seems as though there is no home on earth & no need of one, for there is room enough to wander on forever." They spent the first night in Geneva as guests of a "homespun" Unitarian minister, Augustus Conant, who with the help of his father had built his own comfortable house and uncomfortable furniture. When Fuller heard his Sunday sermon, she was critical. He "preach[ed] *finely . . .* saying what he does not feel." But she noticed how highly his congregation regarded him and realized why the settlers loved him. "[T]his preaching [is] a pleasure to them for it binds them to their home, and the people of this place are New Englanders in tastes, feelings, & objects; of course, to be preached and lectured to is their music."[8]

One evening, after a picnic "on an oak shaded knoll," she wrote in her journal about the pleasure "all through the journey [of] taking care of ourselves and going in so independent a manner." She was much taken with William Hull Clarke, who was two years younger than she. Endowing him with the qualities she had hoped to find in the new western race, she enjoyed sitting beside him as he drove the wagon; there is some evidence that she became enough attached to him during the journey in northern Illinois to hope for a romance. Commending him for his part in the journey's success, she wrote:

W[illiam] C[larke] was the pleasantest person one could be with in such a way, for he has the spirit of light fun and adventure, delicate perception and a good deal of wit, knows every anecdote of the country whether of man or deer, drove admirably, with a coolness and self-possession in all little difficulties. . . . He knows his path as a man, and follows it with the gay spirit of a boy. We do not see such people in the East; it requires a more varied life to unfold their faculties.[9]

As the journey continued, Fuller gloried in the beauty of nature, writing into her journal an idyll that had echoes of Spenser's *Faerie Queene* as well as Goethe's *Wilhelm Meisters Wanderjahre.* The group picnicked on fresh fish and wild fowl; Sarah sketched while Margaret collected wildflowers—moccasin plant, wake-robin, torch plant, Indian pink, and "magnificent varieties of milk weed, like large bunches of cut coral." Just beyond the Fox River, they spent a night at the farm of a hospitable English gentleman, Mr. Stevenson. He lived in English gentry style with his sister and his two "insipid daughters" who entertained him every afternoon at teatime with piano duets, "in a style equally correct and monotonous."[10]

The stopover that captured Fuller's imagination completely—she called it "Elysium"—was the three-day rest at Hazelwood, the stately home of Alexander Charters overlooking the Rock River a few miles beyond Dixon's Ferry. The house was surrounded with acres of parkland as manicured as the best-kept European estate. This natural sanctuary—a sweeping lawn studded with towering conifers, a deer park, a river path with overhanging greenery, and a warren of garden paths meandering through fields of wildflowers—represented for Margaret her dream of America, the building of a new Eden in the wilderness.[11]

Like the little trellised garden behind her childhood home in Cambridgeport, Hazelwood seemed the perfect, safe haven for dreamers and poets. As she continued along the Rock River, Fuller's enthusiasm continued to grow. She thought she could live here and be "*as* happy as fate permits mortals to be." She wrote Richard proposing that the two of them consider setting up housekeeping together on an Illinois farm, "which would not be a twentieth part of the labor of a N[ew] England farm, and would pay twenty times as much for the labor."[12]

As a shortcut to the town of Oregon, they followed Black Hawk's trail, noting the earth-mound sites of Indian villages and kicking up arrowheads and pottery that lay only an inch or two beneath the soil. The Indians had lived in this natural garden for hundreds of years without deforming the land in any way, Margaret observed; it was clear that in less than twenty years the settlers would "obliterate the natural expression of the country."[13]

Fuller and the Clarkes reached Oregon, Illinois, in time to join in the settlers' celebration of the Fourth of July. Many nationalities were represented in the crowd who listened to "the usual puffs of Ameriky" followed by a picnic on the banks of the Rock River with music and fireworks. While visiting with her relatives and observing their family and community life, she began to develop themes for her book. She was struck with "the unfitness of the women for their new lot." The "joylessness, and inaptitude" in the women led her to wonder if the girls "would grow up with the strength of body, dexterity, simple tastes, and resources that would fit them to enjoy and refine" their lives. Why was life in this abundant natural garden so spiritually withering and culturally dull?[14]

After stopping at Belvidere to make inquiries about Arthur's chances of establishing a school, the Clarke prairie schooner returned to Chicago. Fuller and Sarah Clarke then went together to Milwaukee. Hundreds of immigrants, mostly from Germany and the Scandinavian countries, were arriving there every day. After bedding down for a few days in a shanty town for new arrivals, they would make their way—usually by foot—into the backcountry to stake out a piece of unclaimed land.

Margaret and Sarah made a foray into the hinterland and visited a few of the recent settlers, most of whom had been working people in their home countries and had no expectation of an easy life. But many were unprepared for the hardships and the isolation. The only contented woman Margaret met was an Englishwoman who proclaimed that the hardships of the Wisconsin Territory were "nothing" compared to those at home.[15]

In her book, Fuller described the small bands of disheveled Potawatomi Indians that she saw wandering helplessly over their former lands; they had found it impossible to survive farther west and were creeping back to their homelands to beg. During a sudden downpour on Silver Lake, she and Sarah took shelter in a destitute Potawatomi encampment, where they saw the old and sick huddled miserably together on dirty mats. Back in Milwaukee, they were shocked to come upon a band of homeless Indians—vagrants now in the teeming immigrant city—reduced to performing a "wild and grotesque" begging dance in order to get enough to eat. The band's chief did not join this humiliating performance; instead, with the "grand gait and gesture" of "a real Roman," he strode through the streets, but looking "as if he felt it was no use to strive or resist."[16]

On returning to Chicago, Fuller found a letter from James Freeman Clarke, enclosing fifty dollars so she would not cut short her trip for lack of funds. With it, she was able to spend nine days at Mackinac Island observing the annual encampment when hundreds of Chippewa and Ottawa arrived from all over the Great Lakes to receive their government payments of a few blankets and kettles. A letter from Emerson announcing the death of Washington Allston saddened Sarah Clarke, who had already fallen ill, leaving Fuller to make her journey alone. When she arrived at Mackinac, she found over 3,000 Indians already on the beaches and 2,000 more expected. While watching the flotillas of canoes arrive, she mingled with the arrivals, playing with the babies, conversing in sign language, and joining the women in the daily ritual of pounding corn. She enjoyed the Indians' fascination with her umbrella, her gold locket, and her folding eyeshade. When she learned that the Chippewas had recently petitioned the state of Michigan for citizenship, she sadly predicted that only second-class citizenship would be possible since "the white man, as yet, is a half-tamed pirate, and avails himself, as much as ever, of the maxim, 'Might makes right.' "[17]

After a few days she discovered she could make a round trip to Sault Ste. Marie on the *General Scott*. In *Winter Studies and Summer Rambles in Canada,* Anna Jameson had written an enticing description of riding the rapids of the river; Fuller yearned to do the same. While fogbound for two days near St. Joseph Island, she coaxed the captain into taking her on several rowboat excursions up the side rivers. When the skies cleared, she was able to match Anna Jameson's exploit: Her only complaint was that her white-water ride was over too quickly. Before she could enjoy a "gasp of terror and delight," before she had time "to feel anything but the buoyant pleasure," the two calico-shirted Chippewas in whom she had put her trust had maneuvered her expertly through the rapids in their birchbark canoe. It was a beautiful climax to her western journey.[18]

Thanks to James, Fuller had enough money to return home by way of New York where William Henry Channing, now a leading activist in the American Union of Associationists, introduced her to several of his socialist friends, including Horace Greeley, the editor of the *New-York Daily Tribune*. At William Channing's church, she ran into Henry Thoreau, who was now living on Staten Island as tutor to the children of William Emerson, Waldo's older brother. In New York she also met Waldo Emerson's friend, the Swedenborgian Henry James, who later wrote Emerson that he was impressed with Margaret's insights.

Back home again in Cambridge, Fuller found her younger brothers awaiting her with their usual problems. She nursed Arthur through his decision to establish his school in Belvidere, and she helped him finance his trip and make the arrangements to invest in the school building and land. Once he departed, she turned her attention to Richard, who had failed to win academic recognition at the end of his third college year and was apprehensive as he began the final stretch.

In late October she went to Brook Farm for two weeks to check on Lloyd, visit Charles King Newcomb, and catch up with old friends. As soon as she returned to Cambridge, she began her fifth season of Conversation classes. In keeping with the practical attitude that her western trip had inspired, she chose "Health" as the general theme. The attendance was much lower than in any previous year; in order to keep up her income, she was forced to increase the hourly tuition for her special language and literature classes from sixteen to twenty-five dollars for the season. Even at that high price, she managed to attract six pupils for the year.

Once she had her routine settled, she started work on her travel book. She got permission—the first woman to do so—to use the Harvard Library for her research. Thomas Wentworth Higginson remembered seeing her "sitting, day after day, under the covert gaze of the undergraduates who had never before looked upon a woman reading within those sacred precincts."[19]

It was her first totally original work of book length; other than her two short stories, a few poems, and her mystical pieces, she had published only reviews, essays, and translations. She had never finished her Goethe biography or managed to complete the original plays she had started. "Dont expect any thing from the book about the West. I cant bear to be thus disappointing you all the time," she wrote Emerson. "No lives of Goethe, no romances. . . . I cannot promise any thing."[20]

It took her all winter to finish. While she was writing, she was in a querulous, disjunctive state of mind, hardly the self-possessed woman who had finished "Lawsuit" on such a high note the previous spring and impressed Emerson with her self-possession. She was frequently at odds with her friends. On a Brook Farm visit with Elizabeth Hoar, Fuller's "rude impetuous conduct" caused Hoar to leave abruptly for home. When Waldo—supported by Ellery and Henry Thoreau—turned down one of Margaret's translations for the *Dial*, she responded with a hectoring letter criticizing Emerson's editorial policy.

In December, Fuller even had a quarrel with Anna Ward—probably brought on by the news that the Wards were moving to Lenox in the western part of the state. (Sam, long attracted to Waldo's lifestyle, had finally won his father's support for a plan to spend a few years as a farmer–literary man.) Her letter of apology, typical of the appeals for understanding she had used publicly in the schoolroom and in her Conversations as well as privately in her journal outpourings, begged forgiveness for her "childishness," which she blamed on the years of "inward conflict" that sapped her "vital energy" and on her overactive "imagination" and sensitivity to old wounds. She would never be free of these liabilities until she was "translated either into a sphere or into a body, better fitted for free and mature existence."[21]

She was touchy and worried all winter. Richard's graduation from Harvard would mark the end of her seven years' devotion to the welfare of the younger children. She frequently complained about her family's demands on her; yet the responsibility had given her life a center. With that center withdrawn, she would be more dependent than before on making her way as a writer. Anxiety plagued Margaret all the time she was writing *Summer on the Lakes,* and her mood crept into the style and spirit of the book.

Summer on the Lakes, in 1843 is a meandering, fragmentary, subjective book, almost a diary. Employing the voice of a traveling companion rather than that of a guide, Fuller invites the reader to join in her spontaneous thoughts, her self-exploration, her moods and misgivings. As a travelogue, the form she chose was not unusual. Washington Irving's *Sketch Book of Geoffrey Canyon, Gent* was the most popular contemporary example of the genre. In Fuller's case, the relaxed tone and the eclectic, pluralistic method reinforce her major theme: the dislocation and disjointedness that western settlement had forced on the lives of the newcomers and the Native Americans alike. She mourns the despoiling of the land and the displacement of the Indians, the insensitivity of the newcomers to natural beauty and to human suffering, and the futility of the settlers' clinging to old identities and forms in the new environment.

In her chapter on Niagara Falls, Margaret included a striking episode that occurred while she was sitting on Table Rock overlooking the falling water. "[A] man came to take his first look. He walked close up to the fall, and, after looking at it a moment, with an air as if thinking how he could best appropriate it to his own use, he spat into it." For Margaret, this was a disturbing reminder of "love of *utility*," a trait that all the recent British authors—Dickens, Martineau, Trollope, and Jameson—had pinpointed as the quintessential American quality. It pained her to consider that they might be right.[22]

As an example of how the treatment of the Indians dehumanized the settlers, she told of a Wisconsin farmer who was incensed when an Indian who had once lived on "his" hill returned, and, driven by homesickness, hung around the property and could not be chased off. "This gentleman, though in other respects of most kindly and liberal heart, showed the aversion that the white man soon learns to feel for the Indian on whom he encroaches, the aversion of the injurer for him he has degraded."[23]

The condition of the women settlers had surprised her, she wrote. Instead of finding a new race of women flourishing in an atmosphere free of worn-out restrictions, she saw many who were discontented and overwhelmed with the hard work. Many were still clinging nostalgically and pointlessly to the patterns of their former lives. She may have been thinking of the drawbacks of her own education when she pointed out that "methods copied from the education of some English Lady Augusta, are as ill suited to the daughter of an Illinois farmer, as satin shoes to climb the Indian mounds." The first rule of a western education should be that it "meet the wants of the place and time." Using the same critical standard to measure the western way of life as she had devised for reviewing books, she wrote, "It is always thus with the new form of life; we must learn to look at it by its own standard."[24]

She used the same criteria in her mediation of popular attitudes in regard to Native Americans. Scoring the whites for assuming that their "superior civilization and religious ideas" justified taking over the country and only proving thereby how faulty were both their civilization and their religion, she argued that, "[l]ooked at by his own standard, [the Indian] is virtuous when he most injures his enemy, and the white, if he be really the superior in enlargement of thought, ought to cast aside his inherited prejudices enough to see this,— . . . and do all he can to mitigate the doom of those who survive his past injuries." And doom was her prediction. Voicing one of the more benign assumptions of the theories of scientific racism developing at the time, she forecast:

Amalgamation would afford the only true and profound means of civilization. But nature seems, like all else, to declare, that this race is fated to perish. Those of mixed blood fade early, and are not generally a fine race. They lose what is best in either type, rather than enhance the value of each, by mingling. There are exceptions, one or two such I know of, but this, it is said, is the general rule.[25]

Throughout the book, Fuller introduced material unrelated to her trip, insertions that could be seen as serving the theme of the dislocations that accompanied the making of a protean, ever-changing, unstable culture in the West: occasional poems of her own as well as one on love's transience that James Freeman Clarke had enclosed with the fifty-dollar gift; a few paragraphs from a letter Sam Ward had sent from the West four years earlier; her review of a case study of a German hysteric, *The Seeress of Prevorst;* and her short story, "Mariana," based in part on a personal experience at Miss Prescott's School in Groton but extended to tell of Mariana's miseries in an incompatible marriage. In one conversational episode, in which Fuller represents Emerson as "Self-Poise" and herself as "Free Hope," she set at rest her differences with Emerson, telling him grandly,

You, Self-Poise, fill a priestly office. Could but a larger intelligence of the vocations of others, and a tender sympathy with their individual natures be added, had you more of love, or more of apprehensive genius, (for either would give you the needed expansion and delicacy) you would command my entire reverence. As it is, I must at times deny and oppose you, and so must others, for you tend, by your influence, to exclude us from your full, free life. We must be content when you censure, and rejoiced when you approve; always admonished to good by your whole being, and sometimes, by your judgment.

Whether or not she intended this to serve as a declaration of independence from his influence, she could be quite certain he would recognize himself in the sobriquet.[26]

Perhaps Fuller intended these insertions to support themes that are implicit in the book: the interaction of civilization with nature, reality's power to undermine the ideal, the disappointments inherent in fantasy, and lost opportunities in the meeting of minds, souls, and civilizations. In any event, many of the fragments, as well as her travelogue ruminations, reveal her sustained preoccupation with the social concerns introduced in "The Great Lawsuit."

Her interest in the prospects for women making a fresh start in the new West was connected with her heightened sensitivity to women's psychological collusion in their situation, one of the main themes of "Lawsuit." Another theme, the indictment of racism with respect to "the black man," is continued in *Summer on the Lakes* in her mounting outrage at the condition of "the red man," whose image haunts the narrative from a momentary threatening illusion at Niagara Falls of an Indian brave wielding his tomahawk to her final appeal for compassion. She calls on the missionary to direct his preaching not to the Indian but "to the trader who ruins him"; on legislators, if they "cannot undo the effects of past sin," to "save us from sinning still more deeply"; and on "every man and every woman, in their private dealings with the subjugated race, [to] avoid all share in embittering, by insult or unfeeling prejudice, the captivity of Israel."[27]

On the last page of her book she made a recommendation that heralds her open support of reform activism. On the boat returning home from Detroit, she overheard a group of passengers discussing "the doctrines of Fourier."

It seemed pity they were not going to, rather than from, the rich and free country where it would be so much easier, than with us, to try the great experiment of voluntary association, and show, beyond a doubt, that "an ounce of prevention is worth a pound of cure," a maxim of the "wisdom of nations," which has proved of little practical efficacy as yet.[28]

Emerson had arranged with his Boston publishers, Little and Brown, to publish the book, paying Fuller ten cents a copy for the seventy-five-cent book, a generous arrangement that pleased her. When she sent the first sheets of *Summer on the Lakes* to the printer on May 9, she wrote Emerson that she felt "a little cold at the idea of walking forth alone to meet that staring sneering Pit critic, the Public at large, when I have always been accustomed to confront it from amid a group of 'liberally educated and respectable gentlemen.'" Her *Dial* articles had appeared without bylines. Unprotected by her male associates, she was now setting out under her own name. Even for the self-confident and self-determined Fuller, the prospect of public exposure brought on a frisson of fear.[29]

Published on June 4, 1844, *Summer on the Lakes* was well received. Lydia Maria Child congratulated Fuller on her "highly agreeable book, full of touches of beauty, and original piquant sayings," but she thought it necessary to add that Fuller wrote with "too much *effort.*" "Your house is too full," she added; "there is too much furniture in your rooms. This is the result of a higher education than popular writers usually have; but it stands much in the way of extensive popularity."[30]

Orestes Brownson's comments in his *Quarterly Review* were the glaring exception. Brownson, who was undergoing a religious crisis in 1844, was acutely sensitive to Fuller's radical critique of Christian institutions and to her ironic comments on missionary activities with the Indians, on woman's place in the emerging society, and on church authority. He called her "a heathen princess, though of what god or goddess we will not pretend to say."[31]

Although *Summer on the Lakes* never became a big seller, the first two printings of the first edition sold briskly. Fuller wrote to William Channing, urging him to promote *Summer on the Lakes* among his Philadelphia and Cincinnati friends. "Outward success in this way is very desirable to me, not so much on account of present profit to be derived, as because it would give me advantage in making future bargains, and open the way to ransom more time for writing."[32]

Such a bargain came more quickly than she could have hoped, from Horace Greeley, who had admired her pieces in the *Dial* and republished many of them in his newspaper. The *New-York Weekly Tribune*'s review of June 15 proclaimed that *Summer on the Lakes* embodied "the observations of one of the most original as well as intellectual of American women." Greeley was impressed with Fuller's ability to look beneath the surface appearances of American life to uncover troubling areas of concern. In the late spring or early summer of 1844, he asked her to expand her "Lawsuit" article for publication in book form. At the end of the summer he also offered her the job of literary editor of the *New-York Daily Tribune*. The rumor was that her salary would be a generous $500 a year.[33]

Though her book's success was satisfying, Margaret was still in a slump, suffering possibly from William Hull Clarke's rejection. There is some evidence that during a trip east in March, Clarke renewed his friendship with her, raising her expectations, only to complicate their relationship by showing a preference for the company of Sturgis. Her brother Richard wrote of a rupture at about this time between Fuller and "some lady friends of beautiful artistic taste and rare culture." He explained that Fuller's "heart had become so much knit to them that it was a long and cruel work to disengage her affection." Sturgis and her sister Ellen Hooper would answer to Richard's description, as would her life-long friends, Elizabeth Randall Cumming and her sister, Belinda. But if Fuller's low spirits at this time stemmed from her belief that Sturgis had stolen William Clarke's affection, though the pain may have been great, there was no rupture with her.[34]

At the same time Fuller was worrying about her future. After five years the novelty and excitement of her Conversations had worn thin and the attendance was dwindling. She suspected that it was only a matter of time before she would have to find another means of support. But by all the customs of her class and country, her duty as the only unmarried daughter was to follow the examples of her Aunt Abby Crane in Canton and her Aunt Elizabeth Fuller in Merrimack and devote herself to the companionship and care of her aging mother. Aware "that this time is one of especial importance, and I wish to mark each day as it goes by," she started a new journal at the beginning of May.[35]

On May 23, 1844, Margaret's thirty-fourth birthday, Ellen gave birth to a daughter, who was named Margaret Fuller Channing. "I . . . hoped it would have been a boy," Margaret wrote Caroline. "However," she reasoned, "my star may be good for a girl, educated with more intelligence than I was. Girls are to have a better chance now I think."[36]

While Margarett Crane Fuller was in Concord helping with the new baby, Sturgis came to stay with Fuller in Cambridge. For the moment, they were getting along very well, but Fuller knew that the volatile Sturgis could turn away from her at any moment. During the summer she had a disturbing dream in

1. Margaret Fuller, July 1846. Courtesy of the Schlesinger Library, Radcliffe College.

2

3

4

5

6

7

2. Margarett Crane Fuller, oil portrait by an unknown artist, 1820s. Courtesy of Edward Cushing.

3. Timothy Fuller, oil portrait, probably painted with that of his wife in the 1820s, at the time of the family's prominence and prosperity. Courtesy of Willard P. Fuller, Jr.

4. George Thomas Davis, 1858. Courtesy of the Harvard University Archives.

5. James Freeman Clarke, 1858. Courtesy of the Harvard University Archives.

6. Caroline Sturgis Tappan, about 1850. Courtesy of the International Museum of Photography, the George Eastman House, Rochester, N.Y.

7. Samuel Gray Ward in his twenties. From an oil portrait by William Page. Courtesy of John H. Mansfield.

8. Anna Barker Ward at age seventeen. From an oil painting by Henry Inman. Courtesy of John H. Mansfield.

8

9

9. Giovanni Angelo Ossoli, late 1840s. Courtesy of the Houghton Library, Harvard University.

10. James Nathan, from a picture accompanying a 1902 review of *The Love Letters of Margaret Fuller* in *Literary Digest*.

11. Lidian Jackson Emerson with her son, Waldo, 1838 or 1839.

12. Elizabeth Barrett Browning, 1858.

13. Adam Mickiewicz, 1842, from a charcoal portrait by Witold Pruskowski.

10

11

12

13

14. Margaret Fuller, an engraving from an idealized painting by Alonzo Chappel. Published in Evert A. Duyckinck, *Portrait Gallery of Eminent Men and Women with Biographies* (New York, 1873).

15. Fuller family members. *Standing left to right:* Eugene Fuller, Margarett Crane Fuller. *Seated:* Arthur Buckminster Fuller, Ellen Kilshaw Fuller Channing, Richard Frederick Fuller. Courtesy of Willard P. Fuller, Jr.

16. Margaret Fuller in Italy, 1848. Engraving of painting by Thomas Hicks. Fuller is portrayed in a Venetian setting with a statue of Eros behind her, a nosegay of flowers at her feet, and a courting couple in the arcade.

14

15

17

18

17. Ralph Waldo Emerson in 1847.

18. Margarett Crane Fuller, early 1840s. Courtesy of Willard P. Fuller.

which Sturgis was lost at sea. When Fuller tried to save her, she found her feet "rooted to one spot," and her red robe kept falling off her as the waves washed up Sturgis's "dead body on the hard strand & then drew it back again." Earlier in the summer, after she and Sturgis had slept together, she compared their friendship to that of Ceres and Persephone in Greek myth, and, recalling the spiritual affinity of the two great holy women of Christianity, Elizabeth and Mary, "on the hills of Judea," when the two women were pregnant, she saw a similarity with them also.[37]

Fuller had been so schooled in the beauty of Platonic love that she could not acknowledge openly her sexual responses, either to men or to women. In "Lawsuit," in her discussion of marriage, she had ignored its physical aspects in the interest of emphasizing its spiritual possibilities. She expressed her ideal in terms of mutual development: "Two persons love in one another the future good which they aid one another to unfold." If man thought of himself as a "brother and friend," instead of "the lord and tutor of woman," and both sexes thought of married love as "a love of spirit for spirit" and " 'a stair to heaven,' " there would be no need to specify the rules of marriage or woman's functions and employments. "A great majority of societies and individuals are still doubtful whether early marriage is to be a union of souls, or merely a contract of convenience and utility," she wrote. In her pre-Freudian world, the carnal side of marriage, sharply separated from the spiritual, fell into the category of a utility, but it was also a very private utility; even when recognized and treasured, its place was in the private world. Fuller called upon women to find their liberation by seeking "Truth and Love in their universal energy." Once this goal was attained, a woman "would never be absorbed by any relation; it would be only an experience to her as to man."[38]

But she was unable to maintain the stance of self-dependence she advocated. Caught between her feelings and her ideology, she fell victim to overwhelming loneliness. On July 4, after Sturgis left and she was alone in the house, she wrote in her journal, "O I need some help. No, I need a full, a godlike embrace from some sufficient love. I know not why, but the wound in my heart has reopened yesterday & today." The next day, while arranging papers, she came upon the letter Sam Ward had written her five years earlier about Platonic love. He had observed "how widely apart are the points from which life is surveyed by those whose personal experience of passion has been thorough, and those in whom it has (though giving brightness to the fancy and earnestness to the thoughts) remained comparatively undeveloped." His psychological assessment that in such people "all the higher classes of emotion[,] all the noble views of life exist, but in a shape that seems sublimated and idealized to the more experienced" irritated her anew. As usual when she felt betrayed, she took refuge in a contemptuous epithet. In her journal she put Ward down as "the sentimental man of the world." Possibly because his analysis implied an experience that evaded her, she regarded it as written proof that he had capitulated to worldly values; nevertheless, she copied the passage into her journal for safekeeping.[39]

In July Sophia Hawthorne invited Fuller to Concord with Sarah Clarke. As an artist herself, Sophia was curious to see the western sketches Sarah was preparing for the second issue of the first edition of *Summer on the Lakes*. Margaret had seen little of the Hawthornes since the summer of their marriage. Once, in January 1843, before her trip to the West, she had asked Hawthorne if he would be interested in having Charles Newcomb as a farm helper and boarder, but Hawthorne turned her down without mentioning that the reason was that Sophia was pregnant. Although Sophia lost that baby, she bore a healthy daughter in March 1844, a few months before Margaret's visit.

After ten happy days at the Old Manse, during which Hawthorne was unfailingly kind and attentive to her, Margaret moved to Ellen and Ellery's house where she soon discovered that Ellery was reverting to his churlish behavior; the responsibilities of parenthood were too much for him. She worried that her namesake, nicknamed Greta, was affected by the discontent in the household. Compared to the Hawthorne daughter, Una, Greta was sickly and pale. Ellen had no milk and brought Greta every day to the Old Manse for Sophia to nurse, a fairly common practice between good friends at the time. Una was a perfect beauty. "She will have a good chance for freedom and happiness in the quiet wisdom of her father, the obedient goodness of her mother," Margaret wrote.[40]

The Hawthorne marriage met Margaret's criteria for the highest type of marriage: two accomplished artists dedicated to the development of each other's aspirations in a peaceful home. Living with them revived her yearning for a close relationship. Her only consolation was that her "curse" was "nothing compared with that of those who have entered into those relations but not made them real: who only *seem* husbands, wives & friends."[41]

In the summer of 1844 the Emersons were not as accessible as usual because Lidian gave birth to a son, Edward, on July 10. Waldo had just finished his second volume of essays, and he read them aloud whenever his friends assembled. His "Essay on Life" was "grand" but "cold," Fuller wrote. She was weary of his "transcendental fatalism," his maddening facility for keeping all the world's ills at a distance. "But lure me not again too near thee, fair Greek, I must keep steadily in mind what you really are." Describing him in her journal condescendingly as a "Sweet child.—Great Sage—Undeveloped Man!" she was delighted when he told her that the device of her coat of arms should be "a ship at sea in a gale" and her motto "Let all drive."[42]

He had said this when she had enclosed in a letter to him sketches of a sistrum, a symbol of the Egyptian goddess Isis, and of an occult emblem comprising two overlapping triangles, one black, one white, encircled within a figure of a serpent emanating rays of energy. Two poems in her journal describing these figures show that she was continuing to develop her personal mythology of feminine power as expressed in several of her *Dial* essays, particularly "Leila," as well as honoring a mystical concept of androgyny far more radical than the challenges to gender stereotypes that she had made in "The Great Lawsuit."

In Fuller's "Leila" poem, she compares a "dusky, languishing and lone" Leila to the goddess Isis, who has the power to civilize even the most brutal men. Other "children" of Leila are the Greek goddesses Hecate and Hebe, both of whom ruled from lonely heights.

> Leila in the Arabian zone
> Dusky, languishing and lone
> Yet full of light are her dark eyes
> And her gales are lover's sighs.
> So in Egyptian clime
> Grows an Isis calm sublime.
> Blue black in her robe of night
> But blazoned o'er with points of light
> The horns that Io's brow deform
> With Isis take a crescent form,
> And as a holy morn inform.
> The magic Sistrum arms her hand
> And at her deep eyes' command
> Brutes are raised to thinking men
> Soul growing to her soul filled ken.
> Dean of the lonely life
> Hecate fed on gloom and strife.
> Hebe on her throne of air
> Only Leila's children are.
>
> Patient Serpent, circle round
> Till in death my life is found
> Double form of godly prime
> Holding the whole thought of time
> When the perfect two embrace,
> male and female, black and white
> Soul is justified in space
> Dark made fruitful by the light,
> And centered in the diamond sun
> Time, eternity are one.[43]

Using phrases that would resound in her revision of "Lawsuit," she described the conflict between her feminine yearnings for love and protection and her "manly" will to dedicate herself to some sort of heroic action. "My history presents much superficial, temporary tragedy. The Woman in me kneels and weeps in tender rapture; the Man rushes forth, but only to be baffled. Yet the time will come, when, from the union of this tragic king and queen, shall be born a radiant sovereign self." She appropriated Emerson's image of the New World's fully mature and self-reliant Man as the new American royalty to her vision of a new Woman embracing the attributes of both kings and queens. In

1838 Emerson wrote, "I wish society to be a Congress of Sovereigns without the pride but with the power." He often spoke of his chosen friends as "kings and queens." His vision was that the American Revolution would be fulfilled when the spiritual power that came to the individual from self-trust would replace the European hierarchical authority derived from force. From childhood Fuller had played with fantasies of royalty. "Incedit regina," her father would call out to her when she assumed a royal distance while nursing a hurt. "Queen Margaret," the Peabody sisters dubbed her in response to her role among the women attending her Conversations. She conceived of her problem now as one of reconciling the male and female elements in her character so as to be able to use the power of both. In "To the Face Seen in the Moon," another poem written that summer when she decided she would turn all her disappointments "to Muse," she wrote:

> But, if I steadfast gaze upon thy face
> A human secret like my own I trace,
> For through the woman's smile looks the male eye

Observing the infants around her that summer, she queried:

And yet where lies this difference between male and female? I cannot trace it. How all but infinite the mystery by which sex is stamped in the germ. . . . Impossible to trace; here am I the child of masculine energy & Eugene of feminine loveliness, & so in many other families.[44]

In the middle of August she jotted in her journal the lines that Mary Ann Evans, the future George Eliot, would find "inexpressibly touching" a few years later: "With the intellect I always have—always shall overcome, but that is not the half of the work. The life, the life, O my God! shall the life never be sweet?" Evans, whose life would parallel Fuller's in many ways and who admitted that she was "not a little desponding now and then," identified with the phrase. "It is a great help to read such a life as Margaret Fuller's," she wrote her friend. Understanding how succinctly the phrase expressed Fuller, Emerson, after her death, selected it from her journal for publication.[45]

She struggled once more that summer with her attraction to Emerson. On August 1, 1844, the tenth anniversary of the emancipation of the slaves in the West Indies, he gave an address for the Concord abolitionists in which he called for full human and constitutional rights for American slaves. The "beautifully spoken" oration excited her, she wrote, "to a new life, and a nobler emulation by Waldo." Yet she still found him an enigma. She was certain that if she could "once know him" she would not be disappointed in him. "But he is hard to know, the subtle Greek!" she concluded.[46]

Early in the summer Sophia Ripley told the Fullers that Brook Farm could no longer put up with Lloyd; he was unable to fit into the new Fourieristic structure of the life there. Elizabeth Palmer Peabody gave him a job in her bookstore, but the trial did not succeed—his "slowness of mind" was too great. During the summer Margaret found him a place in a school in Andover, but no one believed that he would ever become self-supporting. Several years later Peabody wrote Emerson that Hawthorne always said that Lloyd "explained the faults of Margaret."

I don't know if you ever saw that creature. He seems to be the Fuller organization, Fullerism unbalanced, unmixed with the oversoul, which sweetens and balances the original demon, and yet he is unquestionably what the Scotch people call "innocent"; for he is so self sufficient, and exacting, and insolent, unawares, unconsciously, and in the purest good faith. He acts and feels according to his Constitution, and God is responsible for his ugliness. He was sent, perhaps, as a sign that original ugliness could be overcome by a glorious spirit which had a vision of the good and true and beautiful, with a will and determination to conquer. Margaret's life was the result of this strange association.[47]

When George Davis offered Richard a job in his Greenfield law office, the family decided to sell the old Fuller house on Cherry Street in Cambridgeport where they all—except Lloyd—had been born. The sale would bring everyone in the family a windfall of a few hundred dollars. Margarett Crane Fuller decided to live in Canton with her mother and Abby, but she wanted her family to know she was always ready to help with new babies.

The coast was now clear for Fuller to take up Horace Greeley's job offer in New York, but she hesitated. On September 10 she was still unable to "see clearly what course to take," but on September 13, when Greeley came to Cambridge to discuss her final decision, she agreed to start work in December. Sturgis agreed to go with her to stay in Fishkill on the Hudson River where she would revise "Lawsuit." Fuller's last days in Cambridge were spent with the Farrars. She made a quick trip to Concord (made simple now with direct rail service). She had tea with the Hawthornes, spent two hours with the Emersons, and had an "affecting" farewell with Ellen. "I will always be just and tender to her," she wrote.[48]

She also spent a day at Brook Farm where her friends showered her with gifts. Theodore Parker briefed her on what to expect in New York. As her departure approached she had a recurrence of bad dreams, including the one of her mother's death and burial that always accompanied times of stress or separation. The following night, Joe Angier came over to the Farrars with Elizabeth Randall Cumming and her sister Belinda. They sang trios, and Margaret found it "indeed like old times." When she left Boston on October 1, 1844, friends and students came to the station to wave goodbye. One of the last faces she saw from the train window was of the loyal, admiring, effusive Elizabeth Palmer Peabody.[49]

Years before, the Reverend Mr. Channing had chided Fuller for her treatment of Peabody, saying, "Miss Fuller, when I consider that you are and have all that

Miss Peabody so long wished for, and that you scorn her, and that she still admires you,—I think her place in heaven must be very high." In most of Fuller's relationships she had suffered "because the sympathy, the interest, were all on [her] side," as she had recognized by the time she was twenty. Now, as she was leaving New England with her obligations to friends and family paid in full and overpaid, and with the confidence to start a new life on her own, Peabody's selfless faithfulness made her feel guilty. "I admit I have never done you justice," Margaret confessed to her in a letter from New York. Admitting that she would always be in Elizabeth's debt, she asked her to "pardon all that must be to you repressing—and unpleasant in me." Fuller faulted Peabody for her "tendency to extremes" and to infatuation, weaknesses Fuller had always blamed herself for in her private journals. She thought she had finally vanquished these demons in herself, but she would soon discover in New York that they would reappear in different guises.[50]

Persist to ask, and it will come, / Seek not for rest in humbler home; / So shalt thou see, what few have seen, / The palace home of King and Queen.

Woman in the Nineteenth Century

WHILE LIVING in a boardinghouse with a view overlooking the Hudson River, Fuller and Sturgis spent their days walking in the hills, taking excursions on the river, and writing: Fuller on her revision of "The Great Lawsuit," and Sturgis on a collection of stories for children. In November Ellery Channing joined them for a three-day junket into the Catskills. Horace Greeley had also added Ellery to the *Tribune*'s literary department, and after settling Ellen and Greta with his family in Boston, he stopped over on his way to the new job. Another visitor was Christopher Pearse Cranch, who had forsaken his divinity school education to become a poet-artist. He came with his wife, Elizabeth De Windt Cranch, whose parents owned Locust Grove, a nearby estate. The Cranches were now living on Amity Place in New York, and their large house was a haven for artists and poets. William Henry Channing boarded with the Cranches when he was in town. William, too, visited Margaret and Caroline at Fishkill Landing.

Another of Fuller's friends nearby was Georgiana Bruce, the adventurous Englishwoman whom she had met at Brook Farm. She was now working as an assistant warden of women prisoners under the innovative Eliza Farnham at Sing-Sing Prison in Ossining, New York, on the Hudson, about forty miles south of Fishkill Landing. Fuller, with the thought that she might one day write a self-culture novel for women based on the *Wilhelm Meister* model, had been encouraging Bruce to send her sketches of the life histories of her charges, many of whom were prostitutes. "[T]heir degradation" highlighted the plight of women in general, Fuller explained in a letter to Bruce, "for a society beats with one great heart." She arranged to visit the prison the last weekend in October with Sturgis and William Channing, who was experienced in prison visiting. The plan was that he would talk to the men prisoners while Fuller talked to the women.[1]

Writing in advance for advice on how to handle herself, Fuller was curious to know whether she was right in assuming that the black women would speak more freely than the whites, and she wondered how the prostitutes viewed the whole concept of chastity. "Do they see any reality in it," she asked Bruce, "or look on it merely as a circumstance of condition, like the possession of fine clothes? You know novelists are fond of representing them as if they looked up to their more protected sisters as saints and angels!" Bruce thought the question was naive; she took the view that chastity was a state of mind that depended on one's options more than anything else. Fuller did not manage to "touch" the level of the prisoners during her talk with them, Bruce wrote later, even though she told them earnestly that she was writing about women and wanted to understand their situation.[2]

Whether or not Fuller inspired the prisoners, the Sing-Sing visit inspired her with new ideas for the revision of "Lawsuit." In her plea on behalf of prostitutes and suggestions as to how genteel women should respond, she added her voice to the reform discourse on a problem that was arousing increasing public concern as prostitution was becoming more openly visible on the streets, in the theaters and places of amusement. "[S]till a street trade of independent work-ers," prostitution was rapidly becoming urbane and accepted as endemic to city life. (Robert Carter in his 1845 book, *Life in New York,* noted that "a committee of the board of aldermen estimated" that there were "ten thousand of the bad women residing among us.")[3]

Basing her analysis on prison interviews, Fuller put forth an argument that placed some of the responsibility on middle-class women. When Fuller asked women prisoners to explain how they had come to Sing-Sing, she found that "love of dress, love of flattery, love of excitement," was the cause. "They had not dresses like the other ladies, so they stole them; they could not pay for flattery by distinctions, and the dower of a worldly marriage, so they paid by the profanation of their persons," she wrote, asking if the privileged, were "not answerable for those women being in prison." While the Female Moral Reform Society had long faulted envy of fine clothes as a leading cause of woman's fall, Fuller's argument moved the debate into the dangerous arena of class when she suggested that some women might choose prostitution as an alternative to the dreariness of a home life of poverty and family stress. At a time when pros-titutes were viewed as either innocent victims or depraved reprobates, Fuller's appeal for greater understanding of the underlying causes of prostitution was an extension of the social criticism and reform spirit that had been emerging in her writings beginning with the publication of "Lawsuit." She not only indicted frivolous women of fashion for providing a "pernicious example," but for the first time she urged women to express their Muse quality in social action— either to join in "organized measures of reform" or to act in private by seeking out "these degraded women, give them tender sympathy, counsel, employment. Take the place of mothers, such as may have saved them originally."[4]

Fuller's attack on the double standard as the major cause of prostitution and the standard's relation to the sexual subordination of women of all classes is stated unequivocally. Were not men as guilty of the crime of seduction as women were of a "proneness" to being seduced? Recalling the well-advertised case of a New York prostitute, Amelia Norman, who had been arrested for stabbing her seducer on the steps of Astor House, Fuller predicted that the decision in the case would become an important legal precedent. (Norman was acquitted, partly as a result of the support of Lydia Maria Child, who attended the trial and publicized it in her "Letter from New York," a regular column in the *Boston Courier*.) No change could be expected until men understood their responsibility.[5]

In response to the controversy brewing among the Transcendentalists over the means of transforming society—changing social institutions versus changing individual values—Fuller was now taking a middle course. Horace Greeley, who had commissioned her work, was one of the best-known institutional reformers of the day, but her message was geared to awaken the consciousnesses of individual women, so, while she faulted patriarchal institutions for women's restrictions, the locus for reform remained the inner life of the solitary soul.

These bad institutions, indeed, it may always be replied, prevent individuals from forming good character, therefore we must remove them. Agreed, yet keep steadily the higher aim in view. Could you clear away all the bad forms of society, it is vain, unless the individual begin to be ready for better. There must be a parallel movement in these two branches of life.[6]

One of Greeley's enthusiasms was Fourierism or some form of voluntary associationism as a way of maintaining harmony between employers and workers without disturbing the capitalist system, which he believed could be made to work for the benefit of all. From 1841 to 1843 he had given the American promoter of Fourierism, Albert Brisbane, front-page space to advertise Americanized forms of the Phalanx program to a mass audience. Whether at Greeley's suggestion or because her visits to Brook Farm and the proselytizing of William Henry Channing had aroused an interest, she read Fourier before going to New York and took notice of him in her revision of "The Great Lawsuit," commending him for placing "Woman on an entire equality with Man" and contrasting his social theory with Goethe's. "Fourier says, As the institutions, so the men!" Warning Fourier that no "flourish of trumpets for attractive industry" can reform "unready men," she turned to Goethe's motto, "As the man, so the institutions," and rebuked him with, "Ay! but, Goethe, bad institutions are prison walls and impure air, that make him stupid so he does not will."[7]

When Greeley first urged Fuller to expand her *Dial* essay for publication as a book, he noted particularly that she had not said enough about "the need of providing a greater range of employment for women." She added a section on this theme, but she steered clear of making specific recommendations; women, she believed, should be free to try any occupation that appealed to them. "But if you ask me what offices they may fill; I reply—any," she wrote exultantly. "I do not care what case you put; let them be sea-captains, if you will." This was the phrase that Greeley seized upon afterward as the keystone remark of Fuller's book. He quoted it whenever he wrote about her. Though it became the watch-word of her feminism in the public mind, the offhand quality of the remark in the autumn of 1844 indicates how little Fuller was then concerned with the specific problems of women and work.[8]

The insertions in *Woman in the Nineteenth Century* directed at immediate social problems did not distract from the original message of "The Great Law-suit." Even more strongly, she urged women to be wary of entering into mar-riages that would lead to excessive dependence. An honorable celibacy was not only infinitely preferable but recommended as an important stage in self-realization with apotheosis as a final goal.

I wish woman to live, *first* for God's sake. Then she will not make an imperfect man her god, and thus sink to idolatry. Then she will not take what is not fit for her from a sense of weakness and poverty. . . .
   By being more a soul, she will not be less Woman, for nature is perfected through spirit. Now there is no woman, only an overgrown child.[9]

To strengthen her claim that throughout history and in every culture wom-en's strengths had been recognized, Margaret added dozens of new literary allusions and quotations, ranging from Xenophon to John Quincy Adams, and expanded her chronicle of famous queens in history. She inserted a paragraph on women and mysticism and an appendix of references to archetypal women in religion, myth, and literature, including a description of her own mystic fascination, Isis. Central to her stream of thought was the idea that the man-ifold positive versions of women in ancient myth, especially the virgin god-desses, held a key to the possibilities for women who had the courage to begin life on a new course. Fuller's vision was one of feminine empowerment through which women could participate equally with men as the two sexes moved forward into an era of unlimited possibilities. Throughout the book, she spoke of a "new era," "the coming age," "the reign of love and peace," "an era of freedom and new revelations."[10]

She was not happy about dropping "The Great Lawsuit: Man *versus* Men, Woman *versus* Women" as her title, but she gave in to advice that she find something less perplexing. The new title, *Woman in the Nineteenth Century,* emphasized her prophecy that a new era for women was in the making, but it forfeited her wish to illuminate how the "prejudices and passions" of the time obstructed "the growth of the individual." In her preface, added at Emerson's suggestion, she explained that her reference to "Man *versus* Men, Woman *versus* Women" was so worded only to draw attention to a principal point.

By man I mean both man and woman: these are the two halves of one thought. I lay no especial stress on the welfare of either. I believe the development of the one cannot be effected without that of the other. My highest wish is that this truth should be distinctly and rationally apprehended, and the conditions of life and freedom recognized as the same for the daughters and the sons of time.

She hoped that her women readers would use her suggestions as a starting point from which they could begin to "search their own experience and intuitions" for even more ideas on the subject of women's position. She wanted them to "fill up with fit materials the trenches that hedge them in" and develop leaders from their own ranks in order to expand woman's sphere. From her men readers she asked only for "earnest attention."[11]

Holding firmly to her theories of sexual difference and gender multiplicity, she retained her call for greater development of the Minerva qualities in women, while at the same time speaking in greater support of the Muse side of woman's nature than she had in "The Great Lawsuit." Now she claimed that the "unimpeded clearness of the intuitive powers," as expressed in poetry, prophecy, and particularly the ability to inspire others, was the most promising feminine quality; she predicted that when women were free to make full use of this gift in a wide range of endeavors they would take their place among the great creative artists. Women were "especially capable" of poetic insights, she pointed out. "Even without equal freedom with the other sex, they have already shown themselves so, and should these faculties have free play, I believe they will open new, deeper and purer sources of joyous inspiration than have as yet refreshed the earth."[12]

Woman in the Nineteenth Century was intended for a much wider audience than the Transcendentalist sympathizers who read the *Dial*, and many of Margaret's friends had complained that her meaning was sometimes lost in "The Great Lawsuit"; nonetheless, she made no effort to soften the millennial tone of her discourse or to tighten the logical progression of her arguments. She wrote in a rush of inspiration, just as she spoke. Speaking and prophesying from direct experience, she felt under no obligation to be strictly coherent. For her, in this case, the essential elements of communication were the steadiness and intensity of the inspiration, spontaneity and sincerity, not the order of thought. She made only a few changes in the original text, and her insertions and additions did not help to clarify her argument: It proceeded as before, marked by unexpected leaps, digressive eruptions, provocative juxtapositions, loose associations, and a disruptive multiplicity of voices.[13]

Toward the end, hoping to help her readers follow what she called "the stream which is ever flowing from the heights of my thought," she introduced a rough summary of her "points"—why she believed that the hope of equality "would receive an ampler fruition, than ever before, in our own land." She ended with a prayer and a poem asserting her faith in the golden age to come in America, when both sexes would reign as equal monarchs in a land dedicated to the constant improvement of mankind. Her poem concludes:

> Persist to ask, and it will come,
> Seek not for rest in humbler home;

So thou shalt see, what few have seen,
The palace home of King and Queen.[14]

On November 17, when Fuller completed her manuscript, she wrote Emerson matter-of-factly that she had at last "spun out [her] thread." She reserved the expression of her triumphant sense of accomplishment for William Henry Channing on the same day: "I felt a delightful glow as if I had put a good deal of my true life in it, as if, suppose I went away now, the measure of my foot-print would be left on the earth."[15]

She asked Channing to contact Greeley as soon as possible about the publishing arrangements. She was willing to pay for the expense of publication herself but thought that her sales would be higher if a publisher would back the book. But she would turn over the rights for only a single edition, she wrote, because she intended to "make it constantly better" and wanted to "retain full command of it, in case of subsequent editions." The book had already taken on a life of its own; she wanted full control of its growth.[16]

For all her enthusiasm and high expectations, Fuller was not deceived about the potential commercial value of her product. She told William Channing—who had encouraged her the previous summer to think in terms of an edition of 1,500—that a more realistic figure would be 1,000. She knew that the many literary and historical allusions made the book difficult going for the average reader. "I shall be satisfied if it moves a mind here and there and through that others; shall be well satisfied if an edition of a thousand is disposed of in the course of two or three years."[17]

When Horace Greeley first discussed the book with Fuller, he said the publishing terms would be better if she could persuade Emerson to write an introduction. When asked, Emerson pleaded that he was preoccupied with the publication of his second collection of essays and could oblige her only if she could delay publication for several months. His response was fully in character. Although *Woman in the Nineteenth Century* can be read as an application of Emerson's doctrine of self-culture to the woman question, it would have been surprising had he readily agreed to add his name to the work. Like Margaret herself in her earlier years, he avoided being associated with causes, even on such issues as slavery, where he felt deeply. He viewed reform movements as superficial skirmishes, a reshuffling of the cards. Reforms in institutions came about when a majority of those affected changed from within and insisted on external changes to accommodate the new reality. While recognizing that there was substance in the agitation for a wider sphere of action for women, Emerson took the view that where women were concerned biology was destiny. "I find them all victims of temperament," he wrote. "Nature's end of maternity,— maternity for twenty years,—was of so supreme importance, that it was to be secured at all events." Thus had nature dictated woman's role irrevocably. Endowed with special spiritual and moral gifts, she provided "the heart and sanctuary of our civilization," Emerson wrote. Inasmuch as he put such a high value on the inner life, he saw woman as more than adequately compensated for nature's physical limitations.[18]

Among the lectures Emerson was preparing for publication while Fuller was finishing her book was "Manners." In it he took notice of the woman's rights movement and agreed with Fuller's recommendation in "The Great Lawsuit" that woman must take the lead in discovering what changes were in order. "Certainly let her be as better placed in the laws and in social reforms as the most zealous reformers can ask," he offered, "but I confide so entirely in her inspiring and musical nature, that I believe only herself can show how she is to be served." Since Emerson believed that few women would wish to change their favored and natural situation, this was a shrewd response to the mounting agitation.[19]

At the time *Woman in the Nineteenth Century* was ready for publication, Horace Greeley and his business partner, Thomas McElrath, were publishing a series with the remarkably saccharine title of "Cheerful Books for the People." Fuller's book was introduced as a paperback book in this series; it appeared in the bookstores in mid-February 1845 at fifty cents a copy. Margaret had enough friends among New York's reviewers to give *Woman,* as she called her book for short, a good sendoff. In a notice that appeared in the *Broadway Journal* on February 15, Margaret's old friend Maria Child, praised it for its "noble aspirations" and its "free energetic spirit" but cautioned that certain passages—those alluding to "subjects which men do not wish to have discussed, and which women dare not approach"—would offend some readers. But as the motive was to ennoble human nature the "clean-minded" would not sneer.[20]

The *Tribune* review elaborated on Fuller's noble doctrine of marriage and plea for a single standard in sexual relations. In *Graham's Magazine,* Horace Greeley welcomed the "discussion of the position, capacities and opportunities of women in our age and in Christendom, by one of the most independent, free-spoken, and large-souled of the sex." William Cullen Bryant's *Evening Post* conceded that there was some "pretty strong" language in the book, but "the thoughts it puts forth are so important that we ought to rejoice to know it read by every man and woman in America." Surprisingly, the *Knickerbocker,* which had often ridiculed the *Dial,* conceded that *Woman in the Nineteenth Century* was "a well-reasoned and well-written treatise." At the end of February, Charles Fenno Hoffman, the former editor of the *Knickerbocker* who kept a close eye on New York's literary events, wrote that "Miss Fuller's 'Women [*sic*] in the Nineteenth Century' begins to make some talk." In Boston, Elizabeth Palmer Peabody, Sr., wrote to her daughter Sophia Hawthorne that "Margaret's book has made a breeze." George William Curtis made a joke of Fuller's suggestion that women remain single until they are sure of their needs. He wrote his fellow

Brook Farmer John S. Dwight that he had every intention of marrying in order to "spite" Miss Fuller's theory that "celibacy is the great fact" of the age.[21]

By the time Eugene wrote from New Orleans in early March that he had seen a notice of the book in a local newspaper, Margaret was beginning to feel that she was on the brink of a successful literary career. On March 2 she wrote to Richard (who was still burdening her with all the family problems):

> I have now a position when if I can devot[e] myself entirely to use its occasions, a noble career is before me yet. I want to be unimpeded by cares which I cannot, at this distance, attend to properly. I want that my friends should *wish* me now to act in my public career rather than towards them personally. I have given almost all my young energies to personal relations. I no longer feel inclined to this, and wish to share and help impel the general stream of thought.[22]

But even as she was establishing herself, some of the wind was being taken out of her sails. On March 1 Charles Frederick Briggs, the erstwhile coeditor with Edgar Allan Poe of the *Broadway Journal,* began an attack on *Woman* that Poe later characterized as "silly." Briggs, who was nicknamed Harry Franco after the hero of his one successful novel, *The Adventures of Harry Franco* (1839), had a reputation for being a gentleman-humorist in New York literary circles. The March 8 issue was illustrated with a cartoon entitled "Portrait of a Distinguished Authoress"; it showed a lean, ringleted woman squinting into a magazine. The caption—written by Poe—explained that the woman was reading "one of our criticisms upon her penultimate ode 'To the Universe.' "[23]

Briggs was a close friend of James Russell Lowell, who along with other members of his Cambridge Brother and Sister Club thought that Fuller had too high an opinion of herself. Whether Briggs thought it a joke to ridicule Fuller or wished to diminish her as a favor to Lowell, the *Broadway Journal* review was among the most negative to appear in a respected New York journal. Briggs charged Fuller with "wasting the time of her readers" and ignoring "the law that woman shall reverence her husband, and that he shall be her head." Since she was unmarried and "Woman is nothing but as a wife," Fuller could not be relied upon; "she sees things through a false medium" and could not "truly represent the female character."[24]

Sensible Maria Child wrote Francis Shaw in Roxbury that Briggs's "squibs on Margaret Fuller are, I think, very ungentlemanly. Not because she is a *woman*—but ungentlemanly from one human being to another." She abhorred the name-calling, "the rabid desire for *personalities*" in the press. Briggs "knows no more how to judge of Margaret Fuller, than I do of Goethe's theory of colors," she snapped. "His ideas of women are at least a century behind the age." But Child had to admit that Fuller's work suffered from a major drawback. "Margaret's egotism is a fault much to be regretted. It mars the nobleness of her views, and of her expression. But it is the consequence of her father's early injudicious culture, never *allowed* to forget *herself*."[25]

If Fuller took Briggs's squibs seriously, she did not admit it to Eugene when she wrote him in March that "[a]buse[,] public and private," was "lavished" on the book's "views" but "respect" expressed for her personally. She took heart in the fact that within two weeks of publication the whole first edition was sold out and the publishers presented her with eighty-five dollars. "Not that my object is in any wise money, but I consider this the signet of success. If one can be heard, that is enough!"[26]

The most thorough condemnation came in April from her old adversary Orestes Brownson in his *Quarterly Review*. This time he attacked Margaret as "the chieftainess" of the Transcendentalists, guilty of false pride and a pagan belief in "a terrestrial paradise."

Miss Fuller would have all offices, professions, callings, pursuits thrown open to women as to man; and seems to think that the lost Eden will not be recovered till the petticoat carries it over the breeches. She is quite sure the ancient heathen understood this better than we do.[27]

The *Christian Examiner* called the book "a collection of clever sayings and bright intimations." The *Southern Quarterly* was shocked—Fuller's treatise encouraged women to begin

mingling with man in the pursuit of knowledge, assuming a masculine tone of mind, tracing out Greek roots like a mad Dacier, telescoping the stars like a Mrs. Somerville or settling the destinies of nations like a Miss Martineau. When a woman begins to do this she is quoad [*sic*] hoc no longer a woman.[28]

Fuller wrote home that "the only notice . . . of the book, I thought worth keeping" was by Charles Lane, an English friend of Bronson Alcott, for the New Hampshire newspaper, the *Herald of Freedom*. Lane had returned to the United States with Alcott and convinced him to establish in Harvard, Massachusetts, a vegetarian community that they called Fruitlands. When the Fruitlands experiment failed after seven months, Lane turned to journalism. His review emphasized the "spiritual tendency" and "the catholic spirit in which the book is penned, the warm enlightened affection, the practical piety, which breathes on every page." It was a book such "as to quicken the reader's soul for immediate action," Lane claimed. He heartily underwrote her conclusion that women must take the responsibility themselves to work their way to a freer life. This was exactly the kind of commentary Fuller felt the book should have evoked.[29]

It disappointed her that, other than Lane, the reviewers failed to catch the religious flavor of her book. To her it was a fervent expression of her religion of aspiration and hope, not only for women but for her country and for the future of the species. She was also depressed that in the midst of her book's growing success so many of her friends had found fault with it. "I have found the stranger more sympathizing and in my belief intelligent than some of my private friends," she wrote Richard. It was not only the usual objections to her style and method that tempered even the most approving reviews, it was the personal comments as well, she confided. Indeed, many of the letters from friends were wounding. When Caroline Sturgis wrote her that it was "not a book to take to heart and that is what a book upon woman should be," she knew that was Caroline's code way of saying that a book about women should deal only with a woman's emotional life. "Are you not inconsistent to reproach me for writing such outside things," she asked Caroline, "and then fear that I will reproduce, even in veils, what I have known that is most interesting? Of what shall I write then?"[30]

John Neal, who had long been associated with "the Woman Question," disappointed her in another way. He thanked her for what she was doing for women, but he criticized her for going "for thought" rather than "for action." As far as he was concerned, "there is no life for woman, till she has a hand in making the law—no chance for her till her *vote* is worth as much as the man's vote. When it is, women will not be fobbed off with six pence a day for the very work a man would get a dollar for." His practical suggestions were just what Margaret had avoided. Her aim was to establish a long-range philosophical and psychological program for women. The greatest hurt of all was hearing from Richard that Waldo Emerson had commented recently that she "ought not to write" because she "*talked* so well."[31]

All Margaret's psychic wounds were as naught in December when she had the great satisfaction of receiving a copy of her book from England, where it had been republished in Clarke's Cabinet Library. Even though she would not receive a penny from the pirated edition, this recognition was a sign of real success. "I . . . am very glad to find it will be read by women there; as to advantage to me the republication will bring me no money but will be of use to me, here, as our dear country folks look anxiously for verdicts from the other side of the water." She had copies sent to three English women writers who had shown interest in the theme in their own writings: Elizabeth Barrett Browning, Anna Jameson, and Harriet Martineau, and she hoped the English edition would spur Thomas McElrath to put out a second New York edition. She suspected he was holding back because "the boldness" of her thinking did not suit his "narrow mind."[32]

Fuller was thirty-five when she gained a solid place among the New York literati with the success of *Woman in the Nineteenth Century*. At the same age, her father had just been elected to the Massachusetts Senate, the first office of his political career. She had already done her best to see that Timothy's determination to give his children the best possible educations and establish them in life had paid off. In her book she had paid homage to her father for believing in "the equality of the sexes" and for instilling in her his own virtues of clear judgment, courage, honor, and fidelity. Now she meant to make a new life for herself on her own terms. Though she could not speak from a lectern in

Congress, she was nevertheless very much in the public eye. Shortly before he died in 1842, the Reverend William Ellery Channing conceded that "[t]he press is a mightier power than the pulpit," and her column was front-paged in the *New-York Daily Tribune*. Horace Greeley claimed that his paper had "half a hundred thousand readers" a day. While Fuller was still far from the fulfillment of her personal aspirations, her book's success was a sign that she could succeed in her public ambitions.[33]

Living with Mary and Horace Greeley and their infant son, "Pickie," in a ramshackle farmhouse on Turtle Bay, a half-hour ride on the omnibus from downtown New York, she could combine the advantages of both country and city life. When Maria Child came out to visit in February 1845, she wrote that she followed Margaret's directions and rode the Harlem omnibus to "*forty-ninth street.*"

But instead of a street, I found a winding zigzag cart-track. It was as rural as you can imagine, with moss-covered rocks, scraggly bushes, and a brook that came tumbling over a little dam, and run [*sic*] under the lane. After passing through three great swing-gates, I came to the house, which stands all alone by itself, and is as inaccessible, as if I had chosen it, to keep people off. It is a very old house, with a very old porch, and very old vines, and a very old garden, and very old summer-houses dropping to pieces, and a very old piazza at the back, overgrown with very old rosebushes, which at that season were covered with red berries. The piazza is almost *on* the East river, with Blackwell's Island in full view before it. Margaret's chamber looks out upon a little woody knoll, that runs down into the water, and boats and ships are passing her window all the time. How anything so old has been allowed to remain standing near New York so long, I cannot imagine. I spent three or four delightful hours with Margaret and then trudged home in the mud, afoot and alone. . . . I like Margaret very much.[34]

The house is kept in a Castle Rackrent style, but there is all affection for me and desire to make me at home, and I do feel so.

Mary and Horace Greeley

THE VERY OLD house at Turtle Bay where Fuller lived with the Greeleys was built as a summer residence by Isaac Lawrence, a president of the United States Branch Bank. Left empty and allowed to decay after the banker's death, the Greeleys moved there after the 1844 presidential election in which the Democrat James Polk soundly defeated the Whig candidate Henry Clay. Having thrown himself vigorously behind his old hero Clay, Greeley described himself as "the worst beaten man on the continent," and moved his family to Turtle Bay from downtown New York where he had lived for thirteen years, "usually within sixty rods" of City Hall.[1]

He claimed that his wife was the one who first proposed Fuller for the job of literary editor and suggested that she live with them and their eight-month-old son, Arthur (nicknamed Pickie). Mary Young Greeley had taken a liking to Fuller when she attended a few sessions of the Conversations in Boston, and their friendship had deepened when visits to Brook Farm coincided. Mary, who had given up a teaching career when she married, was a constant reader and committed to self-improvement. She had a nervous temperament, needed companionship, and thought of Fuller as "a monitor and friend." Horace thought Fuller would have a stabilizing effect.[2]

It was really Mary who forced the move to the country. After losing two children and suffering two miscarriages, she was determined to bring up Pickie in the country air. The family was barely settled when Fuller joined them. People said that the grief and pain of losing her babies had turned Mary into a hypochondriac and ruined her disposition. The "cruel surgical delivery" of one miscarriage in particular had kept her bedridden for six months. At times she went off on tangents and had frequent temper tantrums, and one observer wrote, "Her words had a kind of crack like the report of a rifle." Compulsive about cleanliness but with no taste for domesticity, her housekeeping was as frantic as it was aimless. After several weeks, Margaret admitted that her life was "a queer one" and presented "many daily obstacles of a petty sort," but it did not really matter to her that the house was "kept in a Castle Rackrent style," as she wrote Eugene, since "there is all affection for me and desire to make me at home." Her friends were free to come and go as they pleased, her own eccentricities were tolerated, and the Greeleys even invited Margarett Crane Fuller to visit whenever she wished.[3]

Horace, who worked late and often slept in his office at the corner of Nassau and Ann streets in the Battery, called the farmhouse "an old, desolate rookery" but found it useful as a retreat. He talked of starting a vegetable garden but never got around to it. His *Tribune* was his full-time passion. The first *New-York Tribune* had hit the streets on April 10, 1842, and in less than four years he had turned his dream of a Whig penny daily into a profitable business and a political power. By founding a progressive newspaper capable of mirroring the needs and dreams of a great city in the great new nation, he had hit on the formula for success.[4]

In spite of his dedicated efforts on behalf of Whig candidates, Horace Greeley was not a reliable Whig; the conservatives thought him too radical. He called himself a Democratic Whig. He loved the common folk, the worker, and democracy, but he was excessively afraid of the masses. What kept him in the Whig line was his belief in hierarchical authority. His Bible was Thomas Carlyle's *Past and Present,* which called for an "Industrial Aristocracy, and a class of Noble Masters among Noble Workers." A former journeyman printer himself, he understood decreasing wages and unemployment as social disorders that could be controlled by social arrangements. He was concerned about workers but much more interested in "redeeming" than in "liberating" them. So focused on his causes and getting out the paper, he was a poor businessman; it was not until he took on Thomas McElrath, a dependable Whig conservative, as a partner that the *Tribune* began to make a profit.

A New Hampshire farmboy who left home at fifteen to begin his newspaper career as an apprentice printer in East Poultney, Vermont, Greeley never regretted his lack of a college education. "Of all horned cattle," he growled once, "a college graduate in a newspaper office is the worst."[5] He made jokes about intellectuals, but he respected those he spotted as having literary talent or original ideas. When everyone else was ridiculing the Transcendentalists, he was their most devoted champion in New York. He saw them as educators who were doing the country a service, and he believed they were sincere and unconventional without seriously disturbing the peace. He worshiped Waldo Emerson for his gospel of self-help and admired Thoreau for shunning literary success in favor of literary excellence; later, Greeley was Thoreau's literary agent in New York. A close friend of William Henry Channing, he served with him on the board of the American Union of Associationists (he invested heavily in the Brook Farm community) and—when he went to church—attended Channing's Church of the Future on Crosby Street. "Not that I agree with all that is taught and received as Transcendentalism," he wrote, "but I do like its spirit and its ennobling tendencies."[6]

Soon after settling in with the Greeleys, Fuller wrote Anna and Sam Ward that she was meeting all kinds of new people and getting "a far more various view of life" than ever before. She liked Greeley. "He is a man of the people, and outwardly unrefined, but he has the refinement of true goodness, and a noble disposition. . . . We have an excellent mutual understanding."[7]

Years later, when Horace was asked to comment on his relationship with Fuller, he described it as one of "friendly antagonism." He could not understand how "the best instructed woman in America" could be so obtuse about her health. He and his wife were health enthusiasts, hydropaths and Grahamites whose diet was restricted to cold vegetables and brown bread. It annoyed him that she drank cup after cup of tea and then complained about spinal afflictions, nervousness, and headaches. To Greeley, obeying the laws of health was akin to obeying the moral law. When he drew attention one day to the connection between her severe headache and "her strong potations of the Chinese leaf the night before," she told him that she " 'declined being lectured on the food or beverage she saw fit to take.' "[8]

He made fun of her inconsistencies. While demanding "absolute equality" for women in her writings, she still "exacted a deference and courtesy from men to women, *as* women," Greeley complained. When she asked him to escort her into a room or asked for his company through the dark thickets surrounding the farm, he was apt to quote her "*Let them be sea-captains if they will!*" He backed the idea of "regarding all alike as simply *persons,*—as human beings," but he thought it was "preposterous" to even consider woman suffrage. Greeley had one serious bone of contention with Fuller. He found it hard to accept her lack of "capacity for incessant labor." She told him she could work only when she was in the mood. To an "inveterate hack-horse of the daily press," who could do ten articles to her one, this was heresy. Looking back on her year and a half at the *Tribune,* he was forced to say that her "earlier contributions" were not "her best."[9]

But he put up with her, in part because Mary liked her company and Pickie adored her but also because he needed her in his literary department. The *Tribune* was a Whig newspaper, and the Whigs, suffering badly from the 1844 defeat, had to increase their efforts to appeal to a wider sector of voters. Greeley, with the blessing of Thurlow Weed, was putting on a drive to show the public that Whigs were for the underdog, for the workingman, the immigrant, the homesteader, even the antirenter.

Not that Greeley needed any encouragement. From the start the *Tribune* had been dedicated to "Anti-Slavery, Anti-War, Anti-Tobacco, Anti-Seduction, Anti-Grogshop, Brothels, Gambling houses." Unlike the New England reformer, he did not believe in the essential goodness of mankind. He was fearful of the people, of their capacity to break out and tear society apart. To abate that possibility, Greeley's solution was to build a national ethos of social harmony.[10]

That was why he called his newspaper "The Tribune of the People" and went overboard for reforms. Brotherhood was his watchword, and progress was his gospel. Greeley wanted the Whigs to confront the problems of close conflict, to find a way to preserve some of the harmony between employer and employee that existed in the passing artisan system of labor. Following a program of universal education and equal opportunity, one and all would build together the glorious American future. But, first of all, the people needed those who had seen the light to lead them in the right direction. With this aim in mind he hired Fuller. In his *Tribune* "Prospectus for the Year 1845," he announced that he had just engaged a person "already eminent in the higher walks of Literature" and looked forward to "a decided and gratifying change" in the literature department.[11]

Greeley had republished several of Fuller's *Dial* pieces in his *Weekly Tribune,* but it was *Summer on the Lakes* that convinced him that she was what he needed for his paper. Years after its publication, he was still praising it as "unequaled, especially in its pictures of the Prairies and of the sunnier aspects of Pioneer Life." He thought she had caught the American experience in a moment of transition and given wise warnings of the dangers ahead. When he published *Woman in the Nineteenth Century,* he boasted to his friend, the editor Rufus Griswold: "Margaret's book is going to *sell.* I tell you it has the real stuff in it." Later he repeated: "I tell you it will make its mark. It is not elegantly written, but every line talks."[12]

He admired the gusto with which Fuller wrote about the plight of prostitutes and her ability "to arouse and quicken intellect." She was, he wrote later, "a philanthropist, preeminently a critic, a relentless destroyer of shams and out-worn traditions." Convinced that with some discipline on his part, he could make a newspaperwoman of her, he placed her columns on the first page. Instead of a by-line, she signed herself with a star. Her assignment was to review the important new books, to keep the public informed on new trends in Euro-pean literature, and to cover cultural events in New York. As a part of his effort to instill a sense of mutual responsibility between the classes, Greeley gave her the special task of visiting the city's benevolent institutions and alerting her readers to the conditions in New York's prisons, hospitals, and almshouses.[13]

When Fuller began at the *Tribune,* she worried that her style would be too literary for its general readership; Greeley assured her that she would provide "a vigorous and purifying" element. She explained to Anna and Sam Ward: "[I]t is emphatically an American journal. Its readers want to know about our affairs and our future."[14] Within a short time she demonstrated her grasp of the new cultural situation coming into being in New York: the formation of a metro-politan sensibility that was eager for advice and guidance on how to think about social and cultural events. She became the first full-time practitioner of literary journalism in a city that would later attract to the craft such original thinkers as her friends George Ripley and George William Curtis and the man who was to become her admirer, Walt Whitman, at the time twenty-four years old, earning his living as a printer, and publishing his fiction in the *Star* and the *Democratic Review.*

While Fuller was setting her "plough" in a new direction, as she put it to her mother, Greeley assigned subjects to her. She began her New York career with a review of Emerson's second series of essays (the book that had prevented his writing a preface to *Woman in the Nineteenth Century*) and used her new forum to pay homage to her teacher, to display him, at a time when most writers were catering to public taste and using their talent to earn as much money as possible, as "a father of the country" for his "pure" use of literature—"the discernment and interpretation of the spiritual laws by which we live." She compared Emerson to "the early poets and civic legislators of Greece—men who taught their fellows to plow and avoid moral evil, sing hymns to the gods and watch the metamorphoses of nature." Once having established his preeminence, she agreed with the charges commonly made against him: that his style was obscure and overly subtle and fanciful. She ended with her old complaint against her old friend, his lack of passion and engagement. "We [think] this friend raised himself too early to the perpendicular," she wrote, "and did not lie along the ground long enough to hear the secret whispers of our parent life. We could wish he might be thrown by conflicts on the lap of mother earth, to see if he would not rise again with added powers." It must have been difficult for Emerson, who had suffered so many losses, to read this explanation of his shortcomings.[15]

In her first months on the job, Fuller managed to schedule writing at least two articles a week on a wide variety of subjects. She praised the concerts of Ole Bull, the Norwegian violin virtuoso who was thrilling American audiences with his compositions *Niagara* and *Solitude of the Prairie;* marveled that the New York Philharmonic orchestra had more than fifty instruments; and in her enthusiastic review of the *Liberty Bell,* the annual publication of the Anti-Slavery Society, lauded the high quality of the contributions of Frederick Douglass, "who was only six years since a fugitive from a southern cornfield."[16] In some cases she embraced Greeley's gospel of brotherhood with more moral indignation than optimism. In her review of Henry Schoolcraft's *Oneonta; or, The Red Race of America,* she confessed that she had been brought up like most other Americans to believe "that the Indian obstinately refused to be civilized." It had never occurred to her until her trip to the West, she wrote, "that the white man had no desire to make the red owner of the land his fellow citizen, but [rather] to intoxicate, plunder, and then destroy or exile him." The time had unfortunately passed when "the possessors of the soil might have been united as one family with their invaders," she charged, and went on to instruct that the

Indians were a profoundly religious people whose tales and legends were a priceless part of the American heritage.[17]

In her New York's Day column, she began with a beautiful image of an Indian tribe celebrating the new year with a ceremony in which all the fires were extinguished, and, after "a day of fasting and profound devotion," a new fire was lit "afresh" on the altar and the hearth. In the jeremiad that followed, Fuller looked in vain for signs that "this modern Christian nation" was celebrating the season with any rites of devotion. After denouncing the imminent annexation of Texas as imperialist and as a contrivance to extend the boundaries of slave-holding territory, and commiserating with "ye, sable bands," she prayed to the "All-Wise" to lead the country out of "this labyrinth." She reminded Americans that their nation was chosen for a special destiny: "The whole history of its discovery and early progress indicates too clearly the purposes of Heaven with regard to it." Comparing Americans to the "Chosen People," she added, "We too have been chosen, and plain indications [have] been given, by a wonderful conjunction of auspicious influences, that the ark of human hopes has been placed for the present in our charge." This theme remained the moral under-pinning of much of Fuller's discourse during her career as a journalist. She constantly reminded her readers of the responsibility that Americans bore for the future; it was her obligation, she believed, to identify all who offend against "a heritage like ours."[18]

In January 1845 Fuller came down with the flu and began working at home, another indulgence that annoyed Horace Greeley, but after February 5, when the *Tribune* building on Ann Street went up in flames and the staff was forced into tight temporary quarters on Nassau Street, her preference was tolerated. The manuscript of *Woman in the Nineteenth Century* was in the hands of the printers and escaped the fire. Fuller thought the fire might slow Greeley down a bit, but he continued on with "smiling courage." Ellery was boarding with a series of acquaintances. She hardly ever saw him but had heard that he was complaining about the work.[19]

In late January Fuller began a series of weekly treatments for the back trouble that had plagued her from time to time ever since her father's death. Dr. Theodore Leger, a French doctor, used a form of mesmerism that he called "psychodunamy." Georgiana Bruce, who accompanied Fuller to one of the sessions, described the technique. While Margaret sat on a stool with her back bared, Leger moved his right hand with fingers pointed—but not touching—up and down the vertebral column. "There was a slight trembling of his arm as he *willed* that power should flow from him to the patient." Fuller told Bruce that she felt as if "a rod of iron" was at work in her spine. "Nothing wonderful" happened to her during the sessions, she wrote Caroline, but she seemed to get a great deal of strength from them, and she was interested in everything going on in the establishment while enjoying at the same time the conversation of the "*insouciant* robust" doctor. Skeptical of the many claims for what was generally called "animal magnetism" at the time and aware that most educated people looked on the researches as "folly," Fuller believed nevertheless that there did exist a "super-sensual element" by means of which people could communicate more completely and precisely than was as yet understood. She expected that sometime in the future the mysterious workings of this force would be explained by science.[20]

Ever since her year in Providence at the Greene Street School when the phrenologist Orson Fowler had examined her head and the "blind somnabulist" Loraina Brackett had located the exact spot of her headache, she had been following the experimenters with interest. She had participated in at least one session with Anna Parsons, a Brook Farmer who was credited with unusual "psychometric" powers—the supernormal ability to read character or past history from handling a subject's possessions—and went out of her way to collect material on clairvoyance. The monumental study *The Seeress of Prevorst* especially fascinated her, and she summarized the story of Frederica Hauffe in *Summer on the Lakes* and referred to it again in *Woman in the Nineteenth Century.*[21]

Within two months the results were remarkable: Fuller was so improved that she sometimes walked to the Battery from Turtle Bay. According to the doctor's measurements, her height increased four inches and her shoulders were now equal. Sam and Anna Ward, who came to New York in February to visit Anna's grandparents, were so astonished by her appearance that Anna too put herself under Dr. Leger's care. Sam told Caroline Sturgis that Margaret had grown two inches. Caroline sent her congratulations, along with the wish that Margaret should now "progress in height until your head strikes the stars."[22]

By the time this remarkable transformation was astounding Fuller's friends, she had been seeing almost daily a young man she had met at a New Year's Eve party. James Nathan was a German immigrant with literary ambitions who made his living as a textile wholesaler. A few months younger than Margaret, tall and dark, with piercing blue eyes and a confident manner, he played the guitar, loved going to concerts, and enjoyed sightseeing. In early February, he began inviting her out, and she fell in love with him almost immediately.

Perhaps it is that I was not enough a child at the right time, and now am too childish, but will you not have patience with that?

James Nathan

IN HIS AUTOBIOGRAPHY, *Recollections of a Busy Life,* Horace Greeley remarked that Fuller had all the makings of a great actress. "She had marvellous powers of personation and mimicry," he wrote, "and, had she condescended to appear before the footlights, would soon have been recognized as the first actress of the Nineteenth Century." He mentioned her rich social repertoire, from her "somewhat stately and reserved" manner among strangers to her marvelous and unaccountable "magnetic sway" that attracted intimacies, revelations, and "the most jealously guarded secrets" from chambermaids and seamstresses as well as from those of "her own plane of life." Emerson too was fascinated by her skill at drawing people to her: "Persons were her game; a marked person—marked by fortune or character,—these were her victims," he wrote, implying a certain helplessness on the part of her quarry, himself included.[1] Yet, in her five-month affair with James Nathan, she set aside her sophisticated strategies and gave herself up to her vulnerabilities. Now that her professional career required that she perform as Minerva in public, she found release in giving free rein to the Muse in a private relationship. She may have felt that she was in control of the emotions that interacted between the two poles of the Minerva–Muse spectrum, but the experience was to reinforce her warnings of the dangers of unchecked emotional involvement.

Fuller's nineteenth-century biographers made no mention of her romance with James Nathan. Several of her friends knew about the interlude but kept all reference to it out of their reminiscences. Like Mrs. Gaskell (Elizabeth Cleghorn Stevenson) faced with Charlotte Brontë's love for Constantin Heger, for them the evidence was partial and the situation complex. The public could easily misconstrue the episode which, in any event, did not reflect well on the subject; moreover, memoirs of literary women were written under myriad constraints of propriety.

After Fuller's death, at the time her friends and family were planning to write a memoir of her, Fuller's brothers commissioned William Henry Channing to ask Nathan, who was living in New York, to return Fuller's letters. He refused, and, according to Caroline Sturgis (Tappan), who heard about the negotiations at second hand, Nathan remarked that no one can "write a biography of Margaret without his letters to her; he wishes to have them himself." At the end

of the century, her letters, somewhat expurgated, were published with an introduction by Julia Ward Howe, comments from Emerson and Greeley, and a
preface by James Nathan, who had changed his name to Gotendorf. If Caroline
Sturgis Tappan's hearsay information was correct, his letters written to Fuller in
early 1845 were presumedly in his possession after Fuller's death. They have
never been discovered. Without them, the story of Fuller's relationship with
him, as told, is one-sided and perhaps totally deceptive. One hears in them a
Fuller voice that had not spoken for years, not since George Davis had stopped
visiting the Dana Mansion; it is a beseeching and tentative voice, afraid of
making a fatal mistake. It does not sound like the Fuller who was at the same
time writing bold newspaper copy signed with a star.[2]

When Fuller met James Nathan, he was a prosperous businessman who had
begun to cultivate friendships in New York literary circles. Drawn to him at first
by his "boldness, simplicity and fervor," she wrote, she also admired him as
someone "who combined force with tenderness and delicacy." He had arrived
in New York in 1830 a penniless nineteen-year-old immigrant. "Our education
and relations are so different," she wrote him later. His foreignness, his accent,
his difference from the New England men she had known added to his attrac-
tiveness and the sense of adventure she felt in his company. "My thoughts were
interested in all you told me, so different from what I knew myself," she explained in April after confessing that she felt "a strong attraction" to him. She
had probably never met a Jew before, and if she had a preconception, it was that
he would be exotic, exciting, and experienced—"worldly," in the language of
New England transcendentalism. But she had not expected, as she wrote him
soon after they met, that he would be so "gentle and civilized" and "with blue
eyes!" He played the guitar and loved music and poetry. Certainly he could not
help but offer a rich, new experience, and Fuller still held to Goethe's theories
of personal growth through absorbing personal relationships as expressed in
Wilhelm Meister.[3]

On their first outing together, they went to see a panoramic model of the city
of Jerusalem; thereafter, Margaret wrote him that she hoped he would explain
modern and ancient Jewry to her. He might be her key to understanding the
modern emancipated German Jew she had been reading about in the foreign
reviews: the circle of the Schlegels, Rahel Varnhagen's salon, Heinrich Heine,
Ludwig Börne, and Felix Mendelssohn. In April, when she was meeting Nathan
constantly, she wrote a review for the *Tribune* on "The Modern Jews," providing
background sketches of leading German Jewish literary personalities and noting that many of "the celebrated personages . . . who have had so great an
influence on the present state of literature, are not of Christian birth."[4]

When Fuller and Nathan first began seeing each other, they spent a few
evenings with the Greeleys at the farm, but Mary Greeley objected to Margaret's
having a gentleman caller (an attitude she reversed a month later), and Fuller

steered Nathan into meetings in town. Sometimes they met at the Cranches on Amity Street or at Lydia Maria Child's rooms on East Third Street. (Edmund Benzon, a German-born businessman and devoted friend of Child, was also friendly with Nathan at this time.) Sometimes Fuller and Nathan arranged brief encounters during the workday at some spot between the *Tribune* office on Nassau Street and Nathan's business on Cedar Street. Fuller had free press tickets to all the musical events, and he often accompanied her.

When Nathan, on their first outing, described his condition on arriving homeless in America fifteen years before, Fuller was instantly aroused to sympathy. As he poured out his aspirations for a literary career and his dreams of a better future for his people, she found herself in her element. Here was another idealistic young man whom she could encourage. Calling on her long experience in the role of inspiring mother-figure, she thought he might respond to her ability to "refine, expand, and exalt" him and told him so, but unlike her younger brothers and her New England protégés, Nathan had been self-supporting since his teens. He was poised, self-educated, and experienced; he knew several other women authors in New York; he was not looking for a spiritual guide.[5]

In his preface to her love letters to him, he wrote that Fuller's "high intellectuality, purity of sentiment and winning conversation" captivated him; yet, during their romance in the spring of 1845, he made light of her literary accomplishments, submitting to her repeated requests that he indulge her in what she described as her "pet dream," to walk like a child with a "brave playmate."[6] The secret of Nathan's powerful attraction lay in his willingness to play this role and the release it gave Fuller, now that she was free of the burden of daily family cares and able to live an independent life in the relative anonymity of a big city. She may have seen in him some of the characteristics of the tutor and counselor Ephraim in Bettina von Arnim's *Correspondence of Fraulein Günderode and Bettina von Armin,* the book she had partially translated. Always looking for coincidences in names, Fuller may have hoped that he would turn out to be a Nathan the Wise, who, like the sage in Lessing's famous play, would help her to a deeper self-understanding, a mission that her Concord sage, Emerson, had failed to fulfill.

Careful not to rush their friendship, Fuller addressed him as "Mr. Nathan" until the end of February; through most of March and early April, he was "dear friend." Later he became "mein liebster," the German for "my beloved." By that time she was still attempting to keep the relationship on a spiritual level while showering him with almost daily letters of subjection and surrender. She gave him a copy of *Woman in the Nineteenth Century* soon after they met; she tried desperately to guide the relationship according to the theory there projected that both sexes sought for completion in opposite qualities and that true love was based on a solid foundation of ideal friendship.[7]

She had just fitted Nathan comfortably into her life when she heard from a landlady in his neighborhood the disturbing news that he had a connection with an English girl. The gossip was that he was living with her. Nathan, aware of Fuller's recommendations in *Woman in the Nineteenth Century* and her work rehabilitating women prisoners, gave as his excuse that, in his efforts to help "an injured woman," he had unfortunately " 'broken through the conventions of this world' "; he had taken in the young woman for her own protection—she was his ward. Fuller, hoisted by her own petard, after a thoughtful delay, accepted this explanation but worried that the story would become known and his reputation would suffer. Her magnanimity was faultless:

I am myself exposed to misconstruction constantly from what I write. Also there have been circumstances in *my* life, which if made known to the world, would[,] judged by conventional rules, subject me as probably to general blame, as these could you. They will, probably, never be made known, but I am well prepared for the chance. Blame could not hurt me, for I have not done wrong, and have too much real weight of character to be sunk. . . . As I feel for myself, so do I for a friend. You are noble. I have elected to abide by you.[8]

Assuming an air of disdain for convention for convention's sake, Fuller fell for the deception and even offered to help with the rehabilitation of the young woman. Perhaps she was more aware than appears and had decided to run the risk for the sake of a rich, new experience, but the persona she presented was hardly that of the sophisticated woman of the world; rather, she seemed to insist on appearing as a playful, innocent ingenue, trustingly offering up the freshness of her spirit and the purity of her instincts to a man of experience.[9]

At the end of March, Nathan told her he was planning to leave New York, possibly within the next few weeks. He had an urge to travel—he wanted to fulfill an old desire to see Jerusalem and the Holy Land. It startled her, she told him, that he did not prize her enough to want to stay with her longer, but his imminent departure only made the drama more poignant. She told him repeatedly that she wanted him to be "the actor and the voice," while she (like Bettina with Goethe) followed along "like a child . . . close to the side of my companion listening long to his stories of things unfamiliar to my thoughts." Indeed, if he was using her inexperience to his advantage, she found an opportunity for regression in his indifference to the rules of the New England conscience.[10]

After Mary Greeley changed her mind about Nathan and welcomed him to the farm, he gave Margaret his Newfoundland dog, Josie, with the understanding that she would take care of him while he was on his travels. Interpreting this as a sign of trust and a pledge of his intention to return to her, Margaret's letters became more yielding and suggestive. "I am with you as never with any other," she told him, and compared her thoughts to flower roots preparing for a later bloom when, "lonely in the confidential night, they will return a blessing for all that has been given." When he misunderstood and made physical advances, she was confused. She admitted that his personality had a "powerful magnetic effect" on her and that it did seem that the time had come to express what she felt for him; yet she had always "attached importance to such an act" and found that she simply "could not." A few days later she wrote him that she was ready to give up her reserve and act just as she felt, but she expected him to protect her. She understood he was more worldly and direct than she, a "man of the world." He looked at things with more "common sense," but he was "less refined"; she wished he would put aside his "prudence and calculations, and arrangements." He responded that he had "both a lower and a higher" nature than she "was aware of" and that she had no right to disdain him.[11]

By the middle of April, he had taken the offensive and was accusing her of vanity and moral arrogance and telling her that she lived in an unreal world. Apologizing abjectly for her "self-love, pride, and distrust," she promised to change. To her, these condemnations indicated that they had a good deal to learn from each other. She confessed to him that she had been told before that her views on the physical relations of the sexes would probably change if she had "the experience of passionate life." She realized, she wrote, that he needed her to make his life "more poetic," while she needed him to make hers "more deeply real."[12]

"[M]ust we go opposite ways in the same road?" she asked. To help him understand that her passions were not necessarily sensual, she sent him some of her poetry and two poems written to her by admirers—Ellery Channing and Sam Ward—both of them saluting her for her spiritual aspirations. She also took Nathan to hear William Henry Channing preach; he agreed it was an inspiring experience.[13]

She did not make it easy for him to extricate himself. If he had started out merely interested in a mild flirtation with an intriguing literary woman, he soon found himself with more than he had bargained for. He was fair enough to put her on notice more than once that whatever was going on between them was likely to be temporary. In April he told her bluntly that he thought it unlikely that he would ever give his heart wholly to her, adding that he doubted that she would ever understand him. She repeatedly told him she was determined to do so.

Days passed without his answering her letters or agreeing to a rendezvous. Yet, whenever she was about to resign herself to his neglect, he offered some encouragement, to which she clung anxiously, reading multiple meanings into a slight promise or an ambiguous word. When he stayed on in New York through the month of May, a good month longer than he had originally proposed, she was again encouraged. On May Day, when he failed to come out to the farm as arranged, she sent a bouquet of flowers to his boardinghouse. Throughout the month, he claimed he was preoccupied with making arrangements for his departure, but he could have had no illusion as to the hold he had over her emotions and her imagination. Hoping to catch some glimpse of him, she wrote almost daily, telling him when on the following day she would be strolling on Wall Street or in the neighborhood of the Battery. As the month progressed, her letters laid more complex claims on him. She seems to have believed—or wanted to believe—that they were united by a magnetic attraction, by a force beyond their control. At the beginning of May, she wrote:

I hear you with awe assert the power over me and feel it to be true. It causes awe, but not dread, such as I felt sometime since at the approach of this mysterious power, for I feel deep confidence in my friend and know that he will lead me on in a spirit of holy love. . . . I have deep mystic feelings in myself and intimations from elsewhere.
   . . . I long to be human, but divinely human. . . . Are you my guardian to domesticate me in the body, and attach it more firmly to the earth? Long it seemed that it was only my destiny to say a few words to my youth's companions and then depart. I hang lightly as an air plant. Am I to be rooted on earth, oh choose for me a good soil and a sunny place, that I may be a green shelter to the weary and bear fruit enough to pay for staying.[14]

When he tried to put the relationship on a cooler footing, she was not discouraged. "I observe that it is with you, as it has been with me in many cases. You attract beings so much that after a while it is too much for their good or your pleasure. Then comes the painful retrograde motion." Toward the end of the month, she suggested that he destroy her letters, "as they are so intimately personal." She begged him to come out to the farm and let her hold his hand while they sat in the new grass. "[I]t does me so much good, the soft warm life close to the earth. Perhaps it is that I was not enough a child at the right time, and now am too childish, but will you not have patience with that?"[15]

When he sailed on the first of June, as a goodbye present she gave him a book of Shelley's poems, and, to encourage him to write to her, she also gave him a fine pencil. He gave her an odd present—a white veil—and after presenting it made her promise not to speculate about its significance. She did not go to see him off, which was just as well since he seems to have taken his English mistress with him. From the day he left in June through the summer months, Fuller wrote him faithfully, and he answered with reasonable frequency. When Fuller received his first letters in mid-July, she wrote him a delighted and newsy letter.

I dont know that any words from your mouth gave me more pleasure, a strange kind of pleasure, than these, "You must be a fool, little girl." It seemed so whimsical that they should be addressed to me who was called on for wisdom and dignity long before my leading strings were off and so pleasant too. Indeed thou art my dear brother and must ever be good and loving as to a little sister.[16]

At Nathan's request, Margaret managed—though with some embarrassment since she was now writing for a Whig newspaper—to get him a letter of introduction from her old friend, the Democrat George Bancroft, now secretary of the Navy in President Polk's cabinet. She eagerly offered to get letters from Edward Everett and from the husband of her friend Julia Ward Howe, Samuel

Gridley Howe, who had a loyal following in Greece, where he had served as a doctor with the Greek army in their battle against the Turks. There was hardly anything she would not do to oblige him. When he wrote that he had been unable to find anyone to take the English maiden off his hands, she was foolish enough to suggest that the English relatives of Mrs. Farrar or even Harriet Martineau might be able to find a domestic position for her.

At the end of August she finally burst forth with the realization that the fantasy she had forced on their relationship had been a mistake:

O the summer! "the green and bowery summer" gone, irrecoverably gone!
Yet, all through it, have I been growing in the knowledge of you. You would be surprised to find how much better I know you than when we parted. But I should have been so much more happy in real than in the ideal intercourse! Why! Why? Yes I must fret, *must must* grieve.[17]

In August, and again in three different issues of the *Tribune* in September, she published sections of his travel letters—considerably edited by her—in a column entitled "Wayside Notes." Explaining that he found it impossible to keep up a correspondence while traveling, he sent only one letter from the first of September to the first of December. By the end of the year she cherished only a wan hope that, when he returned to America or she went to Europe, they would meet again. On the last day of 1845 she wrote reminding him that it was just a year since they had met and begged him not to reveal to anyone what had passed between them. As later developments proved, she was right to worry that he would not keep their relationship private.

I want the mysterious tie that binds us to remain unprofaned forever, and that if in this cruel fatal sphere we are in, we have to bury the sweet form of the Past, that we should do it quite alone, we the only ones that could appreciate its budding charms, how lovely it was, and of capacity how glorious. Then we would weep together and part, and go our several ways alone but we would tell no man.
Promise me this.[18]

She tried to pry out of him a clear statement of how things stood between them; this had been an important romantic experience, and it called for a romantic ending. But James Nathan did not respond to the urgency in her request. Once again, when she had let herself follow the side of her nature that she had described in her autobiographical sketch as "fervent, of strong grasp, and disposed to infatuation, and self-forgetfulness," her Muse side, she had brought disappointment on herself. She was certainly infatuated with James Nathan. Blind, self-forgetful, and tenacious, she gave herself up to her feelings with abandon, suspending her Minerva side, as she experimented with her sensibilities. Nathan, at least, understood what Margaret could not accept in herself—that what she was feeling for him was the simplest of physical yearnings. Rogue that he was, he does not bear all of the blame for escaping from the web of contradictory messages into which she had invited him.[19]

Throughout the time she was seeing Nathan, she was reticent about the connection with her friends. Those who knew that she was seeing him, the Greeleys, Lydia Maria Child, William Henry Channing, and her mother, who visited at Turtle Bay for three weeks in June, were discreet about it afterward. When Nathan sent her, after his departure, a book from his friend Thomas Delf, an agent in London for American publishers, she warned Nathan, "Yet, have no confidante to our relationship! I have had and shall have none. I wish to be alone with you in strict communion." In any event, by the time Nathan left for the Middle East in the late spring of 1845, she was an established literary figure in New York, and her friends at the time seemed to have viewed the affair much as James Nathan did—as a passing interlude.[20]

Years later, Caroline Sturgis wrote Emerson that Fuller's experience in New York was "an new era. The persons she knew best there were more vehement, adventurous & various than her friends here; less moral, less poetical, less beautiful than some she had known, but she enjoyed their freedom from the puritanism that had annoyed her here." Sturgis was certainly thinking of Nathan first of all, but there were many others who easily answered to that description.[21]

CHAPTER 16

*I have to exert myself laboriously and unremittingly,
or give up going to Europe.*

New York, 1845–1846

In 1845 Philip Hone, the wealthy former mayor, wrote in his *Diary,* "The city of New York is so overgrown that we in the upper regions do not know much more about what is passing in the lower, nor the things which are to be seen there, than the inhabitants of Mexico or Grand Cairo."[1]

This wide divide was an expanse that Greeley hoped his newspaper could span. In the early months of working for the *Tribune,* Fuller found that New York life taxed her energies. New York's population of 371,000 was almost four times larger than Boston's 99,036. Both port cities faced working-class riots, labor displacement, and a new wave of immigration, but Boston had just passed through its boom years whereas New York, stagnant during the early years of the decade, was about to become one of the fastest-growing cities of the world. Comparing Boston with New York's "vicious" and turbulent atmosphere that year, N. P. Willis, the veteran social commentator, described Boston as "a Utopian beau ideal of efficiency and order."[2]

Though Horace Greeley was impressed with Fuller's versatility and the high quality of her work, he kept prodding her to turn out reviews on short notice and to meet strict deadlines. He wanted his paper to be the first to print the news in the literary department as well as any other. In April he fired Ellery Channing, and a few weeks later he told Fuller that he would have to postpone a summer trip to the West if she did not take more interest in her work. After Nathan left, she applied herself steadily, and, five weeks later, Greeley indicated he was "content." Fuller was now covering concerts, lectures, art exhibits, American books, and foreign literature as well as social issues. She knew that some of her New England literary friends looked down on penny-press journalism, and she may even have heard that Waldo Emerson had written Sam Ward that it was odd that she and Ellery had forsaken the Muse for the "treadmill"—but she liked the influence her job gave her and thought of herself as a public educator.[3]

Not all of her friends were critical. James Freeman Clarke wrote that her columns were "better written" than anything else she had done; he congratulated her on their "ease, grace and freedom" of style and assured her that she was doing much good. Encouraged, she answered immediately:

I was pleased with your sympathizing about the Tribune. I do not find much among my old friends. They think I ought to produce something excellent, while I am well content for the present to aid in the great work of mutual education in this way. I never regarded literature merely as a collection of exquisite products but as a means of mutual interpretation. Feeling that many are reached & in some degree aided, the thoughts of every day seem worth writing down, though in a form that does not inspire me. Then I like to feel so fairly afloat in mid-stream, as I do here. All the signs of life appear to me at least superficially, and, as I have had a good deal of the *depths*, an abode of some length in the *shallows* may do me no harm. The sun beams fall upon me.[4]

It was exciting to be in on the creation of this new literary endeavor: the use of the popular press to influence culture. Literary criticism was just becoming recognized as a full-time profession, and Margaret was writing sometimes three columns a week. Recent improvements in the printing press, the cheap manufacture of paper, and the rapid rise of literacy were turning the book industry into a profitable business. In earlier periods, the appreciation of literature had been a pastime only for the privileged. As recently as 1837, upon being asked to contribute to the *Democratic Review,* John Quincy Adams had replied that "literature was, and in its nature must always be, aristocratic; that democracy of numbers and literature were self-contradictory."[5]

By the middle of the 1840s there were some two million readers in the United States. The book market was a mass market, and the tone of literature was changing to express a wider range of human experience than ever before. Recognizing that literature was now the province of anyone who could read and write, in the summer of 1845 Fuller reviewed the poems of the British poet-weaver William Thom, a man of no formal education, and her article set forth a theory of literary standards that took account of the new situation and impressed the New York literary community.

She concluded that, if a critic could "tolerate only what is excellent" and demanded perfection, she would be content only "with the Iliads and Odysseys of the mind's endeavor." If, on the other hand, "literature may be regarded as the great mutual system of interpretation between all kinds and classes of men," then it made no difference how refined the author or how perfect the product might be, for the work could still have value: "*first,* in proportion to the degree of its revelation as to the life of the human soul; *second,* in proportion to the perfection of the form in which that revelation is expressed."[6]

Her commonsense formulation, in addition to the sureness of her aesthetic definitions, established her as a literary force in New York. She had arrived in the city at a time when literary rivalries had reached a high point. Long-standing quarrels over personalities and issues now divided the city's writers into militant camps. At the center of the controversy was a disagreement over the means, the standards, and the pace American authors could adopt in their effort to rid themselves of dependence on European models and create a national literature consonant with America's destiny. The famous triumvirate,

Washington Irving, James Fenimore Cooper, and William Cullen Bryant, were aging, but no new writers were recognized as their successors. Fuller's position was that the widest possible grounding in literature, foreign and domestic, was needed to encourage the reading and writing of good books. She knew what she was looking for—indeed, she was one of the few in New York who saw from the first the authenticity of Herman Melville's *Typee*—but she was willing to write approvingly of any book if it had the ring of truth.

Even though Fuller was writing for a Whig newspaper, her literary taste had much in common with the literary party known as Young America, most of whose members were Democrats. Its mission, in the words of one of its leaders, Evert Duyckinck, was to prepare "the new, mass public for literature in an age of equality." After reading *Summer on the Lakes*, Duyckinck judged it to be "the only genuine book, I can think of, this season." He tried to persuade the firm of Wiley and Putnam, where he was an editor, to republish Fuller's translation of *Günderode*, and if she had been able to find the time to complete the partial version Elizabeth Palmer Peabody had published in 1842, he might well have succeeded. Nevertheless, he encouraged Fuller, respected her taste, and supported her literary career.[7]

The New York literary community included many women who were supporting themselves as authors and journalists. Anne Lynch, a journalist Fuller had known in Providence who had once been Henry Clay's secretary, had recently moved to New York. At her house on Waverly Place, she conducted a weekly at-home that was the nearest thing in New York at the time to a literary salon. Among the women writers who came regularly to Lynch's evenings were the poet Frances Sargent Osgood; Anne Stevens, who wrote for *Graham's Magazine* and the *Ladies' Companion;* the historian Elizabeth Ellet; Catharine Sedgwick, whose books Margaret had praised in *Woman in the Nineteenth Century;* and Caroline Kirkland, who was writing sketches of western life. (Kirkland had privately berated Evert Duyckinck for backing Fuller, whom she scorned as "a woman so abandoned in religious opinion.")[8]

Lydia Maria Child was Fuller's steadiest and most loyal friend among New York's coterie of women authors. She had moved to New York in 1841 to edit the *National Anti-Slavery Standard*, but bitter battles within the abolition movement forced her to resign in 1843; she continued to run a small publishing house and wrote a column for the *Boston Courier*, "Letter from New York." In 1845 her dispatches covered many of the same cultural events and metropolitan problems as Fuller. Impressed with Fuller's boldness in daring to write about prostitution, she wrote Louisa Loring, "She is a great woman, and no mistake, I like her extremely."[9]

Child boarded in the house of the Quaker activist Isaac Hopper on East Third Street. At the time of Fuller's arrival in the city, Hopper had just taken over the New York Prison Association, which was spearheading reform in the treatment of state prisoners in opposition to an influential civic group that believed frequent beatings and solitary confinement were necessary to control criminals. Margaret's visits to Sing-Sing had already awakened her interest in prison reform. Later that year, she would write an article opposing the death penalty. Now, with Greeley's encouragement, she began to publicize conditions in the city's charitable institutions, not only the prisons but the almshouses, insane asylums, and homes for the blind and the deaf. Partly because she believed that society's dislocations were responsible for deviant behavior, Fuller was supportive of the asylum movement. Although sympathetic to providing a healthy, educational environment for all who required public charity, she was wary of mere caretaking institutions that disregarded the sanctity of the individual soul or encouraged dependence. She condemned treating inmates "by wholesale" as "an evil incident to public establishments, . . . which only a more intelligent public attention can obviate." Advocating programs that elevated self-respect and encouraged self-development, her first requirement was that "Every establishment in aid of the poor should be planned with a view to their education." The one institution that won her wholehearted endorsement was the "beautifully situated" Bloomingdale Asylum for the Insane where there was no "sign of the hospital or the prison." There, as "one of the world's people," she attended a St. Valentine's Eve dancing party and observed the distinctive individuality in each of the inmates. Ending her article with a brief address in the tradition of a morality play, she invited her readers to identify with the dancers and agree that, "while owning that we are all mad, all criminal, let us not despair, but rather believe that the Ruler of all never could permit such widespread ill but to good ends."[10]

William Henry Channing took Margaret on his rounds through the slums of the city. She got a good look at the "loathesome" Five Points district of lower Manhattan where Dickens had visited earlier in the decade. Comparing its "filth and wretchedness" to "Seven Dials, or any other part of St. Giles," in London, he visited a series of tenement houses at night and pronounced, "Where dogs would howl to lie, women, and men, and boys slink off to sleep, forcing the dislodged rats to move away in quest of better lodgings." Many immigrants arriving in the city in 1845 found shelter in the district, one of whose many tenements, the notorious Old Brewery, was reputed to hold a thousand people huddled together in hutches on any given night.[11]

In several of her articles, Fuller publicized the mistreatment and misunderstanding of the new immigrants; she denounced "the flock of harpies who hover about our port," ready to pounce on the innocent new arrivals and trick them into paying exorbitant fees for inland transportation, herding them onto open decks, and leaving them "cruelly exposed and abused." Later, she lashed out at employers who complained that Irish servants and laborers were constitutionally guilty of lying and ingratitude. She put the blame on the insensitivity of the employer who would not take the trouble to educate the victims of a feudal culture in the new American ways. At least one Irish reader objected to her high-minded and simplistic recipes for social harmony. He wrote the *Tribune* criticizing its "*starry*" literary editor for assuming that "certain principles of love and good will" were all that was necessary to bring about "the New Jerusalem."[12]

In the spring of 1846 Fuller wrote a striking ironic parable in which a black Christ, accompanied by his dark-skinned mother, appears before a disputing council. As in the biblical account of Christ "instructing the Doctors," the unrecognized newcomer challenges the racial prejudices of the Pharisees of midcentury America, unmasking the self-deceit and sham of conventional wisdom on the issue.[13]

Fuller's *Tribune* columns continued to press the woman question, but on a more practical level than in her book. When money was raised to establish the first halfway house in New York for women prisoners, her appeals were directly credited. (The resulting Home for Discharged Female Convicts still exists today as the Hopper Home on the lower East Side.) After several hundred women, representing all ranks of the sewing trade, convened in City Hall Park in early March and organized themselves under Elizabeth Gray into the Ladies' Industrial Association, Fuller took notice of working women in a forceful article, "The Wrongs of American Women, the Duty of American Women." She argued that, although much "has been written about Woman's keeping within her sphere, which is defined as the domestic sphere," it is obvious that "[h]undreds of thousands must step out of that hallowed domestic sphere, with no choice" but to go to work. But even as she called for "opening more avenues of employment for women" and emphasized the need for more nurses and teachers, she reminded her readers that the necessary first step for women was the program of self-reliance she had outlined in *Woman in the Nineteenth Century*.[14]

In her literary reviews, Fuller continued to support the work of women artists and writers, praising books by the Americans, Caroline Kirkland, Eliza Farnham, Anna C. Mowatt, and Lydia Sigourney, as well as her favorite Europeans, George Sand, Elizabeth Barrett, and Anna Jameson.

Although she was far less adventurous in undertaking art criticism in New York than she had been in Boston, she kept her readers aware of what was going on at the National Academy of Design and the Art Union. Her standards for assessing the visual arts were similar to those she had applied to literature: "to inquire first, as to the object of the artist; second, his mode of treatment; third, his degree of success."[15]

She devoted commentary to the concerts at the Tabernacle and Castle Hill, but her notices of New York's musical events rarely ventured beyond observations about ticket prices, audience response, and her personal opinions about the social good of the work. She never developed the skill to excel in either art or music criticism. For her, in New York it was enough to be a promoter. "We need unspeakably the beautiful arts to animate, expand and elevate our life which rushes dangerously toward a coarse utilitarianism," she wrote after the Norwegian singer, Ole Bull's farewell concert. "This is their office, not to pamper the pride of wealth . . . but to educate the heart and mind."[16]

In August Waldo Emerson dropped by to see her after visiting his brother William on Staten Island. Margaret took him on an outing to Rockaway, her favorite beach. Since she had moved to New York, their correspondence had fallen off, but Caroline Sturgis was still strongly attached to Emerson, and the two were now carrying on "a high-minded flirtation," somewhat on the order of the three-sided one Fuller had been a party to five years previously. This summer Sturgis went so far as to ask Emerson to find her a place to board in Concord, but when he brought up the matter with Lidian he realized that his relations with young women pained her even when she agreed to welcome them as guests, as she did in this instance. Emerson had told Sturgis earlier that she needed a young love of her own; now he took the matter into his own hands. During his New York visit, he met William Tappan, a member of a wealthy family active in the abolition movement, and decided he would make a good match for Caroline. A romance began that ended two years later in marriage.[17]

In late September, when Horace Greeley finally agreed that Fuller had earned a vacation, she went directly to Concord but discovered at once that the sense of community that she had enjoyed in spite of the tensions during the previous two summers had disappeared. The Hawthornes, unable any longer to pay the rent at the Old Manse, were preparing to move back to Salem. Henry Thoreau was living in a cabin he had built during the spring on Walden Pond. Emerson was distant—"did not enjoy being with Waldo as usual," Fuller wrote Anna Ward, "our moods did not match. He was with Plato, and I was with the instincts."[18]

Fuller stayed with Ellen and Ellery in the cottage Ellery had just finished building on farmland on Punkawtasset Hill on the outskirts of the town. He was brooding and unhappy and seemed embarrassed in Margaret's presence. She thought he was hurt by his failure in New York; even though his "ill success [was] willingly incurred," she noted, it still rankled him. Ellen was pregnant again, but complained of feeling lonely so far from the center of town.[19]

Except for "poor Lloydie," the rest of the Fuller family seemed to be fine. Margarett Crane Fuller had returned to housekeeping in a new house on Prospect Street in Cambridgeport, close to the cemetery where her husband and two children were buried. Both Richard and Arthur were back home again. In March Richard had left George Davis's law office in Greenfield to spend a year at Harvard Law School. And at the end of the summer Arthur gave up his Belvidere school experiment to enter Harvard Divinity School—out West he had gone the rounds as an itinerant lay preacher and had found that the church was his calling. Eugene had heartened the whole family by landing a job on a New Orleans newspaper, where he was still doing well after several months. Lloyd remained the constant family worry. "Poor, *poor* Lloyd," Margaret wrote. "Most deeply do I feel fo[r] him! [H]e is likely to suffer far more from his partial inferiority than he would, if it were complete." He was still unhappy in Andover; her last hope was that he could return to Brook Farm when the farmers completed their reorganization into a phalanstery along the lines set out by the French philosopher Charles Fourier.[20]

When Fuller went out to Brook Farm, she stayed on Spring Street with the Shaws. Frank Shaw was now treasurer of the American Union of Associationists and a student of French socialism. He was translating George Sand's novel *Consuelo* for the *Harbinger*, the new magazine the Brook Farmers were publishing to propagate their ideas for social reform.

Fuller's best friends at home now were several of her old students, most of them younger than she, married, and with young families. Though she worked hard at playing the faithful friend and wise counselor, she was peripheral to their lives. Jane Tuckerman King was having trouble with her marriage and confiding in her. Anna (nicknamed Nony) Loring had just withdrawn from the overamorous attentions of Margaret's brother Richard. Margaret tried to mend matters between them—instructing Richard to be less impulsive and attempting to recruit Anna's help in domesticating him—but by the time she intervened the two were too wary of each other to start anew. Margaret was exasperated, because she was convinced that the match would have been an excellent one for Richard.

When she called on the Farrars in Cambridge, she found them "dolorous beyond description." A physician's attempt to treat John Farrar's heart condition with the electric magnetic machine made him worse for a time and ultimately had no effect at all. Before she returned to New York, Fuller went to New Bedford to see Mrs. Farrar's Aunt Mary Rotch. She ended her vacation with a visit to her ninety-year-old Grandmother Crane in Canton.[21]

Throughout the summer she had been at odds with Mary Greeley. Mary's moody temperament increasingly got on her nerves. "She wishes her feelings to be quite sweet towards me and is not conscious they are not," Fuller wrote James Nathan. Mary was "more dejected than ever," and Horace was now calling the farm "Castle Doleful." In June, when Margarett Crane Fuller visited for three weeks, she could not understand how Margaret could endure the Greeley family dissension and household confusion. Horace was to complain later that Mary had found it impossible throughout her life to keep even "one wise, devoted and helpful friend." Margaret thought that Mary was jealous of her, resenting the freedom and variety of her life and forgetting "the dark side of my lot, of which once she thought with so much tenderness."[22] Shortly after

Fuller returned from New England in October, she moved into a boarding-house on Warren Street, on the opposite side of City Hall Park from the *Tribune*'s new offices at the corner of Nassau and Spruce streets. She was able to make the move without causing a breach with the Greeleys. They expected her to visit them on weekends and invited her for a longer stay in the spring.

Fuller's maternal grandmother, Elizabeth Jones Weiser Crane, died in early December; her death revived Margaret's guilt over leaving her mother, who had received emotional support from the old woman's affection and gratitude. During her visit with her family in Cambridgeport, Margaret had been irritated to find her brothers often insensitive to their mother. She wished they could "learn to be, in part, daughters also." It was time for them to free her, she told them, from the gnawing sense of responsibility for her mother's welfare.[23]

Her concern grew in January when she received a letter from Ellery Channing, telling her of his preparations to go to Rome at the beginning of March. Ellen was expecting their second child in April, and Ellery, who disliked the disruption babies brought to the household, purposely chose this moment for his departure; he took it for granted that during his absence Margarett Crane Fuller would move in and help Ellen. Ellery's blatant self-centeredness disgusted Fuller. And she was enraged by his request that she help him get a position as a foreign correspondent on the *Tribune* and use her influence to aid in the collection of a purse generous enough to cover his expenses for several months.

It infuriated her even more when she learned that Caroline Sturgis, Anna and Sam Ward, and Waldo Emerson all justified Ellery's decision on the grounds that he was a poet. "He is driven by fate or his genius, or both," Sturgis explained. Fuller was expected to accept the situation even if she considered the scheme "a wild & even a ruthless one." Even Ellen realized it was better to let him go, Fuller heard from home. "[N]ow we have to take every spare dollar for Ellery," Caroline wrote to show how firmly the Concord group had rallied behind him. Ellery sailed for Europe on March 3, 1846, and on April 13 Ellen gave birth to a daughter, Caroline Sturgis Channing.[24]

That winter, Fuller's reaction to the outpouring of support for Ellery's trip was further complicated by a project of her own which would also require financial help from her friends. Early in the fall of 1845, Marcus and Rebecca Spring, Quaker friends of William Channing and Horace Greeley, whom she had met at a Valentine party given by Anne Lynch, told her of their plan to go to Europe in the summer of 1846 if Marcus could arrange matters with his business associates. They invited her to accompany them and offered to pay part of her expenses in return for her tutoring their nine-year-old son, Eddie. Because of the delicacy of Marcus's negotiations with his associates, Fuller had been asked to remain silent about the possibility of the trip. Now it seemed that her sources of funds were to be exhausted by her brother-in-law.

Furious that her "poor frail Mother" was the one to be sacrificed to Ellery's plans, she sat down and wrote out all her feelings in a letter to him, only to destroy it, but the exercise enabled her to "calm" her mind and "dismiss the subject." She was determined not to let anything interfere with her own plan to go to Europe. "I am going to let every thing go in this world and scud where the wind drives," she wrote Sturgis. "I shall have no chance to think of any body but myself, as I have to exert myself laboriously and unremittingly, or give up going to Europe."[25]

In early February, she was delighted when—through the good offices of her friend, the poet and historian Elizabeth Lummis Ellet—Evert Duyckinck expressed interest in publishing a collection of her writings for Wiley and Putnam's popular series, the Library of Choice Reading. To have another book to her credit would enhance her position in European literary circles and perhaps help with the financial problem.

Margaret's national political views hewed to the Whig line. She refused to mourn Andrew Jackson's death on June 6, 1845—"except on this score, that the flaming old warrior was so downright."[26] But her egalitarian positions on social issues and the humanism of her literary theory continued to win her the friendship of Democratic writers. By now she not only had the admiration of Evert Duyckinck but was on friendly terms with the editor of the *Democratic Review*, John Louis O'Sullivan, the influential political analyst who originated the term "Manifest Destiny" and was the first to publish Nathaniel Hawthorne. Parke Godwin, William Cullen Bryant's son-in-law, a writer for the *Evening Post* and a confirmed Associationist, invited her for a weekend at the family home in Hempstead and, when he heard she was going to Europe, gave her several letters of introduction to European authors. The novelist and essayist Cornelius Mathews was the most controversial of her Democratic friends. He was a brash publicity seeker and self-promoter who had annoyed just about every literary personage in town with the exception of Evert Duyckinck. Fuller supported him because he was such an intrepid advocate of a national literature. Mathews, who was well connected in London, gave Fuller a packet of letters to London literary lights, including Elizabeth Barrett.

In March, in order to save money for her trip, she moved out to Brooklyn to stay with Mary and Richard Manning, a prosperous couple who were close associationist friends of the Springs and William Henry Channing as well as distant relatives of Nathaniel Hawthorne. The Springs also lived in Brooklyn, and she occasionally stayed with them as well. On weekends, when convenient, she went to the Greeley farm. It was the old peripatetic life she had found at once pleasant and tiring in the early forties in Boston, but now she was sustained by the promise of a European voyage. She began to write more frequently and at greater depth about events in Europe. She believed that the social unrest that was manifesting itself in new experiments in social organization was a sure sign that a more equitable social order was emerging, one that would outgrow the injustices of the old European order and come to fruition in the New World. As many of her closest New York friends were committed Associationists, she occasionally visited the North American Phalanx in Red Bank, New Jersey, where sixty Albany shopkeepers and tradesmen were successfully maintaining a community. Horace Greeley, William Henry Channing, Mary and Richard Manning, and Rebecca and Marcus Spring had all invested in the experiment. They all grieved when the newly built phalanstery at Brook Farm was destroyed by fire on March 3, leaving little hope for that community's future.

Though critical of the rigidities of the Fourier blueprint, Fuller continued to support these efforts. In an April 1846 *Tribune* article, she wrote a detailed description of one such community recently established in Brazil. A few years later she would claim that she had been a socialist before leaving America, but while she lived in New York the true believers never considered her one of them. To her, all the experiments in social reorganization were expressions of a yearning for a better life, the same impulse that had motivated her to write *Woman in the Nineteenth Century.*[27]

Albert Brisbane's *Tribune* column promoting the Fourierist program (1842–43) had, by 1845, inspired the founding of twenty-six community experiments. Greeley, obsessed with anxiety about "industrial warfare," enthusiastically supported associationism as a solution to industrial ills. Under his leadership, the *Daily Tribune* had led the way in exposing exploitive labor practices, such as the widespread practice of "sweating" revealed in an 1845 series of reports. Fuller's awareness of social inequities was greatly extended during her period on the paper. Although her analysis of social problems did not penetrate to the fabric of society itself or suggest any radical restructuring, she urged activism in combatting social ills and continued to believe that her challenge to women could bring about the radical changes in the society that would speed it on its way to a golden future.[28]

In her choice of European books to review and her translations of news reports, Margaret kept her readers aware of the signs of change. She noted the importance of the new sociological approach in Michelet's *History of France;* she introduced the authors of the Young France movement and the books written by working people for working people in Germany, England, and France. In January 1846, after describing the radical platform of the German Social-Reform Association in New York, she commented,

But though we ourselves profess to belong to "the extreme left" of the army of Progress, though we hail the spirit of reform wherever it seems to us to be a vital, creative, healthy and not a feverish spirit, yet, precisely for that reason, would we say to all concerned, "you must be sure your light is in proportion to your heat."[29]

In August, in a translation from *Der Deutsche Schnellpost* defining the differences among communism, socialism, and humanism, she introduced her readers to Karl Marx and Friedrich Engels, whose earliest writings were just appearing in Europe. She was especially susceptible to European political exiles and gave positive notice to their books, music, and art whenever she got the chance. In February she took up the cause of Harro Harring, a Danish political exile whose novel *Delores* was first accepted and then rejected by Harper and Brothers. According to Margaret, Harring's story of camaraderie among European revolutionary exiles was ultimately rejected because it romanticized revolutionary activity. Just at the time when she was casting about for financial help from her friends to support her European trip, she impulsively loaned Harring $500 to publish his book privately and publicized his case in her column, calling for a convention of authors and publishers to set up regulations to govern contracts. Harring never repaid the loan.

After more than a year at the *Tribune,* Fuller had become a moral voice in the city of New York. In March her name began to be bandied about in connection with an episode with moral overtones involving Edgar Allan Poe, whose poem "The Raven" had just been published to great acclaim. According to the gossip, Margaret's friend Elizabeth Ellet, accompanied by Anne Lynch and Fuller, arrived unannounced at Poe's cottage in Fordham and demanded the return of a packet of letters sent to him by the poet Frances Sargent Osgood. After Poe's aunt, Mrs. Clemm, and his wife, Virginia, had shown the letters to Ellet on an earlier visit, Ellet had decided they were compromising and undertook the recovery mission without Osgood's knowledge. Poe allegedly threw a tantrum. He called the women "busy-bodies" and insulted Ellet by telling her she would be better occupied requesting the return of her own letters to him.[30]

According to one story, Ellet's brother then went to Fordham and threatened Poe with a pistol. Frances Osgood's husband, a portrait painter who had painted Poe the year before, threatened a lawsuit. In the ensuing clamor, Poe plead temporary insanity, and his doctor ordered a complete rest. A few months later, Poe took his revenge; in his New York Literati series, published in *Godey's Lady's Book,* he insulted Anne Lynch—she was easy to manipulate, he said,—and left Ellet's name off of his list of New York's prominent writers entirely.

If Fuller was indeed included as one of the "busy-bodies," Poe did not hold it against her in his August 1846 portrait for the Literati series. He praised *Woman in the Nineteenth Century* for its "independence" and "unmitigated radicalism." It was "a book which few women in the country could have written, and no woman in the country would have published, with the exception of Miss Fuller." Her style was impossible to categorize because her manner was "infinitely varied" and "always forcible," for she wrote just as she spoke. To help his readers get the "*conversational woman* in the mind's eye," Poe included his scrupulously observed sketch of "the *personal* woman."[31]

She is of the medium height; nothing remarkable about the figure; a profusion of lustrous light hair; eyes a bluish gray, full of fire; capacious forehead; the mouth when in repose indicates profound sensibility, capacity for affection, for love—when moved by a slight smile, it becomes even beautiful in the intensity of this expression; but the upper lip, as if impelled by the action of involuntary muscles, habitually uplifts itself, conveying the impression of a sneer. Imagine, now, a person of this description looking you at one moment earnestly in the face, at the next seeming to look only within her own spirit or at the wall; moving nervously every now and then in her chair; speaking in a high key, but musically, deliberately, (not hurriedly or loudly,) with a delicious distinctness of enunciation . . . imagine all this, and we have both the woman and the authoress before us.[32]

Poe's interest in Fuller was in part gratitude for the complimentary notice she had given to his *Tales* as well as for her support in a controversy he had started years earlier by accusing Henry Wadsworth Longfellow of plagiarizing Tennyson. Fuller, who was acquainted with Longfellow and aware of his popularity, had tried to stay out of the battle; she knew too many of his Cambridge and Boston friends. But under Greeley's pressure she had relented and published her honest opinion: Though not a plagiarist, Longfellow was too much an imitator of European models, she wrote, and did not write from deeply felt personal experience. His reputation was overblown. "Twenty years hence when he stands upon his own merits, he will rank as a writer of elegant, if not always accurate taste, of great imitative power, and occasional felicity in an original way, where his feelings are really stirred." (When Longfellow read the review, he called it "a bilious attack.")[33]

Poe's Literati piece praised Fuller's Longfellow review, recommended *Summer on the Lakes* and her *Dial* essays to readers in search of "Miss Fuller's genius," and added that "high genius she unquestionably possesses." This grandiose appreciation was to be the last good word Fuller got from Poe. After Evert Duyckinck published her *Papers on Literature and Art* in the fall of 1846, Poe stripped her of her genius, accorded her "some general but no particular critical powers," and described her as "an ill-tempered and very inconsistent old maid." She had done the unforgivable. She had failed to include him among the American writers she chose to discuss in her essay "American Literature: Its Position in the Present Time, and Prospects for the Future."[34]

Throughout Fuller's last weeks in New York, John Wiley of Wiley and Putnam kept her busy with the editing problems of *Papers on Literature and Art.* She was infuriated when he decided to omit two essays—one on Shelley and the other on Philip Bailey's *Festus*—because they were " 'controversial' " and might " 'offend the religious public.' "[35]

"Now you well know that I write nothing which might not offend the so-called religious public," Fuller wrote Evert Duyckinck, Wiley's editor. "I am too incapable of understanding their godless fears and unhappy scepticism to have much idea of what would offend them. But there are probably sentences in every piece, perhaps on every page, which . . . will lead to censure." Wiley's final decision was even more disappointing. He decided to publish only one volume instead of the two originally planned. He was not interested in any of her work on foreign authors. In her preface she expressed her regret. It had been "one great object of my life," she wrote, to introduce "the works of these great geniuses" of Europe in the hope that they would inspire the young of America.[36]

At the last minute, just before the book went to press, Duyckinck argued her into including several passages from *Witchcraft; or, The Martyrs of Salem,* a controversial play Cornelius Mathews had recently completed. Because she liked the play, she agreed and put it in her appendix. Later, enemies of Mathews, including Edgar Allan Poe, accused her of toadying to him. By the time Fuller was ready to leave New York, she had been drawn into many of the ongoing literary battles, and she was soon to learn that she was herself not immune to personal invective.

Out of the blue, in early July she had a letter from James Nathan, the first since December. He asked her to find a publisher for his Near East travelogue before she left for Europe. The letter included a tantalizing assurance: If she did not have another letter from him before she left, "you will certainly find something with Mr. Delf in London, from me, if not myself and then thanks to god! in all probability shall we meet either there or here." (Thomas Delf was the English representative of the Appleton publishing house.)[37]

Fuller's reply was addressed to "My friend." She told Nathan that Horace Greeley would help him publish his book if it were well written—"brief and vivid"—but since he was not well known he could not expect "*much* pecuniary profit." At the end she added breezily that she still hoped "to find a good letter if not yourself in London, early in Septr."[38]

Her last days in New York were frantic as she struggled to keep up with her newspaper work, finish editing her book, and collect all her belongings to take back to Cambridge to store with her mother. At the beginning of July, Ellery Channing had arrived back home after only sixteen days in Rome. He had been disappointed in Europe, but at least he was no longer straining the family purse. Richard came to New York to help Margaret settle her financial arrangements. Marcus Spring transferred all her assets ($404.43) to the account of his firm, Wells and Spring, where she was assured 7 percent interest. She had hoped Uncle Abraham would contribute to her journey, but he pleaded being "out of money." Richard told her that both Uncle Abraham and Uncle Henry were proud of her talents and her reputation but not of her views. This came as no surprise. Having other sources of income now, she was free of their power.[39]

Anna and Sam Ward sent her a loan and got permission from Sam's father, the American representative of the British financial house Baring Brothers, to use their services abroad. She also had a loan from the Mannings and a small gift from Aunt Mary Rotch. Her satisfaction was complete when Horace Greeley offered her a position as foreign correspondent at ten dollars an article and gave her an advance of $120. It was possible, she thought, that she could make the entire trip without further aid.

She wrote Anna and Sam, who were now settled at Highwood, their Berkshire estate, that her expectations were of an entirely different order now than ten years ago, when she had hoped to be in Europe with them. A European trip then would have given "wings" to her ambitions and she would have achieved by now far more.

> I do not look forward to seeing Europe now as so very important to me. My mind and character are too much formed. I shall not modify them much but only add to my stores of knowledge. Still, even in this sense, I wish much to go. It is important to me, almost needful in the career I am now engaged in[;] I feel that, if I persevere, there is nothing to hinder my having an important career even now. But it must be in the capacity of a journalist, and for that I need this new field of observation.[40]

Just before leaving New York, she went with Rebecca Spring to Plumb's Gallery because all her friends were caught up in the rage for daguerreotypes and exchanging likenesses. Even though she did not think that the portraits resulting from the new process were satisfactory, she posed leaning over an open book, her eyes downward, with one hand on her brow, the other resting in her lap; her hair was elaborately parted to show off her fine head. Rebecca thought the portrait, which showed "her noble look, and her lovely hair," was "really Margaret."[41]

Horace Greeley had taken pride, he said later, in watching Fuller's writing style improve until it was marked by "directness, terseness, and practicality." The day before she left New York, he brought Pickie to the *Tribune* office to say goodbye. Mary arrived late, but she joined in the farewell at the ferryboat taking Fuller to Brooklyn to pick up her luggage.[42]

She had only two days with her family in Cambridgeport before the *Cambria*, the latest (along with its sister ship, the *Hibernia*) of the Cunard steam packets, was to sail from Boston on August 1, and she was in a flurry to get letters of introduction from her influential friends. Edward Everett turned her down, saying it was against his principles. Waldo Emerson, who had already written Carlyle that he wished him "to give a good & faithful interview to this wise, sincere, accomplished, and most entertaining of women," came in from Concord with a special letter for her to carry by hand. Up to the last minute she worried that she would not see Waldo before she left; his coming was the sign she needed to assure her that—in spite of all their misunderstandings—they were comfortable and loyal old friends.[43]

On the day Fuller sailed to Europe, the *Tribune* published her "Farewell" to her adopted city, New York—"the point where American and European interests converge." New York, she wrote, was where all the new ideas first came to the surface and where everything happened so fast that the thinker was challenged to find a way to be open to the new but "not be carried away with it." In spite of the "Vice and Crime," New York was large enough and "provided occupation enough" that a "person who is independent and knows what he wants, may lead his proper life here unimpeded by others."[44]

She told her readers that during her year and a half in the city she had seen progress in two areas she cared about: the promotion of "National Education by heightening and deepening the cultivation of individual minds, and the part which is assigned to Woman in the next stage of human progress in this country." Now, she wrote, she was off to observe "life in the Old World," from which she hoped to bring back some fresh ideas to hasten progress in the New World. She had written Anna and Sam that it was too late for the experience to impact her in any fundamental way, but circumstances she could not foresee would soon put this assumption to the test.[45]

CHAPTER 17

To the horrors and sorrows of the streets in such places as
Liverpool, Glasgow, and above all, London, one has to grow insensible or die daily.

England and Scotland

MARGARET'S traveling companions, Rebecca and Marcus Spring, were conscientious Quakers who expected to study industrial reform activities in Europe. Rebecca had come by her interest in the welfare of workers from her father, Arnold Buffum, a hat manufacturer who, on several visits to England early in the century, had fallen under the influence of the English reformers William Wilberforce and Thomas Clarkson. Inspired by their example, he became a founder of both the American and the New England antislavery societies and established two mill schools for factory workers, one in Fall River and the other in Uxbridge, Massachusetts.

Before her marriage, Rebecca taught in one of the mill schools; when the family moved to Philadelphia, she became an instructor in the Philadelphia Coloured Infant School. While she was attending a women's antislavery convention in the Pennsylvania Hall of Liberty in Philadelphia in 1838, an opposition mob set fire to the building; the incident stiffened her commitment. Quiet and self-contained, even-tempered and inner-directed, she was at opposite poles temperamentally from Fuller but had been impressed by *Woman in the Nineteenth Century* and by William Henry Channing's stories of Fuller's intrepid acts of generosity during their joint visits to slum households in New York.

She had seen Fuller often during the previous year and had mixed feelings about her. In a journal she kept during their travels in Europe, she wrote that she worried about Fuller's impulsiveness, social blunders, and romantic flights of fancy but, in the end, had invited her on the European trip because of her popularity with Eddie, the Springs' nine-year-old son who was to accompany them. (They left their infant daughter, Jeanie, with a relative in Massachusetts.)

Marcus Spring was a clean-cut, handsome cotton merchant, a self-made man, brought up as a Unitarian, who became a Quaker after marrying Rebecca. He was just Margaret's age, thirty-six; Rebecca was a year younger. Cultivated and attractive, the Springs shared with Margaret many close friends as well as a devotion to human progress. As active supporters of associationism in America (they held stock in Brook Farm and the North American Phalanx), part of their agenda was to study industrial conditions in Europe. It was as ideal an arrangement as Fuller could expect. With their pooled letters of introduction, the three had personal contacts at every major stopping point. Margaret had a packet of letters to literary figures; the Springs had connections to a network of Unitarian and Quaker movers and shakers, dissenters, and nonconformists. So many British writers at the time were social critics that the two groups overlapped considerably.[1]

The *Cambria*'s record run from Boston to Liverpool on its August 1, 1846, voyage—just ten days and sixteen hours—was none too fast for Margaret, who had no taste for sea air. There was a flurry of excitement when the governor general of Canada, Lord Falkland, came aboard at Halifax with Lady Falkland, the illegitimate daughter of William IV, but Margaret told her *Tribune* readers in her first dispatch that her hero of the voyage was the ship's captain, C. H. E. Judkins, who proudly bore the title of "the Nigger Captain." The epithet had been thrown at him the year before, when he had stood up to a group of passengers who objected to the presence on board of the brilliant black orator Frederick O. Douglass, who was traveling to Europe on a lecture tour sponsored by the Massachusetts Anti-Slavery Society.[2]

Alexander Ireland, part owner of two Manchester newspapers and a friend of Emerson, met Fuller and the Springs on their arrival. He took them on tours of the Manchester and Liverpool Mechanics Institutes, showplaces of popular education, where, for five shillings a year, any resident, including women, could attend exhibitions and lectures and take courses in everything from fine arts and landscaping to foreign languages and mathematics. Ireland told Fuller that the *Dial* had many admirers in England and that her writings had been quoted in lectures, a compliment she reported in her first dispatch.

Setting out to use the same style and techniques she had found successful in *Summer on the Lakes*, Fuller titled the first series of her reports, "Things and Thoughts in Europe." She set the stage for a running commentary of eclectic observations, designed to appear in the *Tribune* at frequent intervals so as to keep interest alive. The previous autumn, when she had given Nathan advice on newspaper travel writing, she had suggested that he strengthen his reporting with "direct observations" to "mix in them personal life" and to "see through veils." She had refused to print one of his letters from Rome because his descriptions of the city's landmarks were "too familiar to the reading public." She wished he had written on "Modern Rome" instead, "for your observations on what you personally meet are always original and interesting."[3] Mixing old Europe with the new, spicing up the discourse with occasional jabs at popular opinion and conventional wisdom, and giving the whole text enough personal flavor to be unmistakably Margaret Fuller was her method.

A day trip to the walled city of Chester, between Manchester and Liverpool, gave Fuller her first sense of being in the heart of the Old World. When told that one might still find in the soil Roman tiles or coins bearing the head of Jupiter, she knew she was at last walking the ground of old Europe. The ramparts, the ruined towers, gateways, and "old houses with biblical inscriptions," the town's very configuration in the shape of a cross, responded to her expectations.[4]

While exploring Chester's ramparts, she discovered a sign of the new Europe: In one of the towers there was a newly established local museum whose director was—as she noted in her *Tribune* column—a woman. But more common signs of the times were the swarm of "squalid and shameless beggars of Liverpool," the "coarse" and "rude" mill girls in Manchester, the sight of women, "too dull to carouse," seated in the windows of "gin-palaces." The degradation of women was so widespread, she wrote, that the homes of industrial England had lost their "sweetness." After nine days, the most comforting thought she could rally was that "only the new Spirit in its holiest power" could restore these homes, deserted by women who had been forced into the streets.[5]

After Liverpool, the next stop was Ambleside, where Harriet Martineau had just built herself a stone cottage. Harriet, who had recently been cured by mesmerism of an illness that had kept her bedridden for five years, was now touring on foot and on horseback in all the corners of the Lake District while preparing a guidebook, which promised to be a best seller now that the railroads were revolutionizing tourism. Although *Woman in the Nineteenth Century* had impressed Martineau—she wrote her friend Fanny Wedgwood that it was "Beautiful"—she had not completely forgiven Margaret's stern criticisms of her *Society in America* or her tardiness in embracing the antislavery movement; the two were not completely at ease with each other.[6]

Harriet entertained her four guests by taking them on excursions and introducing them to her famous neighbors: Thomas Arnold, headmaster of Rugby, whose son Matthew was home from Oxford at the time, and the poet William Wordsworth. In her twenties, Fuller had memorized reams of Wordsworth's poetry; she had since decided that he was a poet for the young. He was seventy-six now, the poet laureate of England, but she found him far from her youthful ideal of a poet: "no Apollo, flaming with youthful glory, laurel-crowned and lyre in hand, but, instead, a reverend old man clothed in black, and walking with cautious step." An attentive and courteous host, Wordsworth made a fuss over Eddie Spring and showed his guests about Dove Cottage, and even quoted lines of his poetry, but he disappointed Margaret when he showed no concern for his country's social problems. He lived too protected a life in prosperous Westmoreland, Fuller decided—"he hears not the voice which cries so loudly from other parts of England, and will not be stilled by the sweet poetic suasion or philosophy, for it is the cry of men in the jaws of destruction." Fuller's social conscience was now influencing her literary judgments. Passing through Robert Burns country on the way to Edinburgh, she paid tribute to Burns's "noble, genuine democracy which seeks not to destroy royalty, but to make all men kings." This made him, she wrote her *Tribune* readers, a far "rarer man" than the popular but aristocratic Sir Walter Scott.[7]

As well as being the gateway to the Highlands, Edinburgh was a center of reformist activity. The Springs decided to take rooms there and make side visits before proceeding south to London. As soon as Fuller knew their itinerary, she wrote to James Nathan's London-based friend, Thomas Delf, for news of Nathan. If he should be in England—as he had written he might be—Fuller would like him to accompany her and the Springs on their Highland excursion. During the week that she awaited an answer, she and the Springs led a busy social life meeting civic leaders and reformers: Robert and William Chambers, the self-made men who controlled a publishing empire including the popular weekly, *Chambers's Edinburgh Journal,* and the Reverend Thomas Chalmers, a noted mathematician and theologian, who not only led the separatist movement in the Scottish church but was active in parish work in the slums. Dr. Andrew Combe, founder of the Edinburgh Phrenological Society, persuaded Fuller to ask Horace Greeley to take up his cause against his American publishers, who were refusing to update his popular books on anatomy and digestion because the old ones were steady best sellers. Thomas De Quincy, "the English Opium-Eater," now an old widower living alone, absorbed in writing his *Suspiria de Profundis,* entertained Fuller for hours with reminiscences of his youth, recalling the days when he was a close friend of Coleridge and Wordsworth, two poets who had inspired the youthful Fuller's ambition to be a writer.[8]

A letter from James Nathan, relayed through Thomas Delf in London, arrived just before the party set out for the Highlands. He wrote from Hamburg, explaining to Fuller that he was engaged to be married and would not be able to meet her in Europe in the near future. Resorting to an antisemitism that had been the other side of her having so romanticized Nathan's origins, Fuller made a brief entry in her diary:

Leave Edinburgh on Monday morning, 8th (Sept.) for Perthshire. Letter containing virtual reply to my invitation of 1st Sept. also dated 1st Sept. From 1st June, 1845, to 1st Sept., 1846, a mighty change has taken place, I ween. I understand more and more the character of the *tribes.* I shall write a sketch of it and turn the whole to account in a literary way, since the affections and ideal hopes are so unproductive. I care not. I am resolved to take such disappointments more lightly than I have. I ought not to regret having thought other of "humans" than they deserve.[9]

She tore up Nathan's letter in a fit of anger and started on the trip in a distraught state. On her arrival at Perth she described her journey:

I have been every where on the top of the coach, even one day of drenching rain, and enjoy it highly. Nothing can be more inspiring than this swift, steady progress over such smooth roads, and placed so high as to overlook the country freely, with the lively flourish of the horn preluding every pause.[10]

Rebecca, who knew most of the Nathan story, worried about Margaret's defiance of good sense and propriety, as she watched her working herself up to a frenzy of activity as an antidote to disappointment. When they settled at Trossach Inn near Loch Katrine, Margaret told Rebecca that she was beginning to conquer her disappointment, but Margaret's depressed and reckless state of mind continued to concern the Springs. The following day Fuller found herself lost for the night on Ben Lomond. She and Marcus had climbed the mountain in the late afternoon; after enjoying the view from the top, they could not find the path down, and, as each searched for the way, they became separated. Their calls to each other were lost in the wind and Marcus headed down, certain she must have already started ahead. She wandered about, climbing down to a point surrounded by water. Believing she could reach level ground on the other side, she thought of jumping into the water and tested its depth with a stone, but she could not summon the nerve to jump. Twenty shepherds and their dogs found her in the early morning shivering near a stream. Back at the hotel, she protested that she had another day of strength in her, but the Springs forced her to bed while they entertained the rescue crew at a dinner.[11] For the *Tribune*, Fuller described her night on the mountain as one of "grand solitude"; alone with her "Ossianic visions," she had learned that she could meet danger equably. About the whole episode there was an air of a foolhardy tour de force, as if the pressures of the preceding days had mounted up in her and, like the whirling dervish Mariana in her short story, she could find relief only in some dramatic and taxing escapade.[12]

A visit to Glasgow two days later sobered her. She found the city an "*Inferno,*" and she came away remembering the miserable population shuffling through the streets, "the forsaken, slovenly hopeless gait, gesture, eye"; the spiritual emptiness that she sometimes fought in herself was walking the streets in crowds. Glasgow was to hold its rank throughout the tour of Britain as "the very saddest place I saw in the United Kingdoms." In the big cities, "one has to grow insensible or die daily," she wrote. Yet the sight of "swarms of dirty women and dirtier children" in the "sweet, fresh, green country" around Perth summoned her most fervent statement yet of sympathy with utopian socialism: "Can any man who has seen these things dare to blame the Associationists for their attempt to find prevention against such misery and wickedness in our land?"[13]

After returning to Edinburgh, where they met the philanthropist James Simpson, famous for establishing infant schools and providing public baths, Fuller and the Springs headed south, stopping at all the obligatory shrines— Abbotsford and Sir Walter Scott's grave, York Cathedral, Chatsworth, and Warwick Castle. At Newcastle they visited a coal mine—"an odd sensation to be taken off one's feet and dropped down into darkness by the bucket," Fuller observed. At Birmingham they stopped long enough to hear George Dawson, a popular lecturer who had borrowed Emerson's philosophy, some of his style, and quotes from several of his lectures. Always on the lookout for great communicators serving the cause of the future, Fuller was disappointed in Dawson.

In fact, she decided, none of the British speakers could compare in spiritual eloquence with William Henry Channing or Theodore Parker.[14]

On the day they arrived in London—October 1—Harriet Martineau, who was stopping over on her way to Egypt, gave them a reception. Fuller had already sent from Liverpool Cornelius Mathews's letter to Elizabeth Barrett. Her presumptuousness annoyed Barrett, who had complained to Robert Browning:

[A]n American lady who in her time has reviewed you & me . . . is about to come to see me . . . armed with a letter of introduction from Mr. Mathews. . . . Observe the double chain thrown across the road at my feet—I am entreated to show her attention & introduce her to my friends.[15]

But before Fuller arrived in London, the lovers had eloped; they were somewhere on the Continent and the talk of London.

When Margaret sent out her other letters of introduction on the day after the Martineau reception, Thomas Carlyle came promptly to call. His curiosity could hardly resist the bait in Emerson's letter. He had described Margaret as "this dear old friend of mine" who has been working as "literary editor" for Horace Greeley:

She is full of all nobleness, and with the generosity native to her mind & character, appears to me an exotic in New England, a foreigner from some more sultry & expansive climate. She is, I suppose, the earliest reader & lover of Goethe, in this country, and nobody here knows him so well. Her love too of whatever is good in French & especially in Italian genius, give her the best title to travel. In short, she is our citizen of the world by quite special diploma.[16]

When Carlyle invited Margaret soon afterward to a quiet evening at Cheyne Walk, she found him "in a very sweet humor, full of wit and pathos, without being overbearing or oppressive." His earnestness reminded her of the early Carlyle, who wrote the stirring *Edinburgh Review* articles that in the late 1820s had introduced her to German literature. She had not liked his recent books, but after almost two months in Britain she could "appreciate the strength and hight of that wall of shams and conventions which he, more than any man, or thousand men,—indeed, he almost alone—has begun to throw down."[17]

Later in the month, when the Carlyles gave her a literary party, she saw what she dubbed his "acrid mood." Tennyson was out of town, and John Stuart Mill turned down the invitation, but George Henry Lewes, who was then working on his Goethe biography, came to meet America's "citizen of the world." Margaret dismissed Lewes, who had not yet made his famous alliance with George Eliot, as "a witty french flippant sort of man." She was far more interested in Carlyle's own performance that evening. At first he annoyed her by dominating the conversation and haranguing against the foolishness of romantic poets and those, like Margaret, who held them in reverence. Afterward, when he turned his "railing and raillery" on the modern French writers, he charmed her with his wit and "admirable penetration." She admired his ability to enjoy a deep laugh. "Carlyle is worth a thousand of you for that," she wrote Emerson. "[H]e is not ashamed to laugh when he is amused, but goes on in a cordial human fashion."[18]

For the *Tribune,* Margaret described Carlyle with even deeper appreciation:

Carlyle, indeed, is arrogant and overbearing, but in his arrogance there is no littleness, no self-love: it is the heroic arrogance of some old Scandinavian conqueror—it is his nature and the untamable impulse that has given him power to crush the dragons. You do not love him, perhaps, nor revere, and perhaps, also, he would only laugh at you if you did, but you like him heartily, and like to see him the powerful smith, the Siegfried, melting all the old iron in his furnace till it glows to a sunset red, and burns you if you senselessly go too near. He seemed to me quite isolated, lonely as the desert. . . . He puts out his chin sometimes till it looks like the beak of a bird, and his eyes flash bright instinctive meanings like Jove's bird; yet he is not calm and grand enough for the eagle; he is more like the falcon, and yet not of gentle blood enough for that either. He is not exactly like anything but himself, and therefore you cannot see him without the most hearty refreshment and good will, for he is original, rich and strong enough to afford a thousand faults.[19]

Fuller had little chance to make friends with Jane Welsh Carlyle. "I like her very much;—she is full of grace, sweetness, and talent," Margaret wrote; but they did not meet often.[20]

Thomas Delf, who now represented Wiley and Putnam as well as Appleton publishers in England, helped Fuller and the Springs find inexpensive rooms in a house off Gordon Square, and they settled down to a steady schedule of sightseeing. After years of studying the art of Europe in casts and copies, in etchings, drawings, and cameos, Margaret had her first chance to see large collections of authentic works of art in the London galleries. That season, Turner's impressionistic late style was the subject of a raging controversy in the London art world, and Margaret was brash enough to enter the fray. Many critics had dismissed the paintings as "not pictures at all," but Fuller, who was on principle open to new ideas in the arts, rose to their defense and ventured a criticism in which she sought to define the "mysterious-looking" paintings that required "patience and a devout eye":

Still, these pictures, it seems to me, cannot be considered fine works of Art, more than the mystical writing common to a certain class of minds in the United States can be called good writing. A great work of Art demands a great thought or a thought of beauty adequately expressed.—Neither in Art nor Literature more than in Life can an ordinary thought be made interesting because well-dressed. But in a transition state, whether of Art or Literature, deeper thoughts are imperfectly expressed, because they cannot yet be held and treated masterly. This seems to be the case with Turner. He has got beyond the English gentleman's conventional view of Nature, which implies a *little* sentiment and a *very* cultivated taste; he has become awake to what is elemental, normal, in Nature— such, for instance, as one sees in the working of water on the seashore.[21]

At the Reform Club in London, she both despaired at the "stupidly comfortable" arrangements for single gentlemen and marveled at the male chefs in the kitchen, a sign of progress. "Fourier himself might have taken pleasure in them." Since men called themselves the " 'stronger sex,' " why should not cooking and washing become entirely male preserves? Her greatest enthusiasm was for the large public washing establishment, which provided at a nominal cost water, tubs, drying areas, and ironing facilities where a washing that would take days at home could be finished in three hours.[22]

She went to Hempstead to see the playwright Joanna Baillie, whose moralistic plays she had read in her teens. While at Richmond to view Hampton Court, she had tea with the worldly francophile Mary Berry, close friend of Madame Récamier and Sir Hugh Walpole. Berry, now in her eighties, was the author of the *Comparative View of the Social Life of England and France from the Restoration to the French Revolution.*

A British edition of Fuller's *Papers on Literature and Art* was published shortly before she arrived in London, and favorable reviews soon appeared in the leading literary journals. Word had gotten around London that she was an accomplished linguist, journalist, and lecturer, "one of the most gifted women America had yet produced," famous for "amalgamating in her mind science, art, and general literature in a surprising manner." When Camilla Toulmin, a novelist and magazine editor whose curiosity had been aroused, arrived late one evening at a small party at the home of the playwright Westland Marston, she saw "at a glance who was the cynosure of the evening."

A lady of medium height and size, and of graceful figure, was leaning back in an easy chair, and alternately listening with interest, or talking with animation to the group around her, the American twang in her voice betraying her nationality. Her light hair was simply arranged, and her cheeks showed the fading, so often noticed in her countrywomen when the thirtieth year is passed, yet without exactly ageing the face. The outline of her head was fine, and her blue eyes beamed with candour and intelligence. She wore a dress of lilac silk, enriched with a good deal of black lace drapery. In a few minutes I found myself seated by her side, and very soon any prejudice which I might have entertained against the "strong-minded" woman ebbed away. Though egoistic, certainly, she was wise, genial, and womanly, and when I shook hands with her at parting it was with the hope of seeing her again.[23]

Both William Johnson Fox, the Unitarian leader of the Anti-Corn Law League, and Hugh Doherty, editor of the *London Phalanx,* had dinners for Fuller and the Springs. Emerson's friend Garth Wilkinson, the Swedenborgian doctor, called on them, and Fuller met some of the workingmen poets whose books she had reviewed in the *Tribune*—Thomas Cooper, the poet-editor of the Chartist magazine, *Cooper's Journal,* and the weaver-poet, William Thom, whose *Rhymes and Recollections of a Handloom Weaver* had inspired the *Tribune* essay in which she had presented her latest theory of literary criticism.

The story of Fuller's night on Ben Lomond passed around London, and Thom wrote to the Springs: "Mind you don't lose Margaret again! What simpletons they were in Loch Lomond—didn't keep what they found." Everyone was eager to see her and hear her conversation, but Thomas Cooper complained that she talked in a nasal tone and he could not understand why Americans could not master that "bad habit," and William Fox thought himself somewhat "badgered" with her "shining flow of words."[24]

The best new friends Fuller made in England were Mary and William Howitt, the joint editors of the *People's Journal;* Fuller had cited them in *Woman in the Nineteenth Century* as an example of a professional couple who had achieved an equal marriage. She was often a guest at the Elms, their home in Upper Clapham, and she met through them the journalist Mary Lemon Gillies and her daughter Margaret, an artist, who agreed to keep a box of personal papers for Fuller until she returned to London on her way back to Liverpool. She asked them to destroy the letters in case of her death, a promise that would cause Fuller's friends considerable trouble a few years later.

While Fuller was in England, George Saunders, now coeditor with the Howitts, was adopting an editorial policy in the *People's Journal* that was disturbing to the Howitts. He was publishing articles calling for a restructuring of employee relations, for the creation of workers' associations, and for the removal of middle-class governance from the Mechanics Institutes. These ideas signaled a new phase in socialist thinking, one that was disturbing to middle-class philanthropists like Mary Howitt who believed her editorial policies were progressive when, as she put it, she and her husband made every effort "to induce" the workers "to be prudent, sober, independent; above all to be satisfied to be workers, to regard labour as a privilege rather than a penance."[25]

By the beginning of 1847 the Howitts and George Saunders were quarreling over the journal's stand on labor issues. Fuller thought of herself as a socialist at this time, but she used the term loosely. The American-brand socialism of her Associationist friends was philanthropic and benevolent and, for the most part, paternalistic. Few of them chose to live in the utopian communities they supported. As a matter of Christian conscience, they favored abolition, free education, public washtubs and bathing facilities, humane prisons, cheerful homes for the handicapped and the mentally ill, and the extension of the rights of women. If the specter of class conflict threatened them, they hoped their reforms would ward off serious tensions. But in England the Industrial Revolution was further advanced, and sharp class and political divisions had formed in response to such radical ideas as that the state was responsible for the unemployed or that workers should form associations to promote their interests.

One of the Howitt's contributors was the Italian revolutionary Giuseppe Mazzini, who had been living as an exile in London since 1837. Although engaged in the social movement, he was critical of socialism's all-embracing focus on economic reforms. Regarding economic betterment of the masses as only a means to a subsequent new moral order, he wanted to avoid hostility between the classes, and thus he argued that the social movement should focus on human mutuality and national unity. He led an ascetic life and was occupied with the political exile community in London while enjoying the friendship of many London freethinkers and philanthropists. In spite of theoretical and temperamental differences and many arguments with Thomas Carlyle, he was a frequent visitor at Cheyne Row, often serving as Jane Welsh Carlyle's confidante.

The previous April, in a *Tribune* article, Fuller had recommended an essay by "Mazzini, the celebrated Italian Patriot." Now she met him in London through her old friend Harro Harring, the Danish revolutionary and author of *Delores*, the novel she had financed shortly before leaving New York. Mazzini, the inspiration for one of the novel's characters, had been an instigator along with Harring in a failed insurrection against the Austrian authorities in the Savoy in northern Italy in 1834. They were both captured and imprisoned together for several months.[26]

When Harring turned up in London unexpectedly, Margaret pressed him to arrange a meeting for her with his famous friend. Mazzini was already a legendary figure, fascinating his admirers with his graceful, ascetic appearance, his priestlike garb, and his steadfast devotion to his cause. Margaret had to invite him three times to the Warwick Street apartment before he found the time to come. He wrote her meanwhile that the Carlyles had already told him about her writings, and he eventually arrived on October 26 in the company of Harring. Fuller quickly convinced Mazzini of her enthusiasm for the cause of Italian republicanism as well as her personal interest in him. Throughout the following week, from day to day, he apologized for his inability to meet with her again, but he finally came on Saturday evening. To Fuller's annoyance, the Carlyles also stopped by. She had wanted to talk with Mazzini alone about " 'progress' " and "ideal subjects," but Carlyle, who had little patience with reformers, ridiculed them for their " 'rose-water imbecilities,' " and Mazzini withdrew and grew silent, walking about, according to Rebecca, "with his hands behind him, looking annoyed."[27]

By the winter of 1847, Mazzini's revolutionary movement, Young Italy, had splintered into many groups, each dedicated to the future independence of their country but differing on the means to achieve their ends. They also differed about who would serve as leaders and on the form the future national government should take. Mazzini, exiled in London for six years, threatened with a death sentence at home and a jail sentence in France, and persona non grata in Switzerland, kept his organization alive by establishing "congregations" of sympathizers, not only in Italy but throughout Europe; there were Young Italy congregations as well in Boston, New York, and Buenos Aires.

When Fuller and the Springs offered their help, Mazzini asked if they would be willing to let him accompany them from France into Italy later in the winter if he needed to make the trip at the time. He would have a false identity and an English name. When they agreed, he gave Fuller a letter of introduction to

Giuseppe Lamberti, his contact in Paris. (During the summer he had written Lamberti that Americans and the English were "the best possible intermediaries.") He described Fuller to Lamberti as a distinguished author from the United States whom he regarded highly. Her traveling companions were Mr. and Mrs. Spring, "pure Americans, very active in the cause of the poor Blacks and in every other cause for right and justice." Lamberti was to give them every courtesy and attention; they were carrying letters to several Italian friends and would be willing to take any others Lamberti might add. In particular, he asked Lamberti to give Miss Fuller the address of George Sand.[28]

On November 10, Fuller's last night in London, she went to the fifth-anniversary celebration of Mazzini's Italian Free School on Greville Street. It was said in London that the students there were taught the four R's: reading, writing, arithmetic, and revolution. After being introduced as the author of *Woman in the Nineteenth Century,* "the best work on the subject which has yet appeared," Fuller gave a speech on the importance of an "international moral exchange" and her concern for Italy:

Italy, herself so fair, has bestowed on the rest of the world, beyond any other country, save ancient Greece, those arts which, portraying the beautiful and the graceful, awaken the love of the beautiful and the good, and thus refine the human soul. To the poet and the artist, Italy must ever be most dear; nor can anyone, capable of thought on the subject, be indifferent to the emancipation of this fair land from [its] present degradation.[29]

The next day, November 11, Fuller was on her way to France. She was traveling now as a tourist, a foreign correspondent, and as a courier for the patriotic Italian revolutionary Giuseppe Mazzini.

To themselves be woe, who have eyes and see not, ears and hear not, the convulsions and sobs of injured Humanity.

France

FROM THE TIME Fuller learned in Edinburgh of James Nathan's forthcoming marriage, Rebecca Spring repeatedly urged her to demand the return of her letters, but Fuller denied that there was anything in them other than "spiritual exaltation." Later, in London, she spoke so warmly and naturally of her friendship with Nathan to Thomas Delf that he asked Nathan in a letter if it could be possible that she knew of his engagement. But her controlled public manner veiled a fierce resentment; on October 25 she sent Nathan in Hamburg a sharp note, congratulating him and requesting an exchange of letters, because it was "most fitting for each party to have this part of the record."[1]

Shortly after arriving in Paris, Fuller received a letter from Nathan in which he argued that she had no right to be angry; he reminded her that his "anxiety to be clearly understood" from the "earliest beginning" of their relationship had been the cause of "much insult" to her and "much pain" to him, and he concluded that the only possible act on his part that could have altered the "understanding" that theirs was no more than a friendship was his "fanciful present" of the white veil. But even in that case, he noted, he had taken care at the time to exact a promise from her that she would not give the gift any "ordinary construction." He went on:

The native mysticism of my being, perhaps race, that suggested the idea of the gift, was ever alone enough of a cause, not to let me hope to dare join, so clear, broad and disciplined an understanding as yours, for any length of time; had it even been possible for a moment to forget, my entire deficiency and inferiority of education, the moral and social inequality etc. etc. but if you remember your own remarks on this subject, and *which were very clearly made*, all this saying of mine is useless or rather unnecessary, as those remarks settled the point long since, and really I never should ever have said all this, but for the evident irritation and haste, in which you wish the exchange of letters and which suggest, as though with what happened, I had lost not only all right upon, but even all your confidence to possess them.[2]

Nathan preferred that they each keep the letters in their possession until they returned to New York and could "talk the matter over more fully and fairly." He assured her that her privacy would be respected in his handling of her letters and of his continual high regard for her even though her last letter had "thrown such a cold shower of uncertainty and distrust" over their friendship.[3]

In a scorching reply, Fuller demanded the return of her letters and accused

Nathan of deceiving her. His prompt reaction brought the controversy to a head. He advised her to "keep cool" and rejected "with disdain the reproach" that he had misrepresented himself. He was hurt, he protested, that she had torn up the letter she had received in Edinburgh, having given as her justification that it was written by a person so "changed" and so much "worse" than she had thought him to be that she would have thought the letter "a forgery" but for the fact that it had come to her through Mr. Delf. Nathan attributed Fuller's behavior to other causes. "I call it a want of judgement and experience of life, of which want you have of late, alas! proved yourself too full," he wrote her. "Miss F. you have judged me without a hearing, you have condemned and insulted me, nay! but for the consciousness of innocence, would have destroyed me!"[4]

Nathan now took a much firmer line. He proposed that each should keep the letters now in their possession until death, with the understanding that at that time they would be burned; each was to designate a trusted friend to undertake this mission. For Fuller, it was a humiliating outcome. Nathan managed to keep the upper hand by assuring her that in some future time he would have the opportunity to clear from her "weak and inexperienced Eye" their misunderstandings and that when she knew all the circumstances her "innocent heart" would make atonement for "the chills, contempt and dismay" she was heaping on him. He still held a fund of friendship for her, he asserted, but concluded it was evident they should now terminate their correspondence. Fuller could do nothing but let him have the last word. She had given him a sound scolding and faced him down with her favorite weapon: moral superiority.[5]

In Paris Fuller and the Springs stayed at the Hotel Rougemont on the boulevard Poissonnière, just off the boulevard des Italiens, in the heart of fashionable life and near the theaters and the smartest cafes. Margaret immediately hired a tutor, Monsieur Nicod, to help her gain fluency in French, and she lost no time in contacting, at Mazzini's suggestion, *La Revue indépendante,* the French liberal journal founded by George Sand and Pierre Leroux in 1841. The editor, François Ferdinand, immediately accepted her essay, "American Literature: Its Position in the Present Time, and Prospects for the Future," for the November–December issue. (The piece was prepared for publication so rapidly that the byline listed the author as Elizabeth Fuller.)

She befriended her translator, Pauline Roland, a feminist who had lived for several years in the Saint-Simonian commune, Menilmontant. A friend of George Sand and the poet Béranger, translator of Sainte-Beauve and Chateaubriand, she had recently published articles on the history of woman's position in France and the condition of women and children workers in France's coal mines. The tall, auburn-haired Roland openly opposed marriage and was the main support of her three children; their father, the writer Jean-François Aicard, no longer lived with her. In the winter of 1847 she lived in Pierre Leroux's Fourierist commune at Broussac, a few miles from George Sand's country home in Nohant. At the commune Roland ran a school based on socialist principles, in method and ideology very like Bronson Alcott's Temple School. In the coming years, Roland would be imprisoned and deported to Africa for her advanced opinions; Michelet would praise her; Victor Hugo would celebrate her as one of France's heroes; Verlaine would compare her to Joan of Arc; and a home for unmarried women in Paris would bear her name.[6]

"Madame Pauline Roland I find an interesting woman, an intimate friend of Béranger and Pierre Leroux," Margaret wrote her mother at the end of December. Roland went out of her way to introduce Fuller to the *Revue*'s writers and requested that she continue sending contributions after she returned to America. The idea of writing "a big book" on the changes brewing in Europe was already simmering in Fuller's mind; with Roland's help she began to collect background information and etchings of Sand, Béranger, and Lamennais, three key figures in the humanitarian movement in France.[7]

Bearing an introduction arranged by Mazzini, Margaret visited Félicité Robert de Lamennais, the priest whose *Paroles d'un Croyant* (1834) and *Le Livre du Peuple* (1837) were popular manifestos of worldwide influence calling for a revival of the early Christian ideal of justice and love. Margaret called Lamennais Catholic Europe's "apostle of Democracy"; she admired his courage in continuing to forward a message of republicanism and social responsibility even after he was forced out of the church. When she visited him she found him with Pierre Jean de Béranger, "the great national lyrist of France," the witty poet of the people, whose irreverent, often ribald, ballads and satirical verses—ridiculing the monarchy and reactionary clergy—had won him both great popularity and several prison terms. For Fuller, none of the other great men of France whom she managed to see and hear—Guizot, Thiers, the celebrated Arago, or even Berryer, whose eloquence she admired—had the stature of Lamennais and Béranger. "They are the true kings, the theocratic kings, the judges in Israel," she wrote to the *Tribune*.[8]

Always fascinated by orators and their styles, she enjoyed the spectacle of the Chamber of Deputies, where a dull speaker was always noisily ignored and the room seemed filled with "myriad beehives." She admired the verbal skill of the French deputies and advocated "a corps of the same kind of sharpshooters" to liven things up in the American legislative assemblies. Her greatest pleasure at the Chamber of Deputies was being shown one of its library's treasures, the manuscripts of Rousseau. Though yellow and faded, "at their touch I seemed to feel the fire of youth," she wrote reverently. "He was the precursor of all we most prize."[9]

She went seven times to see performances of the great actress Mlle. Rachel (Elisa Félix), the daughter of wandering peddlers who, at twenty-six, commanded such drawing power that she dictated the policy and program of the Comédie française. A tiny woman, less than five feet tall, she was the toast of

Europe, dominating the stage with her dramatic gestures and attitudes. Fuller, who, in the months before leaving New England for New York, often described her own life as tragic, wrote that no one could surpass the great Rachel in the expression of "the darker passions, and grief in its most desolate aspects." In deploring the lack of any male actor in France who could compare with Rachel, she added another comment, one that the reading public would recognize as quintessentially Fuller: "these men seem the meanest pigmies by the side of Rachel—so on the scene, beside the tragedy intended by the author, you see also the common tragedy, a woman of genius who throws away her precious heart, lives and dies for one unworthy of her."[10]

Paris provided a chance to hear better opera than she had ever heard before, and she heard Grisi and Persiani at the Italian Opera and Duprez in *Ravenswood* at the Grand Opera. She went to the Louvre and admired the Rembrandts and Titians. She visited the Jardin des Plantes to see the wax fungi and moss. At the Hôtel des Invalides, she pondered Napoleon's significance. When she went with Marcus to the Sorbonne to hear the astronomer Leverrier lecture, she was annoyed to find herself excluded because she was a woman. During the lecture, she visited the Hôtel de Cluny. Afterward, when she tried to catch a glimpse of the empty lecture room, she was debarred a second time by the same functionary, who muttered over and over, "It *is the rule*."[11]

Later she did see Leverrier strolling absently about in the Tuileries on the night of the court ball that she and the Springs attended in January 1847 after Fuller and Rebecca Spring were presented at court. (It was "the last Court ball but one" before the fall of Louis Philippe, Spring pointed out in her journal.) While Fuller was forced to admit that her royal evening was like a "flower-garden," she predicted that the regime was faltering; its policy of supporting the wealthy middle class at the expense of the workers and farmers could not continue much longer. In 1845 the food crisis that hit Ireland most tragically came to the rest of Europe. In France, the harvest of 1846 was even worse than that of the year before. As bread prices rose, the rest of the economy suffered and unemployment was rampant. "While Louis Philippe lives, the gases, compressed by his strong grasp, may not burst up to light," Fuller wrote home in a dispatch, "but the need of some radical measures of reform is not less strongly felt in France than elsewhere, and the time will come before long when such will be imperatively demanded."[12]

Fuller informed her readers that she was continuing her "survey" of prostitution and hoped to get out a publication based on her European research. She visited the Deaconess Home in Paris; it served as both a refuge for prostitutes and a hospital for sick children of the poor. She wrote a letter to the *Tribune* extolling the French system of parish crèches—community day-care centers for working women—and she recommended that Americans organize evening schools for working boys on the French model. Her most moving visit was to the School for Idiots near Paris where the young director, by means of an innovative program unknown in America, was teaching the children carpentry as well as reading and mathematics. In New York, Fuller had stressed that education should be a component of all charitable institutions; from France she wrote that she thought sorrowfully of all the children at home who could have benefited from similar care. Perhaps she was thinking of her brother Lloyd, whose condition had deteriorated to the point where Arthur and Richard thought he would have to be sent to the Brattleboro Asylum in Vermont.

It was probably through Pauline Roland that Margaret became acquainted with the legendary "Clarkey," the lively Englishwoman who presided over one of the most distinguished salons in midcentury Paris. But Mary Clarke's circle of English and French friends was so wide that many others could equally well have introduced them. Now in her fifties, a pretty, wide-eyed, snub-nosed, merry woman with a head of unruly curls, Clarke had lived in Paris since her girlhood. A friend of Mme. Récamier and Chateaubriand, she inherited Récamier's salon when the famed beauty retired and had entertained over the years a host of celebrities, including Benjamin Constant, Lafayette, Thiers, Mignet, Cousin, Scheffer, Augustin Thierry, Carrel, Victor Hugo, and Ampère. Clarke was now mourning the death of the poet and literary scholar Claude-Charles Fauriel, who had been her devoted companion for twenty years, a relationship she once described, on his part at least, as a love "sans passion." Clarke had a sharp eye and a candid manner, and she enjoyed Fuller's company enough to give her some useful letters of introduction to friends in Italy and Germany. Her description of Fuller in one of her letters is a vivid study of Fuller as she appeared to a sophisticated European woman:

[S]he is a celebrite (in her own country) and not stuck up and egotistical. She is an American and not always bothering about "our free country." She is enthusiastic and noble minded and yet has plain sense and discrimination of character which I wreckon (I guess) is more rare than all. . . . She has the American drawl . . . but when you get over a little absence of the European graces you will find a grace in her total absence of pretension and in her noble simplicity of character.[13]

Clarke, an able painter and translator, lived on a modest inheritance. She later wrote a book on the history of the salon in France. For her it was a benevolent institution, a way to help remedy the isolation and poverty of literary men and a way for women to make an important contribution to cultural life. As a young woman she had once planned to write a book on accomplished women. George Sand's success she welcomed as "a triumph to the sex," and she applauded Rachel's power over the French theater.[14]

Fuller had to wait until February to meet George Sand, the great woman novelist, who was now forty-three and at the height of her fame. In her novels and her life she had continually challenged social conventions that inhibited the emotional freedom of women. When Mazzini wrote Sand in December asking her to receive Margaret Fuller, she wrote back that she did not expect to return to Paris that winter; family demands and the local hunger riots prevented her from leaving Nohant, her country home. Sand's concern for the starving country people was common knowledge; in January, Margaret wrote Elizabeth Hoar that she had heard that Sand had donated 20,000 francs for the relief of the poor in her home department of Berry. Fuller was able to meet Sand only because Eddie Spring fell ill in January and the Springs postponed their departure for Italy. After Sand returned to Paris on February 5 to prepare the marriage contract of her daughter Solange, Fuller wrote a note announcing that she was coming to call.

She feared that Sand might not receive her and wanted Rebecca Spring to accompany her, but Spring, who shared the usual American distaste for Sand's moral code, refused. So Fuller went alone. Her heart sank when Sand's goddaughter came back to the door, after announcing her to Sand, and said that Sand did not know her. But the problem was soon rectified. The girl had mispronounced her name, and Sand came forward, graciously welcoming her. From that moment they got on famously, even though Fuller's French, as she willingly admitted, was woefully inadequate, especially for situations when she wanted to express herself fully.

Sand was dressed elegantly in a dark violet silk robe with a shawl; she constantly smoked a small cigarette—a custom Fuller observed was common among women in France. Her face was much finer than in the portraits, Fuller reported later, and "[h]er way of talking is just like her writing,—lively, picturesque, with an undertone of deep feeling, and the same skill in hitting the nail on the head every now and then with a blow."[15]

Sand was pleasant, but she did not encourage Fuller's friendship. It is unlikely that she had any idea of the extent to which Fuller had championed her work or the courage it had taken to do so in America. From the time Sand's novels had first appeared in the *Revue des Deux Mondes*, Fuller had read them avidly. They displayed a perception of the inner lives of women that answered to her own concerns: an awareness of the continual interplay in a woman's life "of the passions, and of social institutions," and "the choice which rose above them." Sand was the only novelist Fuller knew who dared to create women characters living "the intellectual life of an artist" without feeling it necessary to show them suffering social ostracism for pursuing "a career to which an inward vocation called them in preference to the usual home duties."[16]

In "The Great Lawsuit," Fuller pointed to Sand as a woman whose views forecast the future: "Women like Sand will speak now, and cannot be silenced; their characters and their eloquence alike foretell an era when such as they, shall easier learn to lead true lives." Later, she praised Sand in two *Tribune* reviews, defending her as a woman who was daring to "probe" the "festering wounds" of her country and helping to find "a cure," and she applauded when Frank Shaw began translating Sand's novels and publishing them in George Ripley's Associationist magazine, the *Harbinger*. But she did not advertise her Parisian interview with Sand in the *Tribune*. In her private journal she wrote:

She needs no defence, but only to be understood, for she has bravely acted out her nature, and always with good intentions. She might have loved one man permanently, if she could have found one contemporary with her who could interest and command her throughout her range; but there was hardly such a possibility of that, for such a person.[17]

Aware of Sand's long affair with the Polish composer Frédéric Chopin, Fuller was under the impression that they were still lovers. But by February 1847 Sand had tired of Chopin; they still had apartments across from each other on the Square d'Orléans, but she was easing him out of her life. Even so, Margaret, by a stroke of luck, managed to meet the great composer through the courtesy of one of his pupils, Jane Stirling, a member of the influential Scottish clan, who had been studying with Chopin for several years. Two days before Fuller left Paris at the end of February, Stirling invited her to sit in on her piano lesson. "I shall be glad to have a lover of *innermost* music with me, for such is Chopin," Stirling wrote when she invited Fuller to accompany her. Margaret found Chopin ill and "as frail as a snow-drop," but his music and his talking were equally satisfying. Intrigued with the gossip that Sand's affair with Chopin had been Platonic, Margaret wished there was a way to discover the truth.[18]

She had personal reasons to be interested in meeting Chopin. By the end of February she had formed an attachment to another Polish exile, a friend of Chopin's, the patriotic poet Adam Mickiewicz. When the Paris visit was extended, Margaret planned to attend Mickiewicz's lectures at the Collège de France, only to discover that he had recently been suspended from his professorship of Slavic literature, charged with using his lectures to advance the mystic message of the blind Polish priest Andrew Towianski, an illuminist mystic who believed himself to be a second Christ and assured his devoted following of Polish exiles in France that the Holy Spirit was working in the political arena to restore Polish nationhood.

In reading Mickiewicz's lectures, Fuller discovered with excitement that she shared many of his philosophical and even some of his religious beliefs: He quoted liberally from Emerson and included feminist themes in his poems; he had written a poem to Emily Plater, the Polish hero whose story Margaret had recounted in *Woman in the Nineteenth Century* and whose picture, she wrote, she would have liked for the book's frontispiece. In his poetry and his lectures, Mickiewicz prophesied a new age of spiritual elevation and social justice, and he called for support of the revolutionary movements in Europe to hasten their realization. To attract Mickiewicz's interest, Fuller sent him a volume of Emerson's poems.[19]

He responded immediately, and during Fuller's last ten days in Paris he spent

many evenings with her and the Springs. Mickiewicz invited Fuller to participated in meetings of the new Circle of God that he was leading himself after
a break with Towianski that did not impair his dedication to the philosophy
and mission of the Lithuanian master. Fuller responded enthusiastically to the
message of universal brotherhood, among whose many sources were Sweden-
borg, the Swedish philosopher who had greatly influenced Emerson, and Louis
Claude de Saint-Martin, the translator of Jakob Böhme, the German mystic
whom Fuller had admired in her early twenties.

After she attended the first Circle meeting, Mickiewicz wrote out for Fuller
his vision of her future role in life. He saw her as a "woman to whom it was
given to touch what is decisive in the present world and to have a presentiment
of the world of the future," and one who had a "mission" to contribute to the
deliverance of womanhood. But he thought that she was perhaps stunting
herself by clinging so strongly to the importance of remaining a virgin so as to
preserve her personal autonomy—the idea she had expressed in *Woman in the
Nineteenth Century*. While conceding that she had every right to her position,
he recommended that she reexamine it. "For you the first step in your deliverance and of the deliverance of your sex (of a certain class) is to know, whether
you are permitted to remain a virgin."[20]

Mickiewicz was a man of tempestuous temperament, and the Puritan idea of
strength through abnegation and denial was foreign to him, if not distasteful.
Yet he was sensitive enough to know that Fuller's sensual education would
require an adjustment that would only come with her consent. His own life had
been one of devotion to the cause of Polish nationalism and a defiance of the
Russian occupation of Polish territories. After he was imprisoned and deported
to Russia as a young man, he managed to exile himself to Paris, where he wrote
the great poems of Polish aspiration—including his epic *Pan Tadeusz*—which
made him a hero to his people and the natural leader of Polish exiles everywhere. Exile and financial uncertainty had been particularly hard on his wife,
Celia Szymanowska, who was emotionally unstable and lived outside Paris with
their two children. He was at the time of Fuller's visit emotionally involved with
the family governess, Xavière Deybel, and had a child by her.[21]

Before meeting Mickiewicz, Fuller had been disappointed that she had been
unable to cement a friendship in France with any public figure who was influencing progressive thought; there was no one, she wrote Emerson, who
could "initiate" her into the special "secrets of the place and time." But when
Mickiewicz befriended her she was sure she had found the representative man
of Europe's midcentury. Far more approachable than Mazzini, Mickiewicz not
only represented his people's sacrifices for national sovereignty but took a
personal interest in her progress. She wrote Emerson that she had found at last
"the man I had long wished to see, with the intellect and passions in due

proportion for a full and healthy human being, with a soul constantly inspiring. . . . How much time had I wasted on others which I might have given to this
real and important relation."[22]

She had formed an alliance with a fiery romantic revolutionary poet-priest, a
hero of the age, who encouraged her confidence, recognized her accomplishments, and even assigned her a role in the coming worldwide revolution. In
him she had found the long-sought friend who promised to perform the service she had taxed Emerson for failing to provide. In one of her letters to James
Nathan in New York, she had written that there were "in every age a *few* in
whose lot the meaning of that age is concentrated," and she felt that she was
"one of those persons." Mickiewicz recognized the power of the presentiments
she had cherished since her childhood of an undefined preordained destiny. By
the time she left Paris on February 25 he had promised to correspond with her
and serve as her spiritual advisor. Certain now that she would find a way to
return to Paris before returning home, she left a box of her winter clothes in the
care of one of Clarkey's friends, a wealthy and elderly Englishwoman, Miss
S. M. Fitton: her velvet bonnet, a brown merino dress, her fur muff, and an oval
watercolor of Faust and Marguerite.[23]

Before Fuller and the Springs left Paris, Mazzini sent word that because the
police were watching him too closely he could not risk a visit to the Continent,
so Margaret and the Springs followed the usual tourist route to the Mediterranean via Lyons without him. As the center of the French home-weaving industry and the site of a violent weavers' uprising in 1835, Lyons had a special interest
for them. In the winter of 1846–47, slackening of demand and technological
improvements had brought about falling wages and widespread unemployment among the home weavers, more than half of whom were women. Some
60 percent of the labor force of 200,000 were out of work. (In March 1848, a
year after Fuller's visit to Lyons, 400 women weavers staged a militant demon-
stration, marching to the Hôtel de Ville and demanding higher wages and
shorter hours.)[24]

The home weavers of Lyons were crowded into houses of seven or eight
stories on narrow, airless streets. Eight or more people often shared a single
room as workplace and living quarters. Fuller took only a short rest on her
arrival in the city before trudging up the steep Fournière hill where the poorest
canuts (the term was derived from the shuttles made of cane used in weaving),
as the weavers were called, lived in huddled misery. She described in her *Tribune* letter the conditions in a typical family workshop of weavers:

Entering the high buildings on this high hill, I found each chamber tenanted by a family
of weavers,—all weavers, wife, husband, sons, daughters—from nine years old upward—
each was helping. On one side were the looms, nearer the door the cooking apparatus,
the beds were shelves near the ceiling: they climbed up to them on ladders.

One teenage mother she interviewed testified to the continual pressure on everyone in the family to work constantly to pay for rent and food. She "knew [to a farthing] the price of every article of food and clothing that is wanted by such a household," Fuller reported. The young woman said that working constantly was her only option in life. "There are but these two ways open to them, weaving or prostitution," Margaret explained. She fumed at those who were complacent in the face of such conditions. "To themselves be woe, who have eyes and see not, ears and hear not, the convulsions and sobs of injured Humanity."[25]

Every one of her columns now made some plea on behalf of "injured Humanity." Her *Tribune* description of the visit to the weavers in their homes was reprinted in the Associationist journal, the *Harbinger*, in June. As she became increasingly devoted to blending social commentary and descriptive material with personal observations, her style became more natural and confident—sometimes too confident, for at times it was supercilious. Occasionally her observations echoed with Timothy Fuller's pompous phrases, especially when she discussed matters of high culture.

These lapses made Fuller an easy target for her old enemy, Charles Briggs, who, as coeditor with Poe of the *Broadway Journal*, had savagely attacked *Woman in the Nineteenth Century*. When the *Broadway Journal* folded—largely because the coeditors found it impossible to work together—Briggs became a columnist for the *New York Mirror*. Without leaving his study on Staten Island, he began writing a series of mock travel letters—signed with the dandyish name of Ferdinand Mendez Pinto—and publishing them as a column intended to parallel those of Fuller. He had in mind to parody the fatuous letters of Nathaniel P. Willis, which had appeared in the *Mirror* a few years earlier, but when Fuller's travel letters began showing up on the front page of the *Tribune*, he saw a fresh lode to exploit.

The owner of the *Mirror* was none other than Fuller's former Providence employer, the headmaster of Greene Street School, Hiram Fuller. From schoolmastering, Hiram Fuller had gone to hack journalism. Marrying well, he was able to buy the newspaper. Now he encouraged Briggs, whose own literary career had suffered many failures, to caricature his enemies and to use the "Pinto" letters as a continuing column of literary and social comment.

During the fall of 1846, while Fuller's *Papers on Literature and Art* was receiving attention on both sides of the Atlantic—mostly laudatory—the writers she had undervalued as well as those she had ignored were nursing their grudges. Briggs had several reasons to retaliate; she not only had championed his archenemy, Cornelius Mathews, but had dismissed the genius of his dear friend, James Russell Lowell. What is more, she was enjoying more literary renown than his boss, Hiram Fuller. In his "Pinto Letters," Briggs gleefully portrayed a gushing "Miss F." dancing Highland flings in Scottish castles and Yankee gigs in British pubs; he described her engaging in bombastic interviews with minor British authors and pontificating on Shakespeare and Goethe; of course, he did not neglect her "Ossianic" night on Ben Lomond. In a column allegedly describing the Elizabeth Barrett–Robert Browning wedding, he "reported" Fuller's wedding toast: "There was Miss F. . . . who made quite a speech—the only part of which I could distinctly hear was something about 'deep significance, aloofishness, union of immortals, woman's rights &c &c.' "[26]

At the end of February, before Fuller's letters from France began appearing in the *Tribune,* the joke had worn thin, and Briggs abruptly stopped his satires. Despite occasional purple passages and archness, Fuller's columns added up to considerably more than the superficial chattering of a stylish traveler in search of Old World culture and the chance to rub shoulders with nobility. It had become difficult to continue burlesquing a writer whose material was centered on democratic change and reform. In France her interest in the political and economic problems of Europe had become the major focus of her dispatches. The purpose of seeking useful ideas for transplantation in the New World had been swallowed up in her sense of a radical vocation to communicate the monstrous suffering and human waste of the historical moment. The human cost of laissez-faire industrial development met her everywhere; she wished to convey the message back to the United States that the same conditions might well follow at home; only a public sensitized to the misery entailed could be awakened to the need for preventive measures. In France, Fuller's social engagement deepened into a concern that pulsated beneath the surface of all her future dispatches. By the time she left Paris, she had sent the *Tribune* twelve letters. Unsure that Greeley would continue her on the job once she had supplied the fifteen for which he had paid in advance, she decided to send the last three from her beloved Italy.

From Lyons, Fuller and the Springs took a steamer down the Rhone to Avignon; there they tramped through the snow to the tomb of Petrarch's Laura. They took a stagecoach to Arles, where Fuller saw her first Roman amphitheater and admired the "full, earnest" gazes of the Arlesiennes.[27] Continuing on by stagecoach to Marseilles, they embarked for Italy by steamer. Their route was the usual one for American tourists on the way to Rome for Holy Week. No one would have any reason to suspect that there was anything out of the ordinary in their stopover in Genoa for a few days in the first week of March, certainly not that they were carrying a packet of letters from Giuseppe Mazzini and expected to receive further instructions from his mother, Maria Drago Mazzini.

I should always suffer the pain of Tantulus thinking of Rome, if I could not see it more thoroughly than I have as yet even begun to.

Italy at Last

MARIA Mazzini Drago, now in her seventies, had always believed in the sanctity of her son's mission. Throughout the sixteen years of his exile, she had kept up a continual chatty correspondence with him, as if she expected his triumphant return to Genoa at any moment. Her husband, Dr. Giacomo Mazzini, a retired professor of anatomy and a practicing physician, shared Giuseppe's compassion for the poor and the dispossessed, but he believed that his son's cause was "a monomaniacal fixation" that could only enflame the Austrian authorities occupying northern Italy and encourage bloodshed and hate. Italy would never become a republic, and it was foolish, he thought, to throw away everything for a utopian dream.[1]

When Fuller and the Springs arrived in Genoa in the first week of March 1847, Maria was already expecting them. Her son had written, asking her to do all she could to make his American friends comfortable. Fuller had told Mazzini of her plan to write a book about the events in modern Italy, and he had asked his mother to introduce her to several friends who might help. In particular, Fuller was to meet two women friends of the family, Fanny Balbi and Caroline Celesia, Mazzini sympathizers who had suffered persecution from the Piedmontese police. After Fuller heard their stories, she told Rebecca that she could understand why Mazzini had chosen his fugitive life. Mazzini had given Fuller letters of introduction to editors in Milan and Torino who were sympathetic to the republican cause and had instructed his mother to initiate a correspondence with Fuller and keep track of her whereabouts as she traveled in Europe—he never knew when he might need her services.

Maria Mazzini was immediately taken with Fuller, but Fuller's easy familiarity led her to misinterpret the American's friendship with her son. When Maria wrote "Pippo" (her nickname for Giuseppe) asking if Margaret intended to return to London to take care of him, he immediately wrote back:

I tell you not to desire that my American friend should reside in London to take care of me. Don't worry! If I were a man to yield and grow soft in the midst of Capuan delights, I would have all possible opportunities to do so: there are at least half a dozen young women, who contend each other the privilege of surrounding me with loving care. The Lord knows if I feel grateful to them, but I cannot afford to grow soft in the midst of their attentions. Sometimes the excessive affection of these young friends of mine makes me sad! Furthermore, if I yielded I would waste all my time with them.[2]

He also sent along several pages from the letter Fuller had written him in gratitude for Maria's kindnesses to her and the Springs. He was touched that Fuller included some sprigs of lavender picked from a spot under the library window. More important was a clipping from the *New-York Tribune* of February 19, Fuller's dispatch from London in which she had devoted to him and his work six paragraphs of praise. This was the kind of help he needed.

Mazzini had another reason for wanting to keep in touch with Fuller. Certain that she was committed to his cause, he had arranged with the *People's Journal* to publish in advance selections from the book she was preparing. This invitation, coming along with a separate request from the Howitts in London and one from Pauline Roland in Paris, encouraged her to begin thinking of staying on in Europe for another year. Her contacts in the European republican network through Mazzini and Mickiewicz gave her an added sense of purpose. The February 1847 issue of the *People's Journal* contained the flattering notice that both George Sand and S. Margaret Fuller would contribute to "future pages of the *People's Journal*." She was now in important company.[3]

In Leghorn, George Palmer Putnam, partner in Wiley and Putnam, the New York publishing house that issued *Papers on Literature and Art,* and his wife, Victorine Haven Putnam, joined Fuller and the Springs for the journey to Naples on the British steamer, the *Tiger.* George Putnam, who had been representing his publishing house in London for several months, admired Fuller and had arranged his trip so as to enjoy her company. Also an admirer of Mazzini, he had been present at the Italian Free School birthday celebration in London when Fuller gave her impromptu speech. Putnam came to admire her even more when, during one of their first nights on the Mediterranean, a mail steamer collided with the *Tiger,* smashing one of the paddle boxes and the wheel. After the jolt, Putnam rushed on deck to investigate the damage; then he ran down to the women's cabin to reassure them that the hull was not injured. As he described the scene, Fuller, in her nightdress, opened the door to the cabin and, on being told that they were in no danger, replied, "Oh, we—had not—made up our minds, that it was—worth while—to be at all—alarmed!" "Verily," Putnam wrote in his journal, "woman—American woman, at least—is wonderful for her cool philosophy and strong-nerved stoicism in great danger!"[4]

The weather in northern Italy and at sea was cold and overcast, and Fuller had to wait until she reached sunny Naples before she found "*my* Italy." For three weeks the group visited all the shrines in the guidebook: the Grotto of Pausilippo, Vesuvius, Baia, Cumae, Capri, Sorrento, and Paestum. Overcome with the pleasure of seeing at last so many of the hallowed places she had been anticipating for years, Fuller was transported by "the sense of enchantment, of sweet exhilaration." But playing against her insistence on having her expectations met was her newly sharpened awareness of the human misery in "this priest-ridden, misgoverned, full of dirty, degraded men and women, yet still most lovely Naples."[5]

Most Americans touring Europe tried to be in Rome to see the colorful church ceremonies of Easter Week, but this year (1847) the celebrations were twofold. The new pope, Pius IX—elected sovereign ruler of the Papal States in June 1846—had announced the formation of a state council of twenty-four elected lay members as well as a municipal government for the city of Rome. "Nothing could seem more limited than this improvement," Fuller wrote to the *Tribune*, "but it was a great measure for Rome."[6]

Pope Nono, as Pius IX was affectionately called, had raised the hope that he would begin the transfer of power from the papacy to the people. He was known to be sympathetic to the liberal movement in Italy but had to proceed cautiously with concessions. The Austrians, who controlled territories surrounding the Papal States, were watching him closely, and strong forces within the church opposed any abrogation of temporal power. Even so, within the first months of his papacy, Pope Nono granted amnesty to several classes of political prisoners, liberalized censorship measures, and mitigated criminal procedures.

By Easter Week 1847, the spirit of revitalization came at least as much from the changed political climate as it did from the traditional season of spiritual renewal; the patriotic demonstrations—permitted for the first time in decades—provided as much color and emotive power as the beautiful but oft-repeated ceremonies of the church. As Fuller described those days, the "numerous and splendid" Easter Week ceremonials were a rich experience, but nothing to compare with the torchlight procession to celebrate the new representative Council of State. The procession started as a circle of fire around the obelisk and lion fountain at the Piazza del Populo. As the crowd proceeded down the Corso, it became a "river of fire" and mounted the steps of Monte Cavallo toward the pope's Quirinal Palace, illuminating the colossal rampant horses and the monumental torsos of Castor and Pollux. Fuller wrote that she had never seen anything finer in her life.[7]

The same week, friends of Mazzini provided her and the Springs with tickets to the open-air dinner in the Baths of Titus celebrating the restoration of municipal government. With the Colosseum and the triumphant arches in the background, the guests—many were only recently returned from exile—assembled to congratulate Pius IX as the founder of the New Rome. Rebecca Spring wrote in her journal that they attended four festivals celebrating the people's expectation that Pope Nono would restore all their ancient liberties, but Fuller was not at all certain that radical change was on the horizon. After observing the pope carefully throughout one of the civic festivals, "Margaret turned sadly away," Rebecca wrote, saying, " 'He is not great enough. He can never carry out the work before him.' "She feared that his reforms would turn out to be mere palliatives, not drastic enough to accomplish the goal to which she had committed her sympathies: a unified Italian nation under a republican form of government and a church shorn of temporal power.[8]

In her *Tribune* dispatch reporting on the celebrations, she pointed out that the people were giving themselves up to "perpetual hurra, vivas, rockets, and torch-light processions," without stopping to realize how "hampered and inadequate are the means at [the pope's] command." She predicted that "the liberty of Rome" was not yet ready to "advance with seven-leagued boots; and the new Romulus will need to be prepared for deeds at least as bold as his predecessor, if he is to open a new order of things."[9]

Pius IX had been influenced by the controversial program advanced by the exiled abbot Vincenzo Gioberti in his book, *The Moral and Civil Primacy of the Italians* (1843). For many Italians who wished to be free of Austrian rule, the goal of a national Italian federation under the moral leadership of the pope seemed within the range of possibility, and many moderates of the Gioberti stamp were among the returned exiles who crowded into Rome to join in the celebration of the new era. One of the most distinguished of the moderate party was Costanza Arconati Visconti, whom Margaret probably met through the good offices of her Paris friend, Mary Clarke, who was an intimate friend and correspondent. But it is also possible that Margaret carried a letter of introduction from Julia Ward Howe who, on her wedding trip in 1843, had been entertained by Arconati.

Costanza Arconati, the Viennese-born wife of Giuseppe Visconti, scion of the legendary family, had only recently returned to Italy after twenty-five years of political exile in France and Belgium. She supported a step-by-step advancement under the leadership of the pope to an Italian constitutional monarchy. Widely read, politically involved, and internationally connected, she was the model of the European woman Margaret had admired ever since she had read Mme. de Staël's books in her teens.

Arconati shared Fuller's fascination with recent German intellectual history; she had known Bettina von Arnim and Rahel von Ense personally and was collecting material with the hope of writing a book on the latter. Edgar Quinet, who had met Arconati frequently at Mary Clarke's salon, described her as having a German air, the grace of a Frenchwoman, and the patriotism of an Italian Carbonaro, a woman whose charm was one of perfect simplicity, gracious and profound at the same time. For years the Italian patriotic poet Giovanni Berchet had lived with the Arconati family as tutor to their son, all the while cherishing an unrequited love for Costanza. During her rather luxurious exile at Gaesbeck in Belgium, the large estate of the Viscontis, Costanza held a continual open house for literary luminaries and Catholic liberals, among them Claude Fauriel and his companion, Mary Clarke. Both the Arconati–Berchet and the Clarke–Fauriel relationships were accepted as Platonic. Each couple traveled together, lived under one roof some of the time, and wrote each other faithfully in the most affectionate terms when separated. To Fuller, who had so much experience with a similar Muse-like relationship as part mother, part teacher, and part protectress and inspirer to young men of artistic bent, this European institution was both appealing and liberating.[10]

Within a few days of her arrival in Rome, she met by coincidence two other European women whose independent styles of life she had read about for years. On Easter Wednesday, at the Sistine Chapel while waiting to hear the Miserere, she found herself seated next to Ottilie von Pogwisch von Goethe, the daughter-in-law of Fuller's hero. She had come to Rome especially to visit Anna Jameson, who was settled there for the winter preparing the text and illustrations for her forthcoming book, *Sacred and Legendary Art*.

According to Emelyn Story, who was to become Fuller's confidante in Rome, Fuller went to hear vespers at St. Peter's on Holy Thursday, the following day, and afterward lost track of the Springs in the dense crowd. As she wandered about, she was approached by a handsome young Italian in his late twenties who offered help. He tried to get her a horse carriage but, because of the competition of the crowd, discovered there was no way to assist her short of walking her back to her hotel on the Corso. This was how Story later remembered Fuller's description of how she had first met Giovanni Ossoli.

George Palmer Putnam, who claimed to be an eyewitness to their first encounter, told a different version of the meeting, even placing it on Ash Wednesday after the Miserere. He remembered Margaret appearing suddenly out of the crowd in St. Peter's Square. She seemed "quite bewildered" and explained that "she had lost her friends." She had "taken the arm of a young gentleman in the crowd, who politely offered to escort her home, or to a cab." As soon as she saw the Putnams, she summarily dropped the young man's arm and took leave of him. "She certainly did not give her address to him," Putnam insisted. "How and when they met again, we do not know," he reported, but he was certain that this was Margaret's first meeting with the man whose name she would bear two years later. Putnam put so little stock in the incident at the time that, when he next wrote to his editorial colleague, Evert Duyckinck, he made the prurient remark that, "within the precincts of the sanctuary," of St. Peter's, Miss Fuller "received very singular suggestions from the young men of Rome which may afford instructive notes to a future edition of Woman in the Nineteenth Century."[11]

But the encounter was hardly as banal as Putnam assumed. A genuine friendship soon ripened. Rebecca and Marcus later recalled the young man's devoted attendance on Margaret, but they did not know at the time that he was a marchese: Giovanni Angelo Ossoli, the youngest son of an aristocratic family which had distinguished itself in the papal service since the seventeenth century. Although fallen in fortune in recent years, they still maintained a palazzo on the Via Tor de Specchi, where Giovanni lived in a second-floor apartment taking care of his invalid father.

As his mother had died when he was a young child and he was considerably younger than his three brothers and two sisters, he had been brought up apart from them and now was on close terms only with his sister Angela, who, married to the Marchese De Andreis, lived on the first floor of the family palazzo. Giuseppe, his eldest brother, was a high papal functionary with a grown family. Two other brothers, Ottavio and Pietro, were officers in the Papal Guard. Another sister, Matilda Ossoli Macnamara, who was married to an Irishman and living in Limerick, seldom wrote to her Italian relatives. Giovanni Angelo, the youngest Ossoli, had received only a casual education from a priest, consisting mostly of a smattering of Latin and religious instruction. At twenty-six he was without a firm purpose in life or a sense of vocation, but he was courteous, gentle, and responsible. To what extent he was already committed to the cause of Italian national unity is not certain, but Margaret let herself enjoy the relaxation of his easy, uncomplicated companionship.

Before the Ossoli connection had time to ripen, she was faced with deciding whether she could afford to remain in Europe for another year. On April 10 a letter arrived from Adam Mickiewicz that forced the issue. The letter, in answer to one of hers, sent from Naples, advised Margaret to live as much as possible with nature, to immerse herself in everything Italian—the music, the spirit, the conversation. He stressed that she "needed" Italy; that was why he had not encouraged her to stay longer in Paris:

And in everything I told you I had in mind your happiness and your progress. You say I was too occupied (busy)!? My occupations, dear Friend, were not of the type that absorb your compatriots. I was not busy in the American sense. Every day I had matters which demanded the whole man, thus I could not be at your disposal completely. And I did not wish to see you unless all of me could be with you.[12]

When Rebecca Spring read the letter and saw how much store Fuller was putting in some future relationship with the Polish poet, she warned her not to be carried away and was outspoken in her opposition when Fuller said she wanted to return to Paris and be with Mickiewicz. As Spring recorded in her journal, "[W]e talked about it late into the night. The next morning she wrote to me a letter of twenty-four pages which she gave to me when we met at breakfast." Margaret, she recalled, "was impatient of contradiction or opposition, and sometimes liked better to express herself by writing than talking. I begged her not to decide hastily and she said she would go to the Villa Borghese and think about it." The unselfconscious and instinctive quality of Italian life had already influenced Fuller to ignore the emotional risks and surrender to the Muse.[13]

The gist of Fuller's letter was that she wished "to be free and absolutely true to

[her] nature," even if this brought pain, as had been the case in the past. She was willing to pay that price, because no matter how deeply she suffered she always emerged "the gainer, always younger and more noble." She was uncertain whether she had ever felt love as "oneness" with another, but she had "loved enough to feel the joys of presence[,] the pangs of absence, the sweetness of hope, and the chill of disappointment."

You ask me if I love M. I answer he affected me like music or the richest landscape, my heart beat with joy that he at once felt beauty in me also. When I was with him I was happy; and thus far the attraction is so strong that all the way from Paris I felt as if I . . . should return at this moment and leave Italy unseen.[14]

In spite of her history of disappointments, Fuller still held on to the hope that where she loved she would provoke love in return, and, if not, the experience itself was her reward. Even at the moment when she recorded her bitter and vicious response to Nathan's letter informing her of his engagement, she had written that she was determined to turn the experience "to account in a literary way." Rebecca, who had recently witnessed this heartbreak and felt responsible for Margaret's welfare, tried to discourage another reckless involvement.[15]

Once Fuller determined to stay in Italy, she started a campaign to raise some extra money. She wrote Richard, asking him how much he could send her without creating hardships for her mother, and she was shameless in her requests to her friends. She alerted George Davis to her need, hinted to Aunt Mary Rotch and the Mannings how useful a little extra would be, and even approached Waldo Emerson. Of them all, Emerson was the most aware that in Europe she was truly in her element. Greatly impressed with her ability to form liaisons with interesting people anywhere, he congratulated her on "the good & famous men & women" she was enjoying and especially on her meeting with George Sand. His good wishes seemed to capture perfectly her current condition:

It was high time, dear friend, that you should run out of the coop of our bigoted societies full of fire damp & azote, and find some members of your own expansive fellowship. What you sought & found at home only in gleams & sparkles of red & yellow light,—in those older gardens is absorbed & assimilated into texture, form, hue, & savour of flower & fruit. Well speed as you have begun, from the France of France to the Italy of Italy, blessed in nothing more than this, that we at home so heartily feel that we all succeed in your success.[16]

In his journal Emerson mused over Fuller's drive to involve herself in complex relationships with successful people, a fascination that was totally foreign to his own inclination to avoid all entanglements. His calling her Corinne (after the *improvitrice* heroine of Mme. de Staël's novel *Corinne; ou, l'Italie*), as he had often done in the past to pay honor to her gift for improvising spontaneous conversation, took on added significance after Fuller arrived in Italy. "What a spendthrift you are, o beautiful Corinne!" he wrote. "What needless webs you weave, what busy arts you play. It costs you no exertion to paint the image of yourself that lies on my retina. Yet how splendid that benefit! and all your industry adds so little and puts in peril so much." It would seem that Emerson understood Fuller's theory of the emotional peril that accompanied the unleashing of womens' electrical and divinatory powers. Although her friends gained much from her, she squandered heedlessly her energies and talent and took dangerous emotional chances.[17]

He had often told her that her exuberant nature made her a foreigner in cautious New England. "By all means keep the Atlantic between you & us for the present," he advised. "I would fain know the best of your Roman experiences," he wrote, begging her to send him more letters. But he refused to send her money, telling her that unfortunately his "unskillful economics" had brought him recently into debt.[18]

Margarett Crane Fuller offered $100 from a loan Eugene had just repaid, but it hurt her that Margaret, in appealing to her friends and family, had reminded them of her mismanaged childhood as a means of bullying them into sympathy for her cause. Her mother wrote: "I regret that I have not been more to you all the years of your life,—if we are reconciled in future years I will try to redeem the past—I used to think if I gave you the [illegible] use of time it was the greatest good I could bestow." She now realized that she should have paid more attention to Margaret's "physical being" and let her "genius to grow upon a strong body."[19]

Richard rose to the occasion and did all he could to raise the money, even though it was not easy to borrow from one to pay the other—the usual Fuller family technique—at a time when Eugene's new wife was expecting their first child and William was threatened with another business failure in Cincinnati. With Arthur graduating from divinity school without a church placement and Ellen and Ellery living on the generosity of the Channing family, a munificent donation was unlikely. Margarett Crane Fuller wrote that Lloyd had now "acquiesced" in going to the Brattleboro Asylum. Richard was a member of the Massachusetts bar now and working as a partner with Uncle Henry in the old office established by Timothy during the first decade of the century, but his uncle's authoritarian ways and constant preaching were becoming almost unendurable and he was dreaming of going west. Against all these odds, he was just making headway toward putting aside a family loan of $100 for Margaret when Uncle Abraham died suddenly on April 6, two days after Easter. The news took well over a month to reach Italy. By the time Margaret heard of her uncle's death there was no doubt in her mind that she would remain in Europe, at least through the coming winter.[20]

She had written Mickiewicz about her meeting with Ossoli and almost immediately received a reply with the advice she needed: "Do not be too hasty about leaving places where you feel well, one is rarely free to return to them.

Prolong your good moments. Do not leave those who would like to remain near you. This is in reference to the little Italian you met in the Church." She was to keep him "always . . . informed about" herself. "I still hope to see you again in Paris. Give me exact details as to your probable date of arrival here." His final words were, "Try to bring away from Italy what you will be able to take of it in joy and in health. There is nothing else to take!"[21]

For Fuller, Mickiewicz's prompt response was proof of his willingness to be her spiritual guide, and his words were like a divine revelation. For years she had believed—as most of the Transcendentalists believed—that the poet-preacher was at the pinnacle of the human hierarchy. Now she had as her personal advisor the poet-preacher-patriot Adam Mickiewicz.

Artists were arguably on the same level as poets. Michelangelo and Raphael had been early members of Fuller's pantheon, and she never quite forgave Sam Ward, her own "Raphael," for abandoning his teenage hobby of painting. At the end of April, while touring the artists' studios in Rome, she met a young American painter whose work she thought gave promise, and she immediately encouraged his friendship. Thomas Hicks, who shared a studio with John Kensett on the Via Margutta off the Piazza di Spagna, was already, at twenty-four, an associate member of the American National Academy. He had first learned to paint from his cousin, the coach painter Edward Hicks, whose numerous *Peaceable Kingdoms* were popular in Pennsylvania. After studying at the Pennsylvania Academy and the National Academy of Design in New York, Hicks had come to Europe to continue his education, supporting himself by making copies of European masters for American collectors.[22]

After Hicks had entertained Margaret and the Springs in his studio, Margaret asked him to call on her. When she did not hear from him, she sent him a book and a compelling note.

I do not understand why you do not seek me more. You said you were too hard at work and had not time. I tried to believe you, because you seem to me one who always wishes to speak the truth exactly, but I could not. I can always find time to see any one I wish to; it seems to me it is the same with every one.

You are the only one whom I have seen here in whose eye I recognized one of my own kindred. I want to know and to love you and to have you love me; you said you had no friendliness of nature but that is not true; you are precisely one to need the music, the recognition of kindred minds. How can you let me pass you by, without full and free communication. I do not understand it, unless you are occupied by some other strong feeling. Very soon I must go from here, do not let me go without giving me some of your life. I wish this for both our sakes, for mine, because I have so lately been severed from congenial companionship, that I am suffering for want of it, for yours because I feel as if I had something precious to leave in your charge.[23]

Hicks responded cautiously to her invitation. Recognizing, he wrote, that the offer came from "the full heart of a great woman, tender, serene, beautiful," he worried that if he told her all about himself she might be disappointed to find only "a lonely ambitious man," even though "great thoughts and the hope to do good deeds engross[ed]" him.

If we are kindred, as you say, and our horoscope in some respects the same, can we ever be separated?

You spoke of my youth, is it by years then that *Life* is measured? Do you not perceive that my heart has grown grey? . . . It is you who are young for every pulse of your being is full & warm with Love.[24]

His letter was provocative, artful with the confusion and studied bewilderment of a young man with his guard up but flattered by her interest. They were soon good friends; Fuller praised his paintings in the *Tribune,* and he became a frequent companion on outings. "Why was I not born here? Why did I ever live anywhere else?" she asked Rebecca. As the weather grew warmer, they took carriage trips every day to the Campagna—to Tivoli, Frascati, Tusculum, Albano, and Lake Nemi. At the Capuchin monastery at Castel Gandolfo, much to the pleasure of the shy Rebecca, Margaret made friends with the monks, joking with them in Italian and Latin, creating such a mood of happy camaraderie that the monks invited them to a picnic of fresh strawberries and cream. Margaret was "radiant," Rebecca remembered. With the passionate, uncritical Italians Fuller had found freedom from the weight she bore at home of feeling like an outsider.[25]

Eager "to know the common people, and to feel truly in Italy," she threw herself into studying the language. By the time she left Rome with the Springs in mid-June she had her mind set on returning. Although the Springs knew that she was on friendly terms with the young man they knew only as "Giovanni," they had no idea that a serious romance had begun or that, as Margaret wrote her sister later, Giovanni had offered her "his hand through life" and that she loved him but refused because "the connextion seemed so every way unfit." In the meantime, she wanted to see the hill towns between Rome and Florence and visit Bologna, Ferrara, and Venice before making her final decision.[26]

Soon after arriving in Florence, around June 20, the news came from home that Uncle Abraham's death made it likely she would have a windfall, at least enough to see her through a few more months. "I should always suffer the pain of Tantulus thinking of Rome, if I could not see it more thoroughly than I have as yet even begun to," she wrote to Richard on the first of July. "I had only just begun to live with their life when I was obliged to leave." Now it seemed reasonable that Richard would be able to send about $500 for deposit in her Paris bank.[27]

With Rome so strongly in her mind, Florence was something of a disappointment, but she realized that it was a rich place to study the fine arts. She renewed her acquaintance with Costanza Arconati, who was there with her husband to celebrate the Grand Duke Leopold's concession of a free press. Almost certain she would be returning to Rome, Margaret made arrangements to stay with the American sculptor Joseph Mozier and his wife on her way back. Mozier was a Vermonter who had come to Florence to try his hand at sculpture after a successful business career in New Jersey. The American artist colony in Florence also included Horatio Greenough and Hiram Powers, both of whom were famous in the United States. Powers had done a bust of Anna Barker a decade before when she was in Rome with Mrs. Farrar. Now he was presiding over the most popular of the art studios in Florence—it was on everyone's itinerary. In the summer of 1847 Powers was a celebrity because of the astonishing success in America of his nude statue, *The Greek Slave* ("[S]o undressed yet so refined," Henry James described it later). Horace Greeley wrote Margaret that "Powers's Greek Slave is raining him flattery and coin among us. I think it must have raked in some thousands already and it has evidently but begun."[28]

In the studio, Margaret admired another of Powers's respectable nudes, his *Eve*, as well as the "simple and majestic" statue of John C. Calhoun that he was working on at the time, a statue that was to play a fateful role in her future. She admired a head of Napoleon that Horatio Greenough was modeling, but her mind was as much on the political situation in Tuscany as on the study of the fine arts. The new press law had opened the way for a flood of reformist literature. She read enough to inform her *Tribune* readers that although everything in Italy seemed quiet the calm was only superficial—"within, Tuscany burns"—everyone was waiting "for a very different state of things."[29]

In Bologna, famous for its recognition of women scholars and artists, Margaret searched out several monuments honoring women of achievement, including a recent professor of Greek, Matilda Tambroni. She also saw many works by the women artists Properzia di Rossi, Elizabetta Sirani, and Lavinia Fontana. The aristocratic women of Bologna even had their own meeting place for lectures, conversations, and entertainments.

On arrival in Venice in early July, Margaret and the Springs settled in the Europa Hotel, formerly the Giustiniani Palace, on the Grand Canal. They rented their own gondola and, with two devoted gondoliers, were able to watch the splendid entertainments in the nearby palaces. Joining a flotilla of gondolas at night, they watched the guests arrive by water at a celebration given by Mme. de Berri, while a band played from the balcony: " 'Twas a scene of fairy-land; the palace full of light."[30]

Soon afterward, the Springs received news that the cousin who was caring for their four-year-old daughter, Jeanie, in America, was engaged to be married and wished to be relieved of her child-care duties as soon as possible. Rebecca and Marcus had been away from home for almost a year; Rebecca was missing Jeanie; Marcus's health was unreliable. It was clearly time for them to return.

"We urged Margaret to go with us," Rebecca wrote in her journal, "but she had her heart set on going back to Rome." From a gondola, Fuller watched her friends go off on an Adriatic steamer on their way to Trieste, where Rebecca's brother William worked at the American consulate. When she wrote Sturgis, in explaining her decision to stay on in Italy, she was disingenuous. She stated her change of plans in the terms of the psychological theory she had formulated in *Woman in the Nineteenth Century:* Concentrated emotional dependency on others leads to pain and anxiety; the solution is a period of solitary withdrawal.

At Venice, the Springs left me, and it was high time, for I had become qui[te] insupportable I was always out of the body, and they, good friends, were *in.* I felt at times a wicked irritation against them for being the persons who took me away from France, which was no fault of theirs. Since I have been alone I ha[ve] grown reasonable again; indee[d] in [the] first week floating about in [a] go[nd]ola, I seemed to find myself again.[31]

Before Marcus left, he advanced Fuller $500 on the strength of Uncle Abraham's will. She employed a servant, Domenico, to serve as a guide and general factotum; she would travel no longer as the American tourist but in the manner of the successful European women authors, Martineau, Jameson, and Sand. At the end of July, when her young friends left Venice, she embarked at last on the new phase of her life. By way of Vicenza, Verona, and Mantua, she traveled to Riva di Trento on Lake Garda. There she took a room for a few days to rest, write letters, enjoy grand views of the Dolomites, and become accustomed to her recent achievement—independence on her own terms. She noted that she was only a few miles from the castle of the Castelbarco family, where Dante had stayed many times during his long exile from Florence. Here she gathered her forces before beginning her new life as an American expatriate in Italy. She had chosen her own exile.

I have not been so well since I was a child, nor so happy ever as during the last six weeks.

Return to Rome

WHILE Fuller worked her way back to Rome during August and September 1847, she wrote Adam Mickiewicz frequently. When she arrived in Milan on the first of August, she found a letter scolding her for letting "romantic reveries" and "melancholy" take over her imagination. "I tried to make you understand that you should not confine your life to books and reveries. You have pleaded the liberty of woman in a masculine and frank style. Live and act, as you write." Mickiewicz stressed that the key to happiness lay in learning how to express freely one's own experience in the daily acts of life:

I saw you, with all your knowledge and your imagination and all your literary reputa-tion, living in bondage worse than that of a servant. You were obligated to everybody. You have persuaded yourself that all you need is to express your ideas and feelings in books. You existed like a ghost that whispers to the living its plans and desires, no longer able to realize them itself. . . . Do not forget that even in your private life *as a woman* you have rights to maintain. Emerson says rightly: *give all for love,* but this *love* must not be that of the shepherds of Florian nor that of schoolboys and German ladies. The relation-ships which suit you are those which develop and free your spirit, responding to the legitimate needs of your organism and leaving you free at all times. You are the sole judge of these needs.[1]

Fuller instantly replied that she found his words "*harsh,*" but he refused to soften his message. He reiterated that she had to learn how to integrate the happiness and animation of her inner life with her whole physical life so that the shocks of reality would not continue to drive her into moods of melancholy and discouragement:

I know well that you often feel *gay* and always animated *internally,* especially when you meditate or when you dream and compose. But try to get this inner life lodged and established in all your body. . . . I tried to make you understand the purpose of your existence, to inspire manly sentiments in you. Your mind still does not wish to believe that a new epoch commences and that it has already begun. New for *woman* too. . . .
. . . You still live spiritually in the society of Shakespeare, Schiller, Byron. Literature is not the whole life.[2]

Mickiewicz recognized that Fuller was driven by erotic energy that she had not learned to focus on the goals she was pursuing. She had made herself a reputation as a herald of a new age for women, but she had failed to recognize that she was herself still very much a victim of the repression of the old order and of the escape strategies she used to cope with her situation. When he told her that she was placing too high a value on intellectual accomplishment to the detriment of a more balanced life, and that taking pride in self-denial and refuge in unrealistic dreams was sapping her energy and threatening her health, he was only telling her what she had already formulated in her writings but had not yet applied effectively to herself.

In Milan, Fuller had expected to visit Costanza Arconati but was able to see her for only a moment because Arconati was on her way to Livorno to attend to an illness in the family. Margaret was already short of money again, and Arconati loaned her 500 francs. Domenico, her employee, was costing her far more than she had expected—he was constantly cheating her, she said—but she thought she had no choice but to keep him, for a woman of any rank would not travel alone without a manservant. She wrote Marcus Spring, begging him to contact Joseph Mozier and ask him to give her a loan when she arrived in Florence.

Costanza Arconati easily arranged an introduction for Fuller to Italy's most famous writer, Alessandro Manzoni, for his daughter was married to Costanza's younger brother. Of all living Italians, Manzoni was the most revered by Americans. During Emerson's European trip in 1834 following the death of his first wife, he had sought out Manzoni because he admired him as a moralist and as the author of the remarkable novel, *I Promessi Sposi*. In *Woman in the Nineteenth Century,* Fuller cited Manzoni's marriage to Henriette Blondel as an example of an ideal union. She later learned that Manzoni's remarriage after Blondel's death—to Teresa Borri Stampa—had dispelled the legend of his marital devotion. Arconati pictured Borri Stampa to Fuller as a difficult recluse, but after meeting her Fuller wrote Emerson that she liked her and found it easy to understand why Manzoni had married her. "Manzoni has spiritual efficacy in his looks; his eyes glow still with delicate tenderness," Fuller wrote Emerson, but in the *Tribune* she stressed that he did not speak to the new epoch. "Young Italy prizes his works, but feels that the doctrine of 'Pray and wait' is not for her at this moment,—that she needs a more fervent hope, a more active faith. She is right."[3]

Before leaving Milan, Fuller looked up two of Mazzini's friends, the educator and editor Enrico Mayer and the youthful aristocrat Guerrieri Gonzaga; both promised to be of help in her effort to write a book on the events in Italy. At the end of August she caught up with Costanza Arconati for ten days at the Visconti villa at Bellagio on Lake Como. Arconati showed her off to her fashionable friends—including the Polish Princess Radziwill, "one of the emancipated wom[e]n," as Fuller called her, and Lady Jane Franklin, who had recently returned from nine years in Tasmania where her husband, Sir John Franklin—now leading an expedition in search of the Northwest Passage—had been lieutenant governor.[4]

Fuller wrote Sturgis that she was enjoying the company of "duchesses, marquises and the like" and found it pleasant to hear of "spheres" so little like her own. The life on Lake Como reminded her of the old dream she had shared with Sturgis of gathering all their best friends in cottages along the Artichoke River at Newburyport near Curson's Mill:

The life here on the lake is precisely what we once at Newbury imagined as being so pleasant; these people have charming villas and gardens on the lake, adorned with fine works of art; they go out to see one another in boats; you can be all the time in a boat, if you like. If you want more excitement or wild flowers you climb the mountains.[5]

When Fuller told Arconati about her friendship with Adam Mickiewicz and of his advice to live a more balanced life, to respond consciously to her need for sensual pleasure and bodily satisfactions, Arconati, like Rebecca Spring before her, was concerned that Mickiewicz was leading Fuller astray. She thought that there was something limiting about his Slavic mysticism. "I will be very angry if you do as Mickiewicz wishes," she warned Fuller. "Even though I respect him; nevertheless I feel very uneasy in his presence, while I feel nothing of the kind with you even though you are from another country and are separated from me by your beliefs and your extraordinary superiority."[6] Presumably Arconati read Mickiewicz's letters to Fuller and interpreted his message as an invitation to unbridled license and behavior that would compromise her new friend's reputation. Constanza was concerned that she would be swept into what she perceived as the mad mysticism that animated Mazzini and the other revolutionaries, and she felt compelled to give Fuller fair warning.

After stopping in Parma to see the paintings of Corregio, Fuller pushed on to Florence. There the Moziers put her to bed for a few days so she could regain her energy. In Florence she found her first letters from home in two months. The most reassuring news was that Richard had sent $500 to the Greene and Company Bank in Paris and that a letter of credit in her name had already arrived in Florence. Responding to her plea for a loan, her New York friends, the Mannings, the Associationist friends of Greeley and the Springs with whom she had often stayed in New York in 1846, had deposited a generous sum in her name with the restriction that she must draw on it in two parts at stated intervals.

Only one family matter preyed on her mind now. Richard had announced that he was engaged to a young Canton woman whom Fuller did not know, Anna De Rose. She thought that Richard was rushing too hastily into marriage out of the need for sympathetic companionship, and she wrote advising him to defer the marriage for several years. Now twenty-three, Richard was earning a living at the bar, yet Margaret's mothering habit was strongly embedded, and, even at this distance, she could not resist advising him to wait three or four years.[7]

Fuller had recently received news of the separation of her good friend Jane

Tuckerman King from her husband, John, after a union of four years. Jane's step, like Almira Penniman Barlow's divorce, was an unusual one among Margaret's friends; the custom was to perpetuate the relationship no matter how bleak it had become. Sarah Clarke's last letter had mentioned details of Elizabeth Randall Cumming's tormented marriage, and Margaret had watched many of her other friends, notably Ellen Sturgis Hooper (Caroline's sister) and Mary Young Greeley, suffer the bitter disillusionment of their romantic dreams. She had also witnessed the silent distances in the Emerson marriage, and, within her immediate family, the glaring example of Ellen and Ellery's hasty and troubled marriage was a constant reminder. She wrote Richard that she "dreaded" for him "that life-long repentance of a momentary dream, that slow penance of years wasted in unfit relations, which I have seen endured by other men."[8]

As for her own immediate plans, Fuller wrote the family that she intended to remain in Rome until April. She thought her funds would carry her through the winter, and she hoped she might even be able to stay longer. A kind but gruff letter came from Horace Greeley; yes, he wanted her to continue sending letters to the *Tribune* and would even be amenable to her serving as Paris correspondent if she went there to live. Greeley made it clear he was not offering charity. "I do not deal in compliments, and shall not solicit contributions from you or others unless I desire to receive them," he wrote. He even gave her permission to draw on the *Tribune* account at her discretion; he was sending her a bill of credit to make that possible.

I do not wish to urge you to write, but be it understood, once for all, that so many letters as you choose to write will be paid for, in such time and manner as shall be to you most agreeable. . . . All the letters you see fit to send us at $10 each will be more than welcome.[9]

The Greeleys' infant daughter, Mary Inez, had died that May. In the last days of the child's illness, Greeley had summoned Margarett Crane Fuller to New York to nurse the child—even providing an escort—but she arrived too late. She wrote Margaret that Horace Greeley had met her at the door, crying out that "Mrs. G[reeley] had "Hy[dropathy] and Alapathy practiced upon the beautiful little child" but that nothing had worked.[10]

In the same letter Margarett Crane Fuller offered the offhand news that "Mr. Nathan is probably married, and may take part of the [Greeley] house" on his return to New York with his wife. This information could have stiffened Fuller's resolve to remain in Europe. Her mother's letter, written in May, had followed her from Liverpool to Paris to Rome, each postmark adding to the cost; when she finally received the battered envelope, she had to pay seven pounds. The cost of transatlantic mail was a discouraging factor in keeping up her correspondence; she had to pay the postage both ways and was ever on the lookout for someone who could hand-carry her letters back home.[11]

The time lapse between sending letters and receiving answers discouraged many of Margaret's correspondents. Sarah Clarke's letter—also sent from Boston in May and not received until October—complained, "It seems very vague to write to you at all while you are vibrating between the two ends of foreign parts." The letter brimmed with home news, including the report that Carlyle had written Emerson that Fuller could easily "maintain" herself by writing in London and that Carlyle hoped she would settle there for a time on her return. This was comforting news as she faced the prospect of living on her own in Europe.[12]

In Siena she let Domenico go. Although dealing with him had been an unpleasant experience it had taught her a good deal about survival on her own, she wrote. She knew now how to bargain and was determined never again to be forced to depend on someone who was in a position to take advantage of her. On October 13 she arrived alone in Rome, prepared to begin her long-anticipated Roman holiday. Within three days she found an apartment on the Corso. (Rebecca Spring was under the impression that it was Ossoli who found the apartment.) She was close to the Borghese gardens, the French Academy, and the artists' studios and had a perfect view of the narrow street that served as a main route for ceremonial occasions, carnival gatherings, and public demonstrations. She wrote her mother that her only worry was that her landlady—whom she thought looked rather like Aunt Martha Whittier, with her "black eyes and red hair"—might be too interfering, but she preferred to forget that because "every thing else promises so sweetly."[13]

Her rooms were "elegantly furnished, everything in the house so neat, more like England than Italy, service excellent, everything arranged with a reasonable economy, and fixed prices for all the six months." She even found it intriguing that her landlady was a marchioness, not by birth, or even in the eyes of society, but because she had been the mistress of "a man of quality" who married her before his death because of his love for her. The marchioness now had a new lover, an officer in the "newly organized Civic guard," who brought all the latest news to the house. Lest her mother fear that she was a captive of the demi-monde of Rome, Margaret noted that her apartment was completely separate.

I have my books, my flowers, every thing leads me to hope the six months of quiet occupation I want, here in glorious Rome, where all the pleasures I most value, so rich and exalting, are within my reach. . . .

A flood of joy came over me when I was able at last to see Rome again. To live here, alone and independent, to really draw in the spirit of Rome, Oh! what joy! I know so well how to prize it that I think Heaven will not allow anything to disturb me! My protecting ang[els] have been very tender of late and led me carefully out of every difficulty.[14]

Every Monday and Thursday the Villa Borghese gardens teemed with Romans in peasant costumes dancing, singing, and picnicking. Listening to the singers and watching the saltarello dancers during these first October days,

Fuller was initiated into the Roman daily life. At the end of the month she wrote Richard that she was "no longer . . . a staring, sight-seeing stranger riding about finely dressed in a coach to see the Muses and the Sybils." She wanted to slough off the sense of being a part of the foreign world of power politics that allowed Italians to live under the domination of Austria. She was living like a native, taking daily walks but never going out to see the sights. "Yes I *am* happy here," she repeated. "I find myself so happy here alone and free." What Margaret did not reveal was that she was constantly in the company of Giovanni Ossoli.[15]

She continued to chronicle for the *Tribune* every new step in the progress toward democracy in Rome. On October 28 she went out on the Appian Way to watch the maneuvers of the Civic Guard. The pope's concession to the people of a Civic Guard had run into difficulties in the course of the summer, but by mid-October the battalions were forming and the smart uniform of the Civic Guard marked a man as a patriot of the new Italy in the making.

Whether or not Giovanni Ossoli felt strongly about political change in the Papal States before he met Fuller is not clear. Although his family background of generations of papal service, as well as his retiring personality, might argue against his having progressive opinions at this stage of the Risorgimento, he was commissioned a sergeant in the Fifth Company of the Second Battalion on November 15, 1847, only a month after it was organized. The Guard was not yet politicized, but the seeds of future dissension were sown, for the loyalty of a guardsman was to the civic authorities, not to the pope.

The Fuller–Ossoli relationship was not yet an all-consuming one. Margaret was actively participating in the expatriate social life. Following the practice of Mary Clarke, her ebullient Paris friend, she held a weekly at-home on Monday evenings. Like Clarke, she served no refreshments but flooded her drawing room with candlelight and filled it with fresh flowers—her only extravagance. Her friendship with Thomas Hicks was as warm as ever. (Later, he would write that during this winter he "stood in the relationship to her of a brother, drawn ever nearer and nearer.")[16] He included her in many of the parties of the younger group of writers and painters. During the previous year, Hicks had become a close friend of George William Curtis, who had left Rome to travel through Germany with Margaret's old friends Frederic Henry Hedge and George Stillman Hillard; the trio planned to spend the winter in Rome. Another close friend of Hicks's was the American sculptor Thomas Crawford, now married to Julia Ward Howe's younger sister, Louisa. (She had once been engaged to Sam Ward's younger brother, John, and was a bosom friend of Sam's sister Mary, who had studied with Margaret in Boston.) With Lizzie and Christopher Cranch settled in Rome, and with Susan and Frank Parkman there for the winter (Susan was Sarah Shaw's sister), a substantial contingent of Margaret's friends was already built into her Roman life.

In some cases, Margaret's reputation in America as having been judgmental and even intellectually arrogant was coming to haunt her. One artist in Rome who did not welcome her with enthusiasm was the Boston painter William Page, dubbed "the American Titian." Margaret had praised his work in her *Dial* article on the Boston Athenaeum exhibition of 1840. But, perhaps out of loyalty to his close friend James Russell Lowell—who had long felt disparaged by Fuller—Page now avoided her, and they saw each other only occasionally. At the end of October, another American couple, also close friends of Lowell and his wife, Maria White Lowell, arrived in Rome: Emelyn Elbridge and William Wetmore Story. He was the son of the Supreme Court justice Joseph Story, whom Margaret's family had known for years in Cambridge. Young Story had attended the one Conversation series Fuller had opened to men in Boston. Trained as a lawyer, he had practiced for a few years but was now realizing a long-suppressed desire. He had come to Italy to investigate the possibility of establishing himself as a professional sculptor.[17]

Years before, when editing the *Dial*, Margaret had turned down one of Story's first essays on art; she had found it too long. Story was nine years younger than Fuller, but she knew a great deal about him from Jane Tuckerman King, who had grown up with him and with James Russell Lowell as a fellow member of an inseparable group of privileged young people who called themselves "the Band." For many years Margaret had looked down on most of them as frivolous, and in 1839 she had rebuked Caroline Sturgis for wasting her time with them. They, in turn, thought Margaret was forbidding and kept their distance. Emelyn Story, in fact, said later that she had been led to believe that Margaret was "a person on intellectual stilts, with a large share of arrogance, and little sweetness of temper." So it was a surprise to her—as she later wrote—on arriving in Rome with her husband and two young children to receive a warm note from Fuller, offering to help them find an apartment and inviting her and her husband to an evening gathering with the Cranches and several others.[18]

Most of Fuller's American friends, with the exception of Thomas Crawford, already an old Roman hand, were still experimenting with expatriate life. In later years, when the Storys settled permanently in Rome, they would live in a sumptuous apartment in the Palazzo Barberini; their home became a cultural mecca for all the famous traveling Americans: Harriet Hosmer, Charlotte Cushman, Grace Greenwood, the Hawthornes, Henry James, Charles Sumner, and Charles Eliot Norton. But in that winter of 1847–48 they lived in modest rooms off the Piazza di Spagna and, as tourists, climbed the magnificent marble staircase in the museum section of their future home to stare at the two portraits *Murray's Guide* recommended to every visitor: Raphael's *Fornarina* and the fascinating *Beatrice Cenci*, then attributed to Guido Reni. That winter everyone in Europe was uneasy about the threatening political situation. Margaret's American friends still thought of themselves as transients, living unsettled artists' lives. They took coffee at the Café Nono on the Corso and dined at the Café Greco or the Lepre on the Via Condotti. They attended concerts as often as possible and, after the season began in December, the opera every night. On Sunday evenings they took a boat across the Tiber to hear vespers at St. Peter's.[19]

Most of the Americans in Italy that year chose to be spectators of the dramatic events unfolding around them. They belonged to a privileged new nation where most of the troublesome problems beleaguering the Europeans had been resolved in a revolution two generations before; they could afford to look on from the sidelines. In the travel book George Hillard wrote about the Roman winter of 1847–48, he advised Americans to give themselves up to "the imaginative principle" while in Rome, to "leave all [their] notions of progress and reform at the gates," and "learn to look upon pope, cardinal and monk, not with a puritan scowl, but as parts of an imposing pageant."[20]

Perhaps this was an acceptable point of view for affluent artists, but Fuller disagreed. For her *Tribune* New Year's letter she wrote on "[t]he American[s] in Europe," dividing them into three categories. The most numerous were the "servile" and "shallow" Americans who came abroad to spend money and indulge their tastes. They were "parasites of a by gone period" and, as such, caused no more than annoyance. The ones who gave the most offense were "the conceited" Americans who looked upon all vestiges of the past as "humbug," judged pictures and customs by the standard of "the Connecticut Blue-Laws," and deemed everything "silly" that lay outside their immediate experience. The third category was "[t]he thinking American . . . who, recognizing the immense advantage of being born to a new world and on a virgin soil, yet does not wish one seed from the past to be lost." In this description, Fuller was stating her own credo as one who was "anxious to gather and carry back with him all that will bear a new climate and a new culture." In order to know the conditions under which it would be possible to transplant these specimens to the New World, it was necessary "to study their history in this," she explained. Accordingly, she was reading Italian history and preparing notes for her own account of contemporary history. Costanza Arconati kept her supplied with books and newspapers, and she had a rich resource of Italian materials at the English library in the Piazza di Spagna. As she became more absorbed in the political drama, writing a history of Italy's struggle became a way of harmonizing the Muse of emotional identification with the artistic endeavor of shaping current events to her point of view.[21]

Most Americans traveling through Rome arranged to be presented to the pope, but Fuller said she had no interest in such a formality; her interest was of quite a different nature. During her first two months back in the city, she took every opportunity to study the pope's commitment to democratic change. She turned up at all his public appearances and even caught a secret view of him one day on the Appian Way when he was taking private exercise. Whenever he gave a public mass she made an effort to join the celebrants; she scrutinized him carefully throughout the ceremony empowering the Civic Guard; she went to watch him during the mass honoring him on his name day—the Feast of St. John—and on the occasion when he administered the oath of office to the new municipal officers. She was irritated when each officer sealed the ceremony by bending and kissing his foot. "A Heavenly Father does not want his children at his feet, but in his arms, on a level with his heart," she bristled.[22]

Nevertheless, she found his personal magnetism extremely powerful. "His is a face to shame the selfish, redeem the skeptic, alarm the wicked and cheer to new effort the weary and heavy-laden," she wrote. Aware of the great difficulties in his position and the suspicion of him harbored by Mazzini and his followers, she still held the view that Pope Nono might be able to lead Italy into a new era, and she found it astonishing that "after the lapse of near two thousand years" the pope's detractors could call him "Utopian" because he had a sincere desire to "get some food into the mouths of some of the *leaner* of his flock." Her greatest fear was that he meant "only to improve, not to *reform.*"[23]

Caught up in the spirit of new beginnings for Italy—a spirit she compared with her own country's on the eve of its own revolution—she dispatched to William Linton, an English reformer friend of both Mickiewicz and Mazzini, a sonnet entitled "To a Daughter of Italy." In the first week in October, Linton published it in the *People's and Howitt's Journal* (the compromise name now used by the Howitts and George Saunders as their quarrel continued). Returning to the idea of woman as gifted with divinatory insight and electrical powers as formulated in *Woman in the Nineteenth Century,* she calls women now to serve Italy's cause in an inspiring and prophesying Muse role. She noted that an Italian writer, Isabella Rossi, had already made the similar appeal in the new journal, *Auba of Florence.*

To a Daughter of Italy

To guard the glories of the Roman reign,
Statesmen and warriors had toil'd in vain;
If vestal hands had failed to tend the fire;
That sacred emblem of pure strong desire.
If higher honors wait the Italian name—
Vestals anew are call'd that flow to fan,
And rouse to fervent force the soul of man.

Amid the prayers I hourly breathe for thee,
Most beautiful, most injured Italy!
None has a deeper root within the heart,
Than to see woman duly play her part:
To the advancing hours of this great day
A Morning Star be she to point the way;
The Virgin Mother of a blessed birth,
The Isis of a fair regenerate earth,
And, where its sons achieve their noblest fame,
Still, Beatrice be the woman's name.[24]

As a postscript to her poem she wrote several paragraphs in defense of Mazzini, who was now under attack in the British press for advocating revolution rather than diplomacy to achieve Italian unity. Buoyed by her own faith in the power of virtue to overcome all obstacles, Fuller argued that two men of such high moral principles as Mazzini and the pope could not help but come to an understanding if they could only meet together. The obstacle, as she saw it, was the pope's ties to the Italian monarchists and the Austrian Hapsburgs. A man like Mazzini, "so deeply penetrated . . . with the truth . . . that liberty is an inborn right of man . . . [does not] demand it as a boon at the hands of princes. The noble heart of the present pontiff has opened an unexpected door. It remains to be seen whether old bottles will contain new wine."[25]

Fuller's well-meaning article brought a strong reaction from Mazzini. Thinking she might have been helpful to him in Switzerland during the rebellion there, he had been trying to find her all summer. Maria Mazzini—using the name of her servant, Benedetta Rossi—had written Margaret in Rome, but the letter did not come until after she had left with the Springs. When Mazzini finally caught up with her in December 1847 after his return to London, he did not thank her for her "lines and postscript" in the *People's Journal,* though he politely expressed appreciation for the spirit of the piece. At a time when he was putting so much of his efforts into his International League—an association of republican activists in Ireland, Hungary, Poland, and Switzerland as well as Italy—it was totally against his convictions and his strategy to have an impassioned American follower advocating reconciliation with the pope.[26]

He advised Fuller that it was "better to wait" before sending any more articles. She could, however, be of help if she had a friend she could trust at Maquay, Pakenham, the banking company in Rome to which Fuller had all her letters addressed. If so, he would like to send letters through the company to a friend. To her suggestion of an entente between him and Pius IX he responded angrily. "As a Pope he has been sent *to give the last blow to the papacy:* and it will be seen when he dies, 'Old bottles will not contain a new wine.' "[27]

He informed Fuller that he had already communicated with the pope. A follower had flung a Papal Letter into the pontiff's carriage in September. Afterward, copies of the letter were distributed freely in the streets. Mazzini's demands to Pope Nono had been anything but conciliatory. Assuming a tone as pontifical as the pope himself, Mazzini informed him that a unified republican Italy was inevitable. As pope he could only "abridge the road and diminish the dangers," and even that he could not do unless he believed in the ultimate outcome. He would have to renounce playing "King, Politician, Statesman" and appeal directly to the people for support.[28]

In his letter to Fuller, Mazzini's irritation at her interference found expression in a comment he made on Ralph Waldo Emerson, who was traveling through England on a lecture tour during the winter of 1847–48. Mazzini admired Emerson and hoped to meet him, but he did not think that Emerson had any message for Europeans. "His work, I think, is very greatly needed in America, but in our own old world we stand in need of one who will like Peter the Hermit inflame us to the Holy Crusade and *appeal* to the collective influences and inspiring sources, more than to individual self-improvement," he wrote her.[29]

Mazzini's letter did not alienate Fuller, nor did it deter her from what had become a highly subjective view of the Italian situation. When Costanza Arconati wrote her in disgust over what she regarded as Mazzini's presumptuous letter, saying it was "shocking" that he had written as an equal to the Pope and even more shocking that he had done so on purpose, Margaret fired back a sharp defense. "I do not wonder that you were annoyed at his manner of addressing the Pope; but to me it seems that he speaks as he should,—near God and beyond the tomb; not from power to power, but from soul to soul, without regard to temporal dignities." Radical as she had become, the individual soul was still the measure of a human being, exalted pontiff or ordinary person.[30]

One way she could help the cause without endangering her friendship with Mazzini, she thought, was to concentrate on her book. From Emerson she had thoroughly imbibed the idea that words can be used as political acts. On December 16 she wrote her mother that she was spending her evenings "chiefly in writing or study. I have now around me the books I need to know Italy and Rome. I study with delight, now that I can verify everything." The weather was "invariably fine," and her life in Rome was beyond her fondest hopes. "I have not been so well since I was a child, nor so happy ever as during the last six weeks."[31] Clearly, her relationship with Ossoli had deepened.

A week later, Margaret's mood had plummeted. When she wrote Waldo Emerson in London on December 20, she was miserable. Yes, she had found Italy "glorious" and she had "known some blessed, quiet days," but the spell was now broken. She needed "two or three years, free from care and forced labor," to "heal" all her hurts. "Since Destiny will not grant me that, I hope she will not leave me long in the world," she wrote, "for I am tired of keeping myself up in the water without corks, and without strength to swim." She had been right to believe that in Italy she would find "an atmosphere" to develop as she needed, she said, but time was running out. "Soon I must begin to exert myself, for there is this incubus of the future, and none to help me, if I am not prudent to face it."[32]

The twentieth of December was too early for her to be sure she was pregnant, but she may have already suspected it. It was unthinkable that she could confess this worry to Emerson, but she could enlist his sympathy and help. From Giovanni Ossoli she could not expect much in the way of material aid. His father was dying, and the family money was tied up in land. The only money he had came from handouts from his older brothers. As the year 1847 ended, all Fuller could do was hope that nature was playing a trick on her. Her immediate problem was to plan a course that would make sense, whether or not she was pregnant and whether or not she brought the baby to term. Her first thought was that she should plan for a long stay in Italy, perhaps three years. This meant she would have to find a way to support herself. She did not ask Waldo if he were coming to Italy or if he wanted to meet her in Paris, as she might have done if she were free. She asked him instead to find an English publisher who would be interested in articles from Italy. The desperate tone of her letter worried him. It did not make sense that she should insist on staying in Italy when she was so miserable. For the next year and a half, her letters hinted at a dramatic change in her life, but her cryptic allusions were difficult to decipher. He had always found her an enigma. No one could understand why she did not come home.

You would be amazed, I believe, could you know how different is my present phase of life, from that in which you knew me.

1848: On Her Own

ALL the Americans in Rome during the winter of 1847–48 complained of the unremitting cold rain. William Wetmore Story wrote James Russell Lowell that it rained from the end of December through Easter Week. George Hillard, in his travel book, *Six Months in Italy,* complained that the rain's "dispiriting influence" all but ruined the Roman Carnival that year. Fuller's rooms were so dark she kept the lamps lit all day. On New Year's Day, 1848, she wrote Richard that after sixteen days of continual rain she felt "quite destroyed." She had enough money for the next few months, but she needed to know exactly how much would be coming to her in the future. She did not reveal her strong suspicion that she was pregnant.[1]

Two months later she wrote Richard, whose fiancée had just broken their engagement, that she had concluded that the Fuller family luck had run out years before; she quoted a comment she remembered Eugene making at the time their father put the Dana Mansion up for sale to the effect that the family star had taken an unfavorable turn and they would never be lucky in the future. The best words of comfort Margaret could summon were, "We are never wholly sunk by storms, but no favorable wind ever helps our voyages."[2]

Her letters home were consistently morose and dejected. "Rome is no more Rome," she wrote her sister Ellen. "I suffered continually in N[ew] E[ngland]. I suffer in Italy; always it is suffering somewhere." Eugene and Arthur suspected something unusual was the matter and conspired to come to her aid. Eugene wrote Arthur at the end of February, "if you have received mine of the 16th you will perceive that the same idea which you suggest about M. has also occurred to me. I can afford to contribute $150."[3]

She came close to telling Caroline Sturgis Tappan everything in a letter dated January 11, but she only dropped provocative hints. Her letter congratulated Caroline on her marriage a month earlier to William Aspinwall Tappan. It was typical of Caroline that she chose to break the news of her marriage in an offhand manner—she sent out wedding announcements in copies of her book, *Rainbows for Children.* Fuller learned of the marriage only secondhand and was hurt. Now she hinted to Caroline of a romantic involvement of her own. She wrote of two happy months of "passive, childlike well-being." But that phase was now over, she said bleakly.

I have known some happy hours; but they all lead to sorrow, and not only the cups of wine but of milk seem drugged with poison for me. It does not seem to be my fault,—this destiny: I do not court these things, they come. I am a poor magnet with power to be wounded by the bodies I attract.

Many times in the past Caroline had listened while Margaret deplored her luck. But this time her fatalism was far darker:

[W]ith this year, I enter upon a sphere of my destiny so difficult, that I, at present, see no way out, except through the gate of death. . . . I have no reason to hope I shall not reap what I have sown, and do not. Yet how I shall endure it I cannot guess; it is all a dark, sad enigma. The beautiful forms of art charm no more, and a love, in which there is all fondness, but no help, flatters in vain.[4]

Fuller may well have kept her condition from Giovanni for weeks. "I am all alone; nobody around me sees any of this," Margaret continued.[5] She was in a desperate situation with no help and no one to whom she could turn. She feared that she might at any time lose the baby because of her age and her uncertain health, and she may have hoped for this. At some point she consulted a doctor in Rome; just when is not known. But her depressed letters were the only way she could signal her family and close friends that all was not well.

Waldo Emerson responded to the desperate tone of her December letter to him in London. He suggested that she join him in Paris in May and return home with him. "How much your letter made me wish to say, come live with me in Concord," he wrote. But he had received that winter too many "tragic letters" from "poor exhausted" Lidian, who was bedridden during the winter of 1847–48. As an alternative, Waldo suggested that Margaret rent the house of Lidian's sister, Lucy Brown, who was vacating for the coming year her house across the street from the Emersons.[6]

There were more complicated reasons for the secrecy of the Fuller–Ossoli relationship, and they were even further complicated in early February when Giovanni's father died. The wife of Giovanni's eldest brother, Giuseppe, stripped the apartment of its better furniture—to the great annoyance of Angela, who lived downstairs—and Giuseppe rented the apartment to an attorney. Angela, who had no children and was fond of Giovanni, took him to live with her, and an uncle gave him a job managing some inner-city property. Whether Giovanni was entitled to an inheritance or any claim to the rents of the few remaining family properties was questionable, but no one seemed in a hurry to make decisions. One thing was certain, however: In the Papal States, the only situation in which Giovanni would be allowed to marry a Protestant was with a papal dispensation, and he knew that his brothers would never accept Fuller and would oppose any such request. It seemed clear that they would disown him if he took matters into his own hands. Fuller did her best to continue with her life as usual. "[W]hat a Rome!" she complained in her mid-January dispatch to the

Tribune, written on the fortieth day of rain. There was no relief in sight. A week later, she continued the refrain. "Pour, pour, pour again, dark as night."[7]

It was the first month of 1848, the year of revolution all over Europe. Fuller's *Tribune* columns described "excitements" in Leghorn and Genoa, provocations in Milan, the "revolution" in Sicily, and Austrian "[a]ggressions" in northern Italy. Pope Nono's popularity was on the decline, and he was avoiding public appearances. A complicated situation was brewing in Italy. Fuller recommended that the United States send a qualified envoy to the Vatican, someone who was "honest," with some "knowledge of Europe and gentlemanly tact, and able at least to speak French."[8]

The wretched weather helped explain her bouts of morning sickness and lethargy to her friends in Rome. Christopher Cranch wrote home to Theodore Parker that Margaret was "in delicate health" and that the "climate seems not to agree with her." In January she went to the opera a few times. In February she enjoyed watching the famous Carnival of Rome from her apartment window overlooking the Corso. Wrapped in a colorful shawl with a boa around her neck for a costume, she marveled at "the admirable good humor" and the vitality of the crowd braving the mud and rain for the sake of the fun. But, as George Hillard reported, news of the French Revolution of February 1848 "broke in upon the frivolous piping and dancing, like the crashing stride of an earthquake."[9]

Along with her friends, the Cranches, the Crawfords, and especially the Storys, with whom she was becoming increasingly intimate, Margaret entertained a constant stream of visiting Bostonians; various Shaws, Lorings, and Gardners came to tea. To some of them she gave introductions to Costanza Arconati in Milan and to Jane Stirling and Mary Clarke (now married to the orientalist Julius Mohl) in Paris. Her closest friends from home to spend the winter in Rome were Frederick Henry Hedge and George Stillman Hillard. Hillard was taking time out from his Boston law practice; Hedge was enjoying his first European vacation since his boyhood years studying in Germany.

Hedge noticed that Fuller did not look well. She walked so awkwardly that he thought she had some spinal complaint. He was taken aback when he came to say goodbye to her in early March, and she threw her arms around him and burst into tears. Afterward she sent him a note including the sentence, "If I never get back and in my sick moping moods I fancy I shall not; it seems so far off; you must write a good verse to put on my tomb-stone." But she added a quintessential Fuller remark in telling him of "the poor peasant Pietro she had befriended, and who had said he had but two friends, God and herself"; she said, "and I think I am the most active of the two."[10]

Enclosed with the note was a letter of introduction to the startlingly beautiful Princess Cristina Trivulzio Belgioioso, whom Hedge hoped to meet in Naples. The most colorful and notorious of Fuller's new Italian friends, the princess was known for her wraithlike beauty, her anti-Austrian activity, and her friendships with Lafayette, Liszt, Balzac, and Heine. Exiled in 1830, she ran a famous salon in Paris and was long associated with the Italian moderates. Fuller had met Belgioioso in Rome in December 1847 and wrote home that she was seeing the princess frequently and admired her as "a woman of gallantry." Hers was the first translation into French of Giovanni Battista Vico's *Scienza Nuova;* she had edited the *Gazetta Italiana* and, later, the *Ausonia,* two liberal political journals. Like Fuller, Belgioioso was writing a history of the Risorgimento as it unfolded.[11]

By the end of March, all of Italy was galvanized into a state of insurgency. An uprising in Milan began with a tobacco boycott in imitation of the Boston Tea Party and ended with more than sixty dead. A revolt in Sicily forced King Ferdinand II to promise on January 30 a constitution for the Kingdom of the two Sicilies. On March 13 the fall of Metternich in Vienna opened the way for a spontaneous outburst in Milan, one that developed into a five-day insurgency in which people from all parts and classes of the city participated. "The Five Glorious Days," as they became known, ended in the withdrawal of the Austrians from Milan and changed forever "the Italian Question" in Europe. On March 30 King Carlo Alberto of Piedmont declared war on Austria.

With the Austrian withdrawal from Milan, the attitude of a whole generation of Italians, who had felt themselves a subjected people, was transformed overnight. Elated with the sense of living in a time of cataclysmic change, the people in all the small Italian principalities—Lombardy and Venetia, the Kingdom of the Two Sicilies, Piedmont, the central duchies of Tuscany, Parma, and Modena, the Papal States, and the Kingdom of Sardinia—now looked toward Milan and were eager to join the army forming under the king of Piedmont, Carlo Alberto.

By the time of the Five Glorious Days in Milan, the spirit of 1848 had already toppled governments in Paris, Prague, and Vienna. On February 24 Louis Philippe had left the throne of France. In the forty-eight hours before the abdication, throngs of students and workingmen chopped down 4,000 trees and tore up over a million paving stones to erect 1,500 barricades throughout the city. Everyone now addressed each other as "Citoyen." Two days later, a provisional government—a republican government—was formed in the Hôtel de Ville under the leadership of the poet Lamartine.

The cautious ministers of King Carlo Alberto of Piedmont warned him that he could never defeat the Austrians without allies—and none existed. The forty-nine-year-old king had waited all his life for a chance to fulfill his mission for Italy, knowing he would venture his life when the time came. He argued down all the opposition. Hundreds of volunteers were already pouring into Milan from all parts of Italy. Even the republicans were ready to join forces. Piedmont was in an uproar, and everyone was bursting with confidence. All rallied to

Carlo Alberto's gallant watchword: "No allies? It does not matter. Italia farà da sè! [Italy will do it alone!]"[12]

By the end of March, Rome was caught up in the war fever, and Fuller's situation was beginning to clarify. By now, she knew that Ossoli had every intention of standing by her. He would arrange for her to bear the child in some country retreat; foreigners customarily escaped Rome during the summer, and her disappearance would not attract attention. All her friends knew she required solitude to write her book about Italy's struggle for independence. She kept up a brave front, but inwardly she was miserable as she considered the problems ahead.

For several weeks in February and March, Adam Mickiewicz was a comfort to her. He came to Rome to raise a legion of Polish exiles to join the Italians in their fight for national sovereignty. For him and his idealistic colleagues, Italy's liberation was only the first step in a world revolution to liberate all oppressed people and inaugurate a new era of human freedom. Mickiewicz took rooms on the Via del Pozzetto, only a few blocks from Fuller's apartment. He encouraged her to view her condition as a cause for rejoicing instead of guilt and morbid musing. Her depression, he told her, was no more than a fear of the future; a woman who had written so compellingly about the better world ahead should not suffer from melancholia. Pointing out that it was "very natural, very common" to be pregnant, he accused her of carrying on in an "extravagant manner." Once she regained her morale, her physical sufferings would diminish.[13]

Self-preoccupied and ill, Fuller neglected her *Tribune* duties in February and March. When she resumed her dispatches, she gave an eyewitness account of the rapturous response in Rome to the new turn of events. When the news of Metternich's fall in Vienna reached Rome, the Austrian coat of arms was ripped from its ministry building and burned in the Piazza del Popolo. The "double-headed eagle," pulled down from the lofty portal of the Palazzo di Venezia, was replaced with an eagle with a single head in white and gold. Young men eager to enroll filled the Colosseum, and soap-box patriots fired them on with inflammatory speeches.[14]

At the end of March, at the height of excitement after the declaration of war, Fuller wrote William Henry Channing, who was boarding for the winter in Mrs. Fuller's Prospect Street house in Cambridgeport:

I have been engrossed, stunned almost, by the public events that have succeeded one another with such rapidity and grandeur. It is a time such as I always dreamed of, and for long secretly hoped to see. I rejoice to be in Europe at this time, and shall return possessed of a great history. Perhaps I shall be called to act. At present, I know not where to go, what to do. War is everywhere. I cannot leave Rome, and the men of Rome are marching out every day into Lombardy.[15]

Fuller asked her *Tribune* readers to join her in considering what the lesson in all this was for Americans. Like Mazzini and Mickiewicz, she saw these events as only the first wave of a universal uprising, the beginning of a new era of popular sovereignty all over Europe. But for her, another movement was working in tandem with nationalism. She prophesied that the last half of the nineteenth century would be marked by the awakening of political consciousness among the working class. Her March 29 letter to the *Tribune* alerted her readers:

To you, people of America, it may perhaps be given to look on and learn in time for a preventive wisdom. You may learn the real meaning of the words FRATERNITY, EQUALITY: you may, despite the apes of the past who strive to tutor you, learn the needs of a true democracy. You may in time learn to reverence, learn to guard, the true aristocracy of a nation, the only really nobles,—the LABORING CLASSES.[16]

Her April 19 *Tribune* letter, dated on the Patriot's Day of her native Massachusetts, described the triumphal entrances into Milan of her two revolutionary brothers. Mickiewicz, whom the Italians were calling the "Dante of Poland," arrived leading his small troop of Poles bearing a gilded banner blessed by the pope and inscribed with three articles of faith: equal rights for all citizens, entire equality in political and civil rights for Jews, and citizenship and equality of rights for women.[17]

Mazzini's return to his country was poetic justice, she wrote in the *Tribune;* he was returning " 'to see what he foresaw,' " she pronounced, quoting Wordsworth's "Character of the Happy Warrior." But great as Mazzini was, Fuller believed that he did not foresee the future completely.

[H]e aims at political emancipation; but he sees not, perhaps would deny, the bearing of some events, which even now begin to work their way. . . . Suffice it to say, I allude to that of which the cry of Communism, the systems of Fourier, &c., are but forerunners.[18]

Although in most of Fuller's writing about Mazzini she was uncritically favorable, in drawing attention to this flaw in Mazzini's analysis she demonstrated that her Minerva qualities had not been subsumed totally by the Muse in Rome. Later historians were to agree that Mazzini's ambitions were hindered by his stubborn insistence that for his purposes the association model of social action be limited to organizing the Italian working people into patriotic societies, united by common bonds of nationality rather than class. His denial of any affinity with the mainstream socialists of the 1840s such as Fourier was an example of the fierce nationalism at the heart of his thinking. In adopting Mazzini's cause, Fuller did not lose sight of the complexity of underlying causes for the instability throughout Europe. Writing Emerson to decline his invitation to accompany him home, Margaret could easily say, "I should like to return with you, but I have much to do and learn in Europe yet. I am deeply interested in this public drama, and wish to see it *played out*. Methinks I have *my part* therein, either as actor or historian." At the same time, she wrote her brother Richard that she loved the city of Rome "profoundly"; it was truly the "City of the Soul."[19]

In Rome, as in all of Italy, expectations mounted. The dream of unity seemed to be taking on unstoppable momentum. On April 19 the pope, who was both the spiritual leader of the universal Catholic church that extended well beyond Italy and the temporal leader of the Papal States, stunned the public by announcing in a special allocution to his cardinals that his role as the Vicar of Christ, the Prince of Peace, had a far greater claim on him than his political role as ruler over his states. He could not declare war, much less condone warfare or take any responsibility for the volunteers from the Papal States who were running off to battle. "A momentary stupefaction received this astounding performance, succeeded by a passion of indignation," Fuller wrote in her column. "[H]e declared that, when there is a conflict between the priest and the man, he always meant to be the priest, and that he preferred the wisdom of the Past to that of the Future." Clearly, Fuller was convinced that the pope had abdicated leadership, and the power now lay in the people.[20]

In her last two *Tribune* letters before leaving Rome for the summer, Margaret explained why she was remaining in Italy; the message was meant for her friends and family as well as the general reader. It was of "vital interest" to stay on in Italy to witness the "manifestation" of her hopes. In Europe "a nobler spirit" was alive. "Here things are before my eyes worth recording, and . . . I would gladly be its historian." To write a history of events that were engaging her deepest emotions provided an emotional and psychological catharsis that answered to her needs. At the same time, she was following the spirit of Mickiewicz's advice to integrate her private feelings with her public performance.[21]

Rome's reputation for being malarial during the summer drove most of Fuller's expatriate friends out of the city by the end of May. Other than Mickiewicz, Thomas Hicks was probably the only friend who knew the truth of her situation. He was planning to leave Rome for Paris, but before he left, at Mickiewicz's suggestion, he painted a portrait of Fuller. He portrayed her seated in an arcade of the doge's palace in Venice. The shadows of two lovers in the background and the bust of Eros on a pillar behind her testify to Hicks's knowledge. In it, Fuller appears melancholy; the figure does not give the impression of the animated and stimulating woman known to the public as Margaret Fuller. Margaret's friends never liked the picture, but Hicks thought highly of the portrait and kept it in his possession for many years. Henry James remembered seeing it at an exhibition when he was a child: "a small full-length portrait of Miss Fuller seated . . . wrapped in a long white shawl, the failure of which to do justice to its original my companions denounced with some emphasis."[22]

At the end of May, when Hicks was leaving to study in the Paris atelier of Thomas Couture, Margaret looked to the real uncertainty of her future and gave him a sealed box to be delivered to her mother in the event of her death; it contained a lock of her hair, a coral necklace, and a long letter. In the letter she described how close she had been to Hicks during a "difficult" time. Whatever else she wrote—about her pregnancy, Giovanni, or a marriage ceremony—her mother kept in confidence when the letter was ultimately delivered.[23]

Margaret was right to have trusted Hicks to say no more than was necessary. In her goodbye note, she instructed him:

You would say to those I leave behind that I was willing to die. I have suffered in life far more than I enjoyed, and I think quite out of proportion with the use my living here is of to others.

I have wished to be natural and true, but the world was not in harmony with me—nothing came right for me. I think the spirit that governs the Universe must have in reserve for me a sphere where I can develope more freely, and be happier—[24]

Facing the possibility that her death in childbirth in a remote Italian village would cause a scandal, disgrace her family, and bring ridicule on herself, she asked for little mercy. Even if she and the baby lived, her family would certainly feel betrayed when they heard the news. This dilemma was at the heart of her misery. Partly because it made her feel devious not to confide in her mother and partly because Margarett Crane Fuller was visiting in Cincinnati, she sent her family letters at this time to Richard. To prepare others for the shock, she occasionally dropped hints in her letters. In the middle of an April letter to Jane Tuckerman King, she divulged enough to prepare the way for future revelations.

But ah dearest, the drama of my fate is very deep, and the ship plunges deeper as it rises higher. You would be amazed, I believe, could you know how different is my present phase of life, from that in which you knew me; but you would love me no less; for it is still the same planet that shews such different climes.[25]

During May, Fuller wandered from town to town on the outskirts of Rome, sometimes with Giovanni and sometimes alone. She visited Ostia, Albano, Frascati, and Subiaco and finally settled in Tivoli for a few days. Feeling well, she was worrying less about dying and more about how she could support herself during her confinement. She wrote Aunt Mary Rotch and made a special point of telling the heiress to the Rotch whaling fortune that she was "rather sore" at being continually congratulated about her Uncle Abraham's legacy when he had left her less than a thousand dollars, only enough to pay her debts and give her these few extra months in Europe. "You must always love me whatever I do. [I] depend on that," she wrote impulsively. She added that she was "as great an Associationist" as William Channing and hoped "in the silence and retirement of the country to write more at length" on several subjects that interested her.[26]

From the time she knew she was pregnant, she had stopped writing to Costanza Arconati and, on one occasion, avoided seeing a Visconti servant who delivered a letter. In late May, when she finally wrote to thank Arconati for a gift of money that had been sent in January, she included an ambiguous allusion that triggered her friend's instant reply.

What mystery lies in the last lines [of your letter]? Yes, I am faithful and capable of sympathy . . . but just what are you talking about? Someone told me that you have had a lover in Rome, a member of the Civic Guard. I have not wanted to believe it, but your mysterious words arouse my doubts.[27]

Fuller knew that Mickiewicz had stayed with the Arconati Visconti family in Milan and suspected that he had seen no reason to be discreet. But with such rumors bandying about, she had to stay away from Rome. She also had received news of the imminent arrival of Caroline Kirkland, the American author of several books on western life who was a close friend of Rebecca and Marcus Spring. Margaret could not risk being seen by her.

In late May and early June, King Carlo Alberto's army met a series of defeats, and Costanza Arconati wrote of the disappointment of the moderates in Milan who saw their hopes of routing the Austrians disappearing. The failure of the Piedmont king and of the pope to provide leadership was forcing many into the republican camp, but Costanza saw no help in that direction. "I want you to understand that my opposition to an Italian republic has nothing to do with my being a member of the aristocracy," she wrote Margaret. "Nothing so small-minded as that. I am convinced that the attempt to establish a republic would make any future attempt at unity impossible." An all-out effort now to form a republic "would only result in the complete failure of all the hopes and sacrifices of the patriots who looked forward to a strong and united Italy," she added. "I am no bigoted Republican," Margaret answered, "yet I think that form of government will eventually pervade the civilized world. Italy may not be ripe for it yet, but I doubt if she finds peace earlier."[28]

Before he left Europe for home, Waldo Emerson made a last attempt to lure Margaret back with him. On May 31 he wrote commanding her to "come to London immediately & sail home with me!" He had been in Paris during the revolution and had heard Lamartine in the Chamber of Deputies. He had spent an evening with the Tocqueville family and with the Comtesse d'Agoult, who had told him she particularly wanted to see Fuller when she returned to Paris. The comtesse, who wrote under the name of Daniel Stern, had published an article in *La Revue indépendante* on Emerson. She was working on her *Histoire de la révolution de 1848,* covering the French situation. Waldo may well have told her about Fuller's projected study of the Italian revolution.[29]

Before Emerson's letter arrived in Rome, Ossoli had taken Fuller to Aquila, a medieval village deep in the Apennines about seventy miles from the city—a "bird's nest village," Margaret called it, because it was perched on a remote mountainside.[30] Ossoli's Civic Guard duties and his job with his uncle kept him in Rome, but he wrote Fuller often and sent her parcels of mail and newspapers. He also found two sisters, Giuditta and Maria Bonani, who acted as her intermediaries and servants. Concerned that all his arrangements on her behalf would arouse suspicions, she warned him to avoid all appearance of being connected with her. When she needed medicines from her doctor or information from her bank, she instructed him to send a servant, not to go himself.

The disorders in Paris and Rome had disrupted banking and mail services throughout Europe. The letter of credit that Greeley had promised so that Fuller could draw from the *Tribune* account never arrived in Rome. Instead of following her instructions to send her money and credit letter to her Paris bank, Greene and Company, Greeley had sent them to Baring Brothers in Paris because he had been told in New York that Greene and Company had terminated services. When Fuller's brothers heard of Greeley's difficulties in getting money through, they held up the $150 they had told her was on its way. Fuller spent the greater part of the summer straightening out this "imbroglio."[31]

Greeley was annoyed when Fuller's *Tribune* dispatches from Rome ceased. Unable to explain to him why she had placed herself so far from the sources of fresh information, she informed him that she was writing a book and did not wish it to be a repetition of her newspaper articles. Greeley wrote back that he did not see why her *Tribune* letters, which were devoted to "the passing moment," would interfere with a book on the larger issues. He reminded her that she was being paid twice as much as any of his other European correspondents and offered her an additional $2.50 for each column over the two-column standard. None of his letters reached her until well into August; for most of the summer she felt abandoned by him.[32]

Ossoli kept her well informed. He made the rounds of Rome's cafes to pick up the latest rumors and sent her the Roman newspapers—the *Epoca* and Mazzini's *Italia del Popolo*—and Milanese newspapers when available. She settled down to work on her book on the current developments in Italy and found that it was her salvation; while working on it, she forgot her fears. To Charles King Newcomb, she wrote poetically of her Aquila life, of the olive trees, the vineyards, and the valley churches with faded frescoes. But during June and July of 1848 (Fuller had arrived in Aquila in the first week of June) the place was transformed into a noisy barracks town and was hardly the restful hideaway she needed. Army brigades stopped there on the way to do battle in the North, and the town citadel was being used as a billet by stragglers returning to the South after King Ferdinand II of the Two Sicilies had recalled his troops to Naples to subdue new uprisings in Sicily. A desperately lonely Fuller wanted to be closer to Rome so Ossoli could visit her more often. She had made friends with two brothers, the marchesi di Torres, leading citizens of the town who had a magnificent art collection, but she worried that socializing with townspeople would jeopardize her secret. The thought of how her family would react when all was divulged sent her into spells of weeping whenever she had letters from home.

By the end of July she had reestablished access to her dwindling account through J. C. Hooker, the new banker in Rome (she was still unaware of Greeley's generosity), and arranged to move to Rieti in the foothills of the

Abruzzi, only forty-two miles from Rome by way of the Via Salaria. Giovanni could get there in an overnight journey by stagecoach, or even by cart, and the postal service from Rome was much more reliable. Her new three-room apartment—at nine dollars a month—was in a private house with its own private loggia, a covered porch off her rooms, long enough for her evening walk. On the first weekend, August 5 and 6, Giovanni joined her. She had not seen him for a month. As soon as he returned to Rome, he heard talk that the pope might be forced to send the Civic Guard to aid the people of Bologna who were holding off an Austrian siege. When Margaret read of this turn of events she wrote Giovanni:

It seems very strange how everything is going against us. The fact that Bologna has resisted is good, but that this would make it likely for you to leave at this very moment!

But do what is right for your honor. I do not really think that the pope will decide to send the Civic Guard, but if it happens, and if it is necessary for your honor, leave and I will try to be strong.

. . . Your visit did me good and afterward I was calmer. And at least we have had some peaceful hours together, if now everything is over.[33]

A few days later, when the pope ordered the Civic Guard to assemble on Monte Cavallo, everyone expected that he would use the occasion of Bologna's defense to justify military action against Austria. But Giovanni reported that the crowd went away downcast. The pope had merely announced, "I have nothing further to say to you at present except that I renew the Apostolic Benediction." Giovanni was personally disappointed. He had been living for months in Rome's edgy atmosphere, watching the companies of young men his age marching off to the North; he wrote Margaret that he wanted to join, that it would fulfill many of his hopes as well as separate him from his "odious brothers."

My state of mind is deplorable. My inner struggle is continual. But for your condition, I could decide more easily; but in the present moment I cannot leave you, I cannot go so far from you, my dear love; ah! how cruel is my destiny in this emergency.[34]

In the first week of August, King Carlo capitulated to the Austrians in Milan and the city was in a state of mob violence. The Italian cause now depended on British or French intervention. Margaret advised Giovanni to wait "two or three weeks" until the situation clarified. "I think I have nothing else to add but leave what to do to your judgment. Only if you leave, come here first, we must see each other again."[35]

Within a few days the pope suspended the departure of any further troops from Rome, putting Giovanni's indecision at rest. In the meantime, Fuller found a good doctor in Rieti, Dr. Camillo Mogliani who bled her twice in August. Other than an occasional headache and toothache and general lethargy, she was healthy during the last weeks of her pregnancy. She liked her landlord, Giovanni Rossetti, and was relying on Giuditta, Maria, and a local midwife to help her through the birth under the doctor's direction. The medical receipts from Dr. Mogliani were made out to Signora Marchesa Margherita Fuller Ossoli, the correct form of address for a married woman.

Giovanni had a difficult time getting permission to leave Rome for any longer than a Sunday. Margaret feared that she might "die alone without touching a dear hand." Giovanni came the last weekend in August and was there again on September 7 when Margaret gave birth to a baby boy. Two days later, she dictated a letter to be sent to Giovanni, now back in Rome, assuring him that she was feeling much better than she had hoped and that the child was well in spite of much crying. In her concern for surviving childbirth, Margaret had not foreseen the powerful hold the child was to have on her. "The child is very beautiful, everybody says so[;] I enjoy very much looking at him," she wrote when he was four days old. Though he had her blue eyes, he had Giovanni's "mouth, hands, feet." Lest she sound too enamored, she added, "He is very naughty; understands well, is very obstinate to have his will." When the baby— soon named Angelo and called both Angelino and "Nino"—was three weeks old, he was so graceful that she compared him to a dancer.[36]

Thoroughly pleased with her child, with her healthy delivery, and with her quick recovery, Fuller was annoyed when she developed milk fever and could not produce enough milk, and blamed Giuditta for upsetting her when she should have been calm at the beginning of nursing. She sent Giuditta back to Rome and told Giovanni not to have anything to do with the wicked girl. That Giuditta or someone else might spread her story around Rome made Fuller cautious as she began to plan her return. With the landlord's help she found a satisfactory wet nurse, Chiara Fiordiponte, one of the most beautiful young women in the town. Chiara offered to take Angelino with her own baby to stay with her brother in Rome. This way Margaret could see him often but not be compromised. But Giovanni thought the plan too risky, both for the sake of security and because he did not think Chiara's offer was serious since she had a husband and obligations in Rieti. He refused to relent when Margaret pleaded with him. She wrote him:

I feel the truth in what you say that we must be very cautious in hiring a nurse; I will wait about everything to take counsel with you. Only think that if the baby is out of Rome, you can not see him very often. Furthermore, without doubt the air of the country would be better for his health. He is so dear; sometimes I think that for all the misfortunes and difficulties, if he lives, if he is well, he can become a great treasure for the two of us, and a compensation for everything.[37]

Forty days of convalescence after childbirth was then the rule. When Fuller computed her obligatory rest period, she decided to leave as soon as possible after October 15 and by the twenty-fifth at the latest. After four months, she was anxious "to go once again into the world." During her absence, the *Tribune* had published two dispatches from Rome written by a free-lance correspondent. To reclaim her position and to continue her book, she needed to be near the scene of action.[38]

Hoping to find a small apartment—even a single room would do—Fuller sent her lover searching throughout the areas of Rome familiar to her. Because she was not sure she could remain separated from Angelino, and she worried that gossip might make her position uncomfortable, Fuller was insisting on a short-term arrangement. She might be forced to choose between her life as a mother and as a correspondent. "You also know that because of the wicked Giuditta . . . it is possible that it could become very unpleasant for me to be in Rome this winter[;] we cannot know yet," she wrote Giovanni when he tried to persuade her to take a six-month lease.[39]

As a devout Catholic, Giovanni wanted Angelino baptized as soon as possible, not only for religious reasons but as a formal recognition of his legal existence. In recognition of Fuller's eldest brother, Eugene, and Giovanni's father, Filippo, they named their son Angelo Eugenio Filippo Ossoli. Fuller wanted Adam Mickiewicz to be godfather. "He knows about the existence of the baby[;] he is a devout Catholic, he is a distinguished man who could be a help to him in his future life, and I want him to have some friend in case something happens to us."[40]

It was too late to get Mickiewicz's permission, let alone his presence by the end of October. Giovanni's main concern was security; he was even willing at first to accept the landlord, Giovanni Rossetti, but Margaret vetoed that. Finally, Giovanni decided on his nephew, Pietro Ossoli, who was good-natured and trustworthy. Through contacts in Rome, they discovered that the godfather could serve by proxy and the parents' names could be withheld from the document until a later time. Such maneuvering did not mean that Giovanni was reluctant to take full responsibility for his child; indeed, he saw to it that a legal document was prepared—bearing the family crest—giving Angelo every right to the Ossoli name and title.

In the meantime Fuller was in a turmoil over the smallpox epidemic in Rieti. When the overworked Dr. Mogliani did not respond to several calls to inoculate Angelino, she lost all patience. The doctor was "detestable, untrustworthy"—he was even worse than all the other Rietians. When he finally appeared, he was out of serum and advised her to have Giovanni buy some in Rome. On October 29, after three weeks of fussing, she finally wrote to Giovanni in Rome that the serum had come and the inoculation had been accomplished.

Giovanni was present at his son's christening ceremony in Rieti on November 6. Afterward Chiara took Angelino home to her extended family, which included ten other children. Violent autumn rains and flash floods delayed Fuller's return to Rome. When she did venture forth in mid-Novermber, much of the route was under water. Even the Tiber had overflowed, and she enjoyed entering Rome on a sheet of silver under the moonlit sky. Giovanni had found her a large sunny room, one she could rent by the month. Now that her life was more complex than ever, she had to be free to move on a moment's notice.

A happy New-Year to my country! may she be worthy of the privileges she possesses, while others are lavishing their blood to win them.

The Roman Republic

FULLER'S new one-room home in Rome overlooked the Triton Fountain in the Piazza Barberini. In one direction, she could see the Palazzo Barberini; in the other, she could look over the walls of the Quirinal Gardens to the rooftops of the papal palace at the top of Monte Cavallo. Her house even had a claim to literary fame; Hans Christian Andersen had lived there and used it as the background for his story, *The Improvvisatore.* Her room was the very one occupied by the Danish painter in the tale. As Fuller described her living conditions, a "quick, prompt, and kind, sensible and contented" old couple took care of the house and treated her and the Prussian sculptor who occupied rooms on the same floor as their own children. At the top of the building, under the eaves, lived a garrulous, inquisitive priest who came to make Fuller's fire on the days when her maid, Antonia, was out. Antonia kept a few flowerpots, a birdcage, and her black cat, Amoretto, on the balcony overlooking the Square.[1]

Within a week of Fuller's return, Rome became the center stage of Italy's drama. Count Pellegrino Rossi, the pope's newly appointed prime minister, was assassinated on the steps of the Chancelleria on November 16. As he was about to enter the Chamber of Deputies, two lines of *reduci,* a ruffian battalion of returned soldiers from the battles in the North, grouped around him in the formation of an escorting guard. As he mounted the steps, he was stabbed in the throat. At the same instant, the entire band raised their daggers in the air so the murderer could not be identified. The atmosphere of unconcern on the part of officials and the public was as sure a sign as the expert staging that the assassination had been carefully planned and that the plot was known to many in advance. "For me, I never thought to have heard of a violent death with satisfaction, but this act affected me as one of terrible justice," Fuller wrote in her first letter to her mother after several months of silence. Her identification with the Italian people had now become so strong that her critical practice of balancing opposing views was in abeyance. Rossi was certainly unpopular, but he was a man of considerable intelligence and ability. His arrogant, stand-offish manner is what undid him, not evil intent. In a climate of high expectations, his policy of moving slowly was mistaken for one of opposition to any effort to form a representative government.[2]

The morning after Rossi's murder, Fuller joined the crowd of more than

10,000 Romans who gathered at the Quirinal Palace to demand that the pope agree to a declaration of independence from Austria, to the formation of a constituent assembly, and to the relegation of papal authority to the spiritual sphere alone. Representatives of the political clubs, student battalions, Civic Guard, Carabinieri, line regiments, ruffians, and outside agitators, many carrying banners and some 6,000 bearing arms, swarmed in the broad piazza. They overflowed down the hill to the Corso and up to the Via Quattro Fontane, just around the corner from Fuller's apartment. The pope refused to appear, and Fuller, knowing that a confrontation was inevitable, returned home. From her window she saw a wounded man carried away and watched Prince Barberini's coach with its liveried footmen turn hurriedly into the courtyard of the Palazzo Barberini. As the massive gates were barred, Antonia sighed—prophetically of Europe's future, according to Fuller—"Thank Heaven, we are poor, we have nothing to fear!"[3]

In the afternoon, snipers were stationed at nearby vantage points, including the campanile of the Church of San Carlo opposite the Quirinal walls. At about three in the afternoon, three bullets whizzed through the pope's antechamber; one killed Monsignor Palma, a bishop who was serving as a papal secretary. Fuller heard the drumbeat call out the National Guard. Late that night, before she sat down to write her mother, she received the news, probably from Giovanni, that the pope had capitulated; he agreed to a cabinet of ministers dictated by the rebels. "It is almost impossible for any one to act, unless the Pope is stripped of his temporal power, and the hour for that is not yet quite ripe," Fuller wrote her mother, "though they talk more and more of proclaiming the Republic, and even of calling my friend Mazzini. If I came home at this moment, I should feel as if forced to leave my own house, my own people, and the hour which I had always longed for." There was no reason to worry about her, she assured confidently; there were people who would look after her, if necessary, and "besides, I am on the conquering side!"[4]

Her references to her private life remained oblique. "These days are what I always longed for,—were I only free from private care." If she had only 600 a year, she wrote, she could live very well. "Foreigners cannot live so, but I could, now that I speak the language fluently, and know the price of everything." She hinted of "strange and romantic chapters" in her life, of a time when she had been afraid of dying, and of a brotherly friend whom she had commissioned to reveal her story when he returned to the United States. Her final sentence was her broadest hint of all to her mother, who knew her Bible thoroughly:

Were you here, I would confide in you fully, and have more than once, in silence of the night, recited to you those most strange and romantic chapters in the story of my sad life. . . . I am sure you will always love your daughter, and will know gladly that in all events she has tried to aid and striven never to injure her fellows. In earlier days, I dreamed of doing and being much, but now I am content with the Magdalen to rest my plea hereon, "*She has loved much.*"[5]

A week after the skirmish at the Quirinal, Pope Nono—disguised, it was said, as a groom and sitting on the box of the Bavarian ambassador's coach—rode out of the Quirinal gate and was whisked along the Appian Way to the fortress of Gaeta in the Kingdom of the Two Sicilies. This event signaled the beginning of the "days" Margaret Fuller had "longed for"—perhaps ever since, at the age of fifteen, she wrote to Lafayette, telling him that he filled her soul with "a noble ambition" and expressing the hope that someday in the future, if it should be "possible to a female, to whom the avenues of glory are seldom accessible," she would make her name in some glorious way. On December 2 Fuller finished two lengthy articles for the *Tribune*, bringing her readers up to date on the developments through the summer and fall. The hero of her story was the Italian people, who had nobly belied all foreign taunts that "the Italian can boast, shout, and fling garlands, but not *act*." The victim was the poor pope, who meant well but who had "his mind torn to pieces" by the conflicting advice of "the scarlet men of sin" surrounding him. She announced her intention to give a more thorough account of these historic events. "Of all this great drama I have much to write, but elsewhere, in a more full form, and where I can duly sketch the portraits of actors little known in America."[6]

For a second time she appealed to America to send "a good Ambassador—one that has experience of foreign life, . . . a man that has knowledge and views which extend beyond the cause of party politics in the United States." Above all, the American ambassador should be someone who could respond fully to the advantage of living in Rome. "Another century, and I might ask to be made Ambassador myself," she ventured, "but woman's day has not come yet." Ending with her traditional New Year's greeting to America—this was her fifth consecutive New Year's letter in the *Tribune*—she proclaimed, "A Happy New-Year to my country! may she be worthy of the privileges she possesses, while others are lavishing their blood to win them."[7]

In the second of her *Tribune* letters Fuller took a daring step. She published one of the hints that she had been inserting in her private letters. Her readers learned that she had taken a six-month vacation secluded in the Italian countryside. "I left [behind] what was most precio[us]," she confided cryptically, but which "I could not take with me." This bold sentence, published in the February 10, 1849, *Tribune*, seems to have been another move in her strategy to soften the impact when news of Ossoli and Angelino became public.[8]

After the pope's surprise refusal in August to sanction military action against Austria, the Civic Guard, in a show of force, occupied the papal arsenal, the Castle St. Angelo, thus identifying itself unequivocally with the parties determined to wrest temporal power from the pope. From the time of its formation, the Civic Guard had represented a wide spectrum of liberal opinion; by the fall of 1848 anyone wearing the uniform was suspected to be a democrat. Ossoli's political sympathies could no longer be hidden from his brothers. But as they lived outside of Rome and had neglected him for years, he was free to enjoy the intermezzo in Rome's drama with Fuller. In the lull that followed the pope's departure for Gaeta, the two picked up their lives where they had left off before the heavy rains of the previous winter. The warm fall weather continued into December, and they revisited their haunts of the previous autumn. From Fuller's house they could easily walk to the gardens of the Villa Albani or the Villa Ludovisi; on some days they ventured out to the vineyards at Porto maggiore or spent a day wandering over Monte Mario. Because the distance to Rieti was considerable, and the autumn floods made the journey difficult and dangerous, Fuller delayed returning to Angelino. In December she wrote William Story—the Storys were spending the winter in Florence—describing their expeditions and openly mentioning her companionship with Giovanni.

But to you I may tell, that I always go with Ossoli, the most congenial companion I ever had for jaunts of this kind. We go out in the morning, carrying the roast chestnuts from Rome; the bread and wine are found in some lonely little osteria; and so we dine; and reach Rome again, just in time to see it, from a little distance, gilded by the sunset.[9]

In December she decided to share her secret with Caroline Sturgis Tappan. In years past, she and Tappan had often speculated about their children-to-be. In fact, they had been more fascinated with their future children than with their future husbands. To tell Tappan out of the blue was just the sort of stroke that she liked—the utterly unexpected dramatic surprise. But there was a more mundane reason: Fuller was trying to build up her bank account by every means possible, and, if given sufficient reason, Tappan was in a position to help. From the time of the pope's departure, Rome was alive with rumors of a coming military intervention. With no help coming from the Ossoli side, she needed funds in case of an emergency.

By the time she wrote Tappan (in mid-December), she had been away from Nino for almost seven weeks, and the desire to be with him over Christmas was pressing. On December 21 Fuller left Rome. Ten hours later she was in Rieti, holding him in her arms. He was fat and healthy even though the house was freezing; wind whistled through the loose construction, and Margaret shivered in bed at night. "[H]e doesn't seem to have a cold," she wrote Giovanni, and "surely he will be stronger for being so exposed in his first few months." On Christmas Eve she enjoyed watching him respond to all the church bells. After a week in the drafty and smoky house, she returned to Rome reassured that Nino was thriving under Chiara's care.[10]

Upon her return she found a letter from Horace Greeley, announcing the birth of a daughter, Ida—"a very nice girl, with a very black head of hair." They had a "capital nurse . . . and a sister of Mr. James Nathan, a most excellent girl, is also staying as a friend with Mrs. G. and doing a great deal for her, especially with regard to Pickie." He then unburdened his reasons for being "provoked" with her for the last few months. First, Margaret had asked him to advance a much larger sum of money than he found it easy to raise ($600) and then, just as he had "forgotten *that*," along came her notification that she would not be sending any more dispatches. "[T]o have you break off utterly just when Italy and Europe were in the throbs of a great Revolution and when I thought I had made an effort to oblige you, struck me as unkind," Greeley complained. He had decided to "let it all pass now"—they could talk it all out when they met again.[11]

She also had news from Mrs. Farrar that the campaign to raise funds for her had been successful, but in a way she found annoyingly inconvenient. A group of her " 'best and most loving friends' " had raised a purse which would provide her an annuity of $300 a year, but she could not draw on it until she returned to the United States. (In addition to Eliza Farrar, the donors were probably Elizabeth Hoar, Sam and Anna Ward, and James Freeman Clarke.) Indeed, there seemed to be a plot on the part of her friends to lure her home. Sarah and William Clarke, and even James Freeman Clarke, with whom she had been out of touch ever since she came to Europe, all wrote pleading with her to return. "Leave revolutions to revolve alone—Let the good Pia Nona take care of his mad subjects as he can. We want you here—Come and see us soon," James commanded.[12]

James's letter revived in Margaret old memories of when they were young confidantes, planning their futures in a grandiose manner and discussing greatness, the noble life, and how to keep from becoming machines. In her reply, she reverted to the language they had used in the old days. People were asking her to come back, but what was there to come back to? "Here is a great past and a *living* present. Here men work for something besides money and systems, the voice of noble sentiment is understood. . . . Tis a sphere much more natural to me than that the old Puritans and the bankers have made." Nevertheless, she assured him she would not have wished to have been born anywhere else than in America, "the land of promise." To give evidence that her presence in Italy at this time of ferment might be of some use, she sent James a copy of the first letter Adam Mickiewicz had sent her in Paris. She told James that she looked "with great reverence" on Mickiewicz's prediction that her soul would find its sustenance in the Old World, its "activity" in the New World, and its "repose" in the "future" world. This was "really true," she asserted.[13]

"Eternal City—but why stay there eternally?" Horace Greeley asked when he wrote again in January 1849, but he was pleased she had resumed her letters to the *Tribune*. As all her friends read them to get news of her, he suggested that she write at least once a month. But he still wondered when she was coming home: "I cannot comprehend your long term in such a region of the dead. Come back soon to refresh your eyes with . . . our young country, or you will grow old yourself." Greeley held until last the news that her literary reputation in New York had gotten a boost recently from an unexpected quarter. The indefatigable Rufus Wilmot Griswold, editor of *Graham's Lady's and Gentle-man's Magazine* and countless giftbooks and sentimental collections and anthologies, who had panned Fuller in his *Prose Writers of America* (1847), had reversed himself in his recent *Female Poets of America*. The quality of her *Tribune* reviews had forced the change, Greeley wrote her: "Griswold has got out a very good compilation of 'The Female Poets of America,' in which he takes back some poor judgments he passed on you in his Prose Writers. I don't suppose you care for the disfavorment or the retraction."[14]

Of course she cared. She depended on her literary reputation now more than ever before. Greeley knew she cared and was also aware that by the time she received his letter she would have seen the savage attack James Russell Lowell had made on her in his *Fable for Critics,* a collection of humorous verse portraits of many of the major literary figures of the day. The satire was published in October 1848; Greeley was offering what comfort he could. Lowell had never forgiven Fuller for the cavalier comment with which she had disposed of him in her *Papers on Literature and Art:* that he was "absolutely wanting in the true spirit and tone of poesy. . . . [H]is verse is stereotyped; his thought sounds no depth, and posterity will not remember him."[15]

When the Storys wrote the Lowells from Rome in the winter of 1848 telling them how much they were enjoying Fuller's company, Lowell quipped maliciously,

I have it on good authority that the Austrian government has its eye on Miss F. It would be a pity to have so much worth & genius shut up for life in Spielberg [the Austrian maximum-security prison for political prisoners]. Her beauty might perhaps save her. Is the Emperor unmarried? Pio Nono also regards her with a naturally jealous eye, fearing that the College of Cardinals may make her the successor of Pope Joan.[16]

When Lowell first started his picture gallery in light verse, he thought his best revenge was to exclude Fuller entirely. He gave in to the temptation to satirize her only after his wife, Maria, and Charles Briggs, Margaret's old enemy, encouraged him to go ahead. The result was the "most wholly negative characterization" in the whole collection. All his other subjects appeared with their real names, but she was lightly disguised as Miranda, the name she had used in her self-portrait in *Woman in the Nineteenth Century.*

> Here Miranda came up, and said, "Phoebus! you know
> That the infinite Soul has its infinite woe,
> As I ought to know, having lived cheek by jowl,
> Since the day I was born, with the Infinite Soul;
> I myself introduced, I myself, I alone,
> To my Land's better life authors solely my own,
> Who the sad heart of earth on their shoulders have taken,
> Whose works sound a depth by Life quite unshaken,
> Such as Shakespeare, for instance, the Bible and Bacon, . . ."[17]

The attack continues for two more verses. Thomas Wentworth Higginson, who was now married to Ellery Channing's sister Mary, wrote Lowell a strong protest, rebuking him for his "undiscriminating solely contemptuous criticism" of a woman whose courage "to study, think, talk & write" had not earned her such treatment. Edgar Allan Poe, whom Fuller had ignored completely in her *Papers on Literature and Art*, was amused that "so unsurpassable a transcendentalist as Miss Fuller, should . . . have had the power to put a respectable poet in such a passion."[18]

The scurrilous portrait hurt Margaret deeply. When the Storys arrived in Rome from Florence in early March, she expressed her indignation and her helplessness to defend herself. Moved by her distress, William Story took his old friend, Jim Lowell, to task. After praising the *Fable for Critics* as a whole, he added:

There is but one thing I regretted, and that was that you drove your arrow so sharply through Miranda. . . . [B]ecause fate has really been unkind to her, and because she depends on her pen for her bread-and-water (and that is nearly all she has to eat), and because she is her own worst enemy, and because through her disappointment and disease, which (things) embitter everyone, she has struggled most stoutly and manfully, I could have wished you had let her pass scotfree.

Lowell wrote back that he was "more sorry . . . than anyone," but he did not recant. He kept the verses intact in future editions, but later in the year both of the Lowells, James and Maria, were vociferous in their praise of Margaret's loyal and brave support of the Roman Republic.[19]

Margaret vented her outrage in a letter to Caroline Tappan (a good friend of Maria Lowell):

This last plot against me has been too cruel and too cunningly wrought. I shall never acquiesce; I submit because a useless resistance is degrading, but I demand an explanation. I see that it is probable I shall receive none while I live here.[20]

She still had her admirers in New York, however. Evert Duyckinck, now editor of the *Literary World*, frequently reprinted sections of her *Tribune* letters and alerted her readers twice in his "What Is Talked About" column that she was writing a "comprehensive" book on the revolutionary movement in Italy.[21]

Fuller had few social claims on her during the winter of 1848–49, partly because the threat of war kept most American travelers out of Rome. She had a visit from Albert Brisbane, the Fourierism enthusiast who had supervised Brook Farm's transformation into a Phalanx. Brisbane was now in Europe observing the development of new Associations, especially in France, where the enthusiasm of the first days of the Second Republic had encouraged a spate of new socialist experiments. Another friend from her Brook Farm days, Frank Shaw, also passed through Rome. He was still translating George Sand's novels.

Margaret was now disillusioned with her old idol. She had felt deep disappointment when Sand refused to run for the French National Assembly and proclaimed that women were not ready either for the vote or for political responsibility. For women to participate in politics, a total transformation of society was required, Sand asserted. First, society would have to accept equality in marriage as well as intellectual and economic equality. Though weary of battling these "giant wrongs" and hoping that a younger generation of women would take up the cause, Fuller told her *Tribune* readers she would have more to say on this subject in the future.[22]

At the beginning of the year 1849, she started a diary. "Rome has at last become the focus of the Italian revolution and I am here," she wrote in her first entry on January 1. The diary served as a day-by-day calendar of events while she expanded on them in a journal. Noting that democracy had progressed—in form, at least—since the first meeting of the Roman Council fourteen months earlier on November 15, 1847, she outlined the steps leading to the inauguration of the first Roman Constituent Assembly and the proclamation on February 5 of the Roman Republic:

What a vast stride for democracy made since then in this country. How many men of straw have been put up and knocked down. . . . Those who came to the [pope's] council [Consulta] were mostly nobles. The princes of Rome lent them their coaches of state; they rode in them and looked out of the window like Whittington and his cat. The present deputies walked on foot, ornamented only with the tri-colored scarf to the sound of the Marseillaise.[23]

Margaret had no illusion that the unstable coalition that called itself a republican government was now permanent. Yet she knew that the peaceful revolution in Rome was worth celebrating. In her February 20 letter to the *Tribune,* she pointed out that what the 1849 Republican Carnival in Rome lost in splendor because of the absence of dukes and princes and their gilded carriages it more than made up for in the lavish displays of flowers and the exuberance of the people in their fanciful costumes, such as the handsome women dressed in white wearing the red liberty cap. Red had become the color of liberty. On June 21, 1848, Giuseppe Garibaldi, who had served with Mazzini in 1834 in the abortive plot to incite an insurrection in the Savoy, had returned from exile in South America with his Italian legion, the first "Redshirts." On February 12 the Roman Constituent Assembly bestowed Roman citizenship on Garibaldi and also on Mazzini, who was still in Florence awaiting the appropriate moment to come to Rome and, in the meantime, encouraging the shaky constituent assembly there to fuse with Rome into a single state.

Mazzini's eloquent letter accepting Roman citizenship, published in the newspapers, summoned Fuller's Muse qualities to action. She wrote him a letter of consolation and encouragement in which she put to use her feminine theory of woman's special gift. Telling him that she was persuaded "that the best friends, in point of perfect sympathy and intelligence the only friends—of a man of ideas and marked character must be women," she wished to join his mother and other women who performed this service for him. He had returned to see his thought "springing up all over Italian soil." Even if the Roman Republic had a brief life, his moral leadership was invaluable in the chain of events governed by God's plan for mankind.

For your sake I would wish at this moment to be an Italian and a man of action. But *though an American,* I am not even *a woman of action;* so the best I can do is to pray with the whole heart. Heaven bless dear Mazzini, cheer his heart and give him worthy helpers to carry out its holy purposes![24]

There was one other contribution she could make, as she wrote Richard later in the month. "This is to see the end of the political struggle in Italy and write its history. I think it will come to its crisis within this year. But to complete my work as I have begun I must watch it to the end." Mazzini arrived in Rome on March 3. He was only one of 262 deputies, yet from his first day in the Assembly he was its recognized leader, and the policies he favored became the government agenda. On March 8 he appeared at Fuller's door. The next evening she wrote Marcus Spring:

Last night, I heard a ring; then somebody speak my name; the voice struck upon me at once. He looks more divine than ever, after all his new, strange sufferings. He asked after all of you. He stayed two hours, and we talked, though rapidly, of everything. He hopes to come often, but the crisis is tremendous.

Mazzini gave her tickets to hear him speak in the Assembly. "He looks as if the great battle he had fought had been too much for his strength, and that he was only sustained by the fire of the soul."[25]

In a letter to her mother after Mazzini's arrival in Rome Fuller admitted that she had little confidence in his ability to prevail against the overwhelming odds. "I fear the entrance into Jerusalem will be followed by the sacrifice," she concluded. Yet, when she wrote Tappan, she heralded him as Rome's savior:

Speaking of the Republic, you say do I not wish Italy had a great man. Mazzini is a great man; in mind great poetic statesman, in heart a lover, in action decisive and full of resource as Cesar. Dearly I love Mazzini, who also loves me. He came in just as I had finished this first letter to you. His soft radiant look makes melancholy music in my soul.[26]

Fuller knew these expressions of intimacy with Mazzini would intrigue and impress Tappan. She had thought that the sharing of her secret had reestablished their friendship on its old confidential footing. Yet Tappan, who avoided conventional enthusiasms, had kept from Margaret the news of her own pregnancy. She was expecting a child in the summer, and once again it hurt Fuller to hear the news from someone else. She wrote Tappan that she "felt sad" to discover "this great fact" of her life secondhand. Tappan was mourning the loss of her sister, Ellen Sturgis Hooper, who had died of tuberculosis the past

November, leaving three children (one of whom, Clover, became the wife of Henry Adams). Both Fuller and Tappan thought Hooper's life had been too much of a sacrifice, that, in Margaret's words, "she had such an anxious delicate sense of what was due to [her husband], that she could never have any free harmonious life in this world."[27]

It was a great relief to Fuller that Tappan had responded generously to her request for money and had even offered to take Angelino if anything should happen to her or to Giovanni. Ordinarily, Giovanni's sister Angela, who had no children, would be the natural one to take Nino if his parents died in Italy. Although Fuller still had never met Angela and knew about her only from Giovanni's reports, she thought of her, she wrote Tappan, as "a person of great elegance and sweetness but entirely limited in mind." Besides, Fuller wanted her son to have American citizenship, especially if the Italian political situation remained uncertain. Now that her spirits had revived, she thought that there was a very good chance that she was going to "live and carry him round myself as I ride on my ass into Egypt," she wrote Tappan who, in her letter, had played on Margaret's former fancy of sometimes comparing herself to Mary by referring to Angelino as having been born in a manger. Margaret took issue with the comparison, pointing out that, in the case of Mary, Joseph, and Jesus, the "manger" episode had lasted for only a short time. She elaborated on the fancy:

[P]resently came Kings with gold cups and all sorts of things. Joseph pawned them; with part of the money he bought this nice donkey for the journey; and they lived on the rest till Joseph could work at his trade, we have no donkey and it costs a great deal to travel in diligence and steamers, and being a nobleman is a poor trade in a ruined despotism just turning into a Republic.

Tappan wrote that she had told no one about Fuller's affairs but warned that "no secret can be kept in the civilized world." While admitting the risk, Fuller replied, "[I]t is very important to me to keep this, for the present, if possible, and by and by to have the mode of disclosure at my option. For this, I have made the cruelest sacrifices."[28]

She could not escape her preoccupation with money. Her latest disappointment was the news that her beloved Aunt Mary Rotch, who had died the previous September, had divided her estate of $150,000 between her companion Mary Gifford and her lawyer. There were no legacies to any of her relatives, let alone to her devoted friends. Margaret saw this as a careless and cruel disposition when even a small percentage of Aunt Mary's wealth—$5,000 was the figure she chose—would have allowed her to live in peace, if not prosperity.

Throughout March 1849 the cause of Italian independence, let alone republicanism, was rapidly losing ground. In Tuscany and Turin, constitutional governments fell; in Genoa, a democratic revolt was suppressed. Carlo Alberto's defeat on March 23 in his last-ditch drive against the Austrians in the Battle of Novara created a crisis. It was the crisis Mazzini had feared and expected when he took his seat in the Roman Assembly. Austria's victory sparked rumors of negotiations between Austria, France, England, and Russia. Foreign intervention was expected. The pope announced that he was asking help from France, Spain, and Naples against "the enemies of our most holy religion and civil society." The rumors of a coming military action against Rome put further pressure on Fuller. Fuller was deathly afraid of being caught in a besieged city, cut off from Angelino, and with no way of supervising his care or of knowing how he was prospering. She was also nervous because the troops of Garibaldi—she called them "desperadoes" in a letter to Tappan—were stationed in Rieti. In just a few months the legion had grown from a few hundred to a thousand men. Just across the border, the Neapolitan troops were quartered and anything could happen any day.[29]

On March 26 "la cittadina Margherita Ossoli" was issued a travel permit to Rieti by the Office of Public Security of the Roman Republic. She was listed as a native of Rome, twenty-nine years of age. (Margaret would be 39 on May 23, 1839). Other identification blanks on the permit were left empty, as if the document had been hastily prepared by a functionary under orders. If—as was likely—Mazzini facilitated the permit, the ten-year age discrepancy could well have been an act of gallantry; the use of the name Ossoli was in keeping with the name Fuller was known by in Rieti, and the listing of Rome as her native city would have avoided unnecessary delay.[30]

In Rieti, Fuller took no chances. She heard tales of soldiers terrorizing priests; there had been at least one wanton killing, and two corpses were found in the river. She kept close to the Fiordiponte house, where she lived in an upstairs room with Nino. The most frightening experience of her stay took place downstairs one night when Chiara's husband, Nicolá, and his brother Pietro began throwing furniture at one another in a drunken brawl. Nicolá brandished a knife in the air until friends separated them. The incident made Margaret consider bringing Nino back to Rome with her; in the end, she decided that he was less threatened by Fiordiponte family quarrels than by those within the Ossoli family. Chiara was as good as ever to Angelino; Margaret was sure of that. "If it is necessary for him, we will tell our secret, who knows if it will not be the best thing in the end?" she speculated to Giovanni. "But it is necessary to think of everything, because our whole future lives depend upon the discretion of this moment." Giovanni was equally concerned. "Please find out everything that is going on in Rieti," he advised, "and if there is any risk return as quickly as you can—with Angelino if you think fit. Meanwhile plan some course of action for our dear one, so as not to leave him unprotected if the entire clerical party should rise."[31]

Margaret and Giovanni both regretted that he was unable to get to Rieti on April 4. Their exchange of letters indicate that the day had a special meaning. In letters that crossed, they both made mention of the date. "I know full well you will remember what day is April 4th," Giovanni wrote when he discovered he could not get free to join her. She wrote that it was "strange" they could not "spend this day together." In anticipation of his coming, she prepared a special meal of blackbirds and could not eat them alone.[32]

If they had met on Holy Wednesday, 1847, as George Putnam reported, they met on March 31, 1847. Easter that year fell on April 4 and could have been the date of a second meeting in which Ossoli declared his interest in Fuller. It is also possible, as Madeleine Stern has argued in her biography of Fuller, that Fuller and Ossoli were married outside of Rome on April 4, 1848, a few weeks before Margaret went to Aquila for her confinement.[33]

For whatever reason, April 4 was an important anniversary. Ossoli missed the occasion in 1849, but he was able to come to Rieti at the end of that week and see for himself how well Nino was progressing. As Dr. Mogliani had repeatedly failed to respond to Chiara's calls when the baby seemed ill, a new doctor was found, Dr. Luigi Bassin. He agreed to write them in Rome at regular intervals, reporting on Angelino's health. Reassured, Ossoli returned to Rome, and Fuller followed a few days later; she arrived in Rome on April 17 after a three-week absence.

While Fuller was in Rieti, the Roman Assembly—in response to the military threat to the Republic—voted to place the government under the leadership of a triumvirate: Mazzini; the aristocrat and scholar Aurelio Saffi; and Carlo Armellini, the grand old man of Italian jurisprudence. Mazzini was offered quarters in the Quirinal Palace, just around the block from Fuller. At the end of March he moved into two small rooms there, with his guitar and his generous supply of cigars, the only luxuries he permitted himself. He took all his meals at workers' restaurants.

When Margaret returned, she found the new government moving ahead, initiating land and tax reforms and intensifying a program of slum clearance. The Assembly abolished the death penalty and primogeniture and decreed freedom of the press and religious equality. The triumvirate was proceeding cautiously, careful to reject proposals to guarantee wages and employment, socialist measures which were undermining the Second Republic in France. But time was short. After savagely repressing a democratic uprising in Brescia in early April, the Austrian army was quartered in the North, watching developments in Rome. The Spanish government was discussing sending a force to Fiumicino opposite Elba. On the day Fuller returned to Rome, the French government voted to send an expeditionary force under General Oudinot to Civitavecchia, Rome's seaport, sixty miles from the city. On April 25, French troops disembarked on Italian soil.

On April 2 the new American chargé d'affaires to the Papal States, Lewis Cass, Jr., arrived in Rome with orders not to present his credentials to the Roman Republic. He was the son of the defeated Democratic presidential candidate in the 1848 election, General Lewis Cass, and his only diplomatic experience was working as secretary when his father had been minister to France. After serving as a major in the Mexican War, the son had returned home to Detroit and dabbled in the law. Through the dogged efforts of his mother, he was appointed to the Roman post. A bachelor, Cass had a reputation as a dandy and almost instantly won the dislike of Mazzini for predicting that the government of Rome "could not live." On April 9 he wrote the secretary of state in Washington that "in the course of a month the Pontiff will be restored to the Vatican." Less than two weeks later, his dispatches had taken an about-face. He praised the good sense and moderation of the majority of deputies in the Assembly and assured his superiors that most of them expressed "the conviction, that no right or freedom or happiness is possible under the sway of the Cardinals, whom they have always regarded as the real government."[34]

On April 30, the day the French attacked Rome, Cass came to Fuller's apartment to urge her to move to the Casa Diez in the Via Gregoriana, where Americans were being provided sanctuary. Within a short time, she established a rapport with him; he said later that he liked her from the moment he met her. But she had other obligations that day. That morning she had received an assignment from her friend Cristina Belgioioso:

Dear Miss Fuller:
You are named Regolatrice of the Hospital of Fate Bene Fratelli. Go there at twelve, if the alarm bell has not rung before. When you arrive there, you will receive all the women coming for the wounded, and give them your directions, so that you are sure to have a certain number of them night and day.
    May God help us,

Cristina Trivulzi, of Belgioioso[35]

Five years before Florence Nightingale was to take over a similar post in the Crimean War, Belgioioso was appointed director of the military field hospitals of the Roman Republic. During the two weeks before hostilities began, she undertook to ready twelve hospitals, all in disastrous condition. After ordering basic supplies, her first step was to address the problem of personnel. In the excited atmosphere of Rome, many women of the aristocracy were expressing their enthusiasm for Italy's independence and donating jewels, gold, and family plate to the cause. Belgioioso hit on the idea—a new one for the time—of calling on lay volunteers. At the same time she urged the government to establish a central house of instruction for nurses. With the help of Rome's Committee for the Aid of the Wounded, from among a much larger number she selected 300 volunteers. The Fate Bene Fratelli Hospital (now written Fatebenefratelli) where Fuller was director was—and still is—on the Tiber Island. There had been some sort of hospital on the spot since ancient times, when the island was dedicated to the god of medicine, Aescalapius, a detail surely not lost on Fuller as she began her mission of April 30, the day Oudinot's army first attacked Rome.[36]

In the late afternoon of the twenty-ninth, Fuller returned to the sanctuary at Casa Diez where all the Americans were assembled. She reported that seventy wounded had already been brought in. As she had predicted the year before (when she wrote Waldo Emerson that she was not yet ready to return home), she had found her "*part*" to play in Italy's struggle. From the end of April to the beginning days of July—throughout the siege of Rome—she went regularly to her post.[37]

But life is so uncertain, and it is so necessary to take good things with their limitations.

Siege and Escape

FULLER spent the first night after the battle at the hospital and walked home through the city at dawn. About 275 soldiers were hospitalized after Oudinot's April 30 attack. By the first of May the French had withdrawn. Garibaldi, the hero of the day, was leading his troops to the south to head off the army King Ferdinand II of Naples had sent to aid the French. He had been chasing the fleeing French soldiers down the road to the sea when he was ordered to move southward. For the rest of his life Garibaldi argued that he should have been allowed to annihilate the French troops that April day. On the afternoon of April 30 the Americans gathered on the balcony of the Casa Diez to watch the battle through eyeglasses. "[T]he boom and rattle" of the musketry was enough to convince the Storys to move immediately from their lodgings near the Porta Pinciana to the safety of the American sanctuary. Margaret joined them there two days later.[1]

The next day Fuller took an American friend, Frank Heath, to her hospital. Overcome by the sight of the mutilation and suffering, he initiated a collection among the Americans which came to $250. When William and Emelyn Story delivered the contribution to Cristina Belgioioso at the Trinità dei Pellegrini, they found her haggard and exhausted after three sleepless nights. She was living at the hospital, sharing a mattress with her eleven-year-old daughter Maria. Taking care of the sick had become "a sort of a passion" with Belgioioso. The relief of pain was the one "effort of charity" that could not fail, she said; it was a thing "definite and certain" and gave her a sense of wholeness.[2]

No one knew when hostilities would resume. From the Casa Diez balcony at night the Americans could still see the watch fires of the enemy camps. Everyone was waiting to hear whether Garibaldi's legion had been successful in the South, whether the Austrians had been detained at Ancona, whether the Spanish would be joining the French in a second attack, and whether Venice—now in a state of siege—was still holding out. This strained atmosphere led Fuller to confide in Emelyn Story. She wanted someone she trusted, someone she was connected with at home, to look out for Angelino if she were killed, hurt, or caught in the besieged city. One night in early May, when all the Americans were living dormitory-style at the Casa Diez, she told Story that she was married to Ossoli and had a son by him. "[S]he told me where her child was, and when it was born," Story wrote later, "and gave me certain papers and parchment documents which I was to keep, and in the event of her death I was to take the boy to her mother in America and confide him to her care and that of her friend Caroline Tappan." Story did not examine the papers closely. The only paper Margaret read over with her was the parchment document bearing the Ossoli family seal, "saying that Angelo Eugene Ossoli was the legal [illegible] heir of whatever title and fortune should come to his father." Story was under the impression that the document had been prepared by the priest who had married Margaret and Giovanni. With the documents was also a book to be delivered to the Fuller family in case of Margaret's death, which, Margaret told Story, contained the whole story of the Ossoli relationship. Story admitted later that she never actually saw a marriage certificate, nor could she explain the oddity of the existence of a document—said to be prepared by the priest who presided at the marriage ceremony—attesting to Angelino's hereditary rights.[3]

After confiding in Story, Fuller wrote Giovanni telling him what she had done; she assured him that if "by any chance" she should die he could change the arrangements she had made "as from [his] wife." This was the first time she called herself a wife (*moglie*) in writing. As the situation was one in which the legal relationship was decisive, her choice of words might suggest that she and Ossoli were now married, but in the absence of any documentary evidence her choice of language is only provocative.[4]

Story kept Fuller's secret; she did not even tell her husband. But the Storys did not intend to remain long in Italy. The museums and galleries were closed. Barricades shut off six main streets between the Trinità dei Monti and the Santa Maria Maggiore. On the Pincian Hill and in the Villa Borghese grounds, the gardens were ravaged; the great oaks had been cut down to their stumps to make barricades. The Forum was completely despoiled. "Rome is shorn of the locks that lent grace to her venerable brow," Fuller reported to the *Tribune*.[5]

News came on April 19 that Garibaldi had successfully stopped the Neapolitans at Velletri and that the French government was sending a peace envoy, Ferdinand de Lesseps (the engineer who was later to construct the Suez Canal). Mazzini, who had already returned all the French prisoners and had the French wounded taken into the hospitals on an equal basis with the fallen Romans, met de Lesseps with trust. Everyone began to hope for a diplomatic settlement, but the French made two demands that could not be met; they were to occupy Rome, and the pope was to be restored to his former powers. Fuller was in close contact with Lewis Cass, Jr., the American chargé d'affaires. On May 20 Cass notified her that the negotiations had broken down. She had been keeping up with political developments all over Europe and realized that de Lesseps's negotiation positions were ruled by internal French politics—in particular, the upcoming elections in which it was expected that the French Catholic conservatives, including the peasants (who strongly favored the pope's return), would win a majority. Suspecting that the Italian-born president of France, Louis Napoleon, a revolutionary himself in the 1831 French insurrections, was now willing to sabotage the peace talks to strengthen his presidency, Fuller wrote to the *Tribune* that the French elections would decide whether France was prepared "to ruin a Government founded precisely on the same basis as their own."[6]

Cass was convinced that hostilities would soon be resumed, and on May 20 he ordered an American frigate, the *Allegheny,* to come to Ostia, Rome's seaport, to evacuate American citizens. The Crawfords and the Cranches had already left for home. When the Storys decided to go to Germany, the minister of war, General Avezzana, who had spent years in America in exile, provided them with a special pass to leave the city on April 24. Margaret and Giovanni spent a last evening with Emelyn and William before they departed Rome. They asked Margaret to send a bouquet of flowers to Garibaldi. Margaret was now the only one left in the Casa Diez. "Now at evening all seems so blank," she wrote; "the little moon looks in with an air of pensive amore; strange noises haunt the rooms."[7]

For her few free hours when Giovanni was detained in camp, she had a new young companion, Arthur Hugh Clough, a "striking-looking" young English poet and classics don who had befriended Waldo Emerson on his recent visit to England. Clough had arrived in Rome with a letter of introduction to Mazzini from Thomas Carlyle and a desire to study the art of classical antiquity. An admirer of Goethe and George Sand, an intellectual worrying about commitment, and an idealist sympathetic to revolution, he became another of Fuller's aspiring young artist-acolytes; she approved of him "tongue, pen and soul." Although he found her "impossible" at times, he came to the Casa Diez frequently (as he later wrote Emerson).[8]

In the lull, Margaret wrote a birthday letter to Richard, who was twenty-five that month. During the previous fall he had gone west as far as Chicago but, overcome with homesickness, returned home and abruptly married Sarah Batchelder, whom Margaret had never met. Richard complained that he found her response to his marriage cold. Margaret's inability to enthuse over Richard's marriage highlighted her own duplicity. It was now almost impossible for her to keep up her big-sister role with any consistency. She explained that all of her emotions were consumed by indignation against Rome's enemies and fear that the city would be bombarded. "I feel but little about myself," she told him, and if, perchance, she were killed the family "need not regret it."

There must be better worlds than this,—where innocent blood is not ruthlessly shed, where treason does not so easily triumph, where the greatest and best are not crucified. I do not say this in apprehension, but in case of accident, you might be glad to keep this last word from your sister.[9]

On the first of June, Cass informed Fuller that an agreement had been reached: The French would regard the Roman Republic as "a friendly power" and would continue to occupy Roman territory only so long as was necessary to prevent "foreign intervention."[10] De Lesseps was returning to Paris to have the treaty ratified. In his absence, however, General Oudinot declared the understanding invalid. De Lesseps, on arrival in Paris, was informed that he had exceeded his instructions and was summarily fired from the diplomatic service. On Sunday, June 3—in spite of an understanding that no attacks would begin on a Sunday—Oudinot attacked Rome at the Porta Pancrazio with a force of 20,000 men, twice that of the Roman Republic.

In the meantime, just as Fuller had predicted, the French election began to dictate French policy. The conservatives had won a considerable majority. Even if Louis Napoleon had only wanted a show of French presence in Rome when he sent Oudinot's forces, as president of France he could not allow his term of office to be stained by a defeat. His dream of regaining the throne of France for a Bonaparte required a clear victory in Italy. By the last weeks of May, the Italian republicans had completely won over Lewis Cass, Jr. In his dispatches to the State Department, Cass never asked directly for permission to recognize the government, but his praise for republican morale and high purpose clearly expressed his surprised admiration.

Fuller used her *Tribune* letter of May 27 to argue for United States recognition of the Roman Republic. Cass had been sent with instructions not to present his papers until the Roman Republic could prove "it can be sustained." But Fuller argued that it was the American government's obligation to recognize this government "*so long as it can sustain itself.*" Recalling Lafayette's support during the American Revolution, she wrote:

Some of the lowest people have asked me, "Is it not true that your country had a war to become free?"—"Yes." "Then why do they not feel for us?"
. . . I have also a lurking confidence in what our fathers spoke of so constantly, a providential order of things, by which brute force and selfish enterprises are sometimes set at nought by aid which seems to descend from a higher sphere. Even old Pagans believed in that, you know; and I was born in America, . . . freed by eight years' patient suffering, poverty and struggle—America, so cheered in dark days by one spark of sympathy from a foreign shore,—America, first "recognized" by Lafayette. I saw him in traversing our country, then great, rich, and free. Millions of men who owed in part their happiness to what, no doubt, was once sneered at as romantic sympathy, threw garlands in his path. It is natural that I should have some faith.[11]

But events were far outrunning even the fastest packet boats. General Oudinot kept Rome under siege for a month. Once his troops had taken possession of the Villa Corsini, the highest point outside the walls, the battle centered on that key spot. Caught completely offguard before dawn, the defenders now had no choice but to storm this point, funneling up the narrow steps of the Via Porta San Pancrazio, up to the walled-in triangle, "the death angle," leading to the entrance to the Corsini grounds where the French were massed in the thousands among the pine woods and parterres of the garden. Several times during the day the defenders of Rome carried the Corsini, only to surrender it a few moments later. At the end of the day, the French were in possession of the crucial ground. The Italians estimated their killed and wounded between 500 and 1,000; the French admitted to a loss of about 275.[12]

Fuller's next days were spent entirely in the hospitals. Princess Belgioioso, now known as Cittadino Belgioioso, suffering from a chronic fever, had made Fuller her assistant. Hospital beds were set up in the churches in Trastevere near the battlefield so that the wounded would not have to be carted great distances. The Quirinal Palace, with its high cool rooms, was turned into a hospital so the ambulatory patients could enjoy the large hillside garden. Fuller's few stolen moments were spent arranging quick meetings with Ossoli, whose unit was billeted on the other side of the city, close to the Vatican.

"What shall I write of Rome in these sad but glorious days?" she wrote the *Tribune*. "Plain facts are the best; for my feelings I could not find fit words." She could not talk of defeat; she could only worry about the future of all the people who had risked their lives in this courageous and hapless venture. All of her wounded, as well as those like Ossoli who were bearing arms, would very likely be taken prisoner. If the able ones among them were to choose exile, there was nowhere left in Italy where they would be safe; like Rome, Venice was now still holding out under siege, but everyone knew it was only a matter of time. "If Rome falls, if Venice falls, there is no spot of Italian earth where they can abide more," she wrote.[13]

She too would become a double exile with the fall of Rome. By June 10 she knew that a web of difficult choices lay immediately ahead. She wrote Emerson about her hospital work and her admiration for Mazzini and made a poignant plea for his support:

Should I never return,—and sometimes I despair of doing so, it seems so far off, so difficult, I am caught in such a net of ties here,—if ever you know of my life here, I think you will only wonder at the constancy with which I have sustained myself; the degree of profit to which, amid great difficulties, I have put the time. . . . Meanwhile, love me all you can; let me feel, that, amid the fearful agitations of the world, there are pure hands, with healthful, even pulse, stretched out toward me, if I claim their grasp.[14]

Her preoccupation with the immediate future colored all her communications with home. When the news came that Ellen and Ellery had their first son, she wrote a halfhearted letter of congratulation, to which the irony of her own secret motherhood gives another dimension:

As was Eve, at first, I suppose every mother is delighted by the birth of a man-child. There is a hope that he will conquer more ill, and effect more good, than is expected from girls. This prejudice in favor of man does not seem to be destroyed by his short-comings for ages. Still, each mother hopes to find in hers an Emanuel.[15]

She wished she could see Ellen's three children, she wrote, but the journey home seemed "so long, so difficult, so expensive." She would like to lie down and sleep herself into another existence as long as she could take with her

one or two that love and need me.... Those whom I knew and loved,—who, if they had triumphed, would have opened for me an easier, broader, higher higher-mounting road,—are every day more and more involved in earthly ruin. Eternity is with us, but there is much darkness and bitterness in this portion of it.[16]

Mazzini and his advisors refused to discuss surrender. News that sympathetic French people were organizing a protest march in Paris raised hopes that the French legislature would be forced to reverse its policy. Should, by some miracle, the republicans manage to stay in power and peace return, Fuller could imagine for herself a manageable life as an expatriate writer in Rome. Ossoli would have a position in the National Guard or in the administration. The abolition of primogeniture, a primary goal of the republican reform, would assure them a small but steady income from property, possibly enough to relieve them of their continual money worries. But more likely, if she and Giovanni both survived the siege, they would have to escape from the Papal States and find some means of living among strangers, or else return to the United States and take their chances. She had already begun to plan their escape. Mrs. Farrar, responding to the desperation in all her letters, had changed the terms of the friends' annuity so that Fuller could receive $100 every four months through her Rome banker, Maquay, Packenham, and Company. To be certain that all was arranged to the best advantage, Mrs. Farrar had put the matter in Sam Ward's hands. Ward had just left Lenox to take on his retired father's position as American agent for Baring Brothers. Mrs. Farrar said Sam was rather "pompous" and "as grand as a three-tailed Bashaw" in his new job.[17]

Richard sent Margaret a letter of credit on a Genoa bank so she could transfer her funds there, but, during the siege, the banks required such a steep discount on money that she was loath to draw on her account; she was living cheaply at the hospital and the Casa Diez and needed very little. On June 19, the eve of the renewed French bombardment, Ossoli was promoted to the rank of captain in the newly-formed National Guard. The artillery attack continued for the next ten days. Shells tore through the office of the Roman military command in the Spada; the roof of San Pietro in Montorio collapsed; shells fell in the Piazza di Spagna. On June 29 a bomb made a hole in the roof of the Trinità dei Pellegrini and landed in a ward full of the wounded.

"But wounds and assaults only fire more and more the courage of [Rome's] defenders," Fuller wrote in the *Tribune*. She chronicled the individual acts of bravery: the "noble" Trasteverini woman who seized a bomb and extinguished it with her bare fingers; the brigades of citizens who wandered through the city singing the "Marseillaise" collecting unexploded bombs, and dousing them in wet clay; the women who stole into French territory and gathered cannonballs. From June 22 until the end of the month, the French succeeded in making several breaches in the Aurelian Wall.[18]

By June 29 they had lost patience with the Assembly's refusal to discuss capitulation. It was the holy Festival of St. Peter and St. Paul, and while the people celebrated, grenades fell all over the city. Ossoli's company was now stationed on the Pincian Hill. When Fuller visited him there on the twenty-ninth she saw fresh bloodstains on the wall and picked up a piece of a grenade that had blown up close by; she decided to spend the following night (June 30) on the hill. Many women stayed with their men throughout the battle, carrying ammunition, loading rifles, serving as vivandières, sappers, and gunners.

Before joining Ossoli at the battle line, Fuller told Lewis Cass, Jr., about her marriage and entrusted him with the packet of papers Emelyn Story had returned to her when she left Rome. He promised to send the packet to her family if she did not return from her night's vigil. But the Pincian Hill—and all the hills of Rome—were spared on the night of the thirtieth. In the afternoon the Roman Assembly had voted to surrender. On being summoned to the Capidoglio at noon, Garibaldi joined Mazzini in refusing to sign the capitulation statement; they would continue the struggle elsewhere in Italy. "Dovunque saremo, colà sarà Roma [Wherever we go, there will be Rome]," Garibaldi declared. That afternoon, it was agreed that the French occupation forces would enter the city on July 3.[19]

Garibaldi summoned all who wished to follow him to meet in front of St. Peter's the morning of July 2. At least 10,000 thronged into the square to bid their defenders farewell. On his white horse, in his feathered cap, and with his white cape fluttering behind him, Garibaldi rode to the obelisk in the center of Bernini's colonnaded semicircle. The statement he made there would become a classic for Italian schoolchildren and would echo in a similar call to sacrifice in northern Europe almost a century later.

Let those who wish to continue the war against the stranger, come with me. I offer neither pay, nor quarters, nor provisions; I offer hunger, thirst, forced marches, battles and death. Let him who loves his country in his heart and not with his lips only, follow me?[20]

That afternoon Fuller went to the Lateran Gate to hear the final muster roll and watch the troops—some 4,000—march out into the Campagna. She sent her farewell message to the *Tribune*:

Go, fated, gallant band! and if God care not indeed for men as for the sparrows, most of ye go forth to perish. And Rome, . . . [m]ust she lose also these beautiful and brave that promised her regeneration and would have given it, but for the perfidy, the overpowering force of the foreign intervention?[21]

The French ordered all the foreigners who had supported the republicans to leave Rome, but Fuller stayed on for another week. For the first few days

Mazzini walked freely about the city, as if he were daring the French to lay a hand on him. Margaret had seen hardly anything of him for weeks. On July 3 he asked a favor: Could she use her influence to get three American passports, one for Ciceruacchio, the republican gadfly whom many suspected had engineered the death of Rossi, one for Ciceruacchio's son Angelo, and one extra—just in case?

Five days before the surrender of Rome, Secretary of State John M. Clayton, wrote Lewis Cass, Jr., that President Taylor did not wish him to be "bound by instructions too stringent for the occasion" and left to his discretion when he should present his "Letter of Credence" to the provisional government of Rome.[22] The letter came too late to help the republicans, but it enabled Cass to hand out at least a dozen passports to Italians whose lives were in danger. Through Cass, Margaret was able to procure the three passports. A few days later, when Mazzini wrote asking if she could arrange his escape with an American or English family traveling to Switzerland, Cass sent him an American passport, but it turned out to be useless because it lacked a French visa. In the end, Mazzini managed to convince the Corsican captain of a French ship to take him to Marseilles without papers. From there he made his way to Switzerland.

Although Cass offered Garibaldi a small American warship to use in his escape, the charismatic leader would not think of separating from his troops during their retreat. Of the republican leaders, only General Avezzana took advantage of Cass's generosity. With a passport made out in the name of Everett, he escaped to the United States, where the Italian community gave him a hero's welcome. Cass also provided Cristina Belgioioso with an American passport, made out in the name of her daughter's English governess, Mrs. Parker. When Fuller asked Horace Greeley to take Belgioioso on as a foreign correspondent, he agreed reluctantly. "I cannot give her *nor* any stranger to our people so much, as you; her letters would not be worth so much." (Two Belgioioso letters from Constantinople were published in the *New-York Tribune* that fall.)[23]

Greeley wrote Fuller that her articles condemning the pope and the papal government had set off a quarrel in New York.

The Romans and you have deprived me of the light of the countenances of my late friends the Catholic Priesthood who have hitherto been my warm friends and supporters but now are off. I am not sure that my very good friend Bp. Hughes will deem it his duty to curse me at the Astor with "bell, book and candle." Never mind: . . . . The World must move on.[24]

There was considerably more to the "Bp. Hughes" matter. In early July, when Bishop Hughes sent an appeal to his parishioners for the collection of Peter's pence for the support of the pope in Gaeta, Greeley immediately objected in the *Tribune,* arguing that American Catholics should not be encouraged to support Pius IX "in his present struggle against the Roman Republic." Bishop Hughes replied that the money was intended only for the pope's personal use at a time when he was cut off from his resources in Rome. Describing the republicans as outsiders who had established a reign of terror in the city, Bishop Hughes denounced Greeley for assuming that "the phalanx" of plotters was a legitimate government when not a single foreign ambassador had yet recognized these upstarts other than the "female plenipotentiary" who supplied diplomatic correspondence to the *Daily Tribune*.[25]

Before Greeley had time to answer, the *Boston Evening Transcript* entered the fray in defense of "Miss Fuller," saying that the bishop could expect a "blow from a broomstick" for his "ungallant hit. . . . Such a combing as he will get! Crucifixes and paternosters will not avail him." It was at this point that James Russell Lowell stepped in and made his amends to Fuller. He was the first American to acknowledge publicly her personal contribution to the Roman cause. In the July 12 *National Anti-Slavery Standard* he wrote:

Bishop Hughes says sneeringly that the Roman Republic has been recognized only by the "female plenipotentiary of the Tribune." It is a pity that America could not be always as adequately represented. But Miss Fuller has not merely contented herself with the comparatively cheap sympathy of words, though even brave words are much if spoken at the right time. We learn from private letters that, the last American left in Rome, she was doing her duty in the hospitals as a nurse for the wounded, thus performing also her mission as woman. Women have been sainted at Rome for less, and the Bishop is welcome to his sneer.[26]

In Fuller's last dispatch from Rome, written on July 8 just before she left for Rieti, she praised Lewis Cass, Jr., for maintaining a "kind and sympathetic course . . . toward the Republicans," which had "removed all unpleasant feelings." But she would always regret the American government's foot-dragging on the issue of the recognition of the Roman Republic, she wrote. It was too late now for Americans to do anything for Rome, but she beseeched her people to support all future movements toward representative government. Having heard of a New York meeting in support of the Hungarian uprising, she lifted her voice in an urgent plea expressing her identity with suffering humanity:

I pray you *do something;* let it not end in a mere cry of sentiment. . . . Do you owe no tithe to Heaven for the privileges it has showered on you, for whose achievements so many here suffer and perish daily? Deserve to retain them by helping your fellow-men to acquire them. . . . Friends, countrymen, and lovers of virtue, lovers of freedom, lovers of truth!—be on the alert; rest not supine in your easier lives, but remember
  "Mankind is one
  And beats with one great heart."[27]

Cass arranged for Fuller to leave Rome for Rieti on July 12. Before leaving, she wrote home explaining the move: "Private hopes of mine are fallen with the hopes of Italy. I have played for a new stake and lost it. Life looks too difficult. But, for the present, I shall try to waive all thoughts of self, and renew my strength."[28]

When she arrived in Rieti, she found Nino listless and thin as a skeleton. She suspected that Chiara had purposely underfed him because they had been slow in responding to her requests for more money. And Dr. Bassin, whom they had paid well to keep them posted, had misled them. They had only been alerted to the need for fresh vaccine and of a bad cold in May, but by the end of June the doctor's letters had described a happy and jovial baby, "as dear as one of Raffael's cherubs."[29]

Fuller now buried her disappointment in obsessive maternity. She was exhausted. What she called in the *Tribune* "the holocaust of broken hearts, baffled lives that must attend it," haunted her. Her epitaph to Rome's fall was that it would take "the blood and tears of more than one generation" to end the struggle between "the principle of Democracy and the old powers"; republican governments would not prevail until the twentieth century. She was trying to make plans for the future. It would be impossible to travel with Nino in his weakened condition. Giovanni, in the meantime, was occupied with finding out whether he could extract some money from his family by renouncing claims on certain small property holdings. It struck her as an ironic twist that the Villa Santucci—from which General Oudinot had been issuing his dispatches—had belonged to Ossoli's grandmother; in her old age she had willed it to her confessor, Monsignor Santucci, who was Ossoli's godfather. The relationship would do them little good now.[30]

At the end of the first week in August, Ossoli made his way to Rieti, empty-handed. He gave Fuller a scare when he was picked up by authorities in Neapolitan territory—just over the border from Rieti—on suspicion of being a Garibaldi supporter. Fuller intervened and got him freed. Since the Ossoli family had property in the area, this escapade may have had a purpose. Soon after Ossoli joined her, a letter arrived from Horace Greeley announcing Pickie's sudden death from cholera after only a few hours' illness. "Oh Margaret! the world grows dark with us. You grieve for Rome has fallen; I mourn, for Pickie is dead!"[31]

The news unleashed a string of memories of lost children in Fuller's life. Eugene and his Eliza had recently lost their first child; in February, James and Anna Clarke's nine-year-old son, Herman, died of scarlet fever. Seeing how short had been the lives of little Waldo Emerson and Pickie Greeley, Margaret steeled herself to the likelihood that Nino was "only treasure lent." Now she realized that she was denying him a part of his existence in keeping him a secret from her family. Later on, she would say that the news of Pickie's sudden death was what prompted her to reveal her secret. She was also afraid that her mother had already guessed the truth. In response to Margaret's query in a letter as to whether Arthur had "some attachment," Margarett Crane Fuller had replied that she knew of no such "prospect," but he well might not bother to tell her, since, as she wrote, "I have not been present at the marriage of any child of mine yet."[32]

An immediate practical reason, as well, was now forcing the issue. She and Ossoli would be living together openly. He had not been able to secure any family money, so the responsibility for their future rested on her. Before she left Rome she wrote Thomas Carlyle, asking him to help her find a publisher for her still unfinished book. He wrote an enthusiastic letter to John Chapman (Waldo Emerson's London publisher), saying that she was "*considerably* a higher-minded and cleverer woman than any of the Lady Lions yet on your Books; and if you and she could make any arrangement useful to both parties, I should be very glad."[33]

Chapman's answer was "in the negative." Carlyle wrote that he could not arrange for publication in advance, but if she would have her manuscript copied when it was "ready" and send it to him, he would then do all he could to find a publisher. Fuller should not have been surprised that a British publisher refused an advance on a still incomplete book on recent Italian history. The cause of the Roman Republic was not a burning issue in Britain; the British government and the establishment viewed Mazzini and company as troublesome upstarts. The *Illustrated News* gave the siege sympathetic coverage, but there was no widespread support for the republicans.[34]

In early September, Adam Mickiewicz wrote Fuller from Paris asking how she had fared during the siege. He was now writing for the radical journal *La Tribune des Peuples* and requested articles; even excerpts from her letters to New York would be welcome. But he cautioned that she could not expect any significant remuneration. Mazzini and Louis Blanc were fellow contributors, and her Paris friend, Pauline Roland, was one of the editors. Throughout the recent political agitation in France she had been campaigning for woman's suffrage.[35]

Living in penury while writing for the radical press in Europe was not an avenue Margaret was prepared to explore. She did not consider herself, like Mickiewicz, a self-exile out of political protest. She had come to Europe, as she wrote earlier, to look for new ideas worth planting in America, and she was writing a history of the changes she had observed in Europe with an American audience in mind. Within less than a month after Mickiewicz wrote her, *La Tribune* was abolished, so even if she could have found a way to return to Paris, his invitation would not have helped her literary ambitions.[36]

Inasmuch as she realized that she could no longer trust Nino to anyone else's care, there was now no way she could hide his existence. And, if she wanted to live with her husband and child as a family, she had to acknowledge their existence publicly. By the end of August, their plans were in place: They would go to Perugia, where they could live cheaply and privately, and she could continue to nurse Angelino during the hot months; the winter would be spent in Florence; they would probably all go to America in the summer.

Lewis Cass offered to see that Fuller's all-important letters announcing her motherhood and relationship to Ossoli arrived safely in the United States.

During the last week of August, she sent off letters to William Henry Channing, Horace Greeley, and her mother. In her condolence letter to Greeley on Pickie's death, she mentioned that she too had "a little son" just about the age Pickie had been when she was living in New York. Her only reference to Ossoli was that he had been in great danger during the siege of Rome. She signed her letter "M.F.O." and added a postscript: "You may address me in future as Marchioness Ossoli." It was as much news of her private life as she was ready to reveal to the New York literati.[37]

The letter to her mother was a challenge. No matter how she put it, she knew the news would be a shock. She chose to rely on the part-truth that her actions had been dictated by consideration for her mother. "I do assure you, that it was only great love for you that kept me silent," she wrote, pleading that her principal motive was to save her mother from anxiety and vowing that she would have continued her silence had it not become necessary, "on account of the child, for us to live publicly and permanently together." Ossoli was "a Roman, of a noble but now impoverished house," who was "not in any respect such a person as people in general would expect to find with me." Though his education had been neglected and he had no "enthusiasm of character," he had "an excellent practical sense; . . . a nice sense of duty, . . . a very sweet temper, and great native refinement." In fact, she wrote, he reminded her of her brother Eugene.[38]

"In him I have found a home, and one that interferes with no tie," she continued, and thus revealed the kernel of their successful relationship. "Amid many ills and cares, we have had much joy together." He was considerably younger, she explained, and when "the difference will become, in a few years, more perceptible than now," he might not love her as much. "But life is so uncertain, and it is so necessary to take good things with their limitations." There were troublesome reticences in Margaret's letter, omissions that could not help but raise questions. Angelino's claim to the Ossoli title was precisely mentioned: "He is a fair child, with blue eyes and light hair; very affectionate, graceful, and sportive. He was baptized in the Roman Catholic Church, by the name of Angelo Eugene Philip, for his father, grandfather, and my brother. He inherits the title of marquis."[39]

But there was no reference to a preceding marriage ceremony. Was Margarett Crane Fuller to infer the ceremony from a child's right to inherit that turned on his legitimacy? Does the silence reflect a defiance of convention or an assumption of a mother's trust in her daughter? Emelyn Story recalled later that, when Fuller gave her the little book in which she had written the story of her marriage, she said that if she did not survive to tell the story herself the book would be "invaluable" to her family. If she lived, it would be of little value because her "word" would be all that was necessary.[40] "Your mind must be much relieved," Lewis Cass, Jr., wrote Margaret after he had sent off her letters. "Withholding confidence when it is due brings ugly feelings." (Cass's remarks indicate that he believed that Fuller was married.)[41]

Her depression lasted for weeks. When William Henry Channing wrote her saying how glad he was that she had found in Rome's defense "this great opportunity" to carry out her principles, she could only shy away from the compliment as inappropriate in the wake of so much human suffering. "I knew not how to bear the havoc and anguish incident to the struggle for these principles," she replied. "I forget the great ideas, to sympathize with the poor mothers," who had brought up their sons "only to see them all lopped and gashed." Mourning and pity for mankind had taken over her spirit.[42]

As Costanza Arconati was now living in Florence during the winter, it was important for Margaret to forewarn her that she would appear there with another name. Even after the republicans had forced the pope from Rome, Arconati had continued their correspondence in a lighthearted vein. "In the moment when politics cease to be a speculation, one cannot exercise toleration with tranquility," she wrote Fuller, "and if you become Minister or President or Popess, I forewarn you that I shall be obliged to break with you. Meantimes I adopt this motto 'Hearts may agree, though heads differ.' "[43]

Margaret now informed Costanza that she was "more radical than ever" and that she had "united . . . [he]r destiny" with an "obscure young man," younger than herself, "of no intellectual culture," a person whom most people would consider an unlikely choice. In addition, "this union" was of long standing, and they had a child a year old.

If you decide to meet with me as before, and wish to say something about the matter to your friends, it will be true to say that there have been pecuniary reasons for this concealment. But *to you* in confidence I add, this is only half the truth; and I cannot explain or satisfy my dear friend farther—I should wish to meet her independent of all relations; but as we live in the midst of "society," she would have to inquire for me now as *Margaret Ossoli* that being done, I should like to say nothing farther on the subject.[44]

Toward the end of August Nino was well enough to travel, and they moved on to Perugia, where Margaret could recapture for a time the old dream of Arcady that had drawn her to Italy in the first place. She wrote Lewis Cass that she wished she could go on living forever in one Italian provincial town after another. On September 21 she requested that her banker in Rome transfer the balance of her account to Florence; she added that it would be under another name—she now called herself "M. Ossoli."[45]

At the end of September the Ossolis moved to Florence. But as soon as they found a small apartment on the Piazza Santa Maria Novella, Ossoli was denied a residence permit because he was traveling under an American passport, which marked him as a Republican fugitive from Rome. He was given a week to get proper identification papers. He immediately wrote to an influential Roman friend, Gaeto Suàrra, who knew something of his affairs, begging him to get from the Roman police a proper "Pontifical passport" to be made out in the name of "Gio Angelo Marchese Ossoli with wife and family." Significantly, he wrote Suàrra that there was no point in applying to the officials in his home parish—the Church of the XII Apostles in the Piazza Santi Apostoli, off the Corso—because he had never told them about his marriage; any passport they could provide would be for him alone. "I never informed them that I had married an American woman outside of Rome," he wrote. He gave no information about the marriage but included the passport he had used to go to Aquila the previous year as well as Margaret's passport. If nothing else worked, he instructed, Suàrra was to take the matter up with his sister Angela and her lawyer husband. And Suàrra must act quickly; he would probably receive the letter on Saturday, October 6. If the passport did not arrive by Wednesday, October 10, Ossoli would be sent away, and that, he observed, would be an "enormous misfortune."[46]

At the same time, Margaret wrote Cass that the police required "fresh papers for Ossoli as a Roman . . . or they will not let us stay. To go would be to us a great source of pain and annoyance." They had no place to go and were strapped for money, she wrote, since they had leased their apartment for six months. A few days later she wrote Cass again, telling him that the American sculptor Horatio Greenough had brought the matter to the attention of a personal friend, Prince Corsini, the Tuscan secretary of state. Could Cass ask the American consul for Tuscany to intercede? When Gaeto Suàrra replied from Rome, he told Ossoli that his "wife should go to the American Ministry immediately—they are extremely interested."[47]

Three weeks later, Ossoli was granted a two-month residence permit with the possibility of extension, but with the warning that he would be under surveillance. A proper "Pontifical passport" would have solved many problems, but Ossoli's request seems to have been disingenuous. With such a passport their marriage would be recognized, and they would be assured passage from state to state in Italy and through France on their way to the United States— even the chance to return to Rome if the climate became more favorable.

That Ossoli's efforts produced only a severely restricted document proved not only that pontifical authorities were not inclined to be lenient to those who had fought on behalf of the Roman Republic but that Ossoli was probably unable to produce evidence of a marriage recognized by the Catholic church. To legally marry a Protestant at the time would have required a papal dispensation. There were, of course, priests sympathetic to the Republic who might have performed the ceremony. During the brief republican period, there were many irregularities, and such marriages may have had a certain local legality. The bishop of Rieti, for instance, supported the establishment of a republic and led the election to the Roman Assembly in his see by casting the first vote "and then watched whether his clergy followed his example."[48] Fuller may have found a Protestant clergyman to do the honors with the understanding that they would have a Catholic ceremony later in the United States. Yet Ossoli ran a risk in telling people in authority that he was married if that were not the case, and Fuller must have had some plausible explanation to offer both Cass and Greenough, who interceded on her behalf. But married or not, they were a devoted couple. Their circle of respectable friends in Florence accepted them at their word as man and wife.

I was not a child. I had lived in the midst of that blessed society in a way that entitled me to esteem and a favorable interpretation, where there was doubt about my motives or actions.

Florence

AFTER Fuller settled in Florence she decided to call herself "Marchesa Ossoli," at least while living in Italy. Although she thought it "silly" for a "radical" like her to carry a title, she did not want to create the impression that she was distancing herself from Ossoli. "[I]t is a sort of thing that does not naturally belong to me," she reasoned, "and unsustained by fortune, is but a *souvenir* even for Ossoli." Yet she worried that if Ossoli dropped the title Angelino might lose some advantage. She found the choice difficult and thought that a "suitable moment" to drop the title would be when Ossoli became "an inhabitant of republican America."[1]

She explained her situation to Costanza Arconati Visconti, who had replied warmly to her last letter; "Just so long as it is not Mazzini you have married, our political differences will separate us no more than in the past," she wrote. Now they had a new tie to unite them, their motherhood. In 1839 Arconati had lost her first child, a son in his late teens. Soon afterward, at the age of thirty-eight— the same age Fuller had been when Angelino was born—she had a second son, Gianmartino, her pride and joy.[2]

Margaret Ossoli's arrival in Florence with her new name and her husband and child caused some "surprise" and "mute astonishment" among the Americans and English. "Nobody had even suspected a word of this underplot," Elizabeth Barrett Browning wrote.

The husband is a Roman marquis . . . appearing amiable & gentlemanly, & having fought well, they say, at the siege, but with no pretension to cope with his wife on any ground appertaining to the intellect. She talks, & he listens—I always wonder at that species of marriage; but people are so different in their matrimonial ideals, that it may answer sometimes.[3]

It was answering very well for Margaret Ossoli, although she reflected from time to time that it might not always be so. For the moment, her daily life was happier than at any time she could remember. The family settled into their three-room apartment on the third floor of the Casa Libri, overlooking the campanile of the Santa Maria Novella Church. Only steps from the Arno River, they were located centrally and had no need of a carriage. Just beyond was the Cascine, the old hunting preserve of the Medici family, now a public park; there

Shelley had written his "Ode to the West Wind." With the miniature greens-ward in front of the great church on their doorstep, family outings with Nino were one of the great pleasures of life.

From Rieti they had brought with them a new wet nurse. Gradually Margaret Ossoli returned to her manuscript, now grown to two volumes. Reviewing her work in tranquillity, she realized it needed much revision; soon she was writing again and searching out new background reading.

When she wrote Anna and Sam Ward in October to tell them of her marriage and to congratulate Sam on his new job, she said she was glad to hear that Sam was leaving his "green retirement." It was "better to mix often with the struggling suffering crowd; it is a more generous life and culture." As head of an international investment house, Sam was hardly mixing with common people, but Margaret was making a point that was in direct opposition to the stance she had taken in their early years of friendship, when she held to the importance of keeping free from worldly taint.[4]

She told Sam that Florence was not her favorite Italian city. It was "a kind of Boston: . . . it is a place to work and study in." She was considering writing a series of letters from Florence on art. If this plan succeeded she might earn enough to extend her stay in Italy. She recommended to Sam—who had just prepared an essay on art criticism for Elizabeth Palmer Peabody's *Aesthetic Papers*—that he should visit Thomas Hicks's studio when he was in New York. "I have loved him very much; we have been very intimate; I should like to have you see him." After a long bout with cholera in Paris, Hicks had returned to New York in September, where he was making a living as a portrait painter.[5]

She was greatly relieved when her mother responded joyfully and without a word of criticism to her dramatic revelations. Margarett Crane Fuller blessed the union with Ossoli and accepted Margaret's explanation that she had withheld the news of her marriage and pregnancy in order to shield her from concern. She wrote: "I should have suffered tortures to have known that you were to become a mother and I so far from you. Blessed be the good God who carried you safely thru this ordeal and gave you the unutterable joy to call one of his angel's sons."[6]

Margarett Crane Fuller wrote that Margaret's letter arrived on October 1, "the anniversary of your father's death." Within two weeks of that first letter's arrival, the Ossoli marriage was common knowledge among her friends. On October 21 Lydia Maria Child wrote Louisa Loring in Boston:

What think you of Margaret Fuller's marriage and motherhood? Cranch, who called upon me on his return from Italy two months ago, knew nothing of it. Eliza Robbins, who you know has a quaint satirical way of saying things, says, "She *bought* the boy, I *know* she did! Never tell me again that Aaron's rod did not blossom nor the dry bones live!" For my own part, I approve of Margaret's taste in having a private marriage all to herself, and thus keeping a little of the *romance* of the tender sentiment.[7]

Two weeks later, Child wrote Loring again, repeating her stand. "As for Margaret's marriage, love *never* seems to me ridiculous. I reverence it everywhere, as life's best blessing."

On November 10 the *Literary World* announced the marriage to the public:

Miss Margaret Fuller, the bright particular star of the *Tribune* is married, and has been for nearly two years, to a Roman count. She is the happy mother of a thriving boy. Doubtless her attainments which, in Italy, where female education is so much neglected, would naturally excite interest, and her intelligent sympathy with the people and their country—have won the affection of some titled *savan* or patriot; at least, this is our conjecture.[8]

By that time there was a great deal of conjecture. Margaret Ossoli's closest friends had noticed that she had avoided mentioning a wedding ceremony or a wedding date. If she had hoped that they would interpret this as an assertion of her right to privacy, she underestimated their fascination with analyzing personalities, a pastime in which she herself had been an adept in the old Concord days. Fredrika Bremer, the Swedish novelist, was making an American tour that year. As a good friend of Rebecca and Marcus Spring, and of William Henry Channing and the New York circle interested in socialist reforms, she listened to constant speculation about the marriage. When she visited Concord, where she met the Emersons, Elizabeth Hoar, and Ellen Channing, she came away astonished at how coolly they seemed to be taking the latest news, "convinced that it will justify itself in the open light of day." She explained the story to her sister in Sweden:

Margaret Fuller went to Italy with my friends, the S[pring]s, about two years since, and remained there when they left. A report has now reached this country that she has connected herself with a young man (she herself is no longer young, being upward of forty), and a Fourierist or Socialist marriage, without the external ceremony, is spoken of; certain it is that the marriage remained secret, and that she has a child, a boy. She herself has written about it, and about her maternal joy, but not anything about her marriage, merely that she shall relate what further concerns her when she returns to America. . . . All this has furnished subject for much conversation among her friends and her enemies.[9]

Margaret Ossoli's radicalism became even more evident when she resumed her *Tribune* letters. On November 15 she sent a letter describing the dying liberal movement in Italy, the French occupation of Rome, and increasing repression in Tuscany and Piedmont. Now that armed revolution had failed, she looked to some sort of new social organization as the means of redressing "the frightful" social ills of Europe, by a peaceful though radical revolution instead of bloody conflict."

[K]ings may find their thrones rather crumbling than tumbling; the priests may see the consecration wafer turn into bread to sustain the perishing millions even in their astonished hands. God grant it. Here lie my hopes now. I believed before I came to Europe in what is called Socialism, as the inevitable sequence to the tendencies and wants of the era, but I did not think these vast changes in modes of government, education and daily life, would be effected as rapidly as I now think they will, because they must. The world can no longer stand without them.[10]

Her prophecies of the coming social changes in Europe irritated Elizabeth Barrett Browning who, thanks to George William Curtis, invited the Ossolis to Casa Guidi soon after they arrived in Florence. Curtis had paved the way two years earlier by bringing the Brownings Fuller's complimentary *Tribune* review of Robert's *Bells and Pomegranates.* He had failed to bring her review of Barrett's *Drama in Exile, and Other Poems;* there Fuller ranked Barrett "above any female writer the world has yet known." At their first meeting, Margaret Fuller Ossoli found Elizabeth Barrett Browning "too gentle and faded" to arouse interest, but as time went on—"over a great gulf of differing opinion," as Elizabeth put it—they were strongly drawn together. Although not Mazzinian republicans, both the Brownings were fervent champions of Italian unity. Elizabeth's *Casa Guidi Windows,* one of the books she was working on while Margaret knew her in Florence, was in part a plea to the British public to take a greater interest in the Italian cause; it was also a detailed account of the political history of Florence from 1847 to 1849.[11]

Both women were humanitarians, but Elizabeth sniffed at Fuller's *Woman in the Nineteenth Century* when Philip Bailey, the author of *Festus,* sent her a copy of it in January 1846. She protested to Robert Browning, "[H]ow I hate those 'Women of England.' 'Women and their Mission' & the rest. As if any possible good were to be done by such expositions of rights & wrongs." But later she thanked Fuller for the book and pronounced it "full of excellent thought & noble sentiment." While she refused the image of reformer, Elizabeth Barrett Browning nevertheless wrote poems that served effectively as propaganda for social change. Her "Runaway Slave at Pilgrim's Point," republished in the American antislavery journal, the *Liberty Bell,* gave great respectability to the cause. And her "Cry of the Children" was later credited, as were Dickens's novels, with hastening the passage of the British Factory Acts.[12]

For both women authorship was a necessary part of life. Elizabeth did not think that Margaret had written anything yet that showed her capacity; later Elizabeth wrote that Margaret herself agreed that "[t]he only work to which she had given time & labour . . . was the unfinished one on Italy." They also had in common their irregular marriages, and both of them presented an image of nonconformity. Both admired, and were influenced by, George Sand. After Elizabeth eloped, she liked to think of herself as living a Bohemian life in her spacious Casa Guidi apartment, with the meals sent in from trattorias and with only her personal maid, Wilson, and a daily charwoman to manage the house while she lived as an invalid on her couch—"the *divine bed-rid*," Emerson called her.[13]

By the time Margaret Fuller Ossoli was a welcome guest at the Casa Guidi,

Elizabeth Barrett Browning had survived one miscarriage (and was about to have another) and had given birth—at the age of forty-three—to Robert Weideman Browning, later known as Pen, who was six months younger than Nino Ossoli. She had added a cook and a wet nurse to the household.[14]

At Christmastime, 1849, Pen was just learning to crawl, and the Brownings delighted in placing his new toys just out of reach so they could watch his eager pursuit. Nino, at the time, was just mastering walking, and Margaret enjoyed watching "his little foolish legs" as he struggled to learn.[15]

Children were an important part of expatriate life in Florence that year. Louisa and Horatio Greenough had a baby daughter, Mary Louise, two months older than Angelino, as well as an older daughter. Teatime with children playing on the rug was a part of the social ritual. Horatio Greenough, who had studied with Washington Allston in Cambridge, was the leader of the American colony in Florence, distinguished for his artistic achievement as well as his championship of Italian liberty. His family lived in the Casa Baciocchi at what is now the Piazza Independenza. Hiram Powers and his wife, Elizabeth Gibson Powers, were near neighbors. They had five children, one of whom, a seven-year-old, was named after Anna Barker. Because of the astonishing financial success of the traveling exhibition of Powers's *Greek Slave* throughout the United States, he was now a rich man with many more commissions than he could fill. Even so, he found time to do a bust of "Margaret Fuller Ossoli, [later] lost at sea."[16]

The Ossolis' most intimate friends among the American colony were the Moziers, the couple who had taken care of Fuller on her way back to Rome in the fall of 1847. Although Joseph Mozier was not highly respected by his fellow sculptors—and was openly disliked by Thomas Crawford—he had made a financial success in less than five years by specializing in female figures swathed in elaborate drapery. In January he gave Ossoli a job in his studio, and Margaret Fuller Ossoli agreed to tutor the Moziers' daughter. She often joined their weekly social evenings, escorted by Ossoli, but he rarely stayed because his English was so poor. Two other faithful friends were two Englishwomen, Catherine Black, who was married to an agent for several British museums, and Julia Smith, a pianist friend of Jane Stirling, the Scotswoman in Paris who had introduced Margaret to Chopin.[17]

In late October George William Curtis, on the last leg of his Grand Tour, stopped in Florence to see the Brownings and the Ossolis. He was curious to meet Giovanni and found him "a tall, slight, dark, quiet, gentlemanly man" who treated Margaret with a "very touching deference." Another Brook Farmer was already on the scene when Curtis arrived: Horace Sumner, the twenty-four-year-old brother of the lawyer and eloquent lyceum speaker Charles Sumner. "As I was coming past the Duomo the other day at set of sun, I saw a pale, erect, narrow little figure, which made all my nerves tingle with old associations," Margaret Fuller Ossoli wrote. "Imagine Brook Farm walking the streets of

Florence." Horace, who had traveled as far as Leningrad on his Grand Tour, attached himself to the Ossolis, stopping by almost every evening to exchange language lessons with Giovanni.[18]

Margaret Fuller Ossoli had foreseen that her revelation would be "an unpleasant surprise" to her friends in America and she waited apprehensively for the reaction. Aware that she was putting her closest friends in a difficult position by giving out such a sketchy account—one that was bound to raise questions—she hoped that they would let criticisms pass, put in a good word for her, and not "admit" for her, as she would not for herself, "the rights of the social inquisition of the U.S. to know all the details" of her circumstances. "You and I know enough of the U.S.," she wrote Emelyn Story in Switzerland, "to be sure that many persons there will blame whatever is peculiar." There would always be those who "are sure to think that whatever is mysterious must be bad."[19]

Even though her friends in Florence—after the initial surprise—accepted her situation with ease, she was soon learning, she wrote home, that the moral philosophers were right when they warned "about the dangers and plagues" of keeping secrets. When William Story first heard about the marriage at a Venice restaurant in October, he was understandably put out. Caroline Tappan wrote from home about the "meddling curiosity of people." Arthur was curt with his congratulations, while Richard was sanctimonious and expressed amazement at his sister's "worldliness." Ellen wrote that she could not agree that protecting their mother from anxiety was an adequate excuse for withholding such important family information. Rebecca and Marcus Spring felt hurt and excluded after having been so close to her during their year together in Europe.[20]

Forced to mend her fences as best she could without revealing more facts, she apologized to William Story and thanked him for continuing to regard her sympathetically. Using Costanza Arconati's response as a model, she pointed out to Caroline Tappan that her European friends had accepted her news "in the kindliest and most refined manner"; Arconati, she wrote, "might be qualified in the court Journal as one 'of the highest rank.'" To Richard she wrote that she was surprised at his accusations and could only hope that someday he could have the opportunity to see Italy and enjoy the rich experiences that had been hers. In reply to Ellen's bid for more news she revealed that Ossoli's membership in the Roman Catholic church was an important factor in explaining why she could not "go into all the matter of fact history." She had met Ossoli during her first visit to Rome in the spring of 1847, she noted, and added:

Very soon he offered me his hand through life, but I never dreamed I should take it. I loved him and felt very unhappy to leave him, but the connexion seemed so every way unfit, I did not hesitate a moment. He, however, thought I should return to him, as I did. I acted upon a strong impulse. I could not analyse at all what passed in my mind. I neither rejoice nor grieve, for bad or for good I acted out my character. Had I never connected myself with any one my path was clear, now it is all hid, but in that case, my development must have been partial. As to marriage I think the intercourse of heart and mind may be fully enjoyed without entering into this partnership of daily life, still I do not find it burdensome. We get along very well.

She now spoke specifically of marriage; her care to make a comparison with relationships outside this "partnership of daily life" would argue that she was using the term precisely and from experience. But her reluctance to provide particulars continued to inflame widespread speculation. The situation improved somewhat when Emelyn Story stepped in with a grand gesture.[21]

In December Story wrote a letter to Maria Lowell, revealing that she had known of Margaret's marriage for more than six months and that both she and William knew the "Marquis Ossoli" and appreciated his character. Because his family supported the pope—he had two brothers in the papal household—and he had taken the radical position, he was looked upon "as the black sheep in the family," Story explained. It was "on account of family difficulties that the marriage was not sooner made known." Story insisted that, even though others might judge that it would have been better to have announced the marriage earlier, "I know enough of their affairs to say that they were prevented solely by family matters from declaring it at the time it occurred."[22]

The Lowells showed Story's letter around in Boston so effectively that by February 1850 Lydia Maria Child decreed that all the gossips had been put in their place. Quincy Adams Shaw, who had visited the Ossoli household in Florence, sent back to Boston the news that Angelino was "the image of his mother." Fredrika Bremer, who continued to follow public opinion on the case, now accepted the marriage as a respectable one. Fascinated with Margaret's story and the discussions of her character, Bremer decided that "Margaret Fuller is a figure strongly characteristic of the ambiguity in woman's position and consciousness in this age of transition."[23]

But Child and Bremer were exceptions. Sarah Clarke wrote Margaret of Fredrika Bremer's interest in her, noting that Bremer's arrival in the United States had coincided with the news of Margaret's marriage, so that Fredrika could not help but hear a great deal about her. Clarke had received a note from Maria Lowell with excerpts from Emelyn's letter, but the explanations did not mollify her.

You say your friends appear to lay extraordinary stress upon your marriage. It is not exactly that but we were placed in a most unpleasant position—because the world said injurious things of you which we were not authorised to deny—not one of us could say that we knew of your marriage beforehand, nor could we tell when it occurred or answer any question about it—If people chose to make unpleasant inferences from this secrecy we had nothing to say beyond expressing our respect for you. This was annoying—To me it seemed that you were more afraid of being thought to have submitted to the ceremony of marriage than to have omitted it.[24]

In a note to Emelyn thanking her for her letter's "happy effect," Margaret explained her reactions:

I was not a child. I had lived in the midst of that blessed society in a way that entitled me to esteem and a favorable interpretation, where there was doubt about my motives or actions. I pity those who are inclined to think ill, when they might as well have inclined the other way. However let them go: there are many in the world who stand the test, enough to keep us from shivering to death.[25]

In January and early February in Florence it was as cold as a Boston winter. The Casa Libri apartment had only one fireplace; Margaret and Nino both suffered from chilblains. William Henry Hurlbut, a Harvard Divinity School friend of Arthur Fuller, stayed in Florence through the winter, enjoying many evenings with Margaret while Giovanni, in his Civic Guard uniform, sat in an armchair reading. When guests joined them, Giovanni usually would escape to a cafe, since he spoke no English. Hurlbut wrote to Thomas Wentworth Higginson that he thought Margaret Fuller had married Ossoli "as a representative of an imagined possibility in the Italian character." In the light of Fuller's lifelong reverence for all things Italian, this was a shrewd observation, but though Ossoli might fulfill her ideal of a being at one with nature, her American friends still found it difficult to pair her with a man who was not her intellectual equal. She went to some pains to describe Ossoli to her friends as a natural, steady, cheerful man, of "simple and uniform" character—not mercurial and forever restless like herself. His "affections are few, but profound, and thoroughly acted out," she wrote. She referred to him as untainted by the nervous anxieties of the fragmented, ambitious society she knew at home. She took for granted that many of her friends, including Waldo Emerson, would not be able to see what she had "in common" with him, but she was sure, she wrote, that her family at least would understand when they saw them together.[26]

In describing the attraction to the Springs, she resorted to the language of phrenology, by now as common among her friends as the vocabulary of psychoanalysis is today. "I have expected that those who have cared for me chiefly for my activity of intellect would not care for him, but that those in whom the moral nature predominates would gradually learn to love and admire him, and see what a treasure his affection must be to me." She gave William Henry Channing the fullest and in modern terms the most easily acceptable explanation. When she first wrote him, she emphasized that Ossoli left her "mentally free" and was not possessive of her time, her interests, or her outside relationships. Later, from Florence, she wrote that only her mother and a few children had loved her "as genuinely" as Ossoli.

He loves me from simple affinity; he loves to be with me, and serve and soothe me. Our relation covers only a part of my life, but I do not perceive that it interferes with anything I ought to have or be; I do not feel anyway constrained or limited or that I have made any sacrifice.

She valued his love, she wrote, far more than the kind of love her intellectual ability had attracted: "a mixture of fancy and enthusiasm excited by my talent at embellishing subjects," as she put it. If she were younger, she speculated, she could imagine herself being attracted at some time or another to a different kind of person, but at this stage of her life she was not afraid of that. "There is more danger for him, as he is younger than I; if he should, I shall do all that this false state of society permits to give him what freedom he may need."[27]

William Hurlbut reported that Margaret Fuller Ossoli spent most of her evenings writing. Costanza Arconati was keeping her informed about the covert activities of the moderate liberals in Turin and Milan who were working to bring about the end of Austrian rule by peaceful means. Lewis Cass, Jr., was sending reports from Rome. In January, Margaret Fuller Ossoli sent a letter to the *Tribune* describing the consequences of Italy's recent struggles for autonomy. "The barbarities of reaction" have sown "[t]he seeds for a vast harvest of hatreds and contempts," she advised. "The next revolution here as elsewhere will be radical." Not only must the Austrians and every foreign potentate be deposed, but everyone who assumes an "arbitrary lordship" over others must be driven out. "It will be an uncompromising revolution." The New Era she had announced in *Woman in the Nineteenth Century* was now at hand:

The New Era is no longer an embryo; it is born; it begins to walk—this very year sees its first giant steps, and can no longer mistake its features. Men have long been talking of a transition state—it is over—the power of positive, determinate effort is begun.[28]

She was reading Lamartine's *Histoire des Girondins* and Louis Blanc's *Histoire de Dix Ans, 1830–1840* that winter, and her writings had the style and intensity of their fervent language, but there is no indication that she read Karl Marx's *Communist Manifesto* (1848) or based her prophecies of future change on materialist theory. Although she was sophisticated about class conflict and realized that expectations had been unleashed that would change the future of Europe, she considered republican governments the radical political form within which mankind would realize its individual aspirations. She continued to view the impetus to socialist thinking and the basis for reform as embedded in the individual's internalization of moral and spiritual law, and it is significant that, of the socialist models under discussion among mainstream intellectuals in Europe in the late 1840s, Fourierism with its program adapted to individual preference and talent was the concept that appealed to her. She believed that, after military force had put down all the peaceful revolutions of 1848 and the new constitutions had been revoked and the kings returned to their thrones, the dream of reorganizing life more equally in Europe would remain alive, but she predicted that it would not be until the twentieth century that republican forms of government would prevail.

Content with the orderly routine of her family life, she took heart from her faith in the future. She expected there would be many changes in Italy by the time Nino grew up; and she liked "to go out and watch the rising generation who will be his contemporaries." She hoped Nino would "retain some trace in his mind of the perpetual exhilarating picture of Italy."[29]

"I have become an enthusiastic Socialist; elsewhere there is no comfort, no solution for the problems of the times," she wrote Rebecca and Marcus Spring in December. She congratulated Marcus on building a public washhouse at Croton on Hudson (in imitation of the Scottish model they had seen on their trip) and, unaware that Fourierism in the United States was all but moribund, she congratulated him on the "practical study" at the North American Phalanx at Red Bank, New Jersey. As a Quaker, Rebecca had criticized Margaret's backing of a military action in Rome, forcing Margaret to defend her support of bloodshed and violence. The challenge put her on the spot; she agreed that "the peace way" was the "best," but it would take centuries to change the world by such means:

Yet the agonies of that baptism of blood I feel oh how deeply in the golden June days of Rome. Consistent no way I felt I should have shrunk back. I could not have had it shed. Christ did not have to see his dear ones pass the dark river; he could go alone; however, in prophetic spirit no doubt, he foresaw the crusades.

The pacifist is justified only if he is "sure he is . . . really and ardently at work undermining [giant wrongs] or better still sustaining the rights that are to supplant them." She also felt obliged to counter the idea that the passion of motherhood was absorbing her completely. Her concern for Nino did indeed give "hue to all the current" of her present life, she admitted to Rebecca.

Yet in answer to what you say, that it is still better to give the world this living soul than a portion of my life in a printed book; it is true; and yet of my book I could know whether it would be of some worth or not, of my child I must wait and see what his worth will be.[30]

By February the Ossolis decided that they would go to live in the United States for three or four years and then consider returning to Italy. Margaret Fuller Ossoli's attempts to get advance terms for her manuscript had not been successful and were complicated by the fact that the British had passed a regulation making it impossible for a foreigner to hold a copyright there. Her best chance for the future was to publish her book at home and establish herself as a serious writer of history. She wanted to be on the spot to make the best possible contract with the publisher and to see the manuscript through the press.

Deciding to go home was not easy. In January she wrote the Wards a nostalgic letter recapitulating their long years of friendship and telling them that she had never been so well or so happy since her father had died. She wrote Lewis Cass, Jr., that she was now experiencing the greatest happiness she had ever known. Still, she wanted to see her family and friends again. She sent home a daguerreotype of Ossoli so he would not seem strange to the family. All along she had compared the tenderness of his love for her with that of her mother, and she was certain they would love one another, especially since he had lost his own mother at an early age.

Ossoli seems to have kept the secret of his marriage until the last minute. Later, his sister Angela would write that she had not known of her brother's marriage to Fuller until they were living together publicly in Florence. She was aware that Fuller had been living in Rieti beforehand and had given birth to Angelino there, and she was certain that Angelino was properly baptized. She was under the impression, she wrote, that the couple were married after they moved to Florence.

On March 11 one of Ossoli's friends, Augustus Lauream, wrote him from Rome congratulating him on the news of his marriage to an American woman. "All your friends send their greetings and all express displeasure that you are about to take such a long voyage." Lauream had broken the news to Angela about his friend's "imminent departure from our peninsula," and she had burst into tears. On March 30 Ossoli wrote his sister in Limerick, Ireland, that he "had been married for some time" to an American woman. They were very much in love and had a beloved child named Angelo, who provided them with "the greatest pleasure"—as well as worry about providing for him. Ossoli conjectured that Matilda was now speaking English very well, whereas he continued to find it "very difficult," but his wife spoke Italian very well.[31]

When Rebecca and Marcus Spring first learned of the marriage, they did not realize that the Marchese Ossoli was the young man they remembered as Margaret's friend Giovanni. When Thomas Hicks informed them of this, Marcus wrote Margaret that while in Rome he had noticed the growing attachment between her and Giovanni. Not remembering Ossoli's family name or that he had a title, he had assumed that she had forsaken him for another. They were glad to hear that it had turned out "right."[32]

Whatever else Rebecca and Marcus remembered about Giovanni Ossoli, it was not such as to encourage them to believe he would be a successful breadwinner in America. Marcus knew how close to the margin financially Margaret was accustomed to living. In December she asked him to go to Wiley and Putnam and try to "squeeze" something from the proceeds of *Papers on Literature and Art*. She was "sore pressed" to find some way to earn her "daily bread, with milk and pearlbarley for my boy." She kept writing to all her faithful circle hinting for loans to help pay the family's passage home. W. H. Channing, who saw the Springs frequently at Associationist meetings and at his church in New York, still worried that Margaret had put herself beyond the pale in the way she had handled the news of her marriage. When Rebecca and Marcus thought seriously about her future, they decided her "best interests" required her to stay in Italy.[33]

During the winter Margaret Fuller Ossoli had written an impressionistic essay, "Recollections of the Vatican," which she sent to Caroline Kirkland who was an editor of the *Union Magazine of Literature and Art*. As Margaret had signed the article only with the star she used for her *Tribune* letters, Kirkland consulted the Springs, for she thought she could sell the essay more easily with Margaret's full name. Marcus suggested that she use "Marchioness Ossoli (late Margaret Fuller)." Kirkland also advised Marcus that Margaret's writings would be much more salable "if sent from Italy" and that the owner of the magazine, John Sartain, would welcome a monthly letter from Florence. Since the Springs knew that Greeley was still eager for Margaret's letters, they concluded that she could support her family in Italy, whereas in the United States she would have greater difficulty finding work. (As it turned out, her article appeared in the July issue of the *United States Magazine and Democratic Review*, signed by her star but listed in the table of contents as written by "Countess Ossoli.")[34]

Marcus was genuinely concerned about the Ossoli family and made a point of contacting Waldo Emerson. When Waldo passed through New York on a lecture tour in early April, Marcus and Rebecca won him over to their point of view. The Springs were convinced that, if Waldo could guarantee to find a publisher for her book on the Roman Republic, Margaret would stay in Florence. During the months after the news of Margaret's marriage was generally known, neither Waldo Emerson nor Elizabeth Hoar contacted her; Margaret guessed it was because they did not know what to say. In April, after conferring with Marcus, Waldo wrote her that he would "make the best terms" for her with a publisher, either with his own new Boston publisher, Phillips and Sampson, or with a New York firm, if she preferred. It was "needless" for her to cross the ocean "only to make a bargain" for her book. Continued residence in Italy would add "solidity" to her "testimony" and "new rays of reputation and wonder" to her "as a star." Her close friends in Concord, all of whom hoped she would live there permanently someday, were willing to postpone their claim in the knowledge that she would join them eventually. His only reference to her new situation was the comment, "but surprise is the woof you love to weave into all your web." The image of an industrious spider continued in his mind when he thought of her.[35]

Marcus enclosed Waldo's letter with one from Rebecca and one from himself, all of them urging Margaret to stay in Italy. She could do so much good if she continued to write of Italy's aspirations with her "enlightened and mature views of true republican freedom." Her "truest welfare" would be promoted "by a one or two years longer sojourne." Rebecca stated the case bluntly: "[M]uch as we should love to see you, and strange as it may seem, we, as well as all your friends who have spoken to us about it, believe it will be undesirable for you to return at present."[36]

"Your packet did not reach me till I had taken passage for America," Margaret wrote back hastily on the eve of departure. The letters contained the first offers of practical help that anyone had sent her from home—"the first glimpse of aid in case I wished to remain," she wrote gratefully. All she had needed to convince her to stay was "a narrow maintenance," but now that she was about to leave she felt "tranquil."[37]

The letter was a godsend because she needed someone in New York to stand surety for her on a hundred-day loan she was taking out on her Florence bank, Fonzi and Hall, in order to pay for the passage home on an American merchantman, the *Elizabeth*. Costanza Arconati Visconti was her Italian guarantor, she explained. She wrote Marcus that she was using his name but that he should not worry that the loan would be dishonored. Should she "perish," she added, he was to get in touch with her other friends:

Mrs. Farrar writes that she has one hundred dollars for me—A letter from Mother that she has placed a hundred at Baring's for me; for the rest the means I propose to raise it by would go to the bottom with me, but Mother, or my brothers would in such a case raise it I am sure if you show this letter.

As usual, Margaret was pulled in two directions. "[T]hough I suffer much in leaving Italy—yet I long too to embrace my loved friends at home." She instructed the Springs to tell William Channing he must "not feel anxious about people's talk concerning me. It is not directed against the real Margaret, but a phantom." She sincerely believed that her European experiences had changed her, had made her more modest and humble.[38]

A few weeks earlier, she had written to Emelyn Story that she would have liked to have returned home on a Cunard liner from Liverpool, but the cost was prohibitive and she had made other arrangements. At the end of March, Joseph Mozier, who was the absentee American consul in Ancona and was privy to shipping news, told her that the American merchant freighter *Elizabeth*, now docked at Leghorn (Livorno), had passenger accommodations and would depart at the end of April. Mrs. Mozier went with her to inspect the vessel. The ship was a sturdy, wide-bottomed bark, broad in the beam, three-masted, and only five years old. The forecastle sat behind a short poop, the passenger cabins in the stern; between them was the deep hollow of the deck.

Margaret liked the captain and his wife, Seth and Catherine Hasty. They were both New Englanders from Maine. She wrote the Springs that Captain Hasty seemed "among the best and most highminded of our American men," and his wife "an excellent woman." They told her that the only passenger booked was a twenty-three-year-old Italian girl, Celeste Panolini, who had worked for a New York artist, Henry Peters Gray, and was returning to take up her job again. She would be willing to help the Ossolis with their child. The Hastys asked only $350 passage money, less than half the cost of returning by way of England.[39]

When Fuller wrote Costanza Arconati informing her of her departure, she told her that her one reservation about the *Elizabeth* was the placing of the passenger cabins. They were grouped like little chapels around the semicircular lounge in the stern of the ship, "terribly exposed in the case of a gale." When Horace Sumner decided to accompany them, Margaret decided that the advantages of traveling as a single party with a trusted captain in a new, well-kept ship and the ease of transferring her property—Leghorn was only a few hours by train from Florence—provided an unexpected and favorable opportunity. She committed the family to the Hastys in a friendly contract that seemed advantageous to both sides.[40]

Because of heavy rains, the loading was delayed for three weeks. The Moziers invited the Hastys to visit them in Florence during part of the delay, so Margaret and Giovanni knew them very well by the time they became passengers. The bulk of the cargo consisted of slabs of Carrara marble, 150 tons of it. The most valuable item was Hiram Powers's statue of John Calhoun, who had died on March 31.[41]

No sooner had Margaret made the final arrangements for their passage than she began to worry. In mid-April she read that the ship "Westmoreland bearing Powers's Eve" had been wrecked off the French coast; during the following two weeks, both a British steamer and an American packet were sunk; she poured out her misgivings to Costanza Arconati, who was visiting in Turin. Costanza told her that two months in the open air would rejuvenate her and that she herself had presentiments that the voyage would be a happy one. Hoping to have some influence on Margaret's book, Costanza filled her last letter with an evaluation of the character and motivations of King Carlo Alberto during the events of 1848 in Milan and Piedmont.[42]

Ossoli's sister Angela sent him an affectionate letter of farewell, telling him she was very upset at the thought of his long voyage. She was glad that he had taken up sculpting, she wrote, but could not see how he could succeed when he had never studied drawing. She sent him some catechism books for Nino, a cross, and a rosary. The return of the pope on April 12 was the big news in Rome. She described Pope Nono's triumphal entrance through the Lateran Gate where he was met by the full diplomatic corps, representatives of all the religious orders, and crowds of supporters shouting their welcome. For three days the whole city was illuminated, especially the Campidoglio. Angela sent greetings to Margaret, a kiss to Angelino, and instructions to write. Ossoli's friend Augusto Lauream, who had gone to great trouble to send him a trunk, also wrote commending him on learning the profession of sculptor, which he was sure would come in handy when he was living in America. He too sent fond farewells.[43]

The night before the Ossolis expected to leave Florence, Robert Browning carried Elizabeth up the six flights to the Ossolis' apartment in the Casa Libri on the Piazza Santa Maria Novella. "We loved her and she loved Ba," Browning wrote a few weeks later ("Ba" was his pet name for Elizabeth). Horatio and Anna Greenough came with Horatio's brother Henry and his wife, Frances.

Although Henry and Frances were leaving on June 1 to return to Boston by a Cunard ship, they encouraged Margaret in her choice. Frances reported that, considering "the superior economy and convenience of embarking, the choice seemed a wise one to all present."[44]

With her "head full of boxes, bundles, pots of jelly & phials of medicine," as Margaret described her departure to the Storys, the family boarded the *Elizabeth* at the end of the first week of May. They also brought along a nanny goat to provide Nino's milk supply. Barely settled, they were told that there was to be a further delay. "The Elizabeth, look out for news of shipwreck, cannot finish taking in her cargo till come one or two good days," Margaret wrote the Storys. The marble was still being brought down the mountain in ox carts, as it had been for hundreds of years, and the driving rains had washed out the paths. The Ossolis returned to Florence.[45]

On the evening of May 15, which was at last to be their final night in Florence, Margaret and Ossoli crossed the Arno to the Brownings. In the high-ceilinged salon, hung with Italian primitives, overfurnished with bookcases, Renaissance settees, a spindle-legged desk on rollers for Ba, and a child's armchair for Pen, the two couples said goodbye. In deference to Elizabeth Barrett Browning, Margaret swept away all talk of ill omens, stating that she took the name of the ship *Elizabeth* as a good one. As a parting gift Ba gave Margaret a carbuncle ring. Margaret gave Pen a Bible, inscribed "*In memory* of Angelo Eugene Ossoli." Her choice of phrase struck Elizabeth later as a "strange, prophetical expression!"[46]

Our thoughts are the epochs of our lives; all else is but as a journal of the winds that blew while we were here.—Thoreau

Return

THE OSSOLIS set sail on the morning of May 17. For the first few days the weather was perfect. The captain and the crew made a pet of Nino, and with the help of Celeste and the companionship of Horace Sumner, it was as if they were on their private yacht skirting westward along the coast of the Mediterranean. About a week out, Captain Hasty complained of chest and back pains. The next day he developed a fever. Catherine Hasty and Margaret Ossoli believed at first that he was suffering from the fatigue and annoyance of loading. But when he developed pustules all over his body and was racked by a convulsive cough, they diagnosed his disease as confluent smallpox and treated him with hot poultices and a light diet. On the night of June 1, as they prepared to anchor in sight of the Gibraltar rock, he seemed to revive. But, shortly after daybreak on June 2, he began to weaken and "passed gently away," Margaret Ossoli wrote, like "a little infant."[1]

The harbor authorities refused to allow a physician on board and ordered the *Elizabeth* to fly the quarantine flag for a week. Before the day was out—it was a Sunday—the mates placed the body in a lifeboat, which proceeded to the American consul's barge waiting a safe distance away. The boat was attached to the barge and towed into deep water; there they buried their captain at sea. The next morning Margaret Ossoli described the scene:

the decent array and sad reverence of the sailors, the many ships with their banners flying, the stern Pillars of Hercules, all veiled in roseate vapor; the little angel-white sails diving into the blue depths with the solemn spoil of the poor good man.[2]

On June 8, after the week in quarantine, they sailed forth under the command of the mate, Henry Bangs. Two days later, Nino, in spite of his multiple vaccinations, came down with the same symptoms that had prostrated the captain. For five days his eyes were completely closed, his whole body covered with pox. No one on board believed he could recover, but under the constant care of his parents he slowly improved and by the last days of the voyage was completely restored to health with only a few scars remaining to concern his mother.

The ship proceeded slowly for a month; then, after the first week of July, the winds shifted. A lively southwest breeze swept them swiftly on their course. By the morning of Thursday, July 18, Henry Bangs believed they were nearing landfall. In the early afternoon he ordered the trunks brought on deck. As the passengers finished their final packing, he informed them that they were between Cape May and Barnegat, New Jersey; he expected to be at Sandy Hook the next morning. There a pilot boat would lead them into New York Harbor. At nine o'clock, even though the brisk winds had swelled to a decided gale, everyone went to bed. They had no way of knowing that the day before a tropical hurricane had begun to move slowly up the Atlantic coast. On Wednesday, July 17, it had hit Elizabeth City, North Carolina, damaging wharves and houses, leveling trees and cornfields. Thursday morning the streets of Richmond, Virginia, were suddenly flooded; the inhabitants of the houses on the flats took to the upper stories of their dwellings. The storm swept away along the Cape Fear River, leveling crops throughout Maryland. The Susquehanna was filled with trees, lumber, and bridge timber. The Cumberland Valley railroad bridge was washed away. Near Lewis, Delaware, the schooner *Adelaide* went aground with 126 tons of coal. In Easton, Pennsylvania, the canal above Mauch Creek was out of commission. The water rose twenty-four feet along the Leish River. All shipping from Augusta, Georgia, northward stopped on Thursday. On Thursday night—as the *Elizabeth* prepared for landing the next morning—the New York mail boat from Boston through Long Island Sound to Stonington, Connecticut, did not run, and the Fall River mail boat to New York put in at Stonington.

At 2:30 A.M. on Friday, July 19, as his passengers slept, Henry Bangs took soundings and reported twenty-one fathoms. This depth assuring safety, he turned in again. A little over an hour later the ship struck a sandbar with a resounding crash; a second thud broke a great hole in its side. As it listed sideways and settled in the stern, the passengers heard the cry, "Cut away!" In their nightclothes, they rushed from their staterooms into the passenger lounge; they found the door wrenched off and water streaming through the hole in the broken skylight. They propped themselves up against a dry wall, bracing themselves against a table; they soothed the whimpering Nino, calmed the hysterical Celeste, and prayed together. Every so often, hoping to attract the attention of someone in the forecastle, Catherine Hasty went to the doorway to shout and gesture across the waist of the ship. In the darkness amid the crashings of the storm her efforts were fruitless. While they waited, Catherine and Margaret divided their money and placed it in small bags, which they tied to their clothing. The inexperienced mate, Henry Bangs, had been driven completely off course by the storm. Later it was said that he "mistook the Fire Island light for that on the Highlands of Neversink" off the New Jersey coast. In the heavy current and hurricane conditions, the *Elizabeth* had wrecked on a sand dune off what is now Point O'Woods, Fire Island.[3]

In the dry forecastle, Charles Davis, the second mate, had for some time been ordering the crew of sixteen to go to the rescue of the passengers. None of them obeying, he went himself in the first light of the morning. He managed to bring them singly across the debris and fallen timber of the passageway. He tied the baby in a bag around his neck and led Margaret across. He almost lost Catherine Hasty down a hatchway but rescued her just in time by seizing her hair. When all were momentarily safe, he returned a last time for Captain Hasty's watch, a jewelry pouch of Margaret's, and a hoard of figs and wine.

Huddled together in the forecastle, as dawn came they were encouraged by the sight of figures moving on the beach. They were only 400 yards from the shore, but the sea was still boiling and the wind strong. Margaret had a serviceable life preserver, which she relinquished to a sailor who offered to go for help. After watching him arrive safely, they launched experimental spars tied with bright clothing to test their chances for safe arrival by this means; shore figures quickly despoiled those that reached the shore. Judging that at any moment the ship could break up, Henry Bangs urged the passengers to agree that the best means of survival was to lash themselves to a plank with a seaman behind to keep them upright. Although Margaret agreed on behalf of the others, she refused to try the plank herself, saying repeatedly that she could not be separated from her husband and child. When Catherine Hasty plunged in with Charles Davis, the strong western current carried them three-quarters of a mile down the beach where, badly bruised, they were rescued by an islander, James Thompson. He took them home, restored them, and gave them money. Henry Bangs, clinging to a hatch, was washed up on shore "insensible." He was resuscitated by another islander, Smith Oakes, who hospitably opened his house to the rescued.[4]

By the middle of the morning, all of the crew except the cook, Joseph McGill; an old Swedish seaman, George Sanford; the steward, George Bates; the ship's carpenter; and a seaman had abandoned ship. These five waited loyally with the Ossolis, urging them to try for land before the tide rose again in the afternoon. At one o'clock, they watched a lifeboat being dragged down on the beach and waited in vain for it to be launched. About 2:30 in the afternoon the breakers rose again, and the gale increased. Just before the ship broke up, George Bates jumped in with the baby in his arms. The rest of the crew followed. The gale tore Ossoli and Celeste out of a tangle of rigging.

Mr. Jonathan Smith, agent for the ship's underwriters, had arrived on the Great South Beach by eleven o'clock on Friday morning. Cargo from the *Elizabeth* had already washed up and covered the shore: straw goods, castile soap, olive oil, bolts of silk, and oil paintings. For a distance of over a mile along the shore salvagers in carts and wagons were busy carrying away the loot. The land sharks and pirates were even carrying off the chests and clothing of the sailors, who were wandering around half-naked searching among the debris for their possessions. "Between 12 and 1 o'clock," Smith reported, "the life-boat and the gun arrived, but the ship was too far off to throw a shot over her, and the surf too high and the wind too strong to allow the life-boat any chance of reaching the wreck." Smith could see some of the crew on deck. The only hope was that the vessel would hold together until low tide "when there might be a chance of boarding her."[5]

The ship broke up shortly afterward. Only a few minutes after the *Elizabeth* went to pieces, two sailors were dragged up on shore alive; they were followed by the bodies of Nino and George Bates. Smith wrote that he and his companion, Mr. Leroy, "picked up the child and were carrying it up on the beach when, we met one of the sailors, who took it from us with a great deal of feeling, placed it behind some cargo, took off his neck cloth and covered him up." An hour later the body of Celeste Panolini, "a very handsome young woman about 22 years old, was picked up about half a mile to the east of the wreck." Smith's account included the statement: "I gather from some of the crew that when the wreck broke up there remained on the forecastle five of the crew, Marquis D'Ossoli, Celeste Pardina [*sic*], and the child—the Marchioness D'Ossoli having previously drowned in the forecastle."[6]

Horace Greeley sent his star reporter, Bayard Taylor, to the scene of the wreck. Taylor had made a name for himself covering the forty-niners in California the year before. He arrived on Wednesday morning, July 24. Taylor's account of the disaster, the one most widely republished and quoted thereafter, mingled Catherine Hasty's reminiscences with the testimony of the crew, the lighthouse keeper, Selah Strong, and onlookers. He reported that the bodies of two more sailors had been found on Monday and that "[a]ll have now come to land but those of the Ossolis and Henry [*sic*] Sumner." The dead were now listed as all of the passengers and three sailors. Taylor found the beach "strewn for a distance of three or four miles with fragments of planks, spars, boxes and the merchandise with which the vessel was laden." In among the sand hills were broken cases of almonds, sacks of juniper berries, and oil flasks, the contents spilling into the sand. "On Sunday there were nearly a thousand persons here, from all parts of the coast between Rockaway and Montauk, and more than half of them were engaged in secreting and carrying off everything that seemed to be of value." For his description of the last moments before the forecastle sank, Taylor relied on the testimony of the cook, Joseph McGill, "the last person that reached the shore alive." As the crew determined to leave, McGill said, the steward grabbed the child "by main force and plunged with it into the sea." Soon afterward Ossoli was washed away; Margaret, unaware of the fate of her husband and child, was heard to say, "I see nothing but death before me,—I shall never reach the shore." In an interview with an anonymous reporter, Catherine Hasty gave an account of Margaret's last moments that contradicts McGill's story. She was told by the last survivors that Margaret had just been persuaded "to trust herself to a plank, in the belief that Ossoli and their child had already started for the shore, when, just as she was stepping down, a great wave broke over the vessel and swept her into the boiling deep."[7]

Henry Thoreau, who considered himself "but little salted . . . accustomed to make excursions to ponds within ten miles of Concord," arrived at Smith Oakes's house on Wednesday just a few hours after Bayard Taylor left. Waldo Emerson had sent Henry down from Concord, charging him with obtaining "all the intelligence &, if possible, any fragments of manuscript or other property." Thoreau spent a day interviewing everyone near the scene of the wreck, corroborating the facts reported by Taylor, and adding that four bodies were still missing: "the two Ossolis—Horace Sumner—& a sailor." He listed and described meticulously the salvaged Ossoli property: a trunk, a carpetbag, a broken desk, none of them intact. All the papers found in the trunk would barely cover a small table, and there was no sign of a manuscript.[8]

Learning that most of the plunderers came from Patchogue, a nearby village where flasks of oil from the *Elizabeth*'s cargo were selling for "6 ½ cents apiece," Thoreau persuaded three sailors to take him there in an oyster boat. The trip was unsuccessful except for a possible gentleman's shirt and "a rumor of a child's petticoat." Back on Fire Island, he interviewed a man who had found a lady's shift, which "he thought had the letters S.M.F. on it," and a coat of the Marchese Ossoli. Thoreau ripped a button off the coat and put it in his pocket.[9]

On Saturday he walked five miles down the beach to view a body that had washed up that morning—"simply some bones washed up on the beach. They would not detain a walker there more than so much seaweed." The form was unrecognizable, either as a man or as a woman; he hired the light keeper to bury it and put a marker on it. He left on Sunday morning with little to show for his trouble. When he returned to Concord, he wrote in his journal:

I have in my pocket a button which I ripped off the coat of the Marquis of Ossoli, on the seashore, the other day. Held up, it intercepts the light,—an actual button,—and yet all the life it is connected with is less substantial to me, and interests me less, than my faintest dream. Our thoughts are the epochs in our lives; all else is but as a journal of the winds that blew while we were here.[10]

Arthur and Richard Fuller brought Margarett Crane Fuller to New York on the Tuesday after the wreck. They left her with Rebecca Spring in Brooklyn while Marcus accompanied them to Fire Island, where the collector of the Port of New York, Hugh Maxwell, was supervising the salvage of the *Elizabeth*. The brothers stayed on the island until the surf boaters assured them that there were no bodies lodged in the wreck. After seeing how extensively the wreckage had been vandalized, Arthur and Richard decided that the bodies of Margaret and Giovanni had probably washed ashore and been plundered by pirates before being secretly buried. A few weeks later, a strange story began to be told in Long Island, one that persisted for years. The story went that, after everyone had gone home, Captain James Wicks found a body cast up on the beach. He was told that Margaret's brothers had left word that, if a body were found, Horace Greeley should be notified. Captain Wicks claimed he delivered the body to Greeley, only to have it rejected, whereupon he buried it on Coney Island. In 1854 Eugene and Arthur were summoned to New York to identify, "through the teeth," a buried body that had been found, but their journey proved fruitless.[11]

The Fuller family did not hold a public funeral service. Margaret's friends mourned her individually. Waldo Emerson fantasized a funeral service: "There should be a gathering of her friends & some Beethoven should play the dirge." He called upon three of Fuller's old Concord friends to give brief commentaries. "Her life was romantic & exceptional: So let her death be," said Almira Barlow, the beautiful divorced schoolteacher who had known Margaret since childhood. "Mrs. Ripley thinks that the marriage with Ossoli was like that of De Stael in her widowhood with the young *De Rocca,* who was enamoured of her," Emerson noted, quoting Sarah Ripley, the woman he considered the most learned in New England. He then called on Elizabeth Hoar, who said, "Her heart, which few knew, was as great as her mind, which all knew," and "she was the largest woman; & not a woman who wished to be a man." In his journal, Emerson wrote his own eulogy for her: "To the last her country proves inhospitable to her; brave, eloquent, subtle, accomplished, devoted, constant soul! If nature availed in America to give birth to many such as she, freedom & honour & letters & art too were safe in this new world."[12]

He realized that he had lost his most perceptive and reliable listener. "I have lost in her my audience," he mourned, openly acknowledging how much he had depended on her responses. When James Freeman Clarke read the news of her death in the paper, he too was struck with the idea of America's inability to appreciate someone like Margaret and thought that hers was a merciful death. He called her drowning "Margaret's Euthanasia—for so it must seem on reflexion. . . . [I]t was manifest that she was not to come back to struggle against poverty, misrepresentation, & perhaps alienated friendships and chilled affections." Now that she was dead, her friends could speak openly about the discomfort her unconventional behavior had imposed. Clarke was able to rationalize her loss as a solution to a difficult problem. "There seemed no position for her like, & her life was complete as far as experiences and development went," he concluded.[13]

Margaret's brother William Henry comforted Margarett Crane Fuller by reasoning that the family's grief was "tinctured with selfishness for if Margaret had lived there would be a thousand trials and cares for her to encounter, and in her peculiar position, she could not have felt much ease or quiet."[14]

Caroline Tappan expressed her sorrow in a letter to Elizabeth Hoar. Tappan remembered that Fuller always dreaded the water. She had been alarmed when the waves at Cohasset—where they had often swum together—threw her against the rocks. "The waves do not seem so difficult to brave as the prejudices she would have encountered if she had arrived here safely. She was always so sensitive to coldness & unkindness, even from strangers.... Her return seemed like tearing a bird's nest from a sheltering tree and tossing it out on the waves." Tappan had read all the accounts of the disaster. She wrote:

How characteristic are all the things told of Margaret on board, giving her only life-preserver to a sailor to seek for help, when a less sanguine or more selfish person would not have done [so]—her refusing to part with her child when she could not have saved him ... ; her securing the money about her showed how much she had felt the need of it—One who had always been taken care of would not have done so when lives were in danger.

Caroline threw up her hands when she considered Margaret's reluctance to be separated from Nino. "[B]ut why should we all be afraid to lose everything? It is not sorrow but tedious days that we fear—that is why we cannot lose those we love."[15]

At the first national Woman's Rights Convention in Worcester, Massachusetts, in October 1850, the delegates observed a moment of silence in memory of Fuller. The president, Paulina Wright Davis, had heard that she was on her way home and had written in hopes that she would attend. "To her, I, at least, had hoped to confide the leadership of this movement," Davis wrote later. "It can never be known if she would have accepted it ... ; she was, and still is a leader of thought; a position far more desirable than a leader of numbers."[16]

In 1853 the Fuller family bought two plots on Pyrola Path in Mount Auburn Cemetery in Cambridge. Margarett Crane Fuller wanted the family "to mingle our dust together as we have our hearts." By 1855 she had erected a large marble sarcophagus, inscribed with the name of Timothy Fuller. On each end of it were the graves of the two children who had died in infancy, Julia Adelaide and Edward Breck. Beside the sarcophagus was a monument to Margaret and Ossoli, and, in front, the stone of Angelo Eugenio Filippo. Founded in 1831, Mount Auburn Cemetery, with its 135 acres of wooded land with ponds, streams, hills, and valleys, was the first garden cemetery in the United States; by 1855 it was a major tourist attraction. Up to 3,000 visitors came daily by omnibus—after 1856 by horsecar—or by private carriage. The guidebooks pictured the Ossoli monument prominently and described it as one of the cemetery's most popular "contemplation spots."[17]

In an environment like mine, what may have seemed too lofty or ambitious in my character was absolutely needed to keep the heart from breaking and enthusiasm from extinction.

Aftermath and Debate

WITHIN A WEEK of the wreck of the *Elizabeth,* Horace Greeley wrote Waldo Emerson suggesting that he prepare a biography of Fuller. Greeley was anxious to get the book out "before the interest excited by her sad decease has passed away." While Emerson was considering the matter, Greeley sent William Henry Channing to Concord to encourage him. The idea was that the book should be based on Fuller's private letters and journals and be called *Margaret and Her Friends.*[1]

At first the idea appealed to Emerson. He thought "a most vivacious book" could come out of it, one that would have some of the charm of Bettina von Arnim's books, but that to do the job well would require the concurrence of all her friends. He first approached Sam Ward with the idea, but Ward replied that he saw too many contradictions in Fuller. Emerson did not see this as a stumbling block. "[C]ontradictions and surprise are the apples of the eyes of Nature," he replied. "And if there be any combination that is improbable & impossible, that is the one which will next appear." Sam was not convinced. "How can you describe a Force? How can you write the life of Margaret?"[2]

"Well, the question itself is some description of her," Emerson responded. But by the time Sam went off to Europe in the fall of 1850 Emerson's enthusiasm for the book had waned. The Fuller family had not been sufficiently cooperative. In early September, Ellery Channing told Emerson that "the Journals contain so many allusions to people, that they can hardly be seen." Two weeks later, when Emerson had all the manuscripts the family was willing to release, he noted that they had been "much mutilated by the knife, &, I suppose, the fire."[3]

Emerson still thought something could be done, but he did not feel up to taking on the job alone. By December he had convinced William Henry Channing to take over, even though he worried that Channing was "too much her friend to leave him quite free enough." When Channing enlisted James Freeman Clarke, James agreed that no single person could "do justice to all sides of her character." George Davis and Sam Ward promised to contribute; "H[enry] Hedge, Mrs. Farrar, some of her European and Italian friends, & a multitude more" would be approached. Caroline Sturgis Tappan remarked that "no one, except [Margaret] herself, could write a life so multitudinous." Thomas Hicks promised to have "the box and bundle of papers" Margaret had entrusted to him sent to Marcus Spring. He refused, however, to supply any of Margaret's letters to him. They were "on subjects, thus far, sacredly confidential." James Nathan refused to give up the letters in his possession. Tappan reported to Emerson that Nathan said, "you cannot write a biography of Margaret without his letters to her; he wishes to have them himself."[4]

Throughout the winter Channing, Clarke, and Emerson collected material. In July 1851 they met in Concord to pool their findings and make final editorial decisions. All three assumed that they were writing a memoir, partly to commemorate a friend and partly, in Emerson's words, to build "a monument, because crowds of vulgar people taunt her with want of position." They understood that the aim was to smooth over the rough edges, to ignore her skepticism and freethinking on religious and gender issues, and to impose on the story the inevitability of a Greek tragedy with the barely hidden moral that her fate was the price she had to pay for "stepping outside the bounds of personal aspiration." Occasionally, in this context, they included quotations from her journals that to the modern reader, aware of the price women pay for the protection of patriarchy, belie the editors' purpose: "In an environment like mine, what may have seemed too lofty or ambitious in my character was absolutely needed to keep the heart from breaking and enthusiasm from extinction"; or, when accused of arrogance, her reply, "The word 'arrogance' does not . . . appear to me to be just. . . . I . . . feel as if there was plenty of room in the universe for my faults, and as if I could not spend time thinking of them, when so many things interest me more."[5]

Emerson and Clarke were anxious to have the book out in time for the Christmas trade, but Channing was proceeding slowly. The delicate problem of how to handle the Ossoli marriage was his responsibility. He had told Emerson confidentially that he did not believe that Fuller had married, "that a legal tie was contrary to her view of a noble life." Emerson disagreed.

I, on the contrary, believed that she would speculate on this subject as all reformers do; but when it came to be a practical question to herself, she would feel that this was a tie which ought to have every solemnest sanction; that against the theorist was a vast public opinion, too vast to brave; an opinion of all nations & of all ages.[6]

When he established a chronology in the Margaret Fuller Ossoli notebook he was using to collect material for his part of the *Memoirs*, Emerson placed her in Rome in October 1847 and underneath wrote: "Married perhaps in Oct. Nov. or Dec"; later he crossed out the word "perhaps." He gave the notebook a Latin epigraph: "Et quae tanta fuit Romam tibi causa videndi? *Libertas*. [And what was the great occasion of your seeing Rome? *Freedom*.]"[7]

Fuller's family and friends continued the search for more information about her life in Europe. In October Sarah Clarke went to Rome and Florence with Julia Ward Howe. They questioned her expatriate friends but could only report that Mrs. Mozier remembered her as "full of sympathy," "and Mrs. Crawford spoke of M. as a mild saint and ministering angel."[8]

They carried a personal letter containing details of the wreck of the *Elizabeth* from Ellen Channing to Ossoli's sister, Angela De Andreis. A few months later, in May 1851, De Andreis answered. She thanked Ellen for the information concerning the tragic death of her beloved brother, who, she wrote, had lived with her "up to the time of his marriage with your sister, Margaret, whom neither I nor my husband ever met." She had no possessions or papers belonging to Margaret or any knowledge of a copy made of a manuscript. Nor did she have any pictures of either Margaret or the child, neither of whom the family had ever seen or known. The letter to Ellen included a disturbing paragraph, which may have been the reason Ellen was anxious about how William Henry Channing would handle the marriage in the *Memoirs:*

Your sister, Margaret, was for a long time in Rieti, and then came to Florence where, my brother Giovanni Angelo told me, she was married, having given birth beforehand to their baby, Nino, who was baptized, and it was with surprise that I learned this, knowing nothing about it previously.[9]

Whether or not Ellen showed this letter to William Channing, he was certainly aware that the marriage question was of great concern to the family. As soon as he completed the section on Margaret's Roman life for the *Memoirs,* he wrote Ellen: "Margaret's marriage is exquisitely beautiful and noble as it works itself out. . . . I have added the finest possible words of my own. Have no fears—all goes well.[10]

In the last weeks before publication, Emerson grew weary. He had come to the conclusion that Fuller represented only "an interesting hour & group in American cultivation. . . . [Q]uantities of rectitude, mountains of merit, chaos of ruins, are of no account without result." Emerson's attitude was not untypical. None of the three regarded Fuller as a historical figure whose achievements would be of value and interest to future generations. And all were careless with the letters and journals they used as source material, erasing, cutting, smudging, and destroying at will. Nor did they see reason to be scrupulous as to facts or dates or personality. The two ministers, Channing and Clarke, treated her as a worthy parishioner to whose aspiring personal life they had been privy as personal counselors. Channing was overly protective of her reputation to the point of near apotheosis, whereas Emerson, in his effort to capture her "contradictions and surprise," drew a concise portrait that many, especially Fuller's family, considered unnecessarily harsh. Challenged by the original approach Carlyle had used in his recently published biography of the poet John Sterling, Emerson made a conscious effort to avoid the tone of pious praise that characterized conventional memoirs of a departed friend. His sketch was honest, revealing Fuller's hold over his imagination and the difficulties her challenging personality had presented; at times it was sharp to the point of caricature, but he was the only one of the three who tried to convey the "alienated intensity" of her character. He understood to some degree how much it cost her to be an outsider.[11]

They did not make the Christmas deadline. Carlyle had promised that letters from Mazzini and the Brownings were on their way; when these failed to appear, they went to press in February 1852. To everyone's surprise, *The Memoirs of Margaret Fuller Ossoli* was a great success on both sides of the Atlantic. It established Fuller as a colorful American personality. When George Eliot finished reading it in March, she wrote to a friend:

[I]t is a help to read such a life as Margaret Fuller's. How inexpressibly touching that passage from her journal—"I shall always reign through the intellect, but the life! the life! O my God! shall that never be sweet?" I am thankful, as if for myself, that it was sweet at last.[12]

Harriet Martineau hastened to let Emerson know that the parts written by Channing and Clarke only confirmed the "unhappy impressions" of Fuller in Britain, adding that only the Italian portion and Emerson's could be expected to correct "existing prejudices." As for her personal opinion, she wrote:

I had no idea how far Margt had gone in mysticism,—nor how very far she was from peace. I had no idea that she was another instance of the old fate,—of a woman of strong nature, debarred from a home of her own, & seeking a refuge in mysticism. How plain this becomes when we see her marry as she did, & become so thoroughly the mother;— so rational & humble too![13]

The book sold briskly. The *New York Home Journal* reported that "the first thousand . . . was sold in twenty-four hours." James Freeman Clarke noted that two more editions "were hurried through the press . . . when, *presto,* the sale stopped. . . . *Uncle Tom's Cabin* was published. The retail book market never can take two enthusiasms at one time." Even so, until *Phineas T. Barnum's Life, by Himself* was published in 1856, *The Memoirs of Margaret Fuller Ossoli* was the best-selling biography of the decade.[14]

Emerson was amazed. "Margaret[']s book has had the most unlooked for & welcome success." All the popular press were praising it. Margarett Crane Fuller was not so enthusiastic, especially about Emerson's section of the book. "The 'Memoir' is not an elegy," she wrote Richard. She thought James's account was "fine" and William Channing's was "just," but "Mr. E. never understood Margaret—that is evident enough." Richard agreed that parts of the book were very "unjust," but they were "neutralized" by the whole, he thought. He was more impressed with the sales figures: "*the first edition is all sold* and the second will be issued Saturday next," he wrote two days after publication. In all, there would be thirteen editions before the end of the century, plus a German translation of parts of the book.[15]

The book helped quell speculation about the marriage, but the question still lingered. Ellery Channing's sister Barbara went to Italy in 1854 and, as her predecessors had done, questioned Margaret's expatriate friends and visited Angela De Andreis. ("She is a stout middle aged woman of plain appearance with a bright face & manner.") But no new information seems to have emerged.[16]

Ever since Fuller's death, Greeley had been pressing for a new edition of *Woman in the Nineteenth Century*. In the summer of 1853 he urged Richard to get Emerson or Channing to write an introduction and to make an average-sized book with all her writings "which allude to the Woman question." To help scan Margaret's papers this time, Richard employed a copyist who agreed, as he put it, "to show or communicate nothing." Richard wrote Ellen, assuring her that he would himself extract and copy out "the parts objectionable" from the papers in his possession and saying that the other members of the family should do the same.[17]

Both Emerson and Channing declined to write the foreword. The woman's rights movement had taken such strides since Fuller's book had been published thirteen years earlier that Emerson gave as his excuse that "the accumulated ripeness and interest of the topic" would now require "considered" and "deep" treatment. Greeley suggested both Lydia Maria Child and Elizabeth Hoar as possible editors of the book. In the end, Arthur Fuller undertook the editing of what became *Woman in the Nineteenth Century and Kindred Papers* (1855) and then went on to edit a collection of Margaret's *Tribune* articles and personal letters from Europe as *At Home and Abroad* (1856). After collecting additional pieces from the *Dial* and from her New York years in *Life Within and Life Without* (1860), Arthur announced to the family, "Margaret's debts are all paid, every dollar!"[18]

In 1863 the family considered sponsoring a new biography. They discussed the project with Caroline Healey Dall, who had been the youngest member of Fuller's Conversation classes in the 1840s. She had become a writer and lecturer and was interested in undertaking the authorship. In hopes of recouping a still outstanding cache of letters, in February 1863 Richard began negotiations with James Nathan, who, encouraged by Horace Greeley, had changed his name in 1855 to Gotendorf, the name of a place in Germany where his forebears had owned land. He had been in banking for some years on Wall Street and returned to Germany to live just about the time Richard hoped to retrieve his sister's letters. The effort failed.

The family's plans for the new biography and a new edition of Margaret's major writings were soon abandoned. In December 1862 Arthur Fuller, who served for a year and a half as chaplain to the Sixteenth Massachusetts Regiment, was killed in the Civil War Battle of Fredericksburg. (He had been honorably discharged for reasons of health the day before, but the next morning he had impulsively grabbed a musket and answered a call for volunteers to cross the Rappahannock and clear the town; he was killed shortly after taking up his position.)

By the time of Arthur's death, few of the Fuller children remained. Ellen, after separating from Ellery in 1853, died of tuberculosis in 1856. (Just before she died, she invited Ellery back but only on condition that he sign a strict marriage contract.) In 1859 Eugene, who was on his way home by sea from New Orleans to visit his dying mother, disappeared overboard the first day out. The family explanation is that he had been suffering from "softening of the brain" from sunstroke. Margarett Crane Fuller died after a long illness in 1859. Richard died a decade later, in 1869, leaving only William Henry, who returned from the West after his mother's death and died in 1878, and Lloyd, who was institutionalized for life; he outlived all the others, dying in 1891.[19]

In 1869 Horace Greeley supervised a six-volume *Tribune* edition of Fuller's writings. Twelve years after her death, on May 23, 1870, several of her old friends, with the encouragement of Julia Ward Howe and other women activists, joined in a gala commemorative sixtieth birthday party for Fuller at the New England Woman's Club on Tremont Place in Boston. Tickets for the event sold out weeks in advance. James Freeman Clarke, Henry Hedge, and William Henry Channing stressed Fuller's importance as a literary critic. Marcus and Rebecca Spring, Elizabeth Palmer Peabody, and Thomas Wentworth Higginson shared their memories and read letters sent for the occasion from George Davis, Thomas Hicks, and Harriet Martineau. Julia Ward Howe closed the celebration with a verse that Lydia Maria Child described in her newspaper report as "a very pearl of a poem." Waldo Emerson was unable to come, but Lidian was present, as was Bronson Alcott. (Henry Thoreau had died of tuberculosis in 1862 at the age of forty-five.) Thereafter, Fuller's celebrity gradually diminished. Bronson Alcott and Ednah Dow Cheney kept her name alive on the lecture circuit, but she was remembered almost entirely as a Transcendentalist, a reformer for woman's rights, and an inspiring personality.[20]

In the early 1880s, Fuller enjoyed a revival. Julia Ward Howe and Thomas Wentworth Higginson published biographies of her in 1883 and 1884, respectively. Howe explained that she called her book "*Margaret Fuller* simply because it is by this name that its subject is most widely known and best remembered" and it "was as Margaret Fuller that she took her place among the leading spirits of her time, and made her brave crusade against its unworthier features." "I am to treat her career as a chapter in the development of American literature," Higginson wrote while writing *Margaret Fuller Ossoli*. He wanted to rectify the prominence that previous biographers had given to "her desire for self-culture." She "was not framed by nature for a mystic, a dreamer, or a bookworm . . . but a career of mingled thought and action, such as she finally found."[21]

With her name once again before the public, in 1884 Fuller became the center of a spirited literary battle that revived speculation about her character. Six months after Higginson's *Margaret Fuller Ossoli* appeared, Nathaniel Hawthorne's son Julian published in his biography of his parents, *Nathaniel Hawthorne and His Wife*, a scathing indictment of Fuller. The damaging passage was an excerpt from Nathaniel Hawthorne's *French and Italian Notebooks*, which Sophia Peabody Hawthorne had chosen to expurgate in her earlier editions of her husband's unpublished journals. (Nathaniel Hawthorne died in 1864.)

Fuller's Florence friend, the sculptor Joseph Mozier, lay behind the affair. While in Rome in the spring of 1858, the Hawthornes befriended the Moziers. Even though Hawthorne found Mozier singularly lacking in "the polish or refinement" one might associate with a sculptor and, in due course, decided that Mozier was "a very poor type of scandal-monger," nevertheless, Mozier's "very curious" revelations about Fuller caught Hawthorne's attention at the time and set him to write some comments which were to become, according to Thomas Woodson, the most recent editor of Hawthorne's journals, the most "notorious" entry in them.[22]

After describing Ossoli as "the handsomest man [he] ever saw," Mozier went on to lampoon him as "half an idiot" who could hardly read or write and who, after four months' work as a sculptor in Mozier's studio, produced "a copy of a human foot" with the toe on the wrong side. The Ossoli family position was, in spite of the title, of no account whatsoever, and Ossoli himself "had something to do with the care of [Margaret's] apartments." What could have been the attraction between the two posed itself as a "riddle" to Hawthorne, one that he resolved by a reading of Margaret's character, which he believed was marked by a hunger for experience at any cost.

But she was a person anxious to try all things, and fill up her experience in all directions; she had a strong and coarse nature, too, which she had done her utmost to refine, with infinite pains, but which of course could only be superficially changed. The solution of the riddle lies in this direction; nor does one's conscience revolt at the idea of thus solving it; for—at least, this is my own experience—Margaret has not left, in the hearts and minds of those who knew her, any deep witness of her integrity and purity. She was a great humbug; of course with much talent, and much moral reality, or else she could not have been so great a humbug. But she had stuck herself full of borrowed qualities, which she chose to provide herself with, but which had no root in her.[23]

Mozier's further assertion that Margaret had lost all capacity for "literary production" while in Rome and that the much lamented "History of the Roman Revolution" never existed drew Hawthorne to the conclusion that Margaret had suffered a complete moral and intellectual collapse in Europe—her "tragedy" all "the sadder and the sterner, because so much of the ridiculous was mixed up with it, and because she could bear anything better than to be ridiculous."

It was such an awful joke, that she should have resolved—in all sincerity, no doubt—to make herself the greatest, wisest, best woman of the age; and to that end, she set to work on her strong, heavy, unpliable, and, in many respects, defective and evil nature, and adorned it with a mosaic of admirable qualities. . . . She took credit to herself for having been her own Redeemer, if not her own Creator; and, indeed, she was far more a work of art than any of Mozier's statues. But she was not working on an inanimate substance, like marble or clay; there was something within her that she could not possibly come at, to re-create or refine it; and, by and by, this rude old potency bestirred itself, and undid all her labor in the twinkling of an eye. On the whole, I do not know but I like her the better for it;—the better, because she proved herself a very woman, after all, and fell as the weakest of her sisters might.[24]

The extraordinary vituperation of the passage, along with its implications— that Margaret Fuller, whom the women in the Peabody family had once called Queen Margaret, had been undermined by female sexuality—provoked an immediate response. After a few early book reviews commented on Hawthorne's solution to the riddle of Margaret Fuller, Fuller's friends rallied to her defense. A letter from Sarah Clarke that appeared in the Boston Transcript on December 12, extolling Fuller's many acts of "kindness and generosity, her sympathy and goodwill," was followed by a conciliatory explanation from James Freeman Clarke, now a famous churchman with a national reputation: Hawthorne "wrote in his notebooks all sorts of hints and suggestions, as they occurred to him, as the ground for future imaginative characters. These notes were not his final judgements on persons, and were the last things he himself would ever have thought of printing."[25]

Thomas Wentworth Higginson, in his review of Nathaniel Hawthorne and His Wife for the Atlantic Monthly, wrote the most virulent retort. Not only did Julian "confuse and becloud" his father's memory, but his description of his parents' marriage showed it to be one of mutual selfishness. With two exceptions "the married pair lived with almost literal exclusiveness for themselves and their children. . . . Had either of these gifted people been of eminently charitable judgment, the case would have been different." Sophia and Nathaniel "clearly abetted each other in the practice of extremely sharp criticisms on the very slightest grounds," he wrote. Higginson quoted the insulting epithets that the couple had cast at Thoreau, Emerson, and Theodore Parker as well as Margaret Fuller. "Mr. Julian Hawthorne seems to share in the family animosity," he concluded.[26]

Christopher Cranch accused Julian of using the diatribe to give the book "a much wider sale" and Elizabeth Cranch added that the notes were taken "from the lips of one who was noted in his day, as being one of the social gossips of Rome."[27]

Richard Fuller's son Frederick wrote a lawyerlike article for the Literary World, based on his aunt's letters and journals and designed to prove that Fuller's relations with the Hawthornes had been for the most part cordial. Searching for a cause for the "pique" that had triggered Hawthorne's negative feelings, as many would do in the future, he looked to the character of Zenobia in The Blithedale Romance—supposedly based on Fuller—for a key to the "dislike." Hawthorne was put off by Fuller's strong ties to Emerson's genius in preference to his own. He also made the shrewd observation that Hawthorne's notebooks contained uncomplimentary remarks about his sister-in-law, Elizabeth Palmer Peabody, who shared some of Margaret's characteristics. In the last week of January, George Curtis, who now sat in the "Easy Chair" at *Harper's Weekly*, dismissed the Hawthorne extract as a whim. "MARGARET FULLER affected HAWTHORNE unpleasantly, and therefore injurious gossip about her naturally lodged in his mind as probable."[28]

When Julian Hawthorne replied, he put the blame on "the old Pharisaic spirit, which says, 'I am holier than thou.'" Margaret's arrogance was a common fault among "respectable people," he wrote. Because most people thought it was better to keep "an evil or imperfect side to an otherwise admirable character . . . mercifully veiled from public knowledge," he was being pilloried for making public Margaret's one egregious sin.[29]

In Nathaniel Hawthorne's mind Fuller's sin was probably not simple arrogance alone; more likely, he considered her guilty of insincerity, or hypocrisy for propogating views that she did not hold personally or for, like Alice Pyncheon in *The House of the Seven Gables*, refusing to recognize the force of her sexual nature: "This fair girl deemed herself conscious of a power—combined of beauty, high unsullied purity, and the preservative force of womanhood—that could make her sphere impenetrable, unless betrayed by treachery within." Treachery within was a major subject for meditation in Hawthorne's works, and with Anne Hutchinson as a prototype he chose several heretic or radical women for scrutiny as heroines. In his major romances, the "trope of the fall," as Lawrence Buell puts it, was important to the story. It may have seemed too obvious in the light of New England gossip about Fuller's European life to cast her too obviously in the role of such a woman. Even though Henry James concluded that "the legend of [Hawthorne] having had [Fuller] in his eye for the figure of Zenobia, while writing "The Blithedale Romance" surely never held water," most of Hawthorne's readers believed otherwise. Likenesses to Fuller had since been found in Hester Prynne in *The Scarlet Letter* and Miriam in *The Marble Faun*. Hawthorne's preoccupation with the type shows that he was aware that a new woman was in the making, but he could not bring himself in his novels to bestow redemption on any but his innocent women characters. If her sexuality caused Fuller to fall into the fate of ordinary womanhood—thus earning Hawthorne's approval—her fall revealed the hypocrisy in her parading of purity in her New England days—thus invoking his charge of evil. The popularity of *The Memoirs of Margaret Fuller Ossoli*, especially Channing's apotheosis of Fuller in the second volume, could well have exasperated him to the point that Mozier's gossip activated an annoyance so grievous as to demand expression. In early March, Christopher Cranch wrote that Julian has his "quietus, for he sees that public opinion is against him." But the senior Hawthorne's words had been too powerfully put, his reputation for insight into human nature too highly revered, and Margaret Fuller's reputation as a pathfinder and admirable person too strongly established to allow the passage to be forgotten by either side.[30]

Five years before the controversy, in 1879, Henry James in his biography of Nathaniel Hawthorne wrote:

It is safe to assume that Hawthorne could not, on the whole, have had a high relish for the very positive personality of this accomplished and argumentative woman, in whose intellect high noon seemed ever to reign, as twilight did in his own. . . . In fact, however, very much the same qualities that made Hawthorne a Democrat in politics—his contemplative turn and absence of a keen perception of abuses, his taste for old ideals, and loitering paces, and muffled tones—would operate to keep him out of active sympathy with a woman of the so-called progressive type. We may be sure that in women his taste was conservative.[31]

In James's *Hawthorne,* Margaret Fuller is portrayed as "a very remarkable and interesting woman" whose "state of mind" defined the cultural atmosphere of New England in the period before the Civil War. James praised Fuller further, noting that some of her writing had "extreme beauty, almost all of it has a real interest"; she had left behind "the same sort of reputation as a great actress." Her life and her "tragical death" had converted her memory into "a sort of legend, so that the people who had known her well grew at last to be envied by later comers."[32]

His own first memory of Margaret was hearing of her death when he was seven years old, sailing with his father on an afternoon boat trip from New York to Fort Hamilton. On the outing they met Washington Irving, who told them "the news of the shipwreck of Margaret Fuller in those very waters." He vaguely recalled that Margaret Fuller "must have been, and probably through Emerson, a friend of my parents," as indeed she had been. She had met Henry James, Sr., in New York in September 1843 on her return from the West, when James Freeman Clarke's gift of fifty dollars made it possible for her to stay over for a few days in the city. Margaret's conversation at this time with Henry James, Sr., a man at least as earnest as she, had a far-reaching result. Quite by accident, it set up an echo of ridicule that would influence her reputation for the worse far more than Nathaniel Hawthorne's diatribe.[33]

Shortly after Henry James, Sr., met Fuller in the fall of 1843, he went to England, where he made the acquaintance of Thomas Carlyle, who had seen the early issues of the *Dial* and had heard about Fuller from Emerson. According to a letter Evert Duyckinck wrote his brother George in 1848, it was the first conversation between Carlyle and Henry James, Sr., that laid the groundwork for the anecdote by which Margaret Fuller became better known than by any of her many remarkable accomplishments. Carlyle reportedly asked James, in his broad Scots accent, "Who is Miss Fooler?" James identified her and then added the comment, "When I last saw Margaret Fuller she told me that she had got to this conclusion—to accept the Universe."[34]

Carlyle replied, " 'God, [deleted] Accept the Universe. Margaret Fooler accept the universe! [with a loud guffaw] Why perhaps upon the whole it is the best thing she could do—it is very kind of Margaret Fooler!" And whenever Carlyle met James afterward, he repeated again, "So! Margaret Fooler is going to accept the Universe!' "[35]

In his *Fable for Critics* (1848), James Russell Lowell made use of the pun on Fuller's name, and the anecdote was bandied about the literary establishment for years. By the end of the century, Carlyle's reply had been abbreviated, but the James family still claimed the story. In his *Varieties of Religious Experience: A Study of Human Nature* (1902), William James, the philosopher son of Henry James, Sr., repeated it, shed of the pun on her name, not as a joke but as a serious theological proposition, and examined its philosophical implications.[36] In the twentieth century a slight variation of William James's version appears regularly in popular collections of famous quotations under "Carlyle," usually in this format:

> *Margaret Fuller:* "I accept the Universe!"
> *Thomas Carlyle:* "Egad, you'd better."

Around the turn of the century, at the same time William James was writing *Varieties of Religious Experience,* Henry James was writing a life of his friend William Wetmore Story. He found that the presence of Fuller hovered over the letters and journals of the Storys that had been written during their early years in Rome. The presence of "the unquestionably-haunting Margaret-ghost," as he called it, challenged him to solve the riddle of how she could manage, after all the years, to have a hold on his imagination. He had by now forgotten his earlier high estimation of her writing and phrased the question entirely in terms of her personality and her story. What was most notable about her, James decided, was "having achieved, so unaided and so ungraced, a sharp identity." And he added to this the "touching and honest" way she responded to being "bitten" by the wolf of Rome and the "underplot" of her marriage:

These things, let alone the final catastrophe, in short, were not talk but life, and life dealing with the somewhat angular Boston sibyl on its own free lines. All of which, the free lines overscoring the unlikely material, is doubtless partly why the Margaret-ghost, as I have ventured to call it, still unmistakenly walks the old passages.[37]

James thought that Fuller would be surprised to know, as he was himself, that "talk may be still, after more than half a century, made about her." He was probably thinking of the surprised stir the publication of her letters to James Nathan aroused in 1903 just at the time James was finishing his biography of Story. Or he might have noticed a newspaper account of the ceremony held at the meetinghouse at Point O'Woods on Fire Island on July 19, 1901, the fifty-first anniversary of Fuller's death, when fifty people, mostly women active in the woman suffrage movement, gathered to dedicate a wooden pavilion on the rocks overlooking the spot where the *Elizabeth* had gone aground in 1850. Unlike the famous authors, they had no problem defining Margaret Fuller. The commemorative plaque on the pavilion described her specifically as "Author, Editor, Orator, Poet." It has taken most of the twentieth century to establish unequivocably the accuracy of this claim.[38]

A major figure in American romanticism, her *Dial* writings and *Summer on the Lakes* expressed in a creative way fresh ideas on self-discovery and self-evaluation. Her original experiments with symbolism and mysticism, misunderstood by her contemporaries as expressions of morbid self-absorption, extended her insight into feminine psychology and the boundaries of religious experience. As a teacher, tutor, and translator, she played an important role in furthering interest in contemporary European literature as pleasurable and instructive in itself, as well as a background to the development of a unique American culture—"an American mind"—a process that she prophesied would develop gradually out of the diversity of the American people. To this end, she made an enduring contribution by giving a national dimension to the role of literary critic, bringing to it a political and social conscience that has been the hallmark of its best practitioners ever since.[39]

Her search for self-expression created a life that touched on many of the major issues of the day, so that her biography transcends the personal tragedy that gave it its force for over a century and becomes an episode in the broader American story, illuminating both the private and the public life of her time, as she so urgently wanted it to do when she started out on her quest.

Notes

Note: Brackets following correspondence indicate material not included in the letter itself.

Introduction

1. Louis Albert Banks, *The Story of the Hall of Fame* (New York, 1902), 404.
2. "The Wreck at Fire Island," *New-York Daily Tribune* (*NYDT*), July 27, 1850, 4.
3. Henry James, *A Small Boy, and Others* (New York, 1913), 61, and *Hawthorne* (New York, 1879), 77.
4. Quoted in Eleanor Flexner, *Century of Struggle* (1959; New York, 1971), 68.
5. Edgar Allan Poe, *The Complete Works of Edgar Allan Poe*, ed. James A. Harrison (1902; New York, 1962), 15: 75; Edgar Allan Poe to George W. Eveleth, Jan. 4, 1848, in *The Letters of Edgar Allan Poe*, ed. John Ward Ostrum (Cambridge, MA, 1848), 2: 355; Julia Ward Howe, *Margaret Fuller* · (*Marchesa Ossoli*) (Boston, 1883), 47–48.
6. Margaret Fuller (MF) to the Marquis de Lafayette, [June 1825?], *The Letters of Margaret Fuller*, ed. Robert N. Hudspeth, 5 vols. to date (Ithaca: Cornell University Press, 1983–), 1: 150 (hereafter cited as *FL*); to Susan Prescott, July 11, 1825, *FL*, 1: 152.
7. Fuller Manuscripts and Works, fMS Am 1086, Houghton Library, Harvard University, Works 3: 303 (hereafter cited as FMW). By permission of the Houghton Library, Harvard University.
8. R. W. Emerson, W. H. Channing, and J. F. Clarke, *Memoirs of Margaret Fuller Ossoli*, 2 vols. (Boston: Phillips, Sampson, 1852), 1: 297 (hereafter cited as *OM*).
9. Quoted in Robert N. Hudspeth, "A Higher Standard in Thought and Action: Margaret Fuller and the Idea of Criticism," in *American Unitarianism, 1805–1865*, ed. Conrad Edick Wright (Boston, 1989), 158; Lawrence Buell, "The Literary Significance of the Unitarian Movement," ibid., 171.

Chapter 1. The Protected Years

1. *OM*, 1:140–41.
2. MF, "Goethe," *Dial* 2 (July 1841): 4. Fuller's "Autobiographical Romance" is in *OM*, 1:11–42, and *The Essential Margaret Fuller*, ed. Jeffrey Steele (New Brunswick, NJ, 1992), 24–43 (hereafter cited as Steele, *Essential*).
3. *OM*, 1:12, 18, 16. Fuller's so-called "Autobiographical Romance" was written at the watershed age of thirty, when she was particularly sensitive to the generational conflict elements in transcendentalism. In need of a firm psychological foothold, she projected her anxieties in the fragment. Although the sketch was not published until two years after Fuller's death, she must have shared it with friends during her lifetime. Some of Horace Greeley's obituary of her in the *New-York Daily Tribune* of July 23, 1850, seems to have been based on parts of it. See Lawrence Buell, *Literary Transcendentalism: Style and Vision in the American Renaissance* (Ithaca, NY, 1973), ch. 10 (hereafter cited as Buell, *Literary Transcendentalism*). For the importance of the thirtieth year in autobiography, see Theodore Ziolkowski, *Dimensions of the Modern Novel: German Texts and European Contexts* (Princeton, NJ, 1969), 262–66.
4. Thomas Wentworth Higginson, *Margaret Fuller Ossoli* (Boston, 1884), 22–23 (hereafter cited as Hig*MFO*).
5. Information on the Crane family in Canton is in Daniel T. Huntoon, *History of the Town of Canton* (Cambridge, MA, 1893), 417–19, 538–39, 638–39.
6. Margarett Crane Fuller (MCF) to Timothy Fuller (TF), [ca. Dec. 27, 1818], Jan. 1, 1819, FMW, 6: 43, 48.
7. MCF to TF, Jan. 26, 1819, FMW, 6: 64; Richard Frederick Fuller (RFF), "Memorial of Mrs. Margaret Fuller," in R. W. Emerson, W. H. Channing, and J. F. Clarke, *Memoirs of Margaret Fuller Ossoli*, 2 vols. with appendix (Boston, 1875), 1, App.: 376 (hereafter cited as *OM-2*); *OM*, 1:12; "Diary of Timothy Fuller," FMW, 2; Edith Davenport Fuller, "Excerpts from the Diary of Timothy Fuller, Jr., an Undergraduate in Harvard College, 1798–1801," *Cambridge Historical Society Publications*, Oct. 1916, 33–53.

8. Family papers on the Reverend Timothy Fuller's controversy are in FMW, 1. Other references appear in Arthur Buckminster Fuller, with additions by Edith Davenport Fuller, *Historical Notices of Thomas Fuller and His Descendants, with a Genealogy of the Fuller Family, 1638–1902* (Cambridge, MA, 1902), 6–7; Francis E. Blake, *History of Princeton*, 2 vols. (Princeton, MA, 1915), 1:61, 82, 146–57, 202. See also Emory Elliott, "The Dove and the Serpent: The Clergy in the American Revolution," *American Quarterly* 31 (Summer 1979): 187–203.

9. "Diary kept by Elizabeth Fuller, daughter of Rev. Timothy Fuller of Princeton," in Blake, *History of Princeton*, 1:302–23; Humphrey Moore, "A Sermon Delivered at the Funeral Service of Timothy Fuller of Merrimac, Formerly Pastor of Princeton, Massachusetts," July 5, 1805.

10. Timothy Fuller's letters and diaries are in FMW, 2. Other information on Timothy Fuller, Jr., appears in A. B. Fuller, *Historical Notices;* James Spear Loring, *A Hundred Boston Orators* (Boston: John P. Jewett, 1852), 494–95; *Biographical Dictionary of the American Congress, 1774–1949* (Washington, DC, 1950), 976; *History of the Bench and Bar, Suffolk County, Massachusetts*, 1: 280; Duane Hamilton Hurd, *History of Middlesex County, Massachusetts* (Philadelphia, 1890), xxxix. For political background, see Paul Goodman, *The Democratic-Republicans of Massachusetts* (Cambridge, MA, 1964), 76–83, 129–55, 203–5.

11. MF to TF, Jan. 16, 1820, *FL*, 1: 95.

12. TF to MCF, Jan. 30, 1816, FMW, 3: 10; MCF to TF, Feb. 22, 1818, FMW, 6: 20; TF to MCF, Sept. 7, 1810, Dec. 21, 1819, FMW, 3:5, 67.

13. *OM*, 1: 13.

14. MCF [1850], FMW, 8:182.

15. *OM*, 1: 62.

16. Ibid., 12.

17. Ibid., 12–13; MF to William Henry Channing (WHC), [Sept. 1? 1844?], *FL*, 3:224. For an explanation of this relationship, I am grateful to Jeffrey Steele, "Freeing the 'Prisoned' Queen," in *Studies in the American Renaissance,* ed. Joel Myerson (Boston, 1992). For concepts of child development, I am influenced by Nancy Chodorow, *The Reproduction of Mothering: Psychoanalysis and the Sociology of Gender* (Berkeley, CA, 1978), and Margaret Homans, *Bearing the Word* (Chicago, 1986), esp. 1–21. Fuller frequently used the term "the golden age" to describe a future age of "perfect freedom." See Christina Zwarg, "Feminism in Translation: Margaret Fuller's *Tasso,*" *Studies in Romanticism* 29 [1990]: 479, 482, and MF, "Torquato Tasso," Margaret Fuller: Visionary of the New Age (Orono, ME., 1994), 301.

18. MCF [1850], FMW, 8:182; TF, Diary, Jan. 1, 1815, FMW, 2:22.

19. TF to Ellen Kilshaw, Apr. 19, 1818, FMW, 2:24; *OM*, 1:22.

20. Thomas Wentworth Higginson, *Cheerful Yesterdays* (Boston, 1898), 12, 9.

21. TF to MCF, Apr. 26, 1814, FMW, 3:7, and July 12, 1814, FMW, 3:9; to MF, Apr. 13, 1820, FMW, 5: 6.

22. MCF to TF, Dec. 13, 23, 1818, [ca. Dec. 27, 1818], Dec. 13, 1818, FMW, 6: 36, 41, 43, 36.

23. *OM*, 1:85; Hig*MFO*, 11.

24. Ellen Kilshaw to MCF, Oct. 27, 1818, FMW, 2: 26.

25. TF to MCF, Mar. 28, 1820, FMW, 3:154.

26. TF to MCF, Apr. 23, 1820, FMW, 3:171; MCF to TF, Jan. 20, 1821, FMW, 6:117; TF to MCF, Apr. 19, 1820, FMW, 3:169.

27. *OM*, 1: 32–39. Fuller family letters to and from Ellen Kilshaw are in FMW, 2:24–28, 30–42, 47–64, 68; MF's "Lillo" is in Steele, *Essential,* 20.

28. Samuel A. Eliot, *A History of Cambridge, Massachusetts, 1630–1913* (Cambridge, MA, 1913), 93–103; Jonathan G. Hales, *Plan of Cambridge from Survey Taken in June 1830,* author's collection; Thomas Wentworth Higginson, *Old Cambridge* (New York, 1899); Higginson, *Cheerful Yesterdays,* 21; James Russell Lowell, "Cambridge Thirty Years Ago," in *Literary Essays* (London, 1890), 1: 53–89; Cambridge Historical Commission, "Report One: East Cambridge" and "Report Three: Cambridgeport," in *Survey of Architectural History of Cambridge* (Cambridge, MA, 1965, 1971).

29. MCF to TF, Feb. 18, 1818, FMW, 6: 16; MCF to TF, Feb. 22, 1818, FMW, 6:20; MF to TF, Jan. 8, 1819, *FL*, 1: 86.

30. MCF to TF, Feb. 15, 1819, FMW, 6: 74.

31. Ibid.

32. TF to MCF, Mar. 27, 1820, FMW, 3: 53.

33. *OM*, 1: 17, 14, 15.

34. Holmes quoted in H. R. Haweis, *Travel and Talk* (New York, 1896), 29; also Oliver Wendell Holmes, "Cinders from the Ashes," *Atlantic Monthly* 23 (Jan. 1869): 116–17.

35. MCF to TF, Dec. 19, 1820, FMW, 6: 103; MF [ca. Nov., 1820], FMW, 6:102.

36. MF to TF, Jan. 16, 1820, FL, 1: 95; TF to MCF, Jan. 27, 1820, FMW, 3: 99; MF to Mary Vose, Aug. 7, 1820, FL, 1: 101.

37. TF to MCF, Jan. 22, 1820, FMW, 3: 94.

38. Eleanor Flexner, Mary Wollstonecraft: A Biography (Baltimore, 1973), 148–49; Gordon Wood, The Radicalism of the American Revolution (New York, 1992), 357.

39. TF to MCF, Dec. 30, 1819, FMW, 3: 74.

40. TF to MF, Dec. 3, 1820, FMW, 5: 7; MCF to TF, Dec. 17, 19, Jan. 9, 1820, FMW, 6: 102, 103, 112.

41. MF to WHC, Oct. 28, 1840, FL, 2: 176.

42. OM, 1: 14.

43. Ibid., 12.

44. Ibid., 18. For a suggestive discussion of recent psychological theory that could apply to Fuller, see Margaret Homans, Women Writers and Poetic Identity: Dorothy Wordsworth, Emily Brontë, and Emily Dickinson (Princeton, NJ, 1980), 14–21.

45. MCF to TF, Nov. 15, 1820, Jan. 28, 1821, Nov. 12, Dec. 12, Nov. 20, Dec. 12, 1820, FMW, 6:88, 120, 87, 100, 89, 100.

46. TF to MCF, May 21, 1820, FMW, 3: 180; Biographical Dictionary of Congress; Leona Rostenberg, "The Diary of Timothy Fuller in Congress, January 12–March 15, 1818," New England Quarterly 12 (Sept. 1939): 521–29.

47. MCF to TF, [Jan. 20, 1821], FMW, 6: 117.

48. For a description of the Boston Lyceum for Young Ladies, see Edward H. Hall, "Reminiscences of Dr. John Park," Proceedings of the American Antiquarian Society, n.s. 7 (Oct. 1890): 69–93; MF to MCF, Dec. 2, 1821, FL, 1: 114.

49. MF to MCF, Dec. 23, 1821, FL, 1: 117.

50. OM, 1: 92–93. For class distinctions in antebellum Boston, see William H. Pease and Jane H. Pease, The Web of Progress: Private Values and Public Styles in Boston and Charleston, 1828–1843 (New York, 1985), chap. 9.

51. OM, 1: 20; MF to Caroline Sturgis (CS), Apr. 17, [1838], FL, 1: 332.

Chapter 2. A Varied Education

1. MF to TF, Mar. 22, 1822, FL, 1: 120.

2. TF to MF, Dec. 15, 1822, FMW, 5: 11; MF to TF, Dec. 22, 1822, FL, 1: 121.

3. TF to MCF, Jan. 26, 1823, FMW, 4: 65; Margaret Fuller Ossoli Collection, Boston Public Library, 22 (hereafter cited as MFOC).

4. OM, 1:91; MFOC, 22; OM, 1: 91. See also Caroline Healey Dall, "Ms. Sketches: Anecdotes of Margaret Fuller," an essay written from Conway, MA, Aug. 7, 1857, Caroline Wells Healey Dall Papers, Schlesinger Library, Radcliffe College, MC 351.90 (hereafter cited as Dall Papers). For biographical information on Hedge, see Orie W. Long, Frederic Henry Hedge: A Cosmopolitan Scholar (Portland, ME, 1940); Bryan F. Le Beau, Frederic Henry Hedge, Nineteenth Century American Transcendentalist: Intellectually Radical, Ecclesiastically Conservative (Allison Park, PA, 1985); Charles Wesley Grady, "A Conservative Transcendentalist: The Early Years (1805–1835) of Frederic Henry Hedge," in Myerson, American Renaissance (1983), 57–87.

5. FMW, box A, 85; OM, 1: 228–29.

6. MF to TF, Dec. 30, 1822, FL, 1:124; TF to MF, Dec. 24, 1823, FMW, 5: 13.

7. TF to MF, Apr. 3, 24, 3, 1824, FMW, 5:15, 16, 15; MF to TF, Apr. 19, May 21, 1824, FL, 1: 137, 139, 139 n., 138.

8. S. Margaret Fuller, Summer on the Lakes, in 1843 (Boston, 1844; rpt., with introduction by Madeleine B. Stern, Nieuwkoop, 1972), 81–102, 83; see also Bell Gale Chevigny, The Woman and the Myth: Margaret Fuller's Life and Writing (Old Westbury, NY, 1976), 94–101. For evidence that the events in "Mariana" may have been based on an actual experience at Miss Prescott's School, see MF to Susan Prescott, Jan. 1830, FL, 1: 160, and to WHC, [June? 1844], FL, 3: 198–99.

9. MF to Susan Prescott, July 11, 1825, FL, 1: 151–52.

10. Josiah Quincy, Figures of the Past (Boston, 1883), 130; Fred Somkin, Unquiet Eagle: Memory and Desire in the Idea of American Freedom, 1815–1860 (Ithaca, NY, 1967), 132.

11. MF to the Marquis de Lafayette, [June? 16? 1825?], FL, 1: 150.

12. Quincy, *Figures,* 137.

13. Dispatch XXX, *NYDT,* June 23, 1849, in Margaret Fuller, *"These Sad but Glorious Days":* *Dispatches from Europe, 1846–1850,* ed. Larry J. Reynolds and Susan Belasco Smith (New Haven, 1992), 284 (hereafter cited as *SGD*). Dispatches are numbered as they were in *NYDT.*

14. *Memoirs of John Quincy Adams,* ed. Charles Francis Adams (Philadelphia, 1874–77), 5: 90.

15. TF, Diary, Nov. 17, 1824, FMW, 2: 13, 101. Timothy Fuller's chances were put in jeopardy when a *New York Patriot* article alleged that Adams had authorized him to make a preelection "arrangement" with Clay. See TF, Diary, Apr. 23, 1824, FMW, 2: 13; see also Adams, *Memoirs of J. Q. Adams,* 6: 303, 314.

16. Richard Frederick Fuller (RFF), *Chaplain Fuller: Being a Life Sketch of a New England Clergyman and Army Chaplain* (Boston, 1863), 18.

17. Dispatch XII, May 15, 1847, *SGD,* 120–21.

18. MF to Susan Prescott, Jan. 10, 1827, *FL,* 1: 154. The best overview of Lydia Maria (Francis) Child's life is Deborah Pickman Clifford, *Crusader for Freedom: A Life of Lydia Maria Child* (Boston, 1992).

19. LMF(C) to Anne Whitney, May 25, 1879, in *Lydia Maria Child: Selected Letters,* ed. Milton Meltzer and Patricia G. Holland (Amherst, 1982), 558 (hereafter cited as *Child Letters*); MF to Susan Prescott, May 14, 1826, *FL,* 1: 154.

20. LMF to MF, [after Oct. 1827?], *Child Letters,* 10.

21. Hig*MFO,* 27.

22. *OM,* 2: 6.

23. Hig*MFO,* 25.

24. *OM,* 1: 95.

25. Clarke quoted in *The Transcendentalists: An Anthology,* ed. Perry Miller (Cambridge, MA, 1950), 44; *OM,* 1: 114.

26. *OM,* 1: 204.

27. Copy in FMW, box A.

28. MF to James Freeman Clarke (JFC), n.d., [ca. Oct. or Nov. 1832], Margaret Fuller Papers, Massachusetts Historical Society (hereafter cited as FP).

29. Hig*MFO,* 36; Eliza Rotch Farrar (ERF) to MCF, Sept. 3, 1850, FMW, 17: 37; see also *OM,* 1: 137–38.

30. For information on Eliza Rotch Farrar, see Elizabeth Bancroft Schlesinger, "Two Early Harvard Wives: Eliza Farrar and Eliza Follen," *New England Quarterly* 38, no. 2 (June 1965): 147–59; Eliza Rotch Farrar, *Recollections of Seventy Years* (Boston, 1865); John M. Bullard, *The Rotches* (New Bedford, MA, 1947), 126–30. Evidence of difficulties within the Rotch family over inheritance is in *Letters of Elizabeth Palmer Peabody: American Renaissance Woman,* ed. Bruce Ronda (Middletown, CT, 1984), 87 (hereafter cited as *Peabody Letters*).

31. MCF to TF, Jan. 24, 1819, FMW, 6: 63; MF's "Lillo," in Steele, *Essential,* 20.

32. *Harriet Martineau's Autobiography,* 3 vols., with memorials by Maria Weston Chapman (London, 1877), 2: 72; *OM,* 1: 91, 228; *The Journals and Miscellaneous Notebooks of Ralph Waldo Emerson,* ed. William H. Gilman, 16 vols. (Cambridge, MA, 1960–82), 11: 91 (hereafter cited as *EJ*).

33. *EJ,* 4: 407. For an analysis of the concept of womanhood to which Fuller was expected to conform, see Nancy F. Cott, *The Bonds of Womanhood: Woman's Sphere in New England* (New Haven, 1977), 64–73, 98–100, 122–25.

Chapter 3. An Unfavorable Turn

1. *Recollections of Richard F. Fuller* (Boston, 1936), 23 (hereafter cited as RFF*Rec*); James Beattie, *Evidences of Christian Religion, briefly and plainly stated* (Philadelphia, 1787); Miller, *Transcendentalists,* 17.

2. See Conrad Edick Wright, "Institutional Reconstruction in the Unitarian Controversy," in Wright, *American Unitarianism,* 4; Buell, "Literary Significance," ibid., 163–80.

3. Lucinda Willard to Joseph Willard, Oct. 1828, "Letters of Rev. Joseph Willard," *Cambridge Historical Society Annals,* Oct. 1916, 30.

4. Ibid., 31; Oliver Wendell Holmes quoted in Eleanor M. Tilton, *Amiable Autocrat: A Biography of Dr. Oliver Wendell Holmes* (New York, 1947), 48.

5. MCF to Arthur Buckminster Fuller (ABF), Jan. 21, 1838, FMW, 8: 16.

6. Sydney E. Ahlstrom, *A Religious History of the American People* (New Haven, 1972), 72; Bryan Jay Wolf, *Romantic Revision: Culture and Consciousness in Nineteenth-Century American Painting and Literature* (Chicago, 1982), 37.

7. MF to George T. Davis (GTD), [Jan. 1830], *FL*, 1: 159.

8. MF to GTD, Jan. 23, 1830, Dall Papers.

9. See, generally, Karen Lystra, *Searching the Heart: Women, Men, and Romantic Love in Nineteenth-Century America* (New York, 1989). Fuller's letters and responses in her relations with both Davis and Clarke follow to a certain extent the formulations set forth in this book. With respect to the George Davis relationship, the pertinent sections are those dealing with "reciprocal demands of personal disclosure" (42 ff.) and "testing" (171–226).

10. Class of 1829 Papers, Harvard University Archives; Francis M. Thompson, *History of Greenfield, Shire Town of Franklin County, Massachusetts*, 3 vols. (Greenfield, MA, 1904–31), 1: 531, 2: 813, 1038, 1172, 1176; Harvard Law School, *Book of Entries*, 1: 1817–40: George Davis, Sept. 1829 matriculation entry, followed by "Time of Departure" and "Remarks"; *Quinquennial Catalogue of the Officers and Graduates of Harvard University, 1636–1925*, 813.

11. MF to GTD, Dec. 29, 1829, Dall Papers.

12. The death of Edward Breck Fuller and Fuller's closeness to him are described in her letters to WHC[?], Dec. 3, 1840, *FL*, 2: 187, and to CS, May 25, [1844], *FL*, 3:197.

13. MF to JFC, [Mar. 28? 1830], *FL*, 1: 163. For biographical information on Clarke, see Arthur Bolster, *James Freeman Clarke: Disciple to Advancing Truth* (Boston, 1955), James Freeman Clarke, *Autobiography, Diary and Correspondence*, ed. Edward Everett Hale (Boston, 1891), and John Wesley Thomas, *James Freeman Clarke: Apostle of German Culture to America* (Boston, 1949).

14. For a description of the Cambridge social life in which Fuller and Clarke participated, see Christina Hopkinson Baker, *The Story of Fay House* (Cambridge, MA, 1929); Caroline H. Dall, "Studies Toward the Life of a Business Woman, being conversations with Mrs. R. P. Clarke in the winter of 1864–65," Dall Papers.

15. MF to JFC, [1832?], FP; *OM*, 1: 88–89.

16. Sarah Ann Clarke (SAC) to JFC, Jan. 26, 1834, in Sarah Clarke, "Letters of a Sister," bMS Am 1569, Houghton Library, Harvard University (hereafter cited as ClLetSister). By permission of the Houghton Library, Harvard University.

17. MF to GTD, Feb. 3, 1831, MFOC, 18. This letter is a copy in the hand of Thomas Wentworth Higginson, whose abbreviations have been written out. The author's reading of Higginson's handwriting is slightly different from the reading in *FL*, 1: 174. Copies of two letters to GTD that seem to have followed this one are in *OM*, 1: 79–80.

18. JFC, "Diary of Facts," [mid-Apr. 1832], 43: 112, in Perry–Clarke Manuscript Collection, Massachusetts Historical Society (hereafter cited as PCMHi).

19. Ibid.; MF to GTD, n.d., MFOC, 18. The emphasis on sincerity at this time is explored in Frances B. Cogan, *All American Girl: The Ideal of Real Womanhood in Mid-Nineteenth Century America* (Athens, GA, 1989).

20. See again Lystra, *Searching*, for a partial explanation of some of the dynamics at work here.

21. JFC to MF, Jan. 10, 1831, in *The Letters of James Freeman Clarke to Margaret Fuller*, ed. John Wesley Thomas (Hamburg, Germany, 1957), 30 (hereafter cited as ClLetMF); see also MF to JFC, Jan. 18, 1831, FP.

22. MF to JFC, May 5, 1830, FP; also in part in *FL*, 1: 166–67.

23. JFC to MF, [Nov.? 1830?], ClLetMF, 25; JFC, "Journal of People and Things," Sept. 12, 1831, PCMHi.

24. For Hedge's situation at this time, see Grady, "Conservative Transcendentalist," 57–87.

25. TF, Diary, Aug. 27, 1832, FMW, 2: 11, 15. See Paul Goodman, *Towards a Christian Republic: Antimasonry and the Great Transition in New England, 1826–1836* (New York, 1988), chap. 2, and Ronald P. Formisano, *The Transformation of Political Culture: Massachusetts Parties, 1790s–1840s* (New York, 1983), chap. 9.

26. MF to RFF, Mar. 17, 1848, *FL*, 5: 57.

27. MF to JFC, May 3, 1833, FP; Hig*MFO*, 54.

28. RFF*Rec*, 9.

29. JFC, Diary, Sept. 12, 1831, ClLetMF, 7. See also Stanley Vogel, *German Literary Influences on American Transcendentalism* (New Haven, 1955), 22; JFC, "Diary of Facts," Feb. 28, 1832, PCMHi.

30. MF to Jane Tuckerman, Oct. 21, 1839, *FL*, 1: 347.

31. Ibid.

32. Vogel, *German Literary Influences*, 65.

33. John Wesley Thomas, *James Freeman Clarke: Apostle of German Culture in America* (Boston, 1949), 29–30; Philip Allison Shelley, "A German Art of Life in America: The American Reception of the Goethean Doctrine of Self-Culture, in *Crosscurrents* (Charlottesville, VA, 1937) 1:243; *OM*, 1: 133. See also Henry A. Pochman, *German Culture in America: Philosophical and Literary Influences, 1600–1900* (Madison, WI, 1957).

34. Margaret Vanderhaar Allen, *The Achievement of Margaret Fuller* (University Park, PA, 1979), 59; MF to JFC, Nov. 1, 1830, FP.

35. David M. Robinson, "Margaret Fuller and the Transcendental Ethos," *PMLA* 97 (Jan. 1982): 84.

36. MF to JFC, [Aug. 1832], *FL*, 1:177.

37. JFC to MF, [1832?], ClLetMF, 35. For an insightful study of Fuller's *Tasso* in relation to her predicament as a writer, see Zwarg, *Tasso*, 463–90; MF to JFC, [ca. Oct. or Nov. 1832], FP.

38. MF to JFC, [ca. Oct. or Nov. 1832], FP. Mary Kelley, in *Private Woman, Public Stage: Literary Domesticity in Nineteenth-Century America* (New York, 1984), penetrates the complexities of this conflict in the lives of several American women writers in the nineteenth century ("society's expectations" versus "personal goals"). For an interesting analysis of the psychological dilemma of eighteenth- and nineteenth-century women authors, see Cora Kaplan, *Sea Changes: Culture and Feminism* (London, 1986), 78–93.

39. Eleanor M. Tilton, "The True Romance of Anna Hazard Barker and Samuel Gray Ward," in Myerson, *American Renaissance* (1987), 57.

40. MF to CS, Oct. 7, 1839, *FL*, 2: 93; JFC to MF, July 17, 1835, ClLetMF.

41. Chevigny, *Woman and Myth*, 112.

42. Eliza Farrar, *The Young Lady's Friend* (Boston, 1836), 269. For a discussion of the nature of friendships between women in America in this period, see Cott, *Bonds*, 160–96. Also useful here is Nancy F. Cott, "Passionlessness: An Interpretation of Victorian Sexual Ideology," in *A Heritage of Her Own: Toward a New Social History of American Women*, ed. Nancy F. Cott and Elizabeth H. Pieck (New York, 1979). A very influential treatment of female friendship in the nineteenth century is Carroll Smith-Rosenberg's "Female World of Love and Ritual: Relations between Women in Nineteenth-Century America," *Signs* 1, no. 1 (Autumn 1975): 1–29. Recent discussions of the limitations of the ideology on "woman's sphere" appear in Nancy A. Hewitt, "Beyond the Search for Sisterhood: American Women's History in the 1980s," *Social History* 10 (Oct. 1985): 299–321, and Linda K. Kerber, "Separate Spheres, Female Worlds, Woman's Place: The Rhetoric of Women's History," *Journal of American History* 75 (June 1988): 9–39.

43. MF to JFC, May 5, 1830, FP.

44. MF to JFC, Aug. 7, 1831, FP.

45. "Camillus and Lelio," FMW, box A; JFC, Journal, March 22, 1833, PCMHi, vol. 45.

46. MF to JFC, "Going to Groton," [1833], May 3, 1833, FP.

Chapter 4. Vain World Begone

1. FMW, Works 3:383; RFF, *Chaplain*, 19.

2. RFF *Rec*, 15–32.

3. MF to JFC, May 1, 1833, FP.

4. MF, Journal, "Groton, May 7, 1833," FMW, box 4; MF, "Thurs. aft., May 9, 1833, FP.

5. MF to JFC, Aug. 17, 30, 1833, FP.

6. MF to JFC, [May 1833], FP.

7. John Neubauer, *Novalis* (Boston, 1980), 63; FMW, 1:685.

8. JFC to MF, Sept. 13, 1833, ClLetMF, 62.

9. MF to JFC, July 27, Nov. 26, 1833, FP.

10. JFC to MF, Dec. 19, 1833, ClLetMF, 70; MF to JFC, Jan. 11, 1834, FP.

11. MF to JFC, Aug. 17, 1833, FP.

12. Frederic Henry Hedge (FHH) to MF, June 24, 1833, Hedge Papers, Andover-Harvard Theological Library (hereafter cited as HedgeMH-AH).

13. MF to JFC, Nov. 26, 1833, FP; Joel Myerson, "A True & High Minded Person, Transcendentalist Sarah Clarke" *Southwest Review* 59 (Spring 1974), 164 (hereafter cited as Myerson, "Sarah Clarke").

14. MF to JFC, Dec. 24, 1833, FP; to Amelia Greenwood, Mar. 20, 1834, *FL*, 1: 201.

15. *OM*, 1: 149.

16. FMW, box A. See Benjamin Disraeli, *Contarini Fleming: A Psychological Autobiography*, 4 vols. (New York, 1832). The young Fleming claimed "ambitions great" to do "something great, and glorious and dazzling." He described himself as "convinced I was a hero and heroes are never forlorn." "A desire for distinction and of astounding action raged in my soul." He wanted to "release beautiful things from his brain" and had a "wish to influence poetic feeling and men" (1:26, 33, 40, 156).

17. Amariah Brigham, *Remarks on the Influence of Mental Cultivation and Mental Excitement on Health* (Hartford, CT, 1832), 50, 81, 73.

18. FMW, box A. References in Fuller's journal entry to two articles by FHH which appeared in the *Christian Examiner* in the March and November issues, 1833, establish the date of these passages as the spring of 1834. Fuller dated her comments on *Contarini Fleming* March 8, 1834. A review of Brigham's book by F. W. Pitt Greenwood, the brother of Fuller's friend, Amelia Greenwood, appears in the March 1834 issue of the *Christian Examiner*.

19. MF to JFC, Nov. 26, 1833, Feb. 7, 1834, FP; JFC to MF, Feb. 24, 1834, ClLetMF.

20. MF to JFC, Apr. 17, 1834, FP.

21. *OM*, 1:18, 19.

22. MF to JFC, Sept. 21, 1833, FP.

23. MF to JFC, Apr. 17, 1834, FP.

24. JFC to MF, Sept. 8, 1834, ClLetMF, 78–80.

25. MF to JFC, Sept. 28, 1834, *FL*, 1:206–7.

26. MF to JFC, Nov. 13, 1834, FP.

27. MF to Almira P. Barlow, Oct. 6, 1834, *FL*, 1: 209; to JFC, Nov. 13, 1834, FP.

28. *Boston Advertiser and Patriot*, Nov. 27, 1834, 2.

29. MF to FHH, Mar. 6, 1835, *FL*, 1: 226; Miller, *Transcendentalists*, 67.

30. FHH, "Coleridge," ibid., 68–69.

31. Ibid., 70–72.

32. William R. Hutchison, *The Transcendental Ministers: Church Reform in the New England Renaissance* (New Haven, 1959), 23; MF to FHH, Nov. 30, 1834, *FL*, 1:213.

33. FHH to MF, Dec. 10, 1834, HedgeMH-AH. For an evaluation of Eichhorn and the Harvard–Göttingen axis of students, see Elisabeth Hurth, "Sowing the Seeds of 'Subversion': Harvard's Early Göttingen Students," in Myerson, *American Renaissance* (1992), 91–120; MF to JFC, Feb. 1, 1835, FP; to FHH, Feb. 1, 1835, *FL*, 1:223–24.

34. MF to JFC, [Feb. 1, 1835], FP; Feb. 1, 1835, *FL*, 1: 221.

35. Ibid.

36. FHH to MF, Feb. 20, 1835, HedgeMH-AH; MF to FHH, Mar. 6, 1835, *FL*, 1:226.

37. JFC to MF, Feb. 20, 1835, ClLetMF, 88; MF to JFC, Mar. 29, 1835, FP.

38. JFC to MF, May 12, 1835, ClLetMF.

39. MF to JFC, Apr. 28, 1835, FP. For a study of the problems women authors experienced in getting their work published in the nineteenth century, see Susan Margaret Coultrap-McQuin, *Doing Literary Business: American Women Writers in the Nineteenth Century* (Chapel Hill, 1990).

40. Robert D. Habich, *Transcendentalism and the "Western Messenger"* (Rutherford, NJ, 1985), 66.

41. MF, "Review of the Rev. George Crabbe and William Roberts, 'Memoirs of the Life and Correspondence of Mrs. Hannah More,'" *Western Messenger* 1 (June 1835): 24, 22–23.

42. MF, "The Pilgrims of the Rhine," *Western Messenger* 1 (Aug. 1835): 101.

43. MF, "Philip van Artevelde," *Western Messenger* 1 (Dec. 1835): 398–408.

44. Ibid.

45. MF to JFC, June 27, 1835, FP.

46. MF to TF and MCF, June 2, 1835, *FL*, 1: 230.

47. RFF*Rec*, 14.

48. MF to Samuel Gray Ward (SGW), Feb. 24, 1850, Barker–Ward Papers, bMS Am 1465, n. 934, Houghton Library, Harvard University, 934. By permission of the Houghton Library, Harvard University; *EJ*, 11: 48.

49. David Baldwin, "The Emerson–Ward Friendship: Ideals and Realities," in Myerson, *American Renaissance* (1984), 308; Samuel Gray Ward, "Long Letter to His Grandchildren," 102, in Thomas Wren Ward Papers, Massachusetts Historical Society (hereafter cited as TWWardMHi).

50. Vera Wheatley, *The Life and Work of Harriet Martineau* (London, 1957), 147–83; Robert K. Webb, *Harriet Martineau: A Radical Victorian* (London, 1960); Una B. Pope-Hennessy, *Three English Women in America* (London, 1929), 215–301.

51. FMW, Works, 3:369; *Martineau's Autobiography,* 2:72; FMW, Works 3:373.

52. MF, "Lost and Won," *New England Galaxy,* Aug. 8, 1835, 1–2; JFC to MF, ClLetMF, Sept. 15, 1835, 103–4.

53. FMW, Works, 3:377; MF to Almira Barlow, Feb. 1, 1836, *FL,* 1:243–44; also FMW, Works, 3:379.

54. RFF*Rec,* 25; Georgiana Bruce Kirby, *Years of Experience: An Autobiographical Narrative* (1887; New York, 1971), 213; Arthur W. Brown, *Margaret Fuller* (New Haven, 1964), 31. See Carroll Smith-Rosenberg, "The Hysterical Woman: Sex Roles and Role Conflict in 19th Century America," *Social Research* 39, no. 1 (Winter 1972), for a discussion of how conflicting role pressures may cause hysterical behavior; see also Elizabeth Zetzel, "The So-called Good Hysteric," *International Journal of Psychoanalysis* 49 (1968): 256–60. Zetzel's description of the family history and life situation common to those whom she characterizes as most amenable to treatment closely parallels the known facts of Fuller's early childhood and her situation as a young adult.

55. FMW, Works, 3:377, 379.

56. Accounts of Timothy Fuller's death are in RFF*Rec,* 20–21, and RFF, *Chaplain,* 31–34; Hig*MFO,* 54.

Chapter 5. A Trial to Fortitude

1. FMW, Works, 3:381; MF to RFF, Aug. 11, 1842, *FL,* 3: 85; FMW, Works, 3:385; also *OM,* 1: 156.

2. RFF*Rec,* 25; FMW, Works, 3:381; *OM,* 1:155.

3. MF to JFC, Nov. 6, 1835, FP.

4. MF to CS, Oct. 22, 1840, *FL,* 2: 168.

5. Ibid., 168–69.

6. MF to JFC, Nov. 6, 1835, Mar. 19, 1836, FP.

7. MF to JFC, Jan. 29, Mar. 14, 1836, FP.

8. MF to JFC, Mar. 14, 1836, FP; to FHH, Mar. 6, 1836, *FL,* 1: 226.

9. MF to JFC, Apr. 19, 1836, FP.

10. JFC to MF, May 4, 1836, ClLetMF, 119; MF to JFC, Apr. 19, 1836, *FL,* 1: 248.

11. MF to [?], Nov. 3, 1835, *FL,* 1:237.

12. RFF, *Chaplain,* 36.

13. MFOC, 145.

14. MF to GTD, Feb. 9, 1836, Dall papers.

15. MF to Eugene Fuller (EF), Jan. 30, Feb. 17, 1836, *FL,* 1: 243, 246.

16. Franklin Benjamin Sanborn, *Recollections of Seventy Years,* 2 vols. (Boston, 1909), 2:406–7.

17. MF to [?], May 23, 1836, *FL,* 1: 254; MF, "Journal," box 4.

18. Margaret Fuller Ossoli, *Life Without and Life Within,* ed. Arthur B. Fuller (Boston, 1860), 357–65 (sheaf of poems); see Steele, "Freeing," 137–43. For a discussion of the German model of romantic friendship, see Henri Brunschwig, *Enlightenment and Romanticism in Eighteenth-Century Prussia,* trans. Frank Jellinek (Chicago, 1974), 208–13.

19. Kenneth Cameron, "Margaret Fuller's Poem on the Death of Charles Emerson," *Emerson Society Quarterly* 18 (1960): 49–50.

20. Charles Chauncey Emerson to Elizabeth Hoar (EH), Mar. [5], 1836, in "Elizabeth of Concord: Selected Letters of Elizabeth Sherman Hoar to the Emersons, Family, and the Emerson Circle," ed. Elizabeth Maxfield-Miller, Part 2 (hereafter cited as Hoar), in Myerson, *American Renaissance* (1985), 136 n.; *Martineau's Autobiography,* 2:72–73.

21. Lidian Jackson Emerson (LJE) to Elizabeth Palmer Peabody (EPP), [late July 1836], in *The Selected Letters of Lidian Jackson Emerson,* ed. Delores Bird Carpenter (Columbia, MO, 1987), 49.

22. *OM,* 1: 202–3.

23. Gay Wilson Allen, *Waldo Emerson: A Biography* (New York, 1981), 220, 242–43 (hereafter cited as Allen, *Emerson*).

24. Ralph Waldo Emerson (RWE) to William Emerson, Aug. 8, 1836, in *The Letters of Ralph Waldo Emerson,* ed. Ralph L. Rusk, 8 vols. (New York, 1939), 2: 32 (hereafter cited as *EmL*).

25. *OM,* 1: 203.

26. *FL,* 1: 260.

27. "Bronson Alcott's 'Journal for 1837,' " Part 1 (hereafter cited as BAJ-1837), in Myerson, *American Renaissance* (1981), 102.

28. Madelon Bedell, *The Alcotts: Biography of a Family* (New York, 1980), 123.

29. Ibid.; EPP to Amos Bronson Alcott (ABA), Aug. 7, 1836, *Peabody Letters,* 181. For Peabody's philosophical differences with Alcott, see ibid., 27–34, 88–91.

30. FMW, 9:41; RWE to MF, Oct. 20, 1836, *EmL,* 2: 41. This arrangement was evidently never fulfilled; see Madeleine B. Stern, *The Life of Margaret Fuller,* rev. ed. (New York, 1991), 76, 81.

31. Otto Friedrich, *Clover* (New York, 1979), 29; "Letters of Caroline Sturgis to Margaret Fuller," ed. Francis B. Dedmond (hereafter cited as Sturgis Letters), in Myerson, *American Renaissance* (1988), 201.

32. Queenie M. Bilbo, *Elizabeth Palmer Peabody, Transcendentalist* (Ann Arbor, University Microfilm 1973, film W2766), 28.

33. *OM,* 1: 176; MF, Journal, FMW, box 3.

34. For the Ripley–Norton controversy, see Charles Robert Crowe, *George Ripley: Transcendentalist and Utopian Socialist* (Athens, GA, 1967), 158–60; Henry L. Golemba, *George Ripley* (Boston, 1977), 38–42.

35. "Prospectus of the *American Monthly Magazine,*" *American Monthly Magazine* (*AMM*), Jan. 1836, vii; MF, "The Life of Sir James Mackintosh," *AMM,* June 1836, 575, 577.

36. MF, "Modern British Poets," *AMM,* Sept. 1836, 235, Oct. 1836, 41.

37. BAJ-1837, Part 1, 48.

38. MF, Journal, FMW, box 3.

39. MF quoted in Bedell, *Alcotts,* 128; BAJ-1837, Part 1, 93.

40. BAJ-1837, Part 1, 51.

41. Odell Shepard, *Pedlar's Progress: The Life of Bronson Alcott* (Boston, 1937), 53.

42. BAJ-1837, Part 1, 30.

43. Miller, *Transcendentalists,* 168; BAJ-1837, Part 2, 54.

44. RWE to ABA, Mar. 24, 1837, *EmL,* 2:61; MF to FHH, Apr. 6, 1837, *FL,* 1: 265.

45. FHH to MF, May 23, 1837, HedgeMH-AH; BAJ-1837, Part 2, 76.

46. BAJ-1837, Part 1, 100.

47. Habich, *Transcendentalism,* 86.

48. MF to JFC, May 13, 1837, FP; MF to FHH, Apr. 6, 1837, *FL,* 1:266.

49. *EJ,* 5:308.

50. Ibid., 319; *Emerson in His Journals,* ed. Joel Porte (Cambridge, MA, 1982), 120; RWE to Convers Francis, Apr. 24, 1837, *EmL,* 2:72.

51. MCF to ABF, Sept. 3, 1837, FMW, 8:9.

52. MF to JFC, May 13, 1837, FP.

53. MF to EPP, May 26, 1837, *FL,* 1:275–76.

Chapter 6. Schoolkeeping in Providence

1. Barbara Welter, *Dimity Convictions* (Athens, OH, 1976), 163; MF to ABA, June 27, 1837, *FL,* 1:287.

2. Allen, *Emerson,* 297; Henry L. Greene, "The Greene-Street School of Providence and Its Teachers," *Publications of the Rhode Island Historical Society* 6 (Jan. 1899): 207.

3. *OM,* 1:177; MF to RWE[?], July 3, 1837, *FL,* 1:288.

4. Judith Strong Albert, "Margaret Fuller and Mary Ware Allen: 'In Youth an Insatiate Student'— a Certain Kind of Friendship," *Thoreau Quarterly Journal* 12 (July 1980): 19; see also Harriet Hall Johnson, "Margaret Fuller as Known by Her Scholars," in *Critical Essays on Margaret Fuller,* comp. Joel Myerson (Boston, 1980), 137 (hereafter cited as *MFCrEssays*); Laraine R. Fergenson, "Margaret Fuller in the Classroom," in Myerson, *American Renaissance* (1987), 135; Edward A. Hoyt and Loriman S. Brigham, "Glimpses of Margaret Fuller: The Greene Street School and Florence," *New England Quarterly* 29 (Mar. 1956): 95. For a record of Fuller's day-by-day performance as a teacher, see Laraine R. Fergenson, "Margaret Fuller as a Teacher in Providence: The School Journal of Ann Brown," in Myerson, *American Renaissance* (1991), 59–117.

5. MF to ABF, July 5, 1837, *FL,* 1:291.

6. MF to RWE, Aug. 14, 1837, *FL,* 1:295; Mason Wade, *Margaret Fuller: Whetstone of Genius* (New York, 1940), 63–64.

7. Allen, *Emerson*, 300.

8. Ibid., 301.

9. Ralph H. Rusk, *The Life of Ralph Waldo Emerson* (New York, 1949), 266.

10. Hutchison, *Transcendental Ministers*, 59.

11. MF to CS, Nov. 16, 1837, *FL*, 1:314–15.

12. Barlow quoted in Joel Myerson, *New England Transcendentalism and the "Dial"* (New York, 1980), 26.

13. MF to CS, Nov. 16, 1837, *FL*, 1:315.

14. Harriet Martineau, *Society in America* (London, 1887), 3:31, 175. For a general view of Martineau's contribution to the sociology of American society, see Seymour Martin Lipset's introduction to his abridgment of Martineau's *Society in America* (New York, 1962).

15. MF to Harriet Martineau, [ca. Nov. 1837] *FL*, 1:309.

16. *Martineau's Autobiography*, 2:71.

17. MF to MCF, Sept. 5, 1837, *FL*, 1:300–301.

18. Fergensen, "Fuller as a Teacher," 84. Ann Brown's school journal notes that Fuller was absent with illness for a day or two the last week of each month. This could indicate that the severe headaches of which she complained were related to her menstrual period.

19. *OM*, 1:183, 197; *EJ*, 11:505; MF to Charles K. Newcomb, Feb. 24, 1840, *FL*, 2:122; see also MF to CS, Feb. 7 [1839], *FL*, 2:47.

20. John D. Davies, *Phrenology, Fad and Science: A 19th Century Crusade* (New Haven, 1955), 1–11; Madeleine B. Stern, "Margaret Fuller and the Phrenologist-Publishers," in Myerson, *American Renaissance* (1980), 229; JFC, "Journal of People and Things," PCMHi; see *Pseudo-Science and Society in Nineteenth-Century America*, ed. Arthur Wrobel (Lexington, KY, 1988), esp. Wrobel, "Introduction," and Harold Aspiz, "Sexuality and the Pseudo-Sciences."

21. MF to CS, Oct. 14, 1837, *FL*, 1:304.

22. MF, *Woman in the Nineteenth Century* (New York, 1845), 91 (hereafter cited as *WNC*); also *EJ*, 9:471; Charles R. Crowe, "Transcendentalism and the Providence Literati," *Rhode Island History* 14 (July, 1955): 73. Since Whitman's record of the evening was written many years after the event, it is likely that Fuller's subsequent reputation colored Whitman's memory.

23. *OM*, 1:181; Windsor P. Daggett, *A Down-East Yankee from the District of Maine* (Portland, ME, 1920), 32; see also John Neal, *Wandering Recollections of a Somewhat Busy Life* (Boston, 1869), and Benjamin Lease, *That Wild Fellow John Neal and the American Literary Revolution* (Chicago, 1972).

24. Crowe, "Transcendentalism," 66.

25. RWE, "Historic Notes of Life and Letters in New England," in Miller, *Transcendentalists*, 494; Tess Hoffman, "Miss Fuller among the Literary Lions: Two Essays Read at 'The Coliseum' in 1838," in Myerson, *American Renaissance* (1988), 45, 49–50.

26. MF to RWE, Mar. 1, 1838, *FL*, 1:327.

27. MF to JFC, Mar. 18, 1838, FP.

28. *The Collected Works of Ralph Waldo Emerson*, ed. Robert E. Spiller and Alfred R. Ferguson, 4 vols. to date (Cambridge, MA, 1971–), 2: 153 (hereafter cited as *CWRWE*).

29. RWE to MF, June 28, 1838, *EmL*, 2:142–43.

30. SGW to Mary Ward, Nov. 8, 1836, TWWardMHi.

31. MF, "fragment of the journal," Aug. 1838, MFOC, 122.

32. SGW, "Long Letter," 143, TWWardMHi.

33. For the description of Anna Barker in Europe, see Farrar, *Recollections*, 273–75.

34. Miller, *Transcendentalists*, 198.

35. MF to Jane Tuckerman, Sept. 21, 1833, FL, 1: 341; MF to JFC, Sept. 15, 1838, FP.

36. MCF to ABF, Mar. 26, 1838, FMW, 8:18. See William Charvat, "American Romanticism and the Depression of 1837," *Science and Society* 2 (Winter 1937): 67–82.

37. MF, "Karl Theodor Koerner," *Western Messenger* 4 (Jan. 1838): 309. MF, "*Letters from Palmyra*," *Western Messenger* 5 (Apr. 1838): 26.

38. JFC to MF, Mar. 1, 1838, ClLetMF, 129; MF to JFC, May 13, 1838, FP; JFC to MF, May 21, 1838, ClLetMF, 132. A valuable discussion of "impressionism" in Fuller is in Henry Lawrence Golemba, *The Balanced View in Margaret Fuller's Literary Criticism* (Ann Arbor, MI, 1983), 75–79.

39. MF to Jane Tuckerman, Sept. 21, 1838, *FL*, 1:341–42.

40. MF to Charles F. Newcomb, Sept. 28, 1838, *FL*, 1:342.

41. Albert, "Fuller and Allen," 13; Frank Sheffelton, "The Journal of Evelina Metcalf," in Myerson, *American Renaissance* (1985), 42.

42. Julia Ward Howe, *Reminiscences* (Boston, 1900), 250; Bolster, *Clarke*, 144.

43. MF to WHC, Dec. 9, 1838, *FL*, 1:354.

Chapter 7. Episodes in the Crusade

1. MF to George Ripley, Feb. 25, [1839], *FL*, 2:52.

2. JFC to Thomas Wentworth Higginson, Sept. 19, 1883, MFOC, 198; RFF*Rec*, 43.

3. MF to Charles Newcomb, Mar. 4, 1839, *FL*, 2:56–57.

4. MF to ABF, [Mar. 10, 1839], *FL*, 2:62.

5. EH to RWE, Mar. 27, 1841, Hoar, Part 3 (1986), 120; EH to Hannah L. Chappell, Apr. 3, 1839, Hoar, Part 2 (1985), 151–52.

6. EH to Mary Moody Emerson, Apr. 3, 1839, Hoar, Part 2 (1985), 151–52. For Emerson's relationship with Mary Moody Emerson, see Evelyn Barish, *Emerson: The Roots of Prophecy* (Princeton, NJ, 1989), 36–53. For Moody's views on Fuller, see *The Selected Letters of Mary Moody Emerson*, ed. Nancy Craig Simmons (Athens, GA, 1993), 523, 527, 551–52.

7. For a modern biography of Varnhagen that captures the spirit that appealed to Fuller, see Clara Malraux, *Rahel, ma grande soeur: un salon littéraire à Berlin au temps du romanticism* (Paris, 1980); also Kate Vaughan Jennings, *Rahel: Her Life and Letters* (London, 1883); Ellen Karolina Sofia Key, *Rahel Varnhagen: A Portrait* (London, 1913).

8. MF to Sarah Helen Whitman, June 10, 1839, *FL*, 2:75; to [?], May 13, 1839, *FL*, 2:66; to Charles K. Newcomb, May 29, 1839, *FL*, 2:68. For the influence of William Ellery Channing's Unitarianism on Washington Allston's paintings, see Wolf, *Romantic Revision*, 25–45.

9. MF to CS, Jan. 10, 1839, *FL*, 2:35.

10. Ibid.

11. MF to CS, Feb. 7, [1839], Feb. 2, 1839, *FL*, 2: 46, 45.

12. MF to CS, Oct. 7, 1839, *FL*, 2:94, note.

13. MF to EF, June 8, 1839, *FL*, 2:73; RWE to MF, June 7, 1839, *EmL*, 2:202; Frederick Augustus Braun, *Margaret Fuller and Goethe* (New York, 1910), 173; Joel Myerson, *Margaret Fuller: An Annotated Secondary Bibliography* (New York, 1977), 2 (hereafter cited as Myerson, *Sec. Bib.*); MF to EF, June 8, 1839, *FL*, 2:73. For a description of the censure Fuller courted, see Hig*MFO*, 283.

14. MF to SGW, July, 1839, *FL*, 2:81.

15. MF to [?], May 13, 1839, *FL*, 2:66; to SGW, [Sept. 1839], *FL*, 2:91.

16. See Tilton, "True Romance," 64.

17. MF to CS, Feb. [21?], 1839, *FL*, 2:49. For Emerson's friendship with Ward, see Baldwin, "Emerson–Ward." The footnotes to the Ward letters in *EmL*, vols. 7 and 8, ed. Eleanor M. Tilton, are very helpful.

18. "Margaret Fuller's 1839 Trip to Bristol," ed. Robert N. Hudspeth, *Harvard Library Bulletin* 27 (Oct. 1979): 456, 467–68, 464 (hereafter cited as FJ39).

19. MF to SGW, [early Sept. 1839], *FL*, 2:94. Tilton points out that this letter exists only in a partial copy that Fuller made and kept. "One would like to think that she had the wit not to mail it or that this portion did not get into the final letter" (Tilton, "True Romance," 65).

20. *EJ*, 7:259–60.

21. " 'The Impulses of Human Nature': Margaret Fuller's Journal from June through October 1844," ed. Martha L. Berg and Alice de V. Perry, *Proceedings of the Massachusetts Historical Society* 102 (1990): 77 (hereafter cited as FJ44). For a discussion of how the concept of "Platonic love" may have influenced Fuller's sexual distancing, see Cott, "Passionlessness," 162–81.

22. MF to SGW, Oct. 15, 1839, *FL*, 2:95.

23. MF to CS, Oct. 7, 1839, *FL*, 2:93.

24. RWE to CS, Sept. 6, 1840, *EmL*, 7:402; *EJ*, 7:274.

25. MF, "Lines October 1839," FMW, box A. For an analysis of Fuller's poems, see Steele, "Freeing," 137–76.

26. MF to RWE, [Apr. 25], 1840, *FL*, 2:133. For the story of the carbuncle as a talisman in Novalis, see "*Heinrich von Ofterdingen*: Ein nachgelassener Roman von Novalis," in *Novalis: Das dichterische Werk, Tagebücher, und Briefe*, ed. Richard Samuel (Munich: Carl Hanser, 1978), 1:265; see also *EJ*, 11:259, where Emerson notes that Fuller inscribed a Novalis hymn in her Bible.

27. FMW, box A.

28. FMW, box A.

29. Ibid.

30. *OM*, 1:247.

31. FMW, box A. For American opinion on George Sand, see Howard Mumford Jones, "American Comment on George Sand," *American Literature* 3 (Jan. 1932): 389–407.

32. FMW, Works 3:303–5. Fuller's perception of a clear distinction between the subject matter of men and women writers and her concern that her desire to write one way or the other indicated male or female qualities in her personality raise questions that are discussed in several recent studies of women and authorship in nineteenth-century America. On Fuller in particular, see Ann Douglas, "Margaret Fuller and the Disavowal of Fiction," in *The Feminization of American Culture* (New York, 1977), 259–88; Susan Phinney Conrad, "The Beauty of a Stricter Method: Margaret Fuller, Interpreter of Romanticism," in *Perish the Thought: Intellectual Women in Romantic America, 1830–1860* (New York, 1976), 45–92. For "the literary domestics," see Kelley, *Private Woman;* for the influence of marketplace values on women writers, see Coultrap-McQuin, *Doing Business;* see also Nina Baym, *Woman's Fiction: A Guide to Novels by and about Women in America, 1820–1870* (Ithaca, NY, 1979).

33. Margaret Fuller Scrapbook, 1836–1844, PCMHi (hereafter cited as FS), "Notes from October 1839," 173.

34. Sophia Ripley to John S. Dwight, Aug. 1, 1840, in Zoltan Haraszti, *The Idyll of Brook Farm as Revealed by Unpublished Letters in the Boston Public Library* (Boston, 1940), 13; MF to [Sophia Ripley?], Aug. 27, 1839, *FL*, 2:86–87.

35. Patricia Dunlavy Valenti, "Sophia Peabody Hawthorne: A Study of Artistic Influence," in Myerson, *American Renaissance* (1990), 12. For contemporary accounts of the Conversations, see *OM*, 1:317 ff.; Caroline W. Healey Dall, *Margaret and Her Friends* (Boston, 1895); and Elizabeth Palmer Peabody, *Reminiscences of Rev. Wm. Ellery Channing, D.D.* (Boston, 1880), 403–5; James Freeman Clarke, "Notes on Grecian Mythology—Class with S. M. Fuller," PCMHi, vol. 67.

36. *OM*, 1: 329.

37. Ibid. For an imaginative study of how Fuller's use of Greek myths contributed to her developing vision of "woman's being" freed "from inhibiting patriarchal assumptions," see Jeffrey Steele, *Representation of the Self in the American Renaissance* (Chapel Hill, NC, 1987), 101–33; see also Julie Ellison, *Delicate Subjects: Romanticism, Gender, and the Ethics of Understanding* (Ithaca, NY, 1990), 240–60; Charles Capper, "Margaret Fuller as Cultural Reformer: The Conversations in Boston," *American Quarterly* 39 (Winter 1987): 517–18.

38. MF to [?], Nov. 25, 1839, *FL*, 2:102; Myerson, "Sarah Clarke," 165.

39. Dall, *Margaret*, 13; Joel Myerson, "Caroline Healey Dall's Reminiscences of Margaret Fuller," *Harvard Library Bulletin* 22, no. 4 (Oct. 1974): 416; Dall, *Margaret*, 42, 78.

40. MF to [?], [ca. Autumn? 1839?], *FL*, 2:97; Joel Myerson, "Mrs. Dall Edits Miss Fuller: The Story of *Margaret and Her Friends*," *Papers of the Bibliographical Society of America* 72 (1978): 191; Myerson, "Dall's Reminiscences," 416.

41. MF to [?], Nov. 25, 1839, *FL*, 2: 101; to [?], [ca. Autumn 1839], *FL*, 2: 97.

42. RFF*Rec*, 65; MF to WHC, Nov. 8, [1840], *FL*, 2:184. For an analysis of Fuller's theatricality, see Ellison, *Delicate Subjects*, 241–56.

43. Peabody, *Reminiscences*, 403–4; MF to Maria Weston Chapman, Dec. 26, 1840, *FL*, 2:197.

44. *Martineau's Autobiography*, 2:71.

45. RWE to MF, Nov. 14, 1839, Mar. 3, 1840, *EmL*, 2:234, 259.

46. *OM*, 1:350.

47. Chevigny, *Woman and Myth*, 213; MF to Sarah Helen Whitman, Jan. 21, 1840, *FL*, 2:118.

48. MF to Jane Tuckerman, Aug. 1839, *FL*, 2:82–83.

Chapter 8. The Dial

1. See Myerson, *Transcendentalism and the "Dial,"* chaps. 1–3.

2. RWE to MF, [Nov. 14, 1839], Dec. 12, 1839, *EmL*, 2:234, 243.

3. MF to WHC, Jan. 1, 1840, *FL*, 2:111; to FHH, Jan. 1, 1840, *FL*, 2:113; to JFC, Jan. 1, 1840, FP.

4. MF to FHH, Mar. 10, 1840, *FL*, 2:125.

5. Ibid.; MF to JFC, Jan. 1, 1840, FP. For Hedge's position, see Myerson, "Frederic Henry Hedge and the Failure of Transcendentalism," *Harvard Library Bulletin* 33 (Oct. 1975): 396–410; Doreen Hunter, "Frederic Henry Hedge, What Say You?" *American Quarterly* 32, no. 2 (Summer 1980): 186–

201; Alfred G. Litton, "The Development of the Mind and the Role of the Scholar in the Early Works of Frederic Henry Hedge," in Myerson, *American Renaissance* (1989), 95–113.

6. Theodore Parker to Convers Francis, Dec. 6, 1839, Ms c.1.6., Boston Public Library; FS, 168. For speculation on the relationship between Fuller and Parker, see Myerson, "Dall's Reminiscences," 420.

7. MF to WHC, Mar. 22, 1840, *FL*, 2:126.

8. MF to WHC, Apr. 19, 1840, *FL*, 2:130–31.

9. Myerson, *Transcendentalism and the "Dial,"* 44.

10. RWE to MF, Apr. 8, 1840, *EmL*, 2:275; Journal 1840, box 3.

11. MF to WHC[?], 1840, *FL*, 2:109, 108.

12. FMW, Journal, box A; "Chat in Boston Bookstores," *Boston Quarterly Review* 3 (Jan. 1840): 127–34 (July 1840): 323–31.

13. FMW, 1: 593, 589. For the problems of finding language and literary forms to express feminine thought, see Homans, *Bearing the Word*, passim, and Kaplan, *Sea Changes*, 69–84.

14. RWE to Thomas Carlyle, Apr. 12, 1840, in *The Correspondence of Emerson and Carlyle*, ed. Joseph Slater (New York: Columbia University Press, 1964), 261 (hereafter cited as *E&C*).

15. HigMFO, 152–53.

16. Myerson, *Transcendentalism and the "Dial,"* 51; RWE to MF, July 2, 1840, *EmL*, 2:311, 316; Myerson, *Transcendentalism and the "Dial,"* 56, 201, 50.

17. RWE to MF, Aug. 4, 1840, *EmL*, 2:322, Nov. 27, 1839, *EmL*, 7:239, 240; MF, journal fragment, [ca. Jan. 22, 1840?], *FL*, 2: 161 n.

18. RWE to MF, Feb. 21, 1840, *EmL*, 2:255; *EJ*, 8; RWE to CS, July 21, 1840, *EmL*, 7:396. For the details of Ward's journey and difficulties, see Tilton, "True Romance," 57–71. See also David Baldwin, "Puritan Aristocrat in the Age of Emerson: A Study of Samuel Gray Ward" (Ph.D. diss., University of Pennsylvania, 1961), 106–13. Commentary on Jacob Barker is in Nelson Frederick Adkins, *Fitz-Greene Halleck: An Early Knickerbocker Wit and Poet* (New Haven, 1930), 335–37, 109, 133–35, 167–69; Donald Fitch, "The Ward–Perkins Papers," *Soundings* (Santa Barbara, CA, 1985), 42.

19. MF to CS, July 12, 1840, *FL*, 2:150; FS, 172.

20. MF to CS, [1840?], *FL*, 2:107, 105.

21. *EJ*, 7:509.

22. Ibid.

23. Ibid., 512.

24. RWE to MF, Aug. 29, 1840, *EmL*, 2: 327–28.

25. MF to WHC, Nov. 8, [1840], *FL*, 2:183; to CS, Oct. 18, [1840], *FL*, 2:163; to WHC, Oct. 25, 28, 1840[III], *FL*, 2:174. There is some question as to whether Fuller attended the Barker–Ward marriage (see Tilton, "True Romance," 70). Emerson noted in his "Notebook, Margaret Fuller Ossoli," *EJ*, 11:487, that "She went, from the most joyful of all bridals, to attend a near relative during a formidable surgical operation." This would suggest that Fuller attended the wedding and then accompanied her brother Arthur to an operation on the eye he lost during the early days at Groton in 1833.

26. *EJ*, 7:509.

27. RWE to MF, Sept. 25, 1840, *EmL*, 2:336–37.

28. Ibid., 336; *EJ*, 7:400.

29. MF to RWE, Sept. 29, 1840, *FL*, 2: 159–60.

30. RWE to MF, Oct. 1, 1840, Nov. 14, 1839, *EmL*, 2:340, 235–36.

31. MF to CS, Oct. 22, 1840, *FL*, 2:167.

32. RWE to MF, Oct. 24, 1840, *EmL*, 2:352–53.

33. RWE to CS, [ca. Aug.? 20?, 1840?], *EmL*, 2:326. In analyzing the friendship debate, I have found most useful the following articles: Christina Zwarg, "Emerson as 'Mythologist' in *Memoirs of Margaret Fuller Ossoli*," *Criticism* 31 (Summer 1989): 213–33; Dorothy Berkson, " 'Born and Bred in Different Nations': Margaret Fuller and Ralph Waldo Emerson," in *Patrons and Protegees: Gender, Friendship, and Writing in Nineteenth-Century America*, ed. Shirley Marchalonis (New Brunswick, NJ, 1988), 3–30; George Sebouhian, "A Dialogue with Death: An Examination of Emerson's 'Friendship,' " in Myerson, *American Renaissance* (1989), 219–39; Carl F. Strauch, "Hatred's Swift Repulsions: Emerson, Margaret Fuller, and Others," *Studies in Romanticism* 7, no. 2 (Winter 1968): 65–103; Marie Olesen Urbanski, "The Ambivalence of Ralph Waldo Emerson towards Margaret Fuller," *Thoreau Quarterly Journal* 10 (1978): 26–36.

34. *OM*, 1:268.

35. RWE to MF, Sept. 25, 1840, *EmL*, 2:336–37.

36. *EJ*, 8:131.

37. Nicholas Boyle, *Goethe: The Poet and the Age* (Oxford, 1991), 608; MF to CS, [ca. Oct. 1840], *FL*, 2:170.

38. MF to CS, Sept. 8, [1840], *FL*, 2:157; to WHC, Oct. 25, 28, 1840[I], *FL*, 2:171; to CS, Oct. 22, 1840, *FL*, 2:167–68.

39. For Goethe's poem "Daemon," see Johann Wolfgang Goethe, *The Eternal Feminine: Selected Poems of Goethe* (bilingual ed.), ed. Frederick Ungar (New York, 1980), 152–55; for occultism and the supernatural in Goethe, see Albrecht Schöne, *Götterzeichen, Liebeszauber, Satanskult: neue Einblicke in alte Goethetexte* (Munich, 1982).

40. MF to WHC, Oct. 25, 28, 1840[I], *FL*, 2:171; Myerson, *Transcendentalism and the "Dial,"* 58.

41. MF to RWE, Dec. 6, 1840, *FL*, 2:189.

42. Myerson, *Transcendentalism and the "Dial,"* 57.

43. MF to WHC, [Apr. 5, 1841], *FL*, 2:206; MF, Journal, Jan. 5, 1841, MFOC, 132.

44. MF to WHC, Feb. 19, 1841[I], *FL*, 2:202.

45. Crowe, *Ripley*, 121.

46. MF to WHC[?], Mar. 29, 1841, *FL*, 2:205.

47. MF to WHC, Oct. 25, 28, 1840[III], *FL*, 2:173; to JFC, Mar. 18, 1838, Oct. 1, [1837], FP; see also *OM*, 1:99 ("that there would be none on whom I could always lean, from whom I could always learn; that I should be a pilgrim and a sojourner on earth, and that the birds and foxes would be surer of a place to lay the head than I"); MFOC, 120, and Hig*MFO*, 232–33 ("I have no home on earth.... But driven from home to home as a Renouncer ...").

Chapter 9. A Sojourner on Earth

1. Fuller's "Autobiographical Romance"—the title assigned the fragment in *OM*—appears as *OM*'s first chapter (*OM*, 1:11–42). See also Steele, *Essential*, 24–43. For the importance of friendships in women's identity formation as expressed in autobiographies, see Paul John Eakin, *Touching the World* (Princeton, NJ, 1992), 80–82; Sidonie Smith, "Resisting the Gaze of Embodiment: Women's Autobiography in the Nineteenth Century," in *American Women's Autobiography: Fea(s)ts of Memory*, ed. Mary Culley (Madison, WI, 1992).

2. For Charles Newcomb at Brook Farm, see Kirby, *Years*, 105–6. See also the introduction to *The Journals of Charles King Newcomb*, ed. Judith Kennedy Johnson (Providence, 1946).

3. John Weiss, *The Life and Correspondence of Theodore Parker*, 2 vols. (New York, 1864), 1: 99.

4. RF to MF, July 17, 1841, *FL*, 2: 218 n. 4. For Ellen Fuller's problems with the Keats family, see Madeleine B. Stern, "Four Letters from George Keats," *PMLA* 56 (Mar. 1941): 207–18.

5. MF to MCF, July 20, 1841, *FL*, 2:217.

6. "'A Tale of Mizraim': A Forgotten Story by Margaret Fuller," attributed by Jeffrey Steele, *New England Quarterly*, Mar. 1989, 82–104; MF to JFC, [Mar. 29, 1835], *FL*, 1:229.

7. Robert N. Hudspeth, *Ellery Channing* (New York, 1973), 22; see also William Ellery Channing to MCF, Sept. 5, 1841, in Francis B. Dedmond, "The Selected Letters of William Ellery Channing the Younger (Part One)," in Myerson, *American Renaissance* (1989), 159.

8. MF to RWE, Sept. 16, 1841, *FL*, 2:232.

9. CS to MF, Sept. 8, 1841, Sturgis Letters, 219; CS to RWE, Oct. 16, 1841, Tappan Family Papers, bMS Am 1221, n. 334, Houghton Library, Harvard University, 334. By permission of the Houghton Library, Harvard University.

10. MF to CS, [1840?], *FL*, 2:107.

11. MF to WHC[?], ca. Oct. 31, 1840, *FL*, 2:179.

12. RWE to MF, July 31, Aug. 2, 1841, *EmL*, 2:438.

13. MF to RWE, [Oct. 1841?], Letter no. 323, *FL*, 2:233.

14. MF to RWE, [Oct. 1841?], *FL*, 2:236.

15. *EJ*, 8:109.

16. *OM*, 1:228.

17. RFF*Rec*, 50; MF to RFF, May 25, 1841, *FL*, 2:210.

18. EF to MF, Dec. 5, 1841, FMW, 17:6.

19. MF to RWE, Nov. [9?], 1841, *FL*, 2:250.

20. For a description of Boston in the early 1840s, see Oscar Handlin, *Boston's Immigrants: A Study in Acculturation*, rev. and enl. ed. (Cambridge, MA, 1979), chap. 1; Justin Winsor, *Memorial History of Boston, including Suffolk County, Massachusetts, 1630–1880* (Boston, 1881), Vol. 4.

21. For the development of Boston's musical culture, see Michael Broyles, *"Music of the Highest Class": Elitism and Populism in Antebellum Boston* (New Haven, 1992), 182–268.

22. SGW, "Long Letter," 103, TWWardMHi. E. Digby Baltzell, *Puritan Boston and Quaker Philadelphia* (New York, 1979), is helpful in understanding class attitudes in Boston at this time.

23. RWE to MF, Jan. 28, 1842, *EmL*, 3:8.

24. MF to RWE, [Mar. 17? 1842], *FL*, 3:54.

25. For the evolution of Fuller's critical theory, see Hudspeth, "Higher Standard," 145–62.

26. MF to [Sophia Ripley], Aug. 27, 1839, *FL*, 2:87; [George Bancroft], "Goethe: His Character as a Writer and as a Man," *Christian Examiner* 26 (July 1839): 361–68.

27. Steele, *Representation*, 100–33; Jeffrey Steele, "The Call of Eurydice: Mourning and Intertextuality in Margaret Fuller's Writing," in *Influence and Intertextuality in Literary History*, ed. Jay Clayton and Eric Rothstein (Madison, WI, 1991), 271–97.

28. MF to JFC, Jan. 9, 1845, FP.

29. RWE to MF, Mar. 21, 1842, *EmL*, 3:35; MF to RWE, Apr. 9, 1842, *FL*, 3:58.

30. MF to RWE, Apr. 9, 1842, *FL*, 3:58.

31. MF to RWE, June 23, 1842, *FL*, 3:70.

32. Sophia Dana Ripley to MF, [July 1842?], FMW, 17:48; Haraszti, *Idyll*, 18.

33. For the Dorr Rebellion, see Marvin E. Gettleman, *The Dorr Rebellion: A Study in American Radicalism, 1833–1849* (New York, 1973), 132.

34. MF to WHC[?], July 1842, *FL*, 3:72, 74. An explanation of Fuller's fastidious reaction is given in Ellison, *Delicate Subjects*, 261–63.

35. David M. Robinson, "The Political Odyssey of William Henry Channing," *American Quarterly* 34, no. 2 (1982): 167; O. B. Frothingham, *Memoir of William Henry Channing* (Cambridge, MA, 1886), 280.

36. *OM*, 2: 7–8.

37. Frothingham, *Memoir*, 181, 161.

38. Ibid., 181.

39. MFOC, 97; Braun, *Fuller and Goethe*, 257. Fuller's credo (1842) is published in full in Braun, *Fuller and Goethe*, 248–57, and in part in Chevigny, *Woman and Myth*, 170–71.

40. MF to WHC[?], Aug. 25, 1842, *FL*, 3:91–92.

41. MF to RWE, Aug. 10, 1842, *FL*, 3:83; RWE to MF, Aug. 12, 1842, *EmL*, 3:80.

Chapter 10. Marriage Studies

1. RWE to Charles King Newcomb, May 7, 8, 1842, *EmL*, 3:51; to MF, Aug. 12, 1842, *EmL*, 3:81.

2. "Margaret Fuller's 1842 Journal: At Concord with the Emersons," ed. Joel Myerson, *Harvard Library Bulletin* 21 (July 1973): 322 (hereafter cited as FJ42-1).

3. Bedell, *Alcotts*, 161.

4. *The Centenary Edition of the Works of Nathaniel Hawthorne*, ed. William L. Charvat et al., 20 vols. to date (Columbus, OH, 1962–), 8:315, 316 (hereafter cited as *Centenary*).

5. James R. Mellow, *Nathaniel Hawthorne in His Time* (Boston, 1980), 211–12.

6. *EJ*, 11: 482; Sophia Peabody Hawthorne (SPH) to MF, FMW, 16:20.

7. Nathaniel Hawthorne (NH) to SPH, Apr. 13, 1841, Dec. 5, 1839, *Centenary*, 15:527, 382.

8. FJ42-1, 325.

9. Ibid.; *Centenary*, 8:343.

10. *Centenary*, 8:343.

11. NH to MF, Aug. 25, 1842, *Centenary*, 15:646–47; FJ42-1, 328. The Hawthorne marriage is analyzed in T. Walter Herbert, *Dearest Beloved: The Hawthornes and the Making of the Middle-Class Family* (Berkeley, CA, 1993); several of the themes there explored have a bearing on Nathaniel Hawthorne's relationship to Fuller.

12. *OM*, 1:350.

13. FJ42-1, 328. For the Alcott marriage, see Bedell, *Alcotts*, passim; Anne C. Rose, *Transcendentalism as a Social Movement* (New Haven, 1981), 198–202 (hereafter cited as Rose, *Social Movement*).

14. FJ42-1, 330. A valuable discussion of Emerson's philosophy of love and marriage is in Erik Ingvar Thurin, *Emerson as Priest of Pan* (Lawrence, KS, 1981), 26–47, 64–70, 96–111, 221–29.

15. *EJ*, 7:48.

16. FJ42-1, 335.

17. *EJ*, 8:95, 7:336, 8:144.

18. *EJ*, 8:34.

19. FJ42-1, 324.

20. Ibid., 331.

21. Ibid.

22. Ibid., 331–32.

23. Ibid., 336, 337, 339.

24. Ibid., 329.

25. Ibid.

26. Ibid., 334–36.

27. Robinson, "Political Odyssey," 171. At this time Hedge was writing "Conservatism and Reform," an address that considered the role of the scholar in society. See Litton, "Development," 95–114.

28. FJ42-1, 336–37.

29. Ibid.

30. MF, "Bettina Brentano and Günderode," *Dial*, Jan. 1842, 314–15; FJ42-1, 340. On the marriage of Lidian Jackson and Ralph Waldo Emerson, see Rose, *Social Movement*, 165–74, and Joel Porte, *Representative Man: Ralph Waldo Emerson in His Time* (New York, 1974), 214–21, 348 n.4; Ellen Tucker Emerson, *The Life of Lidian Jackson Emerson,* ed. Delores Bird Carpenter (Boston, 1980).

Chapter 11. "The Great Lawsuit"

1. MCF to MF, Apr. 20, 1841, FMW, 17:4a.

2. "Margaret Fuller's Journal for October 1842," ed. Robert D. Habich, *Harvard Library Bulletin* 33 (Summer 1985): 291 (hereafter cited as FJ42-2); MF to EH, Jan. 30, 1843, *FL*, 3:118.

3. FJ42-2, 285; MF to EH, Jan. 30, 1843, *FL*, 3:118; to RWE[?], [Dec.] 26, 1842[II], *FL*, 3:110.

4. MF to JFC, Sept. 9, 1842, FP; to EH, Jan. 16, [1843], Jan. 30, 1843, *FL*, 3: 114, 118.

5. MF to GTD, Dec. 17, 1842, *FL*, 3:105.

6. FJ42-2, 286–87. Fuller probably read about the friendship of de Staël and Récamier in Albertine Neckar de Saussure, *Notice sur le caractère et les écrits de Madame de Staël* (London, 1820), of which there were two copies in Elizabeth Palmer Peabody's Foreign Library. See Madeleine B. Stern, *Books and Book People in Nineteenth Century America* (New York, 1978), 128, 131. Citations to recent works dealing with same-sex relationships among women in the antebellum period are given in chap. 3, n. 42, herein, and in Lee Chambers-Schiller, *Liberty, a Better Husband: Single Women in America, the Generations of 1780–1840* (New Haven, 1984), 43, 203, 206–7, 212 (of particular relevance to Fuller's musings in her journal).

7. FJ42-2, 287.

8. For an illuminating discussion of Fuller's discomfort with the traditional gender divisions of her time, see Mary E. Wood, "With Ready Eye: Margaret Fuller and Lesbianism in Nineteenth-Century American Literature," *American Literature* 65 (Mar. 1993): 1–18.

9. FJ42-2, 290.

10. SAC to JFC, July 20, 1840, Jan. 26, 1834, Nov. 17, 1839, ClLetSister; Myerson, "Mrs. Dall Edits Miss Fuller," 189.

11. MF to RWE, Dec. [4?], 1842[II], *FL*, 3:103.

12. For Fuller's friendship with Bruce, see Kirby, *Years*, 101–2, 113, 115, 190, 205–14; see also Lindsay Swift, *Brook Farm* (New York, 1961), 212–13.

13. MF to EH, Jan. 30, 1843, *FL*, 3:119.

14. *Westminster Review* 35, no. 1 (Jan. 1841): 50.

15. Sophia Ripley, "Woman," *Dial* 1, no. 3 (Jan. 1841): 362, 363.

16. MF, "The Great Lawsuit: Man *versus* Men, Woman *versus* Women," *Dial* 4 (July 1834): 4, 8.

17. Ibid., 7.

18. Ibid., 12.

19. Ibid., 22, 15, 16, 18, 35, 43.

20. Ibid., 43, 32, 43.

21. Ibid., 44, 43, 14.

22. Ibid., 38, 14, 38.

23. Ibid., 28, 29–31.

24. Ibid., 23, 44. For a discussion of single lifestyles in Boston, see Pease and Pease, *Web of Progress*; for the advantages and satisfactions of single women in the period, see Chambers-Schiller, *Liberty*.

25. *EJ*, 8:368–69.

26. RWE to MF, Apr. 29, 1843, *EmL*, 3:170; MF to RWE, May 9, [1843], *FL*, 3:124.

27. RWE to MF, July 11, 1843, *EmL*, 3:183. For the relationship of "talking with pen in hand" to transcendental prose, see Lawrence Buell, *Literary Transcendentalism*, 77–101. See also Henry David Thoreau to RWE, July 8, 1843, in *Familiar Letters of Henry David Thoreau*, ed. Franklin B. Sanborn (Boston, 1894), 44.

Chapter 12. Summer on the Lakes

1. Elizabeth McKinsey, "An American Icon," in *Niagara: Two Centuries of Changing Attitudes* (Washington, DC, 1985), 92–93.

2. Jeremy Elwell Adamson, "Nature's Grandest Scene in Art," ibid., 50; MF, *Summer*, 11.

3. MF, *Summer*, 13, 5, 234–35. For an analysis of responses to Niagara in the 1830s and 1840s, see John F. Sears, *Sacred Places: American Tourist Attractions in the Nineteenth Century* (New York, 1989), chap. 1.

4. MF, *Summer*, 18. In *The Western Experiment: New England Transcendentalists in the Ohio Valley* (Cambridge, MA, 1973), Elizabeth R. McKinsey describes the hopes and disillusionment of Fuller's friends.

5. MF, "Western Journal, 1843," FP, 4–5; MF, *Summer*, 28.

6. MF, "Western Journal, 1843," FP, 6; MF to RWE, June 16, 1843, *FL*, 3:129.

7. MF, "Western Journal, 1843," FP, 7–8.

8. Ibid., 8, 9–10.

9. Ibid., 18–19.

10. Ibid., 9, 12–13.

11. MF, *Summer*, 46. For a history of Hazelwood as well as a commentary on the area Fuller covered on her wagon trip in Illinois, see Richard V. Carpenter, "Margaret Fuller's Visit to Northern Illinois," *Journal of Illinois State Historical Society* 2 (Jan. 1910): 7–22.

12. MF to RFF, July 29, 1843, *FL*, 3:133.

13. MF, *Summer*, 47.

14. Ibid., 58, 61–62; see also Marcia Noe, "The Heathen Priestess on the Prairie: Margaret Fuller Constructs the Midwest," *Old Northwest* 16, no. 1 (Spring 1992): 3–12.

15. MF, *Summer*, 116.

16. Ibid., 120–21.

17. Ibid., 195.

18. Ibid., 246.

19. Hig*MFO*, 194.

20. MF to RWE, Nov. 12, 1843, *FL*, 3:159–60.

21. MF to Anna Barker Ward (ABW), Dec. 26, 1843, *FL*, 3:164–65.

22. MF, *Summer*, 6. Two recent editions of *Summer on the Lakes, in 1843* contain useful introductions: the facsimile edition, with introduction by Madeleine B. Stern, (Nieuwkoop, 1972), vii–xxxv; a 1991 edition, with introduction by Susan Belasco Smith (Urbana, IL, 1991), vii–xxii. The book's position in the travelogue genre is skillfully explained in William W. Stowe, "Conventions and Voices in Margaret Fuller's Travel Writing," *American Literature* 63, no. 2 (June 1991): 242–62. For two perspectives on how Fuller's themes proved adaptable to the travelogue form, see Annette Kolodny, *The Land before Her: Fantasy and Experience of the American Frontiers, 1630–1860* (Chapel Hill, NC, 1984), 118–30; Stephen Adams, " 'That Tidiness We Always Look For in Woman': Fuller's *Summer on the Lakes* and Romantic Aesthetics," in Myerson, *American Renaissance* (1987), 247–64.

23. MF, *Summer*, 115.

24. Ibid., 63, 35.

25. Ibid., 234, 195; see Reginald Horsman, "Scientific Racism and the American Indian in the Mid-Nineteenth Century," *American Quarterly*, no. 2 (May 1975): 152–68.

26. MF, *Summer*, 131, 133.

27. Ibid., 235–36.

28. Ibid., 254–55.

29. MF to RWE, May 9, [1844], *FL*, 3:196.

30. LMC to MF, Aug. 23, 1844, *Child Letters*, 211–12.

31. *MFCrEssays*, 5.

32. MF to WHC, [June? 1844], *FL*, 3:198. By January 1845 some 700 copies of *Summer on the Lakes, in 1843* had been sold.

33. Myerson, *Sec. Bib.*, 7; MF, "Fragments of Margaret Fuller's Journal: 1844–1845," Fruitlands Museum, Harvard, MA (hereafter cited as MHarF); Anne Warren Weston to Caroline and Deborah Weston, [1845?], Weston Papers, 16:13, Boston Public Library.

34. RFF*Rec*, 63. When Emerson compiled his Margaret Fuller Ossoli notebook in preparation for the *Memoirs*, he copied in his calendar of Fuller's life an inscription from her 1844 journal, March 27, " 'time of almost unbearable anguish' " (*EJ*, 11:507).

35. For the evidence that Fuller experienced unrequited romantic expectations in her friendship with William Hull Clarke, see FJ44, 43–51, 56.

36. MF to CS, May 25, [1844], *FL*, 3:197.

37. FJ44, 118–19, 56.

38. Lawsuit, 17, 14, 26–27, 47. Helpful in understanding Fuller's argument is Cott, "Passionlessness," 162–81.

39. FJ44, 71, 77.

40. Ibid., 89.

41. Ibid., 92.

42. Ibid., 83, 93, 105, 94.

43. Ibid., 73.

44. *OM*, 2:136; *EJ*, 7:132, 172–73; *EJ*, 11:463 and *OM*, 1:135; Mellow, 211–12; Steele, *Essential*, 240; see also Steele, "Freeing," 80.

45. E. Marion Evans to Mrs. Peter Alfred Taylor, March 27, 1852, Eliot, 2:15; "Fragments of Margaret Fuller's Journal," 1844–1845, MHarF. See also *Essays of George Eliot*, ed. Thomas Phinney (New York, 1963), 199. The phrase also struck Emerson; it was one of the few he copied from Fuller's 1844 journal into the "Margaret Fuller Ossoli Journal" that he prepared while working on *OM*. See *EJ*, 11:498.

46. FJ44, 107–8; for Emerson's oration and attitude toward abolition, see Len Gougeon, *Virtue's Hero: Emerson, Antislavery, and Reform* (Athens, GA, 1990, 73–85.

47. Lloyd Fuller to MF, June 30, 1844, FMW, XV, 9; *EJ*, XI, 440.

48. FJ44, 115, 118.

49. Ibid., 119.

50. *OM*, 1:239 and *EJ*, 11:259; to JFC, [March 28? 1830], *FL*, 1:163; to EPP, Dec. 26, 1844, *FL*, 3:254.

Chapter 13. Woman in the Nineteenth Century

1. MF to Georgiana Bruce, Aug. 15, 1844, *FL*, 3:223.

2. MF to Georgiana Bruce, Oct. 20, 1844, *FL*, 3:236; Kirby, *Years*, 211; see also MF to EH, Oct. 20 [28?], 1844, *FL*, 3:237. For corroboration in recent research of Bruce's attitude, see Christine Stansell, *City of Women* (New York, 1986), 175–80. The prison reform program initiated by Eliza Farnham is discussed in W. David Lewis, *From Newgate to Dannemora: The Rise of the Penitentiary in New York* (Ithaca, NY, 1965), 241–55. Farnham later embraced Fuller's program for a unique female role in the progress of humanity, transforming Fuller's vision of the Female Savior into a claim to female superiority in her book, *Woman and Her Era* (1864). Farnham's books on western life are also of interest; see Kolodny, *Land before Her*, 97–110.

3. Stansell, *City of Women*, 174; Robert Carter, *Life in New York* (New York, 1845), 164.

4. *WNC*, 132, 133, 138.

5. Ibid., 134.

6. Ibid., 65.

7. Ibid., 111–12.

8. MF, "Fragments," MHarF; *WNC*, 159.

9. *WNC,* 161.

10. Quoted in Elizabeth K. Helsinger et al., *The Woman Question: Society and Literature in Britain and America, 1837–1883* (Chicago, 1983), 47.

11. *WNC,* v–vi.

12. Ibid., 104–5.

13. For a discussion of Transcendental style, see Buell, *Literary Transcendentalism,* chap. 2.

14. *WNC,* 154, 164.

15. MF to RWE, Nov. 17, 1844, *FL,* 3:243; to WHC, Nov. 17, 1844, *FL,* 3:241.

16. MF to WHC, Nov. 17, 1844, *FL,* 3:242.

17. Ibid.

18. *EJ,* 11:445.

19. Ralph Waldo Emerson, *Essays: Second Series,* historical notes and introduction by Joseph Slater (Cambridge, MA, 1983), 3:88.

20. L[ydia] M[aria] C[hild], "Woman in the Nineteenth Century," *Broadway Journal* 1, no. 7 (Feb. 15, 1845): 97; also *MFCrEssays,* 7. See Marie Olesen Urbanski, *Margaret Fuller's "Woman in the Nineteenth Century": A Literary Study in Form and Content, of Sources and Influence* (Westport, CT, 1980); for an illuminating fresh reading of the text, see Ellison, *Delicate Subjects,* 261–87.

21. Horace Greeley, "Review of *Woman in the Nineteenth Century,*" *Graham's Magazine* 27 (Mar. 1845): 143; Brown, *Fuller,* 132; Myerson, *Sec. Bib.,* 9; C[harles] F[enno] H[offman] to Rufus W. Griswold, Feb. 19, 1845, in Homer F. Barnes, *Charles Fenno Hoffman* (New York, 1930), 256; Julian Hawthorne, *Nathaniel Hawthorne and His Wife* (Boston, 1884), 258; George William Curtis to John S. Dwight, Apr. 5, 1845, in *Early Letters of George Wm. Curtis to John S. Dwight,* ed. George Willis Cooke (New York, 1898), 210.

22. MF to RFF, Mar. 2, 1845, *FL,* 4:54.

23. Poe, *Complete Works,* 15:75; *Broadway Journal* 1 (Mar. 8, 1845): 153; see Burton R. Pollin, "Poe on Margaret Fuller," *Women & Literature* 2 (Spring 1977): 47–50.

24. Perry Miller, *The Raven and the Whale* (New York, 1956), 48; Charles F. Briggs, "Review of *Woman in the Nineteenth Century,*" *Broadway Journal* 1, no. 9 (Mar. 1, 1845): 130–31.

25. LMC to Francis Shaw, [Oct. 1846], *Child Letters,* 231.

26. MF to EF, Mar. 9, 1845, *FL,* 4: 56.

27. Orestes A. Brownson, "Miss Fuller and Reformers," *Brownson's Quarterly Review* 7 (Apr. 1845): 253, also in *MFCrEssays,* 22.

28. F[rederic] D[an] H[untington], review of *Woman in the Nineteenth Century, Christian Examiner* 38 (May 1845): 416–17, copy in FMW, box B, also in *MFCrEssays,* 22; M.A.G., "Review of *Woman in the Nineteenth Century,*" *Southern Quarterly,* July 1846, 170.

29. MF to RFF, Dec. [Nov.] 10, 1845, *FL,* 4:166; *MFCrEssays,* 31.

30. MF to RFF, [Mar. 27, 1845], *FL,* 4:64; CS to MF, Mar. 4, 1845, Sturgis Letters, 239; MF to CS, Mar. 13, 1845, *FL,* 4:59.

31. John Neal to MF, Feb. 28, 1845, FMW, 11:117; RFF to MF, July 1, 1845, FMW, 17:15.

32. MF to RFF, Dec. [Nov.] 10, 1845, [ca. Feb. 13, 1846], *FL,* 4:166, 187.

33. *WNC,* 27; David S. Reynolds, *Beneath the American Renaissance: The Subversive Imagination in the Age of Emerson and Melville* (New York, 1989), 15; MF to EF, Mar. 9, 1845, *FL,* 4:56.

34. LMC to Anna Loring, Feb. 6, 1845, *Child Letters,* 217–18.

Chapter 14. Mary and Horace Greeley

1. Horace Greeley, *Recollections of a Busy Life* (New York, 1869), 176.

2. Ibid. For the family life of the Greeleys, see Cecilia Cleveland, *The Story of a Summer* (New York, 1874); Stern, *Life,* chap. 14.

3. Glyndon G. Van Deusen, *Horace Greeley: Nineteenth Century Crusader* (New York, 1968), 176, 148; MF to SGW, Dec. 29, 1844, *FL,* 3: 256; to EF, Mar. 9, 1845, *FL,* 4:56.

4. Van Deusen, *Greeley,* 145.

5. Daniel Walker Howe, *The Political Culture of the American Whigs* (Chicago, 1979), 187; Van Deusen, *Greeley,* 65. For an excellent summary of Greeley's politics, see Howe, *Political Culture,* 184–97.

6. Van Deusen, *Greeley,* 61.

7. MF to SGW, Dec. 29, 1844, *FL,* 3:256.

8. *OM*, 2:153; Greeley, *Recollections*, 171; *OM*, 2:153–54.

9. *OM*, 2:155–56; Van Deusen, *Greeley*, 76; Greeley, *Recollections*, 177; *OM*, 1:154.

10. Van Deusen, *Greeley*, 51. Howe, *Political Culture*, is the best source for an overall view of Greeley's politics. For Greeley's labor policies, see Sean Wilentz, *Chants Democratic: New York City and the Rise of the Working Class, 1788–1850* (New York, 1984).

11. Karen Ann Szymanski, "Margaret Fuller: The New York Years" (Ph.D. diss., Syracuse University, 1980), 138.

12. *OM*, 2:152–53; Constance Rourke, *Trumpets of Jubilee* (New York, 1927), 256.

13. Horace Greeley, "Margaret Fuller Ossoli," in MF, *Woman in the Nineteenth Century and Kindred Papers*, ed. Arthur B. Fuller (Boston, 1874), 406 (hereafter cited as *WNC-KP*).

14. MF to SGW, Dec. 29, 1844, *FL*, 3: 256.

15. MF to MCF, Jan. 12, 1845, *FL*, 4: 43; *Margaret Fuller: Essays on American Life and Letters*, ed. Joel Myerson (New Haven, 1978), 242, 241, 243, 245 (hereafter cited as *Essays*).

16. MF, "The *Liberty Bell* of 1845," *NYDT*, Jan. 7, 1845, 1.

17. MF, "Review of Henry R. Schoolcraft, *Oneonta; or, The Red Races of America*," *NYDT*, Feb. 12, 1845, 1.

18. MF, "New Year's Day," *New-York Weekly Tribune*, Dec. 21, 1844, 1, also in *Essays*, 261–66.

19. MF to [?], [ca. Feb. 9, 1845], *FL*, 4:48.

20. Kirby, *Years*, 213–14; MF to CS, Mar. 13, 1845, *FL*, 4:59; MF, "J. Stanley Grimes, 'Etherology,' " *NYDT*, Feb. 17, 1845, 1, and *Essays*, 271. Kirby was under the impression that Fuller suffered "from a severe spinal curvature, which had developed after she recovered from typhoid fever, perhaps ten years before this." Kirby, *Years*, 213–14. This is the only indication that Fuller's back pains and "peculiar walk" noticed by other observers might be due to the illness she suffered just before her father's death in the autumn of 1836.

21. Evelyn Winslow Orr, "Two Margaret Fuller Manuscripts," *New England Quarterly* (*NEQ*) 11 (Dec. 1938): 794; see also Stern, "Phrenologist-Publishers," 229–37.

22. CS to MF, Mar. 4, 1845, FMW, 10:20.

Chapter 15. James Nathan

1. Greeley, *Recollections*, 179, *EJ*, 11:494.

2. CST to RWE, [Nov. 1850], *EmL*, 8:265 n. 135; Hudspeth mentions W. H. Channing's attempt to retrieve Fuller's letters in *FL*, 4:11 n. 13. A Fuller family file on efforts to retrieve the letters is in FMW, 10:109–21.

3. MF to James Nathan (JN), Apr. 14, [1845], [May 15? 1845], Mar. 14, [1845], Apr. 14, [1845], [ca. Feb. 7, 1845], *FL*, 4: 74, 100, 62, 74, 75, 47.

4. MF, "The Modern Jews," *NYDT*, Apr. 21, 1845, 1.

5. MF to JN, Apr. 14, [1845], *FL*, 4:74.

6. James Nathan, "Prefatory Note," in *Love Letters of Margaret Fuller, 1845–1846* (1903; rpt., New York: AMS, 1970), 4; MF to JN, [Apr. 16? 1845], *FL*, 4:79.

7. MF to JN, [ca. Feb. 7, 1845], [Mar. 7? 1845], Mar. 31, [1845], Apr. 2, [1845], Apr. 14, [1845], Apr. 22, [1845], [Apr.? 24? 1845], [Apr.? 25? 1845], [May? 2? 1845], [May] 7, [1845], May 26, [1845], *FL*, 4: 47, 55, 64, 67, 73, 84, 86, 89, 93, 96, 107.

8. MF to JN, Apr. 6, 1845, Apr. 2, [1845], Apr. 6, 1845, *FL*, 4:68, 67, 69.

9. For an imaginative reading of the record of Fuller's relationship with Nathan, see Cristina Zwarg, "Womanizing Margaret Fuller," *Cultural Critique* 16 (Fall 1990): 161–92.

10. MF to JN, Apr. 9, [1845], Apr. 6, 1845, *FL*, 4: 72, 70.

11. MF to JN, Apr. 9, [1845], Apr. 14, [1845], [Apr. 15, 1845], Apr. 14, [1845], [Apr. 15, 1845], *FL*, 4: 72, 75, 78, 73, 75, 78.

12. MF to JN, Apr. 19, 1845, Apr. 27, [1845], *FL*, 4: 82, 91.

13. MF to JN, Apr. 27 [1845], *FL*, 4: 91.

14. MF to JN, [May? 4? 1845], *FL*, 4:95–96.

15. MF to JN, May 9, 23, 9, [1845], *FL*, 4:99, 104, 98.

16. MF to JN, [July] 22, 1845 (second part of letter of this date), *FL*, 4:137.

17. MF to JN, Aug. 31, 1845, *FL*, 4:154.

18. MF to JN, Dec. 31, 1845, *FL*, 4:179–80.

19. *OM*, 1:18.

20. MF to JN, Sept. 13, 1845, *FL*, 4:159.

21. CS to RWE, Aug. 7, 1850, quoted in *EmL*, 8:256 n. 95.

Chapter 16. New York, 1845–1846

1. Philip Hone, *The Diary of Philip Hone*, 2 vols. (New York, 1889), 2:249.

2. Willis quoted in Edward K. Span, *The New Metropolis: New York City, 1840–1857* (New York, 1981), 44. For information on Boston in 1845, see Handlin, *Boston's Immigrants;* Baltzell, *Puritan Boston;* and Pease and Pease, *Web of Progress.* For New York City, see Wilentz, *Chants*, and Stansell, *City of Women.*

3. MF to JN, [July] 22, 1845 (second part of letter of this date), *FL*, 4:138; RWE to SGW, Dec. 2, 1844, *EmL*, 3:268.

4. JFC to MF, July 26, 1845, ClLetMF, 145; MF to JFC, [Aug. 14], 1845, FP.

5. John Stafford, *Literary Criticism of Young America: A Study in the Relationship of Politics and Literature* (Berkeley, CA, 1952), 5.

6. MF, "Thom's Poems," *NYDT*, Aug. 22, 1845, 1.

7. Thomas Bender, *A History of the Intellectual Life in New York City, from 1750 to the Beginning of Our Time* (New York, 1987), 142–43; Szymanski, "Margaret Fuller," 36.

8. Miller, *Raven*, 171; see Madeleine B. Stern, "The House of the Expanding Doors: Anne Lynch's Soirees, 1846," *New York History* 23 (Jan. 1942): 42–51; *Anne Charlotte Lynch Botta: Memoirs Written by Her Friends, with selections from her correspondence and from her writings in prose and poetry*, ed. Vincenzo Botta (New York, 1894), passim.

9. LMC to Louisa Loring, Feb. 8, 1845, *Child Letters*, 219.

10. MF, "Our City Charities: Visit to Bellevue Alms House, to the Farm School, the Asylum for the Insane, and Penitentiary on Blackwell's Island," *NYDT*, Mar. 19, 1845, 1, reprinted in Steele, *Essential*, 385–91; "St. Valentine's Day—Bloomingdale Asylum for the Insane," *NYDT*, Feb. 22, 1845, 1, reprinted in *Essays*, 277–81.

11. Charles Dickens, *American Notes for General Consultation* (New York, 1842), 36, 32. William Henry Channing's philosophy of philanthropy is discussed in David J. Rothman, *The Discovery of the Asylum: Social Order and Disorder in the New Republic* (Boston, 1971, 1990), 73–75.

12. Szymanski, "Margaret Fuller," 255–56; J.O'C., *NYDT*, July 22, 1846, 1.

13. "What Fits a Man to be a Voter? Is It to be White Within, or White Without?" *NYDT*, Mar. 31, 1846, 1, reprinted in Steele, *Essential*, 400–404.

14. "The Wrongs of American Women, the Duty of American Women," *NYDT*, Sept. 30, 1845, 1, reprinted in Steele, *Essential*, 393–400. For information on the LIA, see Stansell, *City of Women*, 144–49.

15. MF, "Peale's Court of Death," *NYDT*, Dec. 13, 1845, 2. For Fuller's art criticism, see Corlette R. Walker and Adele M. Holcomb, "Margaret Fuller (1810–1850): Her Work as an Art Critic," in *Women as Interpreters of the Visual Arts*, ed. Claire Richter Sherman (Westport, CT, 1981), and Roland Crozier Burton, "Margaret Fuller's Criticism of the Fine Arts," *College English*, no. 6 (Oct. 1944): 18–22.

16. MF, "Ole Bull," *NYDT*, Nov. 23, 1845, 1.

17. Allen, *Emerson*, 449. For the interchange of letters between Emerson and Sturgis, see *EmL*, 8:1–53.

18. MF to ABW, Nov. 16, 1845, *FL*, 4:167.

19. Ibid., 168.

20. MF to RFF, [Aug. 31, 1845], *FL*, 4:158.

21. MF to ABW, Nov. 16, 1845, *FL*, 4:168.

22. MF to JN, July 22, 1845, *FL*, 4:135; Van Deusen, *Greeley*, 148; MF to JN, [July] 22, 1845 (second part of letter of this date), *FL*, 4:136.

23. MF to Anna Loring, Dec. 3, 1845, *FL*, 4:172.

24. CS to MF, [Feb. 22, 1846], Sturgis Letters, 249.

25. MF to CS, [Mar.] 9, [1846], *FL*, 4:195.

26. MF to JN, June 24, 1845, *FL*, 4:121.

27. Sterling F. Delano, *The "Harbinger" and New England Transcendentalism* (Cranbury, NJ, 1983), 68–69.

28. Wilentz, *Chants*, 337, 119.

29. MF, "Der 'Volks-Tribun': Organ der Deutschen Sozial Reform-Association in New York," *NYDT*, Jan. 17, 1846, 1.

30. Thomas Dunn English, "Reminiscences of Poe," *Independent*, Oct. 29, 1896, 1448; see also Joy Bayless, *Rufus Wilmot Griswold* (Nashville, 1943), 140–41; Poe, *Letters*, 3:409 n.

31. Poe, *Complete Works*, 15:74, 77–78, 82.

32. Ibid., 82–83.

33. *Essays*, 323; Samuel Longfellow, *Life of Henry Wadsworth Longfellow* (London, 1886), 2:27; see *The Letters of Henry Wadsworth Longfellow*, ed. Andrew Hilen (Cambridge, MA, 1966–82), 3:93. For a comparison of Poe's and Fuller's criticism of Longfellow, see Sidney P. Moss, *Poe's Literary Battles* (Durham, NC, 1963), 183–84.

34. Edgar Allan Poe, "The Literati of New York City," in Poe, *Complete Works*, 15: 75; Edgar Allan Poe to George W. Eveleth, Jan. 4, 1848, in Poe, *Letters*, 2:355.

35. MF to Evert A. Duyckinck, June 28, [1846], *FL*, 4:212.

36. Ibid.; MF, *Papers on Literature and Art* (London, 1846; rpt., New York: AMS, 1972), vii (hereafter cited as MF*Papers*). For a study of Fuller's writing on foreign literature, see Russell E. Durning, *Margaret Fuller, Citizen of the World: An Intermediary between European and American Literature* (Heidelberg, 1969).

37. JN to MF, June 5, 1846, FMW, 10: 110.

38. MF to JN, July 14, 1846, *FL*, 4:218–19.

39. RFF to MF, July 8, 1846, FMW, 15: 33.

40. MF to SGW and ABW, Mar. 3, 1846, *FL*, 4:192, 193.

41. Rebecca Buffum Spring (RBS) to Thomas Wentworth Higginson, May 25, 1884, MFOC, 257.

42. *OM*, 2:157.

43. RWE to Thomas Carlyle, July 15, 1846, *E&C*, 406.

44. *Essays*, 379–80.

45. Ibid.

Chapter 17. England and Scotland

1. For biographical material on Rebecca Buffum Spring and Marcus Spring, see Rebecca Buffum Spring, "Journal Abroad," Raritan Bay Union Collection, New Jersey Historical Society; Beatrice Borchardt, "Lady of Utopia: The Story of Rebecca Buffum Spring," Huntington Library (copy in New Jersey Historical Society); Marie Marmo Mullancy, "Feminine Utopianism and Domesticity: The Career of Rebecca Buffum Spring, 1811–1911," *New Jersey History* 104 (Fall/Winter 1986): 1–20; Jayme A. Sokolow, "Culture and Utopia: The Raritan Bay Union," *New Jersey History* 94 (Summer/Autumn 1976): 89–95; Carl J. Guarneri, *The Utopian Alternative: Fourierism in Nineteenth-Century America* (Ithaca, NY, 1991), 322–26; Moncure Daniel Conway, *Autobiography: Memories and Experiences* (Boston, 1904), 3:396; Fredrika Bremer, *The Homes of the New World*, 2 vols. (1853; New York, 1968), 70–107, and *Letters of the Fifties* (New York, 1924), 28–29.

2. MF, "Letters from England," *NYDT*, Sept. 24, 1846, *SGD*, 40.

3. MF to JN, Sept. 13, 1845, [ca. Feb. 28, 1846], *FL*, 4:159, 190.

4. MF, "Letters from England," *SGD*, 48.

5. Dispatch II, Sept. 29, 1846, *SGD*, 49; "Letters from England," *SGD*, 47.

6. Harriet Martineau to Fanny Wedgwood, Sept. 29, [1845], in *Harriet Martineau's Letters to Fanny Wedgwood*, ed. Elisabeth Sanders Arbuckle (Stanford, CA, 1983), 85. For Martineau's reaction to Fuller's visit, see *Martineau's Autobiography*, 2:252–53; see also Wheatley, *Life of Martineau*, 247.

7. Dispatch II, Sept. 29, 1846, *SGD*, 53, 57; Dispatch III, Oct. 24, 1846, *SGD*, 61.

8. Dispatch IV, Nov. 5, 1846, *SGD*, 67.

9. *Love Letters*, 187.

10. Dispatch V, Nov. 13, 1846, *SGD*, 69.

11. Borchardt, "Lady of Utopia," chap. 4, "Castles and Hovels Nearby," 59. Robert N. Hudspeth writes in his preface to *FL*, 4 (p. 10), that "the context of depression described by Rebecca Spring raises the possibility of a suicidal gesture, whether it was a conscious one or not. At the least, the night on the mountain bound up with her sense of loss and betrayal."

12. Dispatch V, Nov. 13, 1846, *SGD*, 77. Impressed with Fuller's use of the term, "Ossianic visions," Walt Whitman cut out a paragraph of Fuller's description of her night on Ben Lomond. See

Notebook and Unpublished Prose Manuscripts of Walt Whitman, ed. Edward Grier (New York, 1984), 1806–7.

13. Dispatch VI, Dec. 23, 1846, *SGD,* 79; MF, "Fragment of Tour of Scotland," copy in FMW, Works, 1:203; Dispatch V, Nov. 13, 1846, *SGD,* 72.

14. Dispatch VII, Jan. 5, 1847, *SGD,* 82.

15. Elizabeth Barrett Browning (EBB) to Robert Browning, Aug. 15, 1846, in *The Letters of Robert Browning and Elizabeth Barrett Browning, 1845–1846,* 2 vols., ed. Elvan Kintner (Cambridge, MA, 1969), 1: 961 (hereafter cited as *RB&EBB*).

16. RWE to Thomas Carlyle, July 31, 1846, *E&C,* 407.

17. MF to RWE, Nov. 16, 1846[I], *FL,* 4:246; Dispatch IX, Feb. 19, 1847, *SGD,* 100.

18. MF to RWE, Nov. 16, 1846[I], *FL,* 4: 246, 248, 246.

19. Dispatch IX, Feb. 19, 1847, *SGD,* 100.

20. MF to RWE, Nov. 16, 1846[II], *FL,* 4:248.

21. Dispatch XI, Mar. 31, 1847, *SGD,* 113–14; see Walker and Holcomb, "Margaret Fuller," 138–40.

22. Dispatch IX, Feb. 19, 1847, *SGD,* 96.

23. Mrs. Newton Crosland [Camilla Toulmin], *Landmarks of a Literary Life, 1820–1892* (New York, 1893), 224–25.

24. Spring, "Journal Abroad," 13; Thomas Cooper, *The Life of Thomas Cooper, Written by Himself* (London, 1875), 312; Conway, *Autobiography,* 360.

25. Webb, *Martineau,* 267.

26. MF, "Review of *Le Franco-Americaine,*" *NYDT,* Apr. 7, 1846, 1.

27. MF to RWE, Nov. 16, 1846[II], *FL,* 4:248; Spring, "Journal Abroad," 14.

28. Giuseppe Mazzini (GM) to G. Lamberti, Oct. 23 and Nov. 10, 1846, in Giovanni Mazzini, *Scritti, Editi ed Inediti di Giuseppe Mazzini,* ed. M. Menghini, 94 vols. (Imola, 1906–43), 30: 245, 268.

29. Quoted in "Annals of Progress: Italian School," *People's Journal* 3 (Jan. 16, 1847): 5.

Chapter 18. France

1. Borchardt, "Lady of Utopia," last page of chap. 14; MF note quoted in JN to MF, Nov. 6, 1846, FMW, 10: 109–21, letter no. 2.

2. JN to MF, Nov. 6, 1846, FMW, 10: 109–21.

3. Ibid.

4. JN to MF, Nov. 27, 1846, FMW, 10: 109–21, letter no. 3.

5. Ibid. This discussion of the letters would indicate that Fuller was in possession of Nathan's letters while she was in Paris.

6. MF to MCF, Dec. 26, 1846[III], *FL,* 4:253. For Roland's life and writings, see Pauline Roland, Arthur Ranc, and Gaspard Rouffet, *Bagnes d'Afrique: trois transportés en Algérie après le coup d'état du 2 décembre 1851* (Paris, 1981); Léon Abensour, *Le féminisme sous le règne de Louis-Philippe et en 1848* (Paris, 1913); Marcel Emerit, *Pauline Roland et les déportées d'Afrique* (Algiers, 1945); Victor Hugo, "Pauline Roland," *Les Châtiments,* ed. nationale (*Oeuvres de Victor Hugo*), vol. 4, ed. J. Lemonnyer (Paris, 1885), 269–74; Marguerite Thibert, *Le féminisme dans le socialisme français de 1830 à 1850* (Paris, 1926); Edith Thomas, *Pauline Roland: socialism et féminisme au XIX siècle* (Paris, 1956); Benoît Groult, *Pauline Roland ou comment la liberté vint aux femmes* (Paris, 1991).

7. MF to RFF, Jan. 31, 1847, *FL,* 4: 260.

8. Dispatch X, Mar. 3, 1847, *SGD,* 111.

9. Dispatch XII, May 15, 1847, *SGD,* 120–22.

10. Dispatch X, Mar. 3, 1847, *SGD,* 105–6.

11. Ibid., 109.

12. Spring, "Journal Abroad" ("France," 1); Dispatch X, Mar. 3, 1847, *SGD,* 108; Dispatch XII, May 15, 1847, *SGD,* 119.

13. Margaret Lesser, *Clarkey: A Portrait in Letters of Mary Clarke Mohl (1793–1883)* (Oxford, 1984), 67; Mary Clarke to Leonora Pertz (the English wife of George Pertz of the Berlin Library), Feb. 22, 1847, FMW, 11:125.

14. Lesser, *Clarkey,* 110.

15. *OM,* 2:196.

16. *OM,* 1:248; *WNC-KP,* 238.

17. MF, "Lawsuit," 30; *WNC-KP,* 232–33; *OM,* 2: 197.

18. Jane W. Stirling to MF, [ca. Feb.? 24? 1847?], FMW, 10:145; OM, 2:198.

19. Francis J. Whitfield, *Mickiewicz and American Literature* (Berkeley, CA, 1956), 340–41 (frontispiece). When the author visited the Mickiewicz Museum in Paris in 1976, listed among the museum's holdings was an inscribed copy of Emerson's poems that had been in Mickiewicz's possession; on inquiry, I was told that the copy had disappeared during the German occupation of Paris in the 1940s.

20. Adam Mickiewicz (AM) to MF, [after first meeting, Feb. 15, 1847], in Leopold Wellisz, "The Friendship of Margaret Fuller d'Ossoli and Adam Mickiewicz," *Bulletin of the Polish Institute of Arts and Sciences in America* 4 (1945–46): 93–95; see also FMW, 10:121, and a copy sent to JFC in FP. In Wellisz, Mickiewicz's letters to Fuller are given in the original French with English translations.

21. Jean-Charles Gille-Maisani, *Adam Mickiewicz, poète national de la Pologne: Étude psychanalytique et caractérologique* (Montreal, 1988), 559–602.

22. MF to RWE, Jan. 18, 1847, Mar. 15, 1847[I], *FL*, 4:259, 261.

23. MF to JN, [May? 4? 1845], *FL*, 4:95.

24. Laura S. Strumhingher, *Women and the Making of the Working Class: Lyon, 1830–1870* (Brattleboro, VT, 1979), 32, 35, 61, 106.

25. Dispatch XIII, May 29, 1847, *SGD*, 127–28.

26. Bette S. Weidman, "The Pinto Letters of Charles Frederick Briggs," in Myerson, *American Renaissance* (1979), 114, 116, 118, 122.

27. Dispatch XIII, May 29, 1847, *SGD*, 129.

Chapter 19. Italy at Last

1. Alessandro Luzio, *La Madre di Giuseppe Mazzini* (Turin, 1919), 12 (author's translation).

2. GM to Maria Mazzini, Mar. 27, 1847, Mazzini, *Scritti*, 32:93, as translated in Joseph Rossi, *The Image of America in Mazzini's Writing* (Madison, WI, 1954), 55.

3. "Annals of Progress," *People's Journal* 3 (Feb. 28, 1847): 18.

4. George Haven Putnam, *George Palmer Putnam* (New York, 1903), 400; see 88 n. 1, 399–400, for description of scene.

5. Dispatch XIII, May 29, 1847, *SGD*, 129, 130, 131.

6. Dispatch XIV, July 31, 1847, *SGD*, 136.

7. Ibid.

8. Spring, "Journal Abroad" ("Rome," 3).

9. Dispatch XIV, July 31, 1837, *SGD*, 136, 138.

10. For Edgar Quinet's description of Costanza Arconati, see Charles Augustin Sainte-Beuve, *Correspondance générale*, ed. Jean Bonnerot, 19 vols. to date (Paris, 1935–), 6:88 n. 2. For the relationships of Clarke, Fauriel, Arconati, and Berchet, see Mary Charlotte Mair Senior Simpson, *Letters and Recollections of Julius and Mary Mohl* (London, 1887); Kathleen O'Meara [Grace Ramsay], *Madame Mohl, Her Salon and Her Friends: A Study of Social Life in Paris* (London, 1885); Jean-Baptiste Galley, *Claude Fauriel* (St. Etienne, 1909), 448–53; Claude Fauriel, *Correspondance de Fauriel et Mary Clarke*, ed. Ottmar de Mohl (Paris, 1911); Marion Elmina Smith, *Une anglaise intellectuelle en France sous la Restauration: Mary Clarke* (Paris, 1927); Milano Liceo ginnasio G. Berchet, comp., *Studi sul Berchet* (Milan, 1951), 192–213; *Lettera di Edgar Quinet alla Marchesa Arconati Visconti*, ed. M. Menghini (Castello, 1900), 5–14; Giovanni Berchet, *Lettere alla Marchesa Costanza Arconati*, ed. Robert Van Nuffel, 2 vols. (Rome, 1962), 2:30, 121–27, 191, 214, 229.

11. Emelyn Story's accounts are in MFOC, 178, OM, 1:281–85, and HigMFO, 238–46; George Palmer Putnam's account is in Putnam, *Putnam*, 400; see also Donald Yanella and Kathleen Malone Yanella, "Evert A. Duyckinck's Diary: May 29–November 8, 1847," in Myerson, *American Renaissance* (1978), 225.

12. Wellisz, "Friendship," 99–100.

13. Spring, "Journal Abroad" ("Rome," 3).

14. MF to Marcus Spring (MS) and RBS, Apr. 10, 1846 [1847], *FL*, 4:262–63.

15. *Love Letters*, 187.

16. RWE to MF, Apr. 30, 1847, *EmL*, 3:393–94.

17. *EJ*, 10: 94; see also 4:260 and 8:224. For Fuller as the American Corinne, see *Margaret Fuller: American Romantic*, ed. Perry Miller (New York: Doubleday, 1963), xxi–xxiv (hereafter cited as

MFAmRom); for de Staël's *Corinne* as a model of independence and heroism for women in the nineteenth century, see Ellen Moers, *Literary Women* (Garden City, NY, 1976), 176–212.

18. RWE to MF, June 4, 1847, *EmL*, 3:400–401.

19. MCF to MF, Feb. 7, 1847, FMW, 8:216.

20. MCF to MF, Oct. 8, 1847, FMW, 8:222.

21. AM to MF, Apr. 26, 1847, Wellisz, "Friendship," 102, 103.

22. For biographical material on Thomas Hicks, see George A. Hicks, "Thomas Hicks, Artist, a Native of Newtown," *Bucks County Historical Society; Collection of Papers* (Easton, PA, 1917), 4, 89–92; G. W. Sheldon, *American Painters* (New York, 1879), 35–43; Wayne Craven, *American Painting, 1857–1869* (Newark, 1962), 62–63; James Flexner, *The Wilder Image* (New York, 1970), 218–19; Henry T. Tuckerman, *Book of the Artists* (New York, 1867), 465; Edgar P. Richardson and Otto Witman, *Travellers in Arcadia: American Artists in Italy, 1839–1875* (Detroit, 1951), 40–41; "Thomas Hicks," *Art Journal* 4 (1878): 166–67.

23. MF to Thomas Hicks (TH), Apr. 23 [18]47, *FL*, 4:269.

24. TH? to MF, May 9, [1847], FMW, 11:115.

25. Spring, "Journal Abroad" ("Rome," 3, 5).

26. MF to RWE, June 20, 1847[I], *FL*, 4:276; MS to MF, Apr. 17, 1850, FMW, 11:136; MF to Ellen Fuller Channing (EFC), Dec. 11, 1849, *FL*, 5:292.

27. MF to RFF, July 1, 1847, *FL*, 4:277.

28. Henry James, *William Wetmore Story and His Friends*, 2 vols. (Boston, 1903), 1:114; Horace Greeley (HG) to MF, Sept. 29, 1847, FMW, 10:48. The literature on American artists in Italy in the nineteenth century is considerable. See *"The Lure of Italy": American Artists and the Italian Experience, 1760–1914*, ed. Theodore E. Stebbins, Jr. (Boston, 1992); Madeleine Stern, "New England Artists in Italy, 1835–1855," *NEQ* 14 (June 1940): 243–71; Paul R. Baker, *The Fortunate Pilgrims: Americans in Italy, 1800–1860* (Cambridge, MA, 1969), 127–53; Sylvia E. Crane, *White Silence: Greenough, Powers, and Crawford, American Sculptors in Nineteenth-Century Italy* (Coral Gables, FL, 1972).

29. Dispatch XV, Sept. 11, 1847, *SGD*, 142.

30. Ibid., 144, 145.

31. Spring, "Journal Abroad" ("Venice," 5); MF to CS, Aug. 22, [18]47, *FL*, 4:291.

Chapter 20. Return to Rome

1. AM to MF, Aug. 3, 1847, Wellisz, "Friendship," 105–6.

2. AM to MF, Sept. 16, 1847, ibid., 107–8 ("*harsh*" quoted by AM from MF's letter).

3. MF to RWE, Aug. 10, 1847, *FL*, 4:287; Dispatch XVI, Dec. 25, 1847, *SGD*, 147.

4. MF to [?], Nov. 17, 1847, *FL*, 4:311.

5. MF to CS, Aug. 22, [18]47, *FL*, 4:291–92.

6. Costanza Arconati Visconti (CAV) to MF, Sept. 25, [1847], FMW, 11:43; see also Emma Detti, *Margaret Fuller Ossoli e i suoi corrispondenti* (Florence, 1942), 286.

7. MF to RFF, Sept. 25, 1847, *FL*, 4:296.

8. Ibid.

9. HG to MF, July 27, 1847, FMW, 10:46.

10. MCF to MF, May 27, 1847, FMW, 8:217.

11. Ibid.

12. SAC to MF, May 14, 1847, FMW, 10:38.

13. MF to MCF, Oct. 16, 1847, *FL*, 4:301.

14. Ibid., 301, 302.

15. MF to RFF, Oct. 29, 1847, *FL*, 4:310.

16. TH to MCF, Aug. 2, 1850, FMW, 16:65.

17. Joshua C. Taylor, *William Page, the American Titian* (Chicago, 1957), 89–90.

18. Martin Duberman, *James Russell Lowell* (Boston, 1966), 42–44; *OM*, 2:282.

19. For American expatriate life in Rome, see James, *Story;* William Wetmore Story, *Roba di Roma*, 2 vols. (Boston, 1893); Eric Amfitheatrof, *The Enchanted Ground: Americans in Italy, 1760–1980* (Boston, 1980), 58–75, passim; Baker, *Fortunate Pilgrims;* Van Wyck Brooks, *The Dream of Arcadia: American Writers and Artists in Italy, 1760–1915* (New York, 1958), 110–21; George William Curtis, "Letter from Italy," *Harbinger* 5 (July 3, 1847): 49–50, "Letter from Rome," *Harbinger* 4

(Feb. 13, 1847): 145–46, and "American Travellers," *Putnam's Monthly Magazine* 3 (June 1855): 561–76.

20. George Stillman Hillard, *Six Months in Italy* (Boston, 1853), 1:204.

21. Dispatch XVIII, Jan. 1, 1848, *SGD*, 161–63.

22. Dispatch XXI, Feb. 19, 1848, *SGD*, 184.

23. Dispatch XIX, Jan. 29, 1848, *SGD*, 172; Dispatch XVIII, Jan. 1, 1848, *SGD*, 164; Dispatch XIX, Jan. 29, 1848, *SGD*, 176.

24. MF, "Italy," *People's and Howitt's Journal* 4 (Oct. 1847): 527. For an overview of the position of educated Italian women in public life in the middle of the nineteenth century, see Priscilla Robertson, *Revolutions of 1848: A Social History* (Princeton, NJ, 1952), 312–13.

25. MF, "Italy," 528.

26. GM to MF, Dec. 1847, in Leona Rostenberg, "Mazzini to Margaret Fuller, 1847–1849," *American Historical Review* 47 (Oct. 1941): 75–77; see also Mazzini, *Scritti*, App. 6, 531, 527–28.

27. GM to MF, Dec. 1847, Rostenberg, "Mazzini," 77, 76.

28. "Letter from Joseph Mazzini to the Pontiff," quoted in Dispatch XXI, Feb. 19, 1848, *SGD*, 198, 196.

29. GM to MF, Dec. 1847, Rostenberg, "Mazzini," 77. This letter appears, with some deletions and some minor variations from the text given in Rostenberg, in Mazzini, *Scritti*, App. 6, 524–31.

30. CAV to MF, Jan. 12, [1848], FMW, 11:63; see also Detti, *Ossoli*, 293; MF to CAV, Jan. 14, 1848, *FL*, 5:49.

31. MF to MCF, Dec. 16, 1847[II and I], *FL*, 4:313, 312.

32. MF to RWE, Dec. 20, 1847, *FL*, 4:314–15.

Chapter 21. 1848: On Her Own

1. Dispatch XXIII, May 4, 1848, *SGD*, 209; Hillard, *Six Months*, 2:13; MF to RFF, Jan. 1, 1848, *FL*, 5:40.

2. MF to RFF, Mar. 17, 1848, *FL*, 5:57.

3. MF to EFC, Jan. 12, 1848, *FL*, 5:46; EF to ABF, Feb. 24, 1848, FMW, 10:218.

4. MF to CST, Jan. 11, 1848, *FL*, 5:42, 43.

5. Ibid., 43.

6. RWE to MF, Mar. 2, 1848, *EmL*, 4:28. On March 6, 1848, Lidian Emerson wrote Ralph Waldo that Almira Barlow, who had nursed her through the winter, wished to rent Lucy Brown's house, and it seemed advisable to accept the offer since "I do not on consideration, think Margaret [would] accept the use of the house if offered—because it would not be worth while to [move] furniture into it for a year only." See Carpenter, *Letters of Lidian Emerson*, 142.

7. Dispatch XXII, Mar. 29, 1848, *SGD*, 203, 206.

8. Ibid., 201, 208; Dispatch XXI, Feb. 19, 1848, *SGD*, 188, 189. For a good overview of Fuller's coverage of this period in Europe, see Larry J. Reynolds, *European Revolutions and the American Literary Renaissance* (New Haven, 1988), 54–78.

9. Christopher Cranch to Theodore Parker, Jan. 23, [1848], "An Illustrated Letter from Cranch to Parker," in Myerson, *American Renaissance* (1981), 355; Dispatch XXIII, May 4, 1848, *SGD*, 210; Hillard, *Six Months*, 15.

10. MF to FHH, Mar. 8, 1848, *FL*, 5:55, quoted in *Springfield Republican*, June 1, 1870, 2.

11. For information on Cristina di Belgioioso, see Beth Archer Brombert, *Cristina: Portraits of a Princess* (New York, 1977); Charles Nielson Gattey, *A Bird of Curious Plumage: Princess Cristina di Belgioioso, 1808–1871* (London, 1943); Ludovico Incisa and Alberica Trivulzio, *Cristina di Belgioioso, la principessa romantica* (Milan, 1984); see *Harbinger* 8 (May 20, 1848): 18; MF to RFF, Feb. 8, 1848, *FL*, 5:51. See also Cristina di Belgioioso, *Il 1848 a Milano e a Venezia, con uno scritto sulla condizione delle donne* (Milan, 1867).

12. G.F.H. Berkeley and J. Berkeley, *Italy in the Making: January 1, 1848–November 16, 1848* (Cambridge, England, 1940), 105.

13. AM to MF, May 4, 1848, Wellisz, "Friendship," 115–16.

14. Dispatch XXIII, May 4, 1848, *SGD*, 212.

15. MF to WHC, Mar. 29, 1848, *FL*, 5:58.

16. Dispatch XXIII, May 4, 1848, *SGD*, 211.

17. Dispatch XXIV, June 15, 1848, *SGD*, 223.

18. Ibid., 225.

19. MF to RWE, May 19, 1848, *FL*, 5:66; to RFF, May 20, 1848, *FL*, 5:68. On Mazzini's social theory, see Clara M. Lovett, *The Democratic Movement in Italy, 1830–1876* (Cambridge, MA, 1982), 55–60.

20. Dispatch XXIV, June 15, 1848, *SGD*, 226, 228.

21. Ibid., 230.

22. James, *Boy*, 62. Several years later, Hicks used his portrait of Fuller as a model in his group painting of forty-four prominent American writers of the nineteenth century, entitled "Authors of the United States." Fuller is shown sitting between Richard Henry Dana and William Ellery Channing.

23. MCF to TH, Sept. 9, 1850, MFO Collection, Letter no. 18, MHarF.

24. MF to TH, May 17, 1848, *FL*, 5:66.

25. MF to Jane Tuckerman King, Apr. 1848, *FL*, 5:59.

26. MF to Mary Rotch, May 29, 1848, *FL*, 5:70, 71.

27. CAV to MF, June 3, 1848, FMW, 11:53; see also Detti, *Ossoli*, 300.

28. CAV to MF, June 3, 1848, FMW, 11:53; see also Detti, *Ossoli*, 299; MF to CAV, June 22, 1848, *FL*, 5:73.

29. RWE to MF, May 31, 1848, *EmL*, 4:79.

30. Dispatch XXV, Jan. 19, 1849, *SGD*, 237.

31. HG to MF, July 29, 1848, FMW, 10:53; letter printed in part in Henry Luther Stoddard, *Horace Greeley: Printer, Editor, Crusader* (New York, 1946), 115–17.

32. HG to MF, June 27, 1848, FMW, 10:52.

33. MF to Giovanni Angelo Ossoli (GAO), Aug. 13, 1848, *FL*, 5:99–100. All MF letters to GAO are given in *FL* in the Italian original with an English translation.

34. GAO to MF, Aug. 14, Aug. 17, 1848, FMW, 16:119, 118.

35. MF to GAO, Aug. 18, [1848], *FL*, 5:109.

36. MF to GAO, Aug. 22, [18]48, [Sept. 9, 1848], Sept. 17, [1848], *FL*, 5: 109, 112, 117.

37. MF to GAO, Sept. 23, [1848], *FL*, 5:121.

38. MF to GAO, [Oct. 1848], *FL*, 5:139.

39. MF to GAO, Oct. 18, [18]48, *FL*, 5:133.

40. MF to GAO, Oct. 7, 1848, *FL*, 5:125.

Chapter 22. The Roman Republic

1. MF to MCF, Nov. 16, 1848, *FL*, 5:146.

2. Ibid., 147. For a modern evaluation of Pellegrino Rossi, see Lovett, *Democratic Movement*, 132; Harry Hearder, *Italy in the Age of the Risorgimento* (London, 1983), 115–16.

3. MF to MCF, Nov. 16, 1848, *FL*, 5:147.

4. Ibid., 149–50, 147.

5. Ibid., 147, 145.

6. Ibid., 150; MF to Marquis de Lafayette, [16? June? 1825?], *FL*, 1:150; Dispatch XXV, Jan. 19, 1849, *SGD*, 234; Dispatch XXVI, Jan. 26, 1849, *SGD*, 244; Dispatch XXV, Jan. 19, 1849, *SGD*, 232, 237.

7. Dispatch XXVI, Jan. 26, 1849, *SGD*, 245, 247.

8. Ibid., 238.

9. MF to William Wetmore Story (WWS), Dec. 9, 1848[II], *FL*, 5:161.

10. MF to GAO, Dec. 22, 1848, *FL*, 5:164.

11. HG to MF, Nov. 19, 1848, FMW, 10:54.

12. MF to MCF, Jan. 19, 1849, *FL*, 5:177; JFC to MF, [Dec. 1848], ClLetMF, 146.

13. MF to JFC, Jan. 19, 1849, FP.

14. HG to MF, Jan. 29, 1849, FMW, 10:55.

15. MF*Papers*, Part 2, 132.

16. James Russell Lowell to WWS, Mar. 10, 1848, in *Browning to His American Friends*, ed. Gertrude Reese Hudson (New York, 1965), 229, 231.

17. Duberman, *Lowell*, 99; James Russell Lowell, *Fable for Critics* (Boston, 1848), 72.

18. Duberman, *Lowell*, 100; Edgar Allan Poe, "Review of *Fable for Critics*," *Southern Literary Messenger* 15 (Mar. 1849): 190.

19. WWS to James Russell Lowell, Mar. 21, 1849, in James, *Story*, 1: 170–71; James Russell Lowell to WWS, ibid., 181.

20. MF to CST, Mar. 8, 1849[I], *FL*, 5:198–99.

21. *Literary World* 4 (Jan. 27, 1849): 84; see also 3 (Dec. 2, 1848): 878.

22. For George Sand's position, see Abensour, *Féminisme*, 197–98, 307–9; Dispatch XXVI, Jan. 26, 1849, *SGD*, 245.

23. Leona L. Rostenberg, "Margaret Fuller's Roman Diary," *Journal of Modern History* 12 (June 1940): 211, 216.

24. MF to GM, Mar. 3, 1849, *FL*, 5:196.

25. MF to RFF, Mar. 17, 1849, *FL* 5:213; MF to MS, Mar. 9, 1849[I], *FL*, 5:201.

26. MF to MCF, Mar. 9, 1849, *FL*, 5:202; to CST, Mar. 16, 1849, *FL*, 5:210.

27. MF to CST, Mar. 16, 1849, *FL*, 5:208; to ABF, Jan. 20, 1849, *FL*, 5: 186.

28. MF to CST, Mar. 16, 1849, *FL*, 5:209–10.

29. Hearder, *Italy,* 117; MF to CST, Mar. 16, 1849, *FL*, 5:209.

30. FMW, 11:159.

31. MF to GAO, Mar. 30, 1849, *FL*, 5:220; GAO to MF, Mar. 31, 1849, FMW, 16:133.

32. GAO to MF, [Apr. 3, 1849], FMW, 16:141; MF to GAO, Apr. 4, 1849, *FL*, 5:223.

33. See Stern, *Life,* 430–31. Without making any definite statement because of the absence of proof, Stern believes that "Margaret Fuller and Giovanni Ossoli were married in a civil ceremony on April 4, 1848, in one of the towns near Rome." However, in the Papal States at the time only marriages consecrated in the Catholic church were accepted as legal. For a Catholic to marry a Protestant, a papal dispensation was necessary. This could be obtained through a local bishop, and the records would be kept in the local archives. Stern ascertained that no record exists in "the Vatican Library, in the Protestant archives, in the Vicariate of Rome." This does not preclude a parish archive. In Rieti the bishop was sympathetic to the democratic movement. If an Ossoli marriage was arranged in his diocese, it is unlikely the records survived the bombing of the Rieti region in World War II.

34. Howard R. Marraro, *American Opinion on the Unification of Italy, 1846–1861* (New York, 1931), 71; Lewis Cass, Jr. (LC) to John M. Clayton, Secretary of State, Apr. 9, 21, 1849, in *United States Ministers to the Papal States: Instructions and Dispatches, 1848–1866,* ed. Leo Francis Stock (Washington, DC, 1933), 1: 25, 27. For biographical material on Lewis Cass, Jr., see Frank B. Woodford, *Lewis Cass, the Last Jeffersonian* (New York, 1973), 238; Willis E. Dunbar, *Lewis Cass* (Grand Rapids, MI, 1970), 69–70; W. J. Stillman, *An Autobiography of a Journalist* (London, 1901), 297–98.

35. Cristina Trivulzio Belgioioso to MF, Apr. 29, 1849, FMW, 11:81.

36. For Belgioioso's organization of the Roman hospitals, see Incisa and Trivulzio, *Cristina,* 346–64.

37. MF to RWE, May 19, 1848, *FL*, 5:66.

Chapter 23. Siege and Escape

1. James, *Story,* 1: 153.

2. Ibid., 154–56; Gattey, *Bird,* 138; Incisa and Trivulzio, *Cristina,* 361 (author's translation).

3. MFOC, 178; Chevigny, *Woman and Myth,* 407; HigMFO, 237–41.

4. MF to GAO, [June 1849], *FL*, 5:236.

5. Dispatch XXX, June 23, 1849, *SGD*, 280.

6. Ibid., 279.

7. MF to Emelyn Elbridge Story (EES), May 29, 1849, *FL*, 5:232.

8. Katharine Chorley, *Hugh Clough: The Uncommitted Mind* (Oxford, 1962), 3; MF to EES, Nov. 30, 1849, *FL*, 5:285; Arthur Hugh Clough, *Amours de Voyage,* ed. Patrick Scott (St. Lucia, Queensland, 1974), editor's introduction, 7.

9. MF to RFF, May 22, 1849, *FL*, 5:229–30.

10. LC to MF, June 1, 1849, FMW, 16:144.

11. Dispatch XXX, June 23, 1849, *SGD*, 282–83.

12. George M. Trevelyan, *Garibaldi's Defense of the Roman Republic* (London, 1907), 173, 178–80. For Cass's role at this time, see Rossi, *Image,* 62–74; Stock, *Ministers,* 1:xxiii–xxv, 17–67.

13. Dispatch XXXII, July 24, 1849, *SGD*, 285, 292.

14. MF to RWE, June 10, 1849, *FL*, 5:240.

15. MF to EFC, June 19, 1849, *FL*, 5:241.

16. Ibid.

17. ERF to MF, Mar. 20, 1849, FMW, 11:133.

18. Dispatch XXXI, July 23, 1849, *SGD*, 299.

19. Trevelyan, *Garibaldi's Defense*, 227.

20. Ibid., 231; see also "Garibaldi's Speech to his soldiers in St. Peter's Square, Rome, July 2, 1849," in Denis Mack Smith, *The Making of Italy, 1796–1866* (1968; New York, 1988), 163.

21. Dispatch XXXII, Aug. 11, 1849, *SGD*, 305.

22. John M. Clayton to LC, June 25, 1849, Stock, *Ministers*, 1:45.

23. HG to MF, June 23, 1848, FMW, 10:56. For Belgioioso's escape from Rome, see Incisa and Trivulzio, *Cristina*, 365–67.

24. HG to MF, June 23, 1848, FMW, 10:56.

25. Marraro, *American Opinion*, 58–60; see also *New York Herald*, June 27, 1849, and *Boston Daily Transcript*, June 27, 1849, 2.

26. *Boston Evening Transcript*, June 27, 1849, 2; Chevigny, *Woman and Myth*, 402–3.

27. Dispatch XXXIII, Aug. 11, 1849, 308, 311.

28. MF to RFF, July 8, 1849, *FL*, 5:244.

29. Luigi Bassin to GAO, June 28, 1849, FMW, 11:141 (author's translation).

30. Dispatch XXIX, May 16, 1849, *SGD*, 264; Dispatch XXX, June 23, 1849, *SGD*, 277–78.

31. HG to MF, July 23, 1849, FMW, 10:57, reproduced in Stoddard, *Greeley*, 119–20.

32. MF to EFC, Dec. 11, 1849, *FL*, 5:293; to MCF, Mar. 9, 1849, *FL*, 5:203; MCF to MF, May 21, 1849, FMW, 8:220, quoted in *FL*, 5:307 n. 1.

33. Thomas Carlyle to John Chapman, Aug. 9, 1849, *E&C*, 456 n. 2.

34. [Thomas Carlyle] to MF, Aug. 17, 1849, FMW, 11: 132. Although this letter is unsigned, the handwriting, the subject matter, the "Scotsbrig" return address, and the contents of Carlyle's Aug. 13 letter from "Scotsbrig" to Emerson leave little doubt that Thomas Carlyle is the author; see *E&C*, 454–56. The handwriting can be compared with an example in George Allan Cate, *The Correspondence of Thomas Carlyle and John Ruskin* (Palo Alto, CA, 1982), 124.

35. *La Tribune des Peuples* was published in Paris between April and October 1849. On October 18, 1849, several of the French contributors were arrested. Pauline Roland was accused of professing communist and socialist ideas, being a mother without marrying, and opposing marriage. She was put on parole. In 1851 she was sent to St. Lazare prison for participating in an insurrection. In 1852, after her third arrest, she was deported to prison in Algiers. See Emerit, *Roland*, passim, esp. 13–18.

36. For AM's invitation to Fuller, see Wellisz, "Friendship," 117–21.

37. MF to HG, Aug. 25, 1848 [1849], *FL*, 5:257.

38. MF to MCF, [Aug. 31, 1849], *FL*, 5:260–61.

39. Ibid., 261.

40. MFOC, 178; Chevigny, *Woman and Myth*, 407; see also Hig*MFO*, 239–46.

41. LC to MF, Sept. 5, 1849, FMW, 16:150.

42. MF to WHC, Aug. 28, 1849, *FL*, 5:258.

43. CAV to MF, Jan. 31, [1849], FMW, 11:55.

44. MF to CAV, [Aug. 1849], [I,II], *FL*, 5:250.

45. MF to Edgar T. Welby, Sept. 21, 1849, *FL*, 5:264.

46. GAO to Gaeto Suàrra, [Oct. 1849], FMW, 11:37 (author's translation).

47. MF to LC, Oct. 4, 1849, *FL*, 5:267; Gaeto Suàrra to GAO, Oct. 9, 1849, FMW, 11:32 (author's translation).

48. Robertson, *Revolutions*, 365–66.

Chapter 24. Florence

1. MF to CAV, Oct. 16, 1849 [II,III], *FL*, 5:270.

2. CAV to MF, Oct. 5, 1849, FMW, 11:57.

3. *The Letters of Elizabeth Barrett Browning to Mary Russell Mitford*, ed. Meredith B. Raymond and Mary Rose Sullivan, 3 vols. (Waco, TX, 1983), 3:285 (hereafter cited as *EBB–MRM*).

4. MF to SGW and ABW, Oct. 21, 1849, *FL*, 5:273.

5. Ibid., 274; MF to SGW, Oct. 31 [1849], *FL*, 5:279. For Thomas Hicks as a portrait painter, see *American Portraiture in the Grand Manner, 1720–1920*, ed. Michael Quick (Los Angeles, CA, 1981), 156, 222.

6. MCF to Margaret Fuller Ossoli (MFO), Oct. 5, 1849, FMW, 8:221.

7. Ibid.; LMC to Louisa Gilman Loring, Oct. 21, 1849, *Child Letters,* 250.

8. LMC to Louisa Gilman Loring, Nov. 12, 1849, microfiche 1910 (Cornell University Library, KTO Microfilm, 1979), 764; *Literary World* 5 (Nov. 10, 1849): 406.

9. Bremer, *Homes of the New World: Impressions of America,* trans. Mary Howitt (New York, 1853), 1:170.

10. Dispatch XXXV, Jan. 9, 1850, *SGD,* 320.

11. MF *Papers,* Part 2, 22; MF to George W. Curtis, Oct. 25, 1849, *FL,* 5:275; EBB to Mary Russell Mitford, Sept. 24, [1850], *EBB–MRM,* 3:309.

12. EBB to Robert Browning, Jan. 4, 1846, *RB&EBB,* 1:361; Leona Rostenberg, "Margaret Fuller and Elizabeth Barrett Browning, *American Notes and Queries* 1–2 (1941–43): 165.

13. EBB to Eliza Dick Ogilvy, Sept. 22, [1850], in *Elizabeth Barrett Browning: Letters to Mrs. David Ogilvy,* ed. Peter N. Heydon and Philip Kelley (New York, 1973), 31; Emerson quoted in Louise Greer, *Browning and America* (Chapel Hill, NC, 1952), 31.

14. Edward C. McAleer, *The Brownings of Casa Guidi* (New York, 1977), 6.

15. MFO to CST, [ca. Dec. 17, 1849], *FL,* 5:306.

16. Crane, *White Silence,* 450; see also Nathalia Wright, *Horatio Greenough: The First American Sculptor* (Philadelphia, 1963), 208–62, and *Letters of Horatio Greenough* (Madison, WI, 1972), 352–53.

17. See Rodman J. Sheirr, "Joseph Mozier and His Handiwork," *Potters Monthly Magazine* 6, no. 49 (Jan. 1876): 24.

18. George W. Curtis, *Harper's New Monthly Magazine* 68 (Mar. 1884): 641; MFO to George W. Curtis, Oct. 25, 1849, *FL,* 5:275.

19. MFO to EES, Nov. 30, 1849, *FL,* 5:284–85.

20. MFO to WWS, Dec. 2, 1849, *FL,* 5:286; to CST, [ca. Dec. 17, 1849], *FL,* 5:303; to RFF, Feb. 24, 1850, FMW, 11:135.

21. MFO to CST, [ca. Dec. 17, 1849], *FL,* 5:303; to EFC, Dec. 11, 1849, *FL,* 4:291, 292.

22. EES to Maria White Lowell, [Dec.? 1849?], as copied and sent to Sarah Clarke, Hig *MFO,* 244–46. In 1883, when Thomas Wentworth Higginson was preparing his biography of Margaret Fuller, William Henry Channing, then living in England, sent him "a letter from Mrs. Maria Lowell copying an extract from Mrs. William Wetmore Story's letter testifying to the circumstances of M's marriage, and very minute and exact picture of her Husband's appearance, character, history and relationship"; see EES, "The Private Marriage," MFOC, 178.

23. LMC to Ellis Gray Loring, Feb. 1, 1850, *Child Letters,* 253; Signe Alice Rooth, *Seeress of the Northland: Fredrika Bremer's American Journey, 1849–1851* (Philadelphia, 1955), 218. In Fredrika Bremer's novel *Hertha,* the title character is a humanitarian socialist who believes in the improvement of human institutions as a means to human betterment but also believes that, on a personal level, inner peace can be achieved only through intense individualism. Rooth suggests that Margaret Fuller may have influenced the theme of the book and the portrayal of Hertha; see Rooth, *Seeress,* 138.

24. SAC to MFO, Mar. 5, 1850, FMW, 10:41.

25. MFO to EES, Apr. 16, 1850, FMW, 9:233; letter printed in slightly different versions in Chevigny, *Woman and Myth,* 495, and *MFAmRom,* 314–15.

26. *Letters and Journals of Thomas Wentworth Higginson, 1846–1906,* ed. Mary Thacher Higginson (Boston, 1921), 29; MFO to CST, [ca. Dec. 17, 1849], *FL,* 5:302; to MS and RBS, Feb. 5, 1850, FMW, Works, 1:279, *MFAmRom,* 313; to EFC, Dec. 11, 1849, *FL,* 5:291.

27. MFO to MS and RBS, Feb. 5, 1850, FMW, Works, 1:279, *MFAmRom,* 313; to WHC, [ca. late] July 1849[III], Dec. 17, 1849[II], *FL,* 5:248, 300.

28. MFO, "Italy," *NYDT,* Feb. 13, 1850, Supp., 1, *SGD,* 321.

29. MFO to CST, [ca. Dec. 17, 1849], [Dec.] 29 [internal dating], *FL,* 5:305.

30. For Fourierism in U.S.A. in 1849, see Guarneri, *Utopian Alternative,* 268–91, 340–42; MFO to MS and RBS, Dec. 12, 1849, *FL,* 5:295–96, 294.

31. Augusto Lauream to GAO, Mar. 11, 1850, FMW, 11:15; GAO to Matilda Ossoli Macnamara, Mar. 30, 1850, FMW, 16:138 (author's translation).

32. MS to MFO, Apr. 17, 1850, FMW, 11:136.

33. MFO to MS and RBS, Dec. 12, 1849, *FL,* 5:297, 296; RBS to MFO, Apr. 17, 1850, FMW, 11:136.

34. MS to RWE, Apr. 7, 1850, Raritan Bay collection, New Jersey Historical Society.

35. RWE to MFO, Apr. 11, 1850, *EmL,* 4:199.

36. MS to MFO, Apr. 17, 1850, FMW, 11:136; RBS to MFO, Apr. 17, 1850, FMW, 11:136.

37. MFO to RBS and MS, May 14, 1850, FMW, 9:221.

38. Ibid. See also MF to WHC, [I] [ca. late] July, 1849, *FL*, 5:247.

39. MFO to RBS and MS, June 3, 1850, FMW, 9:221, printed in Sanborn, *Recollections*, 2:413.

40. MFO to CAV, Apr. 12, 1850, *OM*, 2:336.

41. See Dispatch XV, Sept. 11, 1847, *SGD*, 142–43; *Art in the Lives of South Carolinians*, ed. David Molke-Hansen (Charleston, 1979).

42. MFO to CAV, Apr. 6, 1850, *OM*, 2:337; Hig*MFO*, 274; see also *EJ*, 11:459.

43. The letters summarized here are: Angela Ossoli De Andreis to GAO, Apr. 27, 1850, FMW, 11:14; Augusto Lauream to GAO, Mar. 30, Apr. 23, 1850, FMW, 11:15, 16 (author's translation).

44. Greer, *Browning*, 51; *Letters of Horatio Greenough to His Brother, Henry Greenough*, ed. Frances Boott Greenough (Boston, 1887), 218.

45. MFO to WWS, May 10, 1850, FMW, 9:229.

46. EBB to Mary Russell Mitford, Sept. 24, [1850], *EBB–MRM*, 3:303.

Chapter 25. Return

1. MFO to Samuel and Hannah Thompson, June [18], 1850, *American Literature* 5 (Mar. 1933): 69.

2. MFO to MS, June 3, 1850, FMW, 9: 221, printed in Sanborn, *Recollections*, 2:414.

3. *OM*, 2:342; Horace Greeley, "Death of Margaret Fuller," *NYDT*, July 23, 1850, 4, reprinted in MFO, *At Home and Abroad: Things and Thoughts in America and Europe*, ed. Arthur B. Fuller (Boston, 1856), 455 (hereafter cited as *H&A*).

4. Bayard Taylor, "The Wreck on Fire Island," *NYDT*, July 24, 1850, 4, reprinted as "Letter of Bayard Taylor," July 23, 1850, *H&A*, 445.

5. Jonathan Smith, "The Wreck of the *Elizabeth*," *NYDT*, July 23, 1850, 4.

6. Ibid.

7. Taylor, "Wreck on Fire Island," 4; Smith, "Wreck of the *Elizabeth*," *NYDT*, July 24, 1850, 2, reprinted in *H&A*, 448–51.

8. Henry David Thoreau, *Cape Cod*, ed. Joseph J. Moldenhauer (Princeton, NJ, 1988), 3; RWE to HG, July 23, 1850, *EmL*, 4: 219; Thoreau to RWE, July 25, 1850, in *The Correspondence of Henry David Thoreau*, ed. Walter Harding and Carl Bode (New York, 1958), 262.

9. "From the Wreck," *NYDT*, July 26, 1850, 4; "Thoreau's Notes on the Shipwreck at Fire Island," *Emerson Society Quarterly* 52 (1968): 98–99; see also Walter Harding, *Days of Henry Thoreau* (New York, 1965), 277–79.

10. Thoreau, *Cape Cod*, 84, variant version in *The Journal of Henry David Thoreau*, ed. Bradford Torrey and Francis H. Allen (Salt Lake City, 1984), 2: 44; Henry David Thoreau to H. G. O. Blake, Aug. 9, 1850, in Harding and Bode, *Correspondence of Thoreau*, 265, variant version in Torrey and Allen, *Journal of Thoreau*, 2:43.

11. EF to RFF, June 13, 1854, FMW, 16: 163.

12. *EJ*, 11:257, 259, 257, 256.

13. Ibid., 258; JFC to SAC, July 23, 1850, ClLetSister.

14. William Henry Fuller to MCF, July 29, 1850, FMW, 15: 88.

15. CST to EH, [Aug. 1850], FMW, 17: 59.

16. Davis quoted in *The History of Woman Suffrage*, ed. Elizabeth Cady Stanton, Susan Anthony, and Matilda Joslyn Gage (Rochester, NY, 1881), 1:217.

17. MCF to ABF, Mar. 9, 1852, FMW, 8: 134; *Dearborn's Guide to Mount Auburn Cemetery* (Cambridge, MA, 1857); see also Blanche Linden-Ward, *Silent City on a Hill* (Columbus, OH, 1989), 238–39.

Chapter 26. Aftermath and Debate

1. HG to RWE, July 27, 1850, *EmL*, 4:225.

2. RWE to SGW, Aug. 2, Sept. 7, 1850, *EmL*, 4:222, 228; *EJ*, 11:488.

3. *EJ*, 11: 488; RWE to SGW, Sept. 7, 16, 1850, *EmL*, 4:228, 229.

4. RWE to SGW, Sept. 23, 1850, *EmL*, 4:231; JFC to SAC, Oct. 10, 1850, ClLetSister 1161; CST to RWE, May 7, 1851, in George Dimock, *Caroline Sturgis Tappan and the Grand Tour* (Lenox, MA, 1982), 50; TH to MCF, Aug. 2, 1850, FMW, 16:65; TH to EFC, [?], 1851, FMW, 16:65; CST to RWE, [Nov. 1850], *EmL*, 8:265 n. 135. Margarett Crane Fuller thanked Hicks for the box on Sept. 9, 1850. It

contained a lock of hair, a ring, and a "testamentary letter"; MCF to TH, Sept. 9, 1850, MFO Collection, letter no. 18, MHarF.

5. *EJ*, 11:432; David Watson, *Margaret Fuller: An American Romantic* (New York, 1988), 92; *OM*, 2:111–12.

6. *EJ*, 11:463.

7. Ibid., 508, 456.

8. SAC to EH, [Autumn 1850], FMW, 10:42.

9. Angela Ossoli De Andreis to EFC, May 7, 1851, FMW, 16:139, Italian original printed in Detti, *Ossoli*, 192, English translation in Deiss, *Roman Years*, 291–92.

10. WHC to EFC, Nov. 2, 1851, FMW, 15:122.

11. *EJ*, 11:431; Ellison, *Delicate Subjects*, 291.

12. George Eliot to Mrs. Peter Alfred Taylor, Mar. 27, 1852, in *The George Eliot Letters*, ed. Gordon S. Haight (New Haven, 1954), 2: 15.

13. Harriet Martineau to RWE, Feb. 25, [1852], in Harriet Martineau, *Selected Letters*, ed. Valerie Sanders (Oxford, 1990), 122.

14. *New York Home Journal* quoted in Joel Myerson, *Margaret Fuller: A Descriptive Primary Bibliography* (Pittsburg, 1978), 39; Hale, *James Freeman Clarke*, 189.

15. RWE to George Bradford, Mar. 3, 1852, *EmL*, 4:281; MCF to RFF, Feb. 19, 1852, FMW, 8:157; RFF to MCF, Feb. 17, 1852, FMW, 17:32.

16. Barbara Channing to MCF, Apr. 15, [1854], FMW, 15:121.

17. HG to RFF, July 30, 1853, FMW, 16:88; RFF to EFC, Aug. 22, 1853, FMW, 16:168.

18. RWE to RFF, Sept. 7, 1853, FMW, 16:62; RFF, *Chaplain*, 142.

19. A. B. Fuller, *Historical Notices*, 12.

20. "Margaret Fuller: A Birthday Celebration at Boston," in *Transcendental Log: 1973*, ed. Kenneth Cameron (Hartford, 1973), 232.

21. Julia Ward Howe, *Margaret Fuller* (Boston, 1883), Prefatory Note; Thomas Wentworth Higginson to JFC, May 15, 1883, MFOC, 229; Hig*MFO*, 4–5.

22. *Centenary*, 14:154, 493, 155; Thomas Woodson, "Explanatory Notes," ibid., 766.

23. *Centenary*, 14:155–56.

24. Ibid., 156–57.

25. *Boston Evening Daily Transcript*, Dec. 12, 1884, 4, Jan. 2, 1885, 4, quoted in "Hawthorne's Notion of Margaret Fuller," *Springfield Republican*, Dec. 24, 1884, 3, reprinted in Kenneth Cameron, *The New England Writers and the Press* (Hartford, 1980), 211.

26. Thomas Wentworth Higginson, "Nathaniel Hawthorne and His Wife," *Atlantic Monthly* 55 (Feb. 1885): 265, 261–62, reprinted in Kenneth Cameron, *Hawthorne and His Contemporaries* (Hartford, 1968), 269, 267.

27. *Boston Evening Daily Transcript*, Jan. 9, 1885, 6; Leonora Cranch Scott, *The Life and Letters of Christopher Pearse Cranch* (Boston, 1917), 352. In 1852 Mozier entertained the publisher James T. Fields with gossip about the Ossolis. He spoke of Ossoli's stupidity and ineptitude as a sculptor, but he did not disparage Fuller: He "often told me of their manner of life and how much of a woman was poor Margaret & how little of a man was Osseoli [*sic*]." James T. Fields to Edwin P. Whipple, Mar. 15, 1852, in "Five Letters of James T. Fields," *American Transcendental Quarterly*, Spring 1978, 123.

28. Frederick T. Fuller, "Hawthorne and Margaret Fuller," *Literary World* 16 (Jan. 10, 1885): 15, also printed in *MFCrEssays*, 126–27; George W. Curtis, "Margaret Fuller and Hawthorne," *Harper's Weekly Magazine* 29 (Jan. 24, 1885): 15.

29. *Boston Evening Daily Transcript*, Jan. 13, 1885, 6; C. A. Ralph, "With Regard to Margaret Fuller," ibid., Jan. 15, 1885, 6; Julian Hawthorne, "Mr. Hawthorne and His Critics," ibid., Feb. 5, 1885, 4, reprinted in *MFCrEssays*, 129.

30. Nina Baym, *The Shape of Hawthorne's Career* (Ithaca, NY, 1976); 160, Lawrence Buell, *New England Literary Culture: From Revolution through Renaissance* (Cambridge, 1986), 279; James, *Story*, 1:129; Christopher Pearse Cranch to Edward Cranch, Mar. 3, 1885, in Scott, *Life of Cranch*, 352.

31. James, *Hawthorne*, 61–62.

32. Ibid., 68–69, 76–77.

33. James, *Boy*, 61–62.

34. Evert Duyckinck to George Duyckinck, Jan. 28, 1848, quoted in Heyward Ehrlich, "The Origin of Lowell's Miss Fooler," *American Literature* 37 (Jan. 1964): 474.

35. Ibid. Henry James, Sr., told the story to Parke Godwin who, in turn, told it to Evert

Duyckinck. The latter included it in his Jan. 28, 1846, letter to his brother George, who was traveling in Europe.

36. William James, *Varieties of Religious Experience: A Study in Human Nature* (New York and London, 1902), 41: " 'I accept the universe' is reported to have been a favorite utterance of our New England transcendentalist, Margaret Fuller; and when some one repeated this phrase to Thomas Carlyle, his sardonic comment is said to have been: 'Gad! she'd better!' "

37. James, *Story,* 1:128–31.

38. Ibid.; *Poet Lore* 13 (July–Sept. 1901): 457; see also "The Margaret Fuller Centennial," *Bulletin of the Brooklyn Institute of Arts and Sciences* 4 (May 21, 1910): 431.

39. "An American mind" refers to Fuller's use of the term in one of her earliest reviews, "Philip van Artevelde," published in the *Western Messenger* in 1835. In the review she discussed the conditions necessary for such a "mind" to develop; the relevant passages are reprinted in *MFAmRom,* 37–46 (quote on p. 39), under the title "Classical and Romantic."

Index